MW01234531

Descendants of Thomas William Holland and Milley Boyett

Nancy Jackson Pleitt Fenner

AuthorHouse™
1663 Liberty Drive
Bloomington, IN 47403
www.authorhouse.com
Phone: 1-800-839-8640

First published by AuthorHouse 7/28/2009

ISBN: 978-1-4389-9262-4 (sc)

Printed in the United States of America
Bloomington, Indiana

This book is printed on acid-free paper.

DEDICATION

To my children, their spouses, and my grandchildren for their patience, understanding and encouragement during my years of research.

ACKNOWLEDGMENTS

Thanks to my immediate family and those named below who have contributed in various ways to make this book and others a reality; I am grateful for your assistance.

My sister, Jackie Olene, and her husband, Phillip Smith, Aunt Idell (nee Tyndall) Holland, Aunt Freda (nee Holland) Strickland, and cousin, Woodrow Smith. On several occasions, they either walked cemeteries with me and transcribed inscriptions or they graciously sat with me in libraries or courthouses and copied data. These special, loved ones provided data and shared their family memories, often giving me clues that made it easier to tract down an elusive ancestor. Conversations with my sister and our brother, Elon Adel, recalled names of dear individuals and wonderful, as well as sad memories.

I extend a glorious mound of thanks to the wonderful people who work in the offices holding the records of Sampson County, in Clinton, North Carolina, especially the two ladies on the staff where the vital records are kept. Several years ago, on one of my few long visits to Sampson, these two ladies were extremely helpful over a period of several weeks; thank you for your graceful patience and encouragement.

Jerome Tew is mentioned several times in this book. He and other members of the Sampson County Historical Society have worked diligently for many years to preserve the history of Sampson County, North Carolina, and the early families who settled in the area. Thanks Jerome, for reviewing data in my book on the early Hollands, for your confirming research on several events, and for sharing your knowledge and opinions on the events and my research. A message from Jerome about "Millae Holland" named in the will of her father, Moses Boyett, prompted me to remember the same reference I had found a few years ago. We are confident that Millae Holland, named in Moses' Last Will and Testament is the "Milley" named for the wife of Thomas William Holland in the Last Will and Testament of Thomas.

A special thanks goes to Jerome Tew for arranging a visit to the owner of **The Old Holland Record Book** (known as the Old Holland Family Bible) and working with her and her daughter to snap digital images of the old records and thanks to the owner of the book for sharing it with us. The images can be found in the back of this Holland family history.

Woodrow Smith shared with me what he had copied from the Old Holland Record Book, but my sister and I were curious and interested in actually seeing the old records. The current owner was kind enough to let us review and copy the records in this old book and on loose pages placed in the book. I am grateful to her and to Woodrow for sharing data. This old book holds the key to the family found in the history of descendants of Thomas William Holland and apparently has been called "**The Old Holland Family Bible.**" However, recently taken digital images prove that it is not an Old Bible. The title of the book is ***Fifteen Sermons Preached on Various Important Subjects***, by George Whitefield, A. B., late of Pemeroke College, Oxford. Prefixed to the Sermons is "A Sermon, on the Character, Preaching of the

Rev. Mr. Whitefield," by Joseph Smith, V.D.M. This book of sermons was published in 1794 by J. Neilson, for J. Gildies, Book Seller, above the Cross Glasgow (England). Rev. George Whitefield (Whitfield) lived 250 years ago and has been called "one of the most passionate evangelists" of the Great Awakening. Theologically, he was a staunch calvinist and it appears that our ancestor, Thomas William Holland, may have followed Rev. Whitefield's teachings.

It would be unfair of me to fail to mention other dedicated individuals who have worked so industriously to publish historical works on Sampson County and the people who lived there. Many of these books are listed in the sources at the back of this book.

I thank Anthony Schrock, Author Services Representative, Timothy Fitch and others on the Design Team, and Teri Watkins from AuthorHouse for their patience and understanding as they worked with me through the process of publishing my first family history. I have already had conversations with Jared Alexander, Publishing Consultant, and Angela Springer, Marketing, at AuthorHouse about this book and look forward to working with them and others.

CONTENTS

INTRODUCTION

As a child, I especially enjoyed listening to the adults relate stories about family. Over the years, I often wished I knew more about the history of my family lines. Eventually, I realized that perhaps I could learn more, but I didn't actually accomplish much when I started in 1994. I was working full-time Monday through Friday and part-time on the weekends until my retirement in 1998 when I finally had the opportunity to actively pursue genealogical research.

When you live a thousand miles, or more, away from the state and county where the records you need are located, your research proceeds slowly. Several long visits to Sampson County, North Carolina, gave me time to visit libraries where I, and sometimes others with me, found records that included county and family histories, indexes for various state and county records, and transcribed cemetery inscriptions. In county offices I reviewed and copied vital statistics, deeds and wills. I purchased county and family history books, histories and data on CDs, transcribed census records and deed and will abstracts, and historical county and family newsletters. On each visit, interviews and visits with relatives yielded precious data and memories or presented clues for further research.

In the records noted above, I found poor, faded writing, errors on birth and death certificates and marriage records which included strange spellings of names, erroneous dates, and errors in given and maiden names and place names. I found incorrect names and dates on tombstones! Many death certificates name an incorrect burial place. Of course, it wasn't unusual when an informant who was a grandchild or a neighbor wasn't sure of the full name of parents or a birth year for a 90 year old deceased individual.

Computers and the internet have allowed me to find much data on-line and fill in many blanks. Familysearch.org and Ancestry.com and a few other sites paved the way for on-line genelogical research. Ancestry.com has extraordinary records and it continues to add records everyday, but early naming patterns present a challenge for those importing data from those sites directly into their trees; the John Doe found there with about the same year of birth as your John Doe, may not be the correct one.

Almost everytime I confirmed a record, I found a clue that led to another search. When that happened, my desire to leave the best family histories that I could possibly write made me want to continue searching for that other link, but then reality would hit me right in the face and elsewhere. The face in the mirror and my slow moving legs reminded me of my age.

In addition to the Holland family history presented here, my database contains information for paternal lines: **Cannady, Hair, Honeycutt, Jackson, Naylor, Royal**, and a few collateral lines including **Lockamy (Lockerman)**. On my maternal side: **Howell, Carter, Hair, Hudson, Peterson, Tatum, Sessoms**, and a few collaternal lines, including **Tyndall.**

My intent when I started my research was to first search only two lines: Holland and Jackson. Then I found that the other direct and collateral lines intersected like a hugh spider web and within that web was a network of small dense webs. It made sense at the time, to enter all the information and this became more true as time went on and the web of names became denser. There were many times in the beginning of my research when I found myself revisiting the same data for information about individuals I had not thought revelant the first time.

I've enjoyed almost every minute of my research. My heart beats faster and I want to shout everytime I find data that clearly bridges a gap and connects two individuals or families. After almost a year of health problems in 2003, I prayed for time to continue my research and complete a few histories to leave for my family. I thank the Lord for willing me that time.

Since 1998, I have read and studied thousands of records; a large number of these, I have read several times and I've cross-checked, compared and confirmed much of the information in my database. The responsibility for some of the errors you will find are mine and I apologize only for those. I have found a lot of conflicting names, dates and other information and most of our ancestors and others who recorded events, wrote and spelled poorly. A few census enumerators in southern states entered initials for every person they recorded! Nicknames on certificates of death and in census records create at times, an unyielding wall.

You will find various spellings for given or surnames in these records. For instance, "Hair," Hairr," "Haire," and "Hare" can all be found for Hare. This history will sometimes have different spellings of this name in one family and this is the way I found it in my sources. I feel comfortable with most of the families I have linked with data found during my research, especially information found in family Bibles, certificates of death, and other sources, but certificates of death and cemetery records are not always correct and please understand that cousins and aunts or uncles may have the same given name, be about the same age, and live in different counties. Two relatives may provide you with conflicting data. It has not been a fast, easy search to verify many of the names in these records and I suggest to those of you who believe or know incorrect data is presented for your family, please pursue further research and send me corrections.

The Family Tree Maker software format may have entered a first name for the husband and/or wife in some instances when the middle name was the preferred. When I revised the manuscript, I corrected this when I knew which name was used, but I did not always know this. Please bear in mind that full names are preferred when creating a family history. When I found a reference for a nickname, I explained it in the notes.

Children were recorded as orphans in early court records when the father died and when mothers were unable to care for them, they were placed in homes of guardians. One census enumerator might list these children by the surname of their guardian and ten years later they would be recorded by their correct name.

I'm sure that additional data could be found on individuals for whom I have little, but unfortunately, my health does not permit me to pursue a lot of further research.

When I found additional data after I had already generated my book manuscript, I sometimes repeated the names of the parents when entering this information for their children and grandchildren. I had already revised the manuscript and for me to enter the data in my software and create a new manuscript would have further delayed the publishing of the book. Therefore, you will find that **this new data does not follow the mathematical relationship as found for most of the individuals in the book.**

THE + SIGN BEFORE NUMBERS SIGNIFIES THAT THE INDIVIDUAL CAN BE FOUND ELSEWHERE IN THE BOOK WITH A SPOUSE AND CHILDREN. It is easy to follow the numbers back to track ancestors and forward to tract descendants.

Many of the early deeds and Last Will and Testaments have very long sentences, little punctuation and poor spelling and bad grammar can often be found in them. I tried to correct some of these documents to make them easier to read and understand without losing all the historical essence of the record. Unfortunately, to save space, only abstracts are presented for many of the deeds I wanted to share and these include only the basic land description.

We are aware that many early settlers came to the Colony for religious freedom; others came to escape severe punishment for various crimes which may have included murder, fighting for their religious freedom or to overthrow their ruler, and there were those who were led to believe that they would be rewarded with acres of land by agreeing to work for a well-to-do Colonist for a number of years. Later, a large number of men came to the Colony in small organized groups that included families and a variety of occupational skills that would be needed in a new community. In the event they didn't have money to immediately purchase land, they were prepared to settle on vacant land and proceed with a land grant process. Many of those who settled happily within their communites, worked to bring other organized groups to join them.

Thirty Coats of Arm for the Hollands are listed (or recorded) in The General Armory of England, Scotland, Ireland, and Wales. Finding one for our Holland ancestors would be a daunting task for me and it might be impossible to determine the correct one. We may not have one!

NORTH CAROLINA LAND GRANT PROCEDURE 1777-1800

I found "North Carolina Land Grant Procedure 1777-1800," at http://members.tripod.com/abpruitt/id6.htm

The first step in the land grant process was to find vacant land. The man could choose land on which he had been living, an adjoining tract, or a tract far from his current residence. The second step was to have the claim recorded in the land office in the county where the land was and was called "**making a land entry**". In 1778, entry fees, surveying fees and grant fees were required at the time of recording, but this soon changed and only the small entry fee was required when the claim was recorded.

In an effort to keep tories from claiming land, between 1778 and 1781, the individual making an entry was required to pledge allegiance to the state. Next came a waiting period to allow time for others to become aware that the tract of land had been claimed and decide whether the claim included land that was already owned by someone else. "If there were no disputes, the entry taker would issue a land warrant. The warrant was a form letter addressed to the county surveyor instructing him to survey the claim without delay". The surveyor was paid based on the number of acres. When the survey was finished, the land warrant and two copies of the survey were sent to the North Carolina Secretary of State and some would include the name of the surveyor and names of chain carriers. Chain carriers may have been neighbors and/or the person whose land was being surveyed, depending on who was present on that day.

The Secretary was required to make sure that the State Treasurer had received the state's share of the fees before he proceeded with a grant. The state charged 50 shillings per hundred acres between 1778-1781. In 1781 the county entry offices were closed possibly because the state wanted to change the fee structure. The grant process continued and grants were still issued provided the required fees were paid. When the county entry offices re-opened in 1783, the state fee was raised to 10 pounds per hundred acres. Afterward the fee varied; lower fees were charged if the land included a swamp or was mountainous. The Secretary (or one of his clerks) filled out a land grant, the Governor signed the grant and the state seal was attached. One copy of the survey was attached to the grant. The land description was recorded in the land grant books kept by the Secretary of State and the Secretary kept the second copy of the survey and the land warrant. Prior to the Governor signing a grant, a 'last minute' protest could be made. Paperwork survives for petitions dated between 1778 and 1835; these were settled by a jury trial in the county where the land was located.

The grant notification was either returned to the grantee or to the county courthouse where an advertisement was placed in the local newspaper announcing the arrival of grants. The grantee had one year in which to have the grant recorded in books kept by the county Register of Deeds. He paid a small fee for the recording. For at least 50 years, no one was actually in charge to make sure each grant was recorded and some of the grants were never recorded.

Many men never followed through on their land entry; some stayed on the land for a few years and either died or moved on, leaving the land for others to claim. These brave men and women faced a harsh environment; they traveled by river, by walking narrow paths and roads, and many found it difficult to travel to the parish or county governmental office to file necessary paperwork and, of course, when no one was specifically in charge of the recording of the grant process for at least 50 years, it's no surprise we have incomplete records.

After the Revolutionary War, Land Offices disposed of hugh tracts of land confiscated by the states from owners who fought for the British. To save their lives and their families, many of these Tories who were not killed during the war, fled the country never to return; others were later court-martialed.

It is most likely that one or more of our ancestors may have died during the Revolutionary War while defending his family, livestock, and crops. In the event that he was a "Crown-Loyal Tory" and he had not already completed the land grant process, he may have fled with his family to Canada or another safe place, leaving no record of himself and his family. Most of our early ancestors knew little about rotation of crops or how to improve the land; when they had no more forests to clear, they moved on to another forested area nearby or on to another state. There may be no record of an early ancestor for other reasons; the first Federal Census was taken in 1790 and the census records before 1850 only included the names of heads of households and native indians and slaves were not counted. Courthouses burned, sometimes twice over the years, destroying many records.

DESCENDANTS OF THOMAS WILLIAM HOLLAND, AND MILLEY BOYETT, SAMPSON COUNTY NORTH CAROLINA

Generation Number 1

1. Thomas William Holland (Unknown[1]) was born about 1750, and died 08 November 1819 in Sampson County, North Carolina. He married **Milley Boyett**, probably the daughter of Moses Boyett (Boyt, Boyet). She was born about 1755, and died after 21 February 1820 in Sampson County, North Carolina.

See Boyett data elsewhere in this book.

The middle name of this "Thomas Holland" appears to be listed as "William" in records of Thomas. These records of his family and later descendants were either recorded in what we have always called "**The Old Holland Family Bible**" or on loose pages that have been placed in this book. However, recently taken digital images prove that it is not an Old Bible. The title of the book is ***Fifteen Sermons Preached on Various Important Subjects***, by George Whitefield, A. B., late of Pemeroke College, Oxford. Prefixed to the Sermons is "A Sermon, on the Character, Preaching of the Rev. Mr. Whitefield," by Joseph Smith, V.D.M. This book of sermons was published in 1794 by J. Neilson, for J. Gildies, Book Seller, above the Cross Glasgow (England).

To simplify events, in this family history of the Hollands of Sampson County, I will try to refer to this book as "***The Old Holland Record Book.***" **Digital images** from *The Old Holland Record Book* including mages of the names and births of children of Thomas and Milley and of their son, Henry and his wife, Mary, and a few descendants **may be found near the back of this history of the Hollands.**

Recorded in this old record book at the top of one of the images is what appears to be: "Thomas Deceased 8 November _819." This writing is crossed through, but the date of 8 November 1819 probably is the date Thomas William Holland died. It may have been cropped through while in the hands of someone other than a member of the Holland Family. See his will below. The left top corner of the page is torn and unless the publisher crops the left side of this image placed in the back of this book, writing from the page underneath it appears on the left. **Thomas Yrarebery**" is written on the facing page and **Yearbary Autrey** is recorded on the left page of the image. **Yarboro, Yarbough** or **Yarbrough** is probably the name the writer attempted to record and I have no idea whether the Yarbrough family was connected to the Holland.or Autry families. You will notice on this image, "born" is written "Borned."

I'm puzzled by more than one entry in this old record book and by the loose pages, but especially by one entry that says: "September. ... Thomas Holland his Book. Bought of Hugh

McPhail for 10 Shillings in the year 1820." This would have been about one year after the death of Thomas William Holland. Perhaps there was an estate sale for Thomas and "a" Bible" or the old record book was sold, purchased perhaps several months later by Henry Holland and the records are still owned by Henry's descendants. Henry would have been aged 19 in 1820. Whoever purchased the book from Hugh McPhail, thankfully, realized its value to the Holland Family.

Records show that Thomas had a great-grandson named "Theophilus" who was born about 1853 and may have either died or moved from Sampson County before 1870. (Theophilus was the son of Matthew, son of Daniel, son of Thomas William.) This could indicate that Thomas, most likely, was related to Henry Holland (who was born 1758 in Bertie County, North Carolina, and died 28 June 1852 in Georgia. This Henry was a son of Theophilous Holland. Sparse information can be found on Theophilus who is said to have been from Nansemond County, Virginia. Part of southern Nansemond County became part of the northeastern counties of North Carolina when an agreement on the Virginia and North Carolina border was finally reached in 1828.

I have not identified the paren ... or our line of
Hollands tells that we had three H ... npson County.
I have not determined who these ... en mentioned
in my family. However, the oldes ... n John, Apsele
(Apshee), and Dempsey, followed ... miah Holland
began school on 25 November 1 ... pson County's
first known school.

Deeds of Sampson County and ... lliam Holland
indicate that he was a farmer and ... smith tools to
his son, Daniel.

Listed in an old **Holland Record** ... nuary 1800(?).
Henry William may have died yo ... as born; often
a later child was given the name ... ne of Thomas
Willliam's son, Henry, may have be ... and the old Holland Record Book has the only clue for this. It is not actually known whether the Hollands followed naming patterns of that time, but it appears that they did. I know of one old Holland Record Book that is owned by one Holland descendant and loose pages of recorded data are with the Book. Many of the names and dates listed in this old record book were entered more than once; some are faded and, though difficult to read, they provided me with data to confirm data in other records and I proceeded with this family history.

Pension files -
Sampson Ct. &
Duplin
Henry Holland b. 1757
James Holland b. 1744

I have not been able to find a Revolutionary War Record for Thomas William Holland, but it is said that he served and received a pension. It is recorded that "Thomas Holland" from Wake County, North Carolina, served in the American Revolutionary War. His pension was rejected for serving less than six months.

"Thomas Holland," between 21-60 years of age, was listed in Northampton County, North Carolina, as one taxable and head of household in the **State Census of North Carolina**

1784-1787. I found Thomas Holland first recorded in **Sampson County, North Carolina in a deed of 29 April 1789** when he purchased 100 acres from **William Hair** and then he appears as the grantee in a deed of 6 May 1789. The May 1789 deed mentions Thomas as a grantee in one place and Henry Holland as the grantee in another place. This second deed was for 425 acres that Thomas (or Henry) purchased from William McClam (McLamb) in three tracts. The fact that he and this older Henry were mentioned in the deed of May 1789 may indicate a close relationship. See below for abstracts of both of these deeds and others. It is not known whether the Thomas in Northampton County 1784-1787 was the same Thomas who was found in April 1789 in Sampson.

When Duplin County, North Carolina, was formed in 1750 from New Hanover County, Duplin then included what later became Sampson County; At that time in 1750, Duplin contained about 360 white poll taxables and very few other people. It appears Native Americans were not included in the count. Apparently, wives and children were not taxables. In 1755, 628 taxables were reported; this included 460 white men, 168 male and female African Americans and mulattoes. When the Revolutionary War started only about 1,000 taxables were found in Duplin (and Sampson) County; very few were immigrants from Europe. Sampson County, North Carolina, was formed from Duplin in 1784 and had a tax list of 934 heads of families in the 1790 Sampson County census. In 1795, 1847, 1870 and 1872, small areas of New Hanover were added to the southern area of Sampson County.

Sampson County Will Abstracts 1784-1900 by Elizabeth E. Ross records the following on page 57.

> "HOLLAND, Thomas. Written 21 October 1819, and went to probate on 15 November 1819.
>
> "Wife Milley Holland - plantation of 447 acres during Natural Life, then to son HENRY HOLLAND & son THOMAS JAMES HOLLAND feather bed & furn.
>
> "Son DANIEL HOLLAND - my blacksmith tools
>
> "Son JOHN HOLLAND - 1 cow & calf; 1 bed & furn.
>
> "Daughters, MARY, CHARITY, NANEY, ORPAH, & MILLY HOLLAND - have already given them their part
>
> "Exec: DANIEL HOLLAND
>
> "Wit: Fleet Cooper, Ann Duffod (sic) signed Thomas Holland
>
> "NC State Archives"

Ann Duffy (or Ann Duff) may have been the name of the witness.

It appears that Thomas William Holland's estate was not settled until several years later.

I also found a copy of the will on page 99 in Book A, Unprobated Wills of Sampson County, North Carolina and the following is also in that copy of of Thomas' will: "Also to Thomas James Holland's son, **Willis**, a feather bed and calf.

"Witnesses: **Fleet Cooper** and Ann Duffie." This is the only recorded event I have found for **Willis Holland**. Fleet Cooper, witness, was linked through Mary Cooper, wife of Thomas' grandson, Harfrey Holland, son of Daniel. It is not known whether Ann Duffie (Duffy, Duff) was linked to the Holland family. **James Duff** and Gabriel Holmes witnessed a deed of 1 January 1755 when John and Ann Sampson of the County of New Hanover and Town of Wilmington sold 200 acres to William Andrews. George Vaughn of Ireland had conveyed this land to John Sampson by deed of gift. **John Duff** served in the Revolutionary War and North Carolina Army Accounts in Caswell's Journal records that "Messrs Brannock Owens, Henry Hodges and Charles Cook conveyed John Duff, a horse stealer, to New Bern jail from Duplin County's old courthouse." The record actually refers to the jail as "Goal." The three men were paid 1/8/0 pounds for the round trip. It appears that John Duff was not guilty since he remained in Duplin County and was listed in the 1790 census as an adult white male, head of house, with two white females.

Thomas Holland's recorded Estate transactions:

> 15 November 1819. "...Last Will and testament was offered for probate and proved by Fleet Cooper."
>
> 17 November 1819. "Administration on the estate of Thomas Holland, deceased, was granted to Thomas J. Holland. Bond was $1000 with Nathan Jackson, Sr., and Andrew Bass securities."
>
> 21 February 1820. ".. Ordered that Fleet Cooper, Raiford Coore and Robert Butler be a committee to lay off to Mrs. Holland one year's provision from her deceased husband's estate."
>
> 19 May 1820. "...Daniel Holland, administrator, returned an inventory and account of sales of Thomas Holland, deceasedd."
>
> 22 February 1822. "...Ordered William Maxwell, esquire, Robert Butler, Sr. and John Hairr, Sr., be a committee to settle with the heirs of Thomas Holland, deceased, and Daniel Holland, administrator of said deceased, and report to May court term next."
>
> 20 May 1822. "...The committee appointed to settle the estate of Thomas Holland, deceased, returned a report of their proceedings."

The estimated year of Thomas' birth is based upon the year he first paid taxes in North Carolina and when he was first mentioned in a deed of Sampson County, North Carolina.

Willie is not mentioned in his father's Will. He is named in the **Old Holland Record Book** and his year of birth indicates he, most likely, was a son of Thomas and Milley and "Willie" was possibly a nickname for William. Daniel Holland went to court on 22 August 1826 and asked to be appointed administrator on the estate of " William Holland," deceased. Letters of Administration were granted and on 21 November 1826, Sampson County Court records show that Daniel made his report on the estate which was settled a lot quicker than most at that time, leading me to believe that Willie did not marry and his estate was small. Perhaps the "Willie" listed in the **Old Holland Record Book** as born on 15 January 1793 died very young and he and the "William" whose estate is mentioned in court records were not the same person.

The **Old Holland Record Book** mentions that Thomas Holland had 10 siblings in the year 1800. His sons, Henry and John, were born after 1800. The writer may mean that Thomas William had 10 brothers and sisters, but most likely, it refers to his ten children who were born before 1800? Images from this old book may be found near the back of this history of the Holland Family.

Also found in the Old Holland Record Book is "A daughter of Thomas Holland in the year 1814." Milley was probably too old to have had a child at that time and it is not clear where this "unidentified daughter" can be placed. See notes for Orpah.

Evidence is found in the **Old Holland Record Book** of Thomas that supports the marriage of his daughter, Mary, to Daniel Culbreth. This writer copied the following from the old record book:

"Tomzel Culbreath (12-17-1801).

"Millie Culbreath, daughter of Daniel Culbreath and Mary Culbreath. (7-1809 or August 1803?)

"John Culbreath born August 18?5."

Jackie, the sister of this writer, copied the same information. She first copied "Mary Culbreath" and then drew a line through "Mary" and entered "Nancy." As mentioned before, some of the writing was difficult to read. She also copied "August 22 in 1805" for the date of birth for John Culbreath. The will of Daniel Culbreath indicates his wife was "Mary" (no maiden name.) The fact that the above information found in the Old Holland Record Book is the same data found on tombstones in a Culbreath Family Cemetery near Roseboro, North Carolina, strongly indicates Mary Holland married Daniel Culbreath (Culbreth).

The following can also be found in the **Old Holland Record Book**: It appears that multiple entries that sometimes contained conflicting data were made for some names and some of the writing is faded, making it difficult to determine what is actually correct. The year of 1800 for Henry William Holland appears to be incorrect.

HENRY HOLLAND, born 27 February 1801, was the son of THOMAS HOLLAND

HENRY HOLLAND, born 27 February 1802, was the son of THOMAS HOLLAND.

HENRY WILLIAM HOLLAND, born 15 January 18??, was the son of THOMAS JAMES HOLLAND.

HENRY WILLIAM HOLLAND, born 15th day of January 1800.

HENRY WILLIAM HOLLAND, son of THOMAS JAMES HOLLAND, born 25 January 1800(?).

THOMAS JAMES HOLLAND, born 4-1797 was the son of THOMAS WILLIAM HOLLAND

Thomas James Holland, born 15 Januay 18__.

Following are abstracts of Sampson County, North Carolina, deeds naming Thomas Holland:

Sampson County Deed Book 8, page 335. "Deed: **William Hair** to **Thomas Holland.** Dated: **29 April 1789**. Trans.: 25 pounds for 100 acres "On the East side of Little Cohary Swamp beginning at ...James Howard's corner.." ...Wit.: Joel Hair and Thomas Hairr."

9 February 1790. "Deed from William Hare to Thomas Holland was proved and ordered registered."

Orpah, daughter of this Thomas William Holland married a nephew of this William HARE (Hair).

Deed Book 8, page 362. "Deed: **William McClam** to **Henry Holland**. (Grantee is given **as THOMAS HOLLAND in one place**: ... Dated: **6 May 1789**. Trans.: 150 pounds "Current money" for three tracts of land. The first tract consisted of 150 acres "Beginning at a marsh in Cohary swamp then running down the swamp." Etc. Line ran "to a branch of small gums in the marsh." Land was "granted by patent to Thomas Gibbs, said patent Bearing date" 1 July 1758. The second tract consisted of 100 acres "On the West side of Great Cohary and on the head of Flat Branch." Land was "granted by pattent to the said Thomas Gibbs, the said patent bearing date (8 October 1767 or 1768) and conveyed by or from Thomas Gibbs to John Williams and from John Williams to William McClam. The third tract consisted of 175 acres "which was granted by patent to the above said William McClam, said pattent bearing date 1784. On the west side of Great Cohary and south side of Gum Branch beginning... Hollands own line" and a branch..near the head of said branch thence ... to Gibbs Branch or marsh." Etc. Land was granted "by pattent to the said HENRY HOLLAND (SIC). Wit.: Samuel Strickland and Henry King."

I cannot prove it, but I believe that the **Henry Holland** in the above 1789 deed was related to Thomas William Holland. Thomas was recorded in Sampson County deeds eight years after Henry was first mentioned. Henry was most likely the Henry Holland who was a Constable in Capt. Fort's District in 1785, Capt. Toole's District in 1787, paroled in Capt. Hall's Company in August 1795 and again served as Constable in 1801. That Henry may have the Henry who with his son, John Holland, moved to Edgefield District, South Carolina, their neighbors were Monk, Odom, Whitehead, and Kirkland families and it is said that Henry's son, John, and these families later moved to Henry County, Alabama. There was another older Henry who was born 1 March 1757 in Bertie County, moved to an area of Duplin that eventually became Sampson, moved from Sampson County to Georgia in 1787, died in Tattnall County, Georgia on 28 June 1852 and was buried in the Holland Family Cemetery now in Candler County, Georgia.

After the defeat of the Creek and Apalachee Indians in Georgia, many people from Duplin and Sampson Counties, North Carolina, migrated to Georgia between 1820-1840 and settled on land that had been owned by the Indians in Lowndes, Brooks, and Thomas Counties. It is likely that some of the early Holland families found in Alabama also left Duplin and Sampson at that time.

Page 310 in Sampson County Deed Book 9: On 14 May **1793, Daniel Coo**r sold 150 acres in two tracts to **Thomas Holland** for 50 pounds. "The first tract consisted of 100 acres 'On the East side of Little Cohara on the Black Branch Beginning...in little Cohara at the mouth of Juniper branch.' Deed mentions a pond. The second tract consisted of 50 acres 'on the East side of Little Cohara and west side of the Black Branch beginning...in a pond and mentions Needham Dees' Corner." (The Black Branch emptied into Little Coharie) Witnesses: William Honeycutt and William Fowler."

"11 February 1794, Thomas Holland came into court and acknowledged a crop and an under half-moon under the left ear to be his common stock mark." Hogs and other farm animals were not fenced in until years later and those who owned farm animals were required to registered their stock marks.

Page 548 in County Deed Book 11: **Daniel Coor** and **Thomas Holland** witnessed a deed from Southey Fisher to Thomas Fisher, dated 30 March 1799.

Page 160 in County Deed Book 12: **Archibald Culbreath** and **Thomas Holland** witnessed a deed of gift (100 acres) from **Niell Culbreath** to **Daniel Culbreath** (his son). Dated 20 November 1802. It was the custom at the time for a member of the wife's family to witness a deed to protect her rights and I believe that Thomas Holland was protecting the rights of his daughter, Mary, who married Daniel Culbreath (Culbreth). Mary and Daniel's first child was born 1801.

Other deed transactions recorded in court minutes:

19 August 1804: For 50 pounds Thomas bought 100 acres from Sampson Dees. ...on east side of Little Cohara... Deed refers to the "said **John Holland**" and the said **"Thomas Holland"** in different places which seems to indicate that they lived close together and were most likely related. (John Holland, son of Thomas, was not born until 1806).

20 May 1805: James Stewart, Attorney for S. Dees (County of Montgomery and State of Tennessee) to Thomas Holland. $15 for 60 acres on north side of Porters(?) Branch, Catharine Williams' corner...east side of Little Cohara.

The 12 February 1806, the Sampson County, North Carolina Court acknowledged sale of 197 acres from Attorney, John Dickson to Thomas Holland. Thomas bought the land on 23 November 1805 for 25 pounds, 8 shillings and 6 pence. Land lay on east side of Little Cohera joining his own line...Black Branch is mentioned in the deed.

20 May 1808. James Stewart, Attorney for Sampson Dees, deceased, of Montgomery County, Tennessee, sold property to Thomas Holland. Deed Book 14, p. 498). 10 May 1809. Sale of 50 acres from James Stewart, Attorney for Sampson Dees to Thomas Holland was proved.

On 2 Dec (Year not entered?), grant of 100 acres to Thomas Holland... on the east side of Little Cohara joining his own and JAMES' line. ...run of Little Cohara and Holland's old corner ...thence with JAMES' line.

Was this "JAMES HOLLAND'S" line and does it indicate Thomas and James were brothers? James, James F., and James Franklin appear in names of descendants.

Another "James Holland" who was born about 1754 at Moores Creek, New Hanover County, married first Mary Dobson and second to Zilphis Boyette (Boyet) of Duplin County, on 10 May 1807, served in the Revolutionary War and on "26 February 1833, at age 89, appeared before the Duplin County Court and made application for a pension. He was placed on the rolls on 18 March 1834 at $90 per annum and drew a total of $1,125 before his death on 7 February 1843. His widow, at age 78, applied for a pension in Lenoir County, North Carolina, on 10 September 1843 and was granted pension # W 7800. There also was an award of a bounty land warrant # 8447-16055 to them."

An older living relative mentioned that the early Hollands in Sampson County, owned large acreage around Salemburg and County deeds support this. It appears that Thomas' land went to his children, a grandchild and, at least, one son-in-law.

20 May 1812. Two deeds from **Thomas Holland** to **Daniel Holland** were acknowledged. One for 50 acres; the other for100 acres. The deed for 100 acres ($50) mentions East side of Little Cohary...Registered 4 July 1815. The deed for 50 acres mentions North Side of Porter's Branch, Catharine Williams corner... Registered 5 July 1812.

It is said that **Thomas William Holland** served in the **Revolutionary War**. I have not found a record of his service and it's possible that he was living in a county other than Sampson when he served. However the land grant he received could have been in Sampson. The land in the two deeds acknowledged on 20 May 1812 mentioned in the above paragraph may have been from land granted to Thomas William for his service. Tradition erroneously says that Daniel, the son of Thomas William received a land grant from the Kind of England in 1796. **The Revolutionary War ended in 1783**. Deeds of the time and on into the 20th Century, contained a history of prior owners of the land. Many men who served in the War received land grants from the Federal Government. The abstract of land that Daniel received or purchased from his father, or someone else, may have mentioned that one of the prior owners received it in a land grant from the King of England and someone down the line either did not understand or misread the deed. Of course, subsequent deeds may have omitted some pertinent information in describing the history of the land and stories repeated over the years can eventually cloud what eventually happened. These early abstracts presented a wonderful history of the land and the descriptions over time became shorter and shorter and eventually led to the deeds we have today which do not include the names of several prior owners.

25 October 1819. **Thomas Holland** to **Thomas Hairr** 100 acres (a deed of gift). Deed mentions that "Thomas Hair was son of Jonathan Hair. ... land was in the mouth of Black Branch at the run of Little Cohera."

17 November 1819. A deed from **Thomas Holland** to **Thomas Hairr** for 100 acres proved by Raiford Coore. This was proved shortly after Thomas's death and appears to have been the deed of gift to his grandson whom I believe was the son of Milly and **Jonathan Hare**. Thomas Hare (Hairr) was still under age when he received the "deed of gift." See notes for Milly Holland. (Thomas' daughter, Orpah, married John Athae Hair. Say "John Athae" fast and it sounds like "Johnathan" and it probably sounded more so with the earlier accents.)

Court records show Thomas was ordered to serve on the jury for these dates: 17 November 1796, 5 May 1802; 13 May 1805, 17 May 1813, Superior Court, April term 1817. He also served on many other occasions. Every healthy male was also expected to work on the maintenance of the roads and rivers; Thomas shared in this work. Of course, hands on your farm could work in your stead. Sampson County, North Carolina, court minutes show that the early Hollands were active in county government and did their share of work to keep roads open and streams and rivers navigable. There were other Hollands mentioned in the early deeds of Sampson County; several are mentioned in the deed transactions noted above.

Thomas William Holland was listed in the 1790 census with one male 16 and over, three males under 16 and four females of all ages. This census indicates that there were two sons other than Daniel who were born before 1790. In the 1800 census he wass listed with two males and two females under ten, two males and two females 10-16; he and one female are over 45.

Daniel and possibly one other son were married by 1800. Another older son is not mentioned in Thomas's will or in the **Old Holland Record Book**.

Name History and Origin for **Holland**: 1) Irish: reduced Anglicized form of Gaelic O hOileain, a variant of O hAolain, from a form of Faolan (with loss of the initial F-), a personal name representing a diminutive of faol "wolf'. Compare Whelan. 2) English and Scottish: habitational name from Holland, a division of Lincolnshire, or any of the eight villages in various parts of England so called, from Old English hoh "ridge' + land "land'. The Scottish name may also be from places called Holland in Orkney, Houlland in Shetland, Hollandbush in Stirlingshire, and Holland-Hirst in the Parish of Kirkintilloch. 3) English, German, Jewish (Ashkenazic), Danish, and Dutch: regional name from Holland, a province of the Netherlands.

Milley's name appears as "Millie" and as Millzy or Millsey in descendants. I believe she was the "**Millae Holland**," named as a daughter by Moses Boyt in his 1780 Last Will and Testament. Moses also named his wife, Anne, and son, Arther Boyt. The will was witnessed by Thomas Jernigan, Jonathan Gore, and Christopher Martin. John Gore and Chris Martin were found in the 1784-1787 State Census of North Carolina in Capt. Ward's District in Duplin County. Also listed in Capt. Ward's District were **Arthur Boyet, Ephraim Boyet**, Lamuel Boyet (**Samuel Boyet**), and **William Boyet**. Listed in Capt. Hubbard's Company in Duplin County in this census, were Absolom Boyed(sic) (**Absolom Boyet?**), **Elizabeth Boyet**, and **Jones Boyet**. These same seven individuals were listed on the 1785 Tax List for Duplin County.

Arthur Boyt, Ephram and William Boyt are found in the 1790 Duplin County, North Carolina, Federal Census; John Boyt is found in the 1790 Sampson County Census. It appears that Boyt was also entered in records as Boyett, Boyet, Boyette, Boyd, and Boyed. See the back of this book for Boyt (Boyett) data.

Images of the **Old Holland Record Book** appear in the back of this book. The illegible name of a daughter is listed on one image and records that she was born November (illegible) in the year of our Lord Jesus Christ 1781; this may have been "Mary" listed below.

Children of Thomas William Holland and Milley Boyett are:

2 i. **Charity Holland**, died after 1819.

\+ 3 ii. **Daniel Holland, Sr.,** born about 1773; died Between 1850 - 1860 in Sampson County, North Carolina.

\+ 4 iii. **Mary Holland**, born about 1780; died between August 1832 - 1840.

5 iv. **Naney Holland**, born 18 February 1789. Her date of birth was difficult to read.

6 v. **Unknown Son Holland**, born before 1790.

7 vi. Unidentified Son Holland, born before 1790.

\+ 8 vii. **Orpah Holland**, born 27 February 1791; died between 1860 - 1870 in Sampson County, North Carolina.

\+ 9 viii. **Millie Holland,** born 15 January 1793.

10 ix. **Willie Holland** was born 15 January 1793 and appears to have died in 1826. He is mentioned in the **Old Holland Record Book** of Thomas William Holland, but is not listed in his father's will. His name may have been "William." Court minutes record that on 22 August 1826, Daniel Holland went into court and requested administration on the estate of William Holland, deceased. Court ordered that letters of administration be granted after he gave bond and named securities. On 21 November 1826 Daniel made his report on the estate. No other record has been found for this Willie (William?) and it appears that his estate was settled quickly indicating it was probably a small estate and he had no children and probably was not married.

\+ 11 x. **Thomas James Holland**, born 30 April 1797.

\+ 12 xi. **Henry Holland, born** 27 February 1801 in North Carolina; died between 1860 - 1870 in Sampson County, North Carolina.

\+ 13 xii. **John Holland,** born about 1806; died after 1870.

Generation Number 2

3. Daniel Holland, Sr. (Thomas William[2], Unknown[1]) was born about 1773, and died between1850 - 1860 in Sampson County, North Carolina. He married **Elizabeth Sessoms,**

daughter of Solomon Sessoms and Obedience Baker. She was born 27 September 1789, and died after 1880 in Sampson County, North Carolina.

Elma Holland Sollinger states on page 229 of "The Heritage of Harnett County, North Carolina" in the first paragraph of a profile she wrote for The Family of Erastus Holland: "**Daniel Holand** was given a land grant from the King of England in 1796." **America won the Revolutionary War in 1783** when Daniel was about five years old; **the King of England did not own the land in 1796.** It is said that Daniel's father, Thomas William Holland, served in the Revolutionary War and perhaps he was living in another county; I have not yet found a record of his service from Sampson or any other county in North Carolina.

Two deeds to Daniel from his father, Thomas William Holland, were acknowledged on 20 May 1812. The land or part of the land mentioned in these deeds may have been from land granted to Thomas William for his service or he may have received the land through a grant process; I briefly describe this process earlier in this book. Sampson County was formed in 1784 from Duplin County. Deeds of the time and on into the 20th Century, named several prior owners of the land and how the land was conveyed to them..

Many men who served in the War received land grants from the Federal Government; at times this land was in areas other than where they lived. There were young men who met the requirements for the land grants (land warrants) who wanted money in their pockets quickly and sold their promise of warrants cheaply. As in many situations, unethical men could be easily found to take advantage of these young men.

The deed for the land that Daniel received or purchased from his father, or someone else, may have recorded that one of the prior owners received it in a land grant from the King of England and someone down the line either did not understand or misread the deed. Of course, subsequent deeds may have omitted some pertinent information in describing the history of the land which made it appear that Daniel received the land from the King. These early abstracts present a wonderful history of the land and the descriptions over time became shorter and shorter and eventually led to the deeds we have today which do not include the names of several prior owners.

Daniel's father-in-law, **Solomon Sessoms (1753-16 August 1832)**, served in the Revolutionary War for a total of 13 months and received two certificates for his service: one for 85 pounds specie and one for 372 pounds currency. By Acts of Congress on 7 June 1832, in July 1836 and in March 1837, widows and orphans were entitled to balance of money due a pensioner. Solomon's widow, Obedience (nee Baker), applied on 23 February 1837 for his pension at her age of 74 and her application was returned for better identification of Solomon and more marriage information. She did finally receive a pension and died 17 February 1846.

Listed in the 1850 census for Sampson County, North Carolina, with Daniel, (Sr.), aged 72, (blacksmith), and his wife, Elizabeth, aged 61, were: "Elizabeth," aged 33, most likely a daughter; Daniel (Jr.), 28; Milsey, 26; Matthew, 24; Sarah, 13, James, 6, Dicey, aged 1. Daniel, Sr.'s wife, Elizabeth appears to have been too old to have been the mother of Sarah, James (he appears later as James F.), and Dicey and I have not determined the names of their parents. They might have been the children of an older deceased son of Daniel, Sr.

Daniel, Jr., aged 35, (cooper), was head of household in 1860 and listed with him were: his mother, Elizabeth Holland, 67; "Betsey," 33, (weaver), (possibly, Daniel's sister who was actually about 43 years); Wesley, 29, (weaver); James F., 17, (laborer); Dicy A., 13, and Cherry, 8.

James F. Holland, born about 1843, served as Musician-fifer during the Civil War in Co. I, Regt. 46, Infantry. He enlisted on 1 September 1861 in Clinton, North Carolina and was promoted March-April 1862 to Musician-fifer. Pension records show he was wounded at Fort Caswell on 15 September 1861. He surrendered 9 April 1865 at Appomattox Court House, Virginia.

One "**JAMES F. HOLLAND**" was buried in The Old Mill Church of God Cemetery on Penny Tew Mill road (SR 1456) 3.5 miles from Highway 242. He was born 16 June 1812 and died 9 March 1909. I have not found him in the 1880 and 1900 census records, which leads me to believe that either the year of birth in the transcribed census records may be incorrect or he moved from the area after 1870. This older James may be Daniel's son, James listed below.

In 1870, Elizabeth was listed as aged 70; she was more likely about 80 years old. Living with her were: "Elizabeth," 52; Milzie, 45; Cherry, 20 and Dicey, 21 Milzie was not listed in 1860, but was listed as "Milsey," aged 26 in 1850.

"Daniel Hollan" (sic) was listed in the 1830 census of Sampson County, North Carolina as 50-60 years with two males under 5; four males 5-10; two males 10-15; one male 15-20 and one male 20-30. Also one female (Elizabeth?) 40-50; one female under 5; one female 10-15; two females 15-20 and one female 20-30 for a total of 17 in the household. This 1830 census clearly indicates that I have been unable to identify three sons and three daughters of Daniel and Elizabeth. Tradition says that either Daniel and Elizabeth or their son, Harfrey had 17 children. It is difficult to correlate names with ages in these early census records.

March 1820: John Dickson sold 92 acres to Daniel Holland for the sum of $23. ... on east side of Little Cohary Swamp...JOHN HARE'S (HAIR(R) new line.

3 January 1827: Jacob Cooper to Daniel Holland, three tracts for $100. 64 1/2 acres; 4 1/2 acres; 60 acres. Deed mentions run of Great Cohary, T. Crumpler and Cooper's corners, west side of Great Cohary to Crumpler's line....Burnt Island ... to the run of the Swamp.

Daniel Holland sold 242 acres in three tracts on 23 February 1846 to Harphrey (Harfrey) Holland, his son, for the sum of $138.50. Deed mentions Catharine William's corner and the east side of Little Coharie. Proven in May Court Term 1846. Registered 16 July 1846.

In the 1850 Federal Census for Sampson County, North Carolina, Elizabeth (nee Sessoms) Holland was listed as aged 61; in 1860, aged 67, in 1870, she was listed aged 70 and head of household. In 1880 her age was listed as 92 and she was living next door to her son, Harfrey.

The Revolutionary War Pension records for Solomon Sessoms, show that Elizabeth Sessoms, born 27 September 1789, married a "Mr. Holland." The age for Elizabeth, noted as the wife of Daniel Holland in several census records appears to confirm this.

It appears that Daniel and Elizabeth's granddaughter, "Dicy A." who was born about 1846, married her cousin, "JOEL HOLLAND," who was born about 1844, son of John Holland and Dicey Autry, and was probably the "Dicy A. Holland" listed as head of household in 1900 in Honeycutts Township, Sampson County, North Carolina. Listed with Dicy A. was a son, Malet, born in February 1880 and they were living next door to Alger Rose Holland and his first wife, Ida E., and were two doors from Amma Holland, son of Harfrey.

Children of Daniel Holland and Elizabeth Sessoms are:

+ 14 i. **Unknown Child Holland**, born about 1802 in Sampson County, North Carolina.

15 ii. **Unidentified Son Holland**, born between 1805-1815.

16 iii. **Three Unidentified Female Holland**, born between 1805-1815 in Sampson County, North Carolina.

+ 17 iv. **James Holland**, born about 1809 in Sampson County, North Carolina; died after 1880.

18 v. **One Unidentified Male Holland**, born between 1815-1820 in Sampson County, North Carolina.

+ 19 vi. **Harfrey Holland,** born 1816 in Sampson County, North Carolina; died 07 June 1896 in Sampson County, North Carolina.

+ 20 vii. **Elizabeth Holland**, born about 1817 in Sampson County, North Carolina; died after 1880.

+ 21 viii. **Unidentified Child Holland**, born about 1820 in Sampson County, North Carolina.

+ 22 ix. **Thomas James Holland, Sr.**, born 05 February 1821 in Sampston County, North Carolina; died between 1850 - 1860.

23 x. **Maria Holland**, born about 1822 in Sampson County, North Carolina. She married Edwin Green Adams.

+ 24 xi. **Daniel Holland, Jr.**, born between 1822 - 1827 in Sampson County, North Carolina; died after 1880.

25 xii. **Milsey Holland**, born about 1824 in Sampson County, North Carolina, died after 1880 when she was living with her mother. She was, most likely, named for her maternal grandmother, Milley Boyett.

+ 26 xiii. **Nicholas Holland**, born 1826 in Sampson County, North Carolina; died 1886 in Sampson County, North Carolina.

+ 27 xiv. **Matthew Holland**, born about 1827 in Sampson County, North Carolina; died 07 April 1865 in Prison Camp, Elmira, New York.

28 xv. **Wesley Holland**, born about 1831 in Sampson County, North Carolina.

Wesley was not listed with Daniel in 1850, but was listed in the household of his brother, Danie, Jr., in 1860. Their mother was also listed as a widow. A possible sister, Elizabeth (listed as "Betsey) apppears to be listed with an incorrect age of 33. Wesley and his sister,

"Betsey" were weavers. in 1860. It is possible that "Betsey" was Wesley's wife, and not his sister.

I have found no other information about Wesley. My grandfather, Alger, had a brother named (John) Wesley Holland and Alger named his second son, John Wesley Holland.

29 xvi. **Sarah Holland**, born about 1837 in Sampson County, North Carolina.

4. Mary Holland (Thomas William^{2}, Unknown^{1}) was born About 1780, and died Bet. August 1832 - 1840. She married **Daniel Culbreth**, son of Neil Culbreth and Martha Autry. He was born about 1780, and died 1830.

Mary's middle initial is listed as "B" on some internet sources.

The following is entered in the **Old Holland Record Book** of Mary's father, Thomas:

"Tomzel Culbreath (12-17-1801.

"Millie Culbreath, Daughter of Daniel Culbreath and Mary born 7 Aug 1803 (or 1803).

"John Culbreath born August 1805"

The above three children are also found in the names on the stones in the Culbreth Cemetery near Roseboro. The records in the Old Holland Record Book, the names in the cemetery, and the deed recording Mary's father, Thomas, as a witness when Daniel Culbreth received a gift of land from his father, Neil, strongly support the marriage of Mary Holland to Daniel Culbreth. There is no other "known explanation" for Daniel Culbreth and Mary, his wife, and three of their children to have been recorded in the **Old Holland Record Book**.

An old Sampson County, North Carolina deed dated 15 August 1828 and recorded on page 8, Vol. 14, documents that Malcolm Peterson sold (?) to Flora McPhail for $45. The deed names Malcolm Peterson and Catherine Peterson, his wife, Allen Stewart and Nancy Stewart, his wife, Young Autry and his wife, Sarah Autry, and Flora McPhail and Elizabeth McPhail. Young Autry married Sarah McPhail. Perhaps there were two women named "Flora McPail" at the time; it appears that one was single, raising the question: Who was the Anne Flora McPhail who is said to have married Daniel Culbreth. Most likely, there were probably at least two or more Daniel Culbreths at the time.

More often researchers surmise that Daniel, son of Niell Culbreath, married Mary B. Maxwell. The "Daniel" who married Anne Flora McPhail (date of Bond was 08 November 1815 in Cumberland County, North Carolina) may have been a different Daniel. Mary Holland was listed in her father's will that was written in October 1919 and probated in November 1919. The will noted that Mary and her sisters had already received their share of his estate. Thomas Holland was the second witness on the Deed of Gift mentioned below, possibly meaning that he was a witness to protect the interest of his daughter. Of course, we can't ignore the possibility that Daniel was married twice and both wives were named "Mary." In that event,

"Mary Holland" was probably his first wife and, would explain why only three children were recorded in the **Old Holland Record Book**.

A "Culbreth Cemetery" is located on Marion-Amos Road (SR 1301) off Hwy 24, near Roseboro, North Carolina. Cora, John, Allen, Owen, Isaac, O.B., Ned and his wife, Nancy) and Roetta Culbreth are buried there. Only three stones have dates: O. B. Culbreth (Owen Bizzell Culbreth), 1 September 1874-4 November 1942. Nancy Culbreth (wife of Ned,) 30 November 1820-28 July 1899. Roetta Culbreth, died at age 77 on 10 March 1962. A sibling of my mother told me about this cemetery and she, my sister, brother-in-law, and I visited it. This appears to be a black Culbreth family, but my aunt probably was not aware of this. Ned Culbreth, aged 40, male, black, who worked in turpentine and wife, Nancy, aged 37, can be found in the 1870 census of Dismal Township, Little Coharie Township, Sampson County, North Carolina. The ages for Nancy and Ned in this census appear to be incorrect. Seven children were listed with them. At the time, a Native American who had a slightly dark complextion may have been identified as "black."

The following is found in transcribed deed abstracts:

"Deed of Gift: Niell Culbreath to Daniel Culbreath (his son). Dated: 20 November 1802. Daniel Culbreath was given 100 acres "On the East side of "South River and On the west side of the great swamp at a place called Heirs (sic) Fork beginning...about 100 yards from the Swamp and Runs up a small branch." Etc. land was "surveyed (23 February 1772) of which before the signing of these present I have delivered him...an inventory signed by my own hand. Witnesses: Archibald Culbreath and Thomas Holland." "Heirs Fork" mentioned above was likely, "Hair(r)'s Fork."

Orpah Holland married a "Hair."

Page 389 in the first Heritage book of Sampson County, North Carolina, has the following about Daniel Culbreth (born in 1780 and died in 1830):

"... His wife was Mary, surname unknown.

"Daniel Culbreth received on August 14, 1828 from the committee partitioning the lands of Neal (Neil) Culbreth, deceased, "Lot number 2 containing 188 acres on Little Mill Branch valued at $47." Daniel must have been in poor health some time before his father, Neil, died, for his brothers, Alexander and Cornelius, were appointed to administer Neil's estate in 1830, although they were younger than Daniel.

"The minutes of the Court of Pleas and Quarter Sessions contain several entries regarding the property of Daniel Colbreath. On November 15, 1830, the Sampson County Court "Ordered that letters of Administration on the estate of Daniel Culbreath, deceased, be granted to Joel Williams and Young Autry on their entering into bond in the sum of three thousand dollars with John Williams, Raiford Faircloth and Nicholas Sessoms as their securities.

"... November the 3rd 1830. This is to certify that I, Mary Colbraith, widow of Daniel Colbraith deceased, do give into the hands of two sons-in-law, Young Autry and Joel Williams, the whole of the Administration of my husbands property. Signed: Mary (her (X) mark) Colbreath.

"... On motion of petition ordered that William Hall Esqr. Raiford Faircloth and Daniel Williams be a committee to lay off and allot to Mary Culbreath widow of Daniel Culbreath deceased her years allowance of the crop, Stock and provisions of her late husband, deceased."

"The Sampson County Court on August 20, 1832 "Ordered that David Underwood, James White, John C. Williams, Raiford Faircloth, and William Maxwell be a committee to divide the lands and negroes of the estate of Daniel Colbreath Deceasedd." Their report of October 20, 1832, with Charles Butler acting in lieu of David Underwood, was submitted to the November Term 1832 and can be found in Sampson County Deed Book 22, pages 409 to 414.

"Lot No 1 designated as the old Hundred, including the Mansion House (incumbred with the Widow's Dower) and containing 148 acres valued at 50.1/100 (sic) and was appropriated to Young Autry in right of his wife, Millzy, Daughter of said deceased (and Negro girl Jula valued to $200). ... Lot No. 2 containing 2 Fifty acre grants, Consolidated the old lines Containing 87 and 71 acres, was allotted and drawn by John Colbreath, son of said deceased and valued to $62.50 the 87 acres on the East & 71 acres on the west of the Great Swamp (and Violet valued to $300). ... Lot No 3 containing 97 acres denominated (sic) (called?) the road tract, valued to $25 and was allotted and drawn by Tomzelle Williams. wife of Joel Williams & daughter of said deceased (and Hager & Samuel valued to $100). ... Lot No 4 Containing 100 acres adjoining Lot No 3 & Lewis Lucas lines & valued to $25 was allotted and drawn by Daniel Maxwell Colbreath son of said deceased (and man Arch valued to $350). ... Daniel Maxwell Colbreath, miner (his Guardian Joel Williams) received from the (more) valuable dividend or dividends the sum of $15.61 3/4 cents (on the land and pays out $112.50 on the negroes). ... Girl Ren, valued to $300 was allotted and drawn by Mary Colbreath. Widow of said deceased."

"The 1830 Census lists Mary Colbreath as head of household, it appearing that Daniel, although listed in the household, was incapacitated or sick (possibly consumption?). Daniel died after June 1, the census date, and probably after August 16, the date the August Court Term 1830 met, but before November 3, the date of his widow's statement. His widow, Mary, apparently died between August 1832 and 1840 as she has not been located in that census.

"Daniel and Mary had six children."

One of the earlier NEIL GALBRETH's (Culbreth) home was located about three miles in a southeasterly direction from Graham's Bridge and about three miles in a northeasterly direction from the present Clement community near the headwaters of Jones Swamp in Dismal Township, Sampson County, North Carolina. It was about three miles east of Hugh Bain's house, and about one mile east of the Hayes Mill site where today S.R. 1445 crosses Jones Swamp. An exact location has not been determined. This appears to be the home of Daniel's great-grandfather.

Children of Mary Holland and Daniel Culbreath are:

+ 30 i. **Tomzelle Culbreth,** born 17 December 1801 in Sampson County, North Carolina; died 1834 in Green County, Georgia.

+ 31 ii. **Millzy Adelme Culbreth,** born 07 August 1803 in Sampson County, North Carolina; died Bet. 1860 - 1870.

+ 32 iii. **John B. Culbreth,** born 22 August 1805 in Sampson County, North Carolina; died 1854.

33 iv. **Daughter Culbreth,** born between 1810 - 1820 in Sampson County, North Carolina; died before 1830.

34 v. **Son Culbreth,** born between 1810 - 1820 in Sampson County, North Carolina; died before 1830.

+ 35 vi. **Isaac Culbreth, Sr.,** born about 1816 in Sampson County, North Carolina; died before 1900 in Eastover Township, Cumberland County, North Carolina.

+ 36 vii. **Daniel Maxwell Culbreth,** born 13 October 1820 in Sampson County, North Carolina; died 21 February 1865 in Elmira, New York.

8. Orpah Holland (Thomas William[2], Unknown[1]) was born 27 February 1791, and died between 1860 - 1870 in Sampson County, North Carolina. She married **John Athae Hair, Jr.,** son of John Hair and Elizabeth Unknown. He was born 1790, and died between 1846 - 1850 in Sampson County, North Carolina.

See notes for her sister, Millie.

One source shows Orpah's name as "Obedience (Beady). I have found no other record to support that, but it is possible the "**Beady Hair,**" aged 70, listed in the household of her son, **Allen Hair** in the 1880 census records for Sampson County, North Carolina has been mistaken for Orpah. That Beady Hair was "Obedience Howard" wife of Thomas Hair and in 1870, "Beedee Hairr," aged 65 was listed in the household of her son, Daniel Hairr, aged 25, in Sampson County. Census enumerators sometimes, so much altered a name that it wasn't even close to the name it should be.

Her birth of 27 February 1791 is recorded in the **Old Holland Record Book** of her parents. A transcribed copy of the 1850 census for Sampson County gives 55 for "Orphy's" age. The census for 1860 shows age 63 for "Orpha" and age 43 for her daughter, Nancy (Nanny.) Both of them were listed in the household of "Daniel Hair", aged 41, and his wife "Lucindy," aged 34 in Honeycutts Township, Sampson County, North Carolina. This Daniel, most likely, was Orpah's son and his wife "Lucindy (Lucindia, Lucinda) Holland," was the daughter of Henry Holland, Orpah's brother, and would have been Daniel's first cousin. Orpah (Orphy) was not listed in 1870 Federal Census.

The Sampson County, North Carolina, certificate of death for George W. Hair records "Daniel Hair" and "Lucindia Holland" for his parents. This certificate of death, census records and the data in the **Old Holland Record Book** support the data noted here. Images from this old record book may be found near the back of this book.

"**GUIlFORD HAIR**," is mentioned in the will of his grandfather, **William Hair (William Hare)**, a Revolutionary soldier. A report on the sale of property belonging to the estate of William Hair, deceased, was returned to court on 17 February 1829. In 1825, provisions were set aside for Harriet Hair, widow of William. William Hair, (Jr.), Arthur Hair, Felix Hair and Nathan Hale (Hair?) were also mentioned. This Guilford Hair, most likely, was a cousin of John Athae Hair, Jr. Some researchers who have posted data on the internet have inconsistent data about the early "John Hairs" and about **Guilford Hair** and **Gilmore Hair**.

OPRILLA HOLLAND: Page 419 in *The Heritage of Sampson County, North Carolina, 1784-1984,* Editor, Oscar M. Bizzell, reveals that a '"John Athae Hare" born 1790 and wife "OPRILLA," born 1797, were parents of **Stephen Hare**. Stephen Hare was born 12 March 1821 and died 21 May 1881 --- James Elmon Hairr and Rossie Hairr Floyd" submitted this profile on the "Hare Family" and state that the data for John Athae Hare and his wife Oprilla is found in their Family Bible. Stephen's date of birth was also recorded in the **Old Holland Record Book** of Thomas William Holland.

Sampson County court records indicate the Hair(r)s mentioned above lived in the same area as John, Henry and Thomas Holland. The Hollands and Hairs sold land to each other and worked together on the maintenance of the roads and rivers in the area where they lived.

One "**Orphia Holland**" is noted in the court Minutes of Sampson County, North Carolina as having a child by Resin Faircloth. "11-14-1809. Wednesday. Rezin Faircloth came into court as he was bound to do, being charged with begetting a ...child on the body of ORPHIA Holland. Ordered he enter into bond of 200 pounds to keep said ...child from becoming in any ways chargeable to the county. Securities were Robert Magee and William Honeycutt." I have not identified this child.

Listed with Holland Hair, aged 33, a cooper, in the 1860 Federal census of Sampson County, North Carolina, were his wife, Lydia, A. aged 27; Lassister, 8; Jonathan, 4; James, 2; Frances A., 1 month. Holland and his family were living in Dwelling 372 in Hawleys Store, Dismal Township in 1860. His name, age and location of his dwelling lead me to believe that Holland may have been a son of Orpah Holland and John Athae Hair, Jr. or perhaps a nephew, but I have no proof. Holland was a Pvt., in Co. F, Regt 20, Inf, during the Civil War. The transcribed war record gives 1837 for his year of birth indicating that either 1837 or his age of 33 in the 1860 census was incorrect He enlisted on 1 August 1861 at Fort Johnston, was wounded in left arm 17 September 1862 at Sharpsburg, Maryland, captured 19 October 1864 at Cedar Creek, Virginia, and confined to Point Lookout, Maryland. A.W.O.L from 1 December 1862 to 1 June 1864. He was received 30 March 1865 at Boulware's Wharf, Virginia for exchange.

Holland and Lydia were living in Elizabethtown, Bladen County, North Carolina in 1870 with children listed above and Holland, Jr., aged 6. Holland and "Liddy Ann" Hare and all their children except Lassister were living and farming near Clinton, Sampson County, North Carolina, in 1880.

In the **Old Holland Record Book**, the name for John Athae Hair is written as "Jonathan." "John Athae" can sound like the name "Jonathan" when spoken. He may have first married

Millie Holland and then married her sister Orpah and perhaps some of the children listed for Orpah are actually the children of Millie who was alive when their father's will went to probate in November 1819. See notes for Millie Holland.

There appears to be some confusion about which "John Hairr" donated land in 1840 for a school.

The 1830 census of Sampson County records that John, Jr. had six sons and three daughters. Also living in his household in 1830 were one female between the age of 40-50 and one between the age of 50-60. The older female may have been a sister of Orpah.

Children of Orpah Holland and John Athae Hair are:

37 i. **Female Hairr**, born before 1815 in Sampson County, North Carolina.

38 ii. **Nancy Hairr**, born about 1817 in Sampson County, North Carolina; died after 1880. In 1850, Nancy, aged 33, was in the household of her mother, "Orphy Hair" and her brother, Gilmore, and sister, Mary, were still at home. In 1860, "Orpha"(sic), aged 63 and "Nanny," aged 43, were in the household of Orpah's son, Daniel.

She apparently was the "**Nannie Hairr**," aged 54, listed with Blackman (Blackmon) Hair, son of her brother, Stephen, in the 1870 census. **Joel Hairr**, aged 14, was listed with them and appears to have been Nancy's son. See notes below for his sister, Mary.

\+ 39 iii. **Daniel L. Hairr**, born about 1819 in Sampson County, North Carolina, died 17 November 1862 in Hospital in Farmville, Virginia.

\+ 40 iv. **Stephen H. Hairr**, born 12 March 1821 in Sampson County, North Carolina, died 21 May 1881.

\+ 41 v. **Holland Hairr**, born about 1827 in Sampson County, North Carolina, died before 1900.

\+ 42 vi. **Gilmore Hairr** was born between 1828 - 1832 in Sampson County, North Carolina.

\+ 43 vii. **John C. Hair**, born about 1829 in Sampson County, North Carolina, and died of disease in 1865 in New Hanover County, North Carolina.

44 viii. **Unidentified Son Hairr**, born before 1830 in Sampson County, North Carolina.

45 ix. **Mary Jane Hairr**, born about 1830 (or 1835) in Sampson County, North Carolina. Records support her marriage to **Thomas Gautier** who was born about 1830.

In 1880, **Thomas Gotiere** (sic) (**Thomas Gautier**, born about 1830 and Mary J., born about 1835 were recorded in the town of Clinton, Sampson County, North Carolina, with seven children all listed with the surname spelled "Gotiere": 1) **Alexander Gautier**, born 1859; 2) **Orpe E. Gautier;** born about 1862; 3) **Mary F. Gautier**, born about 1864; 4) **John Thomas Gautier**, born about 1867; 5) **William Henry Gautier**; born about 1869; 6) **Molsie A. Gautier**, (**MOLCY ANN GAUTIER**) born about 1872, and 7) **Nancy J. Gautier**, born about 1874.

The following sketch appeared in *The Caucasian* newspaper, Clinton, North Carolina, Thursday, August 1, 1889. Vol. VII # 42. The newspaper presented biographical sketches of the owners of businesses in the town of Clinton, North Carolina:

"Thomas Gautier was born in Honeycutt's Township, Sampson County, July 14, 1830. After age twenty-one, he spent four years wagoning (driving a wagon) in Bladen, Robeson, and Columbus Counties. He returned to Sampson and was married to Miss **Mary Jones Hair** (sic) in 1856, by John C. Williams, Esq. During the year 1861, he acted as overseer for Thomas I. Faison. In 1862 he volunteered and entered the Confederate Army. Since, he has been a tenant of Mssrs. William Kirby, E. L. Faison and others, all of whom consider him as strickly honest, a first-class farmer, and one of their best tenants. He came to Clinton in 1885, opened a business on the corner of Elm and Railroad streets.

"Mr. Gautier has a noted cider resort, and probably sells more than any man in the place. He always keeps a good article and his customer have confidence in him and his cider. He also keeps flour, snuff, candies, peanuts, etc." Transcribed ***Nineteenth Century Vital Statistics of Sampson County and Duplin County, North Carolina. 1871 – 1891,*** by Bradley Lee West records the above biographical sketch about Mr. Gautier.

Mary was living with her son, William in 1910. The "**Jones**" in her name listed in the biographical sketch above, appears to be incorrect. "JANE" was probably spelled incorrectly in either the newspaper or in the transcribed record.

Mr. Bradley Lee West also records in his book that an announcement appeared in *The Caucasion,* Clinton, North Carolina, Thursday, July 16, 1891, Vol. IX # 40: "Mr. Thomas Gautier celebrated his 61st birthday on lst Tuesday, July 14th. He had a number of his friends and relatives to dinner."

NANNIE HARE (NANCY HAIR), Sister-in-law, was in the household of Thomas and Mary in 1880. The ages of Mary and Nancy (Nannie) support their being the daughters of John Athae Hairr, Jr., and Orpah Holland.

Molcy Ann Gautier, named above, married **Loyd Paschail Holland**, son of **Susan McCullen** and her second husband, **William Holland**, who are listed elsewhere in this book.

9. Millie Holland (Thomas William[2], Unknown[1]) was born 15 January 1793. She may have died before 1827. She married **(1) Cornelius Autry** before. 1811, son of Cornelius Autry and Sophia Keen. He was born about 1772. She married **(2) Jonathan Hare** about 1812. He was born between 1780 - 1790.

Her father's **Old Holland Record Book** notes "Thomas Hare, son of Jonathan Hare and Mille, his mother, was born October 3, 1812." Written in the Old Holland Record Book is "Sterling Autry, son of Cornelius Autry and Mille, his mother, was born 1811." Also copied from the record book is "Steven Autry, son of Cornelius Autry and Mille." The writing in this old record book is faded, but enough data can be read to confirm and link records from elsewhere, and most likely, "Steven" was "Sterling" or "Starling." **Sterling Autry**, age 38, was listed in the 1850 census for Sampson County, North Carolina; this census and other records show his wife as Anna Minerva McPhail; other records reveal 30 December1811 for his date of birth. Data posted on the internet name **Theophilus Autry** for the father of Starling (Sterling), not Cornelius as mentioned in the **Old Holland Record Book**. Therefore, there may have been two men named "Sterling (or Starling) Autry;" one, the son of Theophilus and the other the son of Cornelius Autry and Millie Holland The will of Theophilus Autry names Starling for his son.

Records in the **Old Holland Record Book** mentioned above indicate that Millie may have been married twice or Cornelius was the father of Starling (Sterling) and he and Millie were not married. She may have first married Cornelius Autry and they had a son, Sterling (Starling) Autry on 30 December 1811. Cornelius may have died around the time Sterling was born and Millie then married Jonathan Hare (Hairr) and their son, Thomas Hare (Hairr), was born on 3 October 1812. We could say that Millie Holland and Cornelius Autry's son Sterling died young, but I do not think that he did. The date of birth for their son in the old record book of Millie's father and the **date found in sources on the internet** for Sterling Autry the son of Theophilus Autry and Elizabeth Crumpler**, is the same date**! It is highly unlikely that those who posted the data on the internet are even aware of the **Old Holland Record Book.** Autry is spelled "**Autrey**" in this Book.

Thomas Yrarebery" is written on one page of the Old Holland Record Book and **Yearbary Autrey** is recorded on the left page of the image. **Yarboro, Yarbough** or **Yarbrough** is probably the name the writer attempted to record and I have no idea whether the Yarbrough family was connected to the Holland.or Autry families. Was **Yearbary Autrey** a son of Milly and Cornelius?

I have wondered whether **Jonathan Hare** and John Athae Hairr were the same person. Say "John Athae" fast and it sounds like "Jonathan." Milly"s sister, Orpah, married John Athae Hairr. Both Milly and Orpah were mentioned in their father's will. Therefore, if Jonathan and John Athae were the same person, Milly would have died between November 1819 - 1827 and she would have been the mother of some of the children listed for Orpah. See notes for Orpah. However, it is possible that she and **Jonathan Hare** had other children.

Mr. Bundy in his history of the Autry family notes on page 100 that he had been able to locate only one child of Cornelius Autry and Sophia. However, on page 200 he writes that this Cornelius Autry was the son of Cornelius Autry and Sophia (?) and the brother of Theophilus Autry." See will below.

The 1784 tax records of Sampson County, North Carolina, listed: Cornelius Autry, 100-1-0; Cornelius Autry, 100-1-0; Isham Autry, 0-1-0; John Autry, 100-1-0; Theophilus Autry, 100-1-0. "Cornelius" was listed in the Cumberland County, North Carolina taxables of 1815.

The will of one "Cornelious" Autery is on page 200 of Mr. Bundy's book. It was signed on November 19, 1820 and reads:

"Last will and testament of Cornelius Autery of the County of Cumberland and State of North Carolina. I, Cornelious Autery....

" ... First I (give) ... unto my beloved wife, "Clody Autery," all my property consisting of personal and real estate during her natural lifetime to dispose of as she sees proper except my lands and negroes. At the death of my wife, Cloldy Autery, my negroe boy, Pompe, to be set free and likewise my negroe, Guirly Mories, to be set free.

"Also at the death of my wife, Cloldy Autery, the lands whereon I now live is to be sold and the money to be divided equally among my brothers and sisters.

"Also I (give) to (Cloldy's brother ?) half of that track of land above (_?_)

"Also I give unto all my heirs fifty cents, which sums of money is to be paid within six months after my death and lastly as to all the rest ... to my wife.

"Executor: Daniel Maxwell 19th day of November ... 1820

"Witt: Joseph Chaston X signed Cornelius Autery (Seal)

John Steling X

Joseph Chaston Junior X"

Mr. Bundy notes on page 102 about this other Cornelious Autry: "It would appear that this Cornelius Autry with wife, (Choldy) (or Chloe), was a son of either William, Cornelius, or Isam Autry since the children of John, Theophilus, and Drury are listed in their wills and none of them had a child named Cornelius."

Records indicate there were probably at least three men with the name "Cornelius" (or Cornelious) Autry in Sampson County between 1770 and 1832. An older one married Sophia Keen, another married Cloldy (maiden name unknown), as named in the above will, and the third married Millie Holland as recorded in the old record book of Millie's father. Who were the parents of the "Cornelius Autry" who married Millie?

Listed in the household of Jonathan Hare in 1830 were two males under 5, two males 5-10, one male 15-20 and one male 40-50. Also listed were one female under 5, one female 5-10, one female 15-20 and one female 30-40 for a total of 10.

Child of Millie Holland and Cornelius Autry is:

\+ 46 i. **Starling Autry**, born 30 December 1811 in Cumberland County, North Carolina; died October 1897.

Child of Millie Holland and Jonathan Hare is:

47 i. **Thomas Hare**, born 03 October 1812. See notes for Millie's father, Thomas.

It appears that he married **Belinda Howard.** A deed of 25 May 1835 supports the marriage of Thomas and Belinda and indicates she may have been either the daughter or sister of **Benjamin Howard.** See notes below for Henry Holland and his wife, Mary Tew.

11. Thomas James Holland (Thomas William[2], Unknown[1]) was born 30 April 1797. His wife is not known.

An unknown submitter has provided a short family tree history on Ancestry.com for a **"Milly Holland"** who was born in1820 in Sampson County, North Carolina, and died 30 June 1890 in Grady, Alabama. **Thomas Holland and Milly** are entered for her parents. It is noted that Milly married **James H. Howell** about 1838 in Sampson County, North Carolina, son of Osborn Howell, Jr. and **Nancy Strickland.** James was born 1 May 1812 in "W. (western?) North Carolina," and died 2 July 1908 in Grady, Alabama. Milly and James' son, **James Arthur Howell,** was born 8 January 1850 in W. North Carolina and died 18 March 1915 in Rose Hill, Alabama. James Arthur married **Arkansas Missouri Sweat** on 11 January 1880 in Alabama; she was born 18 December 1854 in Alabama and they had a son, **James Franklin Howell** who was born 9 October 1882 in Ramar, Alabma, and died 15 November 1964 in Lake Wales, Florida. James Franklin married **Mary Clara Shields** on 25 December 1901 in Rose Hill, Alabama; she was born 17 August 1884 in Ramar, Alabama.

Another researcher submitted a tree named Robert Allen Kelly. The Robertallenkelley/ Kelly/O'Kelley Tree names **James H. Howell** and **Milly Holland** with ten children:

1) **William T. Howell** was born 1837. 2) **John Howell**, born 1840. 3) **Sallie Howell** born 1844. 4) **Mary Howell,** born 1846. 5) **Ann Howell**, born 1848. 6) **James Arthur Howell** 1850-1915. 7) **Samuel Howell,** born 1854. 8) **Nancy Ann Howell**, born 1856. 9) **Porter Howell**, born 1857. 10) **Robert Howell**, born 1860. I found nine of these children listed with James and "Milley" in the 1860 Federal Census of the 2nd District in Montgomery, County, Alabama, (town of Ramar, Alabama). In 1900, James Howell and his second wife, Martha J. Kirksey (Kirksey probably her married name), with his stepson, Morgan Kirksey, were in Dublin, Montgomery County, Alabama.

   Osborn Howell, aged 30-39 and his spouse, aged 20-29, can be found in the 1830 Federal Census of Johnson County, North Carolina, with two males and two females under five, one male 5-9, one male 10-14 and one female 15-19. **James H. Howell,** named above, may have been the son listed as aged 10-14 in this census, but he would have been a little older; there is also the possibility that he could have been bound out to learn a trade.

The history by the unknown researcher continues with the 25 December 1901 marriage of **James Franklin Howell** to **Mary Clara Shields** who was born 17 August 1884 in Ramar Alabama. Children named for James Franklin and Mary are: 1) **Lula Mae Howell** born 30 May 1903. 2) **Living Howell.** 3) **Wilbur Buren Howell, Sr.** born 16 May 1905. 4) **Gladys Rebecca Howell** born 5 December 1908. 5) **Martha Estelle Howell** born 15 October 1910 in Covington, Alabama. 6) **Vernon Cleo Howell** who was born 3 October 1910. 7) **James Oliver Howell** was born 9 April 1915 in Rose Hill, Alabama. 8) **Living Howell.** 9) **Living Howell.** This tree also appears to have descendants of several of these nine children.

I have not pursued further research on the descendants of Milly Holland and James H. Howell and add **Milly Holland** and **James H. Howell** here in the event that "Milly" may be connected to our Holland line. **Thomas James Holland** appears to be the Thomas who would be the right age to have had a daughter born in 1820. Six of the children of James Franklin and Mary also have families that can be found on Ancestry.com. Someone eventually may also find that the Osborn Howell family may be linked to the Howells in eastern Cumberland County, North Carolina. My grandfather, Alger Rose Holland, (see elsewhere in this book) married Ella Jane Howell, daughter of David James Howell and Catherine Carter, of Cumberland County.

The children below are the only ones referenced in the Old Holland Record Book of Thomas William Holland and I had been unable to find other data for the family, but the data above may indicate that he and his family left Sampson County a few years after his father died.

Children of Thomas James Holland is:

i. **Willis Holland** who was born about 1817 and his descendants lived in Duplin and Sampson County, North Carolina. The will of his grandfather, Thomas William Holland, written in October 1819, leaves a feather bed and furniture to Willis Holland, son of Thomas James Holland.

ii. **MILLY HOLLAND,** born about 1820 may have been a daughter. She may have been a daughter and may have married **James H. Howell.** See above notes for Thomas James Holland.

48 iii. **Henry William Holland,** born 15 January 1821.

The **Old Holland Record Book** of Thomas William Holland, father of Thomas James, records that Henry William Holland, son of Thomas James was born 15 January 1821. I have found no other information for Henry William.

12. Henry Holland (Thomas William[2], Unknown[1]) was born 27 February 1801 in North Carolina, and died between1860 - 1870 in Sampson County, North Carolina. He married **Mary Tew** about 1825, daughter of John Tew and Patience Blackman. She was born 18 May 1806 in Sampson County, North Carolina, and died between 1870 - 1880 in Sampson County, North Carolina.

The names and dates of birth for Henry and Mary's children and a few other descendants are recorded in the **Old Holland Record Book.** Images from that record book may be found near the back of this book.

Monday, 19 August 1822. "**Ordered Bluford Hairr** be overseer of the river beginning at Gabriel Holmes' Mill to Capt. Hall's River and that Owen Owens, Daniel Owen, Henry Owen, Alex Fisher, Thomas Howard, ... Henry Holland, ... work with the usual hands."

Monday, 18 November 1822."Ordered William Vann be overseer of the road instead of Owen Crumpler and Henry Holland, Jonathan Hairr and the usual hands work under him."

In 1826 "Henry Holland," John Crumpler, Blackman Crumpler, Owen Crumpler, ..., Capt. Cooper..., Privates under Capt. Hartwell Porter; each served guard duty for one night.

Transcribed Court Minutes of Tuesday, 22 August 1826. Sampson County, North Carolina: Guards for the Jail: "...And it also appearing that Capt. Hartwell Porter and the following men as his privates: John Crumpler, Blackman Crumpler, Owen Crumpler, Edward Brown, Henry Porter and Henry Holland were regularly called out and each served as a guard for one night. Ordered, therefore, that Capt. Cooper be allowed for four nights at the rate of $1.50 and he received $6. His men should receive $1 each..."

Saturday, 23 February 1828. "Overseers: ... Martin Hairr for that part of the River Coharie from Gabriel Holmes' Landing to Raiford Coore's Upper Landing with the following hands to work: GILFORD HAIRR, ...JONATHAN HAIRR, HENRY HOLLAND, William C. Hairr, Ollen Hairr and Minson Howard's hands."

5 February 1841: Henry Holland sold his interest in all the lands on the East or lower Ssde of the Black Branch to Love Culbreth for $50. No acreage given.

A deed dated **25 May 1835** between the Heirs of **Benjamin Howard**, deceased, to **John Howard**, (Deed Book 24, page 328) mentions the heirs as "Henry Holland and his wife Mary Holland (FORMERLY **Mary Howard**), **Thomas Hair** and his wife, Belinda, and **Sally Howard** ... for the sum of one dollar and fifty cents in hand paid by the said **John Howard**.... containing eighty nine acres... it being their **undivided shares** of said tract of land as the lawful representatives of B. Howard." Land lay on the east side of Little Coharie...on the south side of a branch "a little above Jacob Sessoms.'" Deed also mentions Crumpler's line and corner.

The above mentioned deed of 1835 has led some to question whether Mary Tew was the wife of Henry Holland. It leads me to believe that Mary Tew may have first married a Howard (probably Benjamin Howard as his second or third? wife), but I haven't found a record of any children they may have had. **Benj. Howard, between 26-44 years of age, was listed in the 1810 Federal Census for Sampson County and lived two doors from Daniel Holland, Henry's brother. Benj. (Benjamin?) was the only male in the household and with him were two females under 10 years of age, indicating his wife was deceased.**

I have not been able to link the above mentioned "John Howard" to parents and in the event that he was the son of Benjamin Howard and Benjamin married Mary 'TEW,' **she would have been too young to have been the mother of John** and most likely would have been his third wife .

Benjamin Holland, listed as the oldest child of Henry and Mary might have been a "Howard." Benjamin Howard may have willed land to Mary for her use during her natural life or widowhood and/or she could have been appointed guardian for Benjamin's children. His will also could have stipulated that the children were to receive the property when they became of age.

Henry Holland sold 106 acres on 22 February 1856 to **Jacob C. Howard** for $250. Deed mentioned Martin Hair's old line, Nixon Cooper's line and the east side of Little Coharie. This may have been the Jacob Howard, aged 31, listed in the 1850 census with wife, Elizabeth, 21, with two children.

Another source links Mary as the daughter of Minson Brough Howard, Sr. and his second wife, Dorcus. Records show that women named Mary (nee Howard) of that period married others. Minson, Sr. and his first wife had a daughter named Mary Elizabeth who was born in 1796 and she married Thomas Sessoms Parker. "Benjaman Howard" was at least, aged 21 when he witnessed a deed dated 5 November 1801 from Minson Howard (Jr.) and Dorcus Howard (his wife) to John Simmons, Jr., **meaning he was born by 1780. Mary Tew was born in 1806**. Minson Howard, Sr. can be found in the 1800 Federal Census of Sampson County, aged 26-44 with a spouse 26-44. They had 2 sons and 2 daughters under 10 and 3 sons and 2 daughters, 10-15 years of age. Data found on Ancestry.com notes that Ann Williams, Minson's first Wife died in 1799. He and his second wife, Dorcus (widow of James White, Sr.), had a son, Minson Brough, Jr., in January 1801, and she had two sons by her first husband, James White, deceased. The sons recorded in the 1800 census would have included Minson's three sons by Ann and his two stepsons, if both were still living, but if this was the case, it appears that the ages were incorrect; four sons were under 10 and one was 10-15.

It is interesting that Thomas Allen Howard, Sr. (15 January 1790-2 March 1875), son of Minson Brough Howard, Sr. and his first wife, Ann Williams, named a daughter, "Aholibah E. Howard" in 1818. The **Old Holland Record Book** records "**Aholabah Holland**," born 3 November 1843, daughter of Henry and Mary. **Aheliba** was listed for her name in the 1850 and 1860 census records for Sampson County, North Carolina. She is **listed as "Olivia" below**. See her notes elsewhere in this book for other various spellings of her name.

Mary (only her given name) and her year of birth are recorded in the **Old Holland Record Book** and a profile about Mary's parents and siblings was written for the first Heritage book of Sampson County in which a descendant of John Tew mentions her year of birth, her marriage to Henry Holland and notes that she and Henry had a large family in Sampson County, North Carolina. Mary's parents moved to Pike County, Alabama, in the late 1820s and to Barbour County, Alabama, about 1836 One of Mary's sisters married and settled in Cumberland County, North Carolina; another sister married Reason Lockerman and settled in Sampson County and one brother married Patience Tew (a cousin) and remained in Sampson.

The certificate of death for Henry's daughter, Orpah Caroline, who married Raeford Lockerman (later Lockamy), reveals the name "Mary Howard" for Caroline's mother. The certificate of death for Henry's son, Steven (Stephen) Senter, also states "Howard" for his mother. By naming only "Howard" for Stephen's mother, it appears that the informant, A. Butler, did not actually know the name of his mother. I have found that many informants for data on certificates of death did not know the actual maiden name of the mother of the individual who died. I am inclined to believe that Mary Tew probably first married a "Howard" as I have stated above, and they may have had children who were possibly either adopted or raised as children of Henry Holland. Were the first four children Howards? Mary, Millie, Nancy, Henry, John, Orpah and Stephen are all names found in the Holland families of North Carolina. The deed noted above mentions Benjaman Howard and the name "Benjamin" was not found in my Holland line except for Benjamin T. listed in the Old Holland Record Book who was the Benjamin listed as a son of Henry and Mary in the 1850 census.

On the 4 March 1851 Henry sold 153 acres to **Benjamin Holland** for $250. Two days later, Benjamin sold this same land to James White for $210. I have found no later record in Sampson County for Benjamin Holland.

Transcribed Revolutionary War records reveal another Henry Holland, served as a Private in the 10th North Carolina Continental Line:

"Soldier of Duplin County, North Carolina was listed as # 12 on the pay roll of Captain Elisha Rhodes' Company of the North Carolina Militia, commanded by Col. Sam Jarvis, dated 5 June 1780. On 14 September 1781, he enlisted as a private in Captain Coleman's Company of the 10th North Carolina Regiment for 12 months. He was listed as # 28 on the roll of Lieutenant Wilkinson's Company of the 10th Continental Line on 19 July 1782. He received voucher # 5778 from the Wilmington District and final settlement voucher # 1254 was taken for him by H. Montfort. He received pension # S 31759. On 10 October 1781, he received from Marmaduke Ryal (Royal(l) a deed for 100 acres in return for Holland's 12 months service in Ryal's place in the Continental Army.

"Soldier was born 1 March 1757 in Bertie County, North Carolina to Theophilous Holland. He married 2 September 1783 to Sarah Clay in Duplin County and had a number of real estate transactions in Sampson County before moving to Georgia in 1787. His and Sarah's children were: 1- David. 2- John. 3- Dempsey. 4- William. 5- Frederick. 6- Elizabeth. 7- Mary. 8- Sarah. And 9- James. Soldier died in Tattnall County, Georgia on 28 June 1852 and was buried in the Holland Family Cemetery now in Candler County."

Another "Henry Holland" (a third "Henry Holland") was old enough to be listed in the 1790 census of Sampson County, North Carolina, he had several deed transactions and served as constable in 1801, but I haven't found him in the 1830 census. He was probably born by 1776.

In the 1830 census for Sampson County, North Carolina, one "Henry" appears as head of household, under age thirty with one female under age thirty, one male under ten and two females under age five.

On 12 May 1837, Henry Holland sold 100 acres to John Holland (probably his brother). Dollar amount was blank, but it doesn't say this was a gift. Deed proven in May court Term 1837. Registered 29 June 1837.

Henry's daughter, Mary M. is listed in the **Old Holland Record Book** with a birth date of 15 April 1829; This is the only information I have for Mary and we know Henry recorded in this record book the names of his twins, Millie and Nancy, and their birth date of 22 September 1833. It is said that the twins died young.

Transcribed court minutes for Sampson County, North Carolina, show Henry often worked with others on roads, rivers, and streams and served on juries.

Children of Henry Holland and Mary Tew are:

49 i. **Benjamin T. Holland**, born 18 June 1825 in Sampson County, North Carolina.

'T' was listed for his middle initial in the **Old Holland Record Book**. On the 4 March 1851 Henry Holland sold 153 acres to Benjamin T. Holland, his son, for $250. Deed mentions land on the east side of Little Cohara...run of Little Cohara... Nixon Cooper's line. Benjamin sold this same land two days later to James White for $210. The sale to James White was registered the 28 of September 1852.

I have found no other records in Sampson County for Benjamin T. Holland and it appears that he either died, or moved from the area before 1860.

\+ 50 ii. **Lucinda Holland**, born 05 November 1826 in Sampson County; died after 1880 in Sampson County, North Carolina.

51 iii. **Mary M. Holland**, born 15 April 1829 in Sampson County, North Carolina.

52 iv. **Clarkey Matthew Holland**, born 14 June 1831 in Sampson County.

This name is listed as 'Clarky M.' and 'Clarkey Matthew' in the Old Holland Record Book. It is unclear whether this child was male or female. He/she was not listed with Henry and Mary in the 1850 census. Henry's brother, Daniel, also had a son named "Matthew" who was about three years older.

53 v. **Millie Holland**, born 22 September 1835 in Sampson County. Died young.

54 vi. **Nancy Holland**, born 22 September 1835 in Sampson County. Died young.

\+ 55 vii. **Henry Y. C. Holland**, born 26 March 1836 in Sampson County, North Carolina; died 15 May 1864 in Battle of Wilderness, Virginia.

56 viii. **John R. Holland**, born 12 May 1838 in Sampson County, North Carolina; died 03 May 1863 in Chancellorsville, Va..

The source for his date of death shows: "Holland, John R., Pvt., Co. A, Regt. 30, Infantry. Born 1840, Sampson Co. Farm laborer. Enlisted 1 September 1861, Clinton. Hospitalized 3 October 1862 at Richmond, Va. with wound of head. Killed 3 May 1863 at Chancellorsville, Virginia. Nominated for Badge of Distinction for gallantry at Chancellorsville."

His middle initial in the Old Holland Record Book appears to be "R." "John R." is entered in the 1860 Census for Sampson County, North Carolina.

57 ix. **Emphton B. Holland** is named in the Old Holland Record Book with a birth date of 26 October 1840 in Sampson County, North Carolina, and it appears that he died before 1850. His date of birth is also listed as 16 October 1840.

\+ 58 x. **Olivia Holland**, (**Aholabah Holland**), born 03 November 1843 in Sampson County; died 02 July 1913 in Sampson County, North Carolina.

\+ 59 xi. **Orpah Caroline Holland**, born 03 March 1846 in Sampson County, North Carolina; died 10 April 1925 in Cumberland County, North Carolina.

\+ 60 xii. **Stephen Senter Holland, Sr.**, born 24 June 1848 in Sampson County; died 07 November 1914 in Honeycutts Township, Sampson County, North Carolina.

\+ 61 xiii. **Alderman McKay Holland**, born 24 August 1852 in Sampson County, North Carolina; died 16 July 1925 in Little Coharie Township, Sampson County.

13. John Holland (Thomas William[2], Unknown[1]) was born about 1806, and died after 1870. He married **Dicey Autry** who was born between 1815 - 1820, and died after 1870.

I cannot say with certainty that Dicey's maiden name was Autry. John was mentioned in his father's will and the 1860 census for Sampson County, North Carolina, shows he and his brother, Henry, were living next door to each other. Next door to John was Daniel Hair and his wife, Lucinda, Henry's daughter. Daniel Hair was the son of Orpah, (Henry's and John's sister), and her husband, John Athae Hair, Jr. Daniel Holland, Jr., the son of Daniel Holland, brother of John, Henry and Orpah, was living nearby with his mother. John Holland was listed as aged 43 in the 1850 census for Sampson County, 54 in Honeycutts Township in 1860 and 64 in Honeycutts Township. In 1870 census records. John's son, Thomas B., could have been named for his grandfather and Charity was probably named for her Aunt.

On 29 December 1858, John Holland sold 100 acres to William R. and Thomas N. Culbreath for $59.75. Deed mentions East Side of Little Cohary and both sides of the Marsh Branch joining Thomas Hare's (Hairr) line and corner.

Sampson County, North Carolina court minutes of 18 February 1830, record that John Holland was "fined $.50 and stands committed until fine and costs are paid." He was fined for affray (fighting).

Children of John Holland and Dicey Unknown are:

62 i. **Jane Holland**, born about 1838.

In 1860 she was listed as "Jewry" and in 1870 as "Jinney." She may have been the "Jennie Holland," aged 40, living with Mary Ann Newman in 1880 and Jennie Holland (born 1839) the lodger, in the household of Joseph Parker in 1900. Joseph and his wife had a son born in 1900 and Jane, like many women at the time, was probably staying with the family to help Joseph's wife, Nancy Ellizabeth, with her pregnancy and/or the baby and other household duties. After giving birth, mothers, at that time, stayed in bed much longer than they do today and, as we know, many of them had complications from childbirth.

The Works Progress Administration Historical Records Survey compiled about 1939, records that one "Jinnie Holland," died in June 1909 at 68 years of age and was buried in the Joseph D. Parker Cemetery. This fits the Jinney (Jane?) Holland, daughter of John and Dicey Holland. Joseph D. and other members of his family were also shown as buried there, but later records show that he and his wife have tombstones at McGee United Methodist Church Cemetery. McGee Church has a cemetery that is in the church yard and another one a short distance from the church which may indicate that Joseph D. Parker lived very near the church and that either he or a descendant donated land for the church and cemetery.

\+ 63 ii. **Eliza Holland**, born about 1840 in Sampson County, North Carolina.

\+ 64 iii. **Delila Holland**, born about 1842; died after 1920.

\+ 65 iv. **Joel Holland**, born about 1844; died before 1900.

\+ 66 v. **Charity Holland**, born about 1845 in North Carolina; died after 1910.

\+ 67 vi. **John J. Holland**, born April 1847.

68 vii. **Elizabeth A. Holland**, born about 1849.

69 viii. **Thomas B. Holland**, born about 1851.

He either died before 1870 or he may have been the Thomas, aged 15, living with Marcheston Killett in Clinton, Samspon County, North Carolina, in 1870.

70 ix. **Sarah M. Holland,** born about 1852; died about 1919. She married John Robert Cannady, as his second wife, on the 29 July 1906 in North Carolina. He was born March 1836 in North Carolina and died about 1913 in Sampson County, North Carolina.

"Sarah M. Holland," aged 6, was listed in the 1860 census records for Sampson County as the daughter of John, aged 54, and Dicey, 40. In 1870, "Sarah" was listed as aged 17. In 1900, "Sarah M. Holland" was living in the household of Matthew Holland in Honeycutt Township, Sampson County, North Carolina and was listed as "cousin," placing her father, John, for a brother of Daniel Holland, father of Matthew.

She was buried in Mingo Baptist Church Cemetery, (SR 1002) and (SR 1605), Sampson County, North Carolina.

John Robert Cannady served in Co. I. 46th North Carolina Inf., CSA during the Civil War. He enlisted on 26 April 1862 at Clinton, North Carolina and was hospitalized from 25 August 1862 to 1 January 1863 in Richmond, Virginia and again from 14 June 1864 to 5 September 1864. John was furloughed 5 September 1864, for 40 days. He deserted to federal forces 25 March 1865. Took oath and was furnished transportation to Wilmington, North Carolina. My feeling is that many of the men who were written up as deserters, were probably either just ready for the war to end or may have realized it would end soon, when they turned themselves over to the union forces. Many of the men, when camped near their home, would visit their family and upon returning to camp, would find the men they served with would have moved on and when he was unable to find his company, would simply join another one, and he would be written up as a deserter.

"John R. Canada" pplied for a homestead exemption in February 1869 and it was registered 4 May 1869. He had 117-1/2 acres of land and personal property valued in the amount of $288.25.

Stephen H. Hairr and his wife, Mary Jane, sold to John R. Canady, 2 August 1880, three parcels of land (total of 286 acres) for $800. Deed mentions lands of James H. Porter, Horse Pasture Pocosin, Fann's corner, Isaiah McPhail, ditch by Wootens corner, Mrs. Porters line, Lewis' line, Tew's line and Great Piney Pocosin. Witness was O. L. Chesnutt. Deed registered 2 August 1880.

Deed dated 15 January 1881 records that J. R. Canady and first wife, ELIZABETH J. CANADY sold to N. Q. Grantham, 110 acres for $400...land was located ...east side of Little Coharie...run of the Big Swamp...Fanns corner. Proven 15 January 1881; registered 10 February 1881.

John was the first man buried in the Mingo Church Cemetery. Sources show he and his brother, Samuel, were born only five months apart. The year for one of them is incorrect.

71 x. **Catherine Holland,** born about 1856; died after 1900.

She may have been the Catherine Holland, aged 45, who was working as a domestic in the household of Miles C. Simmons in 1900.

72 xi. **Margaret J. Holland,** born about 1859.

Generation Number 3

14. Unknown Child Holland (Daniel[3], Thomas William[2], Unknown[1]) was born about 1802 in Sampson County, North Carolina.

The children listed for "Unknown Child Holland" are listed under Daniel and Elizabeth in 1850-1870. It appears that they were grandchildren of Daniel and Elizabeth, but I have not determined the actual names of their parents.

Children of Unknown Child Holland are:

i. **Sarah Holland**, born about 1837.

73 ii. **James F. Holland**, born about 1844. He most likely, married Rebecca E. Jackson 16 February 1872 in Sampson County, North Carolina; she was born about 1852 and died 10 February 1921.

He served in the Civil War in Company A., Regiment 30, Infantry. James enlisted on 1 September 1861 in Clinton, North Carolina and was promoted March-April 1862 to Musician-fifer and North Carolina pension records show he was wounded 15 September 1861 at Fort Caswell. He surrendered 9 April 1865 at Appomattox Court House, Virginia.

Thomas B. W. Jackson and his wife, Jinnette Jackson, and Nancy Tew, on 3 August 1881 sold to James F. Holland 45 acres for the sum of $175. This was from the division of the lands of John Tew's estate and "was on the west side of Caesar's Swamp ...runs west ...to a stake in the Two mile swamp". Williams' corner, now Holley's corner, mentioned in the deed.

I found a "**JAMES F. HOLLAND**" in transcribed cemetery records who is buried in The Old Mill Church of God Cemetery on Penny Tew Mill road (SR 1456) 3.5 miles from Highway 242. He was born 16 June 1812 and died 9 March 1909. His middle name was probably "Franklin," a name found in Harfrey Holland's family. Buried next to James F. is a "**JOHN JACKSON**" with no dates, but the remark is, 'John served in "Co A 2NC Arty CSA." I have been unable to link this James F. Holland who has a birth of 16 June 1812 on his gravestone and have not found him in the 1880 and 1900 census records which leads me to believe that the year of birth in the transcribed cemetery records may be incorrect.

\+ 74 iii. **Cherry Ann Holland**, born between 1850-1852.

17. James Holland (Daniel[3], Thomas William[2], Unknown[1]) was born about 1809 (aged 41 in 1850 Census) in Sampson County, North Carolina and died after 1880. He married **Sabra Culbreath**. She was born about 1808.

Sabra was identified as (nee Culbreth) in a transcribed copy of the 1860 census of Sampson County, North Carolina. I have not found other information to support Culbreth for her maiden name. The only certificate available for their children is the one for their son, Thomas James, whose birth is stated 11 September 1842 and who died 24 August 1917. Alex Autry was the informant and Dr. Sikes did not write Sabra's maiden name clearly. It looks like it could be Sabra M. Culbreth, born in Cumberland County.

I found a "**JAMES F. HOLLAND**" in transcribed cemetery records who was buried in The Old Mill Church of God Cemetery on Penny Tew Mill road (SR 1456) 3.5 miles from

Highway 242. He was born 16 June 1812 and died 9 March 1909. His middle name was probably "Franklin," a name found in Harfrey Holland's family. Buried next to James F. is a "**JOHN JACKSON**" with no dates, but the remark is, 'John served in "Co A 2NC Arty CSA." In the event that this James F. Holland listed in the transcribed cemetery records is the "James Holland" named above who was born about 1809, where was he in 1880, and 1900. I have not found him in those census records, which leads me to believe that the year of birth in the transcribed census records may be incorrect.

The 1850 Census for Sampson County, North Carolina shows a "RUFFIN HOLLAND" laborer, aged 19, living with James and Sabra. He was listed at the end and there is a span of about seven years between Ruffin and William leading me to believe that James may have been married twice and Ruffin was the child of the first spouse or Ruffin was either a nephew or related otherwise. James, Sabra, and daughter Nancy were living in Dismal Township in Sampson County, North Carolina when the 1880 census was taken.

On 6 August 1873, James made a gift of 100 acres to his daughters, Nancy J and Sarah J. Holland, in consideration of the love that he had for them. He and his wife had a lifetime right to live on the land.

Children of James Holland and Sabra Culbreath are:

\+ 75 i. **Ruffin Holland**, born about 1831; died 18 February 1863 in Camp Gregg, Danville, Virginia.

\+ 76 ii. **William Holland**, born about 1838; died between 1877 - 1880.

77 iii. **Nancy J. Holland**, born about 1840; died after 1910.

In 1870 "Nancy J." was living with her mother, Sabra, and her sister, Sarah J. She did not marry. It appears that in January 1900, her brother, Thomas James (John Thomas?) Holland, and others, sold the land their father had given to Nancy J. and their sister, Sarah J. In 1910, Nancy J. was living with her brother, Thomas James. and his son, Bernice Culbreth Holland, and Bernice's wife, Lessie. Nancy died after 1910 and before it was a requirement to register deaths in North Carolina.

\+ 78 iv. **Thomas James Holland**, born 11 September 1842 in Sampson County, North Carolina and died 24 August 1917 in Dismal Township in Sampson County.

79 v. **Daniel Holland**, born about 1845.

He served in the Civil War. "Holland, Daniel, Private, 3rd Company B, 2nd Artillery, Regement 36. Born 1845, Sampson County. Laborer. Enlisted 1 July 1863, Clinton. Killed 23 August 1863, in action with enemy gunboats near Fort Fisher."

80 vi. **Sarah J. Holland**, born 1849; died before January 1900.

"Sarah J." was living with her mother and sister, Nancy J., in 1870. She did not marry.

19. Harfrey Holland (Daniel[3], Thomas William[2], Unknown[1]) was born 1816 in Sampson County, North Carolina, and died 07 June 1896 in Sampson County, North Carolina. He married **Mary Sessoms**, daughter of Solomon Sessoms, Jr. and Mary Cooper. She was born

16 March 1827 in Sampson County, North Carolina, and died 30 March 1902 in Sampson County, North Carolina.

His name is also spelled "Harprey" and his tombstone may read "Harffrey." Harfrey's grandson, Harvey, son of Henry Lee, was the informant on Henry Lee Holland's Certificate of Death and named "HARVEY HOLLAND" for the father of Henry Lee.

In the spring of 1874, Harfrey and several other men met in a log cabin used for a three-month term of public school, to draw up a charter and make arrangements for opening the first high school in Salemburg, North Carolina.

23 February 1846: Daniel Holland sold three tracts of land (total of 242 acres) to Harpherey (Harfrey) Holland for $138.50. Deed mentions east side of Little Coharie...Porter's Branch, Catharine Williams' corner.

Rye Swamp mentioned in several deeds for the early Hollands has a tributary that crosses Route 242 in Sampson County and, as seen in a North Carolina Atlas and Gazetteer, the head of the swamp appears to be at Hollandtown Road. This may be why Holland descendants say that Daniel and Henry's families lived across the creek from each other.

To find the Holland Cemetery where he, his wife, Mary, and Lena Holland (daughter of Chester and Emily Holland) were buried, take Old Fayetteville Road for one mile from Salemburg. Turn left on Aaron Road (SR 1413). Go for 0.8 mile and turn right onto Hollandtown Road (SR 1412) for 0.3 mile and then turn right on dirt road. The cemetery is on the right in the field. At least three unknown graves are there. Mary's tombstone is difficult to read.

Harfrey is said to have had 17 children. Eleven of his children, sixteen grandchildren and many neighbors gathered for a family reunion to celebrate his 74th birthday. In the 1900 census for Honeycutts Township, Sampson County, North Carolina, Mary, aged 73, was living with her, son, Henry Lee and his wife, Rachel.

Children of Harfrey Holland and Mary Sessoms are:

\+ 81 i. **Quincy A. Holland**, born about 1839 in Sampson County, North Carolina; died 23 August 1863 in Hospital in Chester, Pennsylvania.

\+ 82 ii. **Bluman Holland**, born about 1846 in Sampson County, North Carolina; died 01 September 1924 in Sampson County, North Carolina.

83 iii. **Lewis Holland**, born 22 February 1848 in Sampson County, North Carolina; died 15 September 1939 in Honeycutts Township, Sampson County. He married **Elizabeth Spell** who was born 12 June 1851 in Dismal Township, Sampson County and died 14 May 1936.

In March 2000, Elma (nee Holland) Sollinger told me that her Uncle Columbus Holland and his wife moved in with his uncle, Lewis Holland, who never married and Lewis gave Columbus his farm. It appears that Lewis did marry, but perhaps had no living children.

On 6 March 1869, Lewis became the highest bidder for 39 acres of land on Rye Swamp. This may have been the 39 acres he sold to his second cousin, Stephen Senter Holland on 4 February 1873. Elizabeth Spell was listed as "Elizabeth," wife of Lewis Holland, in the 1880 and 1930 census records for Sampson County, North Carolina. In other census records, she was listed as "Lizzie."

Lewis and Elizabeth were buried in a Strickland Cemetery on Huntley School Road (SR 1434), Sampson County, North Carolina

\+ 84 iv. **Franklin Holland**, born March 1850 in Sampson County, North Carolina; died 17 June 1927 in Honeycutts Township, Sampson County.

\+ 85 v. **Jordan Holland**, born 18 June 1854 in Sampson County, North Carolina; died 20 June 1938 in Cross Creek Township, Cumberland County, North Carolina.

\+ 86 vi. **Chester Holland**, born 21 September 1856 in Sampson County, North Carolina; died 13 April 1942 in Sampson County, North Carolina.

\+ 87 vii. **Romelia Holland**, born 16 January 1860; died 16 January 1937 in Dismal Township, Sampson County, North Carolina.

\+ 88 viii. **Laura Ann Holland**, born about 1862.

89 ix. **Louiza Holland**, born 1862.

90 x. **Charley Holland**, born 21 May 1866; died 30 July 1899. He married **Minnie Laurence**.

"Charlie Holland" was buried in a Holland Cemetery about 1 1/2 miles from Salemberg, Sampson County, North Carolina, the same Holland Cemetery where his parents were buried.

\+ 91 xi. **Ammie Holland**, born 09 July 1867; died 25 January 1953.

92 xii. **William Allen Holland**, born 02 January 1870 in Sampson County, North Carolina; died 29 January 1941 in Honeycutts Township, Sampson County, North Carolina. He married **Cornelia C. Tew** 01 February 1897 in Sampson County, North Carolina. She was born 30 August 1879 in Sampson County, North Carolina, died 01 April 1939 and was the daughter of L. M. Tew and Adline (maiden name unknown).

William Allen's Certificate of Death records that he died from a gunshot wound of the head. He was buried on 30 January 1941 in the Molton Royal Family Cemetery near Salemburg, Sampson County, North Carolina. "Cordelia" was also listed for her name. His brother, Ammie was the informant named on Willaim's certificate of death.

\+ 93 xiii. **Henry Lee Holland**, born 31 August 1874 in Sampson County, North Carolina; died 16 June 1944 in Cross Creek Township, Cumberland County, North Carolina.

20. Elizabeth Holland (Daniel[3], Thomas William[2], Unknown[1]) was born about 1817 in Sampson County, North Carolina, and died after 1880.

She was living with her mother, Elizabeth, in 1880. I list her as a daughter of Daniel Holland, Sr. and Elizabeth Sessoms, but she may have been the wife of a son of Daniel and Elizabeth. I feel confident, however, that Daniel, Sr., and his wife would have named a daughter, "Elizabeth." In 1850, **Elizabeth Holland, 33**, was listed with Daniel Holland, Sr. and his wife Elizabeth. In 1860, **Betsey Holland, aged 33**, was listed with Elizabeth Holland, aged 67, and Daniel Holland, Jr., aged 35. Wesley Holland, aged 29, was also listed with his mother, Elizabeth and brother, Daniel, Jr. in 1860; he and Betsey were weavers. Wesley was not listed in the Sampson County Census in 1850. Were Elizabeth and Betsey different women? After all, if Betsey was Elizabeth, her age should have been 43 in 1860. Elizabeth was with her mother in 1870 and was aged 52 and her daughter, Dicey was with them! Milsey. aged 45, daughter of Daniel, Sr. and Elizabeth and Cherry, "Cherry Ann Holland," aged 20, were also in the household in 1870. I have not determined the name of Cherry's parents.

Child of Elizabeth Holland is:

\+ 94 i. **Dicey Ann Holland**, born 1847; died 10 August 1915 in Mingo Township, Sampson County, North Carolina.

21. Unidentified Child Holland (Daniel[3], Thomas William[2], Unknown[1]) was born about 1820 in Sampson County, North Carolina.

Child of Unidentified Child Holland is:

95 i. **James G. Holland**, born about 1844; died about 1872. He may have been the James G. Holland who married **Patience Cannady** 17 September 1871 in Sampson County, North Carolina, who was born about 1839 in North Carolina; died after 1910. Patience was the daughter of Hardy Cannady and Nancy Honeycutt.

James, aged 6, was listed in the household of Daniel Holland, 72 and Elizabeth, 61 in 1850 and was probably a grandchild. James F. Holland, aged 17, was listed in the household of Elizabeth, aged 67 and her son, Daniel in 1860 and in 1870, James F., aged 26, was in the household of Joel Jackson. James F. Holland was the right age to be the James G. who married Patience in 1871. Unless someone has better records than those I found, it may not be possible to correctly determine the parents of James G.

The ages of the children of Patience listed in census records indicate that, most likely, Patience was married about 1862 to an Unknown "Hairr," but no record has been found to support that, other than the 1880 census record (see below). The marriage index for Sampson County, North Carolina, records the marriage date of 17 September 1871 for James G. Holland and Patience Canada, born 1839. I can't ignore the marriage record and I have found no other Patience Cannady who was born about 1839 or James G. Holland who was born about 1844 in Sampson County.

The 1880 and 1900 census records show Patience and "Pasie," respectively, as the wife of James T. Hair. Pasie was a nickname for Patience. The James Thomas Hairr born about 1848 would not have been old enough to have been the father of Rhoda Hairr, aged 17, who was in his and Patience's household in 1880. Either Patience was married to an Unknown "Hairr" or Rhoda was related some other way. The Civil War created unusual circumstances; children orphaned by the war lived with various relatives and census enumerators were not always correct when entering surnames.

In the 1860 census of Sampson County, North Carolina, a daughter, "Ursala, 1 yr.," is placed under Patience, 19 yrs, who is listed under Hardy and Jane Cannady. This placement seems to indicate that Ursala was the daughter of Patience rather than Hardy and Jane. However, Ursala is the right age to be "Vestinia," daughter of Hardy and Jane, who is listed in 1870 as age 12, but not listed in 1860. this seems to indicate that Vestina was listed as Ursala in 1860 and she may actually be the daughter of Patience by an unknown father.

IS IT POSSIBLE that **JAMES G. HOLLAND** and **JAMES T. (THOMAS) HAIRR** were used for the name of one man, James Thomas Hair(r), son of John C. Hairr (John C. Hair) who died in the Civil War? See notes for **John C. Hair**.

22. Thomas James Holland, Sr. (Daniel[3], Thomas William[2], Unknown[1]) was born 05 February 1821 in Sampston County, North Carolina, and died between 1850 - 1860. He married **Eliza Crawford Whitfield**, daughter of John Whitfield and Susan Wright. She was born 31 October 1824 in Kenansville, Duplin County, North Carolina, and died about 1878 in Deep Run, Duplin County, North Carolina.

Records appear to show that most of his descendants lived in the southeastern area of Sampson County, North Carolina. Eliza Crawford Holland was head of household in Sampson County in 1870, but apparently, she was not living in Sampson County in 1860. The certificate of death for their daughter, "Catharan Gray" names Eliza Crawford for her mother.

Children of Thomas Holland and Eliza Whitfield are:

96 i. **George Washington Holland,** born 24 July 1848 in Clinton, Sampson County, North Carolina; died 25 August 1938 in Kansas City, Missouri. He married Effie Joseph Irons.

\+ 97 ii. **William Wright Holland,** born 14 April 1850 in Clinton, Sampson County, North Carolina; died 20 June 1926 in Sampson County.

\+ 98 iii. **Catharan Gray Holland,** born 16 June 1853 in Clinton, Sampson County, North Carolina; died 22 August 1923 in Albertson, Duplin County, North Carolina.

\+ 99 iv. **Thomas James Holland, Jr.**, born 23 November 1854 in Sampson County; died 01 April 1906.

24. Daniel Holland, Jr. (Daniel[3], Thomas William[2], Unknown[1]) was born between 1822 - 1827 in Sampson County, North Carolina, and died after 26 September 1889. He married **Mary Manda Autry** 09 February 1869 in Sampson County, daughter of Starling Autry and Anna McPhail. She was born 08 March 1835 and was Daniel's first cousin, once removed.

Mary Manda is said to have first married **Beaufort Faircloth**. See her elsewhere in this book. Professor Bundy names Beaufort Faircloth for the spouse of Mary Manda, daughter of Starling, and a North Carolina Marriage Collection records the marriage of "**Mary Autery**" to Beaufort Faircloth on 20 May 1855 in Cumberland County, North Carolina. I have not been successful in finding any other information for Beaufort and Mary. Jordan Holland, nephew of Daniel, married Mary Manda's sister, Ann Sophia.

Several researchers have posted data for Daniel, Jr. and Mary Manda on Ancestry.com. All of these researchers except one, have named "Mary Manda Autry" for the wife of Daniel, Jr.

The 1850 census for Sampson County, North Carolina, records Daniel with his parents. In 1860, he was listed as aged 35 and was head of household with his mother, Elizabeth. Listed with them were: Betsey, 33; Wesley, 29; James F. 17; Dicy A., 13; Cherry, 8. He did not appear to be married in 1850 and it is not clear whether "Betsey" listed with him in 1860 was his spouse or his sister. It appears that he was not the father of James F., Dicy A., and Cherry, but he may have been. In 1870 "Mary M." was listed as his spouse. Dicy A. and Cherry were in the household of Daniel's mother, Elizabeth in 1870. James F. was living with Joel Jackson.

Most likely, he was the Daniel Holland who served in the Civil War as a "Private in Company I, Regiment. 46, Infantry. His war record tells he was born in 1827 in Sampson County and was a cooper. He enlisted 12 March 1862 in Clinton, North Carolina and was ill and unfit for duty from 22 October 1862 to February 1864. On 21 April 1864, he was assigned to light duty as a nurse in Jackson Hospital, Richmond, Virginia and was later captured there. Another Civil Ward record states he enlisted in Company Battery B., North Carolina Company B and Light Artillery Battery on 1 july 1863 and was mustered out at Fort Fisher, North Carolina, on 23 August 1863 On the **26 September 1889**, he attended the veteran's reunion in Clinton.

Another United States Civil War Soldier Record and Profile records that he was a Cooper and enlisted on 3 December 1862 as a private and also records that he enlisted on 16 April 1862. While he was ill and unfit for duty, he was, most likely at home.

The certificate of death for their son, Hanson G. names "Dan Holland" for Hanson's father and "Unknown" for his mother. Daniel's sons, Hanson and Julius, died of carcinoma of the stomach. Hanson was the informant listed on the certificate of death for his brother, Julius, and names Daniel Holland for Julius' father and Mary Autry for his mother leading me to believe that Mrs. R. B. Wilson the informant on the certificate for Hanson either was not related to the family or she was a younger descendant with little knowledge of the ancestors.

Children of Daniel Holland and Mary Autry are:

100 i. **Addy A. Holland**, born March 1870.

101 ii. **Junious Everett Holland**, born about 1873.

I have found no other information after the 1880 census for him except the date of 17 December 1958 for the birth of Russell Fletcher Holland in Sampson County and Junious Everett Holland was named for Russell's father. The Junious born about 1873 may have had descendants named after him and Russell Fletcher could have been a grandson or great-grandson.

\+ 102 iii. **Hanson G. Holland**, born 20 March 1876; died 07 October 1951.

\+ 103 ✓ iv. **Julius Holland**, born 06 August 1878 in Sampson County, North Carolina; died 07 February 1936. Both Julius and his brother, Junious appear in the 1880 Federal census for Honeycutts Township, Sampson County.

26. Nicholas Holland (Daniel[3], Thomas William[2], Unknown[1]) was born 1826 in Sampson County, North Carolina, and died 1886 in Sampson County, North Carolina. He married **Charity (maiden name unknown)**. She was born about 1825, and died 1891.

Most likely, Nicholas (Nickolas) was a son of Daniel; his maternal great-grandfather was Nicholas Sessoms, Jr. (1731-1813); his great, great, grandfather was Nicholas Sessoms, Sr., (1687-1769.) Neither Nicholas nor Charity are listed in the 1870 census for Sampson County. On 24 September 1863, Nicholas Holland from North Carolina enlisted in the Civil War. Transcribed cemetery records of Sampson County show that he and Charity were buried in Maxwell Cemetery on the southeast corner of Maxwell Road (SR 1006) and (SR 1427), Sampson County, North Carolina.

George W. Autry, aged 4, in 1850 and 15 in 1860 was listed in the household with Nicholas and Charity in 1850 and 1860. It appears that Charity was first married to an "Autry" or her maiden name was Autry. George W. Autry was born in 1845 in Sampson County and enlisted on 26 August 1863 in Cumberland County, North Carolina, to serve in the American Civil War. He served in Company B, 2nd Battalion, North Carolina Local Defense Troops and was appointed on the 1 January 1864 to musician. He died 6 March 1864, in Post Hospital, Fayetteville Arsenal and Armory, of cerebritis.

Children of Nicholas Holland and Charity Unknown are:

104 i. **Nancy Holland,** born about March 1850.

105 ii. **Misouria Holland,** born about 1875. She was probably a grandchild.

27. Matthew Holland (Daniel[3], Thomas William[2], Unknown[1]) was born about 1827 in Sampson County, North Carolina, and died 07 April 1865 in a Union Prison Camp in Elmira, New York. He married **Civil (maiden name unknown)**. She was born about 1827, and died after 1900.

Matthew Holland served as a Private in 2nd Company C, 2nd Artillery, Regiment 36, during the Civil War. He enlisted 9 October 1863 in Clinton, was captured 15 January 1865 at Fort Fisher and confined to the Union Prison Camp in Elmira, New York. He died there on 7 April 1865 of chronic diarrhea and was buried in grave # 2657, Woodlawn Cemetery, Elmira, New York.

Children of Matthew Holland and Civil ?? are:

\+ 106 i. **Hiram M. Holland**, born 05 April 1851 in Sampson County, North Carolina; died 08 November 1937 in Sampson County, North Carolina.

107 ii. **Theophilus Holland** was born about 1853 in Sampson County and either died or left Sampson County before 1870.

\+ 108 iii. **Agnes Matilda Holland**, born 30 November 1856 in Huntley, Honeycutts Township, Sampson County, North Carolina; died 25 March 1947.

\+ 109 iv. **Marshall Holland,** born about 1859 in Sampson County; died after 1930.

\+ 110 v. **Robert Mitchell Holland,** born July 1863 in Sampson County; died 18 May 1935.

\+ 111 vi. **Matthew L. Holland,** born 25 September 1864 in Sampson County, North Carolina; died 20 January 1928.

30. Tomzelle Culbreth (Mary[3] Holland, Thomas William[2], Unknown[1]) was born 17 December 1801 in Sampson County, North Carolina, and died 1834 in Green County, Georgia. She married **Joel Williams, Sr.** before 1820, son of Robert Williams and Susanna Daniels. He was born about 1800, and died 1841. Joel married second **EFFIE MCPHAIL** who was born about 1811.

Tomzelle is also listed as "Tomsil." She and Joel were buried in the Neil Culbreth Cemetery near Roseboro, Sampson County, North Carolina. A book of transcribed cemetery records notes that remarks on her tombstone show she died in Green County, GA. It is possible that she visited family in Georgia and perhaps died there? My sister and I didn't copy this information when we copied the inscriptions in this cemetery. Did Joel and "Tomzelle" move to, and stay in, Georgia for a few years? Did Joel return with his children to Sampson County after Tomzelle died in Georgia or did someone confuse Tomzelle and Joel's second wife, Effie (Effy?) who is said to have moved to Alabama and possibly moved farther west?

This source also shows that the remarks indicate incorrectly that thisTomzelle and her sister, Millzy, were the daughters of Daniel Culbreth and Martha Culbreth and Millzy was the husband of Young Autry. **Martha B. Autry was the mother of Daniel Culbreth.**

Joel left all his land and personal property to his second wife during her widowhood, if she lived a life of good behaviour. At her death, or if she lived a loose character in life, it was to be sold and divided equally among all his children. All the personal property not mentioned in his will was to be sold and the proceeds equally divided among his children. His will was dated September 30, 1840 and was proved before the Sampson County Court on May 17, 1841, when John C. Williams was qualified as executor.

His Will:

"I, Joel Williams of the County of Sampson and State of North Carolina, being of sound mind and memory. but considering the uncertainty of my Earthly Existence do make and declare this my Last Will and Testament in manner and form following.

First, my Executor hereinafter named shall pay all my just debts to whomsoever owing out of the moneys that may first come into his hands as part or parcel of my estate. I give and devise to my beloved wife, Effy Williams, all my lands which I now possess and also one grey mare, two cows and yearlings and also three sows now with pigs, and seven head of sheep, also fifteen barrels of corn and one thousand pounds of pork., two beds and furniture, one table and chest, one wheel and cards, one plow and gear, two hoes and one axe, and all my table furniture, one loom and gear, also one negro girl named Sarah. Also to my wife, one side Saddle and bridle, fifteen dollars in money and all my pots and one oven and skillet (frying pan), one wash tub and all the pails, one pair of candle molds and candle stick, one pair of fire dogs, one bible and hymn book, and all my crop of cotton, fifteen pounds of wool, all my sitting chairs, one smoothing iron, one pork barrel and stand, and one pot stand, to have and to hold to the said Effy Williams for a term during her widowhood state of life or her good behaviour while being a widow. The above mentioned property at the death of my wife, Effy Williams, shall all be sold and equally divided among all my children or before her death if she lives a loose character in life and all the rest of my estate not above named shall be sold and equally divided among all my childrren and I do hereby constitute and appoint my friend, John C. Williams, my lawfull Executor to all intents and purposes, to Execute this my Last Will and Testament according to the true intent and means of the same and every part and every clause thereof, hereby revoking and declaring utterly void all other wills and testaments by me heretofore made in witness where of. I, the said Joel Williams here unto, set my hand and seal this 30th day of September AD, 1840. Joel Williams (Seal).

"Signed, Sealed, published and declared by the said Joel Williams to be his Last Will and Testament in presence of us who at his request and in his presence and in the presence of each other do subscribe our names as witness thereunto.

"Lewis F. Carr

"Daniel M. Culbreath."

The inventory of Joel's estate on June 8, 1841 included "23 head of hogs, 31 head of sheep, 6 cows and calves, 3 steers, 1 heifer, 1 sorrel mare, and 1 gray mare, as well as notes on Joel Williams of Cumberland County, John W. McLaurin, William Hair, and Travis Jackson. In the sale of his personal property on June 10, 1841, his bible and Testament were sold to Thomas Williams for 35 cents"

Minutes of Sampson County court of Pleas and Quarter Sessions, show that in the May Term 1847 "John C. Williams came into Court and renewed his bond as Guardian to John, Molcy, Sarah, Daniel, Joel, Isaac, Susan, Elizabeth, Mary Catherine, and Isabella Williams in the sum of seven Hundred dollars with John Royal and Fleet Cooper as securities who were approved and bond filed."

On 13 May 1848 John C. Williams bought Joel's 273 acres of land for $711.65. The minutes of the November 1850 Court Term of Sampon County, North Carolina records the transfer of guardianship from John C. Williams to Effie Williams for her three daughters.

Some of Joel's family stayed in the Sampson County, North Carolina area; others moved to Alabama and some have disappeared from view. Effie and three of her daughters are listed in the 1850 Census of Division No. 23 of Barbour County, Alabama (Dwelling 1232) with Michael McPhair (McPhail?), aged 43 and born in North Carolina, a silversmith (probably Effie's brother.) This indicates that Effy and her daughters were already in Alabama when the Sampson County Court approved the transfer of guardianship from John C. Williams to "Effie."

Children of Tomzelle Culbreth and Joel Williams are:

112 i. **Sarah Williams**, born between 1820 - 1825.

\+ 113 ii. **John E. Williams**, born about 1822; died before 1870.

\+ 114 iii. **Molcy Williams**, born about 1823; died between 1850 - 1860.

115 iv. **Daniel Williams**, born between 1825 - 1830.

\+ 116 v. **Joel Williams, Jr.**, born about 1828; died 04 March 1865 in Prison, Elmira, New York.

+ 117 vi. **Isaac Williams**, born 19 October 1831; died 09 February 1907 in Sampson County, North Carolina.

+ 118 vii. **Susan Ann Williams**, born 19 May 1833; died 28 December 1900.

Joel's children by his second wife, Effie McPhail: **Elizabeth Ann Williams** was born about 1837; **Mary Catherine Williams,** born about 1838; **Eda Isabella Williams** was born about 1840.

31. Millzy Adelme Culbreth (Mary[3] Holland, Thomas William[2], Unknown[1]) was born 07 August 1803 in Sampson County, North Carolina, and died between 1860 - 1870. She married **Young Autry** about 1821, son of Raeford Autry and Henrietta (maiden name unknown). He was born about 1803, and died after 1880.

She is listed as "**Millie Culbreath**", Daughter of Daniel Culbreath and Mary" in the **Old Holland Record Book**, "Millzy Culbreth" on her monument, and as "Molsey" in the 1850 and 1860 census records for Sampson County, North Carolina. Her year of birth in the record book is difficult to read, but appears to be August 1803 and the year 1803 is shown on her tombstone. See notes above for her sister, Tomzelle, for data listed either incorrectly on Tomzelle's tombstone and/or in a book of transcribed cemetery records.

Millzy Adelme was named after her mother's mother. She and her husband, Young

Autry are recorded as buried in the Leroy Autry Family Cemetery off Autryville Road, about 1.3 miles east of Autryville, North Carolina. Their names and years of birth and death are also inscribed on a stone in the Neil Culbreth Cemetery near Roseboro.

Children of Millzy Culbreth and Young Autry are:

+ 119 i. **Daniel Autry,** born 09 April 1822; died 06 February 1896.

120 ii. **Micajah Autry**, born about 1830; died April 1865. He married **Mary Margaret Matthews;** born 28 November 1839; died 28 December 1918. He appears to have been a Timbercutter, living alone in 1860 in Owensville in Dismal Township in Sampson County. Civil War records state he was a Private in 2nd Company C, 2nd Artillary, Regiment 36. He enlisted on 9 February 1863 in Clinton, North Carolina, was captured 15 January 1865 at Fort Fisher, North Carolina, and confined to Elmira Union Prison in New York where he died in April of chronic diarrhea. He was buried in grave # 2621 in Woodlawn Cemetery in Elmira. Mary Margaret may have been the Mary M. Autry listed as aged 28 and head of household in Dismal Township in 1870 with two children, **Martin Autry**, aged about 10, and **Susan J. Autry**, aged 1.

+ 121 iii. **Rebecca Elizabeth Autry,** born about 1831.

+ 122 iv. **Molsey Autry**, born about 1833; died April 1905.

+ 123 v. **Martha Ann Autry,** born 30 September 1835; died 24 December 1914.

124 vi. **Eliza Anna Autry,** born About 1837; died March 1906.

+ 125 vii. **Miles Costin Autry,** born 08 April 1839; died 07 July 1909.

+ 126 viii. **Jeanette Autry,** born 28 April 1847.

32. John B. Culbreth (Mary[3] Holland, Thomas William[2], Unknown[1]) was born 22 August 1805 in Sampson County, North Carolina, and died 1854. He married **Martha Autry**. She was born about 1803, and died after 1860 in Greene County, Georgia.

"John Culbreth," aged 72, was living in the household of Daniel (David?) Mathews in Cedar Creek Township, Cumberland County, North Carolina in 1870.

My sister and I transcribed notes from the **Old Holland Record Book** and by John's name, Jackie copied Nancy, his wife was born July 1803. She crossed through Nancy and again wrote Nancy above and she also wrote "(Mary)." Some of the names in the Record Book are faded and very difficult to read. The name written in the record book is probably "Martha" with her birth date of July 1803. Other sources support the data in the record book.

John B. and Martha have stones in the Neil Culbreth Cemetery near Roseboro, North Carolina. If Martha died in Georgia, she was probably buried there; I do not have a clear indication of where they both were actually buried.

Children of John Culbreth and Martha Autry are:

127 i. **William W. Culbreth.**

128 ii. **Mary Ann Culbreth.**

129 iii. **Martha F. Culbreth.**

130 iv. **Nancy Culbreth.**

131 v. **Dicy B. Culbreth.**

132 vi. **Lena A. Culbreth.**

35. Isaac Culbreth, Sr. (Mary[3] Holland, Thomas William[2], Unknown[1]) was born about 1816 in Sampson County, North Carolina, and died before 1900 in Eastover Township, Cumberland County, North Carolina. He married **(1) Mary Ann Maxwell** 21 January 1836, daughter of Neil Maxwell and Sophia Matthews. She was born 19 September 1814, and died 25 July 1863. Isaac married **(2) Elizabeth Jane Honeycutt** after July 1863, daughter of William Honeycutt and Penelope Royal. She was born 24 July 1840 in Sampson County, North Carolina, and died 19 October 1920 in Flea Hill Township, Cumberland County, North Carolina.

Elizabeth Jane Honeycutt first married **EVAN FAIRCLOTH** who was born about 1834 and died about 1868. She and Evan had one child, **AMMIE CHESTER FAIRCLOTH,** who was born 1 May 1867 and died 5 August 1944 in Fayetteville, North Carolina. Ammie married **MARY ELIZA BULLOCK** who was born 11 February 1872 and died 31 January 1937, daughter of **John Bullock** and **Margaret Sessoms**. Mary and Ammie had 15 children.

Mr. Rosser identifies Isaac **as the possible son the Daniel Culbreth and Anne Flora McPhail.** Isaac was not mentioned in Daniel's will and I have no proof, but I believe that Isaac Culbreth **was possibly the son of Daniel Culbreth and Mary Holland.** In the event that I have incorrectly named Isaac for a son of Mary Holland and Daniel Culbreth, I pray the information provided will still be useful for those interested in Isaac and his descendants.

Issac, Mary Ann and Elizabeth Jane were buried in Salem United Methodist Church in Eastover Township in Cumberland County, North Carolina.

Professor Bundy states in his book: "There are three Culbreth women listed in the William Maxwell Bible, but I do not know to which family they belong. Some say that they were sisters of Daniel McCulbreth, but I have no proof at this time. They were Mathey "Jane" Culbreth born 9-28-1836, Betsey Ann Culbreth born 5-22-1839, and Phebe Lisa Culbreth, born 8-30-1841... When I asked Cousin Armelia about them she said only that, "They did not belong there.'"

Children of Isaac and Mary listed in the 1850 census of Sampson County, North Carolina: Martha, aged 13; Elizabeth, 11; Phebe, 9; Sophia, 7; William 5; Sabra 1. Perhaps Isaac and Mary reared these three older children as their own; Isaac may have been married twice and the children could have been stepchildren of Mary which could explain the remark made by Professor Bundy's cousin.

Professor Bundy also mentions that Blackman Autry born 1822, married 17 June,1858 to Martha Jane Culbreth born 9-28-1836, daughter of Isaac and Mary Culbreth. Mary Ann Maxwell, spouse of Isaac Culbreth, was the daughter of William Maxwell (owner of the Culbreth Bible mentioned above) who was born 23 January 1786 and Sophia Matthews who was born 1797. Martha Jane's date of birth is the same date listed above for "Mathey 'Jane' Culbreth."

Children of Isaac Culbreth and Mary Maxwell are:

\+ 133 i. **Martha Jane Culbreth**, born 28 September 1836; died 18 February 1908.

\+ 134 ii. **Elizabeth Ann Culbreth**, born 22 May 1839; died 22 March 1908 in Salem United Methodist Church, Eastover, Cumberland County, North Carolina.

135 iii. **Pheby Eliza Culbreth**, born 30 August 1841; died 07 February 1921 in Flea Hill Township, Cumberland County, North Carolina. She married **Daniel James McLaurin**; born 31 December 1840; died 26 April 1917 in Flea Hill Township, Cumberland County, North Carolina. Daniel was he son of **Duncan "McLeran"** and **Charlotte Autry**. Pheby and Daniel had seven children,

1) **DAVID JAMES MCLAURIN** was born 12 September 1869 and died 16 June 1928 in Flea Hill Township. On 12 January 1898 he married in Flea Hill Township, **LENORA ELIZABETH SESSOMS,** daughter of **THOMAS LUCIAN SESSOMS** and **REBECCA E. BAKER.** "Nora" was born 4 August 1876 and died 2 October 1959 in Eastover Township in Cumberland County. Both are buried in The Duncan McLaurin Family Cemetery. David and Lenora had six children. Their **first child, a son** was born 24 Febraury 1900 and died 27 February 1900. The second child, a son, was born and died 28 July 1902. These two sons were buried in the Duncan McLaurin Family Cemetery. David and Lenora's third child, **DAISY G. MCLAURIN** was born 5 June 1905 and died 16 August 1906. She, too, was buried in the Duncan McLaurine Family Cemetery. The fourth child of David and Lenora was **IULA W. MCLAURIN** who was born 17 June 1907 and died 5 April 1989 in Fayetteville. She married **ESTON LEMUEL MCLAURIN** who was born 17 August 1903 and died 1 April 1954 in Fayetteville.

Iula and Eston had three children and were buried in Salem United Methodist Church Cemetery. **ROSE MCLAURIN**, the fifth child of David and Lenora, was born 9 November 1911 and married **ALLEY DAVID SMITH** on 25 December 1932 in Fayetteville. Alley was born 14 December 1910 in Johnston County, North Carolina, died 23 August 1981 in Fayetteville, North Carolina, and was buried in Salem United Methodist Church Cemetery. Rose and Alley had one child. The sixth child of David and Lenora was **RENA CATHERINE MCLAURIN.** She was born 5 August 1916 in Flea Hill Township and her first husband husband was **JAMES FULTON BEARD,** son of **James A. Beard** and **Florida Virginia McLaurin.** James Fulton was born 15 May 1911 and died 21 January 1936 in Fayetteville. One child. Rena married second **AUSBY MARTIN MCLAURIN,** son of **Arthur Adolphus McLaurin** and **Mary Catherine Williford.** Ausby was born 1 January 1902 and died 19 November 1982 in Fayetteville. Two children. Both husbands were buried in Salem United Methodist Church Cemetery.

2) **DUNCAN L. MCLAURIN**, second child of Daniel James and Pheby Eliza, was born 20 July 1871 and died 5 December 1886 and was buried in the family cemetery.

3) **DANIEL CORNELIUS MCLAURIN**, third child, was born 23 March 1873 and died 24 September 1951 in Fayetteville. He married on 26 February 1903 in Flea Hill Township to **ANNIE EVELYN CULBRETH**, daughter of Jennet Culbreth. She was born 13 September 1884 and died 3 November 1913. Both were buried in the family cemetery. Three children. I) **A daughter** was born and died 18 January 1904 was buried in the family cemetery. II) **ISAAC OCTAVIOUS MCLAURIN** was born 2 September 1905 and died 31 January 1978 in Fayetteville. Octavious did not marry and was buried in the Duncan McLaurin Family cemetery. III) **WILLIS FLETCHER MCLAURIN** was born 9 June 1913 and died 2 June 1984. He married **ANNIE LOU AUTRY** in Carvers Creek Township, Cumberland County, on 12 April 1952. She was born 30 April 1919 in Flea Hill Township, daughter of **William Stephen Autry** and **Margaret Elizabeth Geddie**. Willis, a retired Sheriff's Deputy, was buried in Lebanon Baptist Church Cemetery. No children.

4) **LOUIS ROBERSON MALAURIN**, fourth child of Daniel James McLaurin and Pheby Eliza Culbreth, was born 23 June 1875 and died 28 December 1946 at his home in Eastover Township in Cumberland County, North Carolina. He married **FRANCES SESSOMS** on 22 April 1906 in Flea Hill Township. She was the daughter of **William James Sessoms** and **Martha C. Wicker,** was born 18 September 1877 and died 27 December 1939 in Fayetteville. Frances first married on 20 September 1898 in Flea Hill Township to **JULIUS W. CULBRETH,** son of **William Culbreth** and **Sarah Elizabeth Sessoms**. (See William Culbreth and Sarah Elizabeth Sessoms elsewhere in this book.) Frances and Julius were buried at Salem United Methodist Church Cemetery. Louis and Frances had two children: **DUEVEL MCLAURIN** was born 19 August 1909, died 10 June 1911 and was buried in Salem United Methodist Church Cemetery. **ROBERT MCLAURIN** was born 16 July 1912. He married on 5 August 1934 in Seventy-First Township in Cumberland County, to **LOUISE BEARD**, daughter of **Gilliam V. Beard** and **Louise Wingate**. Louise was born 1911.

5) **BUNYAN BLACKMAN MCLAURIN**, fifth child of Daniel James and Pheby Eliza was born 8 July 1877 and died 17 January 1948 in Fayetteville. He was not married at time of death and was buried in the Duncan McLaurin Family Cemetery.

6) **ELIZABETH MCLAURIN**, sixth child, was born 23 December 1880 and died unmarried 10 July 1958 near Fayetteville. She was buried in the Duncan McLaurin Family Cemetery.

7) **MARY LOU DELLA MCLAURIN** was born 7 February 1884 and died unmarried 21 November 1923 in Flea Hill Township. She was buried in the Duncan McLaurin Family Cemetery.

136 iv. **Sophia E. Culbreth,** fourth child of Isaac Culbreth and Mary Maxwell, was born 14 September 1843; died 20 June 1900. She married **Duncan McLaurin, Jr.**; born 12 January 1844; died 18 November 1920 in Flea Hill Township, Cumberland County, North Carolina. Sophia and Duncan were buried in the Duncan McLaurin Family Cemetery. Seven Children.

1) **EMILY MCLAURIN**, their first child, was born about 1869 and appears to have died before 1900. She married **FRANKLIN E. AUTRY,** who was born about 1873, son of **Marshall Thomas Autry** and **Emeline Jones.** Franklin might have died before 1900.

2) **MARY M. MCLAURIN,** second child of Duncan and Sophia was born 7 April 1871 and died 16 June 1913. She married **DANIEL L. BEARD,** son of **Daniel Leonard Beard** and **Eliza Jane Core.** Daniel was born 15 August 1874 and died 26 October 1934 in Eastover Township in Cumberland County, North Carolina. Daniel married second on 11 April 1920 in Fayetteville**, ETTA AUTRY,** daughter of **Marshall Stephen Autry** and **Malissia Lee Bedsole.** Etta was born 14 May 1881 and died 19 August 1964 in Fayetteville. Mary was buried in the Duncan McLaurin Family Cemetery. She and Daniel had two children: I) **ELLA CATHERINE MCLAURIN** was born 3 January 1891 in Cumberland County and died 14 March 1969 in Fyetteville. She married **JOSEPH EDGAR BLACK** who was born 30 October 1883 and died 11 October 1955, son of **Hugh A. Black** and **Sarah Parker** of Dunn, North Carolina. They were buried in Greenwood Cemetery in Dunn. Two children, **JOSEPH EDGAR BLACK, JR.,** and **MYRTLE REID BLACK.** II**) VIRGINIA MCLAURIN,** second child of Mary and Daniel, was born 7 December 1893 and died 15 August 1977 in Fayetteville. She married on 2 January 1916 in Flea Hill Township, **JESSE SPIVEY** who was born 3 June 1892 and died 6 June 1979 in Lumberton. Virginia and Jesse were buried at Salem United Methodist Church Cemetery. Two children: **DUNCAN HAROLD SPIVEY** who was born 19 October 1917 in Flea Hill Township and eid 16 July 1973 in Fayetteville. He married **AGNES MARIE WILLIAMS** who was born 19 April 1923 in Fayetteville and they had two children, **Dennis Harold Spivey** and **Gary Michael Spivey.** Duncan was buried at Salem United Methodist Church Cemetery. The second child of Virginia and Jesse was **MARGARET CATHERINE SPIVEY** who was born 7 March 1921 in Flea Hill Township and died 25 December 1985 in Fayetteville. Margaret married **EARL WINSTON MCDANIEL** on 25 June 1939 in Fayetteville. He was born 11 April 1919 in Little Coharie Township and died 15 September **1979 in Fayetteville, son of Charles Emmitt McDaniel and Minnie Owen.** Margaret and Earl were buried at Salem United Methodist Church Cemetery.

3) **HINTON WILBUR MCLAURIN** who was born 21 June 1873 and died 9 February 1938 in Eastover Township in Cumberland County, was the third child or Duncan and Sophia. He married **CALLIE SESSOMS,** daughter of **Thomas Lucian Sessoms** and **Rebecca E. Baker.** Callie was born in 1874 and died 1895. No Children. Hinton married second **SALLIE INEZ HARRISON,** on 15 March 1899 in Flea Hill Township. She was born 10 November 1878 and died 4 January 1954 in Fayetteville. Hinton and Sallie had eight children; he and both wives were buried in the Duncan McLaurin Family Cemetery.

The first child of Hinton and Sallie was **CLARENCE WILBUR MCLAURIN** who was born 12 December 1899 in Fayetteville and died 19 December 1984 in Fayetteville. He married **MARGARET CLARA ABBOTT** who was born about 1905 and they had one child

The second child of Hinton and Sallie was **ROXANNA TERA MCLAURIN** who was born 19 April 1901 in Fayhetteville and married **WILLIAM ARMIE MORGAN** who was born about 1901. Two children: **TALMAGE MORGAN** and **SHIRLY MAXINE MORGAN.**

The third child of Hinton and Sallie was **LEON MCLAURIN** who was born 5 June 1903 and died 17 May 1907. He was buried in the Duncan McLaurin Family Cemetery.

The fourth child of Hinton and Sallie was **ESTILENE SOPHIA MCLAURIN** who was born 12 February 1906 and died 15 May 1963 in Fayetteville. Estilene married **RAYMOND EDGBERT GUY** on 27 March 1926 in Fayetteville. He was born 31 August 1900 and died 17 October 1963 in Eastover Township. They were buried in Salem United Methodist Church Cemetery. Two children: **GERALDINE GUY** and **ROBERT WAYNE GUY.**

The fifth child of Hinton and Sallie was **SIDNEY PEARL MCLAURIN** who was born about 1909 and married **AARON BARNEY BULLOCK** on 22 November 1931 at Jackson Springs, North Carolina. He was born 6 January 1910 and died 24 July 1962 in Fayetteville and was buried in Salem United Methodist Church Cemetery. Three children.

The sixth child of Hinton and Sallie was **EULACE VERNON MCLAURIN** who was born 12 June 1911 and died 13 November 1972 in Fayetteville. He married **HELEN CULBRETH** who was born about 1914 in Boston, Massachusetts, daughter of **Isaac McDuffie Culbreth** and **Mary Alice Murphy (Mary Alice McNulty?).** Eulace was a deputy sheriff and was buried at Salem United Mathodist Church. Four children: **Frances LeGay McLaurin, Mary Alice McLaurin, Carol Annette McLaurin** , and **Harry Eulace McLaurin, Jr.**(sic).

The seventh child of Hinton and Sallie was **BONNIE REBECCA MCLAURIN** who was born 11 January 1916 in Flea Hill Townhip, in Cumberland County, North Carolina. She married **HENRY DUVALL DAIL**, who was born 1 March 1916 and died 2 May 1977 in Fayetteville. He is buried at McMillan Presbyterian Church Cemetery. Three children: **Vernon Royce Dail, Dennis Howell Dail**, and **Gary Mitchell Dail**.

The eighth child of Hinton and Sallie was **RUBY EVELYN MCLAURIN** who was born 1 September 1919 in Flea Hill Township.

4) **DUNCAN A. MCLAURIN**, the fourth child or Sophia and Duncan, was born 7 October 1875 and died 9 February 1901. He was buried in the Duncan McLaurin Family Cemetery.

5) **MARSHALL FLEET MCLAURIN**, the fifth child of Sophia and Duncan was born 25 August 1878 and died 25 March 1950 in Eastover Township. He did not marry and was buried in the Duncan McLaurin Family Cemetery.

6) **GEORGE MELTON MCLAURIN**, the sixth child of Sophia and Duncan was born 1 June 1883 and died 30 November 1967 in Eastover Township in Cumberland County, North Carolina. He married **PAULINE ELIZABETH BYRD** (BESSIE BYRD) who was born 1 September 1888 in Robeson County, North Carolina and died 23 January 1958. Eight children.

7) The seventh child has not been identified.

\+ 137 v. **William Culbreth**, the fifth child of Isaac Culbreth and Mary Ann Maxwell, was born 31 March 1846; died 23 June 1932 in Eastover Township, Cumberland County, North Carolina.

\+ 138 vi. **Sabra Culbreth**, the sixth child of Isaac and Mary Ann, born 23 December 1850; died 12 August 1920.

139 vii. **James Robert Culbreth**, born 26 January 1852; died 21 August 1922 in Carvers Creek Township, Cumberland County, North Carolina. He married (1) Sarah Bullock 27 September 1873; born 22 May 1851; died 18 March 1916 in Carvers Creek Township, Cumberland County, North Carolina. He married (2) Virginia May McCorquodale 25 October 1917; born 1882; died 22 February 1921 in Carvers Creek Township, Cumberland County, North Carolina.

140 viii. **Thomas N. Culbreth**, born about 1853; died after 1880.

Thomas was living with his father in 1880, had rheumatism and was unable to read and write.

\+ 141 ix. **Jennet Culbreth,** the ninth child of Isaac Culbreth and Mary Ann Maxwell, was born about 1857; died after 1884. In 1880, she was living with her sister, Sophia, and brother-in-law, Duncan McLaurin, Jr.

142 x. **Louisa Culbreth**, born about 1861 was the tenth known child of Isaac Culbreth and Mary Ann Maxwell..

Children of Isaac Culbreth and Elizabeth Honeycutt are:

143 i. **Bernice Culbreth**, born 1871. He married Elizabeth Hubbard; born February 1880.

His first name is also listed as "Burnice." Two children, **LEILA AINSLEE CULBRETH** and **Unknown Child**.

144 ii. **John Culbreth**, born 08 September 1872; died 23 March 1945. He married (1) **Luna Augustus Williford** 16 January 1895 in Flea Hill Township, Cumberland County, North Carolina; born 18 January 1871; died 14 May 1907. Luna was the daughter of **Margaret Jane Williams** and **James A. Williford.** He married (2) **Frances Lee Currie** 26 January 1910 in Lumber Bridge, North Carolina; born 24 December 1876; died 24 July 1924 in Lumberton, North Carolina. He married (3) **Nealie May Smith** about 1930; born 26 October 1899; died 21 March 1982 in Lumberton, North Carolina. Nealie May was the daughter **of Lonnie Smith** and **Helena Davis.**

John and Luna Augustus Williford has six children.

1) **An unidentified child** died before 1900.

2) **MARCUS CULBRETH** was born June 1897 in Robeson County and married **HARRIET ETHEL NORTON** on 6 February 1919 in Raeford, North Carolina. She was born about 1898 in Scotland County, North Carolina and they had four children all born in Hoke County, North Carolina: **Malcolm Bruce Culbreth**, **John William Culbreth**, **Unknown Child**, and **Lottis H. Culbreth.**

3) **HENRY C. CULBRETH** was born in February 1899 in Robeson County.

4) **STACEY LEE CULBRETH** was born 16 September 1901 in Hoke County.

5) **LELLON JANE CULBRETH** was born 18 January 1904 in Shannon, Robeson County, North Carolina. She married **C. DEWEY BOUNDS.**

6) **DAUGHTER CULBRETH** was born and died 12 May 1907.

John and Frances Lee Currie had no children.

John and Nealie May Smith had five children, all born in Hoke County, North Carolina.

1) **JOHN FRANKLIN CULBRETH,** born 08 October 1930.

2) **HELEN LOUIE CULBRETH** born 11 September 1933.

3) **WILTON CULBRETH,** born 12 May 1936.

4) **DANIEL STEVEN CULBRETH,** born 16 November 1937.

5) **CHARLES THOMAS CULBRETH,** born 3 September 1939.

+ 145 iii. **Hinton Culbreth**, the third child of Isaac Culbreth and Elizabeth Honeycutt, was born 28 October 1874; died 31 December 1928 in Flea Hill Township, Cumberland County, North Carolina.

+ 146 iv. **Stephen Culbreth**, born 05 May 1877; died 01 June 1957 in Eastover Township, Cumberland County, North Carolina.

+ 147 v. **Daniel Maxwell Culbreth**, born 12 May 1878; died 11 April 1952 in Eastover Township, Cumberland County, North Carolina.

+ 148 vi. **Isaac McDuffie Culbreth**, born 25 October 1879; died 24 December 1924.

36. Daniel Maxwell Culbreth (Mary[3] Holland, Thomas William[2], Unknown[1]) was born 13 October 1820 in Sampson County, North Carolina, and died 21 February 1865 in Elmira, New York. He married **(2) Jannett Maxwell** about 1841, daughter of Neil Maxwell and Sophia Matthews. She was born 29 March 1821, and died 28 May 1895. Jannett Maxwell was buried in Maxwell Cemetery, Clement, Sampson County, North Carolina.

Daniel Maxwell (Daniel Mc) was a minor when his father died. The report on the partition of the lands of his father was submitted to the court on 20October1832 and registered on 14 January1833. Daniel Maxwell "Colbreath," was a minor living with his sister, "Tomzilia" and her husband Joel Williams and drew Lot No. 4 containing 100 acres.

Page 390 of the Sampson County Heritage source notes this: "Daniel Mc Culbreth died at Elmira, New York after his capture at Fort Fisher on January 15, 1865. He enlisted 13 September 1863, at age 44, in 3rd Company B, 36th Regiment, N.C. Troops for three years. After his capture at Fort Fisher, he was confined at Elmira, New York where he died February 21, 1865 of diarrhea."

His death is well documented. Page 69 in Professor Bundy's book notes that Danial Mc (Maxwell) died on February 21, 1865 in Virginia while serving in the American Civil War and was buried there. An inscription on a stone in Maxwell Cemetery at the intersection of Maxwell Road and SR 1427 in Sampson County, North Carolina, notes he was "captured at Fort Fisher on January 15, 1865" and "confined at Elmira Prison, New York," died there and was "buried in Grave No. 2265 in Woodlawn National Cemetery in Elmira, New York." Transcribed cemetery records note that he and his wife, "Jannet Maxwell Culbreth, have stones in the Neil Culbreth Cemetery off Dunn Road north of Roseboro, North Carolina; an inscription on his stone notes that he died at Elmira, New York.

His three oldest sons, John, William and Daniel also served in the war.

Daniel Maxwell was known as "Daniel Mc." This nickname caused me research problems because sometimes, Daniel Maxwell was used; other times they used "Daniel Mc." Although I eventually found a source that told me Daniel Mc was Daniel Maxwell, I'm not convinced that "Maxwell" was the middle name of this Daniel. It is clear from comments of other researchers that they do not know the maiden name of his father's wife, but they strongly believe it was "Maxwell." It is possible that his father, Daniel, had two wives, both named "Mary," (first **MARY HOLLAND** and second, **MARY MAXWELL**) and the **Old Holland Record Book** of Thomas William Holland proves that one wife was a "Holland." The names of his three older siblings are found in the Old Holland Record Book of Thomas William Holland and in Holland Families.

Court Minutes of Sampson County, North Carolina record: 19 February1840, "(23) State vs Dan M. Culbreath - A.B. (Assault and Battery.)" Defendant comes into Court and submits and is fined five cents and stands committed until fine & costs are paid."

The minutes of the Sampson County Court of Pleas and Quarter Sessions record actions involving Daniel M. Culbreth and his fathering children with women whom he did not marry. Sorces on Ancestry.com show that he married all the women mentioned in court records as noted below, but I have not found any other record to support this and as written elsewhere, Mary was the name of his wife.

19 February 1840, "Daniel M. Culbreath comes into court & admits he is the father of a ... child begotten in the body of **Lilly Faircloth** and is ordered by the Court that he pay the said Lilly Faircloth ten dollars for the first month and five dollars annually afterwards, commencing 1st of November 1839, and that he enter into bond with William Bullard and Young Autry as security." It is said that the child's name was Arbella.

20 August 1840 "(25) State vs. Dan M. Culbreath. William Butler (sic), & Young Autry" "Defendant called and failed on motion. Judgment against Defendant & sureties according to Sci Fai."

26 February 1841. "(42) Dan M. Culbreath comes into open court and acknowledges himself the father of a ... child begotten on **Sylvany Faircloth** & is ordered by the Court that said Culbreath pay unto said Faircloth ten dollars for the first month's support of said child and seven dollars annually afterwards commencing 1st June 1840 and enters into bond with John Fowler & Thomas Bullard securities."

18 May 1841, "(38) Daniel M. Culbreath comes into Court & acknowledges himself the father of a ... child begotten on the body of **Jennet Autery**. Ordered that said Culbreath pay said Jennet Autery ten dollars for the first month's support of said child and seven dollars annually commencing first day of March 1841 & enters into Bond with A. Hall & Love Culbreath Sureties." **Jennet Autry**, daughter of **Archibald Autry** and **Patience Autry,** was born about 1820 and was living in 1880 in Dismal Township. Jennet and son, **James Autry**, are listed in the 1850 Census of the Northern Division of Sampson County (Dwelling 353) as aged 30 and 8 and living with her parents. Jennet and James were listed in the 1860 Census

of Dismal District (Dwelling 32) as aged 35 and 18 and living with her parents. Jennet did not marry and her son, **James C. Autry,** died during the Civil War. (see below.)

16 November1841, "(50) Daniel M. Culbreath in open Court acknowledges himself the father of a ... child begotten on Betsey Hall. Ordered said Culbreath pay unto said Betsey Hall ten dollars for the first month's support of said child and seven dollars annually for seven years commencing on the first day of November 1841 and enters into Bond with Lemon (Simon?) Sessoms & John Sessoms as sureties."

"**Elizabeth Hall (Betsey Hall)** was born about 1810 and died after 1860 Census. She was listed in the 1850 Census of the Northern Division of Sampson County Dwelling) as aged 40 with three children, Schoolfield, aged 13, Charles, aged 8, and Fearby, aged 5. She was listed in the 1860 Census of Little Coharie District, Northern Division (Dwelling 270) as aged 50 with three children."

"**CHARLES H. HALL,** son of Daniel M. Culbreth and **Elizabeth Hall,** was born 24 October 1841. He died 11 October 1907 He married about 1878 as her second husband, **Charlotte Sessoms** who was born 1 March 1837 and died 27 March 1920, daughter of **Gray Sessoms** and **Sabra Hall.**" Charlotte first married a Mr. Fisher. Charles and Charlotte had one son, **GRANT HALL,** who was born 23 May 1881 and died 18 April 1945 in Greensboro. Grant married twice. Data on his family can be found on page 856 in "Coharie To Cape Fear", Vol. 2."

Grant Hall first married "7 October 1905, **Donnie A. Hall** who was born about 1884, daughter of Junious Filmore Hall and Mary Isabella Vinson. Two children."

Grant married second, 27 November 1918, **Mamie Elizabeth Jolly,** born. 29 September 1895, died 26 January 1982 in Greensboro, daughter of **George Washington Jolly** and **Adeline Elizabeth Nunnery.** Four children.

"**JAMES C. AUTRY,** son of Daniel M. Culbreth and Jennet Autry, was born about March 1841 and died about 15 November 1864. He enlisted 21 July 1862 at age 28 (sic) at Camp Holmes, near Raleigh, in Company F, 32nd Regiment Infantry, North Carolina Troops. He was captured on or about 10 May 1864 at or near Spottsylvania Court House, Virginia, and confined 18 May 1864 at Point Lookout, Maryland until transferred 3 August 1864 to (the Union Prison Camp) in Elmira, New York where he died on or about 15 November 1864. - North Carolina Troops, 1861 - 1865, a Roster, Volume IX, pa. 57.

Another source for his Civil War record: James C. Autry: "(He enlisted 14 Aug 1862 in Clinton in Company F, 32nd Regiment Infantry, North Carolina Troops. He was hospitalized 3 July 1862 and 3 January 1863 at Petersburg, Virginia. He was captured 10 May 1864 in the Wilderness, Virginia, and confined at Elmira, New York, where he died 15 November1864 - Sampson County Heritage, p. 217.) He is buried in Grave No. 802 in Woodlawn National Cemetery, Elmira, according to the "List of Confederate Soldiers Buried in Woodlawn National Cemetery, Elmira, New York" by the Chemung County Historical Society, Elmira, New York."

Both of the above Civil War Records for James C. Autry are probably correct. It was not unusal for a person to enlist on one date and when he was camped near home, he would visit his family and upon leaving to return to his company, it would be gone from the area and he would enlist in another company. If this was the case with James, he found Company F again, but in the meantime, he may have been serving in another one.

Professor Bundy mentions in his family history, that to his knowledge at that time, only three living great-great-grandsons of Daniel Mc were of child-bearing age to carry on the Daniel Mc Culbreth name. They possibly were **Christopher Culbreth** and **Johnathan Culbreth** of Fayetteville, North Carolina, and **John Culbreth** of Shrewsbury, Massachusetts, descendants of Daniel L. Culbreth, Sr.

Children of Daniel Culbreth and Jannett Maxwell are:

\+ 150 i. **John Culbreth**, born 06 June 1842 in Sampson County, North Carolina; died 23 November 1889.

\+ 151 ii. **William Culbreth**, born … 1894.

\+ 152 iii. **Daniel L. Culbreth, Sr.**, … ina; died 13 July 1882.

153 iv. **Thomas Culbreth**, born a…

\+ 154 v. **Martha Rebecca Culbret**… 1 November 1929.

155 vi. **Jennetta Culbreth**, born …

\+ 156 vii. **Tomzillia Culbreth**, bor… rch 1913 in Sampson County, North …

157 viii. **Love Culbreth**, born 03 J…

Love died in infancy.

158 ix. **Mary Culbreth**, born 07 September 1858 in Sampson County; died 13 January 1911. She married **Gillead Gainey** before 1891; he was born 10 November 1855 and died 26 April 1935. They had five children. Twins died at birth in 1891 and **Dossie Gainey,** born 12 February 1893 married **ARCHIE SRICKLAND** and they had no children. **Garland Gainey** who was born 9 September 1896 and died 24 September 1974 married on 6 June 1929 to **MITILDA GEDDIE** who died 23 August 1967. They had no children. **Gladys Gainey** was born 16 July 1897 and died 1 February 1899. This family is now extinct. Mary and Gilead were buried in a Family Cemetery in Cumberland County, North Carolina near South River. Gilead's first name is also found as Gaillard.

Gilead (Gillard) married second to **EMMA STARLING** and they had three children.

\+ 159 x. **Virginia Culbreth**, born 16 January 1861 in Sampson County, North Carolina; died 22 May 1940 in Dismal Township, Sampson County, North Carolina.

39. Daniel L. Hairr (Orpah[3] Holland, Thomas William[2], Unknown[1]) was born about 1819 in Sampson County, North Carolina, and died 17 November 1862 in Hospital in

Farmville, Virginia. He married **Lucinda Holland**, daughter of Henry Holland and Mary Tew. She was born 05 November 1826 in Sampson County, North Carolina, and died after 1880 in Sampson County, North Carolina.

Lucinda and Daniel were first cousins. Her first name has been found as "Lucindy" (1860 census) and "Lucindia" on the certificate of death for her son, George Washington. Daniel was a Private in Company I, Regiment 46 during the Civil War. He enlisted 12 March 1862 in Clinton, North Carolina, and died of disease in the hospital in Farmville, Virginia.

John Hair, aged 22 was listed in Daniel and Lucinda's household in 1850. I believe he was a brother of Daniel. John, aged 8, was also listed in 1850, but was not with them in 1860. It is unclear whether the younger John was a son of Daniel and Lucinda. John C. Hair who was born about 1827, John C. Hair, born about 1831, and John Hair, born about 1840, all served in the American Civil War. All three were born in Sampson County and all three died while serving in the war.

In the 1860 census for Sampson County, North Carolina, "Orpha (Orpah. Orphy)," aged 63 was listed with Lucinda and Daniel. "Nanny," aged 43 was also listed. Orpha was most likely Lucinda's Aunt who is found in the **Old Holland Record Book** and Nanny (Nancy) could be Orpha's daughter; "Nancy," aged 33. was living with Orphy, aged 55, in 1850.

In 1870, Lucinda Hairr, aged 44, was head of household with four children listed with her.

In 1880, Lucinda and her three youngest children were living near her son, George W. and his family and next door to Harfrey Holland, Lucinda's cousin. Other Hollands were also near.

"Harphy" (Harfrey) Holland was found near Lucinda and Harfrey's mother, Elizabeth and his sisters, Elizabeth and Milsy, were in a dwelling by him. Listed with Lucinda was Mary, aged 26, "Charly H.," aged 19 and "Archy," aged 12.

Children of Daniel Hairr and Lucinda Holland are:

162 i. **John Hairr,** born about 1842 in Sampson County, North Carolina; died 20 February 1863.

This John Hair was listed in 1850 in the household of Daniel and Lucinda. He was listed under Daniel's brother, John, aged 22, indicating that he may not have been the son of Daniel and Lucinda, but was related in some other way.

He may have been the John Hair, born about 1840 who served as a Private in Company F., Regiment. 20, Infantry in the Civil War and died 20 February 1863. Sgt. W. R. Highsmith stated: "Hair died in camp of smallpox."

\+ 163 ii. **George Washington Hair**, born 06 May 1851 in Sampson County, North Carolina; died 27 April 1934 in Honeycutts Township, Sampson County.

164 iii. **Mary Mariah Gretson Hairr**, born 11 February 1854 in Sampson County, North Carolina, and died 11 December 1929 in Honeycutts Township in Sampson County.

In the 1860 census for Sampson County, Mary was listed as "Mary M.," aged 6 and "Mary" in 1870, aged 14. Her name looks like **Mary Uriah Gretson Hair** in the **Old Holland Record Book**, but some of the writing is faded and difficult to read. Her name probably was

"Mary Mariah Gretson Hairr. Images from that old record book may be found near the back of this book. Most census records show "Mary M." for her name.

In 1880, she was single and living in the household of her mother, Lucindia (Lucinda).

In 1910, she was incorrectly listed as Mary Hair, aged 53, **sister,** in the household of Archie B. Hairr. Archie's first wife was deceased and Mary, was apparently this "Mary Mariah Gretson Hairr," his cousin.

She never maried. Her certificate of death names Arteriosclerosis Myocarditis for cause of death.

\+ 165 iv. **Charles Henry Hair,** born 17 January 1861 in Sampson County, North Carolina; died 23 July 1938 in Sampson County. **Charlie Henry Hair** was also found for his name.

\+ 166 v. **Archie Bradley Hairr,** born in 1866 Sampson County, North Carolina. The 1870 and 1880 Federal Censuses **incorrectly record Archie B. Hairr for a son of Luncinda Hairr.** He was actually the son of **John C. Hairr,** brother of Daniel, Lucinda's deceased husband. Both Daniel and John C. died serving in the Civil War. Archie and his family can be found elsewhere in this book.

40. Stephen H. Hairr (Orpah[3] Holland, Thomas William[2], Unknown[1]) was born 12 March 1821 in Sampson County, North Carolina, and died 21 May 1881. He married **Mary Jane Daughtry**. She was born 10 March 1825, and died after August 1881.

A deed noted below names him as "Stephen H. Hair. Did the H. stand for "HOLLAND?" Mary Jane is entered as "**Janetta Daughtry**" in a source on Ancestry.com; this could have been her middle name, but it possibly was only a nickname.

A few of Stephen's descendants are listed in "The Heritage of Sampson County, North Carolina" by Oscar M. Bizzel, Editor. Certificates of Death for several of his descendants spell the surname "**HARE.**"

A few researchers have incorrectly linked three early men named Stephen Hair (Hare). It appears that children for one Stephen have been linked incorrectly to another Stephen. Records show Stephen "Hare" serving in the Civil War for a short time until it was found that he was 40 years old. "Stephen Hare was a Private in Company C. Regiment 38, Infantry. He was born about1821 in Sampson County and was a f armer when he enlisted on 18 October 1861 in Clinton. He was sick furloughed January to March 1861 and discharged 9 December 1862." The older Stephen would have been about 50 years of age and was an older distant cousin. The youngest Stephen to serve in the Civil War was born in 1838. Men over aged 40 served in the Civil War indicating the discharge may have been for another reason.

On 1 August 1880, "Stephen H. Hairr" and wife, Mary Jane, sold three parcels of land (total 286 acres) for $800 to John R. Cannady. Fann's corner and Horse Pasture Pocosin are mentioned in the deed for the first parcel which joined James H. Porter's land; second parcel mentioned Horse Pasture Pocosin; the third parcel mentioned "Canady's corner in Mrs. Porter's line ... Ditch Wootens corner... Lewis' line ... Tew's line ... great Piney Pocosin."

The submitter for one family tree on ancestry.com shows "Hair" born about 1805 and Obedience "Beady" born about 1810 for the parents of Blackman, Stephen and Mary's son. Other sources show that "Obedience Howard" was the spouse of Thomas Hair who was born about 1798. See notes for Orpah Holland.

Children of Stephen Hairr and Mary Daughtry are:

+ 167 i. **Simon S, Hairr,** born about 1844 in Sampson County, North Carolina; died in Pikeville, Wayne County, North Carolina.

+ 168 ii. **Blackman Hairr,** born 27 August 1845; died 30 January 1920.

+ 169 iii. **William H. Hairr,** born 07 August 1847 in Sampson County, North Carolina; died 25 March 1896.

+ 170 iv. **Eliza Jane Hairr,** born about 1848; died before 1900.

+ 171 v. **Hinton Hairr,** born about 1851.

+ 172 vi. **Mary M. Hairr,** born about 1855.

+ 173 vii. **Fanny C. Hairr,** born 12 June 1855; died 18 July 1902 in Sampson County, North Carolina.

174 viii. **Joel Hairr,** born about 1859.

+ 175 ix. **Henry Stephen Hairr,** born 19 July 1859; died 20 December 1926.

41. Holland Hairr (Orpah[3] Holland, Thomas William[2], Unknown[1]) was born about 1827 in Sampson County, North Carolina. He married **Lydia Ann McLamb** who was born about 1836; I have not identified her parents.

The Certificate of Death for their son, "**HOLLAND HARE**" names **KITTIE MCLAMB** and **HOLLAND HARE** for his parents. Their son, Jonathan, appears to have, at times, used the name "John" rather than "Jonathan" and his Certificate of Death names "Holland Hair" for his father and "Not Known" for his mother.

I have not been successful in finding Holland in the 1850 census. Listed with Holland Hair, aged 33, cooper, in the 1860 Federal census of Sampson County, North Carolina, were his wife, Lydia, A. aged 27; Lassister, 8; Jonathan, 4; James, 2; Frances A., 1 month. He and his family were living in Dwelling 372 in Hawleys Store, Dismal Township in 1860. His name, age, and location of his dwelling lead me to believe that Holland may have been a son of Orpah Holland and John Athae Hair, Jr. or perhaps a nephew, but I have no proof. Holland was a Pvt., in Co. F, Regt 20, Inf, during the Civil War. The transcribed war record gives 1837 for his year of birth indicating that either 1837 or his age of 33 in the 1860 census was incorrect He enlisted on 1 August 1861 at Fort Johnston and served as a Private in Company F of the 20th Regiment, North Carolina Infantry. Holland was wounded in left arm 17 September 1862 at Sharpsburg, Maryland, captured 19 October 1864 at Cedar Creek, Virginia, and confined to Point Lookout, Maryland. A.W.O.L from 1 December 1862 to 1 June 1864. He was received 30 March 1865 at Boulware's Wharf, Virginia for exchange.

Holland and Lydia were living in Elizabethtown, Bladen County, North Carolina, in 1870 with children listed above and Holland, Jr., aged 6. Holland and "Liddy Ann" Hare and all their children except Lassister were living and farming near Clinton, Sampson County, North Carolina, in 1880. I have found no data after 1880 meaning that possibly he and Lydia died before 1900.

Children of Holland Hairr and Lydia McLamb are:

176 i. Lassiter Hairr, born about 1852. He was listed "Lassiter Hair," aged 8, with his parents in Honeycutts Township in Sampson County, North Carolina, in a transcribed 1860 Federal Census, and as "ELAFINDER HAIR," aged 17, with his parents in Elizabethtown Township, Bladen County, North Carolina, in 1870. I have found no other data for him and surmise that he either died young or his actual name did not come close to the spelling of these two names.

177 ii. **Jonathan Hairr** (JOHN HAIRR) was born 9 July 1855 in Sampson County, North Carolina, and died 15 April 1926 in Wolfscrape Township, Duplin County, North Carolina. He first married "Unknown Spouse" and they had one child. He then married Mary F. (maiden name unknown) and they had three children. She was born about 1865 in North Carolina and died 26 December 1943 in Duplin County, North Carolina. Apparently, Jonathan used the name **"JOHN HAIRR"** after 1880. This family lived in Wolfscrape Township in northern Duplin County and had a rural Mt. Olive mailing address; Mt. Olive is in Wayne County, North Carolina.

The first child of Jonathan and his Unidentified first spouse was **LEVIE HAIR** who was born 27 April 1881 in North Carolina and died 22 March 1925 in Wolfscrape Township, Duplin County, North Carolina. His brother, J. W. HARE (John W.), was the informant on his certificate of death and names "JOHN HARE" for Levie's father and he did not know the name of his mother. This and the 1930 census listing Mary in the household of John and his family, apparently mean that Jonathan (John) was married twice. Levie and HIS wife had three children: 1) **EVA HAIR** who was born 1914 in Duplin County; 2) **WILLIE JAMES HARE** who was born 1919 in Duplin County; 3) **UNIDENTIFIED HAIR** who was born 1922 in Duplin County.

This family lived in Wolfscrape Township in northern Duplin County and had a rural Mt. Olive mailing address; Mt. Olive is in Wayne County, North Carolina. Levie's World War I Draft Registration provides his date of birth.

The second child of Jonathan (John) and first child of Mary, his second wife, was **JOHN W. HAIR** who was born about 1893 in North Carolina. In 1930 and one other census record, John W. was listed as "JONAS W. HARE." In 1930, he was head of household in Glisson Township in Duplin County and his mother MARY H. and his brother **JAMES HARE** were with him.

The third child of Jonathan and second of Mary was **JAMES E. HAIR** who was born about 1895 in North Carolina. The fact that he was living with his brother, John, and his mother in 1930 may indicate that he did not marry.

The fourth child of Jonathan and third child of Mary was **VIVIE H. HAIR** who was born about 1897 in North Carolina. No other information is known about her.

178 iii. **James Hairr,** born about 1858 was the third child of **Holland Hare** and **Lydia McLamb.**

179 iv. **Frances A. Hairr**, born about 1860 was the fourth child of Holland Hare and Lydia McLamb.

180 v. **Holland Hairr**, born about 1864, was the fifth child of Holland Hare and Lydia McLamb.

It appears that he was married twice, but I can't place the order of the wives. He married **FANNIE L. HOBBS**, the daughter of **HENRY HOBBS** and **MARY MOORE.** She was born 15 February 1873 in North Carolina and died 15 April 1966 in Mr. Olive, Brogden Township, Wayne County, North Carolina. Fannie died of Bronchial Pneumonia and she had Hypertensive cardiovascular Disease for over 10 years. Holland also married **SARAH E. LEE;** they may have married in February 1888 in Sampson County, North Carolina, or this may have been when Sarah was born. Perhaps there were two men known as "Holland Hairr (Hare)" who were about the same age and the birth of Sarah's child may indicate this.

HOLLAND HARE is entered for his and his father's name on his certificate of death and **KITTIE MCLAMB** is named for his mother. The cause of his death is difficult to read, but it appears that he was in an accident on 11 July 1931 and died on the 7 August from injuries he received in the accident.

Children of Holland Hairr and Fannie Hobbs, all born in North Carolina:

1) **MARY HAIRR** was born 19 October 1893 in Sampson County, North Carolina and died 20 March 1960 in Goldsboro, Wayne County, North Carolina. She married **J. H. EZZELL** who died before 1960. Mary fell and fractured her hip several monts before she died of infected ulcers and malnutrition.

2) **WINNIE HAIRR** was born 7 June 1898 in Wayne County, North Carolina and died 1 March 1951 in Clinton, Sampson County, North Carolina. She married **T. J. HOLLINGSWORTH.**

3) **BLACKMAN HAIRR** was born about 1900.

4) **EFFIE HAIRR**, born about 1903.

5) **ROSY HAIRR**, born about 1905.

6) **NETTIE HAIRR**, born about 1906.

7) **STELLA HAIRR**, born about 1908.

8) **DAISY HAIRR**, born about 1911.

9) **GLADYS HAIRR**, born about 1913.

10) **BESSIE HAIRR**, born about 1916.

Child of Holland Hairr and Sarah Lee:

FANNY HAIRR was born 1915 in Duplin County, North Carolina. Fanny may actually have been the daughter of Holland and his first wife, Fanny.

42. Gilmore Hairr (Orpah[3] Holland, Thomas William[2], Unknown[1]) was born between 1828 - 1832 in Sampson County, North Carolina. He married **Eliza Holland**, daughter of John Holland and Dicey (maiden name unknown). She was born about 1840 in Sampson County, North Carolina, and died after 1900, and was his first cousin.

Gilmore served in the Civil War as a Private in Company H, 20th Regiment, Infantry. He enlisted on 7 August 1861 at Fort Johnston, North Carolina, was captured between 9-11 October 1863 near Brandy Station, Virginia, and confined at Point Lookout, Maryland. Received 15 November 1864 at Venus Point, Savannah River, Georgia, for exchange.

In 1860 "Gilmore Hair" and Eliza were living in Eastern Cumberland County, North Carolina, with a Fayetteville address and C. Holland, aged 18, female, was listed in their household. Eliza's sister, Charity, would have been about 18 years of age, but she also was listed in their father's household in the 1860 census. Cumberland and Sampson County censuses were probably taken on different days and this would explain why Charity was listed in both households. She may have been with Eliza to assist her after the birth of Polly Ann who appeared as P. A. in the 1860 census.

In the 1870 census, Gilmore was entered "Gillmore Hare" in White Oak Township in Bladen County, North Carolina. He and his family were back in Honeycutts Township in Sampson County in 1880.

Much inconsistent data is found in the various records for Gilmore and Eliza's family, but I have yet to find records to disprove the family data entered below.

Children of Gilmore Hairr and Eliza Holland are:

181 i. **Molsey Adline Hairr**, was the first child of Gilmore Hairr and Eliza Holland and was born 18 October 1858 and died 15 April 1931.

In the **Old Holland Record Book**, Mosley is found as "Molsey Adline Holland," born 18 October 1858, daughter of "**Elizar Holland**" and **Gillmore Hairr**. "Molly A." is also found for her name.

Records support Molsey's marriage to **MICAJAH BLACKMAN LOCKAMY**, son of **ODOM LOCKAMY** and **MALINDA AUTRY**. Micajah was born 2 July 1853 and died 18 July 1937 and was the brother the husband of Mosley's sister, Polly Ann. The certificates of death for two sons, names Molsey as "Molsie Hair" or "Mollie Hair." Their daughter, Margaret's certificate of death names "Maveeley Hair" for her mother. The certificate of death for their son, Charlie, incorrectly names Moslay "HORNE" for his mother. Molsey's tombstone records her as "Molcey A. Lockamy." "Micajah Blackman" is found as "Macajah," "Cager," "Kager," and his gravestone records only "C. B. Lockamy." He was a brother of **JAMES O. LOCKAMY** (JAMES DALTON LOCKAMY) who married Polly Ann, sister of Molsey Adline.

They are buried in Mt. Zion Church Cemetery in Sampson County, North Carolina, near his brother, James O., (and her sister,) Polly Ann Lockamy, I believe that Molsey, wife of Micajah, and Polly Ann, wife of James, are sisters, but I cannot actually prove it. However, I have found nothing that disproves it. See notes below for Polly Ann Hairr.

Children of Molsey and Micajah.

GEORGE THOMAS LOCKAMY, the first child of Molsey and Micajah was born 13 May 1875 in Sampson County and died 17 February 1955 in Dunn, Harnett County, North Carolina. He married AQUILLA S. Maiden Name Unknown, who was born 2 April 1895 and died 28 December 1976. Their residence was in Mingo Township in Sampson County, but he died in Dunn in Harnett County.

CHARLIE RANSOM LOCKAMY, the second child of Molsey and Micajah, was born 31 October 1885 (or 1886) in Sampson County and died 15 July 1968 in Fayetteville, Cumberland County, North Carolina. His certificate of death names him Charlie Ransom Lockamy, but "Charlie B." is listed for his name on his tombstone. Charlie married **LILLIE ELLEN BASS** who was born 12 April 1898 and died 4 May 1972. They are buried in Mt. Zion Church Cemetery in Sampson County, North Carolina. He and Lillie had two known children. **FREEMAN ALTON LOCKAMY**, their first child, was born 3 February 1923 in North Carolina and died 3 January 1976 in Fayetteville, Cumberland County. He was buried by his parents in Mt. Zion Church Cemetery. **CRAFTON J. LOCKAMY** was their second child and was born 31 October 1925 in Sampson County. He married **Omia Lee Dudley** who was born 6 October 1924 and died 6 February 1990. She was buried in Mt. Zion Cemetery, but transcribed cemetery records show no date of death for Crafton who is also named on the monument.

ELI LOCKAMY, the third child of Molsey Adline and Micajah, was born 25 May 1891 in Sampson County and died 11 January 1952 in Veterans Hospital in Oteen, Buncombe County, North Carolina. He married Dovie, maiden name unknown, who was born 16 November 1895 and her gravestone at Mt. Zion does not show a date of death. Eli served in World War I. The Veterans Hospital in Oteen was established during World War I. He died there of pulmonary hemorrhage and was buried in Mt. Zion Cemetery. An infant was buried near them.

MARGARET LOCKAMY, fourth known child of Molsey and Micajah, was born 28 May 1888 in Sampson County and died 23 February 1975 in Betsy Johnson Memorial Hospital in Dunn, Harnett County, North Carolina. She married a **CHARLIE A. BASS** who was born 18 February 1882 and died 14 March 1947. At the time of her death, she lived in Wade, Cumberland County, North Carolina. She and Charlie were buried in Mt. Zion Church Cemetery in Sampson County. **Joseph Weldon Bass** was the informant listed on her certificate of death and was probably their son. He was born 3 October 1934 and listed with or near him on a stone in Mt. Zion Cemetery is **Rossie McLaurin** who was born 8 April 1936.

182 ii. **Polly Ann Hairr**, was the second child of Gilmore Hairr and Eliza Holland and was born about May 1860 in Cumberland County, North Carolina.

She appeared as P. A. in the 1860 census for Cumberland County, North Carolina, as "Polly A." in the 1870 census for White Oak Township in Bladen County and was not listed with her parents in 1880. I have not found a certificate of death for Polly Ann. However, census records, vital statistics, and cemetery records I have found support her marriage to **JAMES O. LOCKAMY**, son of **Odom Lockamy** and **Malinda Autry**. James was the brother of the husband of Polly Ann's sister, Mosley. James can be found in 1880 with wife, "Mary A," aged 21, and this appears to be the only time Polly was recorded as MARY. "Polly" was oftern used as a nickname for Mary. James Wesley, James' son by May (or Mary) Jackson, his first wife, was living with James' parents in 1880 which could mean that either May was deceased or she was unable to care for James Wesley. However, Polly Ann was not with her parent in 1880.

The informant, Hassell Sykes, listed on the certificate of death for J. O. Lockamy (James O.), names POLLY ANN LOCKAMY for James' wife, but did not know the names of James' parents. I'm inclined to believe that "JAMES O. LOCKAMY" was **"JAMES DALTON LOCKAMY,"** who is found listed on Ancestry.com as a son of Odom and Malinda Lockamy. All other records show his name as James O., J. O., Jim O. and a certificate of death for their daughter, Mary E., names him incorrectly as "M. O. Lockamy." James' middle name was probably "ODUM" and not "Dalton." I have found no other record for a James Dalton Lockamy and when spoken, Dalton and Odom sound similar.

It appears that about 1872, James married **May Jackson** (Mae Jackson) who gave birth to **JAMES WESLEY LOCKAMY** on 03 February 1873 and May (Mae) apparently died before 1880, when James Wesley was living with his grandparents, Odom and Malinda Lockamy. In 1880, Odom and Malinda also had another grandson in their household, but I have been unable to place that grandson as a child of James O. James Wesley died on 1 April 1949 and was buried in Erwin Memorial Park, Erwin, Harnett County, North Carolina. He married **Alice Orena Dale** who was born 18 August 1874 and died 8 January 1950 and is buried in Erwin Memorial Park. They had ten children.

James O. and "Polly A." are buried next to James' brother, **C. B. (Micajah Blackman Lockamy**) and Molcey A. Lockamy in Mt. Zion Church Cemetery in Sampson County. Their children, Mary E., Emily Jane, and James Claude (and his wife) are buried near them. Several other descendants of Odom Lockamy and Malinda Autry were also buried there. Records indicate that Micajah Blackman (C.B.), James' brother, married Polly Ann's sister, **Molsey Adline Hairr.** I'm inclined to believe that the "C" in C. B. stood for "Cajah" or Cager a nickname for **Micajah**. It is high likely that not many family members actually knew the full name of **Micajah Blackman Lockamy**. See Molsey and Micajah above.

CHILDREN OF POLLY ANN HAIRR AND JAMES O. LOCKAMY:

MARY E. LOCKAMY was the first known child and was born 17 September 1886 in North Carolina and died 10 June 1969 in Golden Years Home in Falcon, Cumberland County, North Carolina. Her certificate of death records 17 September 1879 for her birth and transcribed cemetery records list 17 September 1897 for her birth. Given that the certificate names M. O. Lockamy for her father, the dates are clearly incorrect. I did not find her in the 1880 census; in 1900, she was listed as aged 14 and in 1910, she was aged 22. She never married and was buried near her parents. The informant for data on her death certificate was C. L. Lockamy who might have been her brother, Charles,

EMILY JANE LOCKAMY was the second child of Polly and James and was born 17 August 1887 and died 4 October 1965 in Dunn, Harnett County, North Carolina. Her brother, James Claude, was the listed informant on her certificate of death which states that she was a retired farmer in Sampson County. She died in Betsy Johnson Memorial Hospital in Dunn of pneumonia and a staph infection in wound on left hip and was buried near her parents in Mt. Zion Church Cemetery in Sampson County.

JAMES CLAUDE LOCKAMY, the third known child of Polly and James, was born 27 July 1899 in North Carolina and died 10 January 1979 in Sampson County. He married Maude L. whom I believe was his first cousin once removed and was the daughter of EMMIT WOOD LOCKAMY and ADA JANE SESSOMS. Maude was born 23 July 1910 and ded 27 February 1977. James Claude and Maude and their infants were buried near his parents in Mt. Zion Church Cemetery.

CHARLES LOCKAMY , the fourth child was born about 1902 in North Carolina.

183 iii. **Mary E. Hairr** was the third child of Gilmore Hairr and Eliza Holland and was born about 1867 and died 26 June 1925 in Black River Township in Cumberland County, North Carolina

184 iv. **Harriet Tishie Hairr**, the fourth child of Gilmore Hairr and Eliza Holland, was born 15 February 1868 in Sampson County, North Carolina and died 5 March 1918 in Little Coharie Township, Sampson County. She **married DANIEL H. FAIRCLOTH,** son of **Bluford Faircloth** and **Mary Autry**. He was born about 1858 in Cumberland County, North Carolina, and died September 1936 in Cumberland County, North Carolina.

"Harriet R." was listed for her name in the 1870 Federal Census of Bladen county, North Carolina. The certificate of death for "TISHIE FAIRCLOTH" states she was to be buried in a "Holland Grave Yard," but does not mention where it was located. Daniel was listed as "D. H. Faircloth," aged 62, in the 1920 census for Little Coharie Township in Sampson County and his daughter, **MINNIE LEE FAIRCLOTH**, aged 23, was listed with him.

Children of Harriet Hairr and Daniel Faircloth:

WILLIAM H. FAIRCLOTH, first known child, was born about 1892.

MINNIE LEE FAIRCLOTH, second known child of Harriet Hairr and Daniel Faircloth, was born 21 May 1896 in Sampson County and died 10 November 1950 in Pittman Hospital in Fayetteville, Cross Creek Township, Cumberland County, North Carolina. She married **DAWSON SASSER** who was born about 1889 in North Carolina. Minnie is buried in Fayetteville, North Carolina; the name of the cemetery is not written clearly on her certificate of death. She and Dawson had two children listed in the 1930 census and may have had others after 1930.

ANNIE SASSER was born about 1927 in Eastover Township in Cumberland County.

DAWSON SASSER was born about 1929 in Eastover Township in Cumberland County.

v. **EMMET HAIRR** is found as the fifth child of Gilmore Hairr and Eliza Holland. He was born about 1869 in Bladen County, North Carolina, appears in 1870 Fedearl Census of Bladen County, but does not appear in the 1880 census with Gilmore and Eliza, indicating that he may have died before 1880.

185 vi. **John Oliver Hairr,** sixth known child of Gilmore Hairr and Eliza Holland, was born 30 January 1874 and died 09 August 1962. He married **Annie Lee Horne** who was born 22 September 1878 and died 31 December 1943.

In 1900,**John O. Hairr** was single, lived in Little Coharie Township, Sampson County, North Carolina, and was head of household that included his mother (Elijas - spelled incorrectly), his sister (Susan), and niece, **Vider J. Holland,** aged 12.

He was probably the **John O. Hair**" listed in the 1930 census with Spouse, Annie L. and six children: John died of a Cerebral Hemorrhage due to hypertensive cardiovascular disease and he and Annie L. were buried in Baptist Chapel Church Cemetery on Baptist Chapel Road, Sampson County, North Carolina

John and Annie's known children:

GEORGE WASHINGTON HAIRR, Sr., the first known child of John Oliver and Annie Lee, was born 20 May 1905 and died 21 April 1960. He married first **IDA FLORENCE BEASLEY** about 1924. She was the daughter of J. D(?) Beasley and Nettie (maiden name unknown), and was born 27 May 1904 in Sampson County and died 1 March 1938 in Dismal Township in Sampson County. George married second to **SARAH FRANCIS HALL,** daughter of **Thomas L. Hall** and **Mary Malissa Hall**. Sarah Francis was born 16 May 1914 and died 23 October 1972. George, Ida Florence, and Sarah "Frances H." were buried in Baptist Chapel Cemetry on Baptist Chapel Road in Sampson County, North Carolina.

George and Ida had four children:

1) **ELLA M. HAIRR** was born about 1925.

2) **MARGARET L. HAIRR** was born about 1927.

3) **RUTH ELAINE HAIR**

4) GEORGE WASHINGTON HAIRR, JR.

I found data for Ruth Elaine's family and for George's family, but found no other information for Ella and Margaret. George Washington Hairr, Jr., was born 04 July 1937.

Ruth Elaine Hairr, the third child of George Washington Hairr, Sr. and Ida Florence Beasley was born 21 June 1929 in Dismal Township in Sampson County and married **WILLIAM**

RAEFORD FAIRCLOTH, son of **BOND FAIRCLOTH** and **LESSIE AUTRY**. William was born 19 April 1925 in Dismal Township in Sampson County and died 30 August 1969 near Autryville, North Carolina. He served as a PFC in the 407th Infantry. 102nd Division in World War II. He and Ruth Elaine were buried in Bethabara United Methodist Church Cemetery in Dismal Township.

Ruth Elaine and William had three children:

1) **WILLIAM KEITH FAIRCLOTH**, their first child, was born 17 January 1950 in Roseboro, North Carolina and married **GAILYA LYNN RICH** on 5 September 1971 in Salemburg, Sampson County, North Carolina, daughter of **NORMAN RICH** and

EDNA MCLAMB. Gailya was born 16 August 1952 in Roseboro. William Keith and Gailya had two children who were born in Fayetteville, Cumberland County, North Carolina: **BRIAN KEITH FAIRCLOTH** was born 19 January 1973 and **CHARIS LYNN FAIRCLOTH** was born 20 November 1976.

2) **LARRY ARNOLD FAIRCLOTH**, the second child of Ruth Elaine and William, was born 5 November 1951. He married **HAZEL JOYCE HOUSE** about 1971, daughter of **CARNELL ELTON HOUSE** and **HAZEL EVELINE WRENCH**. Hazel Joyce was born 18 July 1953 in Dunn, Harnett County, North Carolina, and she and Larry had one known child, **CARNELLA JOYCE FAIRCLOTH** who was born 7 October 1972.

3) **JAMES WYMAN FAIRCLOTH**, the third child of Ruth Elaine and William, was born 6 June 1955 and married first, **GLENDA HARISS** about 1976. He married second, **ELIZABETH ALICE EVANS** about 1990 in Dillon, South Carolina. Elizabeth was born 31 January 1962. James and Blenda had one child, **MICHELE LYNN FAIRCLOTH,** who was born 18 October 1976. James and Elizabeth had one child, **REBEKAH FAYE FAIRCLOTH** who was born 27 May 1991.

GEORGE WASHINGTON HAIRR, JR. who was born 4 July 1937 in Sampson County, North Carolina. George, Jr., was the fourth child of George Washington, Sr., and Ida Florence Beasley. He married **JUDY ANN TEW** before 1960. She was the daughter of **PERCY TEW** and **IRUTHA FANN** and was born 15 March 1942 in Sampson County. They had one known child: **FELICIA ANN HAIRR** who was born 21 April 1960.

FRANCIS GERALDINE HAIRR was the second child of George Washington Hairr, Sr and his second wife, Sarah Francis Hall. She married **BOBBY RAY JACKSON**, son of O. C. JACKSON and **BEATRICE HONEYCUTT.** Bobby was born 8 March 1944 in Roseboro in Sampson County. Francis Geraldine and Bobby Ray had four children: 1) **WENDY HOPE JACKSON**, their first child, was born 1 October 1970 in Clinton, North Carolina. She married 5 December 1992 in Mt. Elam Baptist Church to **JAMES WINFRED QUANN** who was born 23 September 1950 in Cumberland County, son of **CHARLES Q. QUANN** and **MARY E. JACKSON**. Wendy and James have one child, **ZACHARY CRAIG JACKSON** was born 16 August 1989 in Clinton. 2) **BOBBIE JO JACKSON** was born 15 June 1972 in Clinton and was the second child of Francis Geraldine and Bobby Ray. 3) **WESLEY ARTIE JACKSON** who was born 24 January 1977 in Clinton, was the third child of Francis Geraldine and Bobby Ray. 4) **GERALD RAY JACKSON** was the fourth child of Francis Gerald and Bobby Ray and was born 30 September 1978 in Clinton.

PERRY ERASCO HAIR, the second child of John Oliver and Annie was born 21 May 1906 in Sampson County and died 29 March 1961 in North Carolina. He married **TERA PEARL BAREFOOT** who was born 20 May 1906 and died 08 Decmeber 1990, daughter of **Jesse Barefoot** and **Cora Pope.** Perry worked in bridge construction with the North Carolina State Highway Department. He accidentally drowned. Both he and Tera were buried in The Clinton Cemetery in Clinton, Sampson County, North Carolina.

It is mentioned that Perry and Tera had two sons; I found only one: **JESSIE DARWIN HAIRR** was born 5 September 1941 in Sampson County. He married **JACKIE MAE ROYAL** on 27 June 1965 in Sharon Pentecostal Holiness Church, Sampson County. She was the daughter of **HOWARD ROYAL** and **OPHELIA HERRING** and was born 18 September 1945 in Herrings Township in sampson County. Jessie and Jackie had three sons, all born in Fayetteville, Cumberland County, North Carolina: **JEFFREY DEWAYNE HAIRR** was born 30 September 1971; **JONATHAN DARWIN HAIRR,** born 24 August 1975; **JASON DWIGHT HAIRR,** born 22 February 1978.

EULA MAY HAIR was the third known child of John Oliver and Annie, and was born 9 April 1908 in Sampson County and died after 23 May 1999. She was the informant listed on her father's certificate of death and it appears that she did not marry and was buried in Baptist Chapel Cemetery on Baptist Chapel Road (SR 1455) in Sampson County, North Carolina.

JAMES STACY HAIR, the fourth child of John Oliver and Annie, was born about 1909 in Sampson County. No other information.

JOHN RAYMOND HAIR, the fifth known child of John Oliver and Annie, was born 24 December 1911 in Sampson County and died 18 September 1975 in Fayetteville, Cumberland County, North Carolina. He married **NORA PEARL PAGE** on 28 December 1935 in Clinton, North Carolina. Nora was born 19 May 1907. John is buried at Magnolia Baptist Church Cemetery in Cumberland County. He and Nora had four known children:

1) **DELBERT PARNELL PAGE** was born 25 April 1925 and died 8 November 1985. He married Edna Mae Lovik who was born 10 August 1928 in Flea Hill Township in Cumberland County, daughter of **EDWARD AUGUSTUS LOVICK** and **LAURA ANN HOLLAND**. Delbert was buried in the Bluff Presbyterian Church Cemetery. He and Edna have two children.

2) **LOIS ARLINE HAIRR** who was born 13 March 1937 in Dismal Township in Sampson County. Lois married **EULON ELLIOT HUBBARD,** son of **WILLIE HUBBARD** and **CARRIE WILLIAMS**. Eulon was born 29 April 1933 in Cedar Creek Township in Cumberland County and died 22 October 1970 in Fayetteville, in Cumberland County. Lois and Eulon had two known children: **DALE ELLIOTT HUBBARD** who was born 22 January 1958 in Fayetteville and **DEBRA ARLENE HUBBARD,** who was born 13 July 1959 in Fayetteville. Debra Arlene first married **TONY VERNON POPE** on 18 June 1977 in Stedman, North Carolina. Tony was born 19 February 1959 in Cumberland County. They divorced and Debra then married **STUART LAVANE COOKE** on 10 January 1981 in Stedman, he was the son of **HERBERT COOKE** and was born 25 May 1953 in Brooks County, Georgia. Debra and Stuart had one known child, **SAMANTHA LEIGH COOKE** who was born 17 November 1981 in Fayetteville, North Carolina.

3) **Unidentified Child Hairr** was born 11 October 1938 in Dismal Township, Sampson County and has a grave marker at Baptist Chapel Cemetery.

4) **John Raymond Hair, Jr.** was born 9 May 1940 in Roseboro, North Carolina.

HENRY HUBERT HAIRR was the sixth known child of John Oliver and Annie and was born 18 July 1913 in Sampson County and died 9 July 1992 in Dunn, Harnett County, North Carolina. He may have married **NELLIE HOLLAND**, daughter of **Bernice Culbreth Holland** and **Lessie Williams**. See Nellie Holland elsewhere in this book and her notes for more information.

LOUISE HAIRR, seventh known child of John Oliver and Annie was born about 1916 in Sampson County. No other information.

WARREN HAIRR was the eighth known child of John Oliver and Annie and was born about 1921 in Sampson County. He may be the **WARREN H. HAIRR** who was born 15 November 1920 and died 14 May 1994 and is buried in Magnolia Baptist Church Cemetery near Stedman in Cumberland County, North Carolina. Warren H. married BERTHA S. (maiden name unknown) who was born 13 May 1926 and is buried by Warren.

186 vii. **Susan Hairr**, born about 1875 was the seventh known child of **GILMORE HAIRR** and **ELIZA HOLLAND.** Her name was not written very clearly in the 1880 census and it is difficult to read. Her brother, John, was head of household in 1900 and she and her mother were living with him. Vider J. Holland, niece, was also listed with them, but her relationship is not known.

43. John C. Hair (Orpah[3] Holland, Thomas William[2], Unknown[1]) was born about 1829 in Sampson County, North Carolina, and and may have died of disease in 1865 in New Hanover County, North Carolina. He married **Sylvania Tew**, daughter of Osborn Tew and Patience Tew. She was born about 1830 in Sampson County, North Carolina.

I believe this John was the one living in the household of Daniel Hair and Lucinda (nee Holland) in 1850. Daniel and Lucinda lived in Dwelling 200/Nor (northern arean of Sampson County) and the parents of Sylvania (Sylvanna) Tew lived in Dwelling 220/Nor in 1850. This strongly suggests that this John Hair was the son of John Athae Hair and Orpah Holland, Lucinda's aunt, and that he was most likely a brother of Daniel. Both John C., and his brother, Daniel, died while serving in the Civil War.

Two men named "John C. Hair" from Sampson County, North Carolina served in the United States Civil War. One was captured and paroled on 2 October 1862 at Leesburg, Virginia. It appears that this "John C.," son of Orpah and John Athae, was the one that went A.W.O.L in January 1863, but apparently he returned to service and died of disease in 1865 in New Hanover County, North Carolina.

The other John C. was born about 1831 and served as a Private in Company I, Regiment 46, Infantry. That John C. enlisted on 12 March 1862 in Clinton and died 23 May 1862, in Goldsboro, North Carolina. This other **John C. Hair** appears to have married **LOUISA SMITH** and they had a son whom they also named **JOHN THOMAS HAIR**, who was born 17 July 1859 and died 16 February 1935 in Pearces Mill Township, Cumberland County, North Carolina. This John Thomas married **LOVEDY CATHERINE PAGE (Lovdia Page)** who was born 21 November 1854 and died 8 November 1935, daughter of **JOHN PAGE** and **MARY AUTRY.**

Sylvania Tew's first name was also listed as Sylvanna, Silvanie, Silvia, and Silvana. Her Aunt Mary Tew married Henry Holland, brother of Orpah Holland, John's mother.

I believe Sylvania probably died before 1870. It appears that her son, Archie, was the Archie Bradley Hair, aged 2(?) living in the household of Lucinda Hair (Lucinda Holland) in 1870. Researchers have incorrectly listed Archie Bradley for the son of Daniel and Lucinda. John and Sylvania's son, John Thomas, is most likely, the "John F.", aged 12, listed in the household of Osborn and Patience Tew, Sylvania's parents in 1870. "John T." (John Thomas), was also listed in their household in 1880.

Children of John Hair and Sylvania Tew are:

+ 187 i. James Thomas Hairr, born about 1848; died after 1910.

+ 188 ii. John Thomas Hairr, born 15 April 1859 in Sampson County, North Carolina; died 05 June 1921 in Sampson County, North Carolina.

ARCHIE BRADLEY HAIRR was born 11 April 1866 in Sampson County, North Carolina, and died 10 Ooctober 1944 in Honeycutts Township in Sampson County, North Carolina. He married **(1) Unknown Spouse** before 1902. She was born about 1857 and died before 1910. He married **(2) Mattie Patterson** about 1912, daughter of **JAMES PATTERSON** and **SUSAN SPELL** She was born 10 July 1878 in Sampson County and died 12 January 1953 in Sampson County.

He was probably the Archie, aged 2, listed in 1870 in the household of Lucinda Hairr (Luncinda Holland) in Honeycutts Township, Sampson County, North Carolina. Lucinda's husband, Daniel Hair(r), was the brother of Archie's father, John C. Both Daniel and John C. died during the Civil War. In 1880, Archie was also in Lucinda Hairr's household and was listed incorrectly as her son. The certificate of death for Archie Bradley Hairr names "**SILVIA HAIR**" for his mother and the name of his father was not known by the informant, "R. C. HAIR." R. C. was probably Archie's son, "ROBBIE CLIFTON HAIRR."

Archie was, most likely, the Archie B. Hairr who was a boarder in the 1900 census, in the household of George Cooper. In 1910, he was listed as A. B., head of household in Honeycutts Township with sons, Lonnie and Robbie Clifton and and his sister, Mary. However, **Mary was not his sister**; her age suggests that she was his cousin, MARY MARIAH GRETSON HAIRR, daughter of Daniel L. Hairr and Lucinda Holland. In 1920 he was listed as "Ardie B. Hair," aged 52, with wife Mattie, Lonnie, Robie C., Annie M., Ruby L. and Neta A. His first name was probably "Archibald."

I have been unable to identify Archie's first wife. His second wife, Mattie, is found listed as Martha, and "**Mattie Peterson**" is also found for her name, but her certificate of death and certificates of her siblings confirm that she was "**Mattie Patterson**," daughter of Dr. **James H. Patterson** and Susan Spell. She had two full brothers, **John Robert Patterson** and **Henry Clay Patterson.** Henry Clay's certificate of death names North Carolina for their father's place of birth and John Robert's certificate of death names Gretna Green, Scotland County, North Carolina, for his father's place of birth. Gretna Green is said to be a community in Halifax County in northern North Carolina; Scotland County is Southwest of Sampson County.

Children of Archie Hairr and Unknown Spouse are:

i. **Lonnie Hairr**, may be the "Lonnie Hairr" buried in Sunrise Memorial Gardens 3 miles north of Roseboro who was born 16 November 1902 and died 11 June 1980. "Willie T.", his wife, was born 7 January 1909 and died 24 December 1993.

ii. **Robert Clifton Hairr**, born 06 November 1904; died 15 November 1990. Robbie married **MYRTLE HOLLAND**, daughter of **RUFUS HOLLAND** and **DELLA A. LEE**. She was born 13 September 1902 and died 18 June 1975. Robert was usually known as as "Robbie." "Robbie" and Myrtle were buried at Zoar Pentecostal Free Will Baptist Church Cemetery near Salemburg, North Carolina.

BETTIE E. HAIRR, the first known child or Robbie and Myrtle was born in 1929.

RUFUS CLIFTON HAIRR, second known child of Robbie and Myrtle was born 31 January 1932 and died 5 August 1991. He married Glenda C. (Maiden name unknown) on 17 June 1956. She was born 1 February 1938. Rufus was buried in Zoar Pentecostal FWB Church Cemetery on Zoar Church Raod (SR 1322) near Salemburg in Sampson County, North Carolina.

Children of Archie Hairr and Martha Unknown are:

i. **Annie May Hairr**, was born 24 January 1913 in Sampson County, North Carolina and died 7 November 1992 in Clinton, North Carolina. She **married OLLIE FRANKLIN NAYLOR** on 30 November 1933 in Herrings Township in Sampson County, son of **JONAH NAYLOR** and **IDA PETERSON** and he was born 30 November 1912 and died 1 December 1971 in Clinton, Sampson County, North Carolina. Ollie's cause of death was stroke and pneumonia. He and Annie were buried in Sunrise Memorial Gardens between Salemburg and Roseboro, North Carolina.

Annie and Ollie had three children:

1) THOMAS EARL NAYLOR, the first child of Annie and Ollie, was born 10 February 1935 in Honeycutts Township,Sampson County, North Carolina, and died 19 September 2005 in Sampson County. He married **JERLENE HUDSON** on 21 June 1959 in Salemburg in Sampson County. She was born 3 July 1935 in Honeycutts Township in Sampson County and was the daughter of **JONAH HUDSON** and **HOSIE CRUMPLER.**

Thomas and Jerlene had three children: 1) **KELLY HOPE NAYLOR** was born 11 November 1960 in Clinton, Sampson County, and married **WILLIAM DONAL WINDERS** who was born 20 November 1958. 2) **THOMAS DERRICK NAYLOR** was the second child of Thomas and Jerlene. He was born 27 November 1966 in Clinton, Sampson County and married **TERRI LYN ABBOTT** on 2 October 1993 in Salemburg Baptist Church, Salemburg, North Carolina. She was born 21 August 1962. 3) **JOAN ELIZABETH NAYLOR,** the third child, was born 24 March 1974 in Clinton, Sampson County, North Carolina.

2) I have not identified the **second child** of Annie Hairr and Ollie Naylor.

3) ROBERT FRANKLIN NAYLOR, the third known child of Annie and Ollie, was born 18 August 1941 in Roseboro, North Carolina, and died 17 March 1988 near Salemburg, North Carolina. He married **ALICE HALL.** Robert was buried in Sunrise Memorial Gardens between Salemburg and Roseboro, North Carolina.

ii. **Katie A. Hairr,** born about 1918. I found a Katie A. Hairr listed as a daughter of Archie, but I believe she and Neta A. were probably the same person.

iii. **Ruby Lee Hairr,** the third known child of Archie Bradley Hairr and Mattie Patterson was born 17 August 1914 in Sampson County, North Carolina; died 15 August 1984 in Sampson County. She married **FLOYD HEDRIE LOCKERMAN** who was born 11 August 1912 in Sampson County, North Carolina and died 14 October 1989 in Sampson County, North Carolina.

In 1920, Floyd was listed as Floyd H.; in 1930 census, he was listed as L. Feloid H. Lockerman. I have listed his name as found in Social Security Index and County records. Ruby Lee and Floyd Hedrie were buried in Zoar PFW Baptist Church Cemetery near Salemburg, North Carolina.

Floyd was the son of Ferdinand Lockerman and Sarah Ann Holden. His sister, Betty Clyde Lockerman, married Arby Herring Carter, son of Levi Herring Carter and Rachel Anne Howard.

iv. **Alice Clyde Hairr** was the fourth known child of Archie and Mattie and was born 1 November 1916 in Sampson County and died 11 June 1996 in Sampson County. She married "Unknown Taylor."

v. **Neta A. Hairr**, born 1919 in Sampson County was probably the "Katie A. Hairr" listed in birth records as the daughter of Archie with a birth year of 1918.

vi. **Mattie Hairr** was born 9 February 1920 in Sampson County and died 10 February 1920 in Honeycutts Township in Sampson County, North Carolina. She was buried in a family cemetery.

46. Starling Autry (Millie[3] Holland, Thomas William[2], Unknown[1]) was born 30 December 1811 in Cumberland County, North Carolina, and died October 1897. He married **Anna Minerva McPhail**, daughter of Daniel McPhail and Elizabeth Hair. She was born 20 July 1816, and died June 1905.

An internet source gives Starling's date of birth as December 30, 1811 in Cumberland County, North Carolina. "Sterling Autrey" was listed for his name in the **Old Holland Record Book** which also recorded his birth as 30 December 1811 in Sampson County. See notes for his mother, Millie Holland.

Family history # 413 on page 285 in the first heritage book of Sampson County mentions Cornelius Autry for Starling's father.

Full dates for "Sterling" and Anna were also found on Ancestry.com.

An infant, Sterling Autry, was listed in the 1850 Mortality Schedule for Sampson County, North Carolina. He died in a fire at age two in December 1849. His parents have not been identified.

An excerpt from page 725 in the 1 January 2004 issue of the "Huckleberry Historian" published quarterly by the Sampson County, North Carolina, Historical Society, provides the following information about Sterling:

"... We then went to school at the Grove Academy to Micajah Autry. Brother Ed, Brother John, and sister Barbara and myself; this school continued for some two-three years. A number of young men finished their education with this school. Mr. Autry brought to the school two grown Brothers, STERLING and JOHN, neither of them knew their letters. This was the second year of the school. We young chaps felt quite large when Sterling and John would ask us to tell them their lessons, which we were permitted to do in that school. In a very short time those young men made such fine progress as to be reading Latin and both made finely Educated young men, they both soon followed teaching school. Sterling when last heard of, was a Methodist Itinerant Preacher. Micajah was killed (with Davy Crockett in the Texas War of 1836 (Alamo). John was teaching school near Kenansville.)"

I find sparse information about Grove Academy. It appears that it was organized in 1785 and located in Kenansville, near the Duplin and Sampson County border and was possibly open from 1785 until about 1823. The academy provided room and board for those who did not live nearby. The writer of the above excerpt was Thomas James Armstrong (1813-1877) and he was about the same age as STERLING and JOHN AUTRY which makes his comment about "two grown brothers" interesting. Micajah was a much older brother of Sterling and John. The writer notes that it was the second year of the school and it continued for two-three years which leads me to believe that the academy may have been closed for some years and I assume that Micajah reopened it for a few years and it may have closed again around the time he moved to Tennessee in 1823 (see below.) The writer, Thomas James Armstrong, and his brother, sister, and Sterling and John Autry were most likely at least seven or eight years of age when they attended the school, placing their attendance between 1818-1823. It is said that Micajah returned to his father's farm in 1815. Therefore, he could have taught at Grove Academy between 1815 and 1823.

Starling Autry was buried in Autry Cemetery on Minnie Hall Road about 1.5 mile from HWY 242, Sampson County, North Carolina

Children of Starling Autry and Anna McPhail are:

\+ 189 i. **Mary Manda Autry**, born 08 March 1835.

190 ii. **William Autry**, born 10 April 1837; died 18 December 1862.

He served as a Private in Company A, Regiment, 30, Infantry during the Civil War. Captured and was paroled 29 September 1862 at Warrenton, Virginia. Died 18 December 1862 in hospital, Gordonsville, Virginia of pneumonia.

191 iii. **Matilda Jane Autry**, born 16 September 1839 in North Carolina; died 02 June 1917 in North Carolina. She married **John Cooper**; born 29 May 1835 in North Carolina; died 06 June 1924 in North Carolina.

Matilda was still living with her parents in 1870. John Cooper may have been the son of Nixon Cooper and Martha Underwood

\+ 192 iv. **Mariah Jetson Autry**, born 12 October 1841 in North Carolina; died September 1917 in North Carolina.

\+ 193 v. **Allen Merdeth Autry**, born 30 December 1843 near Salemburg, Sampson County, North Carolina; died 31 May 1875.

194 vi. **Margaret Elizabeth Autry**, born 10 October 1846.

\+ 195 vii. **Ann Sophia Autry**, born 10 December 1848.

196 viii. **Jennette Autry**, born 30 May 1851; died August 1933.

She did not marry and was living with her mother in 1900. She and her sister, Penelope Eliza were living together in 1910. Jennette was buried in Autry Cemetery on Minnie Hall Road about 1.5 mile from HWY 242, Sampson County, North Carolina

197 ix. **Penelope Eliza Autry**, born 22 May 1854; died June 1929.

She did not marry and was living with her mother and sister, Jennette, in 1900. She was buried in Autry Cemetery on Minnie Hall Road about 1.5 mile from HWY 242, Sampson County, North Carolina

+ 198 x. **Charles Gibson Autry**, born 01 November 1858; died 15 January 1927.

50. Lucinda Holland (Henry[3], Thomas William[2], Unknown[1]) was born 05 November 1826 in Sampson County, North Carolina, and died after 1880 in Sampson County, North Carolina. She married **Daniel Hairr**, son of John Hair and Orpah Holland. He was born about 1819 in Sampson County, North Carolina, and died 17 November 1862 in Hospital in Farmville, Virginia.

Her name has been found as "Lucindy" (1860 census) and is "Lucindia" on the certificate of death for her son, George Washington. She and Daniel were first cousins. In the 1860 census for Sampson County, North Carolina, "Orpha Hairr (Orpah. Orphy)," aged 63, Daniel's Mother and Lucinda's Aunt, was living with them. Orpah is found in the Old Holland Record Book of Thomas William Holland. "Nanny," aged 43, Daniel's sister, was also with them and "Nancy," aged 33, was living with Orphy, aged 55, in 1850. In 1870, Lucinda was head of household with four children living with her. Harfrey) Holland was found near Lucinda and Harfrey's mother, Elizabeth, and his sister's, Elizabeth and Milsy, were living in a dwelling near him. Listed with Lucinda in 1880 were Mary, aged 26, "Charley H.," aged 19, her children and "Archy," aged 12, her nephew.

In 1880, Lucinda, Mary, Charley and "Archy" were living near her son, George W. and his family and next door to Harfrey Holland, Lucinda's cousin. Other Hollands were also nearby.

Daniel Hairr was a Private in Company I, Regiment 46. Infantry in the Civil War. He enlisted 12 March 1862 in Clinton and died of disease in the hospital while serving in the war..

John Hair, aged 22 was listed in Daniel and Lucinda's household in 1850. I believe him to be John C. Hairr, a brother of Daniel. Daniel and Lucinda were living near the parents of Sylvanna Tew in 1850. John, aged 8, was also listed. It is unclear whether the younger John was a son; he was not listed in 1860.

Children are listed above under (39) Daniel Hairr.

55. Henry Y. C. Holland (Henry[3], Thomas William[2], Unknown[1]) was born 26 March 1836 in Sampson County, North Carolina, and died 15 May 1864 in Battle of Wilderness, Virginia. He married **Susan C. McCullen** 29 November 1860 in Sampson County, North Carolina, daughter of Unknown McCullen and Emelia Unknown. She was born about 1838.

Henry Y. C. Holland's Civil war record shows "Holland, Henry Y. C., Private in Company I, Regiment. 46, Infantry. He was born about 1838 in Sampson Co. Farmer. He enlisted on 12 March 1862 in Clinton and deserted 11 June 1862 at Camp Drewry's Bluff, Va. Had not been apprehended by 30 October1862." Another source records that he did return to service and was hit in the back by a mini ball on 7 May 1864 in the Battle of Wilderness, Virginia; died on 15 May 1864.

When fighting or battles occurred near his home, a man would sometimes leave his company, go home for a few days and then rejoin his company. When a man was wounded near his home, he might be sent home and was expected to return when he recovered. These men, and others who were away from their company, were often recorded as deserters and records were not always corrected. Punishment varied for deserters.

Henry Y. C.'s date of birth is difficult to read in the **Old Holland Record Book** , but it is the 26 of either March or May 1836. His middle initial "C" was probably for "Chester." There is only one record that may give us **a clue about the "Y."** The **Old Holland Record Book** records the name "Yranbery," "Thomas Yaraaberry," and Yearbary Autrey," son of Cornelias Autrey was born September the 8 in the year of our Lord 1800. These three spellings of the name starting with "Y" may be "Yarborough" or "Yarbrough" that are mispelled in the record book. The recording of the first name in "Yearbery Autrey" is smeared. See the back of this book for an image of this record.

The following indicates that he married Susan C. McCullen:

"'Fayetteville Observer," Fayetteville, North Carolina, Monday, December 17, 1860 Vol. XLIII #2272:

"Married in Sampson County on the 29th of November, by Jas. A. Warwick, Esq., Mr. Henry C. Holland to Miss Susan C. McCullen." It appears that Susan married another Holland (William Holland?) after Henry died, but he wasn't listed with her in 1870 and 1880 census records.

Susan C. Holland, aged 25 was listed head of household in 1870 in Clinton, Halls Township, Sampson County, North Carolina. Her age would have been about 32. Rhoda J. McCullen, most likely her sister, aged 40, was living with her.

In 1870 and 1880, Susan was listed as head of household with her children and Rhoda, her sister, was listed with her in each census. Most of the 1890 census burned and neither Susan nor Rhoda show up later in 1900. In 1870, Susan's children listed with her were: Lucy J., aged 7 and Lina (Lonnie) Oscar, aged 3. In 1880 Loyd Pascail Holland, born 1871 and Mannie Holland, born 1873 were also with her and Rhoda. Lonnie Oscar Holland married Ella Evaline Best about 1891 and they had 12 children. Loyd Pascail married Joanna Tew and they had one child Loyd A. Holland. Loyd and his second wife, Molcy A.Gautier had six children.

SEE THE BACK OF THIS BOOK FOR THE DESCENDANTS OF HENRY AND SUSAN'S DAUGHTER, LUCY JENE HOLLAND, AND FOR THE FAMILY OF SUSAN MCCULLEN AND WILLIAM HOLLAND, WHO APPEARS TO HAVE BEEN HER SECOND HUSBAND.

Child of Henry Holland and Susan McCullen is:

199 i. **Lucy Jene Holland,** born about 1863. See back of this book for her family.

58. Olivia Holland (Henry[3], Thomas William[2], Unknown[1]) was born 03 November 1843 in Sampson County, North Carolina, and died 02 July 1913 in Sampson County, North

Carolina. She married **Hugh J. Lockerman**, son of Riley Lockerman and Louvicey Peterson. He was born 1845 in Sampson County, North Carolina, and died after 1910 in Sampson County, North Carolina.

Olivia Holland's first name is also found as "**Oliba Holland,**" "**Oliva Holland,**" "**Aheliba Holland,**" and in the **Old Holland Record Book** it was recorded as "**Aholabah Holland,**" and the 1900 census listed "Alita" for her name. The certificate of death for her daughter, Minnie (Miney) listed Olivia as "**Aline Holland.**" These records prove that her name was "altered" over the years and eventually she was known as "**Olivia.**"

Hugh J. Lockerman served as Pvt. in 2nd Co. E, Regt. 2, Infantry. Born in Sampson County, North Carolina. Enlisted "26 February 1864 at Orange County, Virginia. Captured 6 April 1865 at Harper's Farm, Virginia. Confined Point Lookout, Maryland. Released 24 June 1865 by oath."

On 7 March 1912, he and "Oliba" sold to Jasper Holland, for $500 about 41 acres (the life estate of H. J. Lockerman and wife Oliba Lockerman and their son, Sicero (Cisero) Lockerman excepted." Land joined the lands of W. L. White, Alexander Brock and Dr. G. L. Sikes and was on the north edge of Crane Branch.

Olivia and Hugh J. Lockerman were buried in a Lockerman Cemetery about one mile into the woods off Lakewood School Rd (SR 1340.) Several other family members were also buried in the same cemetery. Sand beds and clay pits now make this cemetery difficult to find. Anyone not familiar with these woods should not attempt to find it. "Lela Jane Sessoms," 1889 - 1966, and her husband, Thomas C. Sessoms who was born 10 August 1888 and died 20 November 1948 were buried there, but their relationship to the family has not been determined. The 1900 and 1910 transcribed census data and Thomas' certificate of death identifies Thomas as the son of Amos Sessoms,

Census records often list Lockerman as "Lockamy" and over the years Lockamy was used more often by the families.

Children of Olivia Holland and Hugh Lockerman are:

200 i. **Cornelia Lockerman,** born about 1868 in Sampson County, North Carolina.

\+ 201 ii. **Miney L. Lockerman,** born 06 March 1875 in Sampson County, North Carolina; died 19 August 1921 in Cumberland County, North Carolina.

202 iii. **Cicero Lockerman,** born 04 October 1877 in Sampson County, North Carolina; died 19 February 1925.

Cicero Lockerman's registration card for World War I is difficult to read, but it appears to say that he was physically unable to serve in the war. He was buried in a Lockerman Cemetery near Lakewood High School, between Salemburg and Roseboro, North Carolina.

\+ 203 iv. **Dallie Alice Lockerman,** born 29 May 1881 in Sampson County, North Carolina; died 18 September 1958 in Salemburg, North Carolina.

\+ 204 v. **Louvicia Lockerman,** born 11 January 1885 in Sampson County, North Carolina; died 12 November 1948 in Sampson County, North Carolina.

59. Orpah Caroline Holland (Henry[3], Thomas William[2], Unknown[1]) was born 03 March 1846 in Sampson County, North Carolina, and died 10 April 1925 in Cumberland County, North Carolina. She married **Raeford Lockerman** 19 October 1871 in Sampson County, North Carolina, son of Riley Lockerman and Louvicey Peterson. He was born 09 October 1847 in Sampson County, North Carolina, and died 16 June 1932 in Cumberland County, North Carolina.

"Orpah" was listed for her name in the 1850 census for Sampson County, North Carolina. Apparently, she was listed as Caroline in 1860 and 1870. In 1900 and 1910, she and Raeford were living in Cedar Creek Township, Cumberland County, North Carolina and lived there for the remainder of their lives. It is said that she died of breast cancer.

Most of Orpah Caroline and Raeford's children changed "Lockerman" to "Lockamy." Sources for their data usually listed the name as Lockamy. Orpah Caroline and Raeford were buried in Concord Baptist Church Cemetery on Beaver Dam Road, Cedar Creek Township, Cumberland County, North Carolina. "Raeford" is on his tombstone. I cannot locate him in the 1880 census records for North Carolina; "Raiford" and "Raeford" are found for his first name in other census records. He was living in the household of his son, Vander, in 1930.

Sources found on Ancestry.com name **Julius W. Lockamy, Sr.**, born 1878 in North Carolina, for a son of Raeford Lockamy and Orpah Caroline Holland, but I have found no other record to support this. **Julius Wesley Lockamy** married **Mary Bell Averitt** on 21 December 1908 in Cedar Creek, in Cumberland County, North Carolina. She was born about 1892 in North Carolina.

Children of Orpah Holland and Raeford Lockerman are:

205 i. **Mary E. Lockamy**, born about 1872 in North Carolina.

She was living with her parents in 1900.

206 ii. **Thomas F. Lockamy**, born about 1875. He married Jennie B. (maiden name unknown) who was born about 1878. Known child is **George H. Lockamy** who was born in 1900.

207 iii. **Roney Lockamy**, born About 1877.

\+ 208 iv. **Heman Cashwell** Lockamy, born 21 October 1878; died 03 February 1949 in Cumberland County, North Carolina.

\+ 209 v. **Grover** Cleveland Lockerman, born 30 March 1885 in Sampson County, North Carolina; died 24 April 1971 in Cumberland County, North Carolina.

\+ 210 vi. **Vander B. Lockamy**, born 01 December 1888; died March 1982 in Fayetteville, North Carolina.

60. Stephen Senter Holland, Sr. (Henry[3], Thomas William[2], Unknown[1]) was born 24 June 1848 in Sampson County, North Carolina, and died 07 November 1914 in Honeycutts Township, Sampson County, North Carolina. He married **Nancy Elizabeth Hudson**, daughter of Henry Hudson and Dicey Peterson. She was born 13 January 1855 in Sampson

County, North Carolina, and died 30 December 1940 in Honeycutts Township, Sampson County, North Carolina.

His certificate of death records 24 June 1846 for his birth. Al Butler was the informant for the data on Steven's death certificate. Mr. Butler apparently thought Stephen mother's maiden name was 'Howard'; Records indicate his mother was 'Mary Tew'. The 1860 census shows 'Steven' for his first name; most records list Stephen or Stephen Senter. Some family members also say that 'Senter' should be **'Scenter.'**

Will of Stephen Senter Holland, Sr. in courthouse in Clinton, Sampson County, North Carolina:

"... A paper purporting to be the last will and testament of Stephen Senter Holland, deceased is exhibited before me, the undersigned Clerk of the Superior Court of said County, by Alger Holland, the executor therein mentioned and, the due executor thereof by the said Stephen Senter ... by the oath and examination of F. .. & John Avery, the subscribing witness ... which bears date of the 7th of March, 1912...."

"In the name of God, Amen. I Stephen Seter(sic) Holland, of the County of Sampson and State of North Carolina, and being of sound mind and memory and understanding praise be to God for the same, do make this my Last Will and Testament in manner and form following:

"...I give devise and bequeath unto my beloved wife Nancy E. Holland 39 acres of land, the tract whereon I now live, all houses and other improvements to have and hold to her the said Nancy E. Holland for and during the term of her natural life in satisfaction of and in lieu of her dower and third of, and in, all my real estate.

"I give and bequeath to my youngest son, Stephen Senter Holland, all that tract of land whereon I now live except the life estate of my wife to have and hold to him and his heirs forever, and I give and bequeath to my beloved wife, N. E. Holland all my household and kitchen furniture, 18 head of hogs, 2 head of cattle, one mule and one buggy; one cart and all provisions in kind at the time of my death.

"I give and bequeath to my son, Alger Holland $1.00.

" " " " " , Jasper $1.00

" " " " " , Henry, $1.00

" " " " , Wesley $1.00

" " " " " , Sanford, $1.00

" " " " " , Willis, $1.00

" " " my daughter, Angolda Holland, $1.00

"Whereas my youngest son is a minor now, therefore, my will and desire is that my beloved wife is hereby appointed guardian of this my son.

"I hereby constitute and appoint my trusty friend and son, Alger Holland, my lawful executor ....March 7, 1912."

Will was proved 24 November 1914 in Sampson County, North Carolina. Alger Holland, Executor.

On 4 February 1873 Lewis Holland sold to Stephen Senter Holland 39 acres of land in consideration of $130. Land was on run of Rye Swamp at the mouth of a small branch and ran up the said Branch. This appears to be the land that Stephen Senter Holland, Sr. willed to his wife and son, Stephen Senter, Jr. and is known as the Old Holland Home Place. This writer has been told that Lewis's parents lived just across the creek (stream, ditch). Apparently, the creek or stream is "Rye Swamp."

Stephen Senter was buried on 08 November 1914, in the Holland Family Cemetery at the farm called the Old Holland Place, near Zoar Church and not far from Salemburg, Sampson County, North Carolina. Nancy Elizabeth is also buried there and so are their children who died young. Some of the tombstones in the cemetery are eroded and difficult to read. Ronna and Donna are said to have died in infancy; however, they both are listed in the 1900 Federal Census for Sampson County, aged 6 and 4, respectively. The 1900 census also records that Stephen and Nancy had 15 children with 11 living and the 1910 states that they had 15 children with 8 living. The number of living children in both census records does not agree with the total number of children listed here. Perhaps Emily has been recorded as "Evelyn J." in various family records. Unfortunately, I cannot verify the two names and two different dates of birth I found on notes in the Old Holland Record Book.

Stephen Senter Holland, Jr., was the informant for data on Nancy Elizabeth's certificate of death. Her date of birth was listed as 13 January 1855 indicating she was age 85 years, 11 months and 17 days old. Census records and family members indicate her birth year would be about 1857. Her first name is spelled 'Nancey' on the certificate of death and cause of death was fracture of neck from a fall in home.

Children of Stephen Holland and Nancy Hudson are:

211 i. **Emily Holland** was born 13 January 1873 in Honeycutts Township, Sampson County, North Carolina, died in infancy in Honeycutts Township, Sampson County. The **Old Holland Record Book** also records her name as "Emely;" She was buried in the Holland Family Cemetery at the Old Holland Homeplace near Zoar Church and Salemburg, North Carolina.

212 ii. **Evelyn J. Holland**, born 04 August 1873 in Honeycutts Township, Sampson County, North Carolina, died in infancy in Honeycutts Township, Sampson County, and was probably buried in the Holland Family Cemetery near Zoar Church.

213 iii. **Minnie Holland**, born 22 June 1874 in Honeycutts Township, Sampson County, North Carolina, died in infancy in Honeycutts Township. She may have been called "Minna," and was buried in the Family Cemetery at the Old Holland Homeplace near Zpar Church and not far from Salemburg, North Carolina

214 iv. **Millie Holland** was born 22 June 1874 in Honeycutts Township, Sampson County, North Carolina, died in infancy in Honeycutts Township, Sampson County, and was buried in the Family Cemetery at the Old Holland Homeplace near Salemburg, North Carolina.

+ 215 v. **Alger Rose Holland,** born 20 June 1875 in Honeycutts Township, Sampson County, North Carolina; died 19 July 1965 in Honeycutts Township, Sampson County.

+ 216 vi. **Jasper Lee Holland,** born 12 July 1877 in Honeycutts Township, Sampson County, North Carolina; died 25 March 1944 in Honeycutts Township.

217 vii. **William Arthur Chester Holland,** born 30 July 1879 in Honeycutts Township, Sampson County, North Carolina; died 10 May 1896 in Honeycutts Township, Sampson County, and was buried in the Holland Family Cemetery near Salemburg in Sampson County. **"W. A. C. Holland"** appears for his name in the **Old Holland Record Book.** You may find images from this old book in the back of this book.

+ 218 viii. **Henry Holland,** born 17 March 1882 in Sampson County, North Carolina; died 04 June 1950 in Honeycutts Township, Sampson County.

+ 219 ix. **John Wesley Holland,** born 03 May 1884 in Sampson County, North Carolina; died 06 February 1966 in Bladen County, North Carolina. He is listed as "Willis" in his father's will.

220 x. **Erastus Holland,** born 22 September 1886 in Sampson County, North Carolina; died in infancy in Honeycutts Township, Sampson County. He was buried in the Holland Family Cemetery near Salemburg, Sampson County.

+ 221 xi. **Sanford Holland,** born 26 August 1887 in Sampson County, North Carolina; died 04 April 1957 in Honeycutts Township, Sampson County.

+ 222 xii. **Miles Holland,** born 07 September 1889 in Honeycutts Township, Sampson County, North Carolina, died 30 March 1974 in Sampson County.

+ 223 xiii. **Angolda Holland,** born 23 September 1891 in Honeycutts Township, Sampson County, North Carolina; died 27 October 1958 in Honeycutts Township, Sampson County.

224 xiv. **Rona Holland,** born 08 January 1894 in Sampson County, North Carolina; died between 1900 - 1910 in Honeycutts Township, Sampson County, North Carolina. She was buried in the Holland Family Cemetery near Salemburg in Sampson County. It is said that Ronna and her twin, Donna died in infancy.

225 xv. **Dona Holland,** born 16 September 1895 in Sampson County, North Carolina; died between 1900 - 1910 in Honeycutts Township, Sampson County, North Carolina. She was buried in the Holland Family Cemetery near Salemburg in Sampson County.

+ 226 xvi. **Stephen Senter Holland, Jr.,** born 08 February 1898 in Honeycutts Township, Sampson County, North Carolina; died 19 February 1978 in Honeycutts Township.

61. Alderman McKay Holland (Henry[3], Thomas William[2], Unknown[1]) was born 24 August 1852 in Sampson County, North Carolina, and died 16 July 1925 in Little Coharie Township, Sampson County. He married **Laura Francis Carter,** daughter of John Carter and Jane Hairr. She was born about 1855 in Sampson County, North Carolina, and died 09 December 1924 in Little Coharie Township, Sampson County.

Alderman was not a common given name in the Holland Families. He was possibly named after "Rev. Amariah B. Alderman" who preached over a large area of Eastern North Carolina at the time of Alderman's birth. His name can be found as **Almon H. Holland** and **Almond**

H. Holland and **Almond Holland.** One source shows him to be: Almond H. who was born 15 May 1851 and died 16 July 1925.

The **Old Holland Recod Book** records him as "Alderman McKay, born 24 August 1852. He was listed in the 1860 census of Sampson County, North Carolina as Alderman, aged 7. In the 1870 census he was "ALMAN,' aged 18, under Mary Tew, his mother. His son, Frank, was the informant on his certificate of death and gave Alderman McKay's name as "Almond H.," born 15 May 1851 and named Henry Holland for his father and "unknown" for his mother. Francis can be found as the wife of Almond and Alderman McKay Holland.

Alderman was listed as "Alderman" in the 1880 and 1900 Federal Censuses for Cedar Creek Township, Cumberland County, North Carolina. In 1880, his age was listed incorrectly as 21; in 1900, it was 41. The age for Francis in 1880 was 22; in 1900 it was 38.

Cause of death for Laura Francis was Arteriosclerosis of several years duration.

Children of Alderman Holland and Laura Carter are:

+ 227 i. **Sylvester Holland**, born March 1877 in Cumberland County, North Carolina.

228 ii. Maggie Holland, born May 1880 in Cumberland County, North Carolina.

229 iii. **Hattie Holland**, born March 1882 in Cumberland County, North Carolina; died 28 November 1932.

+ 230 iv. **Archie L. Holland**, born February 1889 in Cumberland County, North Carolina; died 27 May 1925 in Chatham County, North Carolina.

231 v. **Franklin Holland**, born April 1891 in Cumberland County, North Carolina.

232 vi. **Rosanna Holland**, born December 1895 in Cumberland County, North Carolina.

63. Eliza Holland (John[3], Thomas William[2], Unknown[1]) was born about 1840 in Sampson County, North Carolina. She married **Gilmore Hairr**, son of John Hair and Orpah Holland. He was born between 1828 - 1832 in Sampson County, North Carolina and was her first cousin.

C. Holland, aged 18, female, was listed in the household of Gilmore and Eliza in 1860. This would be about the right age for Eliza's sister, Charity, but Charity was also listed in their father's household in the 1860 census. Cumberland and Sampson County censuses were, most likely, taken at different times and this would explain why Charity was in both households. She probably stayed with Eliza to help her with the birth of Polly Ann.

In the American Civil War, Gilmore Hairr served as a Private in Company H, Regiment 20, Infantry. His war record shows he was born in 1833. He enlisted on 7 August 1861 at Fort Johnston, North Carolina, was captured between 9-11 October 1863 near Brandy Station, Virginia, and confined at Point Lookout, Maryland. Received 15 November 1864 at Venus Point, Savannah River, Georgia, for exchange.

In 1880, Gilmore and Eliza were living in Honeycutts Township, Sampson County, North Carolina.

Children are listed above under (42) Gilmore Hairr.

64. Delila Holland (John[3], Thomas William[2], Unknown[1]) was born about 1842, and died after 1920.

Delila Holland was listed as "Lilly" in the census records of 1850 and 1860, Delia in 1870 and Delila in 1900. She was head of household in 1900 with daughter, Melvina, aged 33, and it appears that Melvina was listed as "Nohirna" in 1870 in the household of Delila's father. Delila was a servant in the household Lott Owen in 1880 while her daughter, Melvina, was in the household of Delila's parents and listed as their daughter. Oscar Holland, aged 11, was also living with Delila in 1900 and was identified as a nephew. She was listed as "Lilie Holland," aged 72 in the 1920 Federal Census of Honeycutts Township, Sampson County, North Carolina, with daughter Melvina, aged 50. I can't identify the parent(s) of her nephew, Oscar.

Child of Delila Holland is:

233 i. **Melvina Holland**, born May 1866; died 16 September 1925 in Honeycutts Township, Sampson County, North Carolina.

65. Joel Holland (John[3], Thomas William[2], Unknown[1]) was born about 1844, and died before 1900. He married **Dicey Ann Holland**, daughter of Elizabeth Holland. She was born between 1845 - 1847, and died 10 August 1915 in Mingo Township, Sampson County, North Carolina.

I may have linked Joel to the wrong "Dicey A.", but I believe he married Dicey A. Holland, daughter of Elizabeth Holland who was a daughter of Daniel Holland and Elizabeth Sessoms; Dicey A. would have been a great-niece of Joel's father. Census records appear to support this.

He was a Private in Company I, Regiment 46, Infantry. His service records list 1844 for his birth in Sampson County and he was a student when he enlisted on 26 April 1862 in Clinton, North Carolina. Joel was wounded 5 May 1864 at Wilderness, Virginia, and hospitalized, was furloughed 15 July 1864 for 60 days, and still unable to return to his unit 31 December 1864. Apparently, he eventually returned as he was captured 18 March 1865 in Sampson County and confined at Hart's Island, New York Harbor, until his release 18 June 1865 by oath."

Dicey Ann's certificate of death indicates that she was a widow and names "Betsey Holland" for her mother.. In 1850, "Dicy" was listed as aged 1 and she and her mother, Elizabeth (Betsey), were listed in the household of Elizabeth's parents, Daniel and Elizabeth Holland. In 1860 Dicy A., aged 13 and her mother "Betsey" (Elizabeth) were in the household of Daniel Holland, Jr.

Child of Joel Holland and Dicey Holland is:

+ 234 i. **Malette Holland,** born 16 February 1878 in Sampson County and died 12 April 1948 in Eastover Township in Cumberland County, North Carolina.

66. Charity Holland (John[3], Thomas William[2], Unknown[1]) was born about 1845 in North Carolina, and died after 1910. She married **Daniel W. Lockamy** who was born about 1851 in North Carolina, and died after 1910. Daniel appears to be the son of Odom (Odum) Lockamy (Lockerman) and Malinda (Melinda) Autry.

In 1850, Charity was aged 5; in each of the 1860 and 1870 census records for Sampson County, North Carolina, she was listed as aged 15.

Charity Lockamy, aged 30, was listed as the spouse of Daniel Lockamy, aged 27, in the 1880 census of Honeycutts Township, Sampson County, North Carolina. Daniel, aged 59, was listed as D. W. Lockamy in the 1910 Federal Census of Honeycutts Township, Sampson County, North Carolina, with Charity, aged 65. In 1870, William D. Lockamy was living in the household of Bluman Holland and "Cilva" (Sylvania Lockerman), daughter of Lovet Lockerman and Elizabeth (Maiden name unknown.) His age was listed as 16, but many census records contain errors. Daniel's given name could have been either William Daniel or Daniel William and Lockamy and Lockerman were used interchangeably over the years. I have found no proof that William D. was the Daniel W. married to Charity. John, Charity's father, was a great uncle of Bluman. In 1910, Charity and Daniel were living next door to Bluman's brother, Chester, and his family.

The certificate of death for their daughter, Minnie Lee, names Charity Holland and Daniel W. Lockamy for her parents. Daniel does not appear to have been the brother of Sylvania Lockerman, wife of Bluman Holland, but he was probably the William D. Lockamy who was living with them in 1870. At the time many young men and women lived with families other than their own to learn a trade or a skill; some of these children had lost at least one parent and were placed by the court in homes of relatives or other guardians.

Children of Charity Holland and Daniel Lockamy are:

+ 235 i. **Cornelia Lockamy,** born 1877; died 09 July 1923 in Dismal Township in Sampson County.

236 ii. **Minnie Lee Lockamy,** born 1 August 1880 in Sampson County, North Carolina and died 26 March 1943 in Cross Creek Township, Cumberland County, North Carolina. She married **Mallette Holland (Mallett Holland; Malette Holland**), son of **Joel Holland** and **Dicey Ann Holland (Dicy Ann Holland.**) Minnie was with her parents in 1900. See elsewhere in this book for their children.

237 iii. **Vesker Lockamy,** born about 1879 in Sampson County, North Carolina.

238 iv. **Sarah C. Lockamy,** born about 1886 in Sampson County, North Carolina.

67. John J. Holland (John[3], Thomas William[2], Unknown[1]) was born April 1847. He married **Elizabeth A. (maiden name unknown)**. She was born about 1850.

During the Civil War, John was a Private in Company A, 2nd Jr. Reserves, Regiment 71. His service record shows he was born in April 1847 in Sampson County and was a student when he enlisted in April 1864 in Clinton, North Carolina. He left his company on 15 July 1864 due to illness. In Clinton 26 September 1889 for veterans' reunion.

Children of John Holland and Elizabeth Unknown are:

239 i. **Louiza J. Holland**, born about 1873.

+ 240 ii. **Joseph Tilden Holland**, born about 1877.

Generation Number 4

74. Cherry Ann Holland (Unknown Child[4], Daniel[3], Thomas William[2], Unknown[1])

was born between 1850-1852. She married **James Mack Parker** about 1882. He was born about 1853 and North Carolina Death Records name 11 September 1934 for his date of death. I have not found Cherry Ann after the 1900 census.

In the 1880 Federal Census for Sampson County, North Carolina, her name was spelled "Cheny" and in 1900 it was listed as "Cheria." Cherry Ann is the only Cherry Holland who was the right age to have been the wife of James Mack. James Mack was a teamster and I have not identified his parents. He was head of household in 1930 and his son, Seba S. and Seba's wife, Macy, and seven of their children were living with James Mack.

Children of Cherry Holland and James Parker are:

241 i. **Chalie C. Parker**, born January 1883 and North Carolina Death Records show he died on 8 September 1924 at the age of 41.

242 ii. **Thomas Claude Parker**, born September 1886 and North Carolina Death records say he died in June 1945. He married **Jinie Belle Hall**; born 24 August 1887; died 30 May 1946 in Honeycutts Township, Sampson County, North Carolina.

243 iii. **Seba Swendell Parker**, born 28 May 1892; died 06 September 1949 in Erwin, Harnett County, North Carolina. He married **Macy Mae Hall**; born 28 September 1897; died 09 November 1973. She was the daughter of Tom Hall, Jr. and Matilda Jane Culbreth.

Seba Swendell and Macy Mae were buried in War Memorial Cemetery, Dunn, Harnett County, North Carolina

William S. Parker (William Swendall Parker?) of Erwin, Harnett County, North Carolina, provided data on the family of Seba S. Parker and Macy Mae Hall for Professor Mayo Bundy's book.

Children and grandchildren of Seba and Macy:

1. Nenia Mae Parker, born 14 January 1916 married **Joseph A. Honeycutt**, who was born 06 January 1916 and died 30 May 1959. They had one daughter, **Mary Alice Honeycutt** who was born 10 August 1940. Nenia's name may be found as "Minnie Mae."

2. William Swendall Parker was born 12 November 1917 and married **Ludell G. Parker** who was born 15 May 1916. They had one child, **Robert S. Parker,** born on 22 September 1938

3. Vida Parker was born 9 January 1920 and married **Sherrill William Avery** on 22 July 1938. They had three children, **Jacky Darius Avery,** born on 22 October 1939; **William Paul Avery,** born 07 February 1942; **James Mack Avery** born 15 December 1944.

4. Jesse James Parker was born 08 april 1922 and died 25 December 1970. He married **Elizabeth Gower** who was born 5 December 1924 and they had one son**, Larry James Parker, Sr.**, born 25 April 1942. Larry married **Elizabeth Moore** who was born 08 August 1942.

5. Earl D. Parker was born 01 June 1924 and died 21 March 1964. He first married **Bulah Byrd** and they had one daughter, **Patsy Parker,** born 02 February 1948. Earl married second to **Betty Jean Russell** who was born 31 December 1938; they had three children: **Donald Parker**, born 06 March 1958; **Debra Parker**, born 24 September 1961; **David Parker,** born 27 November 1960.

6. Leddie Jane Parker was born 13 November 1925 and married **Danny Kerble Manness** who was born 03 October 1924. Their six children: **Jonathan Malani Manness,** born 15 September 1955; **Shan Manness,** born 15 July 1956; Jayne **Sharmayne Manness**, born 14 August 1957; **Sharon Jeanette Manness**, born 11 April 1959; **Lydia Kerbelin Manness,** born 06 July 1960; **Thelma Vida Lorainne Manness**, born 19 January 1961.

7. Ruth Mildred Parker was born 10 November 1928 and married **Billy Ray Stewart** who was born 20 October 1925.

8. Nell Barbara Parker was born 10 April 1933 and married first to **Donald M. Valley** who was born 11 January 1930. They had two children: **Randy Mareis Valley** was born 17 March 1952; **Gary Mitchell Valley** was born 25 January 1957. Nell married second to **Jerry Poole Pope** who was born 20 January 1939; they had one child, **Jerry Keith Pope** who was born 08 September 1967.

9. Joyce Glendon Parker was born 04 February 1936 and married **Paul Hurman Jackson** who was born 07 June 1931. Their daughter**, Connie T. Jackson** was born 08 October 1954.

75. Ruffin Holland (James[4], Daniel[3], Thomas William[2], Unknown[1]) was born about 1831, and died 18 February 1863 in Camp Gregg, Danville, Virginia. He married **Katherine Cooke** who was born about 1831.

Records for the American Civil War show: "Holland, Ruffin, a Pvt. in Co. D, Regt. 38, Infantry was born 1834 in Samspon County. He was a farmer and enlisted on 22 October 1861 in Clinton. Hospitalized 19 October 1862 with diarrhea. Transferred 19 November 1862 to hospital # 5 at Richmond, VA from Huguenot Springs, VA. Died 18 February 1863 at Camp Gregg, Danville, Virginia."

"Ruffen" Holland sold 50 acres of land for $150 to Micager Autry on 15 May 1856. On 25 October 1856, "Ruffin" sold 20 acres of land for $80 to Micajah Autry. The second deed mentions the east side of South River.

See notes for his father, James.

Children of Ruffin Holland and Katherine Cooke are:

244 i. **Sarah E. Holland,** born about 1855; died 28 August 1900. She married **Thomas Jackson Strickland** 31 March 1885; born 15 February 1863; died 11 August 1926 in Flea Hill Township, Cumberland County, North Carolina. Their daughter, **KATIE CORNELIA**

STRICKLAND was born 28 May 1890 and died 17 October 1944 in Dunn, North Carolina. Katie married **ERSKINE MATTHEW YARBROUGH** on 7 May 1916 in Wade, Cumberland County, North Carolina. Erskin was the son of **AUGUSTUS BRYON YARBROUGH** and **IDA JOSEPHINE WILLIFORD** and was born 28 January 1886 and died 15 May 1975 near Fayetteville, North Caroline. Katie and Erskine had six children, all born in Black River Township in Cumberland County, North Carolina.

1) **Erskine Walter Yarbrough** was born 7 April 1917.

2) **Thomas Augustus Yarbrough**, born 3 June 1919.

3) **Josephine Adel Yarbrough**, a twin, was born 5 June 1922 (3 June 1922 is on gravestone.) She married **DONNIE G. TEW** who was born 13 June 1928. She is buried in Sunrise Memorial Gardens between Roseboro and Salemburg, North Carolina.

4) **Sarah Maebell Yarbrough**, a twin, was born 5 June 1922 and **married LEON R. WOOD** on 4 January 1942 in Galatia Presbyterian Church. Leon was born about 1914 and was the son of FRANK C. and EMMA H. WOOD of Cape Cod, Massachusetts.

5) **Henry Gray Yarbrough** was born 27 July 1925 and about 1980 died in Dunn, North Carolina.

6) **Maxine Elizabeth Yarbrough** was born 28 October 1928 (17 October 1928 is on gravestone) and died 23 July 1945 in Fayetteville, North Carolina.

245 ii. **Mary B. Holland**, second child of Ruffin and Katherine, was born about 1858 in Honeycutts Township, Sampson County, North Carolina. She married **Neill A. Young** 13 December 1885 in Fayetteville, Cumberland County, North Carolina; he was born about 1859.

\+ 246 iii. **Eli Underwood Holland**, born 03 October 1862 in Sampson County, North Carolina; died 10 July 1937 in Black River Township, Cumberland County, North Carolina.

76. William Holland (James^4, Daniel^3, Thomas William^2, Unknown^1) was born about 1838, and died between 1877 - 1880. He married **Ann Eliza Daniel**, daughter of John Daniel and Civil Hall. She was born 12 September 1833, and died 15 June 1917.

William was not listed in the 1880 census; Eliza was head of household with the four sons.

Ann or "Anna" is named Annie Eliza Holland on her own certificate of death and "Annie E. Daniel" on the death certificate for Lewis Benson Holland, the son named below. She is named "Anna Elizabeth Daniel" on the certificate of death for William J(ames) Holland, their son. "Anneliza Daniel Holland" is on Ann's gravestone in Beulah United Methodist Church Cemetery on Corinth Church Road (SR 326), 1.7 miles from Hwy 242. Sampson County North Carolina.

Children of William Holland and Ann Daniel are:

\+ 247 i. **Calton Walker Holland**, born 20 June 1859 in Sampson County, North Carolina; died 20 April 1938 in Sampson County.

\+ 248 ii. **William James Holland**, born about 1862.

249 iii. **Dennis P. Holland**, born 08 March 1874 in Sampson County, North Carolina; died 28 December 1931 in Little Coharie Township, Sampson County.

Burial: Erwin, North Carolina.

\+ 250 iv. **Lewis Benson Holland**, born 15 July 1878; died 08 February 1963.

78. Thomas James Holland (James[4], Daniel[3], Thomas William[2], Unknown[1]) was born 11 September1842 in Sampson County, North Carolina and died on 24 August 1917 of Uremic Poisoning in Dismal Township in Sampson County. He married **Sarah C. Lucas** 26 November 1869 in Sampson County. She was born about 1850 in Sampson County, North Carolina, and died in Sampson County.

The name of his mother on his certificate of death is difficult to read and appears to be Sabra McClason born in Cumberland County.. The first name of Thomas James' father was erased and James written in and in the event McClason is correct, Sabra may have remarried. However, his mother's maiden name, "Culbreth) may be written incorrectly on the certificate; their son-in-law, Alex (William Alexander) was the informant.

He and Sarah may have had a son, **Frank B. Holland,** born about 1884 who married Josephine (Maiden Name Unknown), born about 1886. Frank B. and Josephine had a son, **Rayman F. Holland,** who was born about 1908. In 1910, Frank and Josephine were living next door to Thomas James Holland, Bernice Culbreth Holland, and Bryant B. Holland.

Civil War Records show: "Holland, Thomas J., Cpl., Co. I, Regt. 20, Inf. Born 1843, Sampson County, Farm laborer. Enlisted 17 September 1861 at Fort Johnston, promoted December 1862 to Full Corporal and was wounded 2-3 May 1863 at Chancellorsville, Virginia. Captured 1 July 1863 at Gettysburg, PA and confined Fort Delaware, Delaware and Point Lookout Maryland. Received 14-15 Feb 1865 at Cox's Wharf, Virginia for exchange. Rank reduced to Private. Captured 25 March 1865 at Fort Stedman, Virginia. Confined Hart's Island, New York Harbor. Released 18 June 1865 by oath. In Clinton 26 September 1889 for veteran reunion."

On 20 January 1900, Thomas James and Sarah C. Holland and F. R. Cooper sold for $320 to B. B. Holland the 80 acres conveyed by James Holland to daughters, Nancy J. and Sarah J., sisters of Thomas James.

Sarah's middle initial may have been "E."

Children of Thomas Holland and Sarah Lucas are:

251 i. **Joseph Holland**, born about 1871.

\+ 252 ii. **Bryant B. Holland**, born 25 February 1872 in Sampson County, North Carolina; died 20 January 1945 in Sampson County, North Carolina.

\+ 253 iii. **Richard Lee Holland**, born 08 October 1873; died 19 November 1948 in Eastover Township, Cumberland County, North Carolina.

+ 254 iv. **William Thomas Holland**, born 05 August 1875; died 31 July 1964 in Honeycutts Township, Sampson County, North Carolina.

+ 255 v. **Louetta J. Holland**, born 18 February 1877; died 23 November 1975.

+ 256 vi. **Frances Elizabeth Holland**, born 18 February 1881; died 16 November 1960.

+ 257 vii. **Bernice Culbreth Holland**, born 13 June 1885; died 12 March 1961 in Dismal Township, Sampson County, North Carolina.

81. Quincy A. Holland (Harfrey[4], Daniel[3], Thomas William[2], Unknown[1]) was born about 1839 in Sampson County, North Carolina, and died 23 August 1863 in Hospital in Chester, Pennsylvania. He married **Unknown Spouse**.

The 1850 census for Sampson County, North Carolina, records "Quince," aged 11, after three younger children in Harfrey Holland's household. It has not been determined how he was related to Harfrey; perhaps Harfrey was married prior to his marriage to Mary, or Quincy may have been his nephew. John Holland, aged 10, Julia Holland, aged 8, and William Holland, aged 6, were living in the household of Harpy (Harfrey) Holland in 1870. These three may have been children of Quincy A. Holland.

The book, *Heritage of Sampson County...* on page 230 reveals his Civil War record. "Holland, Quincy A., Private, Company F, Regiment 20. Infantry. Born 1839, Sampson Co. Farmer. Enlisted 9 May 1861, Clinton. Wounded 27 Jun 1862 at Gaines' Mill, Virginia. Captured 3-5 July 1863 at Gettysburg, Pa. Confined Fort Delaware, Delaware. Transferred 10 Aug 1863 to hospital at Chester, Pennsylvania. Died 23 Aug 1863 of debilities."

Quincy (Quince) was not listed in the 1860 Federal Census for Sampson County, North Carolina.

Children of Quincy Holland and Unknown Spouse are:

258 i. **John Holland**, born about 1860.

259 ii. **Julia Holland**, born about 1862.

260 iii. **William Holland**, born about 1864.

82. Bluman Holland (Harfrey[4], Daniel[3], Thomas William[2], Unknown[1]) was born about 1846 in Sampson County, North Carolina, and died 01 September 1924 in Sampson County, North Carolina. He married **Sylvania Lockerman** about 1869, daughter of Lovett Lockerman and Elizabeth Unknown. She was born about 1842 and died 04 July 1907 in Sampson County, North Carolina.

John M. Lockerman sold 39 acres to Bluman on 30 May 1868 for $100. Land was on "...east side of Rye Swamp..." Bluman was living with his son, Alger, in 1910.

Bluman and Sylvania were buried in the Jernigan and Holland Cemetery on Jernigan Loop Road (SR 1619), Sampson County, North Carolina.

Children of Bluman Holland and Sylvania Lockerman are:

\+ 261 i. **Florence E. Holland**, born 09 July 1868; died 24 June 1910.

262 ii. **Repsie Holland**, born December 1869.

\+ 263 iii. **Lovette H. Holland**, born about 1871.

264 iv. **Mary E. Holland**, born about 1873.

\+ 265 v. **Lalister R. Holland**, born 30 August 1875 in Sampson County, North Carolina; died 28 August 1948 in Dismal Township, Sampson County, North Carolina.

\+ 266 vi. **Rufus Addison Holland**, born 14 January 1878 in Sampson County, North Carolina; died 19 December 1952 in Sampson County, North Carolina.

\+ 267 vii. **Alger Marvin Holland**, born 10 May 1881; died 24 September 1943.

84. Franklin Holland (Harfrey[4], Daniel[3], Thomas William[2], Unknown[1]) was born March 1850 in Sampson County, North Carolina, and died 17 June 1927 in Honeycutts Township, Sampson County, north Carolina. He married **(1) Fanny C. Hairr** before 1880, daughter of Stephen Hairr and Mary Daughtry. She was born 12 June 1855, and died 18 July 1902 in Sampson County. He married **(2) Mary A. Howard** 28 December 1902 in Clinton, Sampson County, North Carolina. She was born about 1866. He married **(3) Mary Anna Crumpler** after 1902, daughter of Matthew Crumpler and Sylvania Dudley. She was born about 1866.

Janie Isabell Hairr was a foster child of Frank Holland. In 1910, she was listed as his niece, aged 25.

The census records for 1850, 1860 and 1870 record 'Franklin' for his name. His death certificate shows 'Frank' which was probably a nickname. Cause of death was chronic interstitial nephritis of several years.

The marriage dates for his second and third wives may be incorrect or perhaps there was another Frank(lin) Holland; however, he is the only Frank(lin) Holland I have found who was born about 1850.

Peggy Tripp (Crouch; Workman.) shows that Franklin's first wife was Fannie Hair, his second cousin.

Franklin Holland was buried on 17 June 1927, at home in family cemetery. The Holland Cemetery about two miles west of Salemburg, North Carolina, where Fanny C., his wife, is buried is probably the same cemetery.

In the 1880 census, Fanny C. was listed as "Fannie C"; in the 1870 census she was "Fanny C.," aged 13. Fannie Hare (Hair,) born November 1886 may have also been a foster child of Fannie C. and Franklin Holland. Both Fannie and Janie I. were listed as nieces and living with Fannie and Franklin in 1900.

Mary appears to be his third wife. The date of death for his first wife, Fannie C. Hair(r), indicates that entries in the marriage register may be incorrect for Mary A. Howard.

Mollie was listed for Mary Anna's first name in the 1910 Federal Census for Sampson County, North Carolina, and she was listed as the wife of Franklin Holland. No maiden name was listed, but her mother, Sylvania Crumpler, was in the household.

Children of Franklin Holland and Fanny Hairr are:

+ 268 i. **Janie Isabell Hairr**, born 22 May 1883.

269 ii. **Fannie Hairr**, born November 1886.

85. Jordan Holland (Harfrey[4], Daniel[3], Thomas William[2], Unknown[1]) was born 18 June 1854 in Sampson County, North Carolina, and died 20 June 1938 in Cross Creek Township, Cumberland County, North Carolina. He married **(1) Ann Sophia Autry** before 1885, daughter of Starling Autry and Anna McPhail. She was born 10 December 1848. He married **(2) Mary Frances Autry** about 1886, daughter of John Autry and Sarah Horne. She was born 09 September 1858 in Autryville, Sampson County, North Carolina, and died 05 November 1910. He married **(3) Charlotte Olivia Vann** 22 January 1914 in Residence of D. J. King, Sampson County, North Carolina, daughter of John Vann and Rebecca McAlpin. She was born 06 April 1883, and died 30 September 1956.

Professor Mayo Bundy notes that Hazelene Bass provided him with the data he presents for Jordan, his three wives, and their descendants. I have added additonal data. Jordan's first wife, Ann Sophia Autry, and her infant probably died about 1885. The death certificate for Jordan records Myocardial Insufficiency and uremia for causes of death. It shows that he also had prostate surgery on 26 March 1938 and died in Highsmith Hospital, Fayetteville, Cumberland County, North Carolina. Jordan and Ann Sophia were second cousins.

Ann Sophia's full date of birth was found on Ancestry.com where her middle name is listed as "Sapphira." Ann died during childbirth as did her baby.

On the certificate of death for Jordan and Mary Frances' daughter, Annie Jane, Jordan's name is entered "John J. Holland." This is the only instance where I have found this and I'm inclined to believe **it may mean that Jordan's full name was John Jordan Holland**. Jordan Holland, his second wife, Mary Frances, and his third wife "Oliva V." were buried in the Holland Cemetery on Fleet Cooper Road (SR 1240) in Sampson County, North Carolina.

Charlotte Olivia Vann first married **Amma C. Peterson** and they had two sons, **Henry Sloan Peterson** born in 1907 and **Howard James Peterson** born in 1909.

Child of Jordan Holland and Ann Autry is:

270 i. **Infant Holland** died at birth.

Children of Jordan Holland and Mary Autry are:

\+ 271 i. **Challie Cleveland Holland,** born 17 October 1886 in Sampson County, North Carolina; died 13 November 1957 in Clinton, Sampson County, North Carolina.

\+ 272 ii. **Tomzil Clide Holland,** born 23 December 1888 in Sampson County, North Carolina; died 07 September 1953 in Sampson Regional Medical Center, Clinton, North Carolina.

\+ 273 iii. **Annie Jane Holland,** born 01 July 1890 in Little Coharie Township, Sampson County, North Carolina; died 19 November 1964.

274 iv. **Marion Holland,** born 13 June 1894; died 17 July 1919.

Marion did not marry. He was buried in the Holland Family Cemetery where his parents were buried; his gravestone may read "**Mack C. Holland.**"

\+ 275 v. **Anderson Holland,** born 30 May 1897 in North Carolina; died 05 June 1966 in Clinton, Sampson County, North Carolina.

276 vi. **Nellie B. Holland,** born 09 November 1899.

Nellie never married.

\+ 277 vii. **Drucilla Holland,** born 15 November 1901; died 09 April 1971.

Children of Jordan Holland and Charlotte Vann are:

\+ 278 i. **Charlotte Elizabeth Holland,** born 13 October 1914; died after 1950.

\+ 279 ii. **Katie Rebecca Holland,** born 02 March 1917; died 19 August 1979.

\+ 280 iii. **David Jordan Holland,** born 07 July 1918; died after 1955.

86. Chester Holland (Harfrey[4], Daniel[3], Thomas William[2], Unknown[1]) was born 21 September 1856 in Sampson County, North Carolina, and died 13 April 1942 in Sampson County, North Carolina. He married **Emily Jane Autry** 19 March 1881 in Sampson County, North Carolina, daughter of John William Autry and Sarah Horne. She was born 21 September 1860 in Autryville, Sampson County and died 02 August 1933 in Salemburg, Sampson County.

All of Chester and Emily Jane's children attended the Salem School, one of the oldest schools in Sampson County. Chester's certificate of death records the dates listed above and notes Uremia (6 days) and coronary occlusion (2 weeks) for cause of death.

Chester was buried on 15 April 1942. He and Emily Jane were buried in Salemburg Cemetery, Salemburg, Sampson County, North Carolina.

Children of Chester Holland and Emily Autry are:

\+ 281 i. **Repsie Holland,** born 02 March 1882 in Sampson County, North Carolina; died 18 June 1938.

\+ 282 ii. **Columbus Holland,** born 02 September 1883 in Sampson County, North Carolina; died 24 January 1963 in Sampson County, North Carolina.

283 iii. **Lena Holland,** born 30 November 1886; died 26 May 1888.

Lena was buried in the Holland Cemetery on Hollandtown Road, near Salemburg, Sampson County, North Carolina.

\+ 284 iv. **Erastus Holland**, born 23 July 1888 in Salemburg, Honeycutts Township, Sampson County, North Carolina; died 26 April 1955 in Erwin, Harnett County, North Carolina.

\+ 285 v. **John Love Holland, Sr.**, born 28 October 1890 in Salemburg, Salemburg, North Carolina; died 04 July 1973 in Clinton, Sampson County, North Carolina.

\+ 286 vi. **Lillie Holland,** born 02 February 1893 in Sampson County, North Carolina; died 03 May 1984 in Dunn, Harrnett County, North Carolina.

\+ 287 vii. **Rosella Holland,** born 23 January 1895 in Sampson County, North Carolina; died 02 November 1988 in Asheboro, Randolph County, North Carolina.

\+ 288 viii. **Charlotte Ann Holland**, born 05 May 1897 in Sampson County, North Carolina; died 24 March 1995 in Salemburg, Sampson County, North Carolina.

\+ 289 ix. **James Monroe Holland**, born 04 July 1899 in Sampson County, North Carolina; died 21 March 1993 in either a Nursing or Rest Home in Mount Olive, Wayne County, North Carolina.

290 x. **Geneva Holland,** born 16 April 1900 in Sampson County, North Carolina; died 18 May 1904 in Sampson County.

Geneva was buried in the Holland Family Cemetery near Salemburg, North Carolina, about one mile from the Justice Academy..

87. Romelia Holland (Harfrey[4], Daniel[3], Thomas William[2], Unknown[1]) was born 16 January 1860, and died 16 January 1937 in Dismal Township, Sampson County, North Carolina. She married **Oliver Spell**, son of Wiley Spell and Mary Lucas. He was born 29 August 1854 in Dismal Township, Sampson County, and died 04 July 1896.

Romelia was called "Rosia." The year of birth for either Oliver or for his sister, Lila Isabell, is incorrect. Romelia and Oliver were buried in a Spell Family Cemetery in Little Coharie Township, Sampson County, North Carolina

Children of Romelia Holland and Oliver Spell are:

\+ 292 i. **Braxton Spell**, born 17 December 1883; died 03 September 1947 in Sampson County, North Carolina.

\+ 293 ii. **George Oliver Spell,** born 02 May 1889; died 25 September 1967.

294 iii. **Joseph Spell**, born 16 January 1894; died 12 November 1939 in Little Coharie Township, Sampson County, North Carolina. He married (1) **Lula Jane Williams** 31 March 1918; she was born 23 December 1898 in Sampson County, North Carolina; died 24 December 1920 in Little Coharie Township, Sampson County, North Carolina. He married (2) **Armelia Cannady** 30 December 1922; born 03 June 1903; died 03 October 1924 in Little Coharie Township, Sampson County, North Carolina. He married (3) **Bessie Kate Ezzell** 14 September 1929; born about 1910.

Lula Jane Williams died in childbirth and is buried with infant daughter, **Dixie Spell**, in a Williams Cemetery on Ernest Williams Road, Sampson County, North Carolina

Armelia Cannady's date of death is also listed as 2 October 1924.

295 iv. **Ader Spell,** born 17 June 1888; died 01 May 1902.

Ader was buried in a Spell Family Cemetery on Dunn Road North of Roseboro, North Carolina.

296 v. **James L. Spell,** born 12 March 1897; died 08 May 1912.

James L. was buried in a Spell Family Cemetery on Dunn Road North of Roseboro, North Carolina.

88. Laura Ann Holland (Harfrey[4], Daniel[3], Thomas William[2], Unknown[1]) was born about 1862. She married **Sion Horne** before 1898. He was born about 1854.

Child of Laura Holland and Sion Horne is:

+ 297 i. **Sophia Horne,** born 15 August 1898; died 17 December 1979.

91. Ammie Holland (Harfrey[4], Daniel[3], Thomas William[2], Unknown[1]) was born 09 July 1867, and died 25 January 1953. He married **Lillie L. Horne** who was born 18 August 1873, and died 26 September 1936. She was the daughter of John Horne and Susan Warren.

Ammie is listed as "Abram" in a transcribed copy of the 1900 census for Honeycutt Township, Sampson County, North Carolina and as "AMY Holland" on the Certificate of Death for Lillie. He and Lillie were buried in McDaniel Family Cemetery on Cedar Creek Road, Cedar Creek Township, Cumberland County, North Carolina.

Child of Ammie Holland and Lillie Horne is:

+ 298 i. **Herman Perry Holland,** born 08 January 1906 in Sampson County, North Carolina; died 29 April 1953.

93. Henry Lee Holland (Harfrey[4], Daniel[3], Thomas William[2], Unknown[1]) was born 31 August 1874 in Sampson County, North Carolina, and died 16 June 1944 in Cross Creek Township, Cumberland County, North Carolina. He married **Rachel Eliza Dudley** in Sampson County, North Carolina. She was born 28 August 1874, and died 19 April 1942 in Honeycutts Township, Sampson County, North Carolina.

Henry Lee was living in Cross Creek Township in Cumberland County, and died in Highsmith Hospital, Fayetteville, Cumberland County, North Carolina. Cause of death was Uremia due to Hypertrophy Prostate with Diabetes Mellitus. His certificate of death listed "Harvey" for his father's name. Henry Lee and Racher Eliza were buried in Salemburg Cemetery, Salemburg, Sampson County, North Carolina; Rachel was buried on 20 April 1942.

Harvey, son of Henry Lee was the informant on Henry Lee's Certificate of Death and "HARVEY HOLLAND" was incorrectly named for the father of Henry Lee by the individual who completed the information. "Harvey" does sound like "Harfrey."

Children of Henry Holland and Rachel Dudley are:

+ 299 i. **Harvey Holland**, born 05 October 1897 in Sampson County, North Carolina; died 22 August 1947 in Honeycutts Township, Sampson County, north Carolina.

+ 300 ii. **Pauline Holland**, born 01 August 1901; died 13 November 1957 in Fayetteville, Cumberland County, North Carolina.

94. Dicey Ann Holland (Elizabeth[4], Daniel[3], Thomas William[2], Unknown[1]) was born between 1845 - 1847, and died 10 August 1915 in Mingo Township, Sampson County, North Carolina. She married **Joel Holland**, son of John Holland and Dicey Unknown. He was born about 1844, and died before 1900.

Her certificate of death indicates that she was a widow and names "Betsey Holland" for her mother. In 1850, Dicy was listed as aged 1, and she and her mother, Elizabeth (Betsey), were listed in the household of Elizabeth's parents, Daniel and Elizabeth Holland. In 1860 Dicy A., aged 13 and her mother "Betsey" (Elizabeth) were in the household of Daniel Holland, Jr.

I may have linked Joel to the wrong "Dicey A.", but I believe he married Dicey A. Holland, who would have been a great-niece of his father and Joel's first cousin, once removed. Census records appear to support this.

Civil War records placed Joel as a private in Company I, Regiment 46 Infantry and listed 1844 for his year of birth in Sampson County. He was a student when he enlisted on 26 April 1862 in Clinton, North Carolina. He was wounded 5 May 1864 at Wilderness, Virginia, hospitalized and later was furloughed 15 July 1864 for 60 days, but was still unable to return to unit by 31 December 1864. On the 18 March 1865, he was captured in Sampson County, confined at Hart's Island, New York Harbor, and released on 18 June 1865 by oath."

Child is listed above under (65) Joel Holland.

97. William Wright Holland (Thomas James[4], Daniel[3], Thomas William[2], Unknown[1]) was born 14 April 1850 in Clinton, Sampson County, North Carolina, and died 20 June 1926 in Sampson County. He married **Louisa Vann** 13 September 1873, daughter of **Henry Vann** and **Eliza Odom**. She was born 20 April 1853 in Sampson County, North Carolina, and died 08 February 1923 in Sampson County.

In 1860 and 1870, William was living in the household of Lott Owen. He and Louisa were buried in a Holland Cemetery on Merritt Road (SR 1944), Sampson County, North Carolina

Children of William Holland and Louisa Vann are:

+ 301 i. **Onie Vendex Holland**, born 14 October 1871; died 30 June 1952 in Sampson County, North Carolina.

302 ii. **Ardella Holland**, born 25 June 1874; died 1938.

+ 303 iii. **Charles Henry Holland, Sr.**, born 15 April 1876; died 25 May 1962.

+ 304 iv. **William Jasper Holland**, born 04 December 1879 in Sampson County, North Carolina; died 26 July 1962 in Sampson County.

305 v. **Odius D. Holland**, born 25 March 1881.

+ 306 vi. **Arthur Braxton Holland**, born 23 March 1883; died 04 September 1971.

307 vii. **George Estelle Holland**, born 30 March 1888; died 11 April 1964. He married **Sallie E. Johnson** 18 December 1915 in Clinton, Sampson County, North Carolina; born about 1897; died 08 October 1932.

George Estelle and Sallie E. were buried in a Holland Cemetery on Merritt Road (SR 1944), Sampson County, North Carolina

308 viii. **Katie Florence Holland**, born 01 January 1890.

+ 309 ix. **Leslie Lee Holland**, born 17 November 1891 in Sampson County, North Carolina; died 19 March 1961 in Sampson County, North Carolina.

+ 310 x. **Elliott Rexford Holland**, born September 1895.

98. Catharan Gray Holland (Thomas James[4], Daniel[3], Thomas William[2], Unknown[1]) was born 16 June 1853 in Clinton, Sampson County, North Carolina, and died 22 August 1923 in Albertson, Duplin County, North Carolina. She married **Nathan Satchell Boyette** 09 November 1887 in Giddensville, Sampson County, son of Nathan Boyette and Mary Lee. He was born 28 April 1821 in Giddensville, Sampson County, North Carolina, and died 02 February 1901 in Giddensville, Sampson County.

"Catherine Grey Boyette can be found for her name; **Catharan Gray Boyette** is recorded on her certificate of death and "Eliza Crawford" was named for her mother; Whitfield, her maiden name was not entered.

In 1900, she was listed as "**Catie G.**" in the census for Duplin County, North Carolina and she, "Satchel" and Vara were living with Nathan and **Sally E. Clifton**. Nathan Satchel had a daughter, Sally E., with his first wife. There may have been some other relationship between the Boyettes and Cliftons. "Satchwell" Boyettee, aged 30, appeared in the 1850 census of Sampson County, North Carolina, with wife, "Ceiney," aged 30, and three children; also listed with them were Mary Andrews, aged 43, and her daughter, Jane, aged 9. In 1860, Satchwell, aged 38, and "Sarria," aged 39, were listed in Piney Grove, Piney Grove Township, Sampson County, with six children. In 1870, "Satchel," aged 49, and wife, **Nancy**, aged 48, were living in Halls Township in Sampson County with three children. It is not clear whether Ceiney, Sarria and Nancy were the names of more than one wife. Their ages suggest that the name was spelled differently in each census and that Nathan Satchel Boyette was married only once before his marriage to Catherine Grey.

In 1920, "Kate C. (G.?), Aunt, aged 66, and Vara I., Cousin, aged 26, were listed in the household of Patrick B. Merritt and his wife, Della, in Scotland Neck Township, Halifax County, North Carolina. Kate C. may have been Catherine Grey. I have not determined the link.

Anna Whitfield, aged 22, was living in Nathan and Nancy's household in 1870.

Catherine was buried in a Harper Cemetery in rural Albertson, Duplin County, North Carolina.

Children of Catherine Holland and Nathan Boyette are:

311 i. **Infant Son Boyette**, born about 1889 in Giddensville, Sampson County, North Carolina; died 1889.

312 ii. **Infant Son Boyette**, born about 1891 in Giddensville, Sampson County, North Carolina; died 1891.

+ 313 iii. **Vara Irene Boyette**, born 29 May 1893 in Giddensville, Sampson County, North Carolina; died 08 February 1962 in Albertson, Duplin County, North Carolina.

99. Thomas James Holland, Jr. (Thomas James[4], Daniel[3], Thomas William[2], Unknown[1]) was born 23 November 1854 in Sampson County, North Carolina, and died 01 April 1906. He married **Addie Lillian Dail**, daughter of Frank Dail and Zilpha Dail. She was born 16 May 1871, and died 03 February 1950.

He is probably the Thomas Holland living in the household of Marcheston Killett in 1870.

Children of Thomas Holland and Addie Dail are:

+ 315 i. **Effie Gray Holland**, born 24 February 1889 in Piney Grove Township, Sampson County, North Carolina; died 14 February 1979.

316 ii. **Mittie Pearl Holland**, born 03 October 1890; died 26 March 1980. She married **Devroah Smith.**

317 iii. **Forest Pender Holland**, born 03 September 1892; died 01 June 1975 in Moore County, North Carolina. He married **Ruth McKay** who was born about 1902. Forest and Ruth were living with his mother in 1920 and she was in his household in 1930, but Ruth was not listed and may have died. It appears that his mother may have been incorrectly listed for his wife in 1830. Also found for his year of birth is 1977 and "Forrest Pender Holland" is recorded for his name in a North Carolina Death Collection. Children: 1) Elizabeth Holland born about 1911; **Houpe Holland**, born about 1914; **Edwin Holland**, born about 1917. The spelling of "Houpe" may be incorrect.

318 iv. **Annie Crawford Holland**, born 03 March 1894; died 12 January 1976. She married **Theophilus H. McLeod, Sr.**

314 v. **Hettie Dail Holland**, born 24 January 1896; died 01 October 1952. She married **William Patrick Raiford.** Dates are from her certificate of death.

319 vi. **Thomas Arthur Holland**, born 17 June 1898; died 29 September 1899.

320 vii. **Ruby Motley Holland**, born 21 July 1901. She married **Leslie Granville Thompson**.

321 viii. **Leslie Waddle Holland**, born 01 October 1904. He married (1) Nettie P. Unknown. He married (2) **Helen Louise Chamberlain.**

102. Hanson G. Holland (Daniel^4, Daniel^3, Thomas William^2, Unknown^1) was born 20 March 1876, and died 07 October 1951. He married **Lillie Mae W. (maiden name unknown)**. She was born 31 July 1886, and died 20 July 1935.

H. E. "Hance" Holland is found for his name in transcribed cemetery records. Middle initial looks like "G." in census records. He was probably the Hance Holland who was boarder , aged 23, in the household of William J. Hudson in Halls Township, Sampson County, in 1900. He was listed **"Hance G. Holland"** in the 1930 census and his certificate of death records "Hanson G. Holland" for his name. He and Lillie Mae were buried in Corinth Baptist Church Cemetery, Sampson County, North Carolina.

Elias Holland and Vestina Holland, born in 1863 and 1861 respectively, were in Hanson's household in 1930 and were entered as father and mother-in-law in a census index. This may indicate that Lillie's maiden name was Holland; it could also be an error. I have not found any children for Hanson and Lillie. I also have been unable to find any data for Elias and Vestina Holland.

The certificate of death for him records "Hanson G. Holland" for his name and names "Dan Holland" for his father and "Unknown" for his mother. Hanson died of carcinoma of the stomach that had metastasized (spread to other areas of the body). His brother, Julius also died from carcinoma of the stomach. Hanson was the informant listed on the certificate of death for his brother, Julius, and names Daniel Holland for Julius' father and Mary Autry for his mother leading me to believe that Mrs. R. B. Wilson the informant on the certificate for Hanson either was not related to the family or she was a younger descendant with little knowledge of the ancestors.

103. Julius Holland (Daniel^4, Daniel^3, Thomas William^2, Unknown^1) was born 06 August 1877 in Sampson County, North Carolina, and died 07 February 1936. He married **Lillie (maiden name unknown)**. She was born about 1887.

He and Lillie were listed in several census records; I have found Lena, their daughter, listed only in the 1920 census. Julius was buried in Salemburg Cemetery on Bearskin Road, Salemburg, Sampson County, North Carolina and transcribed cemetery records list 1878 for his birth. His certificate of death records the dates listed above and carcinoma of the stomach with obstruction for cause of his death; his brother, Hanson, also died from stomack cancer.

His certificate of death names Daniel Holland for his father and Mary Autry for his mother. His brother, Hanson, was the informant.

Child of Julius Holland and Lillie Unknown is:

\+ 324 i. **Lenna Mae Holland,** born 06 September 1912; died 11 October 1979.

106. Hiram M. Holland (Matthew[4], Daniel[3], Thomas William[2], Unknown[1]) was born 05 April 1851 in Sampson County, North Carolina, and died 08 November 1937 in Sampson County, North Carolina. He married **Margaret Jane (maiden name unknown)**. She was born 15 August 1857, and died 12 November 1930 in Sampson County, North Carolina.

Hiram was a carpenter. He and Margaret Jane were buried in a Holland Cemetery in woods off Herbie Road (SR 1486) in Sampson County.

Children of Hiram Holland and Margaret Unknown are:

325 i. **Blackman Holland,** born about 1885 in Sampson County, North Carolina; died 25 February 1956 in Sampson County, North Carolina.

Blackman was living with his parents in 1930.

326 ii. **Rilla Ann Holland,** born about 1887. Her name on census record is difficult to read; Rittie may have been her first name.

327 iii. **Mittie M. Holland,** born about 1889.

328 iv. **Mary B. Holland,** born about 1891.

329 v. **Hillery F. Holland,** born about 1895.

330 vi. **Katie Clyde Holland,** born 14 April 1900; died 25 June 1989. She married **Almond George Grantham** after 1920; he was born 05 January 1891 in Sampson County and died 27 December 1977 in Clinton, Sampson County, North Carolina.

Almond George's name is also shown as Almon, Alman, Allman and Almond Y. Grantham." Katie Clyde and Almond George were buried in a Holland Cemetery in woods off Herbie Road (SR 1486) in Sampson County.

108. Agnes Matilda Holland (Matthew[4], Daniel[3], Thomas William[2], Unknown[1]) was born 30 November 1856 in Huntley, Honeycutts Township, Sampson County, North Carolina, and died 25 March 1947. She married **Henry H. Royals, Sr.,** son of Gabriel Royal and Sarah Crumpler. He was born 10 January 1850 in Huntley, Honeycutts Township, Sampson County, and died 27 April 1918 in Erwin, Harnett County, North Carolina.

"Till" Holland Royal is the name shown on her tombstone. Matilda and Henry H. were buried in Hollands Chapel Pentecostal Holiness Cemetery on Huntley School Road in Sampson County, North Carolina.

Pages 486 and 489 in "Royal Family Legacy, " by Wanda Royals note that Henry Royal (Royals), Sr., was born in 1847. The 1850 Census of Sampson County listed him as aged 3; his sister, Sally (Sallie, Sarah) was listed as aged 3 months. Sallie would have been born about

March 1850? "Henry H." was listed aged 13 in the 1860 Census and "Sarah" (Sallie or Sally) was listed aged 10.

In 1880, he was either in the household of Marshall Newman in Honeycutts Township, Sampson County, North Carolina or living alone next door and listed aged 32, Laborer. Henry, Matilda and their children were living next door to her brother, Robert Mitchell Holland, in 1900 in Honeycutt Township, Sampson County, North Carolina. Robert and Matilda's parents were living next door to Robert.

In a profile on page 369 of "The Heritage of Harnett County, Vol. 1" (North Carolina), by the Harnett County Heritage Committee, I found Henry was born on January 10, 1850. This profile was submitted by Doris Royals Connor. It also says: "**Henry Royals, Sr.** came to Erwin in 1911 as a carpenter -- working to help build the Erwin Mill and the mill houses. He helped build the mill house at 106 North 16th Street in Erwin and in the spring of 1913 moved his family into that house. 'His grandson, Matthew, and wife, Jean, moved into the house and were living there' in 1992. A picture of Henry and Agnes Matilda is on page 369 of the book.

The town of Erwin was called "Duke" in 1911.

He may have been the "**Hardy Henry Royal**", born in May 1847 who served in the Civil War. (Perhaps he gave an incorrect year for his birth. If so, he enlisted in April 1864 in Clinton, North Carolina, and was assigned on 25 September 1864 to service at Wilson on W & W Railroad Bridge. Paroled 1 May 1865 at Greensboro.

Children of Agnes Matilda Holland and Henry Royals are:

\+ 331 i. **Robertson Royals**, born 17 May 1888 in Sampson County, North Carolina; died 24 December 1951 in Honeycutts Township, Sampson County.

332 ii. **Sister Royals**, born in Sampson County, North Carolina.

333 iii. **Sanford Royals**, born October 1889 in Sampson County. He married **Donnie Fann. (Dona Fann).** No children. On page 58 in "Royal Family Legacy Addendum," by Wanda Royal is the following about Sanford:

"When Sanford went to Supply to visit his family, he would drive a black 1950's milk truck. He gathered his cousins in the truck and would drive them around. They remember this even though most are in their 60's now. His milk truck was not his work but just a vehicle for his enjoyment. He was a most enjoyable, cordial, happy man and made everyone around him smile."

Sanford had a first cousin named Ewell Sanford Jackson, son of his father's sister, Mary Jane (Jean) Royal and Wiley Calvin Jackson.

"Royal Family Legacy," by Wanda Royal enters "Dona" for the spelling of Sanford's wife.

\+ 334 iv. **Sally Royals**, born May 1892 in Sampson County, North Carolina.

\+ 335 v. **Lessie Royals**, born January 1893 in Sampson County.

336 vi. **Offie Royals**, born May 1894 in Sampson County, North Carolina.

Offie never married.

+ 337 vii. **Matthew Royals,** born 04 November 1895 in Sampson County; died 05 December 1976 in Erwin, North Carolina.

338 viii. **Lilly Royals**, born in Sampson County, North Carolina. Lilly died as an infant.

+ 339 ix. **Henry H. Royals, Jr.**, born 18 June 1898 in Sampson County; died 29 September 1981 in Erwin, Harnett County, North Carolina.

109. Marshall Holland (Matthew[4], Daniel[3], Thomas William[2], Unknown[1]) was born About 1859 in Sampson County, North Carolina, and died after 1930. He married **Isabelle Hall** 18 July 1904. She was born about 1875.

In 1930, Marshall was in the household of his brother, Robert Mitchell, Sr.

Child of Marshall Holland and Isabelle Hall is:

+ 340 i. **Julius David Holland, Sr.**, born 07 July 1907; died 15 January 2001.

110. Robert Mitchell Holland (Matthew[4], Daniel[3], Thomas William[2], Unknown[1]) was born July 1863 in Sampson County, North Carolina, and died 18 May 1935. He married **(1) Frances Ella Spell** 19 September 1895 in Sampson County, North Carolina, daughter of William Spell and Chelley Tew. She was born July 1872, and died 15 November 1928 in Honeycutts Township, Sampson County, North Carolina. He married **(2) Lisha A. Draughon** 16 February 1929 in Sampson County. She was born about 1875.

In the 1880 and 1930 censuses for Sampson County, North Carolina, Robert Mitchell was listed as "Mitchell." In 1870, he was entered as "Michael." His brother "Marshall, aged 70," was living with Robert and his second wife in 1930.

Lisha A.'s name appears as "Julia A. Strickland" on the Certificate of Death for Claudius, her stepson. Apparently, Claudius' wife did not know his mother's name. The 1930 census for Sampson County, North Carolina listed her name as "Litha A. Halland."

Children of Robert Holland and Frances Spell are:

341 i. **Claudius Holland**, born 25 February 1889; died 01 May 1946 in Sampson County, North Carolina. He married Bertie (maiden name unknown), who was born 22 August 1903 and died 19 January 1995.

Claudius and Bertie were buried in Beulah United Methodist Church Cemetery on Corinth Church Road (SR 1326), Sampson County, North Carolina

+ 342 ii. **Lela Holland**, born July 1891; died 1939.

+ 343 iii. **Julia Holland**, born 31 July 1894; died 22 April 1985.

+ 344 iv. **Coy Holland**, born 20 October 1896; died 22 January 1983 in Fayetteville, Cumberland County, North Carolina.

345 v. **Hattie Holland**, born July 1898; died 1918. Hattie probably died during the flu epidemic of 1917-1918.

346 vi. **Nellie Holland**, born 08 January 1900; died 08 June 1984. She married Herbert Hollingsworth 28 May 1922 in Dismal Township, Sampson County, North Carolina; he was born 08 August 1903 and died 18 December 1984.

\+ 347 vii. **Chellie Holland**, born 19 October 1901; died 26 October 1991.

\+ 348 viii. **Robert Minson Holland**, born 16 January 1908; died 13 February 1942 in Honeycutts Township, Sampson County, North Carolina.

\+ 349 ix. **Jathronia Holland,** born 14 May 1910; died 06 July 1997.

111. Matthew L. Holland (Matthew[4], Daniel[3], Thomas William[2], Unknown[1]) was born 25 September 1864 in Sampson County, North Carolina, and died 20 January 1928. He married **Eunice Butler** 29 April 1900 in Sampson County, daughter of Daniel Butler and Cherry Tew. She was born 16 April 1873 in Sampson County and died 14 October 1923 in Sampson County.

The 1900 U. S. Census records for North Carolina listed Matthew and Eunice living in Honeycutts Township, Sampson County. No children were listed. Civil, his mother, was in his household. Marshall, his brother and Sarah M., his cousin, were also living with him.

On 9 January 1904, he paid $250 to W. E. and Minnie Ann Tyndall for 50 acres in Honeycutts Township, Sampson County, North Carolina. Land was on the run of Little Coharie and joined the lands of Evander Lindley, Rich Honeycutt, Daniel Butler and William Bee Naylor. On 14 October 1909, he and Eunice (Unice) sold this land for $250 to A. R. Tew and Mary E. Tew. It then bordered land of Robert Lockamy and R. A. Honeycutt.

Matthew L. and Eunice were buried in Holland's Chapel Cemetery, near Newton Grove, North Carolina

Eunice's tombstone records dates of 17 March 1873 and 20 Oct 1923.

Children of Matthew Holland and Eunice Butler are:

350 i. **Gladys Holland**, born about 1904.

351 ii. **Felton G. Holland**, born about 1906.

113. John E. Williams (Tomzelle[4] Culbreth, Mary[3] Holland, Thomas William[2], Unknown[1]) was born about 1822, and died before 1870. He married **Sophia Autry** before 1853, daughter of Reason Autry and Sarah Hall. She was born 08 October 1830, and died 06 November 1902.

"John E." may be "John Williams," son of Joel Williams and Tomzelle Colbreath (Tomsil Culbreth), but no proof has been located. Sophia was buried in Bethabara United Methodist Church Cemetery, Dismal Township, Sampson County, North Carolina.

Children of John Williams and Sophia Autry are:

+ 352 i. **John A. Williams**, born 14 March 1853; died 13 December 1924 in Dismal Township, Clement, Sampson County, North Carolina.

+ 353 ii. **Mary J. Williams**, born 17 January 1856; died 10 February 1896.

+ 354 iii. **Joel R. Williams**, born 14 June 1857; died 12 May 1919.

+ 355 iv. **Susan L. Williams**, born 30 May 1859; died 11 June 1930 in Dismal Township, Clement, Sampson County, North Carolina.

+ 356 v. **Isabelle Williams**, born 05 September 1862; died 12 January 1937 in Eastover Township, Cumberland County, North Carolina.

+ 357 vi. **Reason Raiford Robinson Williams**, born 26 May 1864; died 03 August 1937.

114. Molcy Williams (Tomzelle[4] Culbreth, Mary[3] Holland, Thomas William[2], Unknown[1]) was born about 1823, and died between 1850 - 1860. She married **George Robert Daughtry** about 1843. He was born about 1823, and died between1850 - 1860.

Children of Molcy Williams and George Daughtry are:

+ 358 i. **William H. Daughtry**, born about 1844; died between 1898 - 1900.

+ 359 ii. **George Thomas Daughtry**, born 12 October 1849; died 27 April 1920 in Cedar Creek Township, Cumberland County, North Carolina.

116. Joel Williams, Jr. (Tomzelle[4] Culbreth, Mary[3] Holland, Thomas William[2], Unknown[1]) was born about 1828, and died 04 March 1865 in the Union Prison Camp in Elmira, New York. He married **Sarah Daughtry**. She was born about 1830.

During the Civil War, he served in 2nd Company C, 36th Regiment (2nd North Carolina Artillery.) He enlisted 9 February 1863 in Sampson County, was transferred 19 July 1864 to 2nd Company D of the regiment, and was captured at Fort Fisher on 15 January 1865. He died 4 March 1865 of pneumonia after he was confined at Elmira, New York, and was buried in Grave No. 1972 in Woodlawn National Cemetery.

Daughtry was also spelled "Daughtrey" and "Daughertry."

Children of Joel Williams and Sarah Daughtry are:

+ 360 i. **Nathan Williams**, born 06 May 1850; died 24 February 1926 in Dunn, North Carolina.

+ 361 ii. **Joel E. Williams**, born 18 April 1851; died 16 December 1933 in Fayetteville, North Carolina.

+ 362 iii. **Alexander Williams, Sr.**, born 22 August 1855; died 05 December 1920.

+ 363 iv. **John Robert Williams**, born 07 November 1857; died 18 November 1914 in Little Coharie Township, Sampson County, North Carolina.

364 v. **Mary E. Williams**, born March 1860.

Listed in the 1880 census of Little Coharie Township, Sampson County, North Carolina, aged 19 and unmarried.

365 vi. **Sarah E. Williams**, born about 1863.

Listed in the 1880 Census of Little Coharie Township as aged 17, unmarried and disabled.

\+ 366 vii. **Thomas Jefferson Williams**, born about 1865; died after 1913.

117. Isaac Williams (Tomzelle[4] Culbreth, Mary[3] Holland, Thomas William[2], Unknown[1]) was born 19 October 1831, and died 09 February 1907 in Sampson County, North Carolina. He married **Molsey Maria Lockamy**, daughter of Reason Lockerman and Jane Tew. She was born about 1830 in Sampson County, North Carolina, and died 30 January 1900 in Sampson County.

Molsey was spelled "Molcy" in the 1850 Census and was listed as age 20 under her parents. In 1860, she was listed as Molsey, age 32, (nee Lockamy.) One source shows her as "Molly Mariah Lockerman;" and the same source on another page, shows her as "Molsey Maria Lockerman (Lockamy).

Isaac and Molsey Maria were buried in the Williams Cemetery at end of dirt path off Waterpoint Road, Sampson County, North Carolina.

Children of Isaac Williams and Molsey Lockamy are:

\+ 367 i. **Mary Catherine Williams**, born 14 February 1855; died 19 December 1919 in Black River Township, Cumberland County, North Carolina.

\+ 368 ii. **Tomsilla Jane Williams**, born 20 February 1857; died 12 February 1937 in Dismal Township, Sampson County, North Carolina.

\+ 369 iii. **Lovdie Ann Williams**, born 22 January 1860; died 06 May 1956 in Dismal Township, Sampson County.

370 iv. **Joel James Williams**, born 20 June 1862; died 10 July 1871.

Joel James was buried in the Williams Cemetery at end of dirt path off Welcome School Road (SR1441) about 0.3 mile from Maxwell Road (SR1006) in Sampson County.

\+ 371 v. **Daniel Williams**, born 12 April 1864; died 28 June 1933 in Dismal Township, Sampson County, North Carolina.

\+ 372 vi. **Sarah Eliza Williams**, born 23 October 1866 in Sampson County, North Carolina; died 20 January 1938 in Dismal Township, Sampson County, North Carolina.

373 vii. **Infant Williams.**

118. Susan Ann Williams (Tomzelle[4] Culbreth, Mary[3] Holland, Thomas William[2], Unknown[1]) was born 19 May 1833, and died 28 December 1900. She married **John Bain** 07 May 1853, son of John Bain and Catharine Graham. He was born 06 May 1826, and died 06 January 1892.

Susan Ann and John's marriage bond was issued May 7, 1853. He was called "Little Jack.." John was listed as Jno. Bayne, Jr., aged 34, in the 1860 Census of the Eastern Division of Cumberland County, North Carolina. He was a carpenter with real estate valued at $1600 and personal property of $200. They were listed in the 1880 Census of Black River Township, as aged 54 and 47 with three children and it was noted that he had a broken leg.

Children of Susan Williams and John Bain are:

374 i. **Duncan James Bain**, born 04 June 1855; died 07 January 1862.

Duncan James was buried in Bluff Presbyterian Church Cemetery near Wade, Cumberland County, North Carolina

\+ 375 ii. **John C. Bain**, born 14 August 1862; died 11 September 1930 in Eastover Township, Cumberland County, North Carolina.

\+ 376 iii. **Hugh Alexander Bain**, born 12 May 1866; died 03 November 1933 in Black River Township, Cumberland County, North Carolina.

\+ 377 iv. **Catharine Jane Bain**, born 30 December 1868; died 12 February 1906.

119. Daniel Autry (Millzy Adelme[4] Culbreth, Mary[3] Holland, Thomas William[2], Unknown[1]) was born 09 April 1822, and died 06 February 1896. He married **Julia Ann Averitt**, daughter of Daniel Averitt and Mary Riley. She was born 21 October 1845, and died 02 December 1911.

Julia Ann's maiden name is spelled "Averitte" on the certificate of death for their daughter, Milzie Adeline. Daniel and Julie Ann were buried in the Leroy Autry Family Cemetery off Autryville Road, about 1.3 miles east of Autryville, North Carolina.

Children of Daniel Autry and Julia Averitt are:

\+ 378 i. **Edna Autry**, born 21 June 1862; died 29 January 1922.

\+ 379 ii. **Micajah Autry**, born 22 June 1867; died 29 August 1917.

380 iii. **Daniel Young Autry**, born about 1868.

381 iv. **John C. Autry**, born about 1872.

\+ 382 v. **William Ashford Autry**, born 16 July 1874; died 18 February 1959.

383 vi. **Milzie Adeline Autry**, was born 10 January 1877 and died 3 August1963 in Roseboro, Little Coharie Township in Sampson County, North Carolina. She had Chronic Lung Disease for three years and Arteriosclerosis and senile changes for 10 years. "Adline" can be found for her name. She married Archie Lee Lucas who was born 1867 and died 8 March 1949. Census records of Sampson County, name eight children: 1) **Daniel Lucas**, born about 1898; 2) **Perdue Lucas** born about 1900; **Bessie Lucas**, born about 1902; **Roy Lucas**, born about 1907; **Colonel Lucas**, born about 1909; **Al Lucas**, born about 1913; **Ruby Lucas**, born about 1915; **Willie Lucas**, born about 1916.

384 vii. **Julia Rena Autry**, born 25 December 1880 in Cumberland County and died 02 March 1957. She married Enoch Leslie Horne. He was born 13 April 1880; died 27 October 1941

in Cedar Creek Township in Cumberland County, North Carolina. Dr. Starling stated on Rena's certificate of death that cause of death was probably a fall from steps onto her head. He also stated that she had sudden Coronary Thrombosis and had Chronic Myocrditis and Senile Arteriosclerosis for five years. Children listed in the 1920 census for Cedar Cree, Cumberland County, names three children: **Lena Horne**, born about 1905; **Lela Horne,** born about 1907; **Julia Horne**, born about 1913.

\+ 385 viii. **Polly Autry**, born 17 June 1883; died 19 March 1963.

\+ 386 ix. **James Love Autry**, born 27 January 1885; died 03 May 1952.

121. Rebecca Elizabeth Autry (Millzy Adelme[4] Culbreth, Mary[3] Holland, Thomas William[2], Unknown[1]) was born about 1831. She married **William Williams,** son of Thomas Williams and Nanna Stewart. He was born May 1838, and died after 1900.

Children of Rebecca Autry and William Williams are:

\+ 387 i. **Susan Anner Williams**, born 09 May 1857; died 22 October 1929 in Little Coharie Township, Sampson County, North Carolina.

\+ 388 ii. **Mary Lee Williams**, born about 1858; died 1893.

122. Molsey Autry (Millzy Adelme[4] Culbreth, Mary[3] Holland, Thomas William[2], Unknown[1]) was born about 1833, and died April 1905.

Her name was also spelled "Molsay" and "Molcey."

Child of Molsey Autry is:

\+ 389 i. **Wiley C. Autry**, born 23 June 1861; died 27 May 1946.

123. Martha Ann Autry (Millzy Adelme[4] Culbreth, Mary[3] Holland, Thomas William[2], Unknown[1]) was born 30 September 1835, and died 24 December 1914. She married **James Franklin Daniel**, son of John Daniel and Civil Hall. He was born 20 March 1838, and died 19 May 1907 in Sampson County, North Carolina.

Martha Ann and James Franklin were buried in the Maxwell Cemetery at intersection of Maxwell Road (SR 1006) and SR 1427), Sampson County, North Carolina

Children of Martha Autry and James Daniel are:

390 i. **Daniel Mack Daniel**, born 01 May 1871; died 06 December 1948 in Dismal Township, Sampson County, North Carolina. He married (1) **Sarah Elizabeth Autry**; born 06 November 1869; died 05 June 1928 in Dismal Township, Sampson County. He married (2) **Ella May Sill**; born about 1888. No children.

Daniel Mack and Sara Elizabeth were buried in the Maxwell Cemetery at intersection of Maxwell Road (SR 1006) and SR 1427), Sampson County

391 ii. **Marshall Love Daniel**, born 09 June 1880; died 10 January 1958 in Clinton, North Carolina. He married **Hepsia Ann Williams** 12 March 1905; born 02 May 1881 in Sampson County, North Carolina; died 20 November 1957 in Dismal Township, Sampson County.

Marshall Love and Hepsia Ann were buried in the Honeycutt/Matthews Family Cemetery on SR 1442, Sampson County, North Carolina.

392 iii. **Jennette T. Daniel.**

393 iv. **Vestinia R. Daniel.**

394 v. **Willie F. Daniel.**

125. Miles Costin Autry (Millzy Adelme[4] Culbreth, Mary[3] Holland, Thomas William[2], Unknown[1]) was born 08 April 1839, and died 07 July 1909. He married **Nancy Katherine Faircloth**, daughter of Arthur Faircloth and Catherine Fisher. She was born 22 July 1856, and died 04 January 1919.

Miles Costin and Nancy Katherine were buried in the Autry Cemetery off Autryville Road about 0.7 mile east of Autryville, North Carolina.

Children of Miles Autry and Nancy Faircloth are:

\+ 395 i. **Callie Missouri Autry**, born 27 January 1875; died 07 February 1949.

396 ii. **Dockery Autry**, born 10 May 1876; died 23 October 1947. He married **Annie Victoria Johnson**; born 16 July 1887; died 18 September 1965.

Dockery Autry and Annie Victoria were buried in the Autry Cemetery off Mill Creek Church Road in Sampson County, North Carolina.

397 iii. **Roena J. Autry**, born December 1878. She married **Columbus Parker**; born 1882.

\+ 398 iv. **Miles Herman Autry**, born 10 November 1883; died 20 January 1968.

\+ 399 v. **Fountain Autry**, born 10 July 1886; died 14 December 1945 in Little Coharie Township, Sampson County, North Carolina.

400 vi. **Frances K. Autry**, born 27 July 1889; died 16 July 1925. She married **James W. Johnson**; born 09 October 1891; died 27 May 1967.

\+ 401 vii. **Rebecca Autry**, born August 1890; died before 1949.

\+ 402 viii. **Cordelia Autry**, born 15 May 1894; died 25 June 1970.

403 ix. **Perry Autry**, born about 1896.

126. Jeanette Autry (Millzy Adelme[4] Culbreth, Mary[3] Holland, Thomas William[2], Unknown[1]) was born 28 April 1847. She married **John Robert Hall**, son of Alexander Hall and Ann Fisher. He was born about 1845 in Sampson County, North Carolina.

"Jennet" and "Janet" were also found for her name. She and John Robert were buried in a Hall and Faircloth Cemetery off SR 1416, Sampson County, North Carolina.

Children of Jeanette Autry and John Hall are:

\+ 404 i. **Francenia Jane Hall**, born 08 January 1867; died 22 February 1960.

\+ 405 ii. **Alexander M. Hall**, born about 1869.

406 iii. **Callie Etta Hall**, born 03 September 1873; died 24 January 1951.

She was listed as "Cathie E.," aged 37, in the 1910 census and "Callie E.," aged 56, in the 1930 census for Little Coharie Township, Sampson County, North Carolina. In 1930 she was listed with her brother, Alexander H. and his son, John C.

Callie Etta was buried in the Hall and Faircloth Cemetery off SR 1416 in Sampson County, North Carolina.

\+ 407 iv. **Novella Ann Hall**, born 25 June 1873; died 12 September 1966.

\+ 408 v. **Willie Earnie Hall**, born 18 September 1883; died 03 March 1962 in Little Coharie Township, Sampson County.

\+ 409 vi. **Lena Ethel Hall**, born 19 May 1887; died 02 December 1966.

133. Martha Jane Culbreth (Isaac[4], Mary[3] Holland, Thomas William[2], Unknown[1]) was born 28 September 1836, and died 18 February 1908. She married **Blackman Autry** 17 June 1858, son of Archibald Autry and Patience (maiden name unknown). He was born 1822, and died 17 May 1892.

Martha Jane and Blackman were buried in the Blackman Autry Family Cemetery in Dismal Township, Sampson County, North Carolina.

Children of Martha Culbreth and Blackman Autry are:

410 i. **Mary Marenda Autry**, born 30 November 1858; died 16 October 1863.

Mary Marenda was buried in the Blackman Autry Family Cemetery in Dismal Township, Sampson County, North Carolina.

411 ii. **Patience Elizabeth Autry**, born 13 February 1861; died 28 August 1945 in Confederate Women's Home, Fayetteville, North Carolina. She married (1) **Andrew Jackson Cooper** 01 September 1902; born 01 January 1830 in Sampson County; died 07 June 1904 in Sampson County. Andrew Jackson first married **Elizabeth Butler** who was born about 1835. Patience married (2) **Almond Mallette Butler** after June 1904; he was born 12 September 1853; died 15 November 1922 in Roseboro, North Carolina.

She was called "Lizzie." Andrew and three infants of his and Patience Elizabeth were buried in the Nizon Cooper Family Cemetery in Salemburg, North Carolina; no dates are on the tombstones of the infants.

A great-granddaughter relates this story about Andrew:

"...my Daddy, told me that Andrew Cooper had a grist mill. "His mill was up on top of the dam (located one mile southwest of Salemburg.) The mill rock was up in the loft and the shaft came down to the lower floor. There was a water wheel, and from up in the mill house you could raise something that turned the water and that turned the wheel and ground the corn into meal. One day Grandpa Andrew Cooper got too close to the shaft and it caught his clothes and it beat him round and round until someone came and heard him and shut the water off. He never recovered' and on June 7, 1904 he died."

Almond Mallette Butler was buried in Roseboro's Old Hollywood Cemetery in Roseboro, North Carolina

\+ 412 iii. **John Blackman Autry**, born 28 October 1863; died 10 March 1940 in Cedar Creek Township, Cumberland County, North Carolina.

\+ 413 iv. **William Isaac Autry**, born 10 September 1866 in Sampson County, North Carolina; died 27 June 1948 in Sampson County.

414 v. **James R. Autry**, born 07 December 1871; died 30 October 1886.

415 vi. **Daniel Arch Autry**, born 24 November 1875; died 04 December 1877.

134. Elizabeth Ann Culbreth (Isaac[4], Mary[3] Holland, Thomas William[2], Unknown[1]) was born 22 May 1839, and died 22 March 1908 in Salem United Methodist Church, Eastover, Cumberland County, North Carolina. She married **Giles Mitchell Bullard**, son of James Bullard and Sarah Jones. He was born about 1835, and died between 1880 - 1887.

Children of Elizabeth Culbreth and Giles Bullard are:

416 i. **Duncan J. Bullard**, born about 1860. He married **Ida Dees Spell** 13 March 1898; born 27 May 1880 in North Carolina; died 21 December 1952 in Salemburg, Sampson County, North Carolina. Ida married second, **Valentine T. Baggett**. See her elsewhere in this book.

Duncan J. was buried in William A. Baggett Family Cemetery about 1 3/4 miles west of Salemburg at the south side of S.R. 1233 in Honeycutts Township, Sampson County, North Carolina.

417 ii. **Mary Elizabeth Bullard**, born 20 October 1866; died 17 March 1933. She married (1) **Evander James Cook** 23 January 1889 in Flea Hill Township, Cumberland County, North Carolina; born 19 May 1863; died 26 April 1903. She married (2) **Alex S. Wood** 21 January 1914 in Seventy-First Township, Cumberland County, North Carolina; born about 1855. **See back of book for descendants of Mary Elizabeth Bullard and Evander James Cook.**

418 iii. **Della Ann Bullard**, born 25 August 1868; died 10 August 1934. She married **Duncan J. Guy;** born about 1865.

419 iv. **William Love Bullard**, born 02 January 1871; died 16 July 1944 in Kecoughton, Virginia. William Love died in Veterans Administration Hospital in Kecoughton, Virginia.

420 v. **Sarah J. Bullard**, born about 1875. She married John D. Cook 08 February 1891 in Flea Hill Township in Cumberland County, North Carolina; born about 1867.

421 vi. **Thomas Mallett Bullard**, born 31 March 1879; died 17 January 1929. He married **Josie May Bolton**; born 11 May 1882; died 12 August 1928 in Fayetteville, North Carolina.

Children of Thomas and Josie:

1) **Berta Mae Bullard** was born 3 June 1907 in Fayetteville. She married a Mr. Brown on 23 August 1931 in Bennettsville, South Carolina.

2) **Thomas W. Bullard** was born in 1910.

3) Unidentified Child.

4) **Mary Eleanor Bullard** was born 26 may 1914 in Seventy-First Township, Fayetteville, North Carolina.

5) **James C. Bullard** the fifth child of Thomas Mallett Bullard and Josie May Bolton was born 15 July 1916 and died 2 August 1916 in Seventy-First Township in Fayetteville; he was buried at Salem United Methodist Church. His gravestone records 1 August 1916 for his death.

6) **Irbie Bullard** the sixth child was born 9 February 1918 in Seventy-First Township (he was the sixth child with five living.) Irbie married **Evelyn Holmes Taylor** 19 July 1947 in Fayetteville, North Carolina. She was born 13 April 1924 in Fayetteville, daughter of Charles B. Taylor and Katie Sandlin. They had two children: I) **Charles Thomas Bullard** was born 11 February 1948 in Fayetteville. He married **Brenda Elaine Teal** on 30 May 1970; she was born 15 May 1946 in South Carolina, daughter of Vernon F. Teal and Caretha Trexler. II) The second child of Irbie and Evelyn was **Mary Phyllis Bullard** who was born 6 September 1951 in Fayetteville. She married 2 September 1973 in Fayetteville's Hay Street United Methodist Church as his second wife, **Elliott Kai-Kee**, who was born 8 July 1947 in Alameda County, California, son of Mark Kai-Kee and Blossom Ah-Tye.

7) A stillborn son, 11 April 1920 in Seventy-First Township was buried in Salem United Methodist Church Cemetery.

8) **Ethel Ellen Bullard** was born 23 January 1922 in Seventy-First Township in Fayetteville, Cumberland County, North Carolina. She married **David Pernon McLaurin**, son of Albert Robert McLaurin and Attie Mae Thames. Their one child, **Judith Lane McLaurin** was born 12 February 1942 in Eastover Township in Cumberland County, North Carolina. Judith married **Houston Currie Reece Jr.** who was born about 1940. They had two children, **Tana Gay Reece** was born 25 October 1962 and **Houston Currie Reece, Jr.** was born 9 December 1964 in Fayetteville.

9) Unidentified child.

10) A son, stillborn 15 May 1924 in seventy-First Township is the last known child of Thomas Mallett and Josie May. He was buried in Salem United Methodist Church Cemetery

There were ten children of Thomas Mallett Bullard and Josie May Bolton, six living, one born and died, and three stillborn children

137. William Culbreth (Isaac[4], Mary[3] Holland, Thomas William[2], Unknown[1]) was born 31 March 1846, and died 23 June 1932 in Eastover Township, Cumberland County, North Carolina. He married **Sarah Elizabeth Sessoms** 29 August 1876. She was born 19 July 1857, and died 29 January 1929 in Eastover Township, Cumberland County, North Carolina.

William and Sarah Elizabeth were buried in Salem United Methodist Church, Eastover, Cumberland County, North Carolina

Children of William Culbreth and Sarah Sessoms are:

\+ 422 i. **Julius W. Culbreth**, born 28 October 1875; died 29 August 1901.

423 ii. **Walter Marcellus Culbreth**, born 22 May 1877; died 10 May 1962 in Eastover Township, Cumberland County, North Carolina. He married (1) **Laura Elizabeth Geddie** 18 March 1903 in Flea Hill Township, Cumberland County, North Carolina; born 12 August 1884; died 23 August 1928 in Flea Hill Township, Cumberland County, North Carolina. He married (2) **Leila Alice Griffin** 12 May 1929 in Fayetteville, Cumberland County, North Carolina; born 29 October 1897 in Georgia; died 28 December 1971 in Fayetteville, North Carolina.

At least eight children.

1) **Julius Martin Culbreth,** the first child of Walter Marcellus and Laura Elizabeth was born 14 February 1904 and died 14 December 1970 in Fayetteville. He married 21 June 1925 in Fayetteville to **Eva Gertrude Bullock** who was born 6 August 1906 and died 11 may 180 in Fayetteville. She was the daughter of **Caswell B. Bullock** and **Alice McLaurin.** Julius and Eva were buried at Salem United Methodist Church Cemetery. Two children. Stillborn son, 4 August 1926 and **Claire Lynn Culbreth** who was born 25 July 1933 in Eastover Township in Cumberland County and married **Kenneth Harold Sykes** who was born 18 September 1932 in Fayetteville, son of Marion Hassell Sykes and Vannie Holland. "Sykes" was also spelled "Sikes."

2) **James Leon Culbreth** was the second child of Walter Marcellus Culbeth and Laura Elizabeth Geddie and was born 16 November 1906 and died 27 December 1984 in Fayetteville. He first married 27 August 1926 to **Sadie Viola Geddie** and his second wife was **Lizzie L. Beard** who was born in 1910, daughter of James A. Beard and Florida Virginia McLaurin. James and Sadie's childlren: I) **James Donnie Culbreth** who was born 24 December 1926 in Flea Hill Township in Cumberland County. He married Bessie Mae Williams. II) **Dougald Geddie Culbreth** was born 17 May 1929 in Flea Hill Township and married **Pansy Elizabeth Presler** who was born about 1932. Three children. III) **Walter Duvell Culbreth** was born 7 December 1931 in Eastover Township in Culberland and he married first to **Sarah Neal Grey** and second to **Annie Alretta Bunce**. IV) **Kenneth Alexander Culbreth** was born 28 February 1934 in Eastover Township, married **Donna Foss and** had one child. V) **Fulton Ray Culbreth** was born 20 June 1940 in Eastover Township and Cathay **Diane Bryson** who was born 22 February 1955 in Rockfish Township. One child. VI) **Jennie Sylvia Culbreth** was born 11 December 1944 in Fayetteville and married **Norman Timothy McLaurin** who was born 13 March 1945 in Fayetteville, son of Augustus Merrill McLaurin and Thelma Kathryn Melton. Two children.

3) **Ira Eulace Culbreth,** third child of Walter Marcellus and Laura Elizabeth, was born 3 February 1909 and died 12 January 1975 in Fayetteville. He married **Lola Lorenza Culbreth** who was born about 1909, daughter of **Stephen Culbreth** and **Annie Elizabeth Cain.** He was buried at Salem United Methodist Church Cemetery. Two children.

4) **Kenneth Alton Culbreth** was born 24 September 1912 and died 6 December 1973 near Fayetteville, North Carolina. He married **Sarah Carolyn McNeill** who was born 15 August 1917 in St. Pauls Township. He is buried in Salem United Methodist Church cemetery. Two children.

5) **Bonnie Elizabeth Culbreth** , fifth child of Walter Marcellus and Laura Elizabeth was born 4 August 1914 and died 4 July 1979 in Fayetteville. She married **James Vance McLaurin** who was born 30 November 1914 in Flea Hill Township and died 8 March 1983 in Dunn, North Carolina, son of **William Wellington McLaurin** and **Nancy Jane Averitt.** Children listed under James Vance McLaurin.

6) **Lorena Culbreth** was born 14 October 1916 in Flea Hill Township and married 25 December 1946 in Fayetteville, **Joseph Hannibal Godwin** of Clinton, North Carolina. Three children.

7) **Alma Mae Culbreth,** seventh child of Walter Marcellus Culbreth and Laura Elizabeth Geddie, was born 19 April 1918 in Flea Hll Township, Cumberland County and married 18 June 1955 in Salem Methodist Church parsonage, **Thomas Richard Hall** who was born 1 Septembr 1911 and died 8 March 1988 in Fayetteville, son of **Calton English Hall** and **Nettie Jane Smith**. Thomas is buried at Mt. Vernon Baptist Church Cemetery in Grays Creek Township. No children.

424 iii. **Mary Elena Culbreth**, third child of William Culbreth and Sarah Elizabeth Sessoms was born 18 December 1878; died 31 December 1946 in Fayetteville, North Carolina. She married **Sylvester Carl Godwin**; born 21 December 1878; died 11 November 1955 in Fayetteville, Cumberland County, North Carolina.

No children. Mary wass buried at Salem United Methodst Church Cemetery. Sylvester Carl married a second time and was buried in LaFayette Memorial Park, Fayetteville, North Carolina

425 iv. **Laura Culbreth**, born about 1887. She married Unknown Warwick.

426 v. **Isaac William Culbreth**, born 10 April 1892; died 30 September 1947 on Route 1, Fayetteville, North Carolina. He married **Annie Caroline Warwick**; born 06 May 1888; died 10 February 1976 in Fayetteville, North Carolina. They were buried at Salem United Methodist Church Cemetery.

Five children.

1) **William Odis Culbreth** was born 21 October 1915 in Flea Hill Township. He married first 11 April 1937 in Dillon, South Carolina**, Laura Fields Goff** who was born 26 July 1920 in Falcon, North Carolina. Two children. He married second 21 October 1945 in Fayetteville, **Marion Snelgrove** who was born 29 March 1926 in Fayetteville. No children. Odis married third **Ruby Evelyn Dyson** who was born about 1924 and they had one child.

2) **Julius Clarence Clubreth**, second child of Isaac and Annie, was born 18 May 1918 in Flea Hill Township and died 2 June 1981 in Fayetteville. He married **Mary Lois Dyson** who was born about 1924. Divorced. Three children.

3) **James Herman Culbreth**, a twin, was born 6 February 1922 in Flea Hill Township and died 14 March 1960 in Eastover Township, Cumberland County, North Carolina. He married **Virginia Frances Jackson** who was born 15 August 1923 in Mingo Township, daughter of **Wiley B. Jackson** and **Virginia Kyle Dawson**. They were divorced. He is buried at Salem United Methodist Church Cemetery.

4) **Jasper Vernon Culbreth,** a twin, was born 6 February 1922 in Flea Hill Township in Cumberland and married **Dora Leola Bunce** who was born 25 February 1920 in Seventy-First Township, Cumberland County, daughter of **Wiley B. Bunce** and **Dora Ella Capps**. Four children.

5) **Pittman Lee Culbreth** was born 13 April 1925 in Flea Hill Township.

138. Sabra Culbreth (Isaac[4], Mary[3] Holland, Thomas William[2], Unknown[1]) was born 23 December 1850, and died 12 August 1920. She was listed as aged 1 in 1850.

Children of Sabra Culbreth are:

+ 427 i. **Mary Ellen Culbreth,** born 31 July 1872; died 16 July 1961 in Fayetteville, North Carolina.

428 ii. **Anna Jane Culbreth,** born 17 April 1875; died 27 February 1929. She married **Daniel Troy Anderson** after 1894; born 12 May 1863; died 09 May 1929 in Carvers Creek Township, Cumberland County, North Carolina.

Anna Jane was listed as age one in 1850 Federal Census. She was listed in the 1880 Census of Flea Hill Township as living with her father and stepmother and having two children. In 1900, she was in Grays Creek Township (Dwelling 37) and the census noted indicated three children, two living. She and Daniel were buried in the Duncan McLaurin Family Cemetery.

141. Jennet Culbreth (Isaac^4, Mary^3 Holland, Thomas William^2, Unknown^1) was born about 1857, and died after 1884.

Child of Jennet Culbreth is:

429 i. **Annie Evelyn Culbreth,** born 13 September 1884; died 03 November 1913.

145. Hinton Culbreth (Isaac^4, Mary^3 Holland, Thomas William^2, Unknown^1) was born 28 October 1874, and died 31 December 1928 in Flea Hill Township, Cumberland County, North Carolina. He married **Lela Catherine McLaurin,** daughter of David McLaurin and Mary Geddie. She was born 18 January 1882, and died 25 January 1968 in Cumberland County, North Carolina.

Hinton and Lela Catherine were buried in the Salem United Methodist Church Cemetery on SR 1003, three miles west of Delway, Sampson County, North Carolina.

Children of Hinton Culbreth and Lela McLaurin are:

430 i. **Daughter Culbreth,** born 08 November 1907; died 08 November 1907.

Daughter Culbreth was buried in Salem United Methodist Church Cemetery.

431 ii. **Hilma Lorene Culbreth**, born 30 August 1908; died 26 July 1985 in Fayetteville, North Carolina. She married **Sheldon Persis Beard**; born 06 March 1907 in Stedman, North Carolina.

She and Sheldon had two children. **Yvonne Grace Beard** was born on 2 September 1932 in Eastover Township in Cumberland County, and married **Benny Ray Melvin**, son of J. B. Melvin and Elizabeth Horne. Benny Ray was born 27 October 1932 in Fayetteville. Hilma and Benny Ray's son, **Stephen Ray Melvin** was born 4 November 1952 in Fayetteville.

Hilma Lorene and Sheldon's second child, **Hellon Elizabeth Beard** was born 30 December 1938 in Cedar Creek Township in Cumberland County. She married **John Augustus Matthews** who was born 23 August 1939 in Eastover Township in Cumberland County.

432 iii. **Jesse Hazel Culbreth**, born 26 January 1911 in Fayetteville, North Carolina. She married **Stafford Morton Horne** who was born 02 February 1914 in Cedar Creek Township, Cumberland County, North Carolina and died 02 April 1987. Stafford Morton was the son of John Clevin Horne and Sallie May Carter.

Stafford Morton was buried in Salem United Methodist Church Cemetery.

433 iv. **Stanley Colon Culbreth**, born 29 October 1912; died 26 March 1960 in Fayetteville, North Carolina. He married **Anna Lee Penny**; born about 1927 in Harnett County, North Carolina.

Stanley Colon served as a Technician Fifth Class in Company A, 93rd Chemical Mortar Battalion in WW II. Stanley Colon was buried in LaFayette Memorial Park, Fayetteville, North Carolina.

Stanley Colon and Anna Lee had three childre. **Phyllis Culbreth; Karen Stanley Culbreth** was born 17 April 1952 in Fayetteville; **Keith Colon Culbreth** was born 2 January 1954 in Fayetteville.

434 v. **David Rozzell Culbreth**, born 25 November 1914 in Flea Hill Township, Cumberland County, North Carolina. He married **Flora Culpepper McNeill**; born 23 December 1921 in St. Pauls, Robeson County, North Carolina.

Three children were born in Fayetteville, North Carolina. **David Donald Culbreth** was born 13 July 1950; **Hinton McNeill Culbreth** was born 16 May 1953; **Betty Lou Culbreth,** born 29 November 1957 and on 27 March 1977 she married **James Thurlton Page III in Fayetteville**. James was the son of James Thurlton Page, Jr. and Jessie Mae Lee.

435 vi. **Unknown Child Culbreth.**

436 vii. **Wayland Vernon Culbreth,** born 06 October 1917 in Flea Hill Township, Cumberland County, North Carolina. He married **Virginia Lou Williford** 19 October 1957. She was born 02 June 1920 in Flea Hill Township, Cumberland County, North Carolina.

437 viii. **Catherine Elizabeth Culbreth,** born 28 September 1920 in Flea Hill Township, Cumberland County, North Carolina. She married Unknown Beasley.

438 ix. **Dorris Louise Culbreth,** born 07 April 1923 in Flea Hill Township, Cumberland County, North Carolina. She married **James Herbert Webb** who was born 10 March 1926 in Benson, North Carolina.

Dorris and James had two children who were born in Fayetteville. **Sandra Lynn Webb** was born 17 March 1951 and **Pamela Kay Webb** was born 03 May 1953.

146. Stephen Culbreth (Isaac[4], Mary[3] Holland, Thomas William[2], Unknown[1]) was born 05 May 1877, and died 01 June 1957 in Eastover Township, Cumberland County, North Carolina. He married **Annie Elizabeth Cain**, daughter of Alexander Cain and Nancy McLaurin. She was born 17 December 1879, and died 05 September 1954 in Eastover Township, Cumberland County, North Carolina.

Stephen and Annie Elizabeth were buried in Salem United Methodist Church Cemetery on SR 1003, three miles west of Delway, Sampson County, North Carolina.

Children of Stephen Culbreth and Annie Cain are:

439 i. **Letha Merle Culbreth**, born 12 June 1904; died 30 March 1973 in Fayetteville, North Carolina. She married **Marcus McDuffie McLaurin** 13 November 1923 in Fayetteville, Cumberland County, North Carolina; born 31 January 1896; died 09 March 1963 in Fayetteville, North Carolina.

Five children.

440 ii. **Lola Lorenza Culbreth**, born About 1909. She married Ira Eulace Culbreth who was born 03 February 1909 and died 12 January 1975 in Fayetteville, North Carolina.

Two children.

441 iii. **Eulon Bernard Culbreth**, born 14 March 1912; died 29 September 1989 in Fayetteville, North Carolina. He married **Jannie Catherine Sessoms**; born 11 March 1914 in Flea Hill Township, Cumberland County, North Carolina. Jannie was the daughter of Hugh Alexander Sessoms and Sallie Cleveland Geddie.

Six children.

Martha Culbreth, their first child was born on 14 November 1930 in Cumberland County, North Carolina.

Betty Jean Culbreth, second child of Eulon and Jannie was born on 17 April 1933 in Cumberland County, North Carolina.

Wendell Eulon Culbreth, third child was born on 12 September 1938 in Cumberland County.

Larry Holt Culbreth, their fourth child was born on 6 July 1941 in Cumberland County.

Mary Catherine Culbreth, fifth child was born on 24 June 1944 in Cumberland County.

I have not identified the remaining children.

147. Daniel Maxwell Culbreth (Isaac[4], Mary[3] Holland, Thomas William[2], Unknown[1]) was born 12 May 1878, and died 11 April 1952 in Eastover Township, Cumberland County, North Carolina. He married **Julia Sessoms** 28 February 1906, daughter of William Sessoms and Martha Wicker. She was born 10 April 1888, and died 12 January 1974 in Fayetteville, North Carolina.

Daniel Maxwell and Julia were buried in Salem United Methodist Church Cemetery on SR 1003, three miles west of Delway, Sampson County, North Carolina.

Children of Daniel Culbreth and Julia Sessoms are:

442 i. **Ruby C. Culbreth**, born 12 January 1907; died 20 July 1924.

Ruby C. was buried in Salem United Methodist Church Cemetery on SR 1003, three miles west of Delway, Sampson County, North Carolina.

443 ii. **Unknown Son Culbreth**, born 14 September 1908; died 06 October 1908.

Unknown Son was buried in Salem United Methodist Church Cemetery on SR 1003, three miles west of Delway, Sampson County, North Carolina/

444 iii. **Dossie Orman Culbreth**, born 05 November 1909; died 08 November 1972. He married Gladys (maiden name unknown).

Dossie Orman was buried in Salem United Methodist Church Cemetery on SR 1003, three miles west of Delway, Sampson County, North Carolina.

1) John C. Culbreth

2) Sandra Culbreth married Mr. McAlhaney.

445 iv. **David Worth Culbreth**, born 24 September 1912 in North Carolina.

He moved out of state---lived in Texas in 1972.

446 v. **Elma Nadine Culbreth**, born 15 October 1914 in Pembroke, North Carolina. She married Unknown Truelove.

447 vi. **Eunice Elizabeth Culbreth**, born 05 October 1916 in Pembroke, North Carolina. She married **Leo Milton Raynor**; born 04 November 1914 in Carvers Creek Township, Cumberland County, North Carolina, son of James G. Raynor and Nelia Wood.

Four children.

1) **Laurice Molton Raynor**, born 21 January 1937 in Fayetteville, married **Jean Patricia Combs** who was born about 1939. Two children: **Laurice Milton Raynor, Jr**. was born 10 April 1959 in Cumberland County and **Kimberly Ann Raynor** was born 24 July 1962 in Cumberland County.

2) **Daniel James Raynor** was born 4 December 1938 In Eastover Township in Cumberland County and married **Mary Barbara Ray** 18 July 1964 in Salem United Methist Church. She was born 6 November 1942 in Fayetteville, daughter of Lector Elliott Ray and Vara Jane McLaurin. Three children born in Fayetteville: **Kelly Elliott Raynor**, born 20 April 1967; **James Patrick Raynor**, born 4 March 1970; , born 1 February 1974.

448 vii. **William Sessoms Culbreth**, seventh child of Daniel Maxwell Culbreth and Julia Sessoms was born 22 October 1918 in Flea Hill Township, Cumberland County, North Carolina; died 03 October 1974 in Fayetteville, North Carolina. He married **Dixie Alease Autry** 31 July 1939 in Fayetteville, Cumberland County, North Carolina; born 30 December 1920.

William Sessoms was buried in Salem United Methodist Church Cemetery on SR 1003, three miles west of Delway, Sampson County, North Carolina

Three children:

1) **Patricia Ann Culbreth**, born 29 December 1941.

2) **Richard Lilburn Culbeth**, born 31 January 1947 in Fayetteville

3) **William Sessoms Culbreth, Jr.**, was born 8 February 1948 in Faryetteville. He married **Lynda Carole Calhoun** 28 October 1974 in Fayetteville. She was born 28 September 1952 in Dale County, Alabama, daughter of Lynwood Wright Calhoun and Ethel Carolyn Lee.

449 viii. **Olive Maxwell Culbreth,** eighth known child of Daniel Maxwell Culbreth and Julia Sessoms, was born 01 April 1921 in North Carolina.

Olive Maxwell moved out of state.

450 ix. **Marvin Durwood Culbreth**, born 18 December 1923 in Flea Hill Township, Cumberland County, North Carolina.

Marvin was not listed in Dossie's obituary in 1972.

451 x. **Della Mae Culbreth**, born 12 May 1928 in Flea Hill Township, Cumberland County, North Carolina. She married **Billy Turner Matthews** on 04 October 1947 in Dillon, South

Carolina. He was born 01 July 1927 in Wade, North Carolina and died 27 March 1972 in Fayetteville, North Carolina.

Three children.

1) **Carla Elizabeth Matthews**, born 27 September 1948 in Fayetteville, married **James William Stone** who was born about 1945. Four Children born in Fayetteville: **James William Stone, Jr**, was born and died 23 October 1967, and was buried in Harnett Memorial Park; **Stillborn daughter** 25 December 1968; **Rhonda Michell Stone**, born 25 March 1971; **William Scott Stone**, born 25 December 1974.

2)**Julia Sue Matthews** was born 2 January 1950 in Fayetteville and married **Charles Leonard Godwin.** He was born 8 March 1944 in Harnett County, North Carolina, son of Esther Mae Godwin. Two children born in Dunn, Harnett County: **Christopher Lynn Godwin**, born 2 Decembr 1968 and **Melissa Diane Godwin** born 15 December 1970.

3) **Sharon Gail Matthews** was born 2 December 1968 in Fayetteville and married **Jessie Thomas Moore.** He was born in Cedar Creek Township 22 June 1947, son of Clifton Moore and Carrie Pitter. Three children born in Fayetteville: **Jennifer Renae Moore** born 23 June 1977; **Jessica Gail Moore**, born 198 March 1970; **Jessie Thomas Moore II,** born 23 August 1980.

452 xi. **Walter Clifton Culbreth,** eleventh known child of Daniel Maxwell and Julia was born 30 August 1930 in Eastover Township, Cumberland County, North Carolina. He married **Norma Lee Simmons** who was born 02 October 1933, daughter of Elbert Ray Simmons and Letha Belle Faircloth.

Three children either in, or near Fayetteville, North Carolina.

!) **Clifton Scott Culbreth,** born 6 September 1957 married **Sherri Lynette Horne** who was born 18 January 1957, daughter of Daniel Madison Horne and Patricia Stewart Carr. One child, **Cameron Paige Culbreth** was born 10 October 1988 in Fayetteville.

2) **Wanda Jane Culbreth,** born 6 December 1960.

3) **David Brian Culbreth,** born 22 December 1965.

148. Isaac McDuffie Culbreth (Isaac[4], Mary[3] Holland, Thomas William[2], Unknown[1]) was born 25 October 1879, and died 24 December 1924. He married **(1) Mary Alice McNulty (Mary Alice Murphy?)** Before 1912. She was born about 1880 in Ireland, and died 07 March 1919. He married **(2) Nellie Charlotte Cain** 05 March 1922 in Fayetteville, Cumberland County, North Carolina. She was born 27 April 1883, and died 10 July 1960 in Fayetteville, North Carolina.

Children of Isaac Culbreth and Mary McNulty are:

453 i. **Unknown Child Culbreth.**

454 ii. **Ralph Culbreth.**

455 iii. **Helen Culbreth,** born about 1914 in Boston, Massachusetts. She married **Eulace Vernon McLaurin**; born 12 June 1911; died 13 November 1972 in Fayetteville, North Carolina.

456 iv. **Unknown Son Culbreth,** died 05 March 1916.

This son was buried in Salem United Methodist Church Cemetery on SR 1003, three miles west of Delway, Sampson County, North Carolina.

150. John Culbreth (Daniel Maxwell[4], Mary[3] Holland, Thomas William[2], Unknown[1]) was born 06 June 1842 in Sampson County, North Carolina, and died 23 November 1889. He married **Catherine Jane Williams**, daughter of Robert Williams and Margaret Williams. She was born 05 January 1845, and died 24 November 1931.

During the American Civil War, John Culbreth was a Private in Company D, 2nd Battn., Local Defense. He enlisted on 11 April 1864 in Cumberland County, North Carolina and was present to 31 December 1864 and was assigned "light duty."

John and Catherine Jane were buried in Joe Moore Hill Cemetery, Clement, Sampson County, North Carolina. Another source shows that they were buried in a Culbreth Cemetery on Willow Grey Lane off High House Road (SR 1006), Sampson County, North Carolina. The name of the cemetery may have changed over time.

Children of John Culbreth and Catherine Williams are:

457 i. **Mary Louvinia Culbreth**, born 14 February 1866; died 18 August 1940.

She never married, was a grand cook and collector of family history and pictures.

Mary Louvinia was buried in Joe Moore Hill Cemetery, Clement, Sampson County, North Carolina. Anothe source notes that she was buried in a Culbreth Cemetery on Willow Grey Lane off High House Road (SR 1006), Sampson County.

458 ii. **Stillborn Daughter Culbreth**, born 1868.

This daughter was buried in Joe Moore Hill Cemetery, Clement, Sampson County, North Carolina. Another source shows that she was buried in a Culbreth Cemetery on Willow Grey Lane off High House Road (SR 1006), Sampson County.

459 iii. **Tomsilla Jane Culbreth**, born 15 August 1870; died 16 August 1889.

Tomsilla Jane never married. She was buried in Joe Moore Hill Cemetery, Clement, Sampson County, North Carolina. Another source shows that she was buried in a Culbreth Cemetery on Willow Grey Lane off High House Road (SR 1006), Sampson County.

460 iv. **Daniel Maxwell Culbreth**, born 02 March 1872; died 20 May 1893 in Sampson County.

He never married and was buried in Joe Moore Hill Cemetery, Clement, Sampson County, North Carolina or in a Culbreth Cemetery on Willow Grey Lane off High House Road (SR 1006), Sampson County.

\+ 461 v. **Jennette Ida Culbreth**, born 23 March 1874 in Carolina Beach, New Hanover County, North Carolina; died 30 March 1949 in Carolina Beach, New Hanover County.

462 vi. **Margaret Elizabeth Culbreth**, born 30 June 1876; died 09 December 1879.

Her date of death is also listed as 9 July 1877 and 9 July 1879.

Margaret Elizabeth was buried either in Joe Moore Hill Cemetery, Clement, Sampson County, North Carolina, or in a Culbreth Cemetery on Willow Grey Lane off High House Road (SR 1006), Sampson County.

+ 463 vii. **Roberta Culbreth**, born 02 January 1878; died 29 November 1945 in Cumberland County, North Carolina.

+ 464 viii. **Virginia Culbreth**, born 09 April 1880; died 24 September 1946 in Fayetteville, Cumberland County, North Carolina.

+ 465 ix. **Lena Mae Culbreth**, born 24 July 1883; died 20 September 1959.

+ 466 x. **Annie Vara Culbreth**, born 06 November 1886; died 28 June 1963 in Clinton, Sampson County, North Carolina.

+ 467 xi. **Rebeckah Olivia Culbreth,** born 23 December 1888; died 20 June 1950.

151. William Culbreth (Daniel Maxwell[4], Mary[3] Holland, Thomas William[2], Unknown[1]) was born 30 April 1844 in Sampson County, North Carolina, and died 08 December 1894 at home in Cumberland County, North Carolina. He married **Nancy Jane Autry** in 1870, daughter of William Henry Autry and Jane Riley. She was born August 1852 in Sampson County, North Carolina, and died 14 December 1894 at home in Cumberland County, North Carolina.

William served in the Civil War as did his father and brothers, John and Daniel.

He was a Private in 3rd Company B, 2nd Artillery, Regiment 36. On 0 April 1863, William enlisted in Clinton, North Carolina, was captured 15 January 1865 at Fort Fisher and confined to the Union Prison Camp in Elmira, New York. Released 26 July 1865 by oath.

After the war, William lived with his mother until he married Nancy Jane on 5 November 1871. Following his marriage, he and James Lindsay Autry, Nancy Jane's brother, (Captain Jim), were partners in a general naval stores and turpentine business in Autryville. He and James Lindsay bought 259 acres from Daniel McDonald, his wife Zilphia W. Jernigan and their banker, Edmund J. Lilly, on 27 March 1878 for $1150. This land lay around Starling's Bridge over South River in Black River Township in Cumberland County. William, still living in Sampson County, purchased on 15 April 1880, an additional 270 acres from the McDonalds; land lay west of the first purchase. It isn't clear whether William and Nancy built the house, but they and their three children moved in 1882 from the Clement area in Sampson County to the first house known to be built in what eventually became in 1913 the town of Falcon in Cumberland County, North Carolina. William continued to add to his acreage. He bought 287 acres including the old McDonald home place from the McDonalds for $1000 on 21 December 1882. Land was to the west along the Fayetteville-Smithfield Road. On 29 March 1883, James Lindsay Autry and his wife, Tomzill, sold to William for $945, their interest in the 259 acre tract that William and James Lindsay had purchased earlier. William continued to add to his land holdings and in 1897 when his estate was divided among his seven children, the value of his 930 acres was $3500.

Professor Mayo Bundy writes in his book: "William was known as "Cheap Bill" because of his concern for, and his interest in the poor, as well as his more reasonably priced merchandise. William and Nancy Jane acquired most of land which was later to be used in the development of the town of Falcon.

"The Autrys were as strong Baptists as the Culbreths were strong Methodists. ...

"An interesting observation regarding the William Culbreth Cemetery, which is located in the center of the Antioch Baptist Church Cemetery, is that none of the Culbreths buried there were Baptist nor did they attend this church."

In 1894 he went to Richmond, Virginia, for an operation to relieve a nasal condition he had suffered from for some time. Shortly after he returned by railroad to Godwin and traveled to his home, two miles away, he developed pneumonia and died on "Friday night December 8th, 1894 in the 55th year of his age." His memorial published in the Dunn paper "reveals the esteem that he acquired during his years in Falcon.

"Mr. Culbreth was a native of Sampson County where the days of his youth were spent. He later, removed to Cumberland County and engaged in the naval store and general mercantile business. ... Mr. Culbreth succeeded in business because he was diligent and above all was honest.

"There is no man in this section of the State whose death will be so universally mourned as his – because from his hands and his patronage more than a thousand people were fed. The popularity of Mr. Culbreth was illustrated on the afternoon of his burial when more than 500 sorrowing neighbors congregated around his open grave to lay to his final rest their benefactor and friend. ..."

William and Nancy Jane were buried in the William Culbeth Cemetery located in the center of Antioch Baptist Church Cemetery, Falcon, North Carolina,

Children of William Culbreth and Nancy Autry are:

\+ 468 i. **Julius Ainslie Culbreth**, born 08 December 1871; died 14 February 1950.

\+ 469 ii. **Virginia Isabell Culbreth**, born 08 October 1873; died 19 January 1930.

470 iii. **James Mc Culbreth**, born 08 August 1873; died 09 March 1876.

His date of birth is also listed as 18 August 1873. He was buried in Maxwell Cemetery, Clement, Sampson County, North Carolina.

471 iv. **William Love Culbreth**, born 26 September 1876; died 07 November 1878.

The 26 December 1870 is also found for his birth. William Love was buried in Maxwell Cemetery, Clement, Sampson County, North Carolina.

472 v. **Hattie Jane Culbreth**, born 13 July 1881; died 10 May 1936. She married **Thomas Carl Pate** in 1909. The date of 13 July 1879 is also listed for her birth.

Hattie Jane and her nephew, **Laurice McLellan**, were killed in an automobile accident within sight of his home. Antioch Baptist Church Cemetery in Falcon, North Carolina is also listed for her place of burial.

She and Thomas Carl had two children.

Their oldest child, **Thomas Clyde Pate** was born on 28 October 1911 and died on 5 December 1911. He was buried in Antioch Baptist Church Cemetery in Falcon, North Carolina.

Their second child, **Theron Carl Pate** was born on 6 Apri 1913. He married **F. Coy Rankin** who was born on 27 Novemer 1919 and was the daughter of Robert Franklin Rankin and Florence Jane Rackley. Theron Carl and Coy had six children:

1) Baby Girl Pate was born 26 December 1939 and died on 28 December 1939. Buried in Antioch Baptist Church Cemetery in Falcon, North Carolina

2) Thomas Rankin Pate was born on 02 September 1941. He married **Sue Whitley** on 4 May 1963.

3) Andrew Culbreth Pate was born on 13 August 1945. He married **Diane Skipper** on 27 June 1976.

4) David Randolph Pate was born on 3 August 1949. He married **Patricia Gant** on 25 April 1976.

5) Robert Franklin Pate was born on 25 August 1953.

6) Charles Abbot Pate was born on 9 March 1957.

+ 473 vi. **Minnie Nicholson Culbreth,** sixth child of William Culbreth and Nancy Autry was born 22 June 1883 in Falcon, North Carolina; died 30 January 1939.

+ 474 vii. **Clyde Cleveland Culbreth**, born 03 May 1885; died 20 December 1959 in Black River Township, Cumberland County, North Carolina.

+ 475 viii. **Mamie Worth Culbreth**, born 14 February 1888 in Black River Township, Cumberland County, North Carolina; died 17 March 1951.

+ 476 ix. **Lattie Alston Culbreth, Sr.**, born 14 October 1890 in Black River Township, Cumberland County, North Carolina; died 29 May 1971 in Smithfield, North Carolina.

477 x. **William Sexton Culbreth**, born in December 1894 around the time of his father's death in Black River Township, Cumberland County, North Carolina; died 18 December 1894. The exact date of his birth is not listed.

152. Daniel L. Culbreth, Sr. (Daniel Maxwell[4], Mary[3] Holland, Thomas William[2], Unknown[1]) was born 28 July 1847 in Sampson County, North Carolina, and died 13 July 1882. He married **Phebia Autry** 24 January 1867, daughter of William Autry and Jane Riley. She was born 1848 in Sampson County, North Carolina, and died 24 January 1920.

During the American Civil War, Daniel was a Private in Company H, Regiment 16, Infantry. He was a student when he enlisted on 15 October 1863 at Camp Vance. He was captured 2 April 1865 at Hatcher's Run, Virginia, and confined to Hart's Island, New York Harbor. Released 17 July 1865 by oath.

Daniel and Phebia were buried in the George Horne Cemetery on South River Road one mile west from Minnie Hall Road in Sampson County, North Carolina.

Children of Daniel Culbreth and Phebia Autry are:

\+ 478 i. **Matilda Jane Culbreth**, born 19 April 1868 in Sampson County North Carolina; died 18 October 1897 in Sampson County, North Carolina.

\+ 479 ii. **Jannette Maxwell Culbreth**, born 16 August 1870 in Sampson County, North Carolina; died 17 March 1919.

480 iii. **Daniel L. Culbreth, Jr.**, born 18 February 1872 in Sampson County, North Carolina; died 1885.

Daniel L. Culbreth, Jr. died from fever. He was buried in the George Horne Cemetery 1 mile w on South River Road from Minnie Hall Road. Sampson County, North Carolina.

\+ 481 iv. **William James Culbreth**, born 01 November 1873 in Sampson County, North Carolina; died 04 April 1916 in Dismal Township, Sampson County, North Carolina.

\+ 482 v. Mary H. Culbreth, born 22 September 1875 in Sampson County, North Carolina; died 15 January 1911.

\+ 483 vi. **John Thomas Culbreth, Sr.**, born 06 September 1878 in Sampson County, North Carolina; died 14 June 1963.

\+ 484 vii. **Susan Lee Culbreth**, born 06 July 1881 in Sampson County, North Carolina; died 31 January 1968 in Fayetteville, Cumberland County, North Carolina.

154. Martha Rebecca Culbreth (Daniel Maxwell[4], Mary[3] Holland, Thomas William[2], Unknown[1]) was born 13 February 1850 in Sampson County, North Carolina, and died 11 November 1929. She married **Blackman Williams** 21 September 1871, son of Thomas Williams and Anna Hairr. He was born 11 September 1844, and died 23 November 1928.

Blackman Williams served in Company B, "2nd Battalion, N.C. Local Defense Forces" in the Civl War. Enlisted 20 August 1863.

Martha Rebecca and Blackman Williams were buried in Maxwell Cemetery, Clement, Sampson County, North Carolina.

Children of Martha Culbreth and Blackman Williams are:

485 i. **Daughter Williams**, born September 1872.

486 ii. **Mary Alice Williams**, born 11 September 1873; died 10 August 1875.

Mary Alice was buried in Maxwell Cemetery near Clement in Sampson County, North Carolina

\+ 487 iii. **William Perdie Williams**, born 12 February 1876; died 23 November 1961 in Dismal Township, Sampson County, North Carolina.

488 iv. **Laura Virginia Williams,** born 18 September 1878 in Sampson County, North Carolina; died 27 January 1959 in Autryville, Sampson County. She married **Robert Purdie Royal** 17 December 1902 in Residence of Blackman William. Robert Purdie was born 26 December 1871 in Flea Hill Township, Cumberland County, North Carolina and died 05 August 1954 in Eastover Township, Cumberland.

Laura Virginia and Robert Purdie were buried in the Maxwell Cemetery near Clement in Sampson County, North Carolina

No children.

+ 489 v. **Daniel Walter Williams**, born 12 January 1880; died 20 December 1959 near Autryville, Sampson County, North Carolina.

490 vi. **Rev. Thomas Pritchard Williams**, born 23 April 1882; died 12 July 1918 in Dismal Township, Sampson County, North Carolina. Rev. Thomas did not marry, suffered a long illness and died of tuberculosis. He and his sisters, Bessie and Lula Mae, were buried in the Maxwell Cemetery near Clement in Sampson County.

491 vii. **Bessie F. Williams**, born 05 August 1884; died 06 September 1969 near Autryville, Sampson County.

Bessie F. did not marry. She was buried in the Maxwell Cemetery near Clement in Sampson County.

492 viii. **Lula Mae Williams**, born 24 October 1886; died 27 May 1973 near Autryville, Sampson County, North Carolina.

Lula Mae did not marry and was buried in the Maxwell Cemetery near Clement in Sampson County.

156. Tomzillia Culbreth (Daniel Maxwell[4], Mary[3] Holland, Thomas William[2], Unknown[1]) was born 06 April 1852 in Sampson County, North Carolina, and died 29 March 1913 in Sampson County, North Carolina. She married **James Lindsay Autry, Sr.**, son of William Autry and Jane Riley. He was born 22 March 1838 in Sampson County, North Carolina, and died 05 July 1914 in Sampson County, North Carolina.

Tomzillia's name is also spelled "Tomzilia" and her date of birth is given as 13 February 1850. She and James Lindsay were buried in the Clement Missionary Baptist Church Cemetery on Maxwell Road (SR1006) about 0.5 mile west of SR 1425 in Sampson County.

James Lindsay was called "Captain Jim." He headed Company C (Home Guard) for Columbus and Sampson Counties of the Second Regiment in the Civil War.

He was a turpentine distiller. He subscribed to $10,000 in stock in the Cape fear and Yadkin Valley Railroad that went through Autryville, North Carolina.was instrumental in the establishment of Autryville and provided jobs for many people in the area. Progress caused the railroad to be discontinued in 1937. When the turpentine industry declined, he moved from Autryville to a settlement north of Autryville and he later named this area, Clement. He operated a navel store in Clement; most of his largest customers were relatives! See notes for Tomzillia's brother, William.

It is said that at one time the Autrys, Culbreths and Maxwells owned a strip of land from Autryville to Clement that was seven miles long (Dismal Township).

Children of Tomzillia Culbreth and James Autry are:

\+ 493 i. **Ida J. Autry**, born 28 August 1871 in Sampson County, North Carolina; died 21 May 1897 in Sampson County, North Carolina.

494 ii. **Rebecah Hiden Autry**, born 23 October 1872; died 19 November 1872.

Rebecah Hiden was buried in a Horne Cemetery.

495 iii. **James Lindsay Autry, Jr.**, born 06 December 1875 in Sampson County, North Carolina; died 14 February 1878 in Sampson County, North Carolina.

He was buried in the George Horne Cemetery near intersection of South River Road and Minnie Hall Road, Sampson County, North Carolina.

\+ 496 iv. **William Mac Autry, Sr.**, born 12 October 1878; died 10 December 1966.

497 v. **Mary Pritchard Autry**, born 13 June 1882; died 01 February 1950. She married **James Lee Sutton**; born 05 August 1875; died 30 November 1963.

No children. She and James Lee were buried in the Clement Missionary Baptist Church Cemetery on Maxwell Road (SR1006) about 0.5 mile west of SR 1425 in Sampson County, North Carolina. His year of death is also listed as 1879 in transcribed cemetery records.

498 vi. **Libby Lee Roy Autry**, born 11 December 1883; died 08 June 1887.

He was buried in Clement Cemetery in Sampson County.

499 vii. **Albion Alphonso Autry**, born 26 April 1885 in Sampson County, North Carolina; died 07 January 1925. He married (1) **Rosa Anna McPhail** on 19 December 1909; she was born 10 November 1891 in Sampson County and died 12 August 1910 in Sampson County. He married (2) **Nina Cooper** after 1909; she was born 11 October 1897 and died 12 April 1920.

Both spouses and their babies died during childbirth. Albion Alphonso was buried in the Calvary Tabernacle Pentecostal FW Baptist Church Cemetery, on High House Road one mile west of Highway 242, Sampson County, North Carolina. Rosa Anna was buried in the Clement Missionary Baptist Church Cemetery on Maxwell Road (SR1006) about 0.5 mile west of Sr 1425 in Sampson County, North Carolina. Nina was buried in the Clement Cemetery, Sampson County.

\+ 500 viii. **Armelia Bertha Autry**, born 29 August 1887; died 21 May 1983.

501 ix. Virginia Gray Autry, born 17 December 1888 in Sampson County, North Carolina; died 26 December 1896 in Sampson County.

She was buried in the Clement Missionary Baptist Church Cemetery on Maxwell Road (SR1006) about 0.5 mile west of Sr 1425 in Sampson County, North Carolina.

502 x. **Stacy Oates Autry**, born 28 December 1891; died 11 November 1970. He married **Harriett Marie Woodall**; born 07 April 1904.

Two children. Stacy Oates was buried in Roselawn Cemetery in Benson, North Carolina

503 xi. **Julia Grace Autry**, born 16 August 1893; died 19 January 1981 in Lumberton. She married **Henry McDuffie Bolton**; born 03 January 1898; died 22 December 1977.

Julia Grace and Henry were buried in Meadowbrook Cemetery, Lumberton, North Carolina.

159. Virginia Culbreth (Daniel Maxwell[4], Mary[3] Holland, Thomas William[2], Unknown[1]) was born 16 January 1861 in Sampson County, North Carolina, and died 22 May 1940 in Dismal Township, Sampson County, North Carolina. She married **(1) John N. Cooper** before 1885, son of Andrew Cooper and Elizabeth Butler. He was born 22 August 1858 in Sampson County, North Carolina, and died 23 May 1887 in Sampson County, North Carolina. She married **(2) John Blackman Autry** after 1887, son of Blackman Autry and Martha Culbreth. He was born 28 October 1863, and died 10 March 1940 in Cedar Creek Township,Cumberland County, North Carolina.

Virginia, John N. and John Blackman were buried in the Maxwell Cemetery southeast corner of Maxwell Road (SR 1006) and (SR 1427), Sampson County.

In the 1860 census John was listed as "John N." His date of birth is also found as 28 July 1858.

Child of Virginia Culbreth and John Cooper is:

504 i. **Neta Van Cooper**, born 09 February 1885; died 19 February 1975. She married **Oakey Lawrence Lawson** who was born 27 August 1884 and died 26 March 1959. he was the son of Elisa Lawson and Amanda Bullard.

Neta and Oakey Lawrence were buried in the Evergreen Cemetery in Evergreen, North Carolina.

Four children. Their first child, **Lawrence Lawson** was born 1 September 1909 and married first **ZULA GREEN** and second, **ANN POPE**. Lawrence and Zula had one child, **Rue Lawson** who married **Jonnie McKenney**. Lawrence and Ann had one child, **Larry Lawson**.

Neta and Oakey's second child, **Ida Alcase Lawson** was born 13 August 1912 and died 12 January 1983. Ida married **THOMAS GORDON UNDERWOOD** who was born 18 April 1909 and died 20 February 1968; they had four children.

Okie Thomas Lawson was Neta and Oakey's third child. He was born 5 August 1915 and married **RACHEL BOSTIC**; they had two children.

JUANITH CHRISTINE LAWSON, the fourth child was born 24 October 1917 and married

THOMAS LOGAN JUSTICE. No children.

Children of Virginia Culbreth and John Autry are:

505 i. **James Hayden Autry**, born 16 July 1892; died 12 April 1931.

He never married and was buried in the Maxwell Cemetery, southeast corner of Maxwell Road (SR 1006) and (SR 1427), Sampson County, North Carolina.

506 ii. **Mary Vida Autry,** born 30 April 1894; died 17 August 1990.

She was buried in the Maxwell Cemetery near intersectiion of Maxwell Road (SR 1006) and (SR 1427) in Sampson County.

507 iii. **Virginia Ida Autry**, born 19 July 1896; died 24 August 1977. She married Everett Frink; born 29 February 1896; died 12 January 1980.

Virginia Ida and Everett were buried in the Maxwell Cemetery near intersectiion of Maxwell Road (SR 1006) and (SR 1427) in Sampson County, North Carolina.

508 iv. **John Murchison Autry**, born 19 September 1898; died 05 December 1964. He married **Audrienne Bailey**; born 06 April 1901; died 20 December 1990.

They had two children. **GEORGE BAILY AUTRY** was born 14 March 1937 and married **Bess Pearle Powell** who was born 20 June 1939. George and Bess had two children, **GEORGE BAILY AUTRY,** JR, who was born 12 January 1963 and **MARGARET MURCHISON AUTRY** who was born 22 February 1967.

John and Audrienne's second child was **AUDRIENNE ISABEL AUTRY** who was born 17 May 1941. she first married **GEORGE PHILIP KOONCE** who was born 17 April 1936 and they had four children: 1) **AUDRIENNE MARGUERITE KOONCE** who was born 28 July 1964. 2) **GEORGE PHILIP KOONCE, JR**., who was born 3 April 1966. 3) **JOHN EVERETTE CHRISTOPHER KOONCE** who was born 26 December 1969. 4) **CATHERINE EMILIE ELIZABETH KOONCE** was born 26 January 1972.

Audrienne Isabel's second husband was **FRANCIS HAVEN FREEMAN** and they had once child, **VALOREE HAVEN FREEMAN** who was born 26 November 1975.

509 v. **Flossie Merle Autry**, born 20 July 1901; died 13 August 1990. She married **Thaddeus Earl Mobley**; born 31 August 1902; died 17 March 1964.

Flossie and Earl had five children.

1)**FRANCES EARL MOBLEY** was born 31 October 1926 and she married **CLIFTON HENRY JENNE** who was bron 12 June 1915. Frances and Clifton had one child, **DONNA FRANCES JENNE** who was born 12 June 1915 and married **TIMOTHY THOMAN** who was born 10 November 1947. Donna and Timothy had two children, **KATHRYN MERLE THOMAN** who was born 9 January 1974 and **PAUL CLIFTON THOMAN**. Further research may determine whether Mr. Rosser spelled Thoman correctly.

2) THADDEUS EARL MOBLEY, JR. was born 29 September 1928. He married **LORA GALLAGHER** who was born 06 July 1929 and they had three children: **SUSAN LOUISE MOBLEY,** the first child, was born 6 October 1949 and married **John Taggart** who was born 20 June 1949. Susan and John had one child. The second child of Thaddeus and Lora was **PATRICIA ANN MOBLEY** who was born 14 December 1952 married **STEVEN BODENHEIMER** who was born 10 June 1952. The third child of Thaddeu and Lora was **BRIAN EARL MOBLEY** who was born 12 June 1958. He married in 1977 **SANDRA LEE GOUDREAULT** who was born 25 February 1957.

3) VIRGINIA MERLE MOBLEY was born 24 September 1930, died 22 December 1935 and is buried in Maxwell Cemetery.

4) ROLLAS ANN MOBLEY was born 25 April 1933, died 22 December 1935 and is buried in Maxwell Cemetery. Virginia and Rollas were killed in an automobile accident.

5) JOHN EDWARD MOBLEY was born 22 June 1938 and married **MARIETTA HINSHAW** who was born 11 December 1936. No children.

163. George Washington Hair (Daniel[4] Hairr, Orpah[3] Holland, Thomas William[2], Unknown[1]) was born 06 May 1851 in Sampson County, North Carolina, and died 27 April

1934 in Honeycutts Township, Sampson County, North Carolina. He married **Nancy (maiden name unknown)**. She was born about 1857, and died before 1920.

Cause of death: ariteriosclerosis. Apoplexy. His certificate of death lists "Lucindia Holland and Daniel Hairr for his parents. In 1880, he and Nancy and three children were living next door to his mother, Lucinda.

In 1920, he appears to be the George W. Hair, aged 68 and widowed, living in the household of Gaston H. Avery, aged 58, and Lillie Avery, aged 48. His relation to head of household was, Brother-in-law, but I cannot make a connection unless George's wife, Nancy (maiden name unknown) was an "Avery" (Averitt, Averett, Everitt). This could have been another George W. Hair.

Records also can be found for Hair families in Cumberland County and Bladen County in North Carolina and the names for these families suggest a relationship with the Hair families in Sampson County, North Carolina. It was a common practice for our ancestors to give the same name to cousins and other relatives who were born around the same time.

In 1930, George was listed in the household of his brother, "Charlie H. Hair" (Charley.)

George Washington was buried on 30 April 1934 in a Family Cemetery

Children of George Hair and Nancy Unknown are:

510 i. **Adrian D. C. Hair**, born about 1876.

The 1880 census for Sampson County, North Carolina listed his name as "Adrien D. C. Hair."

511 ii. **Anna B. Hair**, born about 1878.

512 iii. **Sanford T. Hair** was born February 1880 and died 4 September 1941 in Harnett County, North Carolina. He may be the Sanford T. Hair who married **FANNIE J. PARKER** on 24 June 1906 in Robeson County, North Carolina, but I have no other record to support this. She was born about 1887. His middle name may have been "Troy." The 1930 Federal Census for Durham, North Carolina, records a Sanford T. Haire, aged 48 and Fannie J. Haire, aged 43.

iv. **Ive Hair** was born about 1881.

v. **Hattie Hair**, born about 1883.

vi. **Mallie Hair**, born about 1883.

vii. **Fannie Hair,** born about 1886.

viii. **Frances Hair,** born about 1888.

ix. **Robert Marvin Hair**, born 25 October 1894 in Sampson County, North Carolina.

165. Charles Henry Hair (Daniel[4] Hairr, Orpah[3] Holland, Thomas William[2], Unknown[1]) was born 17 January 1861 in Sampson County, North Carolina, and died 23 July 1938 in

Sampson County. He married **Martha Ann Hall**, daughter of William Hall and Martha Hall. She was born 04 July 1868, and died 23 December 1947 in Sampson County, North Carolina. Martha may have remarried.

Apparently, Charley (Charly) Henry was listed as "Charity, aged 9, m, w" in the 1870 census for Dismal, Honeycutt Township, Sampson County, North Carolina. In the 1900 census, he was listed under "Hare." In 1930, his brother, George Washington, aged 78, was living with him.

Charles Henry and Martha Ann were buried in the Hairr Cemetery west of Salemburg on Hairr Lane, Sampson County, North Carolina. Martha Ann Hall Hairr is listed on her tombstone. His gravestone shows him as "**Charlie Henry Hairr.**" In the 1900 Federal Census of Sampson County, North Carolina, February 1873 was incorrectly listed for Martha Ann's birth.

Children of Charles Hair and Martha Hall are:

513 i. **Etta Jane Hair** was born 16 June 1888 in Sampson County and died 10 January 1961 in Chapel Hill, North Carolina, and on 21 January 1910 (or 1911), she married **JUNE WILLIAMS** who was born 11 August 1888 and died 17 July 1971 in Clinton, North Carolina. June was the son of **JOHN WILLIAMS** and **CHELLIE WILLIAMS.** Etta Jane and June were buried in Union Grove Baptist Church Cemetery on SR 1438 one mile west of Rebel City, Sampson County, North Carolina. Etta J. and Ida Etta may have been the same person.

I found one child of Etta Jane and June: **CHARLIE DAVID WILLIAMS** was born 12 February 1916 and died 20 March 1970 in Clinton, Sampson County. He married **EDITH JANE AUTRY** on 1 January 1940 in Roseboro, Sampson County, North Carolina, daughter of **WILLIAM AUTRY** and **ROSABELL TEW**. Edith was born 24 January 1921 in Mingo Township in Sampson County and died 2001. Charlie and Edith were buried in Union Grove Baptist Church Cemetery on Vander Road west of Rebel City, in Sampson County.

Four children.

1) **GURTHA ANN WILLIAMS** was born 16 December 1940 in Roseboro and she married **FRANKLIN CORBETT WILLIFORD** on 21 January 1962 in Union Grove Baptist Church. He was born 20 June 1934 in Mingo Township in Sampson County and died 16 October 1984 in Raleigh, North Carolina. Franklin was buried in Union Grove Baptist Church Cemetery.

2) **JANET RONELL WILLIAMS**, second child of Charlie and Edith was born 24 March 1943 in Sampson County. She married **WILLIAM ALLEN DAVIS** who was born 6 April 1942 in Sampson County.

3) **WANDA WILLIAMS** was born in Sampson County and was the third child of Charlie and Edith.

4) **CHARLIE DAVID WILLIAMS, JR.**, the fourth child of Charlie and Edith was born 10 September 1949 in Roseboro and married Patsy Jean Edwards who was born 12 July 1952 in Clinton, Sampson County. They have two children.

514 ii. **Ida Etta Hair**, second child of Charles and Martha was born June 1890.

\+ 515 iii. **William Estel Hair,** born 18 September 1892; died 11 September 1948 in Fayetteville, North Carolina.

516 iv. **Ella Hair,** born January 1896.

517 v. **Henry W. Hair,** born May 1897.

518 vi. **Daniel G. Hair,** born October 1899.

519 vii. **Iola H. Hair,** born about 1905.

\+ 520 viii. **Allen G. Hair,** born 29 August 1906; died 11 March 1970.

521 ix. **FRANKLIN GENTRY HAIR**. Census records list his birth about 1910. It may not be the correct Franklin , but a "Franklin Gentry Hairr, Sr., died on 25 January 1971 in Siler City, Chatham County, North Carolina. The certificate of death records 5 October 1906 for his birth and names Charles H. Hairr and Martha Sessoms(?) for his parents. He owned a Grocery Store in Siler City and **NELL HAMRICK** is named for his wife. I do not know whether this Franklin of Siler City was the son of Charles Henry Hairr and Martha Ann Hall. It appears that his mother, Martha, remarried.

North Carolina Birth Index, 1800-2000 found at Ancestry.com records two children for the Franklin

Gentry Hairr in Chatham County:

1) **FRIDA ANN HAIRR** was born 23 September 1943;

2) **FRANKLIN GENTRY HAIRR, JR**., was born 1 September 1945. Chatham County Marriage Records list a marriage for Franklin Gentry Hairr, Jr., aged 24 and **DIANA LYNN WASSERMAN**, aged 20, on 20 February 1970. Franklin, Jr. and Diana may have been the parents of **MARY KATHLEEN HAIRR** who was born in Chatham County on 13 September 1970 and **EMILY CHRISTINA HAIRR** who was born in Guilford County on 6 January 1978.

522 x. **Charlie Cecil Hair who** was born 06 May 1912 and died 08 May 1945 was the tenth known child of Charles and Martha. He was buried in the Hairr Cemetery west of Salemburg on Hairr Lane, Sampson County, North Carolina.

523 xi. **Jessie Hair,** born about 1915.

167. Simon S. Hairr (Stephen[4], Orpah[3] Holland, Thomas William[2], Unknown[1]) was born About 1844 in Sampson County, North Carolina, and died in Pikeville, Wayne County, North Carolina. He married **Rhoda M. Bass** about 1866 in Wayne County, North Carolina, daughter of Richard Bass and Carolina King. She was born about 1843 in Sampson County, North Carolina, and died 12 July 1918 in Pikeville, Wayne County, North Carolina.

SIMON HAIRR is listed "SIMON HARE" on several of the Certificates of Death for his children. The Certificate of death for their son, Richard, names Simon S. Hairr for Richard's father, leaving me to believe that Simon's middle name may have been "Stephen." The surname is also found as Hair. Simon and Rhoda were buried in Ham Cemetery, Pikeville, Wayne County, North Carolina. I question whether there was a "HAM Cemetery." The way "HAIR) is written on several documents certainly makes it appear as "HAM," but I believe that it may be a "Hair or Hairr Cemetery.

Children of Simon Hairr and Rhoda Bass are:

530 i. **Della Caroline Hairr**, born about 1867 in Sampson County, North Carolina.

\+ 531 ii. **Edward Redden Hare**, born about 1868 in Sampson County, North Carolina; died 02 December 1930 in Wilson County, North Carolina.

532 iii. **Louis Everett Hairr**, born 12 November 1869 in Sampson County, North Carolina and died 6 September 1956 in Wayne Memorial Hospital in Goldsboro, Wayne County, North Carolina. He is listed as **LEWIS HARE** and **LOUIS HARE** ane **LOUIS E. HARE**. He married **MAUDE SEYMOUR** who was born 27 December 1874 in Wayne County, North Carolina, and died 20 October 1959 in Forest Hill Rest Home in Goldsboro, Wayne County, North Carolina.. She was the daughter of Isaiah Seymour and Louisa Exum. Louis was a retired farmer and merchant; he and Maude were buried in Willow Dale Cemetery in Goldsboro, North Carolina.

Children of Lewis and Maude listed in the 1930 Federal Census for Saulston Township, Wayne County, North Carolina:

1) **ALBERT ARTHUR HARE,** the first child, was born 8 October 1898 in Wayne County, North Carolina and died 4 February 1966 in rural Pikeville, Saulston Township, Wayne County, North Carolina from a Heart Attack. He married **CATHERINE PARSONS** who was born 26 December 1898 in Wayne County and died 10 April 1990 in a nursing home in Wayne County. He and Catherine were married on 5 March 1917 in Carteret County, North Carolina. There marriage record shows her as **"Cathleen Parsons"** while North Carolina Death Collection records **"Catherine Parson."**

The children of Arthur and Cathern(sic) listed in the 1930 Federal Census of Saulston Township, Wayne County, are: **ETHEL HARE,** born 1919; **EARL HARE,** born 1921; **ELMA HARE,** born 1922; **WILLIAM HARE,** born 1924; and **KENNETH HARE** born 1929.

2) **CHARLIE HARE** was the second child of Louis E. and Maude. He was born about 1901in Wayne County, North Carolina, and died 7 May 1939 in Goldsboro Hospital, Goldsboro, Wayne County, North Carolina from Potash Poisoning. It appears he was in an accident at a Filling Station (Gas Station). Charlie married **EULA (Maiden Name Unknown.)** Their daughter, **JEWEL HARE,** was aged 8 in the 1930 census for Saulston Township in Wayne County.

3) **FLOYD HARE** (FLOID HARE?) was the third child of Louis and Maude and was born about 1903 in Saulston Township.

4) **SELMA HARE,** the fourth child was born about 1906 in Saulston Township, Wayne County, North Carolina.

5) LEWIS RUSSELL HARE, SR, the fifth child of Louis Hare and Maude Seymour, was born 20 August 1908 in Wayne County, North Carolina, and died in October 1992 in Goldsboro, Wayne County, North Carolina. He married MIRTHA E. (Maiden Name Unknown) who was born about 1908. Two known children, **LADSON HARE,** was born about 1928 in Saulston, Wayne County and **LOUIS RUSSELL HARE, JR.**

6) **LALA HARE,** the sixth child was born about 1911 in Wayne County, North Carolina.

7) **HATTIE MAY HARE,** the seventh child of Louis Hare and Maude Seymour, was born about 1912. in Wayne County.

8) RUBY HARE, the eighth child, was born about 1915 in Wayne County.

9) **SALLIE E. HARE**, the youngest child of Louis and Maude is listed in the 1930 Federal Census of Stony Creek, Wayne County, North Carolina, and was born about 1916.

533 iv. Elizabeth Jane Hairr, daughter of **Simon S. and Rhoda**, was born about 1872 in Sampson **County, North Carolina.**

534 v. **Mary C. Hairr**, born about 1874 in Sampson County, North Carolina.

\+ 535 vi. **George William Hare, Sr.**, the sixth child of Simon S. and Rhoda, was born 02 May 1876 in Sampson County, North Carolina; died 04 April 1955 in Wayne County, North Carolina.

536 vii. **Richard Stephen Hairr, Sr.**, (RICHARD STEPHEN HARE, SR.) was born 08 January 1878 in Sampson County, North Carolina, and died 26 July 1952 in Goldsboro, Wayne County, North Carolina. He married **MATTIE PEARCE ALPHIN**, daughter of **JESSE ALPHIN** and **MARTHA HUFFMAN**. She was born 26 January 1881 in Onslow County, North Carolina and died 24 June 1967 in Goldsboro, Wayne County.

Richard is buried in Deens Cemetery in Wayne County and Mattie (Minnie) is buried in Willow Dale Cemetery in Goldsboro.

Children of Richard and Mattie were all born in Wayne County, North Carolina:

1) **ALBERT HARE**, born about 1907.

2) **LILLIE MAY HARE**, born about 1908.

3) **LELAND** HARE, born about 1911.

4) **ELMA HARE**, born about 1913.

5) **RICHARD STEPHEN HARE, JR.**, was born about 1919.

537 viii. **Louanna Hairr**, daughter of Simon S. and Rhoda, was born September 1879 in Sampson County, North Carolina.

168. Blackman Hairr (Stephen[4], Orpah[3] Holland, Thomas William[2], Unknown[1]) was born 27 August 1845, and died 30 January 1920. He married **Nellie J. Britt.** She was born 25 July 1849, and died 19 September 1908.

First name also listed as "**Blackmon**" and "**Blackman Hare**" is listed on his Certificate of Death. In 1870, he was listed as head of household and with him appears to be his aunt, "Nannie" Hairr (his father's sister, Nancy) and Joel Hairr. It is not known where this "Joel" should be placed; he may have been Nancy's son.

Blackman "Hare" enlisted in April 1864 in Clinton, North Carolina, to serve in the American Civil War. He was a Private in Company I, 2nd Jr. Reserves. Regiment 71.

He and Nellie were buried in Piney Grove Cemetery about 10 miles from Clinton of the Old Goldsboro Road.

Children of Blackman and Nellie are:

\+ 538 i. **Stephen Hardy Hairr**, born 09 December 1873; died 15 January 1944.

\+ 539 ii. **Charlie E. Hairr**, born March 1877; died 11 August 1944 in Nash County, North Carolina.

540 iii. **Ludie Anna Hairr**, born 7 July 1879 in Sampson County, North Carolina, died 4 December 1943 of Cardiac Failure in Duke Hospital, Durham, North Carolina, and is buried in The Clinton Cemetery, Clinton, North Carolina. She married **Charlie Bennett Brewer** (**Charles Bennett Brewer**) who was born 08 February 1871 in Sampson County, died 23 February 1965 in Clinton, Sampson County, and is buried by Ludie. He was the son of **Bennett Brewer** and **Catherine Weeks**. On her certificate of death, she is listed "**Ludie Anna Brewer,**" her husband is listed as **Charlie B. Brewer** and Blackmon Hairr and Nellie Britt are named for her parents. She may have been called "Louanna," but perhaps Louanna Hairr, daugter of Simon Hairr and Rhoda Bass, who was born in September 1879, has been mistaken for Ludie Anna by a few researchers. The fact that they were born within a few weeks of each other adds to the placement problem.

The 1930 United States Federal Census has three children listed for Ludie and Charlie: **ETHEL J. BREWER**; aged 25, **MARY L. BREWER**, aged 23; **EVA M. BREWER**, aged 19. **Ethel Jane Brewer** was born 5 June 1903 and died 1 February 1988; she was buried near her parents, sister, Eva, and brother, Homer and apparently, never married.

Mary Lou Brewer Fowler was buried in The Clinton Cemetery, Clinton, North Carolina. She was born 20 october 1905 and died 30 October 1993. Remarks on her monument inform us that she was the wife of **Miles Beatty Fowler**, Sr, who was born 1903 and died 1939, mother of **Miles Beatty Fowler, Jr.**, and daughter of Charles B. and Ludie H. Brewer.

Eva Brewer Williams, wife of **W. W. Williams**, was buried near her parents in The Clinton Cemetery. She was born 27 April 1910 and died 8 March 1965.

HOMER W. BREWER was born 28 November 1900 and died 16 October 1961. He was buried next to his parents, Charlie and Ludie.

\+ 541 iv. **Giles Jasper Hairr,** fourth known child of Blackman and Nellie, born 04 January 1880; died 10 April 1926.

542 v. **Joey Hairr**, born May 1884.

543 vi. **Ivey Blackmon Hairr**, born 28 May 1884; died 24 January 1956. He married **Annie A. Bell**. She was born 10 October 1884 in Sampson County and died 02 August 1964 in New Hanover County, North Carolina. She was the daughter of **Oscar Bell** and **Jane Bell.** Ivey is listed "**D. Ivey Blalckmon Hairr** on Annie's certificate of death.

Ivey B. Hairr and Annie were buried in Piney Grove Baptist Church Cemetery on N. McCullen Road, (SR 1741), Sampson County, North Carolina. I found birth and or death records for three children. 1) **Leland B. Hairr**, born 9 September 1910 in Sampson County and died 31 March 1988 in Goldsboro, Wayne County, North Carolina. 2) **Atwood Randolph Hairr** was born 31 July 1913 in New Hanover County, North Carolina and died 10 February 1974 in Wilmington, New Hanover County. Atwood married **Pearl Packer**. 3) **Vaden Bell Hairr** was born 19 September 1920 in Sampson County. A North Carolina Birth Index records **Janet Elaine Hairr,** daughter of Vaden Bell hairr was born 29 June 1951.

544 vii. **Allen Hairr**, born October 1887.

545 viii. **Lizzie M. Hairr**, born 30 May 1886 in Sampson County and died 18 March 1937 of Broncho-pneumonia in Salemburg, Honeycutts Township, Sampson County. Apparently, she married a Mr. Roberts; Mrs. Lizzie Roberts is listed on her certificate of death; she was widowed and her husband's given name was not listed.

169. William H. Hairr (Stephen[4], Orpah[3] Holland, Thomas William[2], Unknown[1]) was born 07 August 1847 in Sampson County, North Carolina, and died 25 March 1896. He married **Elizabeth Cashwell** 21 July 1878. She was born 22 December 1859, and died 21 July 1940. He had descendants who used the surname "HARE." He is named "William B. Hair" on the certificate of death for his son, Elmon M.

Children of William Hairr and Elizabeth Cashwell are:

546 i. **Bluford Hairr**, born 27 July 1879; died 10 March 1907.

Never married.

\+ 547 ii. **Elmond M. Hairr**, born 29 March 1884; died 31 October 1957 in Sampson County, North Carolina.

548 iii. **Alice Hairr**, born 28 September 1887; died 06 August 1888.

\+ 549 iv. **Laura Caroline Hairr**, born 31 August 1889; died 06 July 1970.

\+ 550 v. **Albert B. Hairr**, born 17 September 1893 in Sampson County, North Carolina; died 16 November 1944.

170. Eliza Jane Hairr (Stephen[4], Orpah[3] Holland, Thomas William[2], Unknown[1]) was born About 1848, and died Before 1900. She married **Jesse Bradshaw** 21 December 1865, son of Thomas Bradshaw and Eliza Smith. He was born about 1842, and died 02 April 1918.

Jesse Bradshaw served in the Confederate Army during the American Civil War. He and his brother, John, enlisted on 2 November 1861 in Cumberland County where they were residing at the time, to serve in Company G, 33rd Regiment, North Carolina Troops. "Jesse was captured at or near Chancellorsville on 3 May 1863 and was sent to Washington, D.C, paroled and transferred to City Point, Virginia, where he was received on 13 May 1863, for exchange. Reported absent without leave in July-August 1863. He returned to duty in September - October 1863 and was present or accounted for until captured at Wilderness, Virginia, or at Spotsylvania Court House, Virginia, sometime between 5-12 of May 1864. Confined at Point Lookout, Maryland 17 May 1864 and transferred to Elmire, New York on 10 Autust 1864. Paroled at Elmira on 2 March 1865 and transferred to the James River, Virginia, for exchange."

Children of Eliza Hairr and Jesse Bradshaw are:

\+ 551 i. **John William Bradshaw**, born about 1866.

552 ii. **Mary Eliza Bradshaw**, born about 1869; died 09 January 1926. She married William McCullen.

\+ 553 iii. **David L. Bradshaw**, born 05 September 1871 in Sampson County, North Carolina; died 13 March 1955 in Sampson County, North Carolina.

\+ 554 iv. **Franklin Bradshaw**, born 20 December 1873; died 05 August 1924.

555 v. **Ellen Bradshaw**, born about 1875. She married Almond Honrine.

Ellen died during childbirth.

556 vi. **Joseph Bradshaw**, born March 1878; died 28 May 1941.

Never married.

557 vii. **Minnie Catherine Bradshaw**, born 14 May 1878 in North Carolina and died 29 July 1950 in Halls Township, Sampson County. She married John Bass who died before 1950.

558 viii. **Fred Bradshaw**, born May 1882. He married Pearl (Maiden name unknown).

559 ix. **Ida Jane Bradshaw**, born September 1884; died 04 September 1925. She married **William H. Bradshaw** on 23 October 1904.

560 x. **Luther Bradshaw**, born October 1887; died 02 January 1943. He never married.

561 xi. **Livie Bradshaw**, born 31 March 1891 in Sampson County, died 30 December 1959 in Rural Sampson County, North Carolina. He married **Sarah Frances Jackson**. The year 1957 is found for his death, but the year on his certificate of death appears to be 1959 and it was received by the registrar on 4 January 1960.

171. Hinton Hairr (Stephen[4], Orpah[3] Holland, Thomas William[2], Unknown[1]) was born about 1851. He married **D. Ann (maiden name unknown)**. She was born about 1850.

Hinton was a hired laborer for James Warren in Newton Grove in 1900.

Children of Hinton Hairr and D. Unknown are:

562 i. **Betty Jane Hairr**, born about 1876.

563 ii. **William Henry Hairr**, born about 1878.

172. Mary M. Hairr (Stephen[4], Orpah[3] Holland, Thomas William[2], Unknown[1]) was born about 1855. She married **Unknown Ryan**.

She and her son (?) were living with her parents in 1880.

Child of Mary Hairr and Unknown Ryan is:

564 i. **L. J. Ryan,** born about 1875.

173. Fanny C. Hairr (Stephen[4], Orpah[3] Holland, Thomas William[2], Unknown[1]) was born 12 June 1855 and died 18 July 1902 in Sampson County, North Carolina. She married **Franklin Holland** before 1880, son of Harfrey Holland and Mary Sessoms. He was born March 1850 in Sampson County, North Carolina, and died 17 June 1927 in Honeycutts Township, Sampson County.

In the 1880 census, she was listed as "Fannie C"; in the 1870 census she was "Fanny C.," aged 13. Fannie Hare (Hair), born November 1886 may have also been a foster child of Fannie

C. and Franklin Holland. Both Fannie and Janie I. were listed as nieces living with Fannie and Franklin in 1900.

Fanny C. was buried in a Holland Cemetery about 2 miles west of Salemburg, North Carolina. Franklin was buried on 17 June 1927, at home in a family cemetery. They were probably buried in the same family cemetery.

Janie Isabell Hairr was a foster child of Frank Holland. In 1910, she was listed as his niece, aged 25. The census records for 1850, 1860 and 1870 show his name as 'Franklin.' His death certificate shows 'Frank' which was probably a nickname. Cause of death was chronic interstitial nephritis of several years.

It appears that either the marriage dates for his second and third wives are incorrect or there was another Frank(lin) Holland. However, he is the only Frank(lin) Holland I have found who was born about 1850. Peggy Tripp (Crouch; Workman.) shows that Franklin's first wife was Fannie Hair; he and Fannie were second cousins. See Franklin Holland elsewhere in this book.

Children are listed above under (84) Franklin Holland.

175. Henry Stephen Hairr (Stephen[4], Orpah[3] Holland, Thomas William[2], Unknown[1]) was born 19 July 1859, and died 20 December 1926. Apparently, Henry married his first wife, **RACHEL CLIFTON** before 1883. She was born about 1858 in Sampson County, North Carolina. **Rachel Clifton Britt** is listed for her name by Mr. Rosser; the certificate of death for Katie E., child listed below, leads me to ask, did Henry and Rachel divorce and both remarry or did Rachel die young? Was her full name Rachel Clifton Britt?

Ida Jane Butler, Henry's second wife, was born 20 (or the 21) of December 1866 in Pender County, North Carolina, and died 06 August 1960 in Fuquay Springs, Wake County, North Carolina. Ida was the daughter of EDWARD BUTLER and LAURA LEWIS.

Henry Stephen and Ida Jane were buried in The Clinton Cemetery, Clinton, Sampson County, North Carolina.

Child of Henry Hairr and Rachel Clifton is:

565 i. **Katie E. Hairr** was born September 1883 in Sampson County and died 29 April 1962 in Raleigh, Wake County, North Carolina. She married **Jack B. Bonds**. The certificate of death for Katie Hairr Bonds names Henry S. Hairr for her father and Rachel Clifton for her mother.

Children of Henry Hairr and Ida Jane Butler are:

566 ii. **Varo Henry Hairr**, born 22 December 1896.

567 iii. **Vivia Ida Hairr**, born 03 April 1897.

568 iv. **Almon J. Hairr**, born August 1898. His middle initial also listed as "G."

569 v. **Annie Laurie Hairr**, born 17 September 1900.

570 vi. **John William Hairr**, born 22 September 1902; died 16 January 1985.

187. James Thomas Hairr (John C.[4] Hair, Orpah[3] Holland, Thomas William[2], Unknown[1]) was born About 1848, and died after 1910. He married **Patience Cannady** about 1873, daughter of Hardy Cannady and Nancy Honeycutt. She was born about 1839 in North Carolina, and died after 1910.

James and Patia (Patience) were living with their son, Isaiah, in 1910.

The ages of their children listed in census records indicate that, most likely, Patience was married about 1862, but no record has been found to support that. The marriage index for Sampson County, North Carolina, lists the marriage date of 17 September 1871 for **James G. Holland** and **Patience Canada**, born 1839. I can't ignore the marriage record and I have found no other Patience Cannady who was born about 1839 or a second James (G. or F.) Holland who was born about 1844 in Sampson County at that time.

The records of the above marriage and census records indicate that Patience was probably married twice before she married James Thomas.

The 1880 and 1900 census records show Patience and "Pasie," respectively, as the wife of James T. Hair. Pasie was a nickname for Patience. The **James Thomas Hairr** born about 1848 would not have been old enough to have been the father of **Rhoda Hairr**, aged 17, and **Laura Hairr** who was born about 1869, listed with James and Patience in 1880, and Patience had not yet married James G. Holland before Rhoda and Laura were born. In the event she was the same Patience Canada (Cannady?) who married James G. Holland, it appears that they were married only a few years.

IS IT POSSIBLE that **JAMES G. HOLLAND** and **JAMES THOMAS HAIRR** were used for the name of one man, James Thomas Hair(r), son of John C. Hairr who died in the Civil War? See notes for John C. Hair, his children and Daniel Hairr and Lucinda (Holland) Hairr. Orphans sometimes, were incorrectly listed in census records with the surname of the head of household. **"G"** and **"T"** can certainly sound similiar when spoken.

In the 1860 census of Sampson County, North Carolina, a daughter, "Ursala, 1 yr.," was placed under Patience, 19 yrs, who was listed under Hardy and Jane Cannady. This placement seems to indicate that Ursala was the daughter of Patience rather than Hardy and Jane. However, Ursala was the right age to be "Vestinia," daughter of Hardy and Jane, who was listed in 1870 as age 12, but not listed in 1860. this seems to indicate that Vestina was listed as Ursala in 1860 and she may actually be the daughter of Patience by an unknown father. This would be the Vestina Cannady who tradition says was the daughter of Hardy Cannady and Nancy Jane Faircloth and was the wife of William Bee Naylor.

Children of James Hairr and Patience Cannady are:

\+ 571 i. **Isaiah H. Hairr**, (ISAIAH HAIRR), born 26 May 1874; died 01 January 1948.

\+ 572 ii. **Augustus Davis** Hairr, born 06 August 1879; died 08 March 1935 in Sampson County, North Carolina.

+ 573 iii. **George V. Hairr**, born 1878.

+ 574 iv. **Claude Raste Hairr**, born March 1881; died 15 October 1935 in Turkey, Sampson County, North Carolina.

575 v. **Maline A. Wilson**, born about 1888. It is not clear whether or how she was related to the household.

188. John Thomas Hairr (John C.[4] Hair, Orpah[3] Holland, Thomas William[2], Unknown[1]) was born 15 April 1859 in Sampson County, North Carolina, and died 05 June 1921 in Sampson County, North Carolina. His certificate of death spells his name "**JOHN THOMAS HARE**, names "**John Hair**" for his father, "**SILVAINE TEW**" for his mother and Osborn Tew Cemetery for his place of burial. "Doshie Hare" was the informant. He married **Doshia Ann Draughon** 25 October 1902 in Sampson County, North Carolina, daughter of William Draughon and Leeta Hairr. She was born 17 September 1888 in Sampson County, North Carolina, and died 14 April 1957 in Fayetteville, Cumberland County, North Carolina. Doshia married second **Olive O. Dorman** about 1925; she married third **Walter Purdie Barefoot** on 14 December 1929 in Fayetteville, Cumberland County, North Carolina. Walter Purdie was the son of William Cicero Barefoot and Martha Eliza Lee and was born 15 March 1881 in Sampson County and died 16 April 1957. The 1930 Cross Creek Township, Cumberland County, North Carolina Census, records him as **Walter Barefoot.**

John Thomas may have been married prior to his marriage to Doshia, but I haven't found a record to support this. In 1882, John Thomas Hair(r) was deeded 38 acres by Osborn Tew, his grandfather. He and Doshia Ann were buried in Alphine Cemetery, Alphin Road, Dunn, Harnett County, North Carolina.

Doshia Ann Draughon and John Thomas Hair had nine children; She and Olive O. Dorman had one child and with Walter Purdie Barefoot, she had one child.

Children of John Hairr and Doshia Draughon are:

576 i. **Elsie Lee Hairr**, born 03 October 1903 in Sampson County, North Carolina; died 05 December 1903 in Sampson County.

577 ii. **Ardella Hairr,** born 14 October 1904 in Sampson County, North Carolina; died 25 June 1974 in Fayetteville, Cumberland County, North Carolina. She married a "Fowler" and is buried in Cross Creek Cemetery in Cumberland County, North Carolina.

578 iii. **Mellissie Ann Hairr**, born 06 August 1906 in Sampson County, North Carolina; died 07 December 1968 in Fayetteville, Cumberland County, North Carolina.

579 iv. **Hoover James Hairr,** born 08 September 1908 in Sampson County, North Carolina; died 05 June 1991 in Fayetteville in Cumberland County.

His first name is also listed as "Hosea."

580 v. **Penelope Jane Hairr**, born 04 May 1910 in Sampson County, North Carolina; died April 1993 in Lumberton, North Carolina. Penelope Jane was known as "Nellie."

581 vi. **Ida Leona Hairr** was born 11 April 1912 in Sampson County and died 13 August 1971 in Harnett County, North Carolina.

582 vii. **Lila Izonia Hairr**, born 28 April 1914 in Sampson County, North Carolina; died 01 July 1942 in Fayetteville, Cumberland County, North Carolina.

583 viii. **Kathleen Hairr** was born 04 October 1916 in Sampson County and died 09 August 1939 in Fayetteville, Cumberland County, North Carolina.

Jerome D. Tew in his research spells her name "Katherine." In the 1930 census, it is entered as "**Katherleen Hair.**"

584 ix. **Edna Ashley Hairr**, born 31 October 1919 in Sampson County, North Carolina; died 21 May 1990 in Southport, North Carolina. She married Unknown Smith.

Edna Ashley was buried in Calvary Tabernacle PFB Church Cemetery, 1 mile from intersection of Hwy 242 and High House Road, Sampson County.

Child of Olive O. Dorman and Doshia Ann Draughon is:

Olive Dorman, born about 1925. He was listed with Doshia and Walter Purdie Barefoot as **OLIVE HAIR** in the 1930 Federal Census of Cross Creek Township, Cumberland County, North Carolina. He was probably the **OLIVE JAMES DORMAN** listed in a North Carolina Death Collection with a birth date of 3 May 1924 and a death date of January 1985 with Durham, North Carolina, listed as his residence.

Child of Doshia Ann Draughon and Walter Purdie Barefoot is:

Etta Leevon Barefoot who was born 26 September 1930.

189. Mary Manda Autry (Starling[4], Millie[3] Holland, Thomas William[2], Unknown[1]) was born 08 March 1835. She married **(1) Beaufort Faircloth** 20 May 1855. She married **(2) Daniel Holland, Jr.** 09 February 1869 in Sampson County, North Carolina, son of Daniel Holland and Elizabeth Sessoms. He was born between 1822 - 1827 in Sampson County, North Carolina, and died after 1880. Daniel was her first cousin once removed.

Professor Bundy names Beaufort Faircloth for the spouse of Mary Manda, daughter of Starling, and a North Carolina Marriage Collection records the marriage of "**Mary Autery**" to Beaufort Faircloth on 20 May 1855 in Cumberland County, North Carolina. I have not been successful in finding any other information for Beaufort and Mary.

The 1850 census for Sampson County, North Carolina, records Daniel with his father, Daniel Holland, and his mother Elizabeth. In 1860, this Daniel was listed as age 35, head of household with his mother, Elizabeth. Listed with them were: Betsey, 33; Wesley, 29; James F. 17; Dicy A., 13; Cherry, 8. He does not appear to be married in 1850 and it is not clear whether "Betsey" was his spouse in 1860. It appears that he was not the father of James F., Dicy A., and Cherry. In 1870 "Mary M." was listed for his spouse. Dicy A. and Cherry are found in the household of Daniel's mother, Elizabeth in 1870. James F. was living with Joel Jackson.

Most likely, he was the Daniel Holland who served in the Civil War as a Private in Company I, Regiment 46, Inf. His records list 1827 for his year of birth and show he was a Cooper. He enlisted on 12 March 1862 in Clinton, Sampson County, North Carolina. Ill from 22 October1862 to February 1864 with notation, unfit for duty. Assigned 21 April 1864 to light duty as a nurse in Jackson Hospital, Richmond, Virginia and was captured there. In Clinton 26 September 1889 for veteran's reunion."

Another United States Civil War Soldier Record and Profile records that he was a Cooper and enlisted on 3 December 1862 as a private and also records that he enlisted on 16 April 1862. While he was ill and unfit for duty, he was, most likely at home.

Children are listed above under (24) Daniel Holland, Jr.

192. Mariah Jetson Autry (Starling[4], Millie[3] Holland, Thomas William[2], Unknown[1]) was born 12 October 1841 in North Carolina, and died September 1917 in North Carolina. She married **Lewis Carr Spell** 18 March 1869 in North Carolina, son of James Spell and Penelope Bullard. He was born 20 June 1849 in North Carolina, and died 18 September 1917 in North Carolina.

Children of Mariah Autry and Lewis Spell are:

585 i. **Roena Dallis SPELL**, born about 1870 in North Carolina; died after 30 April 1930. She married **Solomon Jonathan FAIRCLOTH**; born about 1853; died after 30 April 1930.

586 ii. **George SPELL**, born about 1873 in North Carolina.

587 iii. **Bessie SPELL**, born about 1875 in North Carolina.

588 iv. **Gaston SPELL**, born about 1876 in North Carolina.

589 v. **Martha SPELL**, born about 1877 in North Carolina.

590 vi. **James Starling SPELL**, born 12 June 1878 in North Carolina; died 10 October 1948. He married **Ida Langdon Maxwell**; born 10 January 1881; died 27 December 1966.

591 vii. **Ida Dees Spell**, born 27 May 1880 in North Carolina; died 21 December 1952 in Salemburg, Sampson County, North Carolina. She married **Duncan J. Bullard**, son of Giles Bullard and Elizabeth Culbreth. He was born about 1860. Ida married second **Valentine T. Baggett**. See **591** for Ida and Valentine's children.

\+ 592 viii. **Narena C. Spell**, born 16 January 1883 in North Carolina; died 24 May 1960 in Fayetteville, Cumberland County, North Carolina.

193. Allen Merdeth Autry (Starling[4], Millie[3] Holland, Thomas William[2], Unknown[1]) was born 30 December 1843 near Salemburg, Sampson County, North Carolina, and died 31 May 1875. He married **Elizabeth Lorenzo Cobb** 16 February 1870. She was born 22 January 1846, and died 07 April 1932.

Shortly after they were married, Allen and Elizabeth moved to Arkansas seeking better government and better economic opportunities, but were disappointed when they found it to be the same as in Sampson County, North Carolina. In 1872 they returned to North Carolina. Their home, White Hall, was near the Black River.

He enlisted in the American Civil War on 22 March 1862 and was a private in Co. I, Regiment 46, Inf. Wounded 5 May 1864 in Battle of Wilderness, Virginia and was hospitalized for five months.

Allen worked as a timberman floating logs down the river to Wilmington. Once while helping with a log jam, he fell into the river and his clothes froze on him before he could get home. Soon after, he died of pneumonia at age 32. He and Elizabeth are buried in the Autry Cemetery on Minnie Hall Road about 1.5 mile from HWY 242, Sampson County, North Carolina.

Children of Allen Autry and Elizabeth Cobb are:

+ 593 i. **Myrtle Irene Autry,** born 20 November 1872 in Sampson County, North Carolina; died 02 February 1952.

+ 594 ii. **Bettie Allen Autry,** born 19 October 1875 near Beulah Church near Salemburg, Sampson County, North Carolina; died 19 December 1939 in Sampson County.

595 iii. **Infant Daughter Autry** died in infancy.

195. Ann Sophia Autry (Starling[4], Millie[3] Holland, Thomas William[2], Unknown[1]) was born 10 December 1848. She married **Jordan Holland** before 1885, son of Harfrey Holland and Mary Sessoms. He was born 18 June 1854 in Sampson County, North Carolina, and died 20 June 1938 in Cross Creek Township, Cumberland County, North Carolina.

Her middle name also listed as "Sapphira." She died about 1885 during childbirth as did her infant.

Professor Bundy writes that Hazelene Bass provided him with the data for the family of Jordan Holland, his spouses and children. Jordon Holland's death certificate names Myocardial Insufficiency and uremia for his cause of death. It shows that he also had prostate surgery on 26 March 1938. He died in Highsmith Hospital, Fayetteville, Cumberland County, North Carolina and was buried in a Holland Cemetery on Fleet Cooper Road (SR 1240) in Sampson County, North Carolina.

Child is listed above under (85) Jordan Holland.

198. Charles Gibson Autry (Starling[4], Millie[3] Holland, Thomas William[2], Unknown[1]) was born 01 November 1858, and died 15 January 1927. He married **Addie L. Spell,** daughter of Owen Spell and Rachel Faircloth. She was born 06 June 1868 in Sampson County, North Carolina, and died 14 April 1948 in North Carolina.

I am unable to read names of his children in 1900 Federal Census for Sampson County, North Carolina. He has been listed as the son of Duncan Autry and Sarah Ann Lockerman, but I haven't found census data to support that. However, it is said that Duncan died about 1860-61. Actually, **Sarah Ann Lockerman**, born about 1832, daughter of Reason Lockerman and Jane Tew, married **Duncan J. Autry** who died in 1864 while serving in the Civil War. Charles G., aged 2, is listed for the son of Starling in the 1860 census for Sampson County, North Carolina.

Children of Charles Autry and Addie Spell are:

596 i. **Rachel B. Autry**, born November 1886.

597 ii. **Theodore Autry**, born 01 November 1888; died 08 October 1918.

Theodore was buried in the Autry Cemetery on Minnie Hall Road about 1.5 mile from HY 242, Sampson County, North Carolina.

598 iii. **Eula C. Autry**, born July 1891.

599 iv. **Brian Autry**, born about 1893.

600 v. **Edgar Allen Autry**, born about 1896.

601 vi. **Janie Autry**, born about 1898.

602 vii. **Alphonso Autry**, born about 1901.

201. Miney L. Lockerman (Olivia[4] Holland, Henry[3], Thomas William[2], Unknown[1]) was born 06 March 1875 in Sampson County, North Carolina, and died 19 August 1921 in Cumberland County, North Carolina. She married **Surrell Faircloth**, son of Blackman Faircloth and Raney (maiden name unknown). He was born 08 April 1871 in Sampson County, North Carolina, and died 11 June 1936 in Sampson County.

Minnie" is the name found on her gravestone which also records 05 March 1874 for her birth and 17 August 1921 for her death. She died of lobar pneumonia in Highsmith Hospital in Fayetteville, North Carolina.

Miney L. and Surrell were buried in a Lockerman Cemetery near Lakewood High School, between Salemburg and Roseboro, North Carolina Surrell's tombstone records "Surell" for his given name.

Children of Miney Lockerman and Surrell Faircloth are:

603 i. **James Thomas Faircloth**, born 25 June 1897; died 17 May 1918.

James was buried in the Lockamy Cemetery in White Woods near Salemburg, North Carolina

604 ii. **Lonnie Lee Faircloth**, born about 1899.

605 iii. **Bonnie Sue Faircloth**, born about 1900.

606 iv. **Baby Faircloth**, born 1901; died 1901.

Baby Faircloth was buried in the Lockamy Cemetery in White Woods near Salemburg, North Carolina.

607 v. **Bessie B. Faircloth**, born about 1903.

\+ 608 vi. **Lesley Faircloth**, born about 1913.

203. Dallie Alice Lockerman (Olivia[4] Holland, Henry[3], Thomas William[2], Unknown[1]) was born 29 May 1881 in Sampson County, North Carolina, and died 18 September 1958 in Salemburg, North Carolina. She married **Jasper Lee Holland** 24 January 1900 in Sampson County, North Carolina, son of Stephen Holland and Nancy Hudson. He was born 12 July 1877 in Honeycutts Township in Sampson County and died 25 March 1944 in Honeycutts Township, Sampson County.

Dallie Alice died from Congested Heart Failure (6 months) due to chronic brochitis, pulmonary fibrosis and emphysema (several years.) Jasper Lee died from cancer of stomach with ?. He and Dallie Alice were buried in Salemburg Cemetery, Salemburg, North Carolina.

Her name was also spelled 'Dollie' and 'Dahlie.' On the certificate of death for her son, Jimmy Minson Holland, she is listed as Dallie Brock. On his application for a social security card, her son, Henry Lee (Coy) Holland gives her name as "Dallie Alice Lockamy" and on the certificate of birth for her daughter, Seawell, "Malissa Seawell Holland" is written with a line across "Malissa" and Dallie's name is shown as "Allie May Della Lockerman" with a line through "Allie May Della" and "Dallie" written above it.

On a certificate of birth for her daughter, Mary Elizabeth Holland, Dallie's name appears as "Alice Madelia Lockamy". Jasper was known as "Jap."

Will of Jasper Holland: Filed 28 March 1944.

"Having conveyed all my real estate to certain of my children without conveying any of it to one of my children and four of my granchildren, I now make provisions for said daughter and granchildren in lieu of real estate.

"1) Seawell Holland Roberts $...

"2) To my four grandchildren: to wit: Pauline Smith and Adel Smith, children of daughter Floy Smith and to Orlando L. Holland and Bobby Brewer Holland, children of my deceased son, Orlando Holland, each $... in cash and ($... to be loaned and invested for them by said ... and paid to them at age 21 to go toward their education.

"Attention: Pauline Smith, 01 February 1946; Adel Smith, 15 September 1947; Orlando L. Holland, 24 September 1955; Bobby Brewer Holland 21 October 1957."

The remainder of his estate was left to his wife, Dallie, if living and if not, to be equally divided between all issues. Dallie and James Minson Holland, Executors. Book 10, Pages 331-335.

Children of Dallie Lockerman and Jasper Holland are:

+ 609 i. **Henry Lee Holland**, born 28 October 1900 in Sampson County, North Carolina; died 1978 in Yulee, Forida.

+ 610 ii. **Floy D. Holland** was born 28 June 1903 in Sampson County and died 09 December 1927.

+ 611 iii. **Jimmy Minson Holland**, born 30 April 1906 in Sampson County, North Carolina; died 01 March 1995 in Sampson County.

+ 612 iv. **Lonie Mae Holland**, born 20 March 1909 in Sampson County, North Carolina; died 10 April 1993 in Highsmith Hospital, Fayetteville, Cumberland County, North Carolina.

+ 613 v. **Ila Marie Holland** was born 27 March 1910 in Sampson County and died 05 May 2003.

+ 614 vi. **Orlanda Lee Holland**, born 16 October 1912 in Sampson County, North Carolina; died 24 December 1940 near Savannah, Georgia.

615 vii. **Mary Elizabeth Holland**, born 23 June 1915 in Sampson County.

A certificate of birth shows that Mary Elizabeth was born on 23 June 1915. Parents: Jaspey Holland and Alice Madelia Lockamy. No family member is aware that Geneva had a twin sister and Geneva's name may have been registered incorrectly.

+ 616 viii. **Geneva Holland**, born 23 June 1915 in Sampson County, North Carolina; died 24 December 1940 near Savannah, Georgia.

+ 617 ix. **Melissa Seawell Holland** was born 10 November 1917 in Sampson County and died 18 January 1990 in Cumberland County, North Carolina.

+ 618 x. **Elizabeth Ozell Holland**, born 23 August 1920 in Honeycutts Township, Sampson County, North Carolina.

+ 619 xi. **Novella Olean Holland** was born 18 February 1922 in Sampson County and died 11 December 1989 in Sampson County, North Carolina.

204. Louvicia Lockerman (Olivia[4] Holland, Henry[3], Thomas William[2], Unknown[1]) was born 11 January 1885 in Sampson County, North Carolina, and died 12 November 1948 in Sampson County, North Carolina. She married **Alexander E. Brock**, son of Kinion Brock and Pherobe Williams. He was born 22 August 1875 in Sampson County, North Carolina, and died 04 June 1933 in Sampson County North Carolina.

In the 1900 census, Alexander's date of birth was listed as May 1878. Louvicia and Alexander were buried in the Lockerman Cemetery near Lakewood High School, between Salemburg and Roseboro, North Carolina

Children of Louvicia Lockerman and Alexander Brock are:

620 i. **Vander Granville Brock**, born about 1906 in Sampson County, North Carolina.

621 ii. **Margie Lee Brock,** born about 1908 in Sampson County, North Carolina.

622 iii. **Bettie Brock,** born about 1911 in Sampson County, North Carolina.

208. Heman Cashwell Lockamy (Orpah Caroline[4] Holland, Henry[3], Thomas William[2], Unknown[1]) was born 21 October 1878, and died 03 February 1949 in Cumberland County, North Carolina. He married **Rettie Swann Cain**, daughter of Mollay Cain and Margaret Johnson. She was born about 1879, and died 1964.

Heman's first name is also listed as "Hemon." In 1910 he was living in Lisbon Twp, Sampson County, North Carolina, and he was living in or near Garland in September 1918 when he registered for the draft in WW I and was Second Master(?) for the A.C.L. Railroad. His registration card shows black for the color of his eyes and hair.

Heman Cashwell and Rettie Swann were buried in a Johnson Cemetery on Parkersburg Road, Sampson County, North Carolina.

Children of Heman Lockamy and Rettie Cain are:

\+ 623 i. **Leola Lockamy**, born 03 October 1907.

624 ii. **Wesley Lockamy**, born 06 January 1909 in Sampson County, North Carolina. He married (1) Pauline Smith. He married (2) Ella Parker.

625 iii. **Coley L. Lockamy**, born 28 April 1910; died 12 October 1987 in Newport News, Virginia. He married **Gracie Bordeaux** who was born 14 October 1908 and died March 1982 in Clinton, Sampson County, North Carolina.

Coley and Gracie had three children.

626 iv. **Lacy Raeford Lockamy**, born 21 October 1914; died 24 October 1930 in Sampson County, North Carolina.

Lacy was buried in the Johnson Cemetery on Parkersburg Road, Sampson County.

627 v. **Annie Evelene Lockamy**, born 07 September 1917; died 1973. She married (1) **Henry Almond Bryant**; born 29 January 1909; died 23 January 1973. She married (2) **Joe Albert Balkcum.**

She is listed as "Evelyn" in the 1920 census. She and Henry were buried in the Carter Cemetery on Hwy 411 about 4.8 miles south of McDaniels Crossroads, Sampson County, North Carolina. Five children.

209. Grover Cleveland Lockerman (Orpah Caroline[4] Holland, Henry[3], Thomas William[2], Unknown[1]) was born 30 March 1885 in Sampson County, North Carolina, and died 24 April 1971 in Cumberland County, North Carolina. He married **Tamar Hall** 03 May 1912 in North Carolina, daughter of Isaac Hall and Berilla West. She was born 09 August 1894 in Cedar Creek Township, Cumberland County, North Carolina, and died 23 January 1983 in Cumberland County, North Carolina.

Most records lists Grover's surname as "Lockamy." His delayed certificate of birth lists "Lockerman." The date of 24 April 1973 can also be found for his death.

Tamar was listed as "Thelma" on Grover's registration card for WW I. The 1920 census records her as "Tammar." "North Carolina Death Collection, 1908-1996," found on Ancestry.

com records that Tamar Hall Lockamy, was born 9 August 1895 and died 23 January 1983 in Fayetteville, Cumberland County, North Carolina at age 87 and shows she was divorced. She was listed as "Tamar" with her parents, Isaac J. Hall and Berilla J. Hall (nee West,) in the 1900 census for Cumberland County, North Carolina. It is mentioned in "The Wests of the Cape Fear Valley," by Fred West, PHD, that "Grover" went to Baltimore.

Clearly, there are problems with the years of birth listed on Ancestry.com for her and her brothers, Hector and Harvey. I have checked years of birth listed in the Social Security Death Index and have changed them to reflect those dates.

Tamar was buried in Cumberland Memorial Gardens, Cumberland County, North Carolina

Children of Grover Lockerman and Tamar Hall are:

629 i. **Leal Lockamy**, born about 1914.

Her name is difficult to make out in the 1920 census, but it appears to be "Lealfene" which might have been "Josephine."

630 ii. **Rossie Darman Lockamy**, born 25 October 1915 in Cumberland County, North Carolina; died February 1971. She married **Alexander House** 19 December 1929.

631 iii. **Clara Belle Lockamy**, born 05 September 1917 in Cumberland County, North Carolina.

632 iv. **Grover Clayton Lockamy**, born 24 August 1919 in Cumberland County.

633 v. **Hazel Berline Lockamy**, born 10 September 1921 in Cumberland County.

634 vi. **Ruth Doris Lockamy**, born 15 October 1923 in Cumberland County, North Carolina. She married Guy Little.

635 vii. **Catherine Elizabeth Lockamy**, born 15 October 1926 in Cedar Creek Township, Cumberland County. She married Living Warren.

210. Vander B. Lockamy (Orpah Caroline[4] Holland, Henry[3], Thomas William[2], Unknown[1]) was born 01 December 1888, and died March 1982 in Fayetteville, North Carolina. He married **Bertha Hair**. She was born about 1896 in Autryville, North Carolina.

His middle name looks like "Smith" in the 1900 Census index records for Cumberland County, North Carolina. In 1910, 1920 and 1930 census records for Cedar Creek Township, Cumberland County, North Carolina, his name is listed as Vander B. Lockamy.

Child of Vander Lockamy and Bertha Hair is:

636 i. **Raeford Bascomb Lockamy**, born 11 December 1921 in Sampson County, North Carolina; died 02 January 1987 in Fayetteville, Cumberland County, North Carolina.

Raeford was single on the 18 December 1945, when he enlisted to serve in WW II. His civilian occupation was Physical Therapy Technician or Chain Store Manager.

215. Alger Rose Holland (Stephen Senter4, Henry3, Thomas William2, Unknown1) was born 20 June 1875 in Honeycutts Township, Sampson County, North Carolina, and died 19 July 1965 in Honeycutts Township, Sampson County. He married **(1) Ida E. Culbreth** about 1899, daughter of Alexander Culbreth and Christain (maiden name unknown). Ida was born July 1879 in Cedar Creek Township, Cumberland County, North Carolina, and died before 1902. Alger married **(2) Ella Jane Howell** before 1905(?), daughter of David James Howell and Catherine Carter. She was born 08 April 1884 in Cedar Creek Township in Cumberland County, North Carolina, and died 28 December 1915 in Honeycutts Township, Sampson County, North Carolina. He married **(3) Tomzil Clide Holland** 08 August 1916 in Residence of Jordan Holland, Sampson County, North Carolina, daughter of Jordan Holland and Mary Autry. She was born 23 December 1888 in Sampson County, North Carolina, and died 07 September 1953. Her certificate of death notes that she died in the City of Clinton. My memory is that she died at home, but perhaps she was taken to the Sampson County Memorial Hospital in Clinton, known today as the Sampson Regional Medical Center.

The 1900 Federal Census for Honeycutts Township, Sampson County, North Carolina, shows Alger as head of household with his first wife, Ida E., who was born in July 1879, aged 20 yrs. A family member has indicated that his first wife was, Ida or Ada, and she either died during the birth of a son or soon after; the son died either during birth or soon after. In 1906, Alger was listed as "Algier Holland," aged 31, in the Voters' Registration for White Oak Township, Bladen County, North Carolina. Both he and his brother, John Wesley, registered in the same township on 26 October 1906.

Alger Rose and "Senter" the middle name of his father, Stephen Senter Holland, and "Alderman" (Almond?) were three unusual names in my Holland line. I also found a "Senter" Holland in Onslow County, North Carolina. Alger (Algier?) Marvin Holland was a grandson of Harfrey Holland. Some descendants of Harfrey adamantly deny any relationship between the descendants of Daniel Holland and Henry Holland, yet members of my family told me that Alger Rose Holland and his third wife, Tomzil Clyde Holland, were distant cousins on the Holland side. Tomzil was a descendant of Harphrey. Finally, I found a transcribed copy of the will of Thomas William Holland; that copy and a copy of the will I found in the Sampson County Courthouse in Clinton, North Carolina, listed Daniel Holland and Henry Holland as sons of Thomas William Holland. Other sources show Daniel Holland was the father of Harfrey (Harphrey) and Henry was the grandfather of Alger Rose.

The 1900 census shows Alger Rose and his wife, Ida, living near "Amma Holland" and his wife, Lillie L. (Lillie L. Horne.) Amma was the son of "Harfrey Holland." Other children of Harfrey and their families were also living nearby. Another descendant says that the families lived across the creek from each other! Cousins of this descendant have indicated that Alger Rose and this descendant had the same great-great-great-grandfather. Records show that this possible common ancestor would have been great-great-grandfather to Alger, not 3rd great-grandfather. A daughter of Alger Rose Holland could not remember all the details, but told me that he explained how the Holland families who settled in the area were related and three Holland Brothers had settled in Sampson County. This daughter remembered writing down some of the data, but she was unable to find her notes.

I also found data on Ancestry.com that states there were three Holland brothers who initially settled in Virginia. I have not determined whether descendants of these three brothers are in any way related to the Hollands in Sampson County, North Carolina. It is interesting that research indicates the Hollands in Virginia and some of the Hollands in Sampson County, North Carolina, tell of descending from three Holland brothers who immigrated to the new world. Many given names were the same in the early Hollands in Virginia as those found in Sampson County, North Carolina; however, more research is needed on naming patterns for these families and this would probably not be conclusive since many early Holland family records in Virginia were burned when most of a town that was once called "Holland," burned. As mentioned elsewhere in notes for early Hollands in Sampson County, at least one of these early Hollands moved to Georgia.

Dicey (Dicy) A. Holland and her son Mallet (Malet, Malette) were also living near Alger in 1900. Her husband, Joel Holland, was deceased and both Joel and Dicey were distant cousins of Alger.

Tradition indicates a document exists that records one Holland ancestor was an indentured servant and four years of his remaining time was apparently bought out by his father-in-law. He may have been bound to someone who was to teach him a trade. This document is very old and I understand it is no longer shared with anyone. Perhaps data from this document could clear up some unanswered questions.

On 25 January 1919, A. R. (Alger) and "Tomzial" Holland sold 25 acres to her brother, Anderson Holland, for the sum of $500. This land was in Little Coharie Township, Sampson County, North Carolina joining the lands of C. C. Holland. Tomzil was examined separately to make sure she sold voluntarily.

About August, 1920, Joseph Jackson (Joel Jackson) asked Alger Rose and Tomzil, his third (fourth?) wife, whether they and their children would like to move into his home and care for him, his wife, Hepsie, and their daughter, Sallie; in return he would give them his farm. Alger and Tomzil agreed. Apparently, Sallie had health problems and died before 1930. Alger Rose's mother and Hepsie were first cousins and apparently, part of the farm Hepsie and "Joel" owned was given to Hepsie by her mother; I have been unable to determine wheather a part of it was owned by the family of Joseph (Joel) Jackson.. It is said that a relative of Joseph lived in a small house near the property and cousins of Oscar Davis Jackson (husband of Alger's daughter, Robertha) visited this man and called him "Uncle." These cousins probably would have visited him between 1930-1935. This man is said to have had a dark complexion and I have been unable to identify him. Descendants of Alger Rose and Tomzil still live on this land.

One tract of land that Joseph (Joel) and Hepsie Jackson deeded to Alger Rose Holland on 18 August 1920 was bounded "on the North by the lands of John Royal, on the East by the lands of A. S. Lockerman, on the South by the lands of John McKenzie and P. B. Lockerman, on the West by the lands of Mr. Gussie Rachels containing 43 acres more or less." The second tract they deeded to Alger Rose was bounded "on the North by the lands of Tom Crumpler, on the East by the lands of said Tom Crumpler, and on the West by the lands of A. S. Lockerman containing 25 acres of land..." Tom Crumpler was "Micajah Thomas Crumpler," father of William Stacy Crumpler. A. S. Lockerman was probably Alexander Stuart Lockerman and P. B. may have been Preston Brooks Lockerman.

On the same day Hepsie was examined to determine whether she freely and voluntarily signed the deed! Deed was filed on 3 September 1920 and Recorded on 7 September 1920.

On 23 September 1921 Joel J. Jackson, Hepsie Jackson, A. R. Holland and Thomsal (Tomzil) Holland sold to Augusta Rachels two acres of land for $100. This land began at "a stake on the run of "**Little Bear Skin**" in the Currie line just above the Bridge at the Rachel overflow and runs S. 25, W. 46 poles to a stake in the Rachel line, thence S. 65, E. 8 poles to a stake, thence N. 25, E. 46 poles to the run of said Little Bear Skin, thence up the run of of the said Bear Skin to the beginning corner." Both wives were examined on 26 September 1921 to determine whether they voluntarily signed the deed. Deed was filed January 25, 1923 and Recorded 29 January 1923.

Little Bear Skin (known today as **BEARSKIN BRANCH)** crosses Crumpler Mill Road, feeds Crumpler Mill Pond, known as Stacy Crumpler's Pond, and the race leading from the dam and Grist Mill crosses again under Crumpler Mill Road and flows into **Bearskin** (Creek or Stream?) that runs for miles through Bearskin Swamp.

Alger Rose purchased 25 acres on 28 March 1922 from A. S. Lockerman and wife, Meliar for the sum of $1,000. This land was across the road from the above mentioned land and was bounded on one side by the road and on the other side by high water marks of Crumplers Mill Pond.

Grandma Tomzil Clide died from a Cardiovascular Accident (2 days) due to Hypertension (15 years.) The certificate of death for Alger Rose Holland shows he died of Generalized Arteriosclerosis (had for years), bronchopneumonia, ASHD and Uremia. On the certificate, his father's name is spelled 'Center.' The correct spelling is Stephen Senter (Scenter) Holland. Alger Rose Holland and his last wife, Tomzil Clyde Holland were buried in Zoar Penecostal Free Will Baptist Church Cemetery near Salemburg, North Carolina

Adaline has also been given for Ida's name. It is said that she died of tuberculosis.

A family member tells, and Ella Jane's certificate of death confirms that her cause of death was consumption (Tuberculosis). The doctor entered "Hereditary" (interesting?) for a contributing factor. The cause of death of daughter, Lucile, was Pots Disease and Tuberculosis.

Mary J. (probably Jane), Mamie Lee, and Lucile were born on the same day. Ella Jane and these triplets daughters are buried in the Stephen Senter Holland Cemetery.

A family member tells that a Black woman whom they called "Aunt Phoebe" was hired to come in and take care of Ella Jane and Lucile. Other family members were not allowed to go into their room and dishes and silverware used by them were kept separated from those used by others in the family.

My notes say Grandma Ella Jane's tombstone records 08 April 1882 for her birth; her certificate of death reads 08 April 1884. It is possible I copied the date incorrectly from her tombstone; some of the stones in the cemetery were eroded.

On 15 December 1915, ten days before her death, Ella Jane and Alger Rose (A.R.), two of her sisters and their spouses and her brother, C. M. (Charles (Charlie), and his spouse sold to her brother, D. J. (David James) forty acres of land for fifty dollars. The following signed the deed:

Dona (Dona Howell) Diker and George W. Diker; Charlotte (Howell) Faircloth and J. H. Faircloth; C. M. (Charlie McPherson Howell) and Blanche Howell.

Excerpts from the deed:

"...the 15th day of December, A.D., 1915, by and between C. M. Howell and Blanche Howell, his wife, both of the County of Bladen, and State of North Carolina, J. H. Faircloth and Charlotte A. Faircloth, his wife, both of the County of Cumberland and State of North Carolina, A. R. Holland and Ella Holland his wife, both of the County of Sampson, and State of North Carolina, and G. W. Diker and Dona Diker, his wife, both of the Town of Randall and State of Iowa, parties of the first part, and D. J. Howell of the County of Cumberland and State of North Carolina, party of the second part.

"...the sum of Fifty Dollars to them in hand paid by the party of the second part...and convey to the said D. J. Howell his heirs and assigns, their entire undivided interest in and to... land, situated ... in Cedar Creek Township, Cumberland County, State of North Carolina, adjoining the lands of H. C. Carter, A. C. Hair and others...

"... Jonathan Carter's corner; thence ... Mary C. Carter's corner; ... containing 40 acres, ..described in a deed from Henry C. Carter and wife to Kitty L. Howell, dated May 18, 1882, and recorded in Book "F" No. 4, page 366, in the office of the Register of Deed for Cumberland County.

"It is the intention of this deed to convey to the said D. J. Howell...land descended to the said...upon the death of the said **Kitty L. Howell** and the interest of each being a one-seventh undivided interest..." This property was near Vander in Cumberland County.

All of the women were examined by a Notary Public to make sure they had signed voluntarily. Dona Diker was examined in the County of Hamilton and State of Iowa, Ella Jane in the County of Sampson, North Carolina and the others in Cumberland County.

Either Grandpa Alger Rose and Grandma Ella Jane had bought land in Bladen County or she also had inherited land from her father that was in "Turnbull Township, Bladen County, North Carolina, adjoining the lands of B. S. Melvin, Tom Avery, W. J. West and others. ...beginning ...Hog Pen Branch ... to Alex Melvin to Wesley Holland's corner. After Grandma Ella Jane died, Grandpa Alger sold this land to his brother-in-law, Uncle Charles McPherson Howell on 17 Janury 1916 for $400." Book 64, page 547, Bladen County, North Carolina. I did not copy the number of acres! This land was very near the Cumberland County border and was probably where the Carter and Howell families lived before moving to the Cedar Creek area in Cumberland County. This may have been the reason, Uncle Charles M. Howell wanted my parents to move to his farm and take care of him and his second wife; in return he offered to build them a house and give them at least part of his large acreage. Uncle Charles'(Charlie) son and his son's wife were not interested in returning to the farm and he probably wanted to keep the land in the family. My dad refused to move where the bears visited the corn field for their share of the corn.

The certificate of death for Alger's son, James Senter Holland, lists James' mother as "**Loraine Howard**" which indicates she would have been the second wife of Grandpa Alger and the mother of Rose Annie and James Senter. This is the only document that shows Loraine's name, but see data below for children of Ella Jane. My mother, Roberta, spoke fondly of the Howards and this may explain why. In the event that Grandfather Alger did marry Loraine Howard, their marriage may have been a short one and I have found no record of this except the certificate of death for James Senter Holland.

Grandpa Alger and Ella Jane had tripletts as noted below and records I have found indicate that several sets of twin were born in the families of his siblings. Grandpa Alger had twin sisters who died young. His brother, John Westley had twins (one of them died young), his brother, Jasper, had twins and one of them died young and a great-granddaughter of Jasper has twins. Several months after I married, I aborted a fetus after only about six or seven weeks of pregnancy. My mother-in-law, told me it looked like I was pregnant with twins. At the time, I clearly believed it was highly unlikely; today, I understand that she may have been correct.

When Alger and Ella Jane's triplett daughters, Mamie Lee, Lucile and Mary J. were born, the certificate of birth for Mamie Lee shows she was born at 3:00 a.m. on the 29 May 1914. The certificate of birth for Mary J. shows 7:45 a.m. on the same day for her birth; it notes she was the sixth child born to her mother including Mary J., and five were living. I only have a certificate of death for Lucile and it does show she was born on 29 May 1914 and a death date of 25 September 1915. The certificate of birth for Mary J. indicates the child not living out of six children must have been Mamie Lee who died between 3 - 7:45 a.m.; we know of no other earlier deceased child of Ella Jane. The number of births and deaths on Mary J.'s certificate of birth also support the information on the certificate of death for James Senter Holland that "Loraine Howard" and Alger Rose Holland were his parents and Loraine must have also been the mother of Annie Rose. When we include Rose Annie and James Senter in the number of children born to Ella Jane, we have eight born to her with seven living which doesn't work with the numbers on Mary J's certificate of birth. This is the data that is recorded.

It is possible that Aunt Lady could not remember correctly, but she did provide the full name "Loraine Howard" for Uncle Senter's (Scenter) mother and other births noted above support it; I'm inclined to believe her. However, others believe that Uncle Senter was the son of Alger and Ella Jane and my data below reflects this.

For about two years after they were married, Grandpa Alger and Grandma Tomzil lived in a large two story home that was in the area where the Howards lived; they then moved to a large, one story home that was in the same area. Grandma Tomzil was pregnant while living in the two story home and commented that she would never again live where she had to walk up and down stairs.

Child of Alger Holland and Ida Culbreth is:

637 i. **Lonnie Perry Holland**, born 16 July 1900 in Bladen County, North Carolina.

He either died at birth or soon after. Written in my mother's old Bible is "Daniel P. Holland. 10 September 1900." This notation could mean that Lonnie Perry Holland's first name was Daniel rather than Lonnie and he lived for about two months. Lonnie's date of birth was provided to me by an aunt. This old Bible appears to have belonged to the parents or grandparents of Ella Jane Howell and was possibly a Carter or Howell Family Bible. See Roberta Holland for a few more notations found in this old Bible.

Children of Alger Holland and Ella Howell are:

638 i. **Rose Annie Holland**, born 14 November 1904.

She was either stillborn or died young. Her middle name may have been 'Marie.' In an old Bible of my mother is a notation: "Rosey A. Holland was born 13 Nov.(?) 1904. Perhaps Rose Annie was born on the 13th and died on 14 November 1904. My Aunt gave me the date of 14 November 1904 from her records.

\+ 639 ii. **James Senter Holland**, born 09 December 1905 in Elizabethtown, Bladen County, North Carolina; died 01 April 1988 in Garland, Sampson County, North Carolina.

\+ 640 iii. **John Wesley Holland**, born 17 October 1907 in Sampson County(?), North Carolina; died 01 April 1998 in Sampson County.

\+ 641 iv. **Roberta Holland**, born 01 September 1910 in Bladen County, North Carolina; died 22 January 1985 in Sampson County Memorial Hospital, Clinton, North Carolina.

\+ 642 v. **Dellar Jane Holland**, born 15 October 1912 near Salemburg, Sampson County, North Carolina; died 05 September 1979 in Clinton, Sampson County.

643 vi. **Mamie Lee Holland**, born 29 May 1914 in Honeycutts Township, Sampson County; records show she must have died between 3:00 – 7:45 A.M. on the day she was born.

644 vii. **Mary J. Holland**, born 29 May 1914 in Honeycutts Township, Sampson County, North Carolina; died before September 1915. She died from tuberculosis.

645 viii. **Lucile Holland** was born 29 May 1914 in Honeycutts Township, Sampson County and died 20 September 1915 in Honeycutts Township, Sampson County. Pots disease and tuberculosis are shown for cause of death. See notes above about these triplets.

Children of Alger Holland and Tomzil Holland are:

646 i. **Raymond Lee Holland**, born 16 August 1914; died 19 March 1986.

"Laymond Lee Holland" and 16 August 1914 are listed on his certificate of birth; his tombstone may read 16 August 1915(?)

The 1920 census lists "Raymond Hall" for his name. He never married and was buried in Zoar Free Will Baptist Church Cemetery near Salemburg, Sampson County, North Carolina.

\+ 647 ii. **Katie Dell Holland**, born 20 April 1917 in Honeycutts Township, Sampson County, North Carolina; died 02 March 1998.

+ 648 iii. **George Bizzell Holland**, born 30 April 1919; died 10 August 1997 in Sampson Regional Medical Center, Clinton, Sampson County, North Carolina.

649 iv. **Lillie Bell Holland**, born 14 January 1921 in Honeycutts Township, Sampson County, North Carolina; died 27 June 1921 in Honeycutts Township, Sampson County, North Carolina.

She is buried in Stephen Senter Holland Family Cemetery. Personal knowledge of living sister shows that her middle name may have been 'Belle.'

650 v. **Ludie Hazelene Holland**, born 15 July 1922 in Honeycutts Township, Sampson County, North Carolina; died 09 April 1923 in Honeycutts Township, Sampson County, North Carolina.

+ 651 vi. **Freda Augustus Holland**, born 25 July 1924 in Sampson County and died 2 April 2008 in Sampson County..

216. Jasper Lee Holland (Stephen Senter[4], Henry[3], Thomas William[2], Unknown[1]) was born 12 July 1877 in Honeycutts Township, Sampson County, North Carolina, and died 25 March 1944 in Honeycutts Township, Sampson County, North Carolina. He married **Dallie Alice Lockerman** 24 January 1900 in Sampson County, North Carolina, daughter of Hugh Lockerman and Olivia Holland. She was born 29 May 1881 in Sampson County, North Carolina, and died 18 September 1958 in Salemburg, North Carolina.

"Jaspey Holland" appears for his name in the **Old Holland Record Book**. You may find images from that book near the back of this book.

Will of Jasper Holland: Filed 28 March 1944:

"Having conveyed all my real estate to certain of my children without conveying any of it to one of my children and four of my granchildren, I now make provisions for said daughter and granchildren in lieu of real estate.

"1) Seawell Holland Roberts $...

"2) To my four grandchildren: to wit: Pauline Smith and Adel Smith, children of daughter Floy Smith and to Orlando L. Holland and Bobby Brewer Holland, children of my deceased son Orlando Holland, each $... in cash and ($... to be loaned and invested for them by said ... and paid to them at age 21 to go toward their education.)

"Attention: Pauline Smith, 01 February 1946; Adel Smith, 15 September 1947; Orlando L. Holland, 24 September 1955; Bobby Brewer Holland 21 October 1957."

The remainder of his estate was left to his wife, Dallie, if living and if not to be equally divided between all issues. Dallie and James Minson Holland, Executors. Book 10, Pages 331-335.

His nickname was Jap. He died from cancer of the stomach with ?, and Dallie Alice died of Congested Heart Failure (6 months) due to chronic brochitis, pulmonary fibrosis and emphysema (several years.). Jasper and Dallie Alice were buried in Salemburg Cemetery, Salemburg, North Carolina.

Her name was also spelled 'Dollie' and 'Dahlie.' On the certificate of death for her son, Jimmy Minson Holland, she is listed as Dallie Brock. On his application for a social security card, her son, Henry Lee (Coy) Holland gives her name as "Dallie Alice Lockamy." On the certificate of birth for her daughter, Seawell, "Malissa Seawell Holland" is written with a line across "Malissa" and Dallie's name is shown as "Allie May Della Lockerman" with a line through "Allie May Della" and "Dallie" written above it. On a certificate of birth for Mary Elizabeth Holland, her daughter, Dallia's name appears as "Alice Madelia Lockamy"

Children are listed above under (203) Dallie Alice Lockerman.

218. Henry Holland (Stephen Senter[4], Henry[3], Thomas William[2], Unknown[1]) was born 17 March 1882 in Sampson County, North Carolina, and died 04 June 1950 in Honeycutts Township, Sampson County. He married **Rossie Davis Royal** 26 February 1908 in Residence of Murd McKenzie in Sampson County, daughter of Marshall Royal and Panolia Lockerman. She was born 05 November 1888 in Sampson County, North Carolina, and died 22 May 1973 in Sampson County Memorial Hospital, Clinton, North Carolina.

On 27 February 1904, this Henry purchased 46 acres on the edge of Crane Branch in Honeycutts Township in Sampson County, from L. M. Tew and his wife, Ellen Tew for the sum of $245. Mentioned in the deed is S. A. Howard and H. J. Lockerman. Crane Branch must have been a small stream near Salemburg in Honeycutts Township that I cannot specifically find on any map;

Rossie's middle name is given as "Davis" on the certificate of birth for Letha Pearl, her daughter. Henry's certificate of death gives his date of birth as 17 March **1883**. Cause of death: Rhumatoid arthritis (20 years). Rossie Davis died from Carcinoma of the Breast with Carcimonatosis (18 months?) She also had ASHD with CHF. She is buried in Zoar Church Cemetery, Salemburg, North Carolina.

Henry Holland and Rossie Davis were buried in Zoar Pentecostal FWB Church Cemetery near Salemburg, Sampson County, North Carolina.

Children of Henry Holland and Rossie Royal are:

+ 652 i. **Clyda Louise Holland**, born 11 January 1909 in Sampson County; died 08 July 1997.

+ 653 ii. **Laudie Mae Holland** was born 20 October 1912 in Sampson County and died 22 August 1993 in Mary-Gran Nursing Center, Clinton, Sampson County, North Carolina.

+ 654 iii. **Letha Pearl Holland**, born 08 April 1915 in Honeycutts Township, Sampson County, North Carolina; died April 2001.

219. John Wesley Holland (Stephen Senter[4], Henry[3], Thomas William[2], Unknown[1]) was born 03 May 1884 in Sampson County, North Carolina, and died 06 February 1966 in Bladen County, North Carolina. He married **Estie Dwight Johnson** who was born 01 March 1881 and died 21 August 1935.

One source records him as "John Wesley Holland." His certificate of death records "John Holland" died of Cardiac Arrest in Dorothea Dix Hospital in Raleigh, North Carolina. When I was young, this institution was known as a state hospital for the insane. His certificate of death **incorrectly names** "Lester S. Holland" for his father and correctly names Nancy Hudson for his mother. When I called the hospital in 2006 about copies of records for a great aunt who had also died there, I was informed that all records between 1935 and 1978 have been destroyed. The hospital was scheduled to permanently close in 2007.

I can understand that the hospital records were probably destroyed to save the expense of storage, but I personally believe a summary of the patients' history should have been placed somewhere, perhaps in the state archives and the state probably has copies.

Names mentioned in Deeds indicate Wesley may have owned either part of the old Tatum property in Bladen County, North Carolina, or his land joined it. A corner of his land joined the property of Grandma Ella Jane's brother, Uncle Charles McPherson Howell. One source on the internet lists his name as "John Wesley Holland." I have found it listed only as "Wesley," but he had an uncle and a great uncle named John.

Deed Book 60, page 51 in Bladen County, North Carolina, records that Uncle Wesley bought 156 acres from L. A. Tatum.

Wesley Holland and wife, Estee held a mortgate note on 285 acres of land owned by Richard Tatum on the NE side of Spring Branch.. The first payment for $166.33 was due 21 October 1912, the second of $166.33 was due on 21 October 1913 and the third in the same amount was due one year later. They probably sold Richard Tatum this land. On 25 November 1935, they sold Richard a tract of 50 acres known as the Margaret and Davis draw in the division of said land that joined the above land.

On 28 March 1923, Uncle Wesley and Estee sold land for $234 to W. W. Watson and Sarah A. Watson on the edge of Cypress Pond that adjoined land of Fowler Hews (sp) and W. W. Watson.

Wesley and Estie Dwight were buried in Windsor United Methodist Church Cemetery in the Ammon Community of Bladen County, North Carolina.

Children of John Holland and Estie Johnson are:

655 i. **Ronnie Maude Holland**, a twin, was born 15 January 1910 and died 26 December 1997. She married **Ottis R. Bordeaux**; born 07 August 1912; died 02 May 1983.

No Children. A nephew, Franklin Bordeaux lived near and he and his family took care of Ottis and Ronnie Maude in their later years. Ronnie Maude fell and broke her hip in October 1992. My sister, her husband, and I, stopped by to see Ronnie Maude a few months before she died. She did not know who we were and apparently didn't remember our parents, but she seemed happy even though she was bedridden. A daughter of Franklin was with her that day. Her room and bed were immaculate. The house was the home place of her father.

Ronnie Maude and Ottis were buried in Windsor United Methodist Church Cemetery on Hwy 242, north of Turnbull Creek in the Ammon Community of Bladen County, North Carolina.

656 ii. **Donnie Holland**, born 15 January 1910.

She died young and was a twin of Ronnie Maude.

221. Sanford Holland (Stephen Senter[4], Henry[3], Thomas William[2], Unknown[1]) was born 26 August 1887 in Sampson County, North Carolina, and died 04 April 1957 in Honeycutts Township, Sampson County. He married **Flora Mae Royal** 23 February 1912 in Horse Pen Branch, Sampson County, North Carolina, daughter of Marshall Royal and Panolia Lockerman. She was born 22 August 1893, and died 18 January 1983.

His World War I Registration Card notes that he lived in Erwin and worked in the Cotton Mills in Duke (now known as Erwin), in Harnett County, North Carolina. Transactions show that when in Sampson County, he lived on land that was part of the R.C. Turlington land near L. B. Owens' corner.

Flora Mae's middle name is also given as "May." On the certificate of birth for son, Earl Gibson, her name looks like "Rlora M. Royal."

Sanford's cause of death was Broncho pneumonia (one week) and Cerebro Vascular Accident (1-1/2 yrs.). He and Flora Mae were buried in Zoar Pentecostal Free Will Baptist Church Cemetery, Salemburg, North Carolina.

Children of Sanford Holland and Flora Royal are:

657 i. **Stacy Clifton Holland**, born 05 February 1918 in Harnett County, North Carolina, USA.

658 ii. **Earl Gibson Holland**, born 15 August 1920 in Harnett County and was murdered in his home on 12 November 1998 in Erwin, Harnett County, North Carolina, USA. He was buried in Erwin Memorial Park in Erwin, Harnett County. He was murdered in his home.

659 iii. **Horrace Latham Holland**, born 29 September 1924 in Harnett County, North Carolina, and died 29 May 2004 in Loris, South Carolina.

660 iv. **Beatrice May Holland**, born 13 September 1926 in Harnett County, North Carolina, USA. She married first **Willie James Benton** who was born 9 August 1918 and died 13 September 1977. They were buried in Salemburg Cemetery on Bearskin Road in Salemburg, Sampson County, North Carolina. Beatrice married second **Allen Carlton Tew**, son of Owen Dallas Tew and Bettie Jane Wrench. Carlton was born 5 September 1922 and died 22 September 2001. He and his first wife, **Melba Merle** Tyner were buried in Sunrise Memorial Gardens on Highway 242 between Salemburg and Roseboro in Sampson County, North Carolina.

661 v. **Charles Linwood Holland** was born 24 November 1929 in Harnett County and died 29 September 2006.

662 vi. **Frances Evonne Holland**.died 29 March 2002 in Orlando, Florida. She married a "Cockerham."

664 vii. **Carolyn Elizabeth Holland**, born 15 March 1936 in Harnett County, North Carolina, USA. She married Donald Wrench.

222. Miles Holland (Stephen Senter[4], Henry[3], Thomas William[2], Unknown[1]) was born 07 September 1889 in Honeycutts Township, Sampson County, North Carolina, and died 30 March 1974 in Honeycutts Township, Sampson County, North Carolina. He married **Cornelia Butler** 12 May 1916 in Residence of M. H. Alexander, Minister; Sampson County, daughter of Bennett Butler and Sarah Royal. She was born between 11 August 1881 - 1882 in Sampson County and died 05 June 1959.

Middle name may have been "Colton" or Clayton. Miles served in World War I and was in France when his son, Miles Clayton was born. He and Cornelia were buried in Zoar Pentecostal Free Will Baptist Church Cemetery, Salemburg, North Carolina.

Children of Miles Holland and Cornelia Butler are:

+ 665 i. **Miles Clayton Holland**, born 30 September 1918 in Honeycutts Township, Sampson County, North Carolina; died 22 August 1993 in Honeycutts Township.

666 ii. **Stillborn Girl Holland**, born 31 January 1921 in Huntley, Sampson County, North Carolina.

667 iii. **Janie Pearl Holland** was born 09 October 1922 in Honeycutts Township, Sampson County and died 28 January 1968. She married **Ernest A. Tyndall** after January 1949; he was born 21 July 1903; died 21 July 1982.

Janie Pearl and Ernest were buried in Owens Grove PFWB Church Cemetery near Kitty Fork, Sampson County, North Carolina. His name is 'Ernie A.' on his tombstone and is found in census and other records as Earnest.

223. Angolda Holland (Stephen Senter[4], Henry[3], Thomas William[2], Unknown[1]) was born 23 September 1891 in Honeycutts Township, Sampson County, North Carolina, and died 27 October 1958 in Honeycutts Township, Sampson County. She married **Ransom Columbus Warren** 30 January 1918 in Sampson County, North Carolina. He was born 14 July 1888, and died 14 August 1961 in Sampson County.

"Goldie" is listed on her tombstone and in transcribed records of the 1920 Federal Census for Sampson County, North Carolina, their last name is incorrectly spelled "Marren." Aunt Angolda and Uncle Ransom were buried in Zoar Pentecostal FWB Church Cemetery on Zoar Church Rd, Sampson County, North Carolina.

Children of Angolda Holland and Ransom Warren are:

668 i. **Almeta Warren,** born about 1914.

669 ii. **Elvin J. Warren**, born 04 June 1920; died 02 March 1937 in Sampson County, North Carolina. He accidentally shot himself and was buried in Zoar Pentecostal FWB Church Cemetery on Zoar Church Rd, Sampson County.

670 iii. **Murkus R. Warren,** born 23 January 1922; died 06 January 1996. He married Lillie (Maiden Name Unknown).

He is buried in Zoar Pentecostal FWB Church Cemetery on Zoar Church Road (SR 1322) near Salemburg in Sampson County.

+ 671 iv. **Eva D. Warren** was born 20 May 1923 and died 3 November 2008.

672 v. **Eunice B. Warren**, born 12 December 1924; died 14 August 1991. She married Unknown Shell. She was buried in Zoar Pentecostal FWB Church Cemetery on Zoar Church Road (SR 1322) near Salemburg in Sampson County, North Carolina.

673 vi. **Clara Mae Warren**, born 21 June 1928; died 01 August 1928.

She was buried in Zoar Pentecostal FWB Church Cemetery on Zoar Church Rd, Sampson County.

674 vii. **James Lester Warren**, born 28 October 1926; died 20 January 2001. He married Joan (maiden name known.) who died 19 April 2008.

Both were buried in Zoar Pentecostal FWB Church Cemetery on Zoar Church Road (SR 1322) near Salemburg in Sampson County.

226. Stephen Senter Holland, Jr. (Stephen Senter[4], Henry[3], Thomas William[2], Unknown[1]) was born 08 February 1898 in Honeycutts Township, Sampson County, North Carolina, and died 19 February 1978 in Honeycutts Township. He married **(1) Sallie Corinn Lewis** 21 November 1921, daughter of John Lewis and Ada Sessoms. She was born 08 March 1905 in Sampson County and died 02 September 1959 near Salemburg, Sampson County, North Carolina. He married **(2) Mattie Ruth Jackson** after 1959, daughter of Haburn Rice Jackson and Molsey Naylor. She was born 01 September 1912 in Honeycutts Township, Sampson County and died 18 May 2006.

He was called 'Bud(d).' cause of death: ASHD with Fibrilation (5 years.) Sallie Corinn died from a Coronary Thrombosis. She and Bud were buried in Salemburg Cemetery, Salemburg, North Carolina.

Mattie Ruth was buried near her first husband, **Miles Simpson Parker,** in Corinth Baptist Church Cemetery on Corinth Church Road (SR 1326), Sampson County, North Carolina

Children of Stephen Holland and Sallie Lewis are:

675 i. **James Frederick Holland**, born 03 October 1925 in Sampson County and died 25 August 2001 in Fayetteville, Cross Creek Township, Cumberland County, North Carolina.

I also have the date of 4 October 1925 for his birth.

+ 676 ii. **Elizabeth Inez Holland**, born 21 October 1927.

677 iii. **Naomi Slylisteen Holland**, born 13 December 1932.

227. Sylvester Holland (Alderman McKay[4], Henry[3], Thomas William[2], Unknown[1]) was born March 1877 in Cumberland County, North Carolina. He married **Jennie (Maiden Name Unknown)**. She was born about 1880.

He served in Spanish American War. Private, Second Regiment, Company A. Lived in Roseboro, North Carolina, for a time, and later in 1910, lived on the Clinton Road in Mars Hill Township, Cumberland County, North Carolina.

Children of Sylvester Holland and Jennie Unknown are:

678 i. **Ethel Holland**, born about 1902.

679 ii. **Lottie Holland**, born about 1908.

680 iii. **Lester William Holland**, born 08 September 1909; died 08 August 1959 in Cumberland County, North Carolina.

230. Archie L. Holland (Alderman McKay[4], Henry[3], Thomas William[2], Unknown[1]) was born February 1889 in Cumberland County, North Carolina, and died 27 May 1925 in Chatham County, North Carolina. He married **Maude L. Ward**. She was born about 1893.

His World War I Draft Registration Cards lists his date of birth as 17 January 1891. Maude's father, Jim Ward, aged 81, was living in her household in 1930.

Children of Archie Holland and Maude Ward are:

681 i. **Bertha W. Holland**, born about 1914.

682 ii. **Jessie R. Holland**, born about 1920.

683 iii. **Franklin Herbert Holland**, born about 1920.

684 iv. **Mabel N. Holland**, born about 1922.

685 v. **Catherine F. Holland**, born about 1926.

234. Malette Holland (Joel[4], John[3], Thomas William[2], Unknown[1]) was born 16 February 1878 in Sampson County and died 12 April 1948 in Eastover Township in Cumberland County, North Carolina. He married **Minnie Lee Lockamy** 06 September 1900 in Residence of Daniel Lockamy in Sampson County, North Carolina. She was born 1 August 1880 in Sampson County and died 26 March 1943 in Cross Creek Township in Cumberland County, North Carolina. She was the daughter of Daniel W. Lockamy and Charity Holland. His name is also spelled "Mallett" and "Malett." Minnie Lee died of lobar pneumonia.

Malette and Minnie Lee were distant cousins. They were buried in McMillan Church Cemetery near Wade, North Carolina.

Children of Malette Holland and Minnie Lockamy are:

i. **Lemoine Holland**, born about 1901 in Sampson County.

686 ii. **Sallie A. Holland**, born about 1906 in Sampson County, North Carolina.

687 iii. **Betty E. Holland**, born about 1908 in Sampson County.

+ 688 iv. **Addie Mae Holland**, born 20 October 1910 in Sampson County, North Carolina; died 14 October 1982 in Fayetteville, North Carolina.

689 v. **M. Melva Holland**, born about 1915 in Sampson County.

"Murusmelva" is listed incorrectly for her name in a transcribed index of the 1920 census records for Mingo Township, Sampson County, North Carolina.

690 vi. **Burnice Holland**, born about 1925 in Sampson County.

235. Cornelia Lockamy (Charity[4] Holland, John[3], Thomas William[2], Unknown[1]) was born 1877, and died 9 July 1923. She married **Nathon Evander Wrench**, son of Joseph Wrench and Ceknak (Senna) Parker. He was born 25 November 1857, and died 10 March 1947.

She was living with her parents in 1900. Nathon was listed as Marion E. Wrench in 1910 census records and he can also be found as Mason, but more often as "Nason E." and on the certificate of death for Cornelia, he was listed as "Dock" Wrench. He is listed "Nathon E. Wrench" on his own certificate of death and Joseph E. Wrench and Seniah Ann Parker are named for his parents.

Cornelia was buried in an unmarked grave in a field (old Julius House farm) off Ernie Road, Sampson County, North Carolina, but she has a tombstone in Baptist Chapel Church Cemetery on Baptist Chapel Road, Sampson County, where **Nathon E. Wrench** (Or Nason E.) was buried.

Children of Cornelia Lockamy and Mason Wrench are:

691 i. **Della Wrench**, born about 1903 in Sampson County, North Carolina.

692 ii. **Millard Wrench**, born 22 April 1906 in Sampson County, North Carolina; died 05 August 1971. He married Lillie W. Williams; born 19 August 1907; died 10 March 1978.

Millard and Lillie are buried in Baptist Chapel Church Cemetery on Baptist Chapel Road, Sampson County, North Carolina.

693 iii. **Ada Wrench**, born about 1908 in Sampson County, North Carolina.

694 iv. **Wilber Wrench**, born about 1912 in Sampson County, North Carolina.

695 v. **Mason Wrench**, born about 1917 in Sampson County, North Carolina.

240. Joseph Tilden Holland (John J.[4], John[3], Thomas William[2], Unknown[1]) was born about 1877. He married **Virgie (Maiden Name Unknown).** She was born about 1891.

He and his family lived in Florida in 1920.

Children of Joseph Holland and Virgie Unknown are:

696 **i. Odel** Holland, born about 1909.

697 ii. **William A. Holland,** born about 1914.

Generation Number 5

246. Eli Underwood Holland (Ruffin[5], James[4], Daniel[3], Thomas William[2], Unknown[1]) was born 03 October 1862 in Sampson County, North Carolina, and died 10 July 1937 in Black River Township, Cumberland County, North Carolina. He married **(1) Alice Ward** before 1893. She was born 15 July 1871, died 20 March 1901, and was the daughter of Stephen Ward and Susan Hollingsworth. He married **(2) Lillie Jones** 05 August 1901 in Flea Hill Township, Cumberland County, North Carolina. She was born 13 July 1880, and died 16 August 1952 in Godwin, Sampson County, North Carolina and was the daughter of Jackson Jones and Lillie Ann Strickland.

Eli Holland, aged 18, was a boarder in 1880 in the household of J. T. Matthews in Black River Township, Cumberland County, North Carolina; he was a "Hireling."

Child of Eli Holland and Alice Ward is:

i. **James Holland** was born about 1891 in Cumberland County.

698 ii. **Mary Catherine Holland,** born 17 April 1893; died 06 June 1977. She married **Martin McDuffy McLaurin** 19 October 1912 in Flea Hill Township, Cumberland County, North Carolina; born 01 March 1884; died 04 August 1973.

She and Martin were buried in Greenlawn Memorial Gardens north of Fuquay-Varina, North Carolina.

Children of Mary Catherine and Martin McDuffy:

Their oldest child, **Winfred McDuffy McLaurin** was born 25 July 1913 and he married on 12 November 1938 in Wade, North Carolina, **May Belle Cook**, daughter of Duncan Sewell Cook and Irene Jane Edwards of Holly Springs. May Belle was born on 11 February 1920. She and Winfred had seven children.

Robert A. McLaurin was the second child of Mary Catherne and Martin. He was born on 15 April 1915 in Black River Township, died 18 July 1916 in Black River Township and was buried in the Bluff Presbyterian Church Cemetery.

Hersey Alvin McLaurin, the third child of Mary Catherine and Martin, was born 16 June 1917 in Sampson County and died 3 January 1978 in Fayetteville. He married 12 October 1940, **Evah Louise Murray**, daughter of Doyle Bunnion Murray and Jessie Evelyn Cook. She was born 27 March 1922 in Wake County. Hersey and Evah had one child. Hersey was buried in LaFayette Memorial Park in Fayetteville, North Carolina.

Mary Isabel McLaurin, the fourth child of Mary Catherine and Martin, was born 23 September 1922 in Flea Hill Township and Mr. Rosser states that her certificate of death names 27 January 1920 for her death in Flea Hill Township. Her tombstone reads 15 January 1923 for death. She was buried at the Bluff Presbyterian Church Cemetery in Cumberland County, North Carolina. Flea Hill Township was changed to Eastover Township in 1929.

Agnes Rubelle McLaurin was the fifth child of Mary Catherine and Martin and was born on 15 August 1924 in Flea Hill Township and died 01 December 1924 in Flea Hill Township. She was also buried in Bluff Presbyterian Church cemetery.

Sula Allene McLaurin, the sixth child was born on 23 October 1925 in Black River Township. She married **William Green Raynor** on 2 June 1945 in Wade, Cumberland County, North Carolina. He was born 20 August 1920 in Banner Township in Johnston County, North Carolina, and was the son of John Green Raynor and Sarah Mandy Hudson. Allene and William have four children.

Eldred Martin McLaurin the seventh child was born on 22 August 1927 and married on 27 November 1948 to **Stella Marie Baker**, daughter of Willie E. and Lusettie Baker. Stella was born 27 December 1929. She and Eldred have two children.

Evander Troy McLaurin, a twin, was the eighth child of Mary Catherine and Martin and was born 21 July 1931 in Eastover Township in Cumberland County, North Carolina. "Tracy" married on 20 February 1955 to **Mary Ree Dickens**, daughter of Theophillus William Dickens and Eunice Arnold. Mary Ree was born 15 November 1934. She and Tracy had one child.

Eli Lacy McLaurin, a twin, was the ninth child and was born on the 21 July 1931 in Eastover Township. He married on 6 November 1955 to **Ernestine Holloman**, daughter of Charles Freeman Holloman and Tessie Fleeter Garner. She was born on 20 August 1933. Eli Lacy and Ernestine have two children.

Charles Clayton McLaurin, the tenth child of Mary Catherine and Martin, was born on 10 December 1935 and he married first on the 20 August 1955 to **Alice Marie Wilson**, daughter of Eugene McKenzie Wilson and Mamie Harris. Alice Marie was born 3 April 1937 and died 7 August 1973 in Greensboro. He was buried in Greenlawn Memorial Gardens. Charles and Alice had three children. He married second on 11 October 1974 to Catherine Bone, daughter of William Edgar Bone. I am not sure about the spelling of Catherine's maiden name, "Bone." Catherine was born 26 April 1929 and she and Charles had no children.

iii. **Clarence Holland,** third child of Eli Underwood Holland and Alice Ward was born about 1896 in Cumberland County, North Carolina.

iv. **Annie Holland, (Laura Ann Holland?**), fourth child, was born about 1898 in Cumberland County. Annie may be the **Laura Ann Lovick** for whom I found a certificate of death that states she was the daughter of Eli Holland and Alice Ward. She was born 24 August 1896 and died 16 August 1944 and, at her death she was married to Edward A. Lovick. She was buried in Old Bluff Church Cemetery near Wade, North Carolina.

Children of Eli Holland and Lillie Jones are:

i. **Sarah Lillie Holland** was born 24 July 1904 in Cumberland County, North Carolina and married **Lemon Thaddeus Starling** on 7 June 1924 in Fayetteville, Cumberland County. He was born 14 January 1902 in Sampson County, North Carolina and died 5 October 1960 in Cross Creek Township in Cumberland County and was the son of James Madison Starling and Julia Catherine Wilkes. Sarah and Lemon Thaddeus had one known child: **Doris Maxine Starling** who was born 14 September 1926 and married **Thomas Edward Lee,** Sr. on 20 January 1959 in Godwin, Cumberland County.

ii. **Alice Holland** was born about 1905 in Cumberland County.

iii. **Lula Holland** was born about 1910 in Cumberland County and about 1932 married James Lee Williams who was born 18 August 1902 and died 12 June 1954 in Eastover Township in Cumberland County, North Carolina. "Buck" was buried at the Bluff Presbyterian Church Cemetery. Lula married second to **Atwood Azzell Pope**, son of **James Daniel Pope** and **Nancy Eliza Starling**. Atwood was born 27 September 1904 and died 12 February 1983 in Dunn and was buried in War Memorial Cemetery in Dunn, North Carolina, with his first wife, Lila Beatrice. Rhye. Lula and Atwood were divorced.

Children of Lula and James Lee:

1) **Ila Ruth Williams** was born 5 September 1933 in Lumberton, North Carolina and maried **Ottis Franklin Jones** on 11 April 1953 in Wade, North Carolina. "Otis" was born 29 December 1931 in Harnett County, North Carolina, and died 30 November 1987 in Fayetteville, Cumberland County. He was the son of **Willard Washington Jones** and **Irene Cochern Thornton** and was appointed Sheriff of Cumberland County in 1974 and was re-elected to four full terms beginning in May 1974. He was buried in LaFayette Memorial Park. Ila Ruth and Ottis had two children, **James Franklin Jones** and **Doris Jones**.

2) **Connie Williams,** the second child of Lula and James Lee was adopted. She married **Richard Cashin.**

i. **William Rufus Holland** fourth child of Eli and Lillie was born 14 June 1912 and died 16 June 1961 in Black River Township in Cumberland County. William first married **Mattie Victoria Williams**, daughter of Martin Roberson Williams and Martha Jane Royal. He and Mattie divorced and he married second, **Inez** (maiden name unknown). He was buried at the Bluff Presbyterian Church Cemetery.

William was a foreman for the railroad. His certificate of death names Eli Holland and Lillie Jones for his parents and records he was killed in a two-truck collision on a highway in Black River Township. He was buried in Gilmont Cemetery in Hope Mills, North Carolina.

Children of William and Mattie:

1) **David Martin Holland** was born 28 october 1935 in Black River Township.

2) **Mary Frances Holland** was born about 1936 and married **Clarence Ward Braswell** who was born about 1936 in Florida. One known child, **Scott Monroe Braswell.**

3) **William Patrick Holland** was born 23 July 1940 and died 26 February 1941.

4) **Laurice Eldon Holland** was born 27 November 1942 in Cumberland County and married Ann (maiden name unknown.)

247. Calton Walker Holland (William[5], James[4], Daniel[3], Thomas William[2], Unknown[1]) was born 20 June 1859 in Sampson County, North Carolina, and died 20 April 1938 in Sampson County. He married **Mary Jelson Sessoms**, daughter of James Sessoms and Jerutha Autry. She was born 19 August 1866 in Sampson County, North Carolina, and died 13 February 1939 in Sampson County.

Mary's middle name also listed as "Jetson."

Calton Walker and Mary Jelson were buried in the Mary Ann Sessoms Family Cemetery on Josh Sessoms Road (SR 1406), Sampson County.

Children of Calton Holland and Mary Sessoms are:

\+ 699 i. **Sabra Jane Holland**, born 16 September 1887 in Sampson County, North Carolina; died 07 December 1961 in Sampson County.

700 ii. **Mamie Holland**, born August 1891 in Sampson County, North Carolina.

701 iii. **William Bluen Holland** was born 16 August 1895 in Sampson County and died 14 July 1971 in Alamance, North Carolina.

He is probably the "**WILLIAM BLANEY HOLLAND**," aged 35, who married **Viola Holland** on 21 January 1931 at the residence of M. A. Warrick, Justice of the Peace, in Sampson County, North Carolina. She was the daughter of **Lonnie Oscar Holland** and **Ella Evaline Best**. See Lonnie Oscar Holland's family elsewhere in this book.

702 iv. **James Futrell Holland**, born 24 July 1896 in Sampson County, North Carolina; died 24 April 1961. He married Maggie (maiden name unknown).

He was buried in the Mary Ann Sessoms Family Cemetery on Josh Sessoms Road (SR 1406), Sampson County, North Carolina.

703 v. **Mary Bruson Holland**, born about 1901 in Sampson County, North Carolina.

Her middle name was difficult to read in the 1910 census and I probably have listed it incorrectly.

\+ 704 vi. **Crayon Dewitt Holland**, born 30 July 1902 in Sampson County, North Carolina.

705 vii. **Roxie Leon Holland**, born 30 April 1906 in Sampson County, North Carolina; died 29 July 1983. She married **Albert Clifton Spell** on 26 March 1938. He was born 17 February 1915, died 04 January 1973 and was the son of **Janie Isabell Hair** and **Hardy Spell.**

Her middle name appears to be "Leon" in the 1910 census. She and Albert were buried in the Spell Family Cemetery on Dunn Road North of Roseboro, North Carolina.

248. William James Holland (William[5], James[4], Daniel[3], Thomas William[2], Unknown[1]) was born November 1862 and died 9 August 1936. He married **Laura Ellen Gautier**, daughter of Peter Gautier and Emily Fann. Emily's nickname was possibly "Millie Fann" or "Molly Fann." She was born 22 December 1867 and died 13 November 1954. Both were born in Sampson County, North Carolina, and died in Mebane, Melville Township in Alamance County, North Carolina.

"Jeams" is given for his middle name on the delayed certificate of birth for his daughter, Lydia.

He and Laura Ellen Gautier are mentioned in one source as the parents of Lewis Benson Holland. Laura Ellen was born about 1867 and, therefore, was not old enough to have been the mother of Lewis. Lewis Benson was living in the household of his brother, James, and Laura, in 1900 and that is probably what leads some to believe that William was his father. William James was listed as "William B. Holland in transcribed 1900 census records. William James and Laura did name a son, Lewis Guilford.

In 1930, William J., 67, and Laura Holland, 60, were in the household of their son, Buddie Holland, aged 28, in Melville, Alamance County, North Carolina. No spouse was listed for Buddie, but three children were in the household: **Cleta May Holland**, aged 6; **Azallee Holland**, aged 3; **Minnie Ola Holland**, aged 1.

Laura Ellen may be listed as "Sarah E." in the Sampson County, North Carolina, census records for 1870. Her certificate of death names William Abner Gautier and Millie Fann for her parents. William Abner, was her brother and was born in late 1859 or early 1860. The certificate names Pine Hill Cemetery in Burlington, North Carolina, for Laura's place of burial. William James' certificate of death names Burlinton for place of burial and he may be in the same cemetery as Laura. They were living in Mebane, Alamance County, North Carolina, at the time of their deaths.

Children of William Holland and Laura Gautier are:

+ 706 i. **Shepard Rose Holland**, born 06 September 1888; died 21 September 1966 in Sampson County, North Carolina.

707 ii. **Bon Sedberry Holland**, born 10 May 1890 in Sampson County, North Carolina; died 23 May 1953 in Roseboro, Little Coharie Township, Sampson County, North Carolina.

708 iii. **Walter Watson Holland**, born February 1894.

709 iv. **Thompson Blen Holland**, born July 1895.

710 v. **Viola Lee Holland**, born July 1896.

711 vi. **Stillars Jeronie Holland**, born April 1898.

712 vii. **Buddie Holland**, born about 1902.

713 viii. **Lewis Guilford Holland**, born about 1904.

714 ix. **Pearlie Snowdon Holland**, born about 1906.

715 x. **Curry Neater Holland**, born about 1908.

+ 716 xi. **Lydia Curl Holland**, born 15 August 1910 in Sampson County, North Carolina.

250. Lewis Benson Holland (William[5], James[4], Daniel[3], Thomas William[2], Unknown[1]) was born 15 July 1878, and died 08 February 1963. He married **Carlessie E. Fann** 03 February 1907 in Residence of A. Fann, Sampson County, North Carolina, daughter of Alpheus Fann and Eliza Honeycutt. She was born 07 September 1885, and died 20 March 1960.

Mary Lou Holland, possibly a daughter, who was born 30 December 1928 and died 11 March 1987 is also buried by him.

Lewis Benson and Carlessie were buried in the Beulah United Methodist Church Cemetery on Corinth Church Road (SR 326), about 1.7 miles from Hwy 242 in Sampson County, North Carolina

Children of Lewis Holland and Carlessie Fann are:

717 i. **Elma Holland,** born 25 October 1907; died 13 July 1908.

She was buried in the Beulah United Methodist Church Cemetery on Corinth Church Road, Sampson County, North Carolina.

ii. **Thelma Earle Holland** was born 25 October 1907 and died 08 August 1990.

In the 1910 Federal census for Honeycutts Township in Sampson County, Thelma was listed as a child of L. B. Holland and Lessie Holland, indicating that Elma and Thelma were twins. Others records show her full name. She married **Dennis Garland Parker** on 24 December 1931; he was born on 07 August 1909 and was the son of Dennis Heman Parker and Cherie Ann Strickland (Cherry Ann Strickland). Thelma and Dennis had five daughters, all born in Sampson County.

1) Helen Rose Parker, the first daughter, was born on 14 September 1932 and married **Edward Barker** of Sampson County and they had two sons, **James Edward Barker** and **Tommy Barker.**

2) Lessie Ann Parker, the second daughter was (born on 7 August 1940?) married **William Brady Parker** on 20 March 1960 in McGee United Methodist Church in Sampson County, North Carolina. William Brady was the son of Coyier Parker and Daisy Naylor and was born 16 February 1934 in Honeycutts Township, Sampson County, North Carolina. Lessie Ann and William Brady had two children, **Deborah Ann Parker** was born on 4 February 1963 in Clinton, North Carolina and **William Kenneth Parker** was born on 4 May 1967 in Clinton.

3) **Norma Jean Parker**, the third daughter of Thelma and Dennis was born on 7 August 1940 and she married **William Walker Bellamy** in 1954. They had one son, William Dennis Bellamy.

4) Martha Grey Parker, the fourth daughter was born on 19 October 1941 and in 1965 she married Bobby Tew;

5) Frankie Marie Parker was the fifth daughter of Thelma and Dennis. Her husband is **William Otis Tyndall, Jr.**, son of William Tyndall and Nadine Hudson and he was born on 31 March 1948 in Salemburg, Sampson County, North Carolina. One source gives 31 March 1945 for his date of birth. Frankie Marie and William Otis had three daughters, all born in Raleigh, Wake County, North Carolina:

Susan Earle Tyndall, the first daughter of Frand Marie and William was born on 27 September 1970, married on the 8 August 1992 in Raleigh to **Christopher Andrew Page** who was born on 6 November 1966. Susan Earle and Christopher had three children, **Allison Noelle Page** was born on 16 April 1995 in Wake County, North Carolina. **Holland Elise Page** was born 31 May 1998 in Wake and a **third child** was born in 2002.

Martha Allison Tyndall, second daughter of Frankie Marie and William Otis was born 12 October 1973 and married **Jonathan Hugh Gregory, Sr.,** on 6 June 1998. He was born in Raleigh, Wake County, North Carolina, on 9 May 1972. Martha and Jonathan's son, **Jonathan Hugh Gregory, Jr.,** was born in 2002.

Julie Ann Tyndall, the third daughter of Frankie Marie Parker and William Otis Tyndall was born 17 January 1978.

718 iii. **Laudie Gibson Holland**, son of Lewis and Carlessie was born 14 December 1908; died 10 October 1992. He married Julia D. (Maiden Name Unknown); she was born 27 June 1916.

He was buried in Roseboro's Old Hollywood Cemetery on 242, Sampson County, North Carolina.

719 iv. **Robie B. Holland**, born 12 December 1910; died 08 June 1918.

He was buried in Beulah United Methodist Church Cemetery on Corinth Church Road, Sampson County, North Carolina.

\+ 720 v. **Percy Benson Holland**, born 09 August 1912 in Sampson County, North Carolina; died 28 October 1996 in Sampson County, North Carolina.

721 vi. **Mossette L. Holland**, sixth child of Lewis and Carlessie was born about 1914.

His full name is listed in the 1920 census, but I cannot read it.

722 vii. **Stacy Franklin Holland**, born 05 April 1915 in Honeycutts Township, Sampson County, North Carolina; died 28 November 1944.

He was buried in Beulah United Methodist Church Cemetery on Corinth Church Road (SR 1326), Sampson County, North Carolina

723 viii. **Annie Elizabeth Holland, (Ann Elizabeth Holland)**,born 15 November 1917 and died 22 November 1999 in Sampson County, North Carolina. One source names 5 November 1917 for her birth and Billie Watson Parker for her husband. Billie was born 29 January 1916 in North Carolina and died 20 December 1984 in Sampson County, North Carolina.

724 ix. **Al Festus Holland,** ninth child of Lewis and Carlessie was born 15 June 1918 in Honeycutts Township, Sampson County, North Carolina.

725 x. **John Benson Holland**, born 1918.

He is not listed in the 1920 census.

\+ 726 xi. **Reba Mae Holland**, born 25 February 1921 in Honeycutts Township, Sampson County, North Carolina.

727 xii. **Evelyn Holland**, twelth child of Lewis and Carlessie was born 08 March 1923; died 02 September 1934. She was buried in Beulah United Methodist Church Cemetery on Corinth Church Road, Sampson County, North Carolina.

728 xiii. **Graham Holland**, born about 1925.

252. Bryant B. Holland (Thomas James[5], James[4], Daniel[3], Thomas William[2], Unknown[1]) was born 25 February 1872 in Sampson County, North Carolina, and died 20 January 1945 in Sampson County, North Carolina. He married **Tomzilla Autry**, daughter of John Autry and Sarah Horne. She was born 02 September 1878 in Sampson County, North Carolina, and died 03 February 1954 in Sampson County, North Carolina.

Bryant and Tomzilla were buried in the Clement Missionary Baptist Church Cemetery, Maxwell Road (SR1006), Sampson County, North Carolina

Children of Bryant Holland and Tomzilla Autry are:

729 i. **Sarah Adeline Holland**, born 03 July 1895; died October 1977. She married **Will Rose**.

No children.

\+ 730 ii. **John William Holland**, born 12 July 1897 in Sampson County, North Carolina; died 01 September 1977 in Selma, Johnston County, North Carolina.

\+ 731 iii. **Lattie Rudesel Holland**, born 23 July 1900; died 1965.

\+ 732 iv. **Robert Elliott Holland**, born 08 September 1903; died 15 December 1973 in Cumberland County, North Carolina.

733 v. **Marvin B. Holland**, born 23 April 1907; died 1908.

734 vi. **Oscar L. Holland**, born 11 February 1909; died 1910.

\+ 735 vii. **Tabitha Hazel Holland**, born 21 November 1911.

\+ 736 viii. **Mildred Holland**, born 12 September 1914.

737 ix. **Katy Holland**, born 02 July 1920; died 03 April 1984.

She was buried in Clement Missionary Baptist Church Cemetery, Maxwell Road (SR1006), Sampson County, North Carolina.

253. Richard Lee Holland (Thomas James[5], James[4], Daniel[3], Thomas William[2], Unknown[1]) was born 08 October 1873, and died 19 November 1948 in Eastover Township, Cumberland County, North Carolina. He married **Margaret Mary Matthews**, daughter of Wiley Matthews and Barbara Williams. She was born 08 January 1878, and died 21 December 1965.

Richard Lee and Margaret Mary were buried in Maxwell Cemetery, Clement, Sampson County, North Carolina.

Children of Richard Holland and Margaret Matthews are:

738 i. **Mary Lee Holland**, born 31 July 1897; died 10 September 1898.

She was buried in Maxwell Cemetery, Clement, Sampson County, North Carolina.

\+ 739 ii. **William Percy Holland**, born 08 January 1899; died 23 March 1965 in Hope Mills, Cumberland County, North Carolina.

740 iii. **Amie B. Holland**, born 16 February 1901; died 19 October 1907.

She was buried in Maxwell Cemetery, southeast corner of Maxwell Road (SR 1006) and (SR 1427), Sampson County, North Carolina. "Amie E. may be the given name found on his tombstone.

+ 741 iv. **Lonnie Edward Holland**, born 16 May 1902; died 03 January 1977 in Fayetteville, Cumberland County, North Carolina.

742 v. **Carson Holland**, born 22 September 1906; died 20 October 1921.

He was buried in Maxwell Cemetery, Clement, Sampson County, North Carolina

743 vi. **Elmon Clayton Holland**, born 01 January 1911; died 06 May 1998. He married **Mary Alice Page** who was born 27 May 1922 in Dismal Township, Sampson County, North Carolina. He was buried in Maxwell Cemetery, southeast corner of Maxwell Road (SR 1006) and (SR 1427), Sampson County, North Carolina.

Three children.

1) **ALICE LORETTA HOLLAND** was born 15 April 1937 in Eastover Township in Cumberland County, North Carolina and she married **EDWARD MARTIN VICK** who was born about 1930. Two children.

2) **PHYLLIS ANN HOLLAND** was born about 1939, married **PETER GUTHRIE JERNIGAN** who was born about 1939, and they have two children.

3) **TONY ELMON HOLLAND** was born 5 October 1940 in Fayetteville, married 16 August 1959 to **JANICE NADENE BARFIELD** in Fayetteville, and they have two children.

744 vii. **Katie Bell Holland**, born 16 September 1915; died 29 June 1916.

She was buried in Maxwell Cemeter, southeast corner of Maxwell Road (SR 1006) and (SR 1427), Sampson County, North Carolina

745 viii. **General Pershing Holland**, born 27 February 1919 in Wade, Cumberland County, North Carolina; died 26 July 1944. He married **Rachel Autry** who was born 08 July 1922 and died 23 August 1993.

His name appears to be "General Pershing Holland." Apparently, someone in the family admired "General Pershing." He and Rachel are buried in Magnolia Baptist Church Cemetery on Magnolia Baptist Church Road (SR 1843), Stedman, North Carolina

254. William Thomas Holland (Thomas James[5], James[4], Daniel[3], Thomas William[2], Unknown[1]) was born 05 August 1875, and died 31 July 1964 in Honeycutts Township, Sampson County, North Carolina. He married **Jeronia Harriett Williams** 27 March 1902, daughter of John Williams and Chellie Williams. She was born 02 August 1884, and died 11 March 1938 in Dismal Township, Sampson County, North Carolina and the gravestone of their son, William E. states that he was the son of W. T. and "Geronia" Holland.

'Tommy' was his nickname. Jeronia is also spelled: "Gearona." William Thomas and Jeronia Harriett were buried in Union Grove Baptist Church Cemetery on Vander Road west of Rebel City, Sampson County, North Carolina.

Children of William Holland and Jeronia Williams are:

+ 746 i. **Lottis Turner Holland**, born 14 December 1902; died 24 November 1988 in Clinton, Sampson County, North Carolina.

\+ 747 ii. **Arizona T. Holland,** born 01 July 1904; died 07 May 1990.

\+ 748 iii. **Ervin C. Holland,** born About 1906.

\+ 749 iv. **Angie Lee Holland,** born 27 November 1907; died 23 July 1979 in Clinton, Sampson County, North Carolina.

\+ 750 v. **Herman Crosby Holland,** born 01 November 1909; died 15 November 1992.

\+ 751 vi. **Euland Randolph Holland,** born 20 June 1912 in Clinton, Sampson County, North Carolina; died 22 July 1989.

752 vii. **Trilman Holland,** born about 1913.

753 viii. **William E. Holland,** born 20 September 1914; died 26 November 1916.

He was buried Union Grove Baptist Church Cemetery on Vander Road (SR 1438) Sampson County, North Carolina.

\+ 754 ix. **Cleo Pearl Holland,** born 15 October 1916 in Salemburg, Sampson County, North Carolina; died 13 November 1985 in Route 1, Salemburg, Sampson County, North Carolina.

\+ 755 x. **Eloise Holland,** born 28 August 1918 in Dismal Township, Sampson County, North Carolina; died 29 October 1978 in Route 1, Autryville, North Carolina.

756 xi. **Charles Linwood Holland,** born 05 November 1921; died 09 December 1922 in Dismal Township, Sampson County, North Carolina.

One source shows his middle name as 'Linwood' and his date of birth as 9 November 1921 while a third source records 5 October 1920 for his birth.

He was buried in Union Grove Baptist Church Cemetery on Vander Road (SR 1438) Sampson County, North Carolina

\+ 757 xii. **Ella May Holland,** born 22 August 1923 in Dismal Township, Sampson County, North Carolina.

758 xiii. **Leroy Holland,** born 05 May 1925 in Dismal Township, Sampson County, North Carolina; died before 1985. He married **Inez Beall.**

255. Louetta J. Holland (Thomas James[5], James[4], Daniel[3], Thomas William[2], Unknown[1]) was born 18 February 1877, and died 23 November 1975. She married **John Bunyan Page,** son of John Page and Margaret Fisher. He was born 03 March 1870, and died 19 August 1949.

Louetta and John Bunyan were buried in Clement Missionary Baptist Church Cemetery, Maxwell Road (SR1006), Sampson County, North Carolina.

Children of Louetta Holland and John Page are:

i. **Johnnie T. Page** was born in November 1896 and was living in 1975.

ii. **Mathew L. Page** was born in March 1898..

iii. **Burnice B. Page,** born April 1900.

iv. **Joe Martin Page**, fourth child of Louetta J. Holland and John Bunyan Page, was born 18 May 1903, died 6 January 1977 in Rural area of Wade in Cumberland County, North Carolina. He married **Ola Florence Autry** on 14 November 1925, daughter of Ransom Murdock Autry and Edith Jane McLemore. She was born 5 October 1907. Joe was buried at Clement Baptist Church Cemetery in Sampson County.

Four children:

1) **Almeta Florence Page** was born 24 March 1927 in Flea Hill Township and first married **Marshall Lloyd Core, Sr.**, son of Ernest J. Core and Mittle Florence Starling. Marshall was born 10 September 1926 in Black River Township in Cumberland County and died 8 January 1971 in Fayetteville, North Carolina; he was buried in LaFayette Memorial Park in Fayetteville. Almeta married second 16 August 1975 in Stedman, North Carolina, as the second wife of **Woodrow Autry** who was born 11 November 1912 and died 13 January 1982 in Fayetteville. He was the son of Newsome Early Autry and Macy Matthews. Almeta and Marshall had two children: **Marshall Lloyd Core, Jr.,** was born 30 July 1947 in Fayetteville and married **Carolyn Lynn Jones** wo was born 10 March 1947 in Fayetteville, daughter of John Wayland Jones and Elizabeth Green. Marshall, Jr. and Carolyn had one known child, **Marsha Lynn Core** who was born 21 January 1967. **Steven Curtis Core** was the second child of Almeta and Marshall, Sr. and he married **Brenda Lee Hood** 20 October 1973 in Cedar Creek Township in Cumberland County. She was born 13 April 1953 in Fayetteville, daughter of Davie George Hood and Jacqueline Cain. Steven and Brenda had two children: **Alan Brandon Core**, born 25 January 1978 in Fayetteville and **Adam Christopher Core**, born 12 August 1981 in Fayetteville.

2) **Helen Wylene Page**, second child of Joe Martin and Ola Florence was born 24 June 1929 in Eastover Township in Cumberland County. She married **Irettis Claydell Matthews** who was born 2 March 1928 in Flea Hill Township and died 3 April 1985 in Fayetteville, son **of Sandy Matthews** and **Fannie Pearl Page**. She was buried at Clement Baptist Church Cemetery in Sampson County, North Carolina. Five children: **I) Helen Fay Matthews** was born 31 August 1947 in fayettevilland and married **Michael Steven Sutton** who ws born 26 February 1946 and they had two children: **Matthew Steven Sutton**, born 30 January 1968 and **Michael Keith Sutton**, born 30 November 1970 in Fayetteville. II) **Vickey Elaine Matthews,** second child of helen and Irettis, was born 28 September 1950 in Fayetteville and married **Sidney Harold Autry** who was born 30 Airl 1949 in Roseboro, son of Lattie Murphy Autry and Della Elizabeth Stewart. Vickey and Sidney had one known child, **Helen Elizabeth Autry** born 17 December 1970. III) **Dennis Clay Matthews**, third child of Helen Wylene and Irettis was born 16 February 1955 in Fayetteville and married 22 December 1976 **Elizabeth Marcelle Jackson,** daughter of Felton Lee Jackson and Sadie Elizabeth Faircloth. Elizabeth was born 17 March 1959 in Fayetteville. IV) **Wendy Lou Mattews**, fourth child of Helen and Irettis was born 1 July 1960 in Fayetteville and married **Bill White**, son of Alvin and Mable White. One child not identified. V) **Pamela Lynn Matthews** was the fifth child of Helen and Irettis and was born 26 December 1966 in Fayetteville, Cumberland County, North Carolina.

3) **Leo Martin Page**, third child of Joe Martin and Ola Florence was born 2 September 1932 in Eastover Township and married **Mary Rebah McLaurin** who was born 20 February 1933 in Eastover Township, daughter of Eugene Leonard McLaurin and Mary Ellen McLaurin.

4) **Lois Evelyn Page**, fourth child of Joe Martin and Ola was born 27 September 1935 in Eastover Township and married a Mr. Lindsey.

\+ 759 v. **Viola Gertrude Page,** fifth child of Louetta J. Holland and John Bunyan Page was born 20 September 1905; anddied 18 June 1988 in Sampson County, North Carolina.

vi. **Eutoka Page** was born about 1909 and was the sixth child of Louetta J. Holland and John Bunyan Page.

256. Frances Elizabeth Holland (Thomas James[5], James[4], Daniel[3], Thomas William[2], Unknown[1]) was born 18 February 1881, and died 16 November 1960. She married **William Alexander Autry**, son of John Autry and Margaret Maxwell. He was born 03 April 1871 in Sampson County, North Carolina, and died 10 May 1931 in Sampson County, North Carolina.

Date of death on gravestone for Frances is 16 Nov 1972. The dates of birth for William Alexander and his brother, Duncan, are five and one half months apart. Clearly one of the dates is incorrect.

Frances Elizabeth and William Alexander are buried in Autry Cemetery on Autry Mill Road, Sampson County, North Carolina.

Children of Frances Holland and William Autry are:

\+ 760 i. **Ethel Elizabeth Autry**, born 22 September 1900 in Sampson County, North Carolina; died 14 December 1979.

761 ii. **Roxie A. Autry**, born 09 September 1902 in Sampson County, North Carolina; died 08 February 1904.

257. Bernice Culbreth Holland (Thomas James[5], James[4], Daniel[3], Thomas William[2], Unknown[1]) was born 13 June 1885, and died 12 March 1961 in Dismal Township, Sampson County, North Carolina. He married **Lessie C. Williams** 25 January 1910 in Residence of J. A. Williams, daughter of John Williams and Chellie Williams. She was born 19 July 1891, and died 11 November 1976 in Clinton, Sampson County, North Carolina.

One source spells his first name as "Burnice." Transcribed cemetery records show Bernice C. Holland incorrectly as wife of Lessie Holland. Sometimes it is difficult to tell which spouse is the husband.

Bernice Culbreth and Lessie were buried in Williams Family Cemetery northeast of Clement in Dismal Township near Dunn Road (SR1002) at SR1441 in Sampson County, North Carolina.

Children of Bernice Holland and Lessie Williams are:

\+ 762 i. **Millard Filmore Holland**, born 09 December 1910; died 27 March 1987 in Clinton, Sampson County, North Carolina.

\+ 763 ii. **James Adam Holland**, born about 1911; died before 1976.

\+ 764 iii. **Ruby Jane Holland**, born 02 December 1913 in Dismal Township, Sampson County, North Carolina.

765 iv. **Rutha Reva Holland**, born 04 January 1916 in Dismal Township, Sampson County, North Carolina; died before 1976(sic). *A North Carolina Death Collection, 1908-2000,* records that "Ruthie Holland Hairr" (Ruthie Holland Holland)(sic) was born 4 January 1916 in Sampson County, and died on 5 September 2000 in Dunn, Harnett County, North Carolina. She was 84 years, was widowed and had attended school for 12 years. I have not determined the name of her husband.

766 v. **Eva Mae Holland**, born about 1919. She married Unknown Autry.

\+ 767 vi. **Nellie Holland**, born 27 August 1920 in Dismal Township, Sampson County, North Carolina.

261. Florence E. Holland (Bluman[5], Harfrey[4], Daniel[3], Thomas William[2], Unknown[1]) was born 09 July 1868, and died 24 June 1910. She married **W. E. Smith**.

The year of birth on her gravestone may be 1864. Florence was buried in Spring Branch Baptist Church Cemetery on Spring Branch Road (SR 1002), Sampson County, North Carolina

Children of Florence Holland and W. Smith are:

768 i. **Alie Smith**, born 03 September 1897 in Sampson County, North Carolina; died 04 June 1898 in Sampson County.

She was buried in Spring Branch Baptist Church Cemetery on Spring Branch Road (SR 1002), Sampson County, North Carolina.

769 ii. **Kattie Smith**, born 20 October 1906 in Sampson County; died 19 May 1907 in Sampson County, North Carolina.

She was buried in Spring Branch Baptist Church Cemetery on Spring Branch Road (SR 1002), Sampson County.

263. Lovette H. Holland (Bluman[5], Harfrey[4], Daniel[3], Thomas William[2], Unknown[1]) was born 9 June 1871 in Sampson County, North Carolina and died 22 August 1944 in Black River Township in Cumberland County, North Carolina. He married **Ella Jane Smith**, daughter of Sidney T. Smith and Martha Jane Williford. She was born about 11 November 1877 in North Carolina and died 19 March 1960 in Dunn, Averasboro Township in Harnett County, North Carolina.

Lovette and Ella were buried in Antioch Church Cemetery in Falcon, North Carolina.

Children of Lovett Holland and Ella Unknown are:

770 i. **Jasper Holland** was born 23 May 1897 in Mingo Township, Sampson County, North Carolina and died 7 August 1966 in the Veterans Administration Hospital in Fayetteville, Cross Creek Township in Cumberland County, North Carolina.

771 ii. **Vinnie Holland**, born about 1899 in Mingo Township, Sampson County.

Vannie is also listed for her name.

772 iii. **Charlie A. Holland,** born about 1902 in Mingo Township, Sampson County. He was possibly the Charlie A. Holland who died at aged 52 on 2 February 1955 in North Carolina. A certificate of death records that Mary Jane Thornton Holland, wife of Charlie Holland was born 17 September 1900 and died at the age of 62 on 19 February 1963 in Clinton, Sampson County, North Carolina. She was the daughter of Guthrie Thornton and Georganna Jackson. Mary Jane lived in Newton Grove at time of death.

773 iv. **Bettie Holland,** born about 1904 in Mingo Township, Sampson County, North Carolina.

774 v. **Joel C. Holland,** born about 1906 in Mingo Township, Sampson County. He might have been the Joel C. Holland who had a Godwin, North Carolina address at time of death. He was born 8 October 1906 in Cumberland County, North Carolina and died 15 November 1998 in Dunn, Harnett County, North Carolina, in Betsy Johnson Memorial Hospital at the age of 92.

775 vi. **Esther Caddie Holland,** born 07 February 1909 in Mingo Township, Sampson County.

776 vii. **Grady Holland,** born about 1912. He was, most likely, the "Lovette Grady Holland" who was born 8 August 1911 and died on 17 February 1995 in Fayetteville, Cumberland County, North Carolina at the age of 83. He was widowed.

777 viii. **Murphy Holland,** born about 1914. He may have been the "Murphy Holland" who was born 1 February 1914 and died 7 March 1987 in Fayetteville, Cumberland County, North Carolina. His wife was possibly, Rosalind L. Holland who was born 6 December 1921 and died 22 December 2008 in Gastonia, North Carolina. One obituary states that her residence at the time of death was Godwin, North Carolina and notes 6 December 1921 for her birth. An obituary in *The Daily Record Newspaper,* Dunn, North Carolina records:

"She was born 12 June 1921 to the late Ivy Luther and Ida Lee Scott Lamm and was preceded in death by her husbnad, Murphy Holland; and a son, Stephen Murphy Hollnad. She was retired from Belk Department Store in Dunn. After retirement, Mrs. Holland delivered Meals on Wheels, and was a member of the Ladies Auxiliary at Betsy Johnson Regional Hospital and Good Hope Hospital. She was the only surviving member of the Godwin Baptist Church. Mrs. Holland lived in Godwin until March 2008. Burial was in LaFayette Memorial Park in Fayetteville.

"Survivors include a son, Gary Henderson Holland and wife, Bonnie of Roanoke, Virginia; a daughter, Joyce Hope Robinson and husband. David of Gastonia, a daughter-in-law, Abby Wood of Erwin, ... grandchildren, Shannon L. Warren of Coats, Whitney Lesniak and husband Mike of Williamsburg, North Carolina, Madonna Ford and husband, Brett of Charlotte, Meredith Butterfield and husband, Corey of Concord, Stephen Holland and wife Holly of Erwin; and great-grandchildren, Ashleigh and Ryan Lesniah, Grace Warren, Reagan and Peyton Ford and Trey Holland"

778 ix. **Challie Holland,** born about 1917. He was possibly the Challie L. Holland who was born 1916 and enlisted on 1 May 1945 in Fort Bragg, North Carolina to serve in World War II.

779 x. **Louise Holland,** born about 1920. Louise may have been the "Louise Saunders" of Rural Route, Godwin, North Carolina, who was named informant on the certificate of death for her mother.

265. Lalister R. Holland (Bluman^{5}, Harfrey^{4}, Daniel^{3}, Thomas William^{2}, Unknown^{1}) was born 30 August 1875 in Sampson County, North Carolina, and died 28 August 1948 in Dismal Township, Sampson County, North Carolina. He married **Ettie S. Williford** 20 January 1907 in Residence of C. A. Jackson, Minister, Sampson County. She was born 27 June 1881, and died 12 June 1957.

Lalister and Ettiie were buried in Calvary Tabernacle PFB Church Cemetery on High House Road one mile from intersection of Hwy 242 and High House Road, Sampson County, North Carolina.

Children of Lalister Holland and Ettie Williford are:

\+ 780 i. **Leslie B. Holland,** born 24 November 1907; died 08 March 1993.

781 ii. **Theresa A. Holland,** born about 1910.

She may be the Theresa Holland Bass buried with her husband, **Mazie Washington Bass,** in Union Grove Baptist Church Cemetery on Vander Road one mile west of Rebel City, Sampson County, North Carolina. Dates on her tombstone are 28 September 1909 - 26 February 1977 and on his tombstone are 25 April 1904 and 28 May 1962.

782 iii. **Fannie Holland,** born about 1915.

She may have been the "Fannie E.," born 12 August 1914 who married **Herman Lee Knowles.**

266. Rufus Addison Holland (Bluman^{5}, Harfrey^{4}, Daniel^{3}, Thomas William^{2}, Unknown^{1}) was born 14 January 1878 in Sampson County, North Carolina, and died 19 December 1952 in Sampson County, North Carolina. He married **Della A. Lee.** She was born 04 June 1881 in Sampson County, North Carolina, and died 26 March 1964 in Sampson County.

In 1910, he and Della were living in Smithfield, Johnston County, North Carolina; in 1920, they were living in Elevation in Johnston County.

Rufus Addison and Della were buried in Calvary Tabernacle PFB Church Cemetery on High House Road one mile from intersection of Hwy 242 and High House Road, Sampson County, North Carolina.

Children of Rufus Holland and Della Lee are:

783 i. **Herman Holland,** born about 1900; died 03 April 1961 in Sampson County.

\+ 784 ii. **Myrtle Holland,** born 13 September 1902; died 18 June 1975.

785 iii. **Mamie O. Holland,** born 09 August 1907; died 19 May 1993. She married **Edgar L. Harris;** born 20 August 1902; died 20 January 1987.

Her name is also listed as Marnie. She and Edgar were buried in Zoar FWBP Church Cemetery Near Salemburg, North Carolina.

\+ 786 iv. **Ransom Bluen Holland,** born 20 April 1910 in Sampson County, North Carolina; died 19 October 1997 in Sampson Regional Medical Center, Clinton, Sampson County.

787 v. **LeRoy Holland,** born about 1914.

788 vi. **Larry Holland,** born about 1914.

"Roy" may have been entered for Larry's name in the 1930 census.

267. Alger Marvin Holland (Bluman[5], Harfrey[4], Daniel[3], Thomas William[2], Unknown[1]) was born 10 May 1881, and died 24 September 1943. He married **Laura Jernigan** 12 February 1905 in Residence of Bride's father, Sampson County, North Carolina, daughter of William Jernigan and Sarah Altman. She was born 01 April 1883, and died 24 March 1964.

He was also listed as "Algery." Laura's name as listed in the 1920 census is difficult to read. They both were buried in the Jernigan and Holland Cemetery on Jernigan Loop Road (SR 1619), Sampson County, North Carolina

Children of Alger Holland and Laura Jernigan are:

789 i. **Howard Holland,** born 14 October 1905; died 18 June 1906.

Howard was buried in the Jernigan and Holland Cemetery on Jernigan Loop Road (SR 1619), Sampson County, North Carolina.

790 ii. **Marvin B. Holland,** born about 1907 in South Clinton Township, Sampson County.

791 iii. **William A. Holland,** born about 1909 in South Clinton Township, Sampson County.

792 iv. **Bertha Holland,** born about 1911 in South Clinton Township, Sampson County, North Carolina.

793 v. **Lillie Florence Holland,** born 02 May 1913 in South Clinton Township, Sampson County.

794 vi. **Perry D. Holland,** born about 1918 in South Clinton Township, Sampson County, North Carolina.

795 vii. **Archie J. Holland,** born about 1919 in South Clinton Township, Sampson County.

796 viii. **Retha Holland,** born about 1922 in South Clinton Township, Sampson County, North Carolina.

268. Janie Isabell Hairr (Franklin[5] Holland, Harfrey[4], Daniel[3], Thomas William[2], Unknown[1]) was born 22 May 1883. After 1911, she married **Hardy Albert Spell,** son of Wiley Spell and Mary Faircloth. He was born 29 August 1879, and died 10 March 1952.

Records show that Janie Isabell Hairr was a foster child of Mr. and Mrs. Frank Holland.

In the 1910 Federal Census for Sampson County, North Carolina, she was listed as a niece and another source shows she was a daughter of Henry Hair and Rachel Clifton Britt.

Janie Isabell and Hardy Albert were buried in a Spell Family Cemetery on Dunn Road north of Roseboro, North Carolina.

Children of Janie Hairr and Hardy Spell are:

797 i. **Henry Stacy Spell**, born 07 August 1912; died 08 September 1973. He married **Betsy Bee Honeycutt** 23 March 1962; born 14 February 1915 in Sampson County, North Carolina. Henry Stacy is buried in a Spell Family Cemetery on Dunn Road, north of Roseboro, North Carolina. No children.

\+ 798 ii. **Lester Frank Spell**, born 07 August 1912; died 11 November 1987.

799 iii. **Albert Clifton Spell**, born 17 February 1915; died 04 January 1973. He **married Roxie Leon Holland** on 26 March 1938. She was born 30 April 1906 in Sampson County, North Carolina, died on 29 July 1983 and was the daughter of **Calton Walker Holland and Mary Jelson Sessoms.** See Calton Walker Holland elsewhere in this book.

Roxie's middle name appears as "Leon" in the 1910 census. Albert Clifton and Roxie Leon are buried in a Spell Family Cemetery on Dunn Road, north of Roseboro, North Carolina.

1) **ALBERT CHARLES SPELL ("A.C." SPELL,)** was born 20 November 1938. he maried **RACHEL SNIPES** who was born 10 August 1938; they have three children.

2) **SARAH JEAN SPELL** was the secnd child of Albert and Roxie. She first married **JIMMY LOVICK** and they had one child; she married second to **TED ALLEN HODGES** who was born 1 November 1938 and they had two children.

3) **RACHEL BERNICE SPELL,** the third child was born 19 September 1942 and married Mr. Hanners. Two children.

4) **ELLEN FAY SPELL,** fourth child was born 22 February 1944 and first married **SIDNEY MCCOY WILKINSON, JR.,** who was born 29 January 1939. They had three children. Ellen married second on 29 August 1979 to TONY TURCI.

5) **MARY ISABELL SPELL,** fifth child of Albert and Roxie, was born 13 December 1949 and married **THOMAS WAYNE DANIELS** who was born 23 March 1948. They have two children.

\+ 800 iv. **David Peyton Spell,** the fourth known child of Janie Hairr and Hardy Spell was born 21 February 1924.

\+ 801 v. **Rometta Spell,** the fifth child of Janie Hairr and Hardy Spell, was born 09 August 1917; died 05 November 1989 in Goldsboro, North Carolina.

271. Challie Cleveland Holland (Jordan[5], Harfrey[4], Daniel[3], Thomas William[2], Unknown[1]) was born 17 October 1886 in Sampson County, North Carolina, and died 13 November 1957 in Clinton, Sampson County, North Carolina. He married **Sabra Jane Holland** 12 February 1908 in Residence of Bride's father, Sampson County, North Carolina, daughter of Calton Walker Holland and Mary Jelson Sessoms. She was born 16 September 1887 in Sampson County, North Carolina, and died 07 December 1961 in Sampson County, North Carolina.

Sabra was called 'Janie.' Challie Cleveland died in Sampson County Memorial Hospital of carcinoma. He and Sabra were buried in Salemburg Cemetery, Salemburg, Sampson County, North Carolina.

Children of Challie Holland and Sabra Holland are:

802 i. **Viola Holland**, born 21 September 1909; died 21 September 1910.

\+ 803 ii. **William Lloyd Holland I**, born 16 October 1911; died 11 September 1953.

\+ 804 iii. **Mary Frances Holland**, born 07 February 1914.

805 iv. **Lillie Carr Holland**, born 01 December 1915; died 01 June 1916.

806 v. **James Dewey Holland**, born 22 May 1917; died 19 May 1965.

His monument records that he served in World War II: NC CPL 2135 Base Unit AAF.

He was buried in Salemburg Cemetery, Salemburg, Sampson County, North Carolina

\+ 807 vi. **Oscar Calton Holland**, born 09 August 1919; died 06 August 1975.

\+ 808 vii. **Jessie Mildridge Holland**, born 30 August 1921; died 12 July 1969.

\+ 809 viii. **Jerutha Veve Holland,** born 01 September 1922 in Honeycutts Township, Sampson County, north Carolina.

810 ix. **Charlie Claxton Holland,** born 31 August 1924 in North Carolina; died 13 January 1925 in Honeycutts Township, Sampson County, North Carolina.

He died at age 4 months and 13 days of tetany. He also had rhickets for 4 hours. His certificate of birth shows a different date of birth and Clayton is found for his middle name. He was buried in Salemburg Cemetery, Salemburg, Sampson County.

811 x. **Edgar Tate Holland**, born 16 July 1927; died 08 February 1928.

He is buried in Salemburg Cemetery, Salemburg, Sampson County, North Carolina

\+ 812 xi. **Margaret Peace Holland**, born 28 December 1928.

272. Tomzil Clide Holland (Jordan^{5}, Harfrey^{4}, Daniel^{3}, Thomas William^{2}, Unknown^{1}) was born 23 December 1888 in Sampson County, North Carolina, and died 07 September 1953 in Sampson Regional Medical Center, Clinton, North Carolina. She married **Alger Rose Holland** 08 August 1916 in Residence of Jordan Holland, Sampson County, North Carolina, son of Stephen Senter Holland and Nancy Elizabeth Hudson. He was born 20 June 1875 in Honeycutts Township, Sampson County, North Carolina, and died 19 July 1965 in Honeycutts Township, Sampson County.

She died from a Cardiovascular Accident (2 days) that was due to Hypertension (15 years.) The certificate of death for Alger Rose Holland shows he died of Generalized Arteriosclerosis (had for years), bronchopneumonia, ASHD and Uremia. On the certificate, his father's name is spelled 'Center.' The correct spelling is Stephen Senter (Scenter) Holland.

Tomzil Clide and Alger were buried in Zoar Penecostal Free Will Baptist Church Cemetery, Salemburg, North Carolina.

The 1900 Federsl Census for Honeycutts Township, Sampson County, North Carolina, shows Alger as head of household with IDA E., his wife, born in July 1879, aged 20 yrs. A family member has indicated that his first wife was, Ida, and she either died during the birth of a son or soon after; the son died also. He was listed as "Algier Holland," aged 31, in the Voters' Registration for White Oak Township, Bladen County, North Carolina. Both he and his brother, John Wesley, registered in the same township on 26 October 1906.

The certificate of death for Alger's son, James Senter Holland, lists James' mother as "Loraine Howard" which indicates she would have been the second wife of Grandpa Alger and the mother of Rose Annie and James Senter. This is the only document that shows Loraine's name, but see data in notes for Alger Rose Holland that supports Alger's marriage to Loraine. My mother, Roberta, spoke fondly of the Howards and this may explain why she felt close to them. In the event that Grandfather Alger did marry Loraine Howard, their marriage may have been a short one and no record exist except the certificate of death for James Senter Holland.

When Alger and Ella Jane's triplett daughters, Mamie Lee, Lucile and Mary J. were born, the certificate of birth for Mamie Lee shows she was born at 3:00 a.m. The certificate for Mary J. shows 7:45 a.m. for her birth with six children born to her mother, including Mary J., and five living. I only have a certificate of death for Lucile and it does show she was born on 29 May 1914 and a death date of 25 September 1915. The certificate of birth for Mary J. indicates the child not living out of six children born to Ella Jane must have been Mamie Lee who died between 3 - 7:45 a.m.; we know of no other deceased child of Ella Jane. Mary J.'s certificate of birth also supports the information on the certificate of death for James Senter Holland that "Loraine Howard" and Alger Rose Holland were his parents. When we include Rose Annie and James Senter in the number of children born to Ella Jane, we have eight born to her with seven living which doesn't work with the numbers on Mary Jane's certificate of birth. This is the data that is recorded. (See notes under number 215 for Alger).

During and after the American Civil War, more unfamiliar names appeared in families and Alger Rose and the middle name of his father, Stephen Senter Holland, still make me think about their origin. When I first found the name "Algier M. Holland," I was perplexed when I couldn't quickly find out whether he was related to Alger Rose. Eventually, I connected Algier M. as a grandson of Harfrey Holland, but I had been told by a few of Harfrey's (Harphrey) descendants that we were certainly not related, yet members of my family told me that Alger Rose Holland and his second wife, Tomzil Clyde Holland, were distant cousins on the Holland side. Tomzil was a descendant of Harfrey. Finally, I found a transcribed copy of the will of Thomas William Holland; that copy and a copy of the will I found in the Sampson County Courthouse in Clinton, North Carolina, listed, Daniel Holland and Henry Holland as sons of Thomas William Holland. Daniel was the father of Harfrey and Henry was the grandfather of Alger Rose.

The 1900 census shows that Alger Rose was living near "Amma Holland" andhis wife, Lillie L. (Lillie L. Horne.) Amma was the son of "Harfrey Holland." Other children of Harfrey and their families were also living nearby. This writer was told by one descendant of Harfrey that there was no kinship between Harfrey and Henry Holland. The families lived across the creek from each other! Cousins of this descendant have indicated that Alger Rose and this descendant had the same great-great-great-grandfather. Records show that this possible common ancestor would have been great-great-grandfather to Alger. A daughter of Alger Rose Holland could not remember all the details, but told me that he explained how the Holland families who settled in the area were related. This daughter remembered writing down some of the data, but she was unable to find her record.

I also found data on Ancestry.com that states there were three Holland brothers who initially settled in Virginia. It has not yet been determined whether descendants of these three brothers are in any way related to the Hollands in Sampson County, North Carolina. It is interesting that research indicates the Hollands in Virginia and some of the Hollands in Sampson County, North Carolina, tell of descending from three Holland brothers who immigrated to the new world. Many given names were the same in the early Hollands in Virginia and in Sampson County, North Carolina; however, more research is needed on naming patterns for these families and this would probably not be conclusive since many early Holland family records in Virginia were burned when most of a town once called "Holland" burned. As mentioned elsewhere in notes for early Hollands in Sampson County, at least one of these early Hollands moved to Georgia.

Dicey (Dicy) A. Holland and her son Mallet (Malet, Malette) were living near Alger in 1900. Her husband, Joel Holland, was deceased and both Joel and Dicey were distant cousins of Alger.

Tradition indicates a document exists that shows one Holland ancestor was an indentured servant and four years of his remaining time was apparently bought out by his father-in-law. Rather than serving time as an indentured servant, he may have been bound to someone who was to teach him a trade. This document is very old and I understand it is no longer shared with anyone. Perhaps data from this document could clear up some unanswered questions.

On 25 January 1919, A. R. (Alger) and "Tomzial" Holland sold 25 acres to her brother, Anderson Holland, for the sum of $500. Land in Little Coharie Township, Sampson County, North Carolina, joining the lands of C. C. Holland. Tomzil was examined separately to make sure she sold voluntarily.

About August, 1920, Joseph Jackson (Joel Jackson) asked Alger Rose and Tomzil, his third (fourth?) wife, whether they and their children would like to move into his home and care for him, Hepsie and their daughter, Sallie, and in return he would give them his farm. Alger and Tomzil agreed. Apparently, Sallie had health problems and died before 1930. Alger Rose's mother and Hepsie were first cousins and apparently, part of the farm Hepsie and "Joel" owned was given to Hepsie by her mother; part of it may have been owned by the family of Joseph (Joel) Jackson. It is said that a relative of Joseph lived in a small house near the property and cousins of Oscar Davis Jackson (husband of Alger's daughter, Robertha,) visited this man and called him "Uncle." These cousins probably would have visited him between 1830-1835. I have been unable to identify this man. Descendants of Alger Rose and Tomzil still live on this land.

One tract of land that Joseph (Joel) and Hepsie Jackson deeded to Alger Rose Holland on 18 August 1920 was bounded "on the North by the lands of John Royal, on the East by the lands of A. S. Lockerman, on the South by the lands of John McKenzie and P. B. Lockerman, on the West by the lands of Mr. Gussie Rachels."The second tract they deeded to Alger Rose was bounded "on the North by the lands of Tom Crumpler, on the East by the lands of said Tom Crumpler, and on the West by the lands of A. S. Lockerman." Tom Crumpler was "Micajah Thomas Crumpler," father of William Stacy Crumpler.

Alger Rose purchased 25 acres on 28 March 1922 from A. S. Lockerman and wife, Meliar for the sum of $1,000. This land was across the road from the above mentioned land and was bounded on one side by the road and on the other side by high water marks of Crumplers Mill Pond.

Children are listed above under (215) Alger Rose Holland.

273. Annie Jane Holland (Jordan[5], Harfrey[4], Daniel[3], Thomas William[2], Unknown[1]) was born 01 July 1890 in Little Coharie Township, Sampson County, North Carolina, and died 19 November 1964. She married **Roberson B. Cannady**, son of John Cannady and Mary Butler. He was born 05 September 1888 in Little Coharie Township, Sampson County and died 26 October 1959.

The data on Annie Jane's certificate of ceath was provided by her daughter, Mable, who named John J. Holland and Mary Autry for Annie's parents. This may indicate that **her father's full name was John Jordan Holland.**

Mr. Bundy, shows his first name as "Robertson." Annie Jane and Roberson B. Cannady were buried in Harrells Cemetery, Harrells, Sampson County, North Carolina.

Children of Annie Holland and Roberson Cannady are:

\+ 813 i. **Zola Cannady**, born 22 February 1910; died 07 December 1991.

814 ii. **Ashford Cannady**, born 08 March 1912; died 08 March 1912.

\+ 815 iii. **Lanty Pearl Cannady**, born 27 September 1914; died 14 August 2000.

816 iv. **Ellen Cannady**, born 11 November 1916; died 26 April 1967. She married **Buck Wilkerson.** She was buried in Harrells Community Cemetery, Wildcat Road and Hwy 421, Sampson County, North Carolina.

\+ 817 v. **Wilbert Cleveland Cannady**, born 13 January 1919; died 03 May 1994.

\+ 818 vi. **Mable Cannady**, born 26 April 1921; died 21 August 1991.

\+ 819 vii. **Elbert Alan Cannady**, born 25 March 1923.

\+ 820 viii. **Julia Ann Cannady**, born between 08 - 29 January 1925; died 23 May 1982.

\+ 821 ix. **James Manly Cannady**, born 05 May 1927; died 21 March 1995.

\+ 822 x. **Herbert Wayne Cannady** I, born 07 August 1929.

\+ 823 xi. **Kenneth Neil Cannady**, born 09 November 1932.

275. Anderson Holland (Jordan[5], Harfrey[4], Daniel[3], Thomas William[2], Unknown[1]) was born 30 May 1897 in North Carolina, and died 05 June 1966 in Clinton, Sampson County, North Carolina. He married **Rebecca Ellen Rich** 05 January 1919 in Roseboro, Sampson County, daughter of Junious Rich and Lide Vann. She was born 29 December 1899 in Sampson County, North Carolina, and died 07 May 1998 in Mary Gran Nursing Center, Clinton, North Carolina.

The tombstone of Anderson Holland notes he served in "WWI. NC PVT BTRY BFA REPL DEPOT." His certificate of death shows cause of death was Myocardial infraction (10 days) due to arteriosclerosis. He was a farmer. Rebecca Ellen died of Bilateral pneumonia, urinary tract infection, dehydration and stroke. She and Anderson were buried in Harmony Church Cemetary on Harmony Church Road (SR. 1235) in Sampson County, North Carolina.

Children of Anderson Holland and Rebecca Rich are:

+ 824 i. **Frances Eliza Holland,** born 06 May 1927.

+ 825 ii. **Hazelene Holland,** born 02 October 1926.

277. Drucilla Holland (Jordan[5], Harfrey[4], Daniel[3], Thomas William[2], Unknown[1]) was born 15 November 1901, and died 09 April 1971. She married **Floyd Barker.** He was born 28 February 1894.

Children of Drucilla Holland and Floyd Barker are:

+ 826 i. **Lottie Mae Barker,** born 06 November 1922.

+ 827 ii. **Janie Frances Barker,** born 1926.

+ 828 iii. **Carl Barker.**

+ 829 iv. **Horace Barker.**

+ 830 v. **Louise Barker.**

+ 831 vi. **Thelma Barker.**

278. Charlotte Elizabeth Holland (Jordan[5], Harfrey[4], Daniel[3], Thomas William[2], Unknown[1]) was born 13 October 1914, and died after 1950. She married **Joseph Arthur Williams, Sr.,** son of Daniel Williams and Betsey Hayes. He was born 31 July 1914, and died 08 June 1951.

Children of Charlotte Holland and Joseph Williams are:

+ 832 i. **Elizabeth Grace Williams,** born 22 April 1933.

+ 833 ii. **Olivia Ruth Williams,** born 11 November 1934.

+ 834 iii. **Norma Jean Williams,** born 11 August 1937.

+ 835 iv. **Joseph Jordan Williams, Sr.,** born 15 April 1940; died 20 February 1965.

836 v. **Elmer Mae Williams**, born 01 October 1942 in Little Coharie Township, Sampson County, North Carolina. She married **Stacy Nelson Tyndall**; born 27 April 1936 in Dismal Township, Sampson County, North Carolina.

Her date of birth is also listed as 14 November 1942 and her name is also found as Elma May.

\+ 837 vi. **Betty Ellen Williams**, born 12 May 1944.

\+ 838 vii. **Jannie Bell Williams**, born 07 January 1946.

\+ 839 viii. **Joseph Arthur Williams, Jr.**, born 03 March 1948.

\+ 840 ix. **Edward Earl Williams**, born 03 July 1950.

279. Katie Rebecca Holland (Jordan[5], Harfrey[4], Daniel[3], Thomas William[2], Unknown[1]) was born 02 March 1917, and died 19 August 1979. She married **Woodrow Delon Strickland** 02 November 1935. He was born 03 October 1911, and died 27 August 1979.

Katie and Woodrow were buried in Harmony Church Cemetary on Harmony Church Road (SR 1235) in Sampson County, North Carolina.

Children of Katie Holland and Woodrow Strickland are:

\+ 841 i. **Albert Lewis Strickland**, born 21 December 1936.

\+ 842 ii. **Wadus Deleon Strickland**, born 02 January 1938; died 28 November 1963.

843 iii. **Charlotte Ann Strickland**, born 02 May 1939; died 02 May 1939.

She was buried in a Holland Cemetery on Fleet Cooper Road (SR 1240) in Sampson County, North Carolina.

\+ 844 iv. **Linda Faye Strickland,** born 25 October 1942.

\+ 845 v. **Carol Rebecca Strickland**, born 18 January 1945.

\+ 846 vi. **Mable Rose Strickland**, born 03 June 1946.

847 vii. **LeRoy Strickland**, born 18 August 1947.

\+ 848 viii. **Ellen Gail Strickland**, born 27 August 1948.

849 ix. **Allen Dail Strickland**, born 27 August 1948. He married **Anna Lee Burnette**.

\+ 850 x. **Jerry Holland Strickland**, born 11 June 1951.

280. David Jordan Holland (Jordan[5], Harfrey[4], Daniel[3], Thomas William[2], Unknown[1]) was born 07 July 1918, and died after 1955. He married **Lottie Byrd**. She was born 25 April 1914.

Children of David Holland and Lottie Byrd are:

\+ 851 i. **Steven Craig Holland**, born 09 January 1941.

852 ii. **Mark Jordan Holland,** born 01 June 1955.

June 02, 1955 is also found for his birth..

281. Repsie Holland (Chester[5], Harfrey[4], Daniel[3], Thomas William[2], Unknown[1]) was born 02 March 1882 in Sampson County, North Carolina, and died 18 June 1938. She married **Daniel Walter Williams** 22 February 1917, son of James Williams and Chelly Tew. He was born 11 November 1881 in Sampson County, North Carolina, and died 03 July 1964 in Sampson County, North Carolina.

One source notes 11 November 1884 for Daniel Walter's birth. He and Repsie were buried in Union Grove Baptist Church Cemetery on SR 1438 one mile west of Rebel City, Sampson County, North Carolina.

Children of Repsie Holland and Daniel Williams are:

+ 853 i. **Lessie Jane Holland Williams,** born 04 August 1905.
+ 854 ii. **Agnes Ruth Williams,** born 01 January 1918; died 14 March 1972.
+ 855 iii. **Chellie Elizabeth Williams,** born 10 December 1919.
+ 856 iv. **Robert Chester Williams,** born 23 September 1923; died 21 June 1998.

282. Columbus Holland (Chester[5], Harfrey[4], Daniel[3], Thomas William[2], Unknown[1]) was born 02 September 1883 in Sampson County, North Carolina, and died 24 January 1963 in Sampson County, North Carolina. He married **Addie Florence Jackson** 08 March 1908 in Residence of Lunda Lee, Sampson County, North Carolina, daughter of James Jackson and Laura Jackson. She was born 02 September 1891 in Sampson County and died 13 October 1974 in Fayetteville, Cumberland County, North Carolina.

Columbus and his wife moved to Dunn in early 1920. He worked for a number of years as a plasterer and brick mason for Mr. Riley West. Elma (Holland) Sollinger told me that her Uncle Columbus and his wife moved in with his "Uncle Lewis Holland" who never married and the uncle gave him his farm. It appears that Lewis did marry, but perhaps had no children. This was "the other Holland Homeplace."

Columbus and Addie were buried in Salemburg Cemetery, Salemburg, Sampson County, North Carolina.

Children of Columbus Holland and Addie Jackson are:

+ 857 i. **Mattie Iona Holland,** born 21 July 1909; died 06 August 1992.
+ 858 ii. **James Albert Holland,** born 22 January 1911; died 25 May 1982.

859 iii. **Almeta Holland,** born 26 November 1914; died 26 September 1916.

One source shows she was born 25 March 1914.

\+ 860 iv. **Mabel Holland**, born 14 October 1917.

\+ 861 v. **Jessie Turlington Holland**, born 31 December 1921.

284. Erastus Holland (Chester[5], Harfrey[4], Daniel[3], Thomas William[2], Unknown[1]) was born 23 July 1888 in Salemburg, Honeycutts Township, Sampson County, North Carolina, and died 26 April 1955 in Erwin, Harnett County, North Carolina. He married **Iona Lee Tew** 17 November 1909 in ... h Tew and Pennie Sinclair. She was born 02 D ... ty, North Carolina, and died 14 July 1964 in Br...

One sources notes that Er... ne reads "April 26, 1955." Erastus and Iona we... , Sampson County, North Carolina.

Children of Erastus Hollan...

862 i. **Matthew Ma...**

863 ii. **Cletha Holla...** **Maxwell, Jr.**; ...

They had no c...

\+ 864 iii. **Chester Aus...** Sampson County, North Carolina, ...

\+ 865 iv. **Aline Holland**, born 13 August 1914.

\+ 866 v. **Elma Holland**, born 11 July 1917 in Sale...

285. John Love Holland, Sr. (Chester[5], Harfrey[4], Daniel[3], Thomas William[2], Unknown[1]) was born 28 October 1890 in Salemburg, Salemburg, North Carolina, and died 04 July 1973 in Clinton, Sampson County, North Carolina. He married **(1) Allie Bertha Warren** 16 November 1915 in Clinton, Sampson County, daughter of Lester Warren and Carrie Carter. She was born 13 May 1896 in North Carolina, and died 03 January 1966 in Salemburg, Sampson County, North Carolina. He married **(2) Lillian Jane Naylor** 07 January 1967 in Salemburg, daughter of Lewis Naylor and Ora Butler. She was born 06 July 1915 in Little Coharie Township, Sampson County, North Carolina, and died 21 March 1987.

Mr. Rosser, Jr. noted that this John Love Holland was a "Jr." He had a son named "John Love Holland, Jr." Elma Holland Sollinger writes in "The Heritage of Harnett County, North Carolina": "At her (sister-in-law's) suggestion, the third son, John Love, came to Dunn and in one week learned to process fruits and vegetables.

"In 1908 the J. L. Holland and Brothers Canning factor was built. All of the family worked together in the fields and preparing the food for canning. The labels were placed on the cans by hand, using a small mop to apply the glue. The cans were boxed and taken to Fayetteville to be sold in the grocery stores."

The certificate of death for Allie shows she died of Cardio Vascular Disease. John Love, Sr. and Allie Bertha were buried in Salemburg Cemetery, Salemburg, Sampson County, North Carolina. Lillian Jane Naylor Holland was buried in Hollywood Cemetery near Roseboro, North Carolina.

Children of John Holland and Allie Warren are:

+ 867 i. **Edna Louise Holland**, born 12 September 1916 in Honeycutts Township, Sampson County, North Carolina; died 29 February 1980 in Wake County, North Carolina.

+ 868 ii. **Ernest Ray Holland**, born 10 December 1919 in Sampson County, North Carolina; died 30 July 1972.

869 iii. **Lemon Grace Holland**, born 17 February 1922 in Honeycutts Township, Sampson County, North Carolina. She married **William James Burton**; born 20 January 1914.

No children.

+ 870 iv. **Lester Floyd Holland**, born 20 January 1924 in Sampson County, North Carolina; died 13 July 1995 in Sampson County Memorial Hospital, Clinton, North Carolina.

+ 871 v. **Alma Inez Holland**, born 18 July 1929 in Salemburg, Honeycutts Township, Sampson County, North Carolina; died 25 May 1984 in Fayetteville, Cumberland County, North Carolina.

+ 872 vi. **John Love Holland, Jr.**, born 30 July 1932 in Sampson County, North Carolina.

286. Lillie Holland (Chester[5], Harfrey[4], Daniel[3], Thomas William[2], Unknown[1]) was born 02 February 1893 in Sampson County, North Carolina, and died 03 May 1984 in Dunn, Harrnett County, North Carolina. She married **Ottis Biggs Naylor** 29 November 1913 in Sampson County, son of John Naylor and Melissa Williford. He was born 01 April 1892 in North Carolina, and died 16 August 1959 in Dunn, Harnett County, North Carolina.

Dr. Bundy in his book has a marriage date of 10 December 1913 for Lillie and Ottis Biggs Naylor. Lillie and Ottis Biggs were buried in Mingo Baptist Church Cemetery, Mingo Township, Sampson County, North Carolina.

Children of Lillie Holland and Ottis Naylor are:

873 i. **Henry Clifton Naylor**, born 30 September 1914 in Mingo Township, Sampson County, North Carolina; died 18 December 1980 in Dunn, Harrnett County, North Carolina. He married **Annie Eldon Barefoot** 14 January 1937 in Erwin, Harnett County, North Carolina; born 11 December 1916 in Mingo Township, Sampson County, North Carolina. No children. He was buried in Mingo Baptist Church Cemetery, Mingo Township, Sampson County, North Carolina.

+ 874 ii. **Charles Hilliard Naylor**, born 09 November 1917 in Mingo Township, Sampson County, North Carolina.

+ 875 iii. **Payton Thomas Naylor** was born 05 November 1919 in Mingo Township, Sampson County and died 22 January 1985 in Wake County, North Carolina.

+ 876 iv. **Graham Willard Naylor**, born 06 May 1921 in Mingo Township, Sampson County, North Carolina.

+ 877 v. **Irene Naylor**, born 26 August 1924 in Mingo Township, Sampson County.

+ 878 vi. **Mary Maxine Naylor**, born 28 June 1926 in Mingo Township, Sampson County.

879 vii. **Ottis Highsmith Naylor**, born 24 June 1929 in Mingo Township, Sampson County, North Carolina; died 11 June 1930.

The tombstone for Ottis Highsmith has June 12, 1930 for his death. He was buried in Mingo Baptist Church Cemetery, Mingo Township, Sampson County.

+ 880 viii. **Malissa Jane Naylor**, born 28 March 1933 in Mingo Township, Sampson County, North Carolina.

+ 881 ix. **Annie Bell Naylor**, born 17 October 1936 in Mingo Township, Sampson County.

882 x. **Young Deceased Daughter Naylor.**

287. Rosella Holland (Chester[5], Harfrey[4], Daniel[3], Thomas William[2], Unknown[1]) was born 23 January 1895 in Sampson County, North Carolina, and died 02 November 1988 in Asheboro, Randolph County, North Carolina. She married **William Hubert Grimes** 27 October 1921 in Honeycutt's Township, Sampson County, North Carolina. He was born 06 February 1895 in North Carolina, and died 08 October 1971 in Asheboro, Randolph County, North Carolina.

Children of Rosella Holland and William Grimes are:

+ 883 i. **Lois Evelyn Grimes**, born 03 August 1922.

+ 884 ii. **Joanne Grimes**, born 23 June 1930.

288. Charlotte Ann Holland (Chester[5], Harfrey[4], Daniel[3], Thomas William[2], Unknown[1]) was born 05 May 1897 in Sampson County, North Carolina, and died 24 March 1995 in Salemburg, Sampson County, North Carolina. She married **Robert Almon Jackson** 22 December 1918 in residence of Chester Holland, Sampson County, North Carolina, son of Almon Jackson and Mary Jackson. He was born 22 February 1888 in Sampson County and died 22 February 1977 in Salemburg, Sampson County.

Robert's middle name is spelled "Almond" on the birth certificate of one of his sons.

Charlotte Ann and Robert Almon were buried in Salemburg Cemetery, Salemburg, Sampson County, North Carolina.

Children of Charlotte Holland and Robert Jackson are:

+ 885 i. **Cleveland DeVane Jackson, Sr.**, born 10 August 1920 in Honeycutts Township, Sampson County, North Carolina.

886 ii. **Lloyd Jackson.**

887 iii. **Ammie Jackson.**

289. James Monroe Holland (Chester[5], Harfrey[4], Daniel[3], Thomas William[2], Unknown[1]) was born 04 July 1899 in Sampson County, North Carolina, and died 21 March 1993 in either a Nursing or Rest Home in Mount Olive, Wayne County, North Carolina. He married **Lou Ina Carter** 21 September 1928 in North Carolina, daughter of Albert Carter and Mamie Best. She was born 07 October 1908, and died 19 June 1981 in Salemburg, Sampson County.

A granddaughter tells that at birth he was named Monroe and he later added James after President James Monroe, but he was always known as "Monroe". He was a bricklayer. Elma Holland Sollinger notes on page 229 in "The Heritage of Harnett County" North Caroline that he was well known for the chimneys he built. They did not "smoke up your house or get cracks in them." Lou Ina was always known as "Ina." She had a dream that she would meet her future husband at her parents' house while she was swearing a pink apron. Monroe went to the Carter home to build a chimney and met Ina, and she was wearing a pink apron just as she had dreamed. They were married in September that same year.

Monroe and Ina were buried in Salemburg Cemetery, Salemburg, Sampson County, North Carolina

Only child of Monroe Holland and Ina Carter is:

\+ 888 i. **Thamer Lee Holland**, born 02 April 1930 in Newton Grove, Westbrooks Township, Sampson County, North Carolina.

292. Braxton Spell (Romelia[5] Holland, Harfrey[4], Daniel[3], Thomas William[2], Unknown[1]) was born 17 December 1883, and died 03 September 1947 in Sampson County, North Carolina. He married **Lela Mae Royal** about 1914, daughter of Enoch Royal and Henrietta Hollingsworth. She was born 07 February 1899, and died 06 May 1982 in Sampson County.

Lela Mae's date of birth is also listed as 02 Jul 1899. Braxton and Lela Mae were buried in a Spell Family Cemetery on Dunn Road North of Roseboro, North Carolina.

Children of Braxton Spell and Lela Royal are:

\+ 889 i. **Lewis Alton Spell**, born 25 July 1915 in Sampson County, North Carolina; died 13 December 1978 in Cumberland County, North Carolina.

890 ii. **Randall Spell**, born 08 August 1918 in Sampson County, North Carolina; died 21 July 1949 in Cumberland County, North Carolina. He married (1) **Edna McLaurin**; born 28 May 1917 in Cumberland County, North Carolina; died 01 October 1938 in Hoke County, North Carolina. He married (2) **Pauline Jackson**; born 22 August 1920 in Cumberland County, North Carolina; died 27 September 1994.

Randall and Pauline were buried in a Spell Family Cemetery on Dunn Road north of Roseboro, North Carolina. Edna was buried in Union Grove Church Cemetery, Sampson County, North Carolina.

\+ 891 iii. **Mae Olive Spell**, born 01 January 1917 in Sampson County, North Carolina.

892 iv. **Amie Vinsion Spell**, born 08 October 1920 in Sampson County. He married **Donnie Mae Myers.**

\+ 893 v. **Pauline Spell,** born 22 October 1922 in Sampson County, North Carolina.

\+ 894 vi. **Ernie Minson Spell**, born 22 September 1924 in Sampson County; died 27 January 1966.

\+ 895 vii. **Almeta Spell**, born 29 August 1929 in Dismal Township, Sampson County, North Carolina.

\+ 896 viii. **James Oscar Spell**, born about 1930 in Sampson County.

\+ 897 ix. **Liston Spell**, born 17 April 1933 in Sampson County, North Carolina; died 03 August 1981 in Sampson County, North Carolina.

\+ 898 x. **Leola Spell,** born 28 July 1934 in Dismal Township, Sampson County.

\+ 899 xi. **Margaret Doris Spell**, born 09 December 1935 in Dismal Township, Sampson County, North Carolina.

\+ 900 xii. **Muriel Grace Spell**, born 11 November 1936 in Sampson County.

901 xiii. **Lathan Spell**, born 23 February 1941 in Sampson County, North Carolina; died 17 April 1980 in Sampson County. He married **Jean Stewart**.

He was buried in a Spell Family Cemetery on Dunn Road north of Roseboro, North Carolina.

293. George Oliver Spell (Romelia[5] Holland, Harfrey[4], Daniel[3], Thomas William[2], Unknown[1]) was born 02 May 1889, and died 25 September 1967 in Lillington, North Carolina. He married **Neta Ann Honeycutt** 19 October 1913, daughter of Wiley Honeycutt and Mary Williams. She was born 10 December 1894 in Sampson County, North Carolina, and died 29 February 1984.

George Oliver and Neta Ann were buried in Union Grove Baptist Church Cemetery on Vander Road (SR 1438) Sampson County, North Carolina.

Children of George Spell and Neta Honeycutt are:

902 i. **Perry Oliver Spell**, born 12 January 1915 in Dismal Township, Sampson County, North Carolina; died 21 March 1980 in Fayetteville. He married **Mary Gladys Blanchard**; born 22 April 1918 in Black River Township, Cumberland County, North Carolina.

He was buried in LaFayette Memorial Park, Fayetteville, North Carolina.

903 ii. **Annie Ruth Spell** was born 17 May 1918 in Dismal Township, Sampson County, North Carolina. She married **Elmon Edison Bradshaw**; born 05 March 1918 in Herrings Township, Sampson County; died 17 September 1982 in Dunn, North Carolina.

+ 904 iii. **Percy Blackman Spell**, born 26 October 1920; died 02 June 1991.

905 iv. **Harold Orman Spell**, born 29 December 1922 in Dismal Township, Sampson County, North Carolina.

906 v. **Mildred Kathalene Spell**, born 10 May 1925 in Dismal Township, Sampson County.

297. Sophia Horne (Laura Ann[5] Holland, Harfrey[4], Daniel[3], Thomas William[2], Unknown[1]) was born 15 August 1898, and died 17 December 1979. She married **Elliott Fletcher Faircloth,** son of William Faircloth and Sarah Autry. He was born 26 April 1898, and died 02 March 1978.

Sophia and Elliott Fletcher were buried in the George Horne Cemetery near intersection of South River Road and Minnie Hall Road, Sampson County, North Carolina.

Children of Sophia Horne and Elliott Faircloth are:

+ 907 i. **Lona Marie Faircloth,** born 02 July 1920.

+ 908 ii. **Eva Faircloth,** born 09 October 1922.

+ 909 iii. **W. J. Faircloth,** born 17 January 1924.

910 iv. **Earl Sion Faircloth,** born 14 January 1928 in Little Coharie Township, Sampson County, North Carolina. He married **Mary Emma Hall**; born 13 November 1928 in Little Coharie Township, Sampson County, North Carolina.

No children. Dr. Bundy gives the year of birth as 1926 for Earl.

911 v. **Nathan Faircloth,** born 21 August 1929. He married **Mattie C. Blount**; born 04 August 1919; died 09 August 1982.

No children. Mattie was buried in George Horne Cemetery on Minnie Hall Road near South River Road, Sampson County, North Carolina.

+ 912 vi. **Sarah Elizabeth Faircloth,** born 12 February 1933.

298. Herman Perry Holland (Ammie[5], Harfrey[4], Daniel[3], Thomas William[2], Unknown[1]) was born 08 January 1906 in Sampson County, North Carolina, and died 29 April 1953. He married **Lenna Mae Holland,** daughter of Julius Holland and Lillie Unknown. She was born 06 September 1912, and died 11 October 1979.

Herman Holland, son of Rufus Holland (another grandson of Harfrey Holland) was born about 1900 and would be a few years older than this Herman Perry. One of these men named Herman may have been the "Herman L. Holland," aged 19 who married Lela Mae Grantham, aged 16 on 22 December 1925 in Clinton, North Carolina. The Lenna Mae Holland listed for the spouse of Herman Perry Holland has a birth date of 6 September 1912 indicating that she would not have been aged 16 in 1925, but Lenna Mae and Lela Mae are such similar names I would suggest that further research is needed to determine the correct name(s). Herman Perry and Lenna Mae were buried in Salemburg Cemetery, Bearskin Road, Salemburg, North Carolina.

Children of Herman Holland and Lenna Holland are:

913 i. **Rupert W. Holland**, born about 1927 in Sampson County, North Carolina.

914 ii. **Symolene Holland**, born 05 September 1934 in Sampson County, North Carolina; died 07 September 1934.

Vital records spell her name as Symoline Holland. She was buried in Salemburg Cemetery on Bearskin Road (SR 1323) in Sampson County, North Carolina.

915 iii. **L. Brown Holland**, born in Sampson County.

299. Harvey Holland (Henry Lee[5], Harfrey[4], Daniel[3], Thomas William[2], Unknown[1]) was born 05 October 1897 in Sampson County, North Carolina, and died 22 August 1947 in Honeycutts Township, Sampson County, North Carolina. He married **Eunice M. Fisher**. She was born 02 May 1897, and died 16 May 1961 in Sampson County.

He was a farmer and carpenter. The cause of his death was Cerebral Hemmorhage (1 hour). Harvey and Eunice were buried in Salemburg Cemetery, Salemburg, Sampson County, North Carolina.

Children of Harvey Holland and Eunice Fisher are:

916 i. **Clyde H. Holland,** born about 1928. He married Daphne Unknown. He died either later 2008 or early 2009.

\+ 917 ii. **Ruby Sykes Holland**, born 08 August 1928 in Honeycutts Township, Sampson County, North Carolina.

918 iii. **Helen Holland.**

\+ 919 iv. **Doris M. Holland**, born 19 May 1934; died 08 May 1998.

300. Pauline Holland (Henry Lee[5], Harfrey[4], Daniel[3], Thomas William[2], Unknown[1]) was born 01 August 1901, and died 13 November 1957 in Fayetteville, Cumberland County, North Carolina. She married **Othi McLamb** 29 April 1922 in Hay Street Methodist Church, Fayetteville, North Carolina, son of Isham McLamb and Adella Jackson. He was born 29 April 1898, and died 01 June 1970 in Elizabethtown, Bladen County, North Carolina.

Child of Pauline Holland and Othi McLamb is:

\+ 920 i. **Isham O'Neal McLamb**, born 02 September 1925 in Honeycutts Township, Sampson County, North Carolina; died 24 May 1984 in Fayetteville, Cumberland County, North Carolina.

301. Onie Vendex Holland (William Wright[5], Thomas James[4], Daniel[3], Thomas William[2], Unknown[1]) was born 14 October 1871, and died 30 June 1952 in Sampson County, North Carolina. She married **John Robert Lockamy** in1891, son of Robert Lockamy and Annie Dudley. He was born 26 July 1874 in Sampson County, North Carolina, and died 19 August 1930 in Sampson County, North Carolina.

Her year of birth is listed as 1877 in "Footprints from Kitty Fork" by Annie Carolyn Tew and Fannie Lee Lockamy Williams. Onie Vendex and John Robert were buried in Owens Grove Pentecostal FWB Church Cemetery, Sampson County, North Carolina.

Children of Onie Holland and John Lockamy are:

+ 921 i. **William Lischer Lockamy**, born 17 February 1897 in Sampson County, North Carolina; died 31 March 1961.

+ 922 ii. **Annie Lockamy**, born 04 September 1898 in Sampson County, North Carolina; died 23 July 1984 in Sampson County.

+ 923 iii. **Ada Lockamy**, born 08 October 1901; died 30 September 1964 in Sampson County.

+ 924 iv. Robert Owen Lockamy, born 02 September 1904 in Sampson County, North Carolina; died 01 July 1966 in Sampson County.

+ 925 v. **Janie Lou Lockamy**, born 22 July 1910; died 30 March 1985.

302. Charles Henry Holland, Sr. (William Wright[5], Thomas James[4], Daniel[3], Thomas William[2], Unknown[1]) was born 15 April 1876, and died 25 May 1962. He married **(2) Mattie V. Sanderson** before 1917. She was born 07 February 1883, and died 07 February 1917. He married **(1) Minnie Griffen**, daughter of George Griffen and Martha Lindsey. She was born 01 June 1894 in North Carolina and died 04 March 1960 of bilateral Broncho-pneumonia and was in a diabetic coma in Duplin County Hospital in Kenansville, Duplin County, North Carolina.

Charles Henry Sr., Mattie V. and Minnie G. were buried in Turkey Baptist Church Cemetery, Turkey, North Carolina.

Children of Charles Holland and Mattie V. Sanderson are:

Nancy P. Holland, born about 1903 in Turkey, Sampson County, North Carolina.

Viola J. Holland, born about 1905 in Turkey, Sampson County.

Katie L. Holland, born about 1909 in Turkey, Sampson County, North Carolina .

Child of Charles Holland and Minnie Unknown is:

926 i. **Charles Henry Holland, Jr.**, born 1927; died 1993.

Charles Henry, Jr. was buried in Turkey Baptist Church Cemetery, Turkey, North Carolina.

304. William Jasper Holland (William Wright[5], Thomas James[4], Daniel[3], Thomas William[2], Unknown[1]) was born 04 December 1879 in Sampson County, North Carolina, and died 26 July 1962 in Sampson County. He married **Ozora Dare** who was born 12 September 1889 and died 16 June 1981.

William Jasper was buried in The Clinton Cemetery, Clinton, Sampson County, North Carolina.

Children of William Holland and Ozora Dare are:

927 i. **Clara Lee Holland,** born 12 October 1908 in Sampson County, North Carolina.

928 ii. **Edna Virginia Holland,** born 20 December 1909 in Sampson County.

929 iii. **W. Theodore Holland,** born about 1912.

930 iv. **Stacy Holland,** born about 1914.

931 v. **James H. Holland,** born about 1920.

932 vi. **William Jasper Holland, Jr.,** born 20 April 1921.

933 vii. **Truman Holland,** born about 1923 in Taylors Bridge.

306. Arthur Braxton Holland (William Wright[5], Thomas James[4], Daniel[3], Thomas William[2], Unknown[1]) was born 23 March 1883, and died 04 September 1971. He married **Lottie Clute Shipp** 24 November 1906. She was born 22 November 1887, and died 19 March 1965.

Braxton Arthur Holland was listed for his name on his delayed certificate of birth. Apparently, he and his parents lived in the southeastern area of Sampson County, North Carolina. Arthur's World War I registration card records 23 March 1881 for his birth. He and Lottie were buried in the Turkey Baptist Church Cemetery on Hwy 24 near Turkey, North Carolina.

The 1920 census lists "Lessie Holland" as a son of Arthur Braxton and Lottie and 1912 for his year of birth, but Lessie is not found in the 1930 census records which may indicate that Fletcher may be listed as Lessie in the transcribed census index. Arthur and Lottie may have had a daughter, "Allie Lee Holland" who was born 11 August 1912 and died 22 November 1915; she was near them.

Children of Arthur Holland and Lottie Shipp are:

i. **William Braxton Holland,** born about 1908 in Turkey, Sampson County, North Carolina. He married **Florence Foye Register** who was born 13 October 1908 and died 19 November 1934. They were buried in Turkey Baptist Church Cemetery on Highway 24 in Turkey, Sampson County, North Carolina. On 26 August 1934, William had a son, **William Braxton Holland,** born in Sampson County.

934 ii. **James Lawrence Holland,** born 13 May 1909 in Sampson County, North Carolina.

935 iii. **Fletcher Grover Holland,** born 18 February 1911 in Sampson County, North Carolina. He is probably the Fletcher "C.?" Holland buried in Trinity United Methodist Church Cemetery on Trinity Church Road (SR 1945) in Sampson County, North Carolina. Shirley J. Holland,

most likely his wife, who was born 6 January 1915 also has a headstone there with no date of death. They were married 6 June 1936. Shirley's Maiden name may have been "Johnson."

iv. **Florine Holland** was born about 1915. Her name appears to be "Florine" in the 1930 census for Turkey, Turkey Township, Sampson County, North Carolina.

936 v. **Paul Crumpler Holland**, born 24 April 1918 in Sampson County, North Carolina. He may have married **KATHLEEN D. MALPASS**. They were the parents listed for **PAUL CRUMPLER HOLLAND, Jr.** who was born 8 July 1947 in Scotland (?) County, North Carolina. Paul Crumpler Holland is named for the father of **DEBORAH ANN HOLLAND** who was born in 1952 in Sampson County.

A birth in 1958 is recorded for **JAMES BRAXTON HOLLAND** son of Paul Crumpler Holland.

937 vi. **Moselle Elizabeth Holland**, born 10 March 1922 in Sampson County, North Carolina; died 02 January 1923 in Turkey Township, Turkey, Sampson County.

vii. **Doris Holland**, the sixth child of Arthur Holland and Lottie Shipp, was born about 1924 in Turkey, Sampson County, North Carolina.

viii. **Jacqueline Holland**, the seventh child of Arthur Holland and Lottie Shipp, was born about 1928 in Turkey, Sampson County, North Carolina.

309. Leslie Lee Holland (William Wright[5], Thomas James[4], Daniel[3], Thomas William[2], Unknown[1]) was born 17 November 1891 in Sampson County, North Carolina, and died 19 March 1961 in Sampson County, North Carolina. He married **Minnie Royal**, daughter of Raiford Royal and Mary Honeycutt. She was born 18 July 1894 in Sampson County and died 07 August 1973 in Sampson County, North Carolina.

Minnie died from chronic lung disease and ASHD due to arteriosclerosis. Leslie Lee and Minnie were buried in The Clinton Cemetery, Clinton, Sampson County, North Carolina.

Children of Leslie Holland and Minnie Royal are:

938 i. **Infant Holland**, born 1910 in Sampson County, North Carolina; died 1910.

She was buried in The Clinton Cemetery, Clinton, Sampson County, North Carolina.

939 ii. **Raymond Holland**, born 1912 in Sampson County, North Carolina.

940 iii. **William Holland**, born about 1922 in Sampson County.

941 iv. **Rufus McKenley Holland**, born 30 April 1926 in Sampson County; died 24 October 1997 in Sampson Regional Medical Center, Clinton, Sampson County, North Carolina.

He never married and he had Chronic obstructive lung disease for years. He was buried in The Clinton Cemetery, Clinton, North Carolina.

310. Elliott Rexford Holland (William Wright[5], Thomas James[4], Daniel[3], Thomas William[2], Unknown[1]) was born 7 September 1895. He married **Molley Frances Honeycutt**

04 November 1912 in residence of Bride's father, Sampson County, North Carolina. She was born about 1894.

Children of Elliott Holland and Molley Honeycutt are:

942 i. **Paul Rexford Holland**, born about 1918.

ii. **Mattie C. Holland**, born about 1920.

943 iii. **Brownie Frances Holland**, born 16 December 1921.

iv. **Junius E. Holland**, born about 1924.

v. **Bettie G. Holland**, born about 1925.

vi. **Doris Holland,** born about 1927.

vii. **Loletta Holland**, born about 1929.

313. Vara Irene Boyette (Catharan Gray[5] Holland, Thomas James[4], Daniel[3], Thomas William[2], Unknown[1]) was born 29 May 1893 in Giddensville, Sampson County, North Carolina, and died 08 February 1962 in Albertson, Duplin County, North Carolina. She married **Ira Grissom Harper** 11 September 1920 in Pikeville, Wayne County, North Carolina. He was born 31 January 1887 in Pink Hill, Lenoir County, North Carolina, and died 01 July 1972 in Kinston, Lenoir County, North Carolina.

Catherine Grey is also found for her mother's name. Vara and Ira were buried in the Harper Cemetery on SR 1543 north of SR 1546, Duplin County, North Carolina.

Children of Vara Boyette and Ira Harper are:

\+ 944 i. **Ivey Gilbert Harper**, born 12 February 1922 in Kinston, Lenoir County, North Carolina.

945 ii. **Milo Warren Harper**, born 12 March 1924 in Pink Hill, Lenoir County, North Carolina. He married Living Alcock. They had ten children.

946 iii. **Jerald Daniel Harper**, born 08 October 1926 in Albertson, Duplin County, North Carolina. He married Living Jones. Six children.

947 iv. **Caroll James Harper**, born 20 June 1928 in Deep Run, Duplin County, North Carolina. He married Living Jones. Seven children.

948 v. **Mildred Irene Harper**, born 21 November 1929 in Deep Run, Duplin County, North Carolina. She married **Gerald David Wood** 26 September 1952 in Salt Lake City, Salt Lake, Utah; born 26 September 1929 in Meridan, Ada, Idaho.

Six children.

949 vi. **Living Harper**.

315. Effie Gray Holland (Thomas James[5], Thomas James[4], Daniel[3], Thomas William[2], Unknown[1]) was born 24 February 1889 in Piney Grove Township, Sampson County, North

Carolina, and died 14 February 1979. She married **Ernest Vanderbilt Woodard, Sr.** 01 August 1912. He was born 31 December 1885, and died 11 June 1965.

Effie and Ernest met "while attending Buies Creek Academy and Business College (later to become Campbell College). While Ernest went on to the University of North Carolina, Chapel Hill, to obtain his pharmacy degree, Effie studied at North Carolina, Normal and Industrial College (UNC-Greensboro) returning to Buies Creek to teach for a year.

"After marriage, Effie and Ernest lived in Selma, North Carolina, where Ernest had his drug store for several years, before joining Creech Drug Company following the depression.

"...Effie's sister-in-law, ...was the Selma Correspondent for the Smithfield Herald and the local paper. When she retired in 1935, Effie took her place, little realizing that for the next forty years she would be writing for newspapers. ... Effie retired in 1975 due to arthritis in her hands.

"Source: Family records --Mrs. Janice H. Smith."

Children of Effie Holland and Ernest Woodard are:

950 i. **Lillian Louise Woodard**, born 13 January 1915 in Selma, North Carolina. She married **Ronald Ernest Herren**; born 18 June 1914 in Harrison, Nebraska.

Lillian and Ronald had two children. **Ronald Ernest Herren, Jr.**, who was born 07 January 1944 in Smithfield, North Carolina and married **Paula Lowry** on 15 June 1968.

Terry Gray Herren, daughter of Lillian and Ronald, Sr, was born 10 May 1947 in Columbus, Ohio. She married **Robert F. Gilead** on 29 June 1974.

951 ii. **Ernest Vanderbilt Woodard, Jr.**, born 29 April 1918 in Selma, North Carolina; died 04 March 1983. He married **Celesta Boyette** 28 February 1946 in Kenly, North Carolina; born 15 June 1918 in Johnston County, North Carolina.

Ernest and Celesta had one child, **Ernest Vanderbilt Woodard III** who was born on 16 October 1950 in Radford, Montgomery County, Virginia, and married **Darlene H. Murray** 25 November 1978.

952 iii. **Thomas Holland Woodard**, born 05 December 1920 in North Carolina. He married **Lanie Gunter** who born 09 February 1922 in Aberdeen, North Carolina.

Thomas and Lanie had two children. **Linda Louise Woodard** was born on 04 October 1946 in Fayetteville, North Carolina and married **Charles Henry Wilson** on 14 June 1968.

Thomas and Lanie youngest daughter, **Sallie Dail Woodard** was born 16 March 1955 in Richmond, Virginia and she married **Bruce Steven Tiso**.

324. Lenna Mae Holland (Julius^5, Daniel^4, Daniel^3, Thomas William^2, Unknown^1) was born 06 September 1912, and died 11 October 1979. She married **Herman Perry Holland**, son of Ammie Holland and Lillie Horne. He was born 08 January 1906 in Sampson County, North Carolina, and died 29 April 1953.

Lenna Mae and Herman Perry were buried in Salemburg Cemetery Bearskin Road, Salemburg, North Carolina.

Herman Holland, son of Rufus Holland (another grandson of Harfrey Holland) was born about 1900 and would be a few years older than this Herman Perry. One of these men named Herman may have been the "Herman L. Holland," aged 19 who married Lela Mae Grantham, aged 16 on 22 December 1925 in Clinton, North Carolina. The Lenna Mae Holland listed for the spouse of Herman Perry Holland has a birth date of 6 September 1912 indicating that she would not have been aged 16 in 1925, but Lenna Mae and Lela Mae are such similar names I would suggest that further research is needed to determine the correct name(s).

Children are listed above under (298) Herman Perry Holland.

331. Robertson Royals (Agnes Matilda[5] Holland, Matthew[4], Daniel[3], Thomas William[2], Unknown[1]) was born 17 May 1888 in Sampson County, North Carolina, and died 24 December 1951 in Honeycutts Township, Sampson County. He married **Maythelia Tew** 08 June 1908 in Peter Jackson's Crossroads, Sampson County, North Carolina, daughter of Newbern Tew and Anna Dawson. She was born 03 July 1888 in Sampson County and died 03 November 1957 in Salemburg, Sampson County, North Carolina.

His name is given as "Robert Royal" in one source. In the 1900 census for Honeycutts Township, Sampson County, North Carolina, his name is given as "Robertson." One source spells her first name, "Maphelia."

Children of Robertson Royals and Maythelia Tew are:

\+ 953 i. **Ivy D. Royal**, born 19 March 1910; died 18 November 1966 in Fayetteville, Cumberland County, North Carolina.

954 ii. **Ora Mae Royal**, born 24 April 1912. She married (1) **Jim Johnson**. She married (2) **Charles Eldridge**; born 27 September 1888.

There were no children from either marriage. "The Heritage of Harnett County," (North Carolina) by The Harnett County Heritage Committee, on page 369 notes her name as "Oramie."

955 iii. **Samuel Maryland Royal**, born 03 July 1914; died 17 February 1975.

He was buried in Sunrise Memorial Gardens, between Roseboro and Salemburg, Sampson County, North Carolina.

\+ 956 iv. **James Evelyn Royal**, born 27 August 1917; died 13 February 2001.

334. Sally Royals (Agnes Matilda[5] Holland, Matthew[4], Daniel[3], Thomas William[2], Unknown[1]) was born May 1892 in Sampson County, North Carolina. She married **George Purdie Honeycutt** 26 April 1919 in Dunn, Harnett County, North Carolina, son of John

Honeycutt and Chelly Honeycutt. He was born 23 July 1874 in Sampson County and died 27 April 1948 in Roseboro, North Carolina.

George first married **Minnie Butler**, daughter of **Haywood Butler** and **Sabra Jane Crumpler.** Minnie was born 10 September 1879 and died 18 October 1918. They had nine children. His Draft Registration Card for World War I shows 1 September 1874 (aged 44) for his birth and Minnie Butler Honeycutt for his spouse. He was an Inspector Hand in Erwin Cotton Mills in Duke, Harnett County, North Carolina.

George Purdie Honeycutt was buried in Honeycutt Cemetery on High House Road near Reynolds Crossroads, Sampson County, North Carolina.

Children of Sally Royals and George Honeycutt are:

957 i. **Minnie Kitchen Honeycutt**, born 03 October 1920 in Harnett County, North Carolina.

958 ii. **Henry Linwood Honeycutt**, born 1923 in Sampson County, North Carolina.

959 iii. **Bruce Melvin Honeycutt**, born 30 March 1931 in Sampson County, North Carolina.

335. Lessie Royals (Agnes Matilda[5] Holland, Matthew[4], Daniel[3], Thomas William[2], Unknown[1]) was born January 1893 in Sampson County, North Carolina. She married **Lorenza Daniel Tew**, son of Ransom Tew and Arrena McLamb. He was born 22 October 1891, and died 04 July 1978.

One source records him as "Lorenzo Dall Tew." The certificate of birth for his daughter, Evelyn, listed "Lorenza Daniel Tew" for his name.

Children of Lessie Royals and Lorenza Tew are:

960 i. **Claxton Tew.**

961 ii. **Crocket Tew.**

962 iii. **Lucille Tew,** born 13 May 1912. She married a Mr. Register.

\+ 963 iv. Blackman Dee Tew, born 19 July 1914 in Little Coharie Township, Sampson County, North Carolina.

964 v. **Henry Ransom Tew,** born about 1917.

965 vi. **Evelyn Tew,** born about 1922. She married a Huff.

966 vii. **Amanda Tew,** born about 1926. She married a Davis.

967 viii. **Herman Tew,** born about 1928.

337. Matthew Royals (Agnes Matilda[5] Holland, Matthew[4], Daniel[3], Thomas William[2], Unknown[1]) was born 04 November 1895 in Sampson County, North Carolina, and died 05 December 1976 in Erwin, North Carolina. He married **Myrtle Williams** 30 June 1927, daughter of Alexander Williams and Cornelia Jackson. She was born 19 May 1903 in Sampson County, North Carolina, and died 14 September 1981 in Erwin, North Carolina.

See Alexander Williams elsewhere in this book.

In the 1900 census for Honeycutts Township, Sampson County, North Carolina, Matthew's name is given as Mathew. He was called "Matt." Matthew and Myrtle were buried in Erwin Memorial Park, Harnett County, North Carolina.

Children of Matthew Royals and Myrtle Williams are:

968 i. **Doris Marie Royals,** born 08 September 1927 in Erwin, North Carolina.

It appears that Doris may have married a "Connor."

969 ii. **Virgiline Royals**.

970 iii. **Matthew Glasgow Royals**, born 22 April 1933 in Erwin, North Carolina. He married Jean (maiden name unknown).

971 iv. **Thomas Wayne Royals**.

339. Henry H. Royals, Jr. (Agnes Matilda[5] Holland, Matthew[4], Daniel[3], Thomas William[2], Unknown[1]) was born 18 June 1898 in Sampson County, North Carolina, and died 29 September 1981 in Erwin, Harnett County, North Carolina. He married **Nora Reaves**.

"The Heritage of Harnett County," by the Harnett County Heritage Committee (North Carolina) notes the following about Henry, Jr.:

"Henry Royals, Sr. came to Erwin (the town at that time was called Duke) in 1911 as a carpenter and worked to help build the Erwin Mill and the mill houses. He helped build the mill house at 106 North 16 Street in Erwin and in the spring of 1913, moved his family into that house. Henry, Sr. and Matilda lived in the house until their deaths. Matt who was Henry, Sr. and Matilda's sixth child, married Myrtle Williams and moved in the house with his parents. Matt and Myrtle lived in the house until their deaths. Following the death of Matt and Myrtle, their son, Matthew, and his wife, Jean, moved into the house.

"Sources: Family Recollections and tombstones. -- Doris Royals Connor."

Children of Henry Royals and Nora Reaves are:

972 i. **Eugene Royals**, born about 1923.

973 ii. **Clifton Royals**, born about 1925.

974 iii. **Cecial Royals**, born about 1928.

975 iv. **Deloris Royals**, born after 1930.

976 v. **Edward Royals**, born after 1930.

977 vi. **Richard Perry Royals**, born after 1930.

978 vii. **Shirley Royals**, born after 1930. She married Hobbs.

Shirley lived in Erwin, North Carolina.

979 viii. **Truman Royals**, born after 1930.

980 ix. **William C. Royals**, born after 1930.

340. Julius David Holland, Sr. (Marshall[5], Matthew[4], Daniel[3], Thomas William[2], Unknown[1]) was born 07 July 1907, and died 15 January 2001.

In 1930, Julius Holland, aged 24, was living with his cousin, Claudius Holland. Social Security records his date of birth as 8 July 1905. His certifice of death records 7 July 1907 for his birth. Julius died in Mary Gran Nursing Center in Clinton, North Carolina. He was divorced. He was buried in Beulah United Methodist Church Cemetery on Corinth Church Road (SR 1326), Sampson County, North Carolina.

Children of Julius David Holland, Sr. are:

\+ 981 i. **Julius David Holland, Jr.**, born 20 September 1942 in Newton Grove Township, Sampson County, North Carolina.

982 ii. **Joel Thomas Holland**, born 1945 in Sampson County, North Carolina.

983 iii. **Nita Louise Holland**, born 1950 in Sampson County.

342. Lela Holland (Robert Mitchell[5], Matthew[4], Daniel[3], Thomas William[2], Unknown[1]) was born July 1891, and died 1939. She married **Harrison Hanstein Royal** 20 February 1915 in residence of C. M. Hall, son of Amos Royal and Atha Honeycutt. He was born 30 November 1893 in Honeycutts Township, Sampson County, North Carolina, and died 02 June 1982 near Clinton in Sampson County.

Lela and Harrison were buried in Calvary Tabernacle Pentecostal FW Baptist Church Cemetery on High House Road one mile west of Highway 242, Sampson County.

Children of Lela Holland and Harrison Royal are:

\+ 984 i. **Roland Duvell Royal,** born 08 December 1916 in Honeycutts Township, Sampson County, North Carolina; died 29 November 1987 in Fayetteville, Cumberland County, North Carolina.

\+ 985 ii. **Coy Aaron Royal**, born 08 August 1918 in Honeycutts Township, Sampson County, North Carolina.

\+ 986 iii. **Amos Harrison Royal**, born 16 January 1921 in Herrings Township, Sampson County, North Carolina; died 28 October 1986 in Clinton, Sampson County.

\+ 987 iv. **Robert Layman Royal**, born 19 January 1923 in Dismal Township, Sampson County.

\+ 988 v. **E. T. Royal**, born 29 July 1925 in Dismal Township, Sampson County, North Carolina.

\+ 989 vi. **Arman Onroe Royal**, born 19 November 1929 in Dismal Township, Sampson County.

343. Julia Holland (Robert Mitchell[5], Matthew[4], Daniel[3], Thomas William[2], Unknown[1]) was born 31 July 1894, and died 22 April 1985. She married **James Columbus Barnes,** son of William Troy Barnes and Molsey Ann Cannady. He was born 12 October 1883 in Johnston County, North Carolina, and died 03 March 1968 in Sampson County, North Carolina.

Her name is also spelled "Julie." Julia and James Columbus were buried in a Barnes Cemetery on a dirt road off Tyndall Bridge Road (SR 1329.) Sampson County, North Carolina. Much of the data for the family of James Columbus Barnes was either confirmed or corrected by Judy Katherine Barnes Jackson, a descendant.

Children of Julia Holland and James Barnes are:

990 i. **Julia Mae Barnes**, born 14 October 1926 in Sampson County, North Carolina; died 14 October 1926.

\+ 991 ii. **James William Barnes**, born 05 November 1927 in Sampson County, North Carolina.

\+ 992 iii. **Lester Lee Barnes**, born 06 September 1931 in Sampson County.

993 iv. **Robert Elger Barnes**, born 24 January 1934 in Sampson County, North Carolina.

Elger was known as 'Gobbay." Never married.

344. Coy Holland (Robert Mitchell[5], Matthew[4], Daniel[3], Thomas William[2], Unknown[1]) was born 20 October 1896, and died 22 January 1983 in Fayetteville, Cumberland County, North Carolina. He married **Naomi Williams** 31 December 1921 in Honeycutt's Township, Sampson County, North Carolina, daughter of Isaac Williams and Lillie Lee. She was born 27 August 1903 in Sampson County, North Carolina, and died 27 April 1989 in Sampson County Memorial Hospital, Clinton, North Carolina.

This "Coy Holland" served in Company K, 27th Division, AEF in WW I. He and Naomi were buried in Roseboro Old Hollywood Cemetery, Hwy 242, Roseboro, Sampson County.

Children of Coy Holland and Naomi Williams are:

\+ 994 i. **James Rupert Holland, Sr.**, born 24 October 1922 in Dismal Township, Sampson County, North Carolina; died 22 January 1985 in Fayetteville, Cumberland County, North Carolina.

995 ii. **Ella Ruth Holland**, born 24 January 1924 in Dismal Township, Sampson County, North Carolina. She married **William Robert Ivey** 17 December 1950 in Sampson County, North Carolina. He was born about 1920 in Sampson County.

Two children.

996 iii. **Alice Freeman Holland**, born 24 October 1926; died 27 January 1941.

Burial: Roseboro's Old Hollywood Cemetery on 242, Sampson County, North Carolina.

997 iv. **Lillie Doris Holland** was born 18 June 1930 in Little Coharie Township, Sampson County and died 15 August 1979. She married **S. Winston Blanchard**.

Burial: Roseboro's Old Hollywood Cemetery on 242, Sampson County, North Carolina.

347. Chellie Holland (Robert Mitchell[5], Matthew[4], Daniel[3], Thomas William[2], Unknown[1]) was born 19 October 1901, and died 26 October 1991. She married **Wiley C. Knowles,** son of William Knowles and Luetta Butler. He was born 28 October 1901, and died 19 October 1959.

Chellie and Wiley C. were buried in Sunrise Memorial Gardens, between Roseboro and Salemburg, Sampson County, North Carolina.

Children of Chellie Holland and Wiley Knowles are:

+ 998 i. **Matthew Mixton Knowles,** born 25 October 1923 in Honeycutts Township, Sampson County, North Carolina; died 19 January 1987 in Clinton, Sampson County.

999 ii. **Retha Knowles,** born 26 August 1925. She married Unknown Hayes.

+ 1000 iii. **Wiley Dixon Knowles,** born 18 October 1928; died 27 June 1984.

1001 iv. **Earl Knowles,** born 14 January 1932; died 22 April 1983 in Sampson County, North Carolina. He married Lillian J. Unknown 07 September 1957; born 18 December 1935.

1002 v. **C. T. Knowles,** born 31 May 1933.

1003 vi. **Francis Knowles,** born 08 August 1934. She married Unknown Guinn.

1004 vii. **Zola Knowles,** born 03 April 1938. She married Unknown Crumpler.

1005 viii. **Sam Knowles,** born 20 January 1941.

1006 ix. **David L. Knowles,** born 22 February 1944 in Sampson County, North Carolina; died 08 December 2004 in Campbellton Health Care Center. He married Joan (Maiden Name Unknown).

348. Robert Minson Holland (Robert Mitchell[5], Matthew[4], Daniel[3], Thomas William[2], Unknown[1]) was born 16 January 1908, and died 13 February 1942 in Honeycutts Township, Sampson County, North Carolina. He married **Nancy Edna Bell McPhail** 23 January 1932 in Dillon, Dillon County, South Carolina, daughter of Daniel McPhail and Ardella Williams. She was born 10 March 1907 in Sampson County, North Carolina, and died 15 April 1979 in Sampson County.

He died of Tuberculosis. Cemetery records show he and Edna were buried at Union Grove Baptist Church Cemetery on Vander Road (SR 1438) Sampson County, North Carolina.

Children of Robert Holland and Nancy McPhail are:

1007 i. **Henry Venton Holland,** born 18 May 1933 in Dismal Township, Sampson County.

+ 1008 ii. **Daniel Robert Holland,** born 24 August 1934 in Honeycutts Township, Sampson County, North Carolina.

+ 1009 iii. **Della Frances Holland,** born 22 October 1937 in Honeycutts Township, Sampson County.

349. Jathronia Holland (Robert Mitchell[5], Matthew[4], Daniel[3], Thomas William[2], Unknown[1]) was born 14 May 1910, and died 06 July 1997. She married **Miles Coston Simmons** 30 January 1932 in Dillon, South Carolina, son of Oscar Simmons and Ada Honeycutt. He was born 17 June 1910, and died 30 April 1990 in Clinton, Sampson County, North Carolina.

Jathronia and Miles were buried in a Honeycutt Cemetery on Huntley School Road, Sampson County, North Carolina.

Children of Jathronia Holland and Miles Simmons are:

\+ 1010 i. **Miles Oscar Simmons**, born 23 October 1932 in Herrings Township, Sampson County, North Carolina.

1011 ii. **Jimmie Aurther Simmons**, born 15 June 1935 in Herrings Township, Sampson County.

His middle name "Aurther" may be spelled incorrectly in my source.

\+ 1012 iii. **Donald Ray Simmons**, born 03 January 1937 in Herrings Township, Sampson County.

1013 iv. **Ada Jenline Simmons**.

352. John A. Williams (John E.[5], Tomzelle[4] Culbreth, Mary[3] Holland, Thomas William[2], Unknown[1]) was born 14 March 1853, and died 13 December 1924 in Dismal Township, Clement, Sampson County, North Carolina. He married **Sarah Georgeanna Faircloth** about 1883, daughter of James Faircloth and Elizabeth Averitt. She was born 04 August 1856, and died 02 July 1928 in Dismal Township, Sampson County.

Certificate of Death for Sarah notes 02 July 1928 for death; transcribed cemetery records list 27 July 1928. She and John have ten unnamed infants buried near them in the Maxwell Cemetery near Clement in Sampson County, North Carolina.

Children of John Williams and Sarah Faircloth are:

1014 i. **Hattie Sloan Williams**, born 03 December 1884 in Cumberland County, North Carolina; died 28 May 1969 in Fayetteville, North Carolina. She married **Duncan Hugh Bain** 15 March 1919 in Fayetteville, Cumberland County, North Carolina; born 03 September 1890 in Cumberland County, North Carolina; died 26 April 1979 in Fayetteville, North Carolina. Duncan was the son of **Duncan Evander Bain** and **Eliza Jane Bain**.

She and Duncan had three children. Hattie and Duncan were buried in Maxwell Cemetery near intersectiion of Maxwell Road (SR 1006) and (SR 1427) in Sampson County, North Carolina.

1015 ii. **Gilespie N. Williams**, born 07 April 1888; died 05 December 1940 in Little Coharie Township, Sampson County, North Carolina. On 14 June 1908 he married **Cordelia Jolly** who born 23 January 1892 and died 01 April 1975. Cordelia was the daughter of **George Washington Jolly** and **Adeline Elizabeth Nunnery.**

He was known as "Glaspie Williams" (Glaspy Williams.) Ten children.

1) **Isaac Marvin Williams** was born 15 January 1911 and died 10 September 1982 in Clinton, North Carolina. He married **Melvia Adelaide Culbreth**, daughter of **Ivey Culbreth**

and **Chellie Matthews**. She was born 17 December 1917 in Dismal Township, Sampson County, North Carolina. She and Gilspie had two children: **Stanley Dixon Williams** was born 30 September 1936 in Dismal Township and married **Joyce Ann Williams,** daughter of Liston Williams and Nina Matthews. Joyce was born 6 November 1940 in Roseboro, North Carolina. **Marvin Ellis Williams**, second child of Isaac and Melvia, was born 19 February 1942 in Dismal Township and married **Brenda Sue Autry** who was born 19 February 1944 in Roseboro.

2) **Lonnie Robinson Williams,** second child of Gilespie and Cordelia was born 8 November 1912 in Sampson County, North Carolina and died 25 August 1977 in Fayetteville, Cumberland County, North Carolina. He married **Lena Ruth Williams**, daughter of **Daniel Williams** and **Alma Spell**. Lena was born 7 August 1905 in Sampson County and died 11 December 1981 near Autryville, North Carolina. Lonnie and Lena had six children. I) **Jean David Williams** was born 14 August 1937 in Dismal Township and died 1 April 1987 near Salemburg, North Carolina. He married **Myrtice Marie Goodrich** who was born 17 July 1939 in Honeycutts Township in Sampson County, North Carolina. II) **Mary Ruth William** was the second child of Lonnie and Lena. She was born 5 June 1940 and married **Jasper LeRoy Baggett**, son of **LeeRoy Baggett** and **Jula Geddie**. Jasper was born 12 April 1939 in Honeycutt Township. Mary and Jasper have two children. III) **Ted Robinson Williams**, thrid child of Lonnie and Lena was born 18 July 1942 in Dismal Townshi and died 27 January 1944. IV) **Trudy Brown Williams**, fourth child of Lonnie and Lena was born 1 August 1943 in Dismal Township and married **Floyd Pearson Hall** who was born 25 September 1936 in Dismal Township, Sampson County. Trudy and Floyd have two children. V**)** **Georgia Bell Williams**, fifth child of Lonnie and Lena was born 6 April 1945 in Dismal Township and first married **Denning Ray Breedlove**. Her second husband, **James Phillip Wrench** is the son of **Quinton Wrench** and **Rochelle Naylor**. Georgia and Denning have two sons. VI) **Robert Eldon Williams** was the sixth child of Lonnie and Lena. He was born 31 January 1947 in Dismal Township and died 31 July 1954. Lonnie and Lena and their two deceased young sons were buried in Union Grove Baptist Church Cemetery on Vander Road one mile west of Rebel City in Sampson County.

3) **James Jennins Williams**, third child of Gilespie and Cordelia, was born 4 October 1914 in Dismal township. He married **Essie Freeman Spell**, daughter of **Grady Spell** and **Rachel Autry.** Essie was born 23 August 1920 and died 30 May 1989 in Durham, North Carolina. One known child, **Janet Leigh William**.

4) **Lula Belle Williams**, fourth child of Gilespie and Cordelia was born 30 June 1919 in Dismal Township. She married **John Andrew Sessoms** on 24 November 1945. He was born 4 December 1913 and died 8 September 1968 near Godwin, North Carolina. Four children: I) **Orpha Blanch Sessoms** was born 22 Novembr 1946 in Roseboro, North Carolina and married **Bobbie Scott** who was born 2 May 1940 in Lumberton, North Carolina. II) **Francee Cordelia Sessoms**, second child of Lula and John, was born 13 January 1949 in Fort Bragg, North Carolina, and married **Thomas Y. Wong**. III) **John Paschal Sessoms**, third child of Lula and John was born 7 August 1950 in Fort Bragg and married **Sheila Denise Brown.** IV) **Faye Imogene Sessoms**, fourth child of Lula and John, was born 7 September 1954 in Roseboro and **Robert William Ratliff.**

5**)** **Sarah Elizabeth Williams** was the fifth child or Gilespie Williams and Cordelia Jolly and was born 7 October 1919 in Dismal Township. She married **Robie Faircloth**, son of **Tony Faircloth** and **Gertie Faircloth**. Robie was born 20 February 1917. Four children: I) **Helen Janette Faircloth** was born 29 June 1942 and married **David Cain**. II) **Robie Dwight Faircloth**, second child of Sarah and Robie, was born 14 May 1944 in Little Coharie Township and married **Gloria Wayne Coates**. III) **Roye Rogers Faircloth** was the third child of Sarah and Robie and was born 21 July 1945 in Little Coharie Township. He married **Sarah Catherine Simmons.** IV) **Addie Phyllis Faircloth**, fourth child of Sarah and Robie, was born 11 May 1955 in Little Coharie Township.

6) **John Rudolph Williams**, sixth child of Gilespie and ordelia, was born 27 August 1927 and married **Helen Lee Matthews**, daughter of **John Matthews** and **Mary Faircloth.** Helen was born 27 July 1932 in Dismal Township. Three children: **Pamela Hope Williams, John Keith Williams and Dennis Dean Williams.**

7) **Berline Williams**, seventh child of Gilespie and Cordelia, was born and died on 3 June 1929.

8) **Mary Louise Williams**, eighth child of Gilespie and Cordelia was born 5 September 1930 in Dismal Township, Sampson County, North Carolina and married **Calvin Collidge Hall** who was born 12 September 1923 in Dismal Township and died 7 November 1983 near Autryville, North Carolina. They had four children.

9) **Ethel Cordelia Williams**, the ninth child was born 7 November 1931 in Dismal Township and married **Lonnie Fletchard McPhail, Jr.**, who was born 6 December 1927 in Dismal Township. Two children.

10) **Baimbridge Lee Williams**, tenth child of Gilsepie and Cordelia was born 3 November 1933 in Dismal Township and married **Senie Wilson** who was born 7 September 1936.

353. Mary J. Williams (John E.[5], Tomzelle[4] Culbreth, Mary[3] Holland, Thomas William[2], Unknown[1]) was born 17 January 1856, and died 10 February 1896. She married **George Lofton Hall** after1880, son of Redden Hall and Martha Hall. He was born 19 June 1860, and died 01 January 1915.

George's middle name is also found as 'Loftin". He and Mary J. were buried in the Hall Cemetery on a dirt road off South River Road (SR 1424), Sampson County, North Carolina.

Children of Mary Williams and George Hall are:

1016 i. **Sophie Jane Hall**, born 06 August 1883; died 04 June 1948 in Dismal Township, Sampson County, North Carolina. She married **John Lee McLaurin** 07 February 1918 in Fayetteville, Cumberland County, North Carolina; born 23 May 1875; died 23 November 1933 in Cedar Creek Township, Cumberland County.

\+ 1017 ii. **Fleet Martin Hall,** born 11 January 1885; died 05 June 1950 in Fayetteville, Cumberland County, North Carolina.

\+ 1018 iii. **Thomas Iverson Hall,** born 08 November 1886; died 02 December 1923 in Dismal Township, Clement, Sampson County, North Carolina.

1019 iv. **Jinie Belle Hall**, born 24 August 1887; died 30 May 1946 in Honeycutts Township, Sampson County, North Carolina. She married **Thomas Claude Parker**; born September 1886; died before 1946.

Jinie Belle and Thomas Claude had five children.

1020 v. **George Evan Hall**, born 07 July 1893; died 12 March 1950 in Dismal Township, Sampson County, North Carolina. He married **Mary Elizabeth Hall**; born 09 February 1898; died 03 May 1966 in Dismal Township, Sampson County, North Carolina. She was the daughter of Raeford Hall and Malinda Jane Hall.

George Evan and Mary Elizabeth were buried in the Hall Cemetery off South River Road near Halltown Road in Sampson County, North Carolina.

Fourteen children.

1) **Brilla Jane Hall** was born 15 May 1918 (tombstone reads 18 May 1918) and died 1 October 1979. On 31 October 1936 she married **Elbra Wilson Williford** who was born 6 September 1912 and died 31 October 1968. They were buried in the Murd Hall Cemetery. Brilla and Elbra had four children: I) **Gladys Fay Williford** who was born 7 October 1937 in Honeycutts Township and died 26 October 1937 in Honeycutts Township (tombstone in Murd Hall Cemetery may read 20 October 1937). II) **George Matthew Williford** was born 30 Janucy 1939 in Honeycutts Township, Sampson County. III) **Gary Williford**. IV) **Jerry Wayne Williford** was born 15 May 1948 in Roseboro.

2) **Cladie Hall** was born 12 November 1919. On 2 February 1946 in Salemburg, North Carolina, she married **Palestine Matthews**, son of **Shadrick R. Matthews** and **Maggie Myrtle Autry**. He was born 30 April 1918. Cladie and Palestine had eight children.

3) **Estel Lee Hall** was the third child of George Evan and Mary Elizabeth and was born 30 October 1921 (or 30 August 1921) in Dismal Township in Sampson County, North Carolina and died 10 November 1922. Buried in Murd Hall Cemetery.

4) **Elizabeth Gray Hall** was born on 19 September 1913 in Dismal Township. She married a Mr. Sessoms.

5) **Alvin Dempsey Hall** was the fifth child of George Evan and Mary Elizabeth and was born 12 March 1925 in Dismal Township and died 26 January 1975 in Fayetteville (DOA). He married **Mittie Girleen Autry** who was born 26 May 1926 in Cedar Creek Township, daughter of **John William Autry** and **Sarah Lee Bledsole**. He was buried in the Murd Hall Cemetery. Alvin and Mittie had two children: i) **Faye Evelyn Hall** was born 26 January 1951 in Roseboro, Sampson County, North Carolina and married a Mr. Cook. ii) **Lois Rebecca Hall** was born 9 March 1954 in Fayetteville, Cumberland County and married Mack Rose Culbreth who was born 13 November 1949 in Dunn in Harnett County, North Carolina. He was the son of **Augustus Rose Culbreth** and **Ellen Maedell Harris**. Lois and Mack have one child.

6) **Jasper Evan Hall** was born and died on 2 July 1926. Buried in Murd Hall Cemetery.

7) **Millard Lofton Hall**, the seventh child of George Evan and Mary Elizabeth was born 17 May 1927 in Dismal Township in Sampson.

8) **Essie Aline Hall** was born 18 December 1928 (tombstone may read 1 December 1928) in Dismal Township and died 28 April 1929. Buried in Murd Hall Cemetery.

9) **Berline Hall** was born 6 June 1930 (tombstone may read 6 January 1929) in Dismal Township and died 22 December 1930. Buried in Murd Hall Cemetery.

10) **George Daniel Hall** the tenth child of George Evan and Mary Elizabeth was born 11 March 1934 (or 11 March 1933) in Dismal Township in Sampson County and died 3 January 1935 (or 8 January 1934?) in Dismal Township. Buried Murd Hall Cemetery.

11) **Hazel Lee Hall** was born 20 November 1935 in Dismal Township. She married **Bobby Dean Matthews**, son of Yveates Matthews and Beulah E. Wrench. He was born 5June 1938 in Dismal Township and died 3 July 1971 in Fayetteville. (DOA). Buried in Murd Hall Cemetery.

12) **George Iler Hall** was born 25 November 1938 in Dismal Township and died before 1966.

13) **Viola Hall** was born 25 March 1940 in Dismal Township and married a first a Mr. Freeman and second, Mr. Spell.

14) **Joilla Hall.**

1021 vi. **Martha A. Hall,** sixth child of Mary J. Williams and George Lofton Hall was born 30 July 1895 and died 03 October 1932 in Dismal Township, Sampson County, North Carolina.

354. Joel R. Williams (John E.[5], Tomzelle[4] Culbreth, Mary[3] Holland, Thomas William[2], Unknown[1]) was born 14 June 1857, and died 12 May 1919. He married **(1) Jennett Autry** about 1885, daughter of John Autry and Margaret Maxwell. She was born 14 April 1866 in Sampson County, North Carolina, and died 02 September 1890 in Sampson County, North Carolina. He married **(2) Mary Eliza Stewart** 22 March 1896. She was born 08 April 1862, and died 18 March 1937.

"B" is listed for his middle initial on his tombstone. Jennett's date of birth is also found as 14 April 1866. Joel R., Jennett, and Mary were buried in the Autry Cemetery about one mile from Clement, North Carolina, on Autry Mill Road.

Children of Joel Williams and Jennett Autry are:

1022 i. **Julia Margaret Williams,** born 20 November 1885; died 19 October 1918. She married **Nathan Alexander Williams** 02 January 1910; born 29 April 1884 in Fayetteville, Cumberland County, North Carolina; died 26 September 1951 in Fayetteville, Cumberland County, North Carolina.

Julia Margaret and Nathan Alexander were buried in the Williams Family Cemetery northeast of Clement in Dismal Township near Dunn Road (SR1002) at SR1441 in Sampson County, North Carolina.

Julia and Nathan had five children; Nathan and his second wife, Mary Jane Geddie had two children, a stillborn child on 25 May 1922 and Grady Maxton Williams who was born 14 April 1926 in Honeycutts Township in Sampson County and died 10 June 1928.

1) **Ora Dixie Williams,** first child of Julia and Nathan, was born 17 October 1910 in Autryville, North Carolina married **Cyrus Earl Autry**, 7 June 1930. He was born 30 August 1908 and died 10 February 1977, son of John Julian Autry and Della Frances Tyndall. He was buried in Cumberland Memorial Gardens in Cumberland County. Three children: **Earl Nixon Autry** born 18 July 1931 in Dismal Township in Sampson County, North Carolina. **Odell Autry** was born and died 16 May 1936 in Pearces Mill Township in Cumberland County and **Candace Elaine Autry**, the third child was born 29 October 1945 in Fayetteville.

2) **Rupert Pearsall Williams** was born 25 September 1912 and died 30 March 1914 in Clinton, North Carolina. He was buried in the Minson M. Williams Memorial Cemetery.

3) **Gladys Holmes Williams**, born 8 October 1914 in Clinton, married **Radford Carl Matthews** who was born 6 June 1899 and died 4 January 1984 in Raeford, North Carolina, son of Julius William Matthews and Virginia Culbreth. Gladys and Radford had two children; He was buried in the Minson M. Williams Memorial Cemetery. See Gladys and Radford Elsewhere in this book.

4) **Grace Goodson Williams** was born 20 July 1916 and died 3 April 1920 in North Clinton Township, Sampson County. She was buried in the Minson M. Williams Memorial Cemetery.

5) **Charles Craddock Williams** was born 22 August 1918 in South Clinton Township. He was the second husband of **Bertha Lemae Taylor** who was born 22 February 1927 in Flea Hill Township (renamed Eastover Township in 1929), Cumberland County, North Carolina. She was the daughter of Lewis Thomas Taylor and Bertie Leona McMillan and she first married as his second wife, **James Carlton Collier**. See James Carlon and Bertha Lemae elsewhere in this book.

1023 ii. **John Kendal Williams,** born September 1887.

He moved to Georgia.

1024 iii. **Isa Mittie Williams,** third child of Joel Williams and Jennett Autry, was born 18 July 1889; died 30 October 1923 in Dismal Township, Sampson County, North Carolina.

Did not marry. Her year of birth is listed as 1883 in transcribed cemetery records.

She was buried in the John Autry Cemetery about one mile from Clement, North Carolina, on Autry Mill Road,

Children of Joel R. Williams and his second wife, Mary Eliza Stewart:

1) **ORIEN OTIS WILLIAMS** was born 6 January 1898 and died 28 December 1964 in Cumberland County, North Carolina. He married and divorced and is buried in the John Autry Family Cemetery.

2) **OVIE STARLING WILLIAMS** was born 1 January 1900 in Sampson County and died 10 September 1973 in Autryville. He married **LUCY DENT PIERCE** on 20 December 1940; she was born in 1910. Ovie is buried in the John Autry Family Cemetery. Two children.

3) **ILA V. WILLIAMS** was born about 1902.

355. Susan L. Williams (John E.[5], Tomzelle[4] Culbreth, Mary[3] Holland, Thomas William[2], Unknown[1]) was born 30 May 1859, and died 11 June 1930 in Dismal Township, Clement, Sampson County, North Carolina. She married **Marshall Love Matthews** 16 August 1893, son of Frederick Matthews and Mary Jackson. He was born 03 February 1859, and died 13 February 1937 in Dismal Township, Sampson County, North Carolina.

Children of Susan Williams and Marshall Matthews are:

i. **Algie Matthews** was born 16 September 1894 and died 21 August 1971 in Clinton, Sampson County, North Carolina.. He married **LILLIE MAE WILLIAMS,** daughter of **William Wesley Williams** and **Sarah Eliza Williams**. Lillie was born 3 May 1893 and died 27 January 1976. They were buried at Bethabara United Methodist Church Cemetery. The 1930 Federal Census for Cypress Creek Township in Bladen County, North Carolina, records Algie Matthews and "Lilly" M. with seven children.

Eleven children:

1) **Dorothy Elmo Matthews** born 25 April 1915 in Dismal Township.

2) **Myrtle L. Matthews** was born 26 June 1919, died 21 April 1920 and was buried in Bethabara United Methodist Church Cemetery.

3) **William Love Matthews,** born about 1917.

4) **Waylon Matthews (Wayland Matthews)** was born about 1920 and it is believed he married **Lenaya Naylor** who was born 9 December 1921 in Herrings Township, Sampson County, North Carolina. It is said Lenaya was the daughter of **John Naylor, Jr. and Amy Ann Naylor**, but I can't find a record that supports John and Amy Ann for her parents. **LENORA Naylor** was born about 1924 and was the daughter of George Washington Naylor III and Laura Ann Bass; it is said that this Lenora married a "Matthis" and they lived in Smithfield, North Carolina. A *North Carolina Death Collection, 1908-2000,* records a "Waylon Matthews" who was born in 1923 in Johnston County and died on 28 May 1975 in Johnston County, North Carolina; also in these records is found "Algie Wayland Matthews" who was born 23 March 1921 in New Hanover County, North Carolina, and died on 16 August 1982 in New Hanover County. Mr. Rosser mentions that "Waylon" Matthews" lived in Pine Bluff Arkansas, in 1976. Apparently, "Waylon" or "Wayland" and "Algie" were popular names in the Matthews (Matthis) families. I have not found birth or death records for either a Lenaya or Lenora Naylor and Lenaya or Lenora Matthews (Matthis); I've searched for various spellings, but a full name or a nickname may be on the death certificates.

5) **Susan Matthews** married Mr. Scronce.

6) **Sarah Matthews** married Mr. Faharney.

7) **Naomi Matthews** married Mr. Jones.

8) **Robert Matthews**.

9) **Lillian Matthews**.

10) **Reba Matthews**.

11) **Shelby Matthews** was born 24 May 1937 and died 30 October 1937 and is buried in Bethabara United Mathodist Church Cemetery.

Alvin Matthews, second child of Susan Williams and Marshall Love Matthews, was born 28 October 1896 and died 17 October 1982 in Falcon, North Carolina. He married 8 November 1916 in Blea Hill Township, **Bessie J. Williams,** daughter of **William Henry Williams** and his second wife, **Mary Magdalene Royal**. She was born 22 August 1898 and died 5 March 1972 in Fayetteville. They had six children.

1) **Edith Ellen Matthews** was born 27 July 1918 (gravestone reads 26 July 1918) in Dismal Township. She married **Bruce Marvin Daniel** on 24 November 1938 in Dillon, South Carolina, son of **Marshall Love Daniel** and **Hepsia Ann Williams**. Bruce was born 11 October 1913 and died 4 July 192 and was buried in the Minson M. Williams Memorial Cemetery. One child.

2) **William Marcus Matthews** was born 15 March 1921 in Dismal Township, Sampson County, North Carolina and died 25 July 1981 in Fayetteville. He married **Dorothy Frances Taylor** on 10 March 1945 daughter of **Walter James Taylor** and **Lida Beatrice Page**. She was born 29 June 1925 in Cedar Creek Township, Cumberland County, and died 26 January 1988 in Fayetteville. William served as a Technical sergeant in the U.S. Army in World War II. He and Dorothy were buried at Oak Grove PFWB Church Cemetery. Six children.

3) **Esther Magdalene Matthews** was born 11 April 1923 in Dismal Township. She married **George Woodrow Besse** who was born 31 March 1917 in Terre Haute, Indiana, and died 26 February 1970 in Fayetteville, North Carolina. He served as a Technician Fifth Class in the U.S. Army in World War II. George was buried in the Minson M. Williams Memorial Cemetery. Three children.

4) Hazel Davis Matthews was born 15 September 1925 in Dismal Towship and married **Clarence Eldridge Bunce** who was born 5 January 1925 in Cedar Creek Township, son of **Clarence Alton Bunce** and **Ada Jane Strickland.** Three children.

5) **Clara Avanel Matthews,** born 24 July 1942 in Dismal Township, married **William Robert Shatterly** who was born about 1828 in Atlanta, Georgia. Five children. Their eldest son, **Robert Wayne Shatterly** married 12 December 1971 to **Jewell Denise Cannady**, daughter of **James Elder Cannady** and **Kathleen Parson**. Other children: **Jeffrey Dale Shatterly, Debra Ann Shatterly, Malanie Beth Shatterly,** and **Sara Annette Shatterly.**

6) **Kinston Ray Matthews** was born 30 November 1935 in Dismal Township and married **Geneva Mae Cox** who was born about 1940 in South Carolina. One child.

i. **John Jenkins Matthews,** third child of Susan Williams and Marshall Love Matthews was born 29 March 1897 and died 26 April 1978 in Clinton, North Carolina. He married **Mary Lou Faircloth**, daughter of **Arthur McCoy Faircloth** and **Repsie Dudley.** Mary Lou was born 11 March 1904. John was buried at Bethabara United Methodist Church Cemetery. Nine children:

1) **Rachel Matthews** was born 9 February 1924 in Dismal Township and married **Grover Cleveland Taylor, Jr.** who was born 10 January 1923 in Flea Hill Township, Cumberland County, North Carolina. Four children.

2) **John Marion Matthews** was born 19 April 1925 in Dismal Township and died 2 January 1989 in Fayetteville, North Carolina. He married 10 February 1946 **Omah Grace Bunce** who was born 6 July 1928 in Cedar Creek Township, daughter of **Clarence Alton Bunce** and **Ada Jane Strickland.** He is buried at Bethany Church of God of Prophecy. One child.

3) **David Calvin Matthews, Sr.** was born 17 October 1925 in Dismal Township. He married **Barbara Anne Jones** who was born about 1930. Two children: **David Calvin Matthews, Jr.** and **David Michael Matthews** who was born 22 July 1957 near Fayetteville. David Michael married **Karen Elaine Hall** daughter of **Henry Troy Hall** and **Clethie Russell Autry**.

4) **Joe Robert Matthews, Sr.,** was born 10 February 1929 in Dismal **Township and married Ruthey Fayden Tew, daughter of Perry Maxwell Tew** and **Irutha Fann.** Ruthey was born 22 October 1936 in Honeycutts Township, Sampson County, North Caorlina. One child, **Joe Robert Matthews, Jr.**

5) **Blackman Matthews** was born 12 March 1930 in Dismal Township. He married **Lettie Alma Honeycutt**, daughter of **Ernie Blackman Honeycutt** and **Jessie Matthew Williams**. Two children.

6) **George Houston Matthews** was born 21 May 1931 in Dismal Township and married **Joyce Ann Honeycutt** who was born 10 December 1937 in Dismal Township, daughter of **William Ferrell Honeycutt and Magdalene Matthews**. One child.

7) **Helen Lee Matthews** was born 27 July 1932 in Dismal Township and married **John Rudolph Williams** who was born 27 August 1927, son of **Gilespie N. Williams** and **Cordelia Jolly** Three children.

8) **Kelly Fredrick Matthews** was born October 1935 in Dismal Township and married **Glenda Diane Blount**, daughter of **J. T. Blount** and Catherine N. Blount. Glenda was born about 1941. Two children.

9) **Jesse Jenkins Matthews** was born about 1937 and married 29 September 1957 **Verdie Ann Brown** who was born 9 February 1938 in Dismal Township, daughter of **Martin Luther Brown** and **Izora Verdie Page.** Two children.

ii. **Major D. Matthews**, fourth child of Marshall Love and Susan Williams, born 20 June 1898, died 24 October 1903 and is buried in Bethabara United Methodist Church Cemetery.

\+ 1025 v. **Jennette Lee Matthews**, fifth child of Marshall Love and Susan Wiliams was born 18 June 1900; died 24 March 1989 near Fayetteville. She married 21 Januaary 1916 (or 22 January 1917) **Minson Marion Williams** who was born 1 May 1892 and died 21 July 1966 in Dismal Township, son of John D. Williams and Emma Alice McLamb. They were buried in the Nathan Williams Family Cemetery, now called the Minson M. Williams Cemetery. Twelve children.

1) **Lawton Gilchrist Williams** married **Dolly Thomason**. One child.

2) **Liston Williams** was born 31 may 1919. He married first 31 October 1936 near Cooper, in Sampson County, **Nina Floy Matthews**, daughter of **Ollen D. Matthews** and **Sarah Ann Autry**. Nina was born 23 August 1916, died 19 July 1966 in Dismal Township and was buried in the Minson M. Williams Family Cemetery. Two children. Liston married second 8 November 1969 in Harnett County, North Carolina, **Hazel Ivey** who was born 28 September 1923 in Averasboro Township in Harnett County, daughter of **Troy E. Ivey** and **Henrietta Hayes**. Hazel Ivey married first **Henry Cleveland House**, son of **John T. House** and **Martha Stencil**..

3) **Newberry Williams** was born 29 May 1921 in Dismal Township, and died 17 March 1982 in Durham, North Carolina. He married **Kathleen Cooke**. Newberry was buried in LaFayette Memorial Park in Fayetteville, North Carolina. Two children.

4) **Nellie Vaughn Williams** was born 23 March 19823 in Dismal Township. She married **Rembert Barnhill** and lived in Maryland. Four children.

5) **Herbert Harrison Williams** was born 16 August 1924 in Dismal Township. He married **Kathy Ainsworth** in Georgetown, South Carolina. Two children.

6) **Gibson Williams**, a twin , was born 13 February 1927 in Dismal Township and married **Sally Gatlin**. Four children.

7) Gertrude Williams, a twin, born 13 February 1927 in Dismal Township, married **James Hall.** 8) **Lois Williams**, a twin, was born 6 January 1929 in Dismal Township and married **Tommy Biladeau** and lived in Maryland. Five children.

9) **Maurice Williams**, a twin, was born 6 January 1929 in Dismal Township and married **Mary Magdaline Gainey** who was about 1936, foster daughter of **Charles Alexander Gainey** and **Addie J. McMillan**. Three children.

10) **Annette Williams**, a twin, was born 17 August 1936 in Dismal Township and married **Roger Harmon** and lived in Florida. Three children.

11) **Jeannette Williams,** a twin, was born 17 August 1937 in Dismal Township married **Arthur Wallace** who was born 13 July 1930 and died 30 May 1982 in Charlotte. He was buried in the Minson M. williams Memorial Cemetery. One child.

12) **Emma Lee Williams** was born 7 November 1938 in Dismal Township and married **Roger Kluckman**. Three children.

356. Isabelle Williams (John E.[5], Tomzelle[4] Culbreth, Mary[3] Holland, Thomas William[2], Unknown[1]) was born 05 September 1862, and died 12 January 1937 in Eastover Township, Cumberland County, North Carolina. She married **John A. Bullard**, son of Alex Bullard and Betsy Everette. He was born 06 June 1861, and died 05 February 1936 in Eastover Township, Cumberland County, North Carolina.

Two unidentified children died before 1900.

Isabelle and John A. are buried in Bethabara United Methodist Church Cemetery, Sampson County, North Carolina.

Children of Isabelle Williams and John Bullard are:

\+ 1026 i. **Alex Robinson Bullard**, born 11 July 1886; died 15 February 1958 in Dismal Township, Sampson County, North Carolina.

1027 ii. **Susan Ella Bullard,** born 12 June 1888; died 30 December 1968 in Fayetteville, Cumberland County, North Carolina. She married **William Rufus Williams, Sr.** on the 08 December 1917 in Flea Hill Township, Cumberland County, North Carolina; he was born 28 May 1849 in Black River Township, Cumberland County, North Carolina and died 12 July 1930 in Black River Township, Cumberland County.

William Rufus first married **Edna Autry** who was born 6 January 1850 and died 25 April 1914 in Black River Township, daughter of George Autry and Fanny Autry. He and Edna had 13 children.

Susan and William Rufus had no children. William and Edna moved from Dismal Township in Sampson County, North Carolina, where William paid $3.23 in taxes for one white poll in 1877, to Cumberland County, Black River Township, (Dwelling 158) before the 1880 Census. In 1880, he and Edna were listed with seven children at home. The children born after 1877 were possibly born in Cumberland County, North Carolina.

Susan Ella and William Rufus, and his first wife, Edna, were buried in the William Rufus Williams Family Cemetery, 4 miles southeast of Wade, Cumberland County, North Carolina.

\+ 1028 iii. **Annie Belle Bullard**, born 15 July 1892; died 14 February 1919 in Flea Hill Township, Cumberland County, North Carolina.

1029 iv. **Joe Tyson Bullard**, born 04 June 1894; died 25 July 1908.

1030 v. **Jessie Martin Bullard**, born July 1896. He married **Thelma Jane Hales**; born about 1908. No other data.

1031 vi. **Mary Void Bullard**, born 09 September 1898; died 14 October 1979 in Fayetteville, North Carolina. She married **William James McMillan, Sr.** on the 22 July 1917 in Wade, North Carolina; he was born 17 June 1897 and died 14 October 1950. She and William were buried in McMillan Presbyterian Church Cemetery. Six children

1) **TREVA EARLINE MCMILLAN**, The first child of Mary Void Bullard and William James McMillan was born 5 April 1924 in Flea Hill Township and married a Mr. Strickland.

2) **HILDA MAGDALINE MCMILLAN,** The second child was born 3 August 1925 in Flea Hill Township and she married "Unknown Autry."

3) **JANIE BELL MCMILLAN,** the third child was born 21 July 1927 and died 19 September 1927 in Flea Hill Township and is said to be buried at South River.

4) WILLIAM JAMES MCMILLAN, JR., the fourth child of Mary Void Bullard and William James McMillan was born 6 May 1929 in Eastover Township, Cumberland County. He married **WANDA LOUISE ROYAL**, daughter of **LANGFORD PAUL ROYAL** and **BERTIE JANE BLAKE** on 26 November 1953 in Cokesbury Methodist Church in Stedman. Wanda was born 24 June 1932 in Stedman. William and Wanda have two children: **WANDA GAIL MCMILLAN** was born 4 May 1957 in Fayetteville and married **ANDY RAY MCCORMICK** on 30 September 1979 in Steman, North Carolina. He was the son of **John Andrew McCormick** and **Reba Ann Smith** and was born 29 May 1960 in Detroit, Michigan. Wanda and Andy have two children. **DEBBIE LOUISE MCMILLAN** was the second daughter of William James McMillan, Jr. and Wanda Louise Royal. She was born 22 August 1959 in Fayettevill and maried 1 July 1979 near Stedman, **JOEL BERNARD STANLEY** who was born 29 March 1961 in Columbus County.

5) LOIS ESTELLE MCMILLAN, the fifth child of Mary Void Bullard and William James McMilland was born 19 April 1932 in Eastover Township in Cumberland County, North Carolina.

6) **LILLIAN MCMILLAN,** the sixth known child of Mary Void Bullard and William James McMillan married a "Knowles."

1032 vii. **Huey James Bullard,** the seventh child of Isabelle and John was born December 1899. No other data.

1033 viii. **C. T. Bullard,** born 01 August 1901; died 22 December 1902.

1034 ix. **Sophia Velma Bullard,** born 25 December 1908; died 19 October 1909.

1035 x. **Murphy Olive Bullard,** tenth child of Isabell and John, was born 31 October 1911; died 15 April 1972. He married **Lillie McQueen McMillan**; born 29 July 1910; died 30 December 1974 in Fayetteville, North Carolina.

They had nine children.

1) Olive Odell Bullard was born 2 Decembr 1930 in Eastover Township in Cumberland County, North Carolina. He married Nancy Lucille Ivey who was born 6 August 1932 in Parkton Township in Robeson County, North Carolina. Olive and Nancy had four children.

2) Margie Velma Bullard was born 29 October 1932 in Eastover Township in Cumberland County, North Carolina. She first married Thomas Burke on 1 December 1949. He was born on the 24 May 1932 in Parkton Township in Robeson County, North Carolina. Velma and Burke had two children. Velma's second husband was Jennings Lafate Barfield whom she married on 23 August 1970 in Fayetteville, Cumberland County, North Carolina. He was born 30 June 1916 in Harnett County, North Carolina and died 22 March 1971 in Fayetteville, Cumberland County, North Carolina. He and Velma had no children. Margie Velma died by lethal injection on the 2 November 1984 in Raleigh's Contral Prison for the murder by arsenic poisoning of Rowland Stuart Taylor, born 13 April 1921 and died 3 February 1978 in Lumberton, Robeson County, North Carolina. Rowland was the son of William Wesley Taylor and Mollie Fisher. Margie was convicted 2 December 1978 in Lumberton of killing Roiwland.

Margie Velma also confessed to the poisoning of John Henry Lee who was born 22 September 1896 and died 4 June 1977 in Lumberton and the poisoning of Dollie Taylor Edwards who was born 14 July 1891 and died March 1977 in Lumberton. Margie confessed also the poisoning of her mother, Lillie.

William and Margie Velma were buried in the Parkton Cemetery. Jennings was buried in Cumberland Memorial Gardens, Cumberland County, North Carolina; his death was determined to be a homicide on 27 May 1973.

3) **John Samuel Bullard,** third child of Murphy Olive Bullard and Lillie, was born 28 April 1935 in Cedar Creek Township, Cumberland County, North Carolina. He married Rogerlene R. Odom and they had two children. **CARRIE BULLARD** and **MIRANDA BULLARD.**

4. **Jesse Earl Bullard** was the fourth child of Murphy Olive Bullard and Lillie. He was born 23 October 1937 in Wade, Cumberland County, North Carolina and married **Gwendolyn Ann Hawley** who was born about 1939. They had three children. **CHRIS BULLARD, MARK BULLARD** and **MATTHEW SCOTT BULLARD.**

5. **Lillie Arlene Bullard** was born 26 December 1941 in Wade, North Carolina and married **ERROL MATTHEWS**. Two children: **STEPHANIE MATTHEWS** and **CHARLA MATTHEWS.**

6. **Rev. James Alex Bullard** was the sixth child of Murphy Olive Bullard and Lillie and he married **JOY CANNADY**. Five children. **MELBA ANN BULLARD, SHERRY BULLARD, PATTIE GAIL BULLARD, ALEC BULLARD** and **KENNY BULLARD.**

7. **Tryon Stanly Bullard.**

8. **Linda Fay Bullard** married first, MIKE MEDINO and they had no children. She married second, **EMANUEL RIVERIA** and they had two children, **ANGELA EMANELE RIVERIA** and the second daughter is not identified.

9. **Linwood Ray Bullard.** Three children, **WAYNE BULLARD, PAUL BULLARD,** and **CECILIA BULLARD.**

357. Reason Raiford Robinson Williams (John E.[5], Tomzelle[4] Culbreth, Mary[3] Holland, Thomas William[2], Unknown[1]) was born 26 May 1864, and died 03 August 1937. He married **(1) Mary Magdaline Autry** about 1887, daughter of Daniel Autry and Rebecca Honeycutt. She was born 14 November 1871 in Sampson County, North Carolina, and died 28 February 1904. He married **(2) Hannah Jane Jessup** 06 April 1922. She was born 14 July 1874 in Central Township, Bladen County, North Carolina, and died 17 May 1968.

Reason and Mary Magdaline had nine children; he and Mary Magdaline were buried in Bethabara United Methodist Church Cemetery near Clement in Dismal Township, Sampson County, North Carolina.

Hannah Jane had no children. Her tombstone indicates she was "Wife of Robert Williams." She was buried at Mt. Horeb Presbyterian Church Cemetery on North Carolina Route 87 in Bladen County.

Children of Reason Williams and Mary Autry are:

\+ 1036 i. **Nora Williams,** born 27 November 1888; died 13 December 1974 in Clinton, Sampson County, North Carolina.

ii. **Venie Williams,** born 12 December 1889 married Ezra Wicker.

One Daughter.

iii. Rena Williams was born 18 June 1892 and died 13 May 1900 in Wake County, North Carolina. She married **Joseph Tyson Whittington** who was born 17 April 1892 and died 31 December 1963 in Coats, Sampson County, North Carolina. They were buried in Erwin Memorial Park in Harnett County, North Carolina.

iv. **Lena Williams** was born 03 October 1894 and died 27 March 1976 in Dunn, Harnett County,

North Carolina. She married **Herman Fentris Ennis** on 25 May 1915 in Lillington, North Carolina. He was born 2 September 1888 and died 28 May 1964 in Grove Township, Harnett County, North Carolina. They had two children: **Hiram J. Ennis** who married **Janet Smith Munn.** Janet was born 12 July 1918 and died 7 November 1957 in Rural Route, Dunn, North Carolina. Their second child, **Pauline Ennis** was born 31 October 1919 in Duke, Harnett County, North Carolina and married **Gordon Leigh Morgan** on 13 December 1941 in Buies Creek, North Carolina. Gordon was born 17 July 1920 in Lillington Township in Harnett County, North Carolina. He and Pauline had two children.

v. **Rona Williams** was born 17 February 1896 and married **John M. Hall**, son of Erastus Hall and Emma Butler. He was born 31 October 1898 and died 3 November 1968 in Raleigh, Wake County, North Carolina.

vi. **Reason Urpha Williams** was born 09 September 1898 and died 27 February 1978 in Fayetteville, Cumberland County, North Carolina. He married **Daisy Ruth Lewis** who was born 20 April 1903. They had three children, **Elizabeth Williams** who was born 25 October 1922 and died 27 April 1967, and **Robert E. Williams** and **Garmond Williams**.

vii. **Clem Murphy Williams** was born 20 October 1899 and died 24 February 1966 in the Veterans Hospital in Buncombe County, North Carolina. He married **Flora Francis Odom** who was born about 1907 in Sampson County, North Carolina.

viii. **Rebecca Williams** was born 17 January 1902 and died 19 January 1989 in Greensboro, North Carolina. She married **Joseph Elder** and they had eight children: **Ann Elder**, **Frances Elder**, **Marcelle Elder**, **J. W. Elder**, **Harold Elder**, **Wayne Elder**, **Jessie Vickie Elder**, and **Margie Elder**.

ix. **Junius Ervin Williams** was born 21 May 1903 and died 06 October 1970 in Erwin, Harnett County, North Carolina. He married **Beatrice O. Michael** who was born 12 October 1905 in Alamance County, North Carolina and died 18 April 1978 in Neills Creek Township in Harnett County, North Carolina. They had two children.

358. William H. Daughtry (Molcy[5] Williams, Tomzelle[4] Culbreth, Mary[3] Holland, Thomas William[2], Unknown[1]) was born About 1844, and died Bet. 1898 - 1900. He married **Narcissus B. Williford**, daughter of Henry Williford and Aley Jackson. She was born July 1858.

Child of William Daughtry and Narcissus Williford is:

1037 i. **William J. Daughtry**, born 02 February 1883 in Rockfish Township, Hoke County, North Carolina; died 27 January 1938 in Rockfish Township, Hoke County, North Carolina. He married (1) **Ida Serena Guy** 20 May 1908 in Sampson County, North Carolina; born 11 February 1888 in Flea Hill Township, (Now Eastover), Cumberland County, North Carolina; died 20 January 1933 in Cumberland County, North Carolina. He married (2) **Jesse Bundy** 09 July 1932 in Cumberland County, North Carolina; born 08 March 1900; died 08 May 1981.

The year of death for Ida Serena Guy is also listed as 1932. She and William had two children.

359. George Thomas Daughtry (Molcy[5] Williams, Tomzelle[4] Culbreth, Mary[3] Holland, Thomas William[2], Unknown[1]) was born 12 October 1849, and died 27 April 1920 in Cedar Creek Township, Cumberland County, North Carolina. He married **Mary Frances Tew** 15 December 1870 in Cumberland County, North Carolina, daughter of Holly Tew and Cherry Lucas. She was born 02 September 1856 in Cumberland County, North Carolina, and died 13 June 1934 in Cedar Creek Township, Cumberland County, North Carolina.

Children of George Daughtry and Mary Tew are:

1038 i. **Lewis Alexander Daughtry**, born 16 October 1872; died 06 February 1940.

\+ 1039 ii. **George Robert Daughtry**, born 31 December 1886; died 21 October 1938 in Fayetteville, Cumberland County, North Carolina.

360. Nathan Williams (Joel[5], Tomzelle[4] Culbreth, Mary[3] Holland, Thomas William[2], Unknown[1]) was born 06 May 1850, and died 24 February 1926 in Dunn, North Carolina. He married **Mary Frances Strickland**, daughter of Sampson Strickland and Edny Starling. She was born 20 August 1853, and died 03 April 1932.

I did not add data for the youngest descendants of Nathan Williams and Mary Frances Strickland. Those of you who wish to add these to your family can find them in ***Coharie to Cape Fear, The Descendants of John Williams and Katharine Galbreth of Sampson and Cumberland Counties,*** by Mr. John C. Rosser, Jr., deceased. Copies of this book are limited, but Mr. Rosser placed copies in local libraries.

Children of Nathan Williams and Mary Strickland are:

1040 i. **Martin Roberson Williams**, born 31 December 1872; died 28 March 1933 in Black River Township, Cumberland County, North Carolina. He married **Martha Jane Royal** 22 November 1894 in Black River Township, Cumberland County, North Carolina; born 25 September 1877; died 16 December 1960 in Dunn, North Carolina. She was the daughter of **Thomas Jefferson Royal** and **Mary Eliza Glover**. Martha Jane and Martin had ten children.

1) **Unidentified Child** was born and died 8 September 1895.

2) **Lola V. Williams** was born about 1897 and died before 1954. She married **H. H. McLeod** of South Carolina.

3) **Mary Belle Williams**, the third child of Martin and Martha was born 16 August 1899 and died 16 October 1970 in Dunn. She married **James Isaac Starling** on 28 October 1935 in Dillon, South Carolina. James (Ike) was born 14 March 1899 in Harnett County and died 26 August 1985 in Dunn, son of **Nathan William Starling** and **Mahalie Elizabeth McPhail.** They are buried at the Bluff Presbyterian Church Cemetery. They had four children: I) **Jerry Mitchell Williams.** II) **James Nathan Starling,** second child of Mary Belle and Isaac was born 6 February 1937 in Black River Township and married **Geraldine Ina Dorman**, daughter of **Elijah Calvin Dorman** and **Nellie Monds Starling**. Geraldine was born 30 August 1928 in Black River Township. She and James Nathan had one child. III) **John Roberson Starling,** a twin and third child of Mary Belle and James Isaac was born 6 February 1937 in Black River Township and died 9 February 1937. He is buried at the Bluff Presbyterian Church Cemetery. IV) **Charles Martin Starling, Sr.,** fourth child of Mary Belle and James Isaac, was born 6 August 1939 in Black River Township and married **Dessie Lee Callahan** on 7 July 1967 in Halls Township. Dessie was born 24 December 1942 and first married **John William Willis III** with whom she had one daughter. Charles Martin and Dessie have two known children.

4) **James Lee Williams,** fourth child of Martin Roberson Williams and Martha Jane Royal, was born 18 August 1902 and died 12 June 1954 in Eastover Township, Cumberland County, North Carolina. "Buck," (apparently his nickname), married **LULA HOLLAND** who was born about 1910, daughter of **ELI UNDERWOOD HOLLAND** and **LILLIE JONES.** See elsewhere in this book for their children.

5) **Beulah Irene Williams,** fifth child of Martin and Martha was born 18 October 1905 in Harnett County and died 4 August 1972 in Wrightsville Beach, New Hanover County, North Carolina. She married **Tom Costas** who was born 1 August 1900 and died 9 October 1970 in Wilmington, New Hanover, son of Anastasia Kostas and Eleni Sotiri. Beulah and Tom are buried in Greenlawn Cemetery in Wilmington.

6) **Sallie R. Williams,** sixth child of Martin and Martha was bouth about 1907 and married **Troy Shaw** who was killed by lightning in South Carolina. Sallie married second to a Mr. Steedly.

7) **Addie Marvin Williams** was the seventh child of Martin and Martha; she married **Hular Foxworth** of South Carolina.

8) Herbert Elton Williams, eighth child, was born 5 August 1915 in Black River Township and died 21 Septembr 1975 in Durham. "Hub" married **Ollie Augustus Hodges** on 2 July 1940, daughter of

James George Hodges and Bessie August Neighbors. Ollie was born 31 January 1922 in Averasboro Township, Harnett County. Three children: I) **Linda Joyce Williams** was born 25 October 1943 and married **Sal Suarez** who was born 6 April 1936 and they had two children. II) **Edith Carol Williams** was born 25 November 1944. III) **Bessie Diane Williams** was born 30 March 1954 and married **James Hubert Williams** who was born 25 July 1948. Bessie and James had one child and are divorced.

9) **Mattie Victoria Williams,** a twin child of Martin and Martha, was born 19 June 1917 in Black River Township and died 29 February 1988 in Fayetteville. Victoria married **William Rufus Holland,** son of **ELI UNDERWOOD HOLLAND and LILLIE JONES.** William Rufus was born 14 June 1912 and died 16 June 1961 in Black River Township. He was buried in Gilmont Cemetery in Hope Mills. "Victoria" was buried in Bluff Presbyterian Church Cemetery. Mattie "Victoria" and William divorced and he married second Inez, maiden name unknown.

Four known children of Mattie Victoria and William: I) **David Martin Holland** was born 28 October 1935 in Black River Township. Name of wife is not known. II) **Mary Frances Holland** was born about 1936 and married **Clarence Ward Braswell**, son of Clarence M. and Pauline Braswell of Waycross, Georgia. He was born about 1936 in Florida. Two children**: Scott Monroe Braswell** and name of second child is unknown. III) **William Patrick Holland** was born 23 July 1940, died 26 February 1941, and was buried in the Bluff Presbyterian Church Cemetery. IV) **Laurice Eldon Holland** was born 27 November 1942 in Black River Township. Names of two children unknown.

10) **Stillborn Twin of** Martin and Martha (19 June 1917) in Black River Township is buried at Black's Chapel United Methodist Church Cemetery.

1041 ii. **Alda L. Williams**, the second child of Nathan Williams and Mary Frances Strickland, was born 02 June 1874; died 19 March 1935 in Wade, North Carolina. She married **George Lee Collier**; born 24 January 1872; died 27 November 1940 in Wade, North Carolina. Alda and George had 12 children. 1) **William Archie Collier** was born 26 August 1897 in Linden in Cumberland County, North Carolina, and died 8 March 1949 in Dunn, Harnett County, North Carolina. He married his first cousin, **Thelma Rosadean Anderson**, on 25 November 1920. She was the daughter of **Henry Beatty Anderson** and **Londinia D. Collier** and was born 22 August 1898 and died 12 May 1968 in Smithfield in Johnston County. They are buried in Four Oaks City Cemetery. Ten children.

I) **Thelma Josephine Collier** was born 10 october 1921 in Goldsboro, North Carolina and married **Wallace Proctor.**

II) **Annie Eugene Collier** was born 17 February 1923 in Goldsboro and married second to **Aldridge Laurence** on 1 August 1950.

III) **William Archie Collier, Jr.** was born 27 september 1924 and died 30 December 1925.

IV) **Milton Bailey Collier** was born 8 November 1926 in Four Oaks, Johnston County, North carolina. He married **Virginia Faircloth** on 9 October 1945 in Four Oaks. She was born about 1929.

V) **George Henry Collier** was born 22 February 1928 in Goldsboro and married **Ethel Andrews** on 26 February 1949.

VI) **Edna Earle Collier** was born 2 January 1930 in Four Oaks and died 6 July 1930 in Johnston County.

VII) **Florence Ellen Collier** was born 5 October 1932 in Four Oaks.

VIII) **Vira Frances Collier** was born 23 January 1936 in Four Oaks.

IX) **Wayman Ernest Collier** was born 9 August 1937 in Four Oaks.

X) **Stillborn Son Collier** on 11 April 1941 in Four Oaks.

2) **John Robert Collier,** second child of Alda and George was born 11 April 1899 in Linden and died 1 November 1969 in Fayetteville. He married **Gladys Matthews**, daughter of **Edwin B. Matthews** and **Margaret Ella Matthews**. She was born 23 July 1902 in Cedar Creek Township, Cumberland

County, and died 6 September 1988. They were buried in LaFayette Memorial in Fayetteville, North Carolina. "Johnnie" and Gladys had two children. **Evelyn Collier** married **Ralph Dixon Tew**, son of **Lewis Frank Tew** and **Mamie Richard Williams**. Ralph was born 21 May 1929 in Dismal Towsnhip in Sampson County. No children. John Robert and Gladys' second child, **Margaret Loriane Collier** was born 1 July 1927 in Flea Hill Township, Cumberland County. Margaret married **Arval Gipson Holland**, son of **Lottis Turner Holland** and Eva Clyde Lewis. He was born 26 April 1926 in Dismal Township as "**Arrel Holland.**" Three children.

3) **Nathan Eugene Collier**, a twin child of Alda and George was born 10 July 1900 in Linden.

4) **Twin Son Colleir,** twin, was born and died 10 July 1900 in Linden.

5) **Harvey Lee Collier**, child of Alda and George was born 28 April 1901 in Linden. He married **Grace Dudley**; four children, names unknown.

6) **Bertha Mae Collier**, sixth child of Alda and George, was born 1 August 1903 in Linden and died 16 Januaru 1990. She married **William Webster Wood**, son of **William Gaston Wood** and **Sarah E. Colvin**. "Webb" was born 9 August 1890 in Cumberland County and died 1 July 1957 in Fayetteville. Bertha and William had four children. I) **William Stewart Wood**, born 14 November 1923 in Carvers Creek Township, Cumberland County, North Carolina. II) **Waymond Worth Wood** was born about 1925 in Cumberland County. III) **Judson Lee Wood** was born about 1928 in Cumberland County and married **Charlotte Ann Ellis** on 25 June 1956. She was born about 1933. IV) **Alda Elizabeth Wood** was born 19 May 1943 in Fayetteville, North Carolina. She married **Robert Evariste Moorhouse** 22 July 1967. He was born 7 September 1943 in Ozone Park, New York.

7) **Nathan Eugene Collier,** seventh child of Alda and George, was born 15 July 1905 and died 14 February 1920 and was buried at the Bluff Presbyterian Church Cemetery.

8) **A son** was born and died 9 December 1906 and was buried at the Bluff Presbyterian Church Cemetery.

9) **Vira Frances Collier**, ninth child of Alda and George, was born 14 October 1907 in Linden and died 8 April 1970. She married **Rev. Edward Pierson Lockamy**, Sr., son of **John C. Lockamy** and **Emma Melissa House** on 25 December 1937 in Fayetteville, North Carolina. He was born 2 December 1908 in Cumberland County and died 8 September 1986 in Lumberton, North Carolina. They were buried in the Ed Lewis Cemetery south of Bladenboro, Bladen County, North Carolina. Edward married second Myrtle Davis (Myrtle first married a "Lamb'). Five children. I) **Edward Pierson Lockamy, Jr.** was born 21 March 1939 and married **Gladys Juanita Callihan**. II) **Alda Mae Lockamy** was born 25 October 1941 and married an "Unknown Shaw." III) **Judy Francis Lockamy** was born 29 August 1944 in Luberton, North Carolina and married an "Unknown Ward." IV) **Willis Gardner Lockamy** was born 6 September 1947 In Lumberton. V) **Larry Eugene Lockamy** was born 15 April 1950 in Lumberton and married **Ellen Daphene Benson** who was born 19 May 1953 in Lumberton. Two children.

10) **George Washington Collier** was born 18 October 1911 in Linden, North Carolina and died 10 June 1975 in Greensboro. He married **Margaret Aleta Autry (Aleta Margaret Autry**?) Two children.

11) **Worth Melvin Collier,** eleventh child of Alda and George, was born 8 August 1913 in Linden and died 8 August 1975. He married **Lona Matthews** on 7 November 1936 in Wade, North Carolina. She was born 30 January 1917 in Flea Hill Township, Cumberland County, North Carolina, daughter of **William Branson Matthews** and **Johnnie Elizabeth Matthews**. Four children. i) **Worth Wingate Collier** married **Janet Rose Warren**. ii) **Raymond Otis Collier, Sr.**, married **Linda McLaurin**, daughter of John McLaurin and Cortez Jackson. iii) **Larry Melvin Collier** died at the age of 12. iv) **Lona Ann Collier** married **John Lambert Horne.**

12) **Raymond Olive Collier**, twelfth child of Alda and George, was born 29 December 1915 in Flea Hill Township in Cumberland County and married **Addielene Matthews** on 10 January 1937. She was born 21 October 1914 in Flea Hill Township, daughter of **William Branson Matthews** and **Johnnie Elizabeth Matthews.**

\+ 1042 iii. **Louida Williams**, was the third child of **Nathan Williams** and **Mary Frances Strickland** and was born 03 July 1877; died 27 June 1955 in Dunn, North Carolina.

\+ 1043 iv. **John Lewis Williams**, fourth child of Nathan Williams and Mary Frances Strickland, was born 25 September 1879; died 25 September 1959 in Fayetteville, Cumberland County, North Carolina.

\+ 1044 v. **Mary Frances Williams**, born 19 October 1881; died 27 February 1919 in Black River Township, Cumberland County, North Carolina.

1045 vi. **Fleet Rose Williams**, sixth child of Nathan and Mary France, was born 16 April 1884; died about 1958. He married **Lilly F. Strickland** 02 November 1904 in Black River Township, Cumberland County, North Carolina, daughter of Isaac Strickland and Mary Baker. Lilly was born about 1874 in Black River Township. Fleet lived, and was buried in New Bern, North Carolina. Three children.

1) **Ava C. Williams** was born about 1906 in Black River Township and was living with her paternal grandparents in 1910.

2) **Lillie Belle Williams** married **Robert Alton Williams** who was born 14 August 1920 in Black River Township.

3) **Unidentified Daughter Williams.**

1046 vii. **Joel Sampson Williams,** born 15 October 1886; died 22 May 1943 in Cedar Creek Township, Cumberland County, North Carolina. He married **Minnie McBryde Williams** 26 September 1909, daughter of **Neill Williams** and **Margaret Gainey.** She was born 17 May 1890 and died 15 March 1972 in Fayetteville, North Carolina. One known child: **Percy Neill Williams** was born 22 October 1912 and died 16 October 1985 in Fayetteville. Percy married **Fannie Williams Averitte** on 6 June 1936 in Wade, Cumberland County, North Carolina. She was born about 1907 in Cumberland County.

1047 viii. **Edna Williams,** born 16 January 1890; died 03 July 1961 in Dunn, North Carolina.

ix. **Nathan Claude Williams** was born 20 July 1893 and died 14 March 1950.

In 1910, **Claudius N. Williams** was in the household of his sister, Alda, and her husband, George L. Collier.

x. **Marion Butler Williams** was born 19 July 1894 and died 18 August 1961 in Benson, North Carolina.

xi. **Isaac William Williams** was born 5 May 1897 and died 12 May 1897.

361. Joel E. Williams (Joel^{5}, Tomzelle^{4} Culbreth, Mary^{3} Holland, Thomas William^{2}, Unknown^{1}) was born 18 April 1851, and died 16 December 1933 in Fayetteville, North Carolina. He married **Amanda E. Raiford** 09 February 1882 in Fayetteville, Cumberland County, North Carolina. She was born 18 May 1859, and died 24 October 1911.

Child of Joel Williams and Amanda Raiford is:

\+ 1048 i. **Janie Williams,** born 20 June 1890; died 01 April 1940 in Fayetteville, North Carolina.

362. Alexander Williams, Sr. (Joel^{5}, Tomzelle^{4} Culbreth, Mary^{3} Holland, Thomas William^{2}, Unknown^{1}) was born 22 August 1855, and died 05 December 1920. He married **(1) Emily Catherine Pope** in 1882. She was born About 1859, and died Bet. 1890 - 1900 in Duke Township, Harnett County, North Carolina. He married **(2) Cornelia Frances Jackson** 25 April 1897 in Black River Township, Cumberland County, North Carolina. She was born 22 February 1865, and died 08 August 1942.

Alexander, Sr. was active in his communtiy in Duke Township, Harnett County, North Carolina and was remembered for his red hair. The southern parts of present day Duke and Averasboro Townships of Harnett County, were in Black River Township of Cumberland County, North Carolina, until 1911.

Children of Alexander Williams and Emily Pope are:

1049 i. **Jessie Williams.**

1050 ii. **Judson Williams.**

1051 iii. **Margaret Williams.**

Children of Alexander Williams and Cornelia Jackson are:

\+ 1052 i. **Alexander Williams, Jr., died 1947.**

1053 ii. **Emma Washington Williams.**

1054 iii. **Marvin B. Williams.**

1055 iv. **Sarah Williams.**

\+ 1056 v. **Myrtle Williams**, born 19 May 1903 in Sampson County, North Carolina; died 14 September 1981 in Erwin, North Carolina.

363. John Robert Williams (Joel[5], Tomzelle[4] Culbreth, Mary[3] Holland, Thomas William[2], Unknown[1]) was born 07 November 1857, and died 18 November 1914 in Little Coharie Township, Sampson County, North Carolina. He married **Matilda Jane Lucas.** She was born 01 November 1859 in Sampson County, North Carolina, and died 21 January 1918 in Little Coharie Township, Sampson County, North Carolina. Matilda may have been the daughter of James Curry Lucas and Martha Spell. In the 1860 census, James Curry Lucas was listed with Martha (nee Spell) in Little Coharie Township, Sampson County, North Carolina; in 1870, he was listed with wife, Patsey, and Matilda, aged 10, was listed with them. Either Martha died or she was listed as "Patsey" with James Lucas in the 1870 census. Patsey Lucas was not listed with her parents in 1860 which may indicate that Martha's nickname was "Patsey."

Most of John Robert and Matilda's children moved from Sampson County, North Carolina, and several of them left the state.

Children of John Williams and Matilda Lucas are:

1057 i. **Charlie D. Williams**, born July 1884; died Before 1952.

1058 ii. **Flora Jane Williams**, born 03 September 1886 in Sampson County, North Carolina; died 25 October 1953 in Pearces Mill Township, Cumberland County, North Carolina. She married **Johnnie Lee Johnson**; born 21 December 1898 in Fayetteville, North Carolina; died 25 November 1947 in Fayetteville, North Carolina. Flora Jane and Johnnie Lee had five children. Ages of the children are not known. One child died young. **JOHNNY LEE JOHNSON, JR.** was born 24 December 1921 in Fayetteville and died 17 April 1973 in La Plata, Maryland. Johnny married Hazel Ray, (maiden name unknown); he and Hazel had five children: **SUSANNE JANE JOHNSON, JAMES S. JOHNSON, ROBERT L. JOHNSON, JOHN W. JOHNSON, AND GARY L. JOHNSON.**

Flora Jane and Johnnie Lee had a stillborn daughter on 18 February 1924. Their son, **JAMES ELLIOTT JOHNSON,** was born 24 September 1926 and died 10 October 1978 in Fayetteville. He served as a Seaman 2nd Class in the United States Navy during World War II. James did not marry. **HELEN ALEASE JOHNSON** may have been the youngest child of Flora Jane and Johnnie. She married a Mr. Miller and, at one time, lived in Hope Mills.

1059 iii. **John Williams,** born 11 March 1890; died 30 May 1952 in Little Coharie Township, Sampson County, North Carolina. He married **VERNA JANE HALL** 05 November 1912 in Residence of Hanes Irvin Hall; born 01 April 1893; died 27 February 1981 in High Point, North Carolina. Verna was the daughter of **Hanes Irvin Hall** and **Susan Adeline Autry.** John Williams was survived by six children and Verna by three children. John was a farmer and sawmill operator and was buried in the Hulda Hall Cemetery; Verna was buried in the George Horne Cemetery.

John and Verna's first child, **CHARLIE DRUE WILLIAMS** was born 13 February 1913 in Sampson County, died 6 May 1958, and was buried in the George Horne Cemetery. Their second child was **THOMAS IVEY WILLIAMS** who was born 2 Augsut 1914 in Autryville and died 23 May 1982 on Rural Route, Autryville. Thomas married Ruby Agnes Willis, daughter of Henry Francis Willis and Bessie Julia Lucas. Ruby was born 23 April 1929 in Little Coharie Township in Sampson County, North Carolina, and she and Thomas had one son and two daughters. Further research may reveal that "Bessie Julia Lucas" mentioned twice above, was the daughter of **Milzie Adeline Autry** and Archie L. Lucas; see them elsewhere in this book.

The third child of John and Verna was **BULA MAYBELL WILLIAMS** who was born 17 May 1916 in Little Coharie Township. Bula married **PAUL W. CLAPP.**

The fourth child of John and Verna was **FLORENCE ELIZABETH WILLIAMS** who was born 22 April 1918 at Hayne, Sampson County, North Carolina. Florence married on 18 December 1944 in Dillon, South Carolina, **ALTON WILLIS**, son of **HENRY FRANCIS WILLIS and BESSIE JULIA LUCAS**. Alton was born 18 August 1920 in Little Coharie Township and he and Florence had four children.

LOTTIE RHUMELL WILLIAMS was the fifth child of John Williams and Verna Jane Hall. She was born 19 September 1920 in Sampson County, died 3 January 1942 in Cedar Creek Township in Cumberland County, North Carolina, and was buried in the McCall Family Cemetery northeast of Stedman.. Lottie married **Douglas V. McCall.**

JOHN LEONARD WILLIAMS was the sixth child of John Williams and Verna Jane Hall. He was born 26 April 1922 in Little Coharie Township, died 2 December 1979 on Route 2, Autryville, and was buried in the George Horne Cemetery. John was called "Occie" and he married **ALENE AUTRY** who was born 18 June 1928 in Little Coharie Township, daughter of **CHARLES ANDREW AUTRY** and **FLORENCE SESSOMS.** John and Alene had three children.

The seventh child of John Williams and Verna Jane Hall was **LEON EDWIN WILLIAMS,** born 6 September 1923 in Little Coharie Township, died 4 July 1951, and was buried in the Hulda Hall Family Cemetery. Three children.

The eighth child of John Williams and Verna Jane Hall was **EARL SIDNEY WILLIAMS,** born 29 July 1925 in Little Coharie Township, died 22 March 1969 in Fayetteville and was buried in the George Horne Cemetery. Earl married **MABEL AMELIA GIBSON** who was born 2 November 1928 in St. Pauls in Robeson County, North Carolina.

1060 iv. **Mary Francis Williams,** born May 1892, was the fourth child of John Robert Williams and Matilda Jane Lucas.

1061 v. **Nora Elizabeth Williams,** fifth child of John Robert and Matilda Jane, was born February 1894. She married **L. S. Johnson**; born about 1893, son of Charlie and Allie O. Johnson.

1062 vi. **Idella Ann Williams,** born 29 November 1896 in Hayne, Samspon County, North Carolina, and did not marry.

1063 vii. **Sarah Etta Williams,** seventh child of John Robert and Matilda Jane, was born 29 November 1896 in Hayne, Samspon County.

1064 viii. **Joel Wesley Williams**, eighth child of John Robert Williams and Matilda Jane Lucas was born 10 January 1898.

\+ 1065 ix. **Pinkie Williams**, born 01 November 1899 in Hayne, Samspon County, North Carolina, was the ninth child of John Robert Williams and Matilda Jane Lucas.

366. Thomas Jefferson Williams (Joel[5], Tomzelle[4] Culbreth, Mary[3] Holland, Thomas William[2], Unknown[1]) was born about 1865, and died After 1913. He married **Leona A. Riley** 18 April 1901 in Fayetteville, Cumberland County, North Carolina. She was born 20 October 1879 in Cumberland County, North Carolina, and died 26 June 1939 in Little Coharie Township, Sampson County, North Carolina.

Thomas Jefferson and Leona had seven children; Three not identified.

Children of Thomas Williams and Leona Riley are:

1066 i. **W. P. Williams.**

1067 ii. **Daniel Williams.**

1068 iii. **Mat McLean Williams**, born 15 November 1905; died 17 November 1956 in Fayetteville, North Carolina. He married **Nena Margaret Butler** 23 January 1942; born 09 August 1902; died 18 February 1961 in Little Coharie Township, Sampson County, North Carolina.

Mat McLean had one stepdaughter.

1069 iv. **Julie Francis Williams**, born 08 October 1914. She married **Edwin Venable Cooper**; born 18 March 1917 in Autryville, North Carolina. Ediwn and Julie had two children.

367. Mary Catherine Williams (Isaac[5], Tomzelle[4] Culbreth, Mary[3] Holland, Thomas William[2], Unknown[1]) was born 14 February 1855, and died 19 December 1919 in Black River Township, Cumberland County, North Carolina. She married **George Washington Starling**, son of Nathan Starling and Amy Strickland. He was born 05 September 1853, and died 25 January 1918 in Black River Township, Cumberland County.

Children of Mary Williams and George Starling are:

\+ 1070 i. **Julia Catherine Starling**, born 21 November 1882; died 25 December 1951 in Black River Township, Cumberland County, North Carolina.

\+ 1071 ii. **Emily Jane Starling**, born 21 June 1885 in Cumberland County, North Carolina; died 19 July 1969 in Fayetteville, Cumberland County.

1072 iii. **Infant Starling**, born 21 June 1887; died 21 June 1887.

\+ 1073 iv. **Arthur Leon Starling, Sr.**, born 14 January 1890; died 21 June 1974 in Rocky Mount, North Carolina.

\+ 1074 v. **Luther Washington Starling**, born 06 November 1891; died 16 January 1982 in Dunn, Harnett County, North Carolina.

\+ 1075 vi. **Mary Eliza Starling**, born 19 August 1893; died 12 August 1934 in Newton Grove Township, Sampson County, North Carolina.

\+ 1076 vii. **Martha Ann Starling**, born 19 August 1893; died 04 November 1987 in Eastover Township, Cumberland County, North Carolina.

\+ 1077 viii. **Leonard Bryan Starling**, born 14 October 1896 in Sampson County, North Carolina; died 31 December 1978 in Rocky Mount, North Carolina.

\+ 1078 ix. **Rev. Hiram Roberson Starling**, was born 12 May 1898 in Godwin, Sampson County and died 29 May 1983.

368. Tomsilla Jane Williams (Isaac[5], Tomzelle[4] Culbreth, Mary[3] Holland, Thomas William[2], Unknown[1]) was born 20 February 1857, and died 12 February 1937 in Dismal Township, Sampson County, North Carolina. She married **Frederick Matthews** after May 1890, son of Shadrick Matthis and Mary McPhail. He was born 06 May 1854 in Sampson County, North Carolina, and died 15 November 1926 in Dismal Township, Sampson County.

Tomsilla is spelled "Tomzil(l)" in Census records.

Child of Tomsilla Williams and Frederick Matthews is:

1079 i. **Neta Campbell Matthews**, born 11 December 1894; died 29 February 1980 in Sampson County, North Carolina. She married **Junious Roscoe Page** 09 October 1918 in Sampson County, North Carolina; born 18 January 1890; died 19 January 1969 in Fayetteville, Cumberland County, North Carolina.

369. Lovdie Ann Williams (Isaac[5], Tomzelle[4] Culbreth, Mary[3] Holland, Thomas William[2], Unknown[1]) was born 22 January 1860, and died 06 May 1956 in Dismal Township, Sampson County, North Carolina. She married **James Bradley Wrench** about 1880, son of Joseph Wrench and Ceknak Parker (Ceknak can be found as Ceiney Parker and Senna Parker.) James was born 31 December 1851, and died 27 January 1933 in Dismal Township, Sampson County, North Carolina.

James Bradley and Lovdie Ann were buried in the Minson M. Williams Family Cemetery at the northeast corner of Dunn Road (SR 1002 and SR 1441) in Dismal Township, Sampson County, North Carolina

I also found the 24 December 1933 for James' death.

Children of Lovdie Williams and James Wrench are:

\+ 1080 i. **Fletcher E. Wrench**, born 01 January 1882; died 22 March 1968 in Near Autryville, North Carolina.

\+ 1081 ii. **Cornelia Wrench**, born 05 September 1884; died 15 July 1969.

371. Daniel Williams (Isaac[5], Tomzelle[4] Culbreth, Mary[3] Holland, Thomas William[2], Unknown[1]) was born 12 April 1864, and died 28 June 1933 in Dismal Township, Sampson County, North Carolina. He married **Susan Ann Evellena Page** About 1888, daughter of Silas Page and Mary Jackson. She was born 15 December 1869, and died 21 January 1951 in Near Godwin, Sampson County.

Daniel and Susan Ann were buried in Williams Family Cemetery northeast of Clement in Dismal Township near Dunn Road (SR1002) at SR1441 in Sampson County, North Carolina.

Children of Daniel Williams and Susan Page are:

1082 i. **Rosa A. Williams**, born 27 September 1889; died 24 April 1890.

\+ 1083 ii. **Viola Beatrice Williams**, born 16 May 1891; died 16 July 1964.

1084 iii. **Venolia Williams**, born 26 May 1892; died 20 December 1961.

She is buried in Williams Family Cemetery northeast of Clement in Dismal Township near Dunn Road (SR1002) at SR1441 in Sampson County, North Carolina,

\+ 1085 iv. **Mary V. Williams**, born 03 December 1893; died 06 April 1964 in Grays Creek Township, Cumberland County, North Carolina.

1086 v. **Molcy E. Williams**, born 02 August 1895; died 02 June 1896.

\+ 1087 vi. **Lela Vira Williams**, born 16 June 1897; died 16 March 1978 in Fayetteville, Cumberland County, North Carolina.

\+ 1088 vii. **Joel Judson Williams**, born 21 January 1899 in Sampson County, North Carolina; died 25 August 1980 in Clinton, Sampson County, North Carolina.

1089 viii. **Lera F. Williams**, born 26 April 1900; died 11 September 1900.

\+ 1090 ix. **Daniel Webster Williams**, born 09 November 1901; died 08 August 1982.

1091 x. **Nettie Clara Williams**, born 02 July 1904; died 25 September 1981 in Fayetteville, Cumberland County, North Carolina. She married **Henry Alton Starling** 01 December 1934 in Wade, Cumberland County, North Carolina; born 05 October 1910; died 26 August 1977.

She and Henry had one known child, **Herbert Eldon Starling** who is listed elsewhere in this book.

Nettie and Henry were buried in a Williams Family Cemetery northeast of Clement in Dismal Township near Dunn Road (SR1002) at SR1441 in Sampson County, North Carolina.

1092 xi. **Ludie M. Williams**, born 25 March 1908; died 24 November 1909.

\+ 1093 xii. **Olive Earl Williams**, born 23 February 1910; died 23 October 1984.

\+ 1094 xiii. **Oleta Gladys Williams**, born 02 November 1913 in Dismal Township, Sampson County, North Carolina; died 17 September 1981 in Clinton, Sampson County, North Carolina.

372. Sarah Eliza Williams (Isaac[5], Tomzelle[4] Culbreth, Mary[3] Holland, Thomas William[2], Unknown[1]) was born 23 October 1866 in Sampson County, North Carolina, and died 20 January 1938 in Dismal Township, Sampson County, North Carolina. She married **William Wesley Williams** 21 January 1886, son of Nathan Williams and Catherine Matthews. He was born 26 March 1862 in Sampson County, North Carolina, and died 11 August 1932 in Dismal Township, Sampson County, North Carolina.

Sarah Eliza and William Wesley are buried in a Williams Family Cemetery northeast of Clement in Dismal Township near Dunn Road (SR1002) at SR1441 in Sampson County, North Carolina.

Children of Sarah Williams and William Williams are:

+ 1095 i. **Elizabeth Jane Williams**, born 17 November 1886 in Sampson County, North Carolina; died 09 November 1935.

1096 ii. **William S. Williams**, born 03 October 1888 in Sampson County, North Carolina; died 11 May 1889. He was buried in a Williams Family Cemetery northeast of Clement in Dismal Township near Dunn Road (SR1002) at SR1441 in Sampson County, North Carolina.

+ 1097 iii. **Molcy Jo Williams**, born 01 September 1890 in Sampson County, North Carolina; died 24 November 1976.

+ 1098 iv. **Lillie Mae Williams**, born 03 May 1893 in Sampson County, North Carolina; died 27 January 1976.

+ 1099 v. **King Sanford Williams, Sr.**, born April 1895 in Sampson County, North Carolina.

+ 1100 vi. **Samuel Tilden Williams**, born 25 May 1898 in Sampson County, North Carolina; died 28 December 1977 in Clinton, Sampson County, North Carolina.

+ 1101 vii. **Raeford James Williams**, born 19 June 1901 in Sampson County, North Carolina; died 26 December 1979 in Dunn, Harnett County, North Carolina.

+ 1102 viii. **Kate Ann Williams**, born 19 June 1901 in Sampson County, North Carolina; died 16 January 1982 in Fayetteville, Cumberland County, North Carolina.

1103 ix. **Nathan Isaac Williams**, born 15 May 1904 in Sampson County, North Carolina; died 03 September 1905. He was buried in a Williams Family Cemetery northeast of Clement in Dismal Township near Dunn Road (SR1002) at SR1441 in Sampson County, North Carolina.

+ 1104 x. **Thera Wesley Williams**, born 20 January 1907 in Sampson County, North Carolina; died 13 March 1986 in Clinton, Sampson County, North Carolina.

375. John C. Bain (Susan Ann[5] Williams, Tomzelle[4] Culbreth, Mary[3] Holland, Thomas William[2], Unknown[1]) was born 14 August 1862, and died 11 September 1930 in Eastover Township, Cumberland County, North Carolina. He married **Sallie Brown** 28 February 1888 in Wilmington, North Carolina. She was born 24 March 1858 in Duplin County, North Carolina, and died 16 September 1937 in Eastover Township, Cumberland County, North Carolina.

Children of John Bain and Sallie Brown are:

1105 i. **John Brown Bain**, born 24 September 1889. He married Lucy Curtis 10 November 1917.

+ 1106 ii. **Edgar Leonidas Bain**, born 01 February 1892; died 03 June 1981 in Lumberton, North Carolina.

+ 1107 iii. **Alma May Bain**, born 28 February 1896; died 08 July 1968 in Raleigh, North Carolina.

1108 iv. **Mary Olivia Bain**, born 18 May 1898.

376. Hugh Alexander Bain (Susan Ann[5] Williams, Tomzelle[4] Culbreth, Mary[3] Holland, Thomas William[2], Unknown[1]) was born 12 May 1866, and died 03 November 1933 in Black

River Township, Cumberland County, North Carolina. He married **Lou Ella Sessoms** 26 January 1899 in Flea Hill Township, Cumberland County, North Carolina, daughter of William Sessoms and Martha Wicker. She was born 29 April 1876, and died 29 June 1949 in Eastover Township, Cumberland County, North Carolina.

Hugh Alexander and Lou Ella were buried in Bluff Presbyterian Church Cemetery near Wade, Cumberland County, North Carolina.

Children of Hugh Bain and Lou Sessoms are:

+ 1109 i. **Anna Lillian Bain**, born 05 October 1900; died 03 August 1955 in Fayetteville, North Carolina.

1110 ii. **Nellie May Bain**, born 08 May 1903; died 10 March 1970 in Fayetteville, North Carolina. She married **James Clinton Maxwell** 16 May 1925 in Black River Township, Cumberland County, North Carolina; born 25 October 1899; died 21 March 1964 in Wade, North Carolina.

Nellie May and Jame had five children. James was the son of William Robert Maxwell and Flora Elizabeth McKethan.

1) **James Alexander Maxwell** was born 13 August 1926 in Wade, Cumberland County and died 14 August 1969 in Hartford, Connecticut. He was buried in Bluff Presbyterian Church Cemetery near Wade.

2) **Vivian Mae Maxwell** was born 15 January 1928 in Flea Hill Township in Cumberland County and first married **James A. Truelock, Jr.**, of Vienna, Georgia. He was born about 1928 and they married on 16 January 1948 in Cross Creek Township in Cumberland County. Vivian married second **W. C. Brooks** and at one time, they lived in Georgia.

3) **Mary Maxwell** first married **Thomas Harold McPhail** who was born 29 November 1926 in Black River Township in Cumberland County, son of James Erastus McPhail and Stella Mae Starling Lewis. Mary married second a **Mr. Sanders**.

4) **Martha Eleanor Maxwell** was born 17 December 1929 and died 19 April 1976 in Fayetteville. She married and divorced a **Mr. Higgins**. Martha served as a 2nd Lieutenant in the United States Army in Korea. She was buried in Bluff Presbyterian Church Cemetery near Wade in Cumberland County.

5) **Carrol Bain Maxwell** was born 28 February 1932 in Eastover Township in Cumberland County and married Mirella DePietrucci who was born about 1932 in North Afirca. Carrol and Mirella had three children.

1111 iii. **Hugh McSwain Bain** was born 21 September 1906, died 13 October 1911 and was buried in Bluff Presbyterian Church Cemetery near Wade, Cumberland County, North Carolina.

1112 iv. **Ruth Washington Bain**, born 04 July 1909. About 1906, she married **Fab Hunter Yates** from Apex, North Carolina.

1113 v. **Seavy Alexander Bain**, born 29 May 1912; died 18 November 1975 in Fayetteville, North Carolina. He married (1) **Mary McLean Andrews** 09 November 1935; born about 1916 and he married (2) **Bernice Elizabeth Swindell** about 1941; born about 1912. Seavy and Mary had no children; he and Bernice Elizabeth had two children.

377. Catharine Jane Bain (Susan Ann[5] Williams, Tomzelle[4] Culbreth, Mary[3] Holland, Thomas William[2], Unknown[1]) was born 30 December 1868, and died 12 February 1906. She married **Neil Washington Bain** 16 December 1896. He was born August 1856, and died 06 April 1937 in Tampa, Florida.

Children of Catharine Bain and Neil Bain are:

1114 i. **Neill James Evander Bain,** born December 1892.

Neill James served as a telegraph operator in France during WW I. Moved to Florida.

1115 ii. **John Stanley Bain,** born January 1895; died Before 1928 in Port of New York.

John Stanley served in the U.S. Navy.

1116 iii. **Catherine Margaret Bain,** born February 1898.

Catherine Margaret did not marry and was a missionary in South Africa.

1117 iv. **Mary H. Bain,** born about 1900.

1118 v. **Samuel Alexander Bain,** born 11 August 1902 in Fayetteville, North Carolina.

Samuel Alexander was serving in the U.S. Navy in 1928.

1119 vi. **Unknown Son Bain,** born 03 February 1906; died 03 February 1906.

378. Edna Autry (Daniel[5], Millzy Adelme[4] Culbreth, Mary[3] Holland, Thomas William[2], Unknown[1]) was born 21 June 1862, and died 29 January 1922. She married **Thomas J. Faircloth** February 1888, son of Sylvania Faircloth. Thomas was born 25 December 1851, and died 18 November 1926; he and Edna were buried in the Leroy Autry Family Cemetery about 1.3 miles east of Autryville, North Carolina.

Elijah Faircloth, aged 8, nephew, was living in the household of Thomas and his mother, Sylvania, in 1880.

Child of Edna Autry and Thomas Faircloth is:

\+ 1120 i. **Julia Elizabeth Faircloth,** born 04 October 1896; died 27 June 1971.

379. Micajah Autry (Daniel[5], Millzy Adelme[4] Culbreth, Mary[3] Holland, Thomas William[2], Unknown[1]) was born 22 June 1867, and died 29 August 1917. He married **Francenia Jane Hall** about 1887, daughter of John Hall and Jeanette Autry. She was born 08 January 1867, and died 22 February 1960.

Micajah and Francenia Jane were buried in the Autry-Hall Cemetery on Edgar Lane, east of Autryville, Sampson County, North Carolina.

Children of Micajah Autry and Francenia Hall are:

1121 i. **Allie Fleet Autry,** born 30 September 1891; died 15 May 1954 in Lee County, North Carolina. He married **Maggie Elizabeth Clark** 30 July 1934; born 12 June 1908 in Moore County, North Carolina. The source mentions that he died in Lee County, North Carolina, and was buried in Shallowell Cemetery in Sanford. The 30 September 1888 is also listed for his death.

1122 ii. **Mary Barbara Autry,** born 01 September 1894. She **married Earl Bishop.**

1123 iii. **Julian Odell Autry,** born About 1909. He married **Pauline Downing.**

382. William Ashford Autry (Daniel[5], Millzy Adelme[4] Culbreth, Mary[3] Holland, Thomas William[2], Unknown[1]) was born 16 July 1874, and died 18 February 1959. He married **Jane Bullard,** daughter of Jones Bullard and Margaret Hair. She was born 02 June 1876, and died 29 October 1948.

William Ashford and Jane were buried in the Leroy Autry Family Cemetery off Autryville Road, about 1.3 miles east of Autryville, North Carolina. She is named "Jennie" Autry on William's certificate of death.

Children of William Autry and Jane Bullard are:

1124 i. **Lela Autry,** born 17 September 1898; died 04 April 1969. She married **Walton Edward Hall;** born 15 September 1894; died 05 March 1982.

Lela and Walton were buried in the Leroy Autry Family Cemetery off Autryville Road, about 1.3 miles east of Autryville, North Carolina.

1125 ii. **Marie Autry,** born 16 October 1899. She married **Spurgeon Moody.**

\+ 1126 iii. **Flossie Autry,** born 09 February 1901; died 01 August 1986.

1127 iv. **Wallace Autry,** born 10 April 1903; died 21 February 1944. Wallace was buried in the Leroy Autry family Cemetery off Autryville Road, about 1.3 miles east of Autryville, North Carolina.

1128 v. **Eugene Autry,** born 24 July 1905. He married **Vistic Murdock.**

1129 vi. **Voshen Autry,** born 29 April 1911; died 25 December 1987. He married Ennis Ruth Butler.

Voshen was buried in the Leroy Autry Family Cemetery off Autryville Road, about 1.3 miles east of Autryville, North Carolina.

1130 vii. **Maggie Autry,** born 27 November 1915.

1131 viii. **Daniel Hubert Autry,** born 20 November 1918; died 30 January 1998. He married **Lola Jackson** 19 July 1941; born 13 December 1919.

1132 ix. **Orville Harding Autry,** born 05 March 1922; died 23 April 1983. He married **Dora Jackson;** born 28 September 1923.

385. Polly Autry (Daniel[5], Millzy Adelme[4] Culbreth, Mary[3] Holland, Thomas William[2], Unknown[1]) was born 17 June 1883, and died 19 March 1963. She married **Allen G. Sessoms,** son of Calton Sessoms and Sarah Cooper. He was born about 1869 in Dismal Township, Sampson County, North Carolina.

Child of Polly Autry and Allen Sessoms is:

1133 i. **Ronnie Sessoms,** born 04 July 1907; died 27 September 1926 in Little Coharie Township, Sampson County, North Carolina. He married **Bessie Kate Ezzell** on 03 July 1926; she was born about 1910. Ronnie was buried in the George Horne Family Cemetery.

386. James Love Autry (Daniel[5], Millzy Adelme[4] Culbreth, Mary[3] Holland, Thomas William[2], Unknown[1]) was born 27 January 1885, and died 03 May 1952. He married **(1) Bertha Bullard**, daughter of Jones Bullard and Margaret Hair. She was born 19 September 1883, and died 25 July 1915. He married **(2) Miranda Jane Hall**, daughter of Isaac Hall and Berilla West. She was born 14 June 1884 in Cedar Creek Township, Cumberland County, North Carolina, and died 09 August 1960.

James Love, Bertha and Miranda Jane are buried in the Leroy Autry family Cemetery off Autryville Road, about 1.3 miles east of Autryville, North Carolina.

Children of James Autry and Bertha Bullard are:

1134 i. **Mamie Autry.** She married **Hillie Barfield**.

\+ 1135 ii. **Maggie Pearl Autry**, born 05 October 1908; died 01 June 1990.

1136 iii. **Mary Ethel Autry**, born 18 October 1910; died 07 May 1973. She married **Alexander Faircloth** 18 October 1924; born 12 November 1900; died 18 April 1986.

Mary Ethel and Alexander were buried in the Autry Cemetery on Autryville Road about 3.5 miles east of Autryville, North Carolina. Her name is listed "Ethel M. Faircloth" on her gravestone.

\+ 1137 iv. **Myrtle Lois Autry**, born 14 November 1912; died 26 February 1982.

1138 v. **James Thurman Autry**, born 25 May 1915; died 15 September 1982. He married **Lena Mae Sessoms**; born 03 May 1915.

Children of James Autry and Miranda Hall are:

1139 i. **Percy Morgan Autry**, born 22 January 1917; died 28 April 1977. He married **Lois Marie Johnson**; born About 1921.

1140 ii. **Elmer Bruce Autry**, born 23 June 1918 in Little Coharie Township, Sampson County, North Carolina; died 22 November 1986 while hunting south of Stedman, Cumberland County, North Carolina. He married **Myrtle Hall**; born 03 May 1925 in Little Coharie Township, Sampson County.

\+ 1141 iii. **Lula Mae Autry**, born 04 January 1920.

1142 iv. **Wilma Estelle Autry**, born 28 October 1921 in Little Coharie Township, Sampson County, North Carolina; died 13 March 1993. She married (1) **Aaron Jolly** before 1961; born 26 April 1914; died 23 August 1961 in Dismal Township, Sampson County, North Carolina. She married (2) **Lottis Turner Holland** after 1961; born 14 December 1902; died 24 November 1988 in Clinton, Sampson County, North Carolina.

Wilma Estelle, Aaron Jolly and Lottis Turner Holland were buried in Halls United Methodist Church Cemetery on Minnie Hall Road north of Autryville, North Carolina.

\+ 1143 v. **Mildred Autry,** born 12 August 1923 in Little Coharie Township, Sampson County, North Carolina; died 15 December 1998.

\+ 1144 vi. **Leroy Autry**, born 21 October 1925 in Little Coharie Township, Sampson County, North Carolina.

387. Susan Anner Williams (Rebecca Elizabeth[5] Autry, Millzy Adelme[4] Culbreth, Mary[3] Holland, Thomas William[2], Unknown[1]) was born 09 May 1857, and died 22 October 1929 in Little Coharie Township, Sampson County, North Carolina. She married **Charles Andrew Williams**, son of Redden Williams and Nancy Faircloth.

He was born 01 February 1860, and died 29 October 1915 in Little Coharie Township, Sampson County, North Carolina.

Susan Anner and Charles Andrew were buried in the Charles A. Williams Family Cemetery (now Jesse Williams Family Cemetery) near SR 1418 and SR 1233, Sampson County, North Carolina.

Children of Susan Williams and Charles Williams are:

+ 1145 i. **William Redin Williams**, born 18 May 1880; died 26 October 1930 in Little Coharie Township, Sampson County, North Carolina.

+ 1146 ii. **Repsie Williams,** born 09 December 1881; died 07 August 1952 in Little Coharie Township, Sampson County, North Carolina.

1147 iii. **Ida Williams**, born 23 October 1883; died 27 June 1943 in Little Coharie Township, Sampson County, North Carolina. She married **C. W. Beal** and they had three children. Ida died at the home of her brother, George and was buried in the Charles A. Williams Family Cemetery (now Jesse Williams Family Cemetery) near SR 1418 and SR 1233, Sampson County, North Carolina.

1) **JULIA P. WILLIAMS**, a twin, was born 14 May 1907 and died 21 May 1907.

2) **ROSA M. WILLIAMS**, a twin, was born 14 May 1907 and died 25 may 1907. Julia and Rosa are buried in the Charles A. Williams Family Cemetery.

3) **JOHN SCOTT BEAL.**

1148 iv. **Susan Lee Williams**, born 22 September 1885; died 04 December 1920 in Little Coharie Township, Sampson County, North Carolina. "Suley" did not marry and was buried in the Charles A. Williams Family Cemetery (now Jesse Williams Family Cemetery) near SR 1418 and SR 1233, Sampson County, North Carolina.

+ 1149 v. **Mollie Williams**, born 24 November 1887; died 22 December 1960 in Little Coharie Township, Sampson County, North Carolina.

+ 1150 vi. **John Frank Williams**, born 28 January 1890; died 15 November 1962 in Little Coharie Township, Sampson County, North Carolina.

+ 1151 vii. **George W. Williams**, born 21 June 1893; died 08 September 1958 in Little Coharie Township, Sampson County, North Carolina.

1152 viii. **Jessie James Williams**, born 17 February 1896; died 15 February 1973 in Near Autryville, North Carolina. He married **Carrie Horne** 20 February 1916; born 26 March 1896; died 06 January 1973 in Clinton, North Carolina. They both were buried in the Charles A. Williams Family Cemetery (now Jesse Williams Family Cemetery) near SR 1418 and SR 1233, Sampson County, North Carolina.

388. Mary Lee Williams (Rebecca Elizabeth[5] Autry, Millzy Adelme[4] Culbreth, Mary[3] Holland, Thomas William[2], Unknown[1]) was born about 1858, and died 1893. She married **Wright L. Faircloth** before 1887, son of Sylvania Faircloth. He was born 28 April 1857, and died 05 July 1918 in Little Coharie Township, Sampson County, North Carolina.

Mary Lee and Wright were buried in a Faircloth Cemetery on Mount Carmel Road near Halls Crossroads, Sampson County, North Carolina. Wood crosses with no dates are placed on the graves where he was buried, except for the grave of his daughter, Claudie; her gravestone has data.

Children of Mary Williams and Wright Faircloth are:

1153 i. **Martha L. Faircloth**, born May 1883.

1154 ii. **William P. Faircloth**, born November 1884.

1155 iii. **Dosha Faircloth**, born 30 April 1888; died 25 October 1967 in Little Coharie Township, Sampson County, North Carolina. She married **Frank Jarvis Faircloth**; born 25 September 1887; died 07 August 1970 near Autryville, North Carolina.

Dosha and Frank Jarvis were buried in the Autry Cemetery on Autryville Road about 3.5 miles east of Autryville, North Carolina.

1156 iv. **Henry G. Faircloth**, born 19 November 1890; died 06 March 1973. Henry was buried in the Autry Cemetery 3.5 miles east of Autryville on Autryville Road (SR 1233), Sampson County, North Carolina.

1157 v. **Claudia Faircloth,** born 06 January 1893; died 01 January 1943. Claudia was buried in the Faircloth Cemetery on Mount Carmel Road near Halls Crossroads, Sampson County, North Carolina.

389. Wiley C. Autry (Molsey[5], Millzy Adelme[4] Culbreth, Mary[3] Holland, Thomas William[2], Unknown[1]) was born 23 June 1861, and died 27 May 1946. He married **(1) Romelia Sessoms** before 1884, daughter of John Sessoms and Penelope Fisher. She was born 06 August 1861 in Sampson County, North Carolina, and died 05 August 1909. He married **(2) Mary Margaret Unknown** after 1910. She was born 23 May 1873, and died 02 November 1944.

Wiley C., Romelia, and Mary Margaret were buried in the Autry Cemetery on Autryville Road about 3.5 miles east of Autryville, North Carolina.

Children of Wiley Autry and Romelia Sessoms are:

1158 i. **Tomzillie Autry**, born 15 December 1884; died 16 April 1956. She apparently did not marry and was buried near her brother, Jefferson, in the Autry Cemetery on Autryville Road about 3.5 miles east of Autryville, North Carolina. "Zillie" is on found on her gravestone and transcribed cemetery records incorrectly name her for the wife of Jefferon.

1159 ii. **Wilbert Autry**, born August 1886.

1160 iii. **Jefferson Autry**, born 04 August 1888; died 01 August 1950.

Transcribed cemetery records show him married to Zille born 15 December 1884. They were buried next each other, but Zille appears to be his sister, Tomzillie, and both of them were still living with their parents in 1930. Jefferson was buried in the Autry Cemetery on Autryville Road about 3.5 miles east of Autryville, North Carolina.

\+ 1161 iv. **Henry Grady Autry**, born 21 June 1890; died 09 November 1979.

1162 v. **Burrell Autry**, born 22 January 1892; died 09 May 1968. He married **Bertie Unknown**; born 25 April 1893; died 29 July 1981.

1163 vi. **Emmer E. Autry**, born September 1893.

\+ 1164 vii. **Ballard Bee Autry**, born 25 June 1896; died 28 August 1984.

1165 viii. **Eullie E. Autry**, born February 1898.

1166 ix. **Pennie Autry**, born March 1900.

1167 x. **Arby Autry**, born About 1904.

395. Callie Missouri Autry (Miles Costin[5], Millzy Adelme[4] Culbreth, Mary[3] Holland, Thomas William[2], Unknown[1]) was born 27 January 1875, and died 07 February 1949. She married **Unknown Spouse**. Callie Missouri was buried in the Autry Cemetery off Autryville Road about 0.7 mile east of Autryville, North Carolina.

Children of Callie Autry and Unknown Spouse are:

1168 i. **Charles A. Autry**, born about 1901. He married **Florence A. Unknown**; born about 1901.

1169 ii. **Brainey Autry**, born about 1903.

1170 iii. **Jerusha Autry**, born about 1904.

1171 iv. **Romie Autry**, born about 1909.

1172 v. **Mellie Autry**, born about 1914.

1173 vi. **Jessie Jame Autry**, born about 1914.

398. Miles Herman Autry (Miles Costin[5], Millzy Adelme[4] Culbreth, Mary[3] Holland, Thomas William[2], Unknown[1]) was born 10 November 1883, and died 20 January 1968. He married **Sarah Elizabeth Faircloth**, daughter of Caleb Faircloth and Rosa Blackman. She was born 22 August 1887, and died 07 August 1960.

Miles Herman and Sarah were buried in a Autry Cemetery 0.7 mile east of Autryville off Autryville Road (1233), Sampson County, North Carolina.

Children of Miles Autry and Sarah Faircloth are:

1174 i. **Linda Autry**. She married **Willie Calton Fisher**; born 12 August 1917 in North Carolina; died 28 April 1970.

1175 ii. **Rosana Autry**. She married **Isaac Sessoms.**

1176 iii. **Rachel Frances Autry**, born 1914 in Sampson County, North Carolina; died 24 March 2000 in Clinton, Sampson County, North Carolina. She married **Albert Blackman Faircloth**; born 12 May 1911 in North Carolina; died 30 April 1987 in Elizabethtown, Bladen County, North Carolina.

399. Fountain Autry (Miles Costin[5], Millzy Adelme[4] Culbreth, Mary[3] Holland, Thomas William[2], Unknown[1]) was born 10 July 1886, and died 14 December 1945 in Little Coharie Township, Sampson County, North Carolina. He married **Mamie Ola Peterson** Before 1923. She was born about 1907. Fountain was buried in the Fountain Autry Family Cemetery near Autryville, North Carolina.

Child of Fountain Autry and Mamie Peterson is:

\+ 1177 i. **Mattie Kate Autry**, born 27 October 1923 in Little Coharie Township, Sampson County, North Carolina; died 22 March 1966 in Clinton, North Carolina.

401. Rebecca Autry (Miles Costin[5], Millzy Adelme[4] Culbreth, Mary[3] Holland, Thomas William[2], Unknown[1]) was born August 1890, and died Before 1949. She married **Frank Sessoms**, son of Cassa Annie Sessoms. He was born about 1880.

Data on Ancestry.com shows Frank as Frank Sessoms Smith; however, he was found in the 1820 census as Frank Sessoms, aged 40, with wife, Rebecca, son, Ransow (Ramsom?), and his mother, Cassie Annie Sessoms, was in the household.

Child of Rebecca Autry and Frank Sessoms is:

1178 i. **Ransow Sessoms**, born about 1915. Adopted. His name may have been "Ransom."

402. Cordelia Autry (Miles Costin[5], Millzy Adelme[4] Culbreth, Mary[3] Holland, Thomas William[2], Unknown[1]) was born 15 May 1894, and died 25 June 1970. She married **James Dawson Sessoms.** He was born 1886, and died 1949.

Child of Cordelia Autry and James Sessoms is:

\+ 1179 i. **Eulie Marvin Sessoms**, born 05 April 1928 in Little Coharie Township, Sampson County, North Carolina; died 18 September 1998 in North Carolina.

404. Francenia Jane Hall (Jeanette[5] Autry, Millzy Adelme[4] Culbreth, Mary[3] Holland, Thomas William[2], Unknown[1]) was born 08 January 1867, and died 22 February 1960. She married **(1) Unknown Spouse Hall** About 1886. She married **(2) Micajah Autry** About 1887, son of Daniel Autry and Julia Averitt. He was born 22 June 1867, and died 29 August 1917.

Francenia Jane and Micajah were buried in the Autry-Hall Cemetery on Edgar Lane, east of Autryville, Sampson County, North Carolina.

Child of Francenia Hall and Unknown Hall is:

\+ 1180 i. **Lonnie Oliver Hall**, born 14 November 1886; died 27 April 1967.

Children of Micajah and Francenia are listed above under (379) Micajah Autry.

405. Alexander M. Hall (Jeanette[5] Autry, Millzy Adelme[4] Culbreth, Mary[3] Holland, Thomas William[2], Unknown[1]) was born About 1869. He married **Doshie Ann Faircloth.** She was born about 1892.

Child of Alexander Hall and Doshie Faircloth is:

1181 i. **John Cay Hall** was born 29 November 1908 and died 01 March 1978; he was buried in a Hall and Faircloth Cemetery off SR 1416, Sampson County, North Carolina.

407. Novella Ann Hall (Jeanette[5] Autry, Millzy Adelme[4] Culbreth, Mary[3] Holland, Thomas William[2], Unknown[1]) was born 25 June 1873, and died 12 September 1966. She married **Nathan Sellers Fisher** 1894, son of Charles Fisher and Charlotte Faircloth. He was born 25 June 1873, and died 06 May 1951.

Children of Novella Hall and Nathan Fisher are:

1182 i. **Laudie M. Fisher**, born about 1896 in Little Coharie, Sampson County, North Carolina.

1183 ii. **Annie May Fisher**, born about 1898 in Little Coharie, Sampson County.

1184 iii. **John C. Fisher**, born about 1900 in Little Coharie, Sampson County.

1185 iv. **Nannie C. Fisher**, born about 1907 in Little Coharie, Sampson County, North Carolina.

1186 v. **Troy A. Fisher**, born about 1909 in Little Coharie, Sampson County.

1187 vi. **Carley L. Fisher**, born about 1909 in Little Coharie, Sampson County, North Carolina.

408. Willie Earnie Hall (Jeanette[5] Autry, Millzy Adelme[4] Culbreth, Mary[3] Holland, Thomas William[2], Unknown[1]) was born 18 September 1883, and died 03 March 1962 in Little Coharie Township, Sampson County, North Carolina. She married **William Redin Williams** 20 April 1907, son of Charles Williams and Susan Williams. He was born 18 May 1880, and died 26 October 1930 in Little Coharie Township, Sampson County, North Carolina.

Children of Willie Hall and William Williams are:

+ 1188 i. **Leon Williams, Sr.**, born 12 July 1909; died 25 May 1975 in Fayetteville, North Carolina.

1189 ii. **Netta Blanche Williams**, born 10 March 1913; died 01 April 1948 in Little Coharie Township, Sampson County, North Carolina. She did not marry, was an invalid and was buried in the William Redin Williams Family Cemetery, Sampson County, North Carolina

409. Lena Ethel Hall (Jeanette[5] Autry, Millzy Adelme[4] Culbreth, Mary[3] Holland, Thomas William[2], Unknown[1]) was born 19 May 1887, and died 02 December 1966. She married **Love Faircloth**. He was born 13 July 1876, died 01 October 1958; he and Lena were buried in the Hall and Faircloth Cemetery off SR 1416, Sampson County, North Carolina

Children of Lena Hall and Love Faircloth are:

1190 i. **Avery Faircloth**, born about 1927 in Sampson County, North Carolina.

1191 ii. **John M. Faircloth**, born 01 September 1920 in Sampson County, North Carolina; died 02 September 1920 and was buried in the Hall and Faircloth Family Cemetery in a field at end of SR 1416 in Sampson County, North Carolina.

1192 iii. **Jennette Faircloth**, born 01 September 1920 in Sampson County, North Carolina; died 08 September 1920 and was buried in the Hall and Faircloth Family Cemetery in a field at end of SR 1416 in Sampson County.

412. John Blackman Autry (Martha Jane[5] Culbreth, Isaac[4], Mary[3] Holland, Thomas William[2], Unknown[1]) was born 28 October 1863, and died 10 March 1940 in Cedar Creek Township, Cumberland County, North Carolina. He married **Virginia Culbreth** after 1887, daughter of Daniel Culbreth and Jannett Maxwell. She was born 16 January 1861 in Sampson County, North Carolina, and died 22 May 1940 in Dismal Township, Sampson County, North Carolina.

John and Virginia were buried in the Maxwell Cemetery, southeast corner of Maxwell Road (SR 1006) and (SR 1427), Sampson County, North Carolina.

One source names May 23, 1940 for Virginia's death. Virginia and John Blackman have five children who are listed above under (159) Virginia Culbreth.

413. William Isaac Autry (Martha Jane[5] Culbreth, Isaac[4], Mary[3] Holland, Thomas William[2], Unknown[1]) was born 10 September 1866 in Sampson County, North Carolina, and died 27 June 1948 in Sampson County, North Carolina. He married **Sarah Frances McPhail** 16 January 1896 in Residence of M. J. Hayes, daughter of Alexander McPhail and Martha Lewis. She was born 02 December 1874, and died 09 June 1955 in Dismal Township, Sampson County, North Carolina.

Sarah Frances was called "Frankie. She and William Isaac were buried in Bethabara United Methodist Church Cemetery near Clement in Dismal Township, Sampson County.

Children of William Autry and Sarah McPhail are:

1193 i. **Janie Lector Autry**, born 23 November 1896 in Sampson County, North Carolina; died 09 August 1965 in Sampson County, North Carolina.

Janie Lector was buried in the Bethabara United Methodist Church Cemetery in Dismal Township, Sampson County, North Carolina.

\+ 1194 ii. **Lessie Dolan Autry**, born 10 August 1899 in Sampson County, North Carolina; died 22 May 1979 in Fayetteville, North Carolina.

\+ 1195 iii. **McKinley Blackmon Autry**, born 28 August 1900 in Sampson County, North Carolina; died 23 March 1969 in Clinton.

1196 iv. **Lizzie Lottie Autry**, born about 1903 in Sampson County, North Carolina.

1197 v. **William Butler Autry**, born 11 May 1905 in Sampson County, North Carolina; died 12 March 1987. He married **Betty Florence Capps**; born 24 June 1907; died 07 April 1984. Betty was the daughter of Edward Benjamin Capps and Betty Forence Taylor. William and Betty were buried in Bethabara United Methodist Church Cemetery. They had three children.

1) **WILLIAM EDWARD AUTRY** was born 20 July 1932 in Dismal Township in Sampson County, North Carolina and married 26 January 1957 in Dillon, South Carolina, **TRAVIS GERTRUDE AUTRY** who was born 20 June 1940 in Fayetteville, daughter of Lattie Murphy Autry and Della Elizabeth Stewart. Two children.

2) **ROBERT EUGENE AUTRY** was born 11 April 1938 in Dismal Township in Sampson County, North Carolina and married 11 September 1957 at Wilson, North Carolina, **VIRGINIA ROSE BROWN** who was born 30 January 1939 in Wilson County, North Carolina. Three children.

3) **BETTIE FRANCES AUTRY** was born 12 March 1949 in Roseboro, North Carolina. She married a **Mr. Boutin.**

1198 vi. **James Taft Autry**, born 18 March 1909 in Sampson County, North Carolina; died 28 May 1911 and was buried at Bethabara United Methodist Church Cemetery.

1199 vii. **Marian Hampton Autry**, born about 1915 in Sampson County, North Carolina. Hampton married 28 April 1940 in South Carolina, **John Daniel Horne** who was born 15 July 1913 in Vander, Cumberland County, North Carolina, son of John Lee Horne and Docia Jackson. One child, **MELBA GAIL HORNE** was born 10 June 1941 in Fayetteville. She married 26 March 1964 **STANCIL DEBERRY BOWLES, JR.**, who was born 6 August 1941 in Fayetteville, son of Stancil DeBerry Bowles and Janie Elizabeth Yates.

1200 viii. **Oleta Autry**, born 21 March 1916 in Sampson County, North Carolina; died 12 June 1985. She did not marry.

1201 ix. **KLIVESTON LIVINGSTON AUTRY** was born 06 October 1917 in Sampson County, North Carolina and died 30 November 1988 on Rural Route, Autryville, North Carolina. He married 6 June 1940 in Florence, South Carolina, **WIXIE MARGUERITE WRENCH** who was born 17 November 1916 in Dismal Township, Sampson County, North Carolina, daughter of FLETCHER E. WRENCH and ANNA BELLE WILLIAMS. Kliveston was buried in the Minson M. Williams Family Cemetery. Two children.

1) **DONALD RAY AUTRY** was born 14 October 1942 in Roseboro, North Carolina. He married 14 July 1962 in Dillon, South Carolina, **JUDITH GREY BULLARD**, daughter of HUBERT MACK BULLARD and MARY EMMA WILLIAMS. Judith was born 14 May 1944 in Fayetteville, Cumberland County, North Carolina. Donald and Judith had two children: **DONNA BULLARD AUTRY** was born 26 February 1963 in North Carolina and married **James Daniel Melvin III** who was born 2 March 1954 in Georgia. **MICHAEL SCOTT AUTRY** was born 28 july 1966 in Fayetteville, North Carolina and was the second child of Donald and Judith.

422. Julius W. Culbreth (William[5], Isaac[4], Mary[3] Holland, Thomas William[2], Unknown[1]) was born 28 October 1875, and died 29 August 1901. He married **Frances Sessoms** 20 September 1898 in Flea Hill Township, Cumberland County, North Carolina, daughter of William Sessoms and Martha Wicker. She was born 18 September 1877, and died 17 December 1939 in Fayetteville, North Carolina.

Julius W. and Frances were buried in Salem United Methodist Church Cemetery, Eastover Township, Cumberland County, North Carolina.

Children of Julius Culbreth and Frances Sessoms are:

AUGUSTA MAE CULBRETH was the first child of Julius and Frances and was born 24 June 1899 in Dillon South Carolina, and died 10 January 1957 in Durham, North Carolina. She married 5 November 1919 in Fayetteville, **WILBERT HAROLD BEARD**, son of DANIEL RAEFORD BEARD and NANCY J. OLIPHANT. Wilbert was born 9 December 1894 and died 7 August 1962. He served as a Sadler in Battery B. 317th Field Artillery Battalion in World War I. He and Augusta were buried in LaFayette Memorial Park in Fayetteville. They had two children: **Lottie Mae Beard**, born 31 January 1924 in Flea Hill Township in Cumberland County and **Omah Gray Beard** who was born 19 February 1927 in Flea Hill Township. Omah first married 12 August 1945 in Eastover Township, **Roger Curtis Williford** who was born 26 November 1925, son of Lattie Leon Williford and Hilma Lesley Bolton. Omah married second a **Mr. Smith.**

1202 ii. **Katie Elizabeth Culbreth** was the second child of Julius and Frances and was born 12 August 1900 in Dillon County, South Carolina; died 04 February 1979 in Fayetteville, North Carolina. She married **Paul Alexander Geddie**; born 15 April 1889; died 22 February 1967 in Fayetteville, North Carolina. She and Paul were buried in LaFayette Memorail Park. Three children: **LOUISE MAXWELL GEDDIE** the first child was born 18 June 1919 in Flea Hill Township. She married **Mr. Eyler**.

The second child of Katie and Julius was **FRANCES SESSOMS GEDDIE** who was born 25 September 1920 in Flea Hill Township. She married **WILLIAM FISKER GEORGE, JR.** He was born about 1918 in Charlottesville, Virginia. Frances and William had two children: **CHERRY ANN GEORGE** and **JANET LYNN GEORGE**.

The third child of Katie and Paul was **JOSEPH WELLINGTON GEDDIE** who was born 29 January 1923 in Flea Hill Township and died 3 August 1984 in Fayetteville. He was buried in LaFayette Memorial Park.

JULIUS WELLINGTON CULBRETH was the third child of Julius W. Culbreth and Frances Sessoms and was born 25 October 1902 and died 18 March 1950 in Fayetteville and is buried in LaFayette Memorial Park in Fayetteville, North Carolina. She married **WILLIAM LEONIDAS WILLIAMS**, son of Nathan Allen Williams and Jennette Howard. He was born 29 June 1892 at Wade in Cumberland County and died 25 December 1973 in Fayetteville, North Carolina. Julius was buried in Cross Creek Cemetery and William was buried in LaFayette Memorial Park Mausoleum in Fayetteville, North Carolina. William married second **Lucile Atkins** who may have first married a Putze.

427. Mary Ellen Culbreth (Sabra[5], Isaac[4], Mary[3] Holland, Thomas William[2], Unknown[1]) was born 31 July 1872, and died 16 July 1961 in Fayetteville, North Carolina. She married **John William McLaurin** 21 January 1892 in Flea Hill Township, Cumberland County, North Carolina, son of John McLaurin and Virginia McLaurin. He was born 06 June 1870, and died 13 September 1928 in Flea Hill Township, Cumberland County, North Carolina.

Flea Hill Township in Cumberland County became Eastover Township in 1929. Eleven children.

Children of Mary Culbreth and John McLaurin are:

i. **Burnice McLaurin** was born 22 August 1892 and died 2 April 1974 in Fayetteville. He married in Flea Hill Township on 14 October 1917 **Sarah Jane Hall**, daughter of Charlie Hall and Katie Horne. She was born 4 June 1893 and died 25 November 1971 in Fayetteville. They were buried in Cross Creek Cemetery in Cumberland County. Five children:

1) **Edward Elwood McLaurin** was born 6 January 1919 in Flea Hill Township and married **Clara Bell Strickland** on 25 December 1946, daughter of Avery Strickland and Emma Brown. She was born 27 October 1927 in Mingo Township in Sampson County, North Carolina. One child.

2) **Mabel Louise McLaurin** was born 18 August 1920 in Flea Hill Township and maried **Alton Preston Strickland,** son of Andrew Jefferson Strickland and Ida Josephine Bunce. Alton was born about 1920. One child.

3) **Stillborn Daughter** born 27 December 1922 in Flea Hill Township was buried in the John A. McLaurin Family cemetery without a marker.

4) **Catherine McLaurin** was born 30 November 1925 in Flea Hill Township and married in Lebanon Baptist Church on 18 March 1950 to **Charles Linwood Chancy** who was born 17 July 1927 in Fayetteville.

5) **John William McLaurin** was born 21 August 1929 in Eastover Township and died 16 August 1985 in Fayetteville. He married **Gladys Mae Carver**, daugher of James Walter Carver and Ethel

Mae Brock. She was born 21 October 1932 in Raeford, North Carolina,. John was buried in Lebanon Baptist Church Cemetery. Four children.

\+ 1203 ii. **William Wellington McLaurin**, second child of Mary Culbreth and John McLaurin, was born 31 March 1894; died 27 October 1957 in Fayetteville, Cumberland County, North Carolina.

iii. Marcus McDuffie McLaurin, third child of Mary Culbreth and John McLaurin was born 31 January 1896 and died 9 March 1963 in Fayetteville. He married **Letha Merle Culbreth** on 13 November 1923 in Fayetteville, North Carolina. She was born 12 June 1904 and died 30 March 1973 in Fayetteville, daughter of Stephen Culbreth and Annie Elizabeth Cain. Marcus and Letha were buried in Salem United Methodist Church Cemetery. Five children.

3) **Millard McDuffie McLaurin** was born 8 October 1925 in Flea Hill Township in Cumberland County.

4) **Lawrence Elbridge McLaurin** was born 6 April 1928 in Flea Hill township.

5) **Leland Duvell McLaurin** was born about 1930 and married Shirley Frances Horne on 17 January 1954 in Pearces Mill Township in Cumberland County. She was born about 1935 in Harnett County, North Carolina, the daughter of Nicholas Horne and Mary Young. Four children.

6) **Deloris Mae McLaurin** was born 5 May 1932 in Eastover Township. On 19 December 1954, "Gertie" married in Salem United Methodist Church, George Laverne Hedges, who was born about 1931 in Nebraska. One child.

7) **Mervin Holt McLaurin** was born 3 December 1938, died 7 May 1939 and was buried at Salem United Methodist Church Cemetery.

iv. **Hughie Alexander McLaurin** was born 4 February 1899 and died 16 February 1968 in Fayetteville. He married in Person Street Methodist Episcopal Church in Fayetteville on 26 October 1919, **Juanita Thrower**, daughter of Charles H. Thrower and Mary Beard. Seven children.

1) **Jesse Franklin McLaurin** was born 22 September 1920 in Flea Hill Township and died 21 July 1971 in Fayetteville, North Carolina. He married **Mary Alma Brafford** on 13 December 1947 in Eastover Townsip. She was born 28 December 1925 in Fayetteville, daughter of Nathan Hawley Brafford and Mary Alma Williams. Jesse was buried in the John A. McLaurin Family Cemetery. Four children.

2) **Dewey Maness McLaurin** was born 6 July 1922 and died 19 September 1977 in Fayetteville. He served in the United States Navy during World War II. He married **Lona Pearl Sewell** who was born 17 July 1920 in Dismal Township in Sampson County, North Carolina. Six children.

3) **Mary Bell McLaurin** , third child of Hughie McLaurin and Juanita Thrower was born 7 August 1924 in Flea Hill Township and first married Frank Gaylord. She married second to Mr. Whitzman. She lived in Connecticut and later in Florida.

4) **Reese Alexander McLaurin** was born 14 May 1926 in Flea Hill Township and died 27 July 1984 in Fayetteville. He married **Rowena Darlene Murphy** on 14 February 1948 in Eastover Township, Cumberland County. Darlene was born 23 May 1930 in Fayetteville, daughter of Raymond Murphy and Margaret Lassiter Baggett. Six children.

5) **Marjorie Cornelia McLaurin** was born 25 April 1928 in Carvers Creek Township and married **Walter Stanford Lovick** on 25 August 1946 in Wade, Cumberland County, North Carolina.

6) **Virginia Lee McLaurin** was born 8 December 1930 in Eastover Township. She married **Oliver Jody Gay** who was born about 1931in Chipley, Florida.

7) **Shirley Juanita McLaurin** was born 19 November 1933 in Eastover Township in Cumberland County, North Carolina, and married **Earl Lester Gay** who was born about 1932 in Chipley, Florida.

1204 v. **Robert Hartford McLaurin**, fifth child of Mary Ellen Culbreth and John William McLaurin was born 30 April 1901; died 16 October 1973 in Fayetteville, North Carolina. He married **Eva Mae Fisher** after 1947; born 19 May 1912; died 07 January 1973 in Fayetteville, North Carolina. She was the daughter of Charlie Clem Fisher and Mollie Sessoms. Eva first married **James Elthon Spell** 17 December 1938 in Clinton, North Carolina. He was born 3 January 1914 in Little Coharie Township and died 14 December 1947 in Fayetteville and was the son of Gaston Spell and Cletha Elena Autry. Robert and Eva were buried in LaFayette Memorial Park in Fayetteville. **James Elthon Spell** was buried in the Charlie Clem Fisher Family Cemetery. Robert and Eva had no children; she and James Spell had three children.

vi. **Lloyd Austin McLaurin** was born 8 August 1904 and died 4 January 1970 in Fayetteville. He did not marry and was buried in the John A. McLaurin Family Cemetery.

vii. **John Almeth McLaurin** , seventh child of Mary Ellen Culbreth and John William McLaurin, was born 3 June 1906 and died 4 October 1964 in Eastover Township. Almeth did not marry and was buried in the John A. McLaurin Family Cemetery.

viii. **Son McLaurin** was born 3 January 1908 and died 4 January 1908 was buried in the John A. McLaurin Family Cemetery.

ix. **Daughter McLaurin** was born and died 15 April 1910 and was buried in the John A. McLaurin

Family Cemetery.

x. **Henry Roosevelt McLaurin** was born 13 May 1912 and died 8 February 1971 in Rural Cumberland County near Fayetteville. He did not marry and was buried in the John A. McLaurin Family Cemetery.

xi. **Hersey Wingate McLaurin** was born 29 January 1916 and died 8 October 1973 in Fayetteville. He served in the United States Army Air Forces in World War II, did not marry, and was buried in the John A. McLaurin Family Cemetery.

461. Jennette Ida Culbreth (John[5], Daniel Maxwell[4], Mary[3] Holland, Thomas William[2], Unknown[1]) was born 23 March 1874 in Carolina Beach, New Hanover County, North Carolina, and died 30 March 1949 in Carolina Beach, New Hanover County, North Carolina. She married **Alvin Ernest Royal** 06 November 1890, son of Molton Royal and Sabra Cooper. He was born 07 October 1866 in Salemburg, Sampson County, North Carolina, and died 09 February 1949 in Carolina Beach, New Hanover County, North Carolina.

Her first name is also found as "Jeanette" and this is the name on her tombstone. She and Alvin were buried in Salemburg Cemetery, Salemburg in Sampson County.

Alvin Ernest was called "A. B." He and Ivey, his brother, opened a general store in Salemburg, and soon opened a second store to keep up with the demand. "Ab kept the Christmas tradition of making "Syllabub" alive for the family after Lonie ceased making the Christmas favorite. Lonie had been convinced by Nixon, her preacher son, to stop making the treat because of the alcohol content in the recipe."

Children of Jennette Culbreth and Alvin Royal are:

1205 i. **Daughter Royal**, born 27 October 1891 in Salemburg, Sampson County, North Carolina; died 27 October 1891 in Salemburg, Sampson County, North Carolina. She was buried in a Culbreth Cemetery on Willow Grey Lane off High House Road (SR 1006), Sampson County, North Carolina This cemetery appears to be also known as Joe Moore Hill Cemetery.

1206 ii. **Mamie L. Royal**, born 09 October 1892 in Salemburg, Sampson County, North Carolina; died 22 May 1894 in Salemburg, Sampson County, North Carolina. Mamie was buried in a Culbreth Cemetery on Willow Grey Lane off High House Road (SR 1006), Sampson County, North Carolina. This cemetery appears to also be known as John Moore Hill Cemetery.

\+ 1207 iii. **Pauline Royal,** born 10 May 1895 in Salemburg, Sampson County, North Carolina; died 09 February 1924 in Salemburg, Sampson County, North Carolina.

1208 iv. **Thomas Earl Royal**, born 15 December 1897 in Salemburg, Sampson County, North Carolina. He married (1) **Helen Pross**. He married (2) **Myrtle Little.**

"Thomas worked in the retail clothing business in New York State. He retired to Kure Beach where he lived until his death. No children. He was buried in Salemburg Cemetery, Salemburg, Sampson County, North Carolina.

\+ 1209 v. **Viola Royal,** born 29 November 1899 in Salemburg, Sampson County, North Carolina; died 03 January 1990 in Salemburg, Sampson County, North Carolina.

1210 vi. **Daughter Royal,** born 1900 in Salemburg, Sampson County, North Carolina; died 1900 in Salemburg, Sampson County, North Carolina. This daughter is buried in the Molton Royal Family Cemetery, 1/2 mile southwest of Salemburg.

1211 vii. **Lattie Gray Royal**, born 03 April 1902 in Salemburg, Sampson County, North Carolina; died 07 February 1910 in Salemburg, Sampson County, North Carolina. Lattie is buried in the Molton Royal Family Cemetery, 1/2 mile southwest of Salemburg.

\+ 1212 viii. **John Robert Royal**, born 04 March 1904 in Salemburg, Sampson County, North Carolina; died 04 October 1984 in Pittsboro, Chatham County, North Carolina.

\+ 1213 ix. **James Molton Royal**, born 13 June 1906 in Salemburg, Sampson County, North Carolina; died 03 February 1988 in Clinton, Sampson County, North Carolina.

1214 x. **Daniel Culbreth Royal**, a stillborn 15 December 1909.

463. Roberta Culbreth (John[5], Daniel Maxwell[4], Mary[3] Holland, Thomas William[2], Unknown[1]) was born 02 January 1878, and died 29 November 1945 in Cumberland County, North Carolina. She married **Hardy Blackman Tew** 22 March 1900 in Sampson County, North Carolina, son of Richard Tew and Aggie Cannady. He was born 07 March 1869 in Sampson County, North Carolina, and died 19 July 1931 in Cumberland County, North Carolina.

Also found for Hardy's date of birth are 7 March 1869 and 7 March 1872. He and Roberta were buried in Cumberland Mills, Cumberland County, North Carolina.

Children of Roberta Culbreth and Hardy Tew are:

\+ 1215 i. **Percy Maxwell Tew**, born 16 January 1901 in North Carolina; died 09 February 1980 in Clinton, Sampson County, North Carolina.

\+ 1216 ii. **Ernest Blackman Tew**, born 22 August 1903 in North Carolina; died 31 March 1979 in Cumberland County, North Carolina.

1217 iii. **Mollie J. Tew,** born 24 October 1906 in North Carolina; died 26 March 1934.

She was buried in Fayetteville, Cumberland Cemetery, North Carolina.

\+ 1218 iv. **John Tew**, born 14 November 1909 in North Carolina; died 16 January 1985 in Cumberland County, North Carolina.

\+ 1219 v. **Sudie Viola Tew**, born 03 March 1912 in Sampson County, North Carolina.

\+ 1220 vi. **Arthur Gibson Tew**, born 14 February 1914 in Dismal Township, Clement, Sampson County, North Carolina; died 09 May 1963 in Fayetteville, Cumberland County, North Carolina.

\+ 1221 vii. **E. Hardy Blackman Tew**, born 24 October 1917 in Honeycutts Township, Sampson County, North Carolina; died 02 May 1982 in Cumberland County, North Carolina.

464. Virginia Culbreth (John[5], Daniel Maxwell[4], Mary[3] Holland, Thomas William[2], Unknown[1]) was born 09 April 1880, and died 24 September 1946 in Fayetteville, Cumberland County, North Carolina. She married **Julius William Matthews** 28 June 1896 in Clinton, North Carolina, son of Wiley Matthews and Barbara Williams. He was born 17 February 1876, and died 22 March 1951 in Fayetteville, Cumberland County, North Carolina.

The date of 9 August 1880 is also found for her birth. She and Julius were buried in Maxwell Cemetery, Clement, Sampson County, North Carolina.

Children of Virginia Culbreth and Julius Matthews are:

\+ 1222 i. **Lela Pearl Matthews**, born 10 July 1897 in Cumberland County, North Carolina; died 13 May 1978 in Harnett County, North Carolina.

\+ 1223 ii. **Radford Carl Matthews**, born 06 June 1899; died 04 January 1985 in Raeford, North Carolina.

\+ 1224 iii. **Irma G. Matthews**, born 24 August 1901; died 31 October 1990.

1225 iv. **Infant Matthews** was born and died on 08 May 1904. Infant was buried in Bethabara United Methodist Church Cemetery.

\+ 1226 v. **William Garland Matthews**, born 09 September 1905.

\+ 1227 vi. **Ola Ann Matthews**, born 21 October 1908.

\+ 1228 vii. **Lula Jane Matthews**, born 14 September 1911 in Dismal Township, Sampson County, North Carolina; died 28 August 2002.

1229 viii. **Lola Belle Matthews**, born 11 February 1914. She married **Robert Matthews**.

1230 ix. **Millard B. Matthews**, born 09 May 1919 in Mingo Township, Sampson County, North Carolina; died 21 August 1988 in Fayetteville, Cumberland County, North Carolina. He married **Mildred Elizabeth Ballance** who was born 07 October 1927 and they had one child. He was buried in the Maxwell Cemetery, Clement, Sampson County, North Carolina.

1231 x. **Olive Virginia Matthews**, born 25 December 1920 in Dismal Township, Sampson County, North Carolina; died Before 1985. She married **Ward Headley Pendley, Jr.**; born 27 November 1924 in Fort Bragg, North Carolina. Olive and Ward had two children.

1232 xi. **Daniel Claxton Matthews**, born 29 December 1922 in Dismal Township, Sampson County, North Carolina; died 29 December 1922.

465. Lena Mae Culbreth (John[5], Daniel Maxwell[4], Mary[3] Holland, Thomas William[2], Unknown[1]) was born 24 July 1883, and died 20 September 1959. She married **Lewis Martin Matthews** 20 January 1903, son of Wiley Matthews and Barbara Williams. He was born 16 October 1879, and died 31 May 1954 in Clinton, Sampson County, North Carolina.

Lena Mae and Lewis were buried in a Honeycutt - Matthews Family Cemetery near Maxwell Road (SR1006) and SR 1442, Sampson County, North Carolina.

Children of Lena Culbreth and Lewis Matthews are:

+ 1233 i. **Atticus Marvin Matthews**, born 16 October 1903; died 09 August 1988 in Clinton, Sampson County, North Carolina.

1234 ii. **Alton Rose Matthews**, born 30 October 1906; died 25 July 1988 in Fayetteville, Cumberland County, North Carolina. He married **Bessie Clyde Matthews**, (daughter of Lonnie Baucom Matthews and Carrie Mae Reynolds), who was born 1912 and they had one child. Alton Rose was buried in LaFayette Memorial Park, Fayetteville, North Caorlina.

+ 1235 iii. **Mabel Inez Matthews**, born 25 November 1908; died 24 June 1995.

+ 1236 iv. **Daniel Crosby Matthews**, born 24 July 1911 in Cumberland County, North Carolina; died 26 December 1987 in Cumberland County, North Carolina.

1237 v. **Lattie Matthews**, born 03 December 1914; died 03 December 1914 in Dismal Township, Sampson County, North Carolina. His certificate of birth and certificate of death apparently lists 03 December 1914, but his tombstone may read 03 January 1914?

+ 1238 vi. **Eupha Mae Matthews**, born 28 April 1917 in Sampson County, North Carolina; died 21 October 1983 in Cumberland County, North Carolina.

+ 1239 vii. **Maggie Nessie Matthews**, born 15 August 1918 in Dismal Township, Sampson County, North Carolina.

1240 viii. **Unknown Son Matthews**, born 10 January 1921 in Dismal Township, Sampson County, North Carolina; died 10 January 1921.

+ 1241 ix. **Adrian Huston Matthews**, born 15 January 1924.

466. Annie Vara Culbreth (John[5], Daniel Maxwell[4], Mary[3] Holland, Thomas William[2], Unknown[1]) was born 06 November 1886, and died 28 June 1963 in Clinton, Sampson County, North Carolina. She married **Carey Martin Tew** 02 January 1907 in Residence of C. J. Culbreth, Sampson County, North Carolina, son of Hiram Tew and Levira Parker. He was born 16 January 1884, and died 21 September 1960 in Dismal Township, Sampson County, North Carolina.

Annie Vara and Carey Martin were buried inChapel Cemetery near Autryville, North Carolina. Carey's date of birth is also found as 16 November 1884.

Children of Annie Culbreth and Carey Tew are:

+ 1242 i. **Macie Tew**, born 13 October 1907.

+ 1243 ii. **Glaspy Elwood Tew**, born 08 October 1916 in Dismal Township, Sampson County, North Carolina.

467. Rebeckah Olivia Culbreth (John[5], Daniel Maxwell[4], Mary[3] Holland, Thomas William[2], Unknown[1]) was born 23 December 1888, and died 20 June 1950. She married **Roscus Honeycutt** 08 January 1919 in Orange, Sampson County, North Carolina, son of

Blackman Honeycutt and Emily Wrench. He was born 20 May 1894 in Sampson County, North Carolina, and died 10 July 1941 in Dismal Township in Sampson County.

Rebeckah Olivia and Roscus are buried in a Culbreth Cemetery on Willow Grey Lane, Sampson County, North Carolina.

Children of Rebeckah Culbreth and Roscus Honeycutt are:

1244 i. **John Culbreth Honeycutt**, born 21 November 1921; died 25 March 1923.

\+ 1245 ii. **Willa Grey Honeycutt**, born 21 January 1929 in Sampson County, North Carolina.

468. Julius Ainslie Culbreth (William[5], Daniel Maxwell[4], Mary[3] Holland, Thomas William[2], Unknown[1]) was born 08 December 1871, and died 14 February 1950. He married **(1) Vinie Irene Bizzell** before 1894. She was born 08 October 1869, and died 23 April 1943 and was the daughter of Hannibal Bizzell who was born in 1847 and died in 1921, and Catherine Underwood who was born in 1851 and died in 1921. He married **(2) Mollie Thornton** 08 September 1945. She was born 15 February 1911 and was the daughter of Henry D. Thornton and Flora Britt.

Professor V. Mayo Bundy writes about Julius in "The Heritage of Sampson County, North Carolina," Editor, Oscar M. Bizzell:

"Julius Culbreth attended the one-room school at Clement in Sampson County from 1878 to 1882 and was taught by Elizabeth (Betty) Howard. When his family moved to Falcon (Starling's Bridge) he attended the Five Oaks School from 1882 to 1888. He met Venie Bizzell, who was teaching music at the Clement School and they married in 1892. From 1890 to 1897 he assisted his father in the operation of his stores in Dunn and Falcon, managed them after his father's death and was also an employee of the First Nationsl Bank of Dunn.

"The year 1896 was the "Aldersgate Street" experience for Julius and Venie Culbreth, for their religious experience at the Rev. Ambrose B. Crumpler's tent revival in May 1896 at Dunn, North Carolina, set the pattern of their lives of service to humanity. According to their daughter, Ruth Culbreth Jones of Raleigh, "At this service when people were asked to donate not only money, but jewelry as well, my mother gave her wedding ring and Merle's small diamond ring. One businessman papa knew has said that if their first child was a girl, he would give her a diamond ring, and did.

"In 1897 Julius and Venie moved from Dunn back to Falcon. He wrote in the Holiness Advocate in 1901:

"...about four years ago (1897) when it became evident that we must leave our home in Dunn and move out here in this country place, our hearts would almost faint when we would think of leaving the Holiness prayer meetings, and breaking away from the sweet fellowship of the saints in Dunn to come here (Falcon) where holiness had never been preached and not a soul even understood what the profession of sanctification meant...'

In the same Field Notes he dates other early landmarks in Falcon when he wrote:

"a nice and comfortable little tabernacle, 1898, our first Camp Meeting, 1900, and a school house was opened to us..., 1902. The school was located in the rear of his father's General Store building.'

"A significate philosophy of Julius Culbreth and one he practiced all his life, and which profoundly affected many others was recorded in this report:

"...a little Tabernacle absolutely independent of every ecclesiasticism, and entirely too broad for any sectarian or denominational narrowness, and the freedom we have is like unto Heaven itself, and through this work, God has not only poured out His blessings upon us in the community, but has sent food to the famine stricken, and the glorious gospel of full salvation to the regions beyond.'

"Many people thought that Julius Culbreth, upon returning to Falcon in 1897, remained there the rest of his life, but this is not the case. In 1916 he returned to the First National Bank in Dunn, and remained there until 1920. From 1920 to 1926 he worked with and helped establish The North Carolina Cotton Association and The North Carolina Credit Corporation in Raleigh. To carry on the work he had started in Falcon, he commuted each weekend from Dunn and Raleigh to Falcon. Most of his earnings were plowed back into the orphanage and the school. After 1926, they made their permanent home in Falcon, and were living there at the time of their deaths.

"...All of Julius' children attended the Falcon Holiness School.

Children of Julius Culbreth and Vinie Bizzell are:

1246 i. **Merle Culbreth**, born 10 December 1894; died 10 January 1981 in Richmond, Virginia. She married (1) **Henry Edward Ragle** Before October 1919. She married (2) **Marvin Belvin** Before 1926.

Merle and Henry Edward had one son, **Henry Edward Ragle, Jr.**, who was born 14 October 1919 and first married **Elsie Wright** on 21 October 1940. Henry, Jr. and Elsie had one child, **Henry Edward Ragle III.** The second wife of Herny Jr. was **Jean French** and they had two children, **Sandra Ragle** who was born on 12 June 1955 and **Joyce Ragle,** born on 29 February 1960.

Merle and her second husband, Marvin Belvin had one child, **Billy Ainsley Belvin** who was born on 19 September 1926 and married **Lottie Beasley** on 18 March 1950. No children.

1247 ii. **William Earle Culbreth** was born 22 September 1898 and died 06 July 1899; he was buried in Antioch Baptish Church Cemetery in Falcon, North Carolina.

1248 iii. **Ruth Catherine Culbreth**, born 27 August 1903; died 28 April 1994. She married **William Davis Jones, Jr.**; born 06 May 1894 in Missouri; died 09 April 1977 in Wilmington, New Hanover County, North Carolina.

Ruth Catherine and William Davis had two children. **William Davis Jones III** was born on 24 November 1926 and married **Susie Burnett**. William Davis and Susie had five children: **Ainslie Ruth Jones** was born 06 October 1954; **William Davis Jones IV** was born on 3 December 1956; **Annetta Burnett Jones** was born on 28 September 1961; **Adam Willie Jones** was born on 24 September 1963; **Della Deaton Jones** was born on 20 June 1966.

Ruth Catherine and William Davis' second child was **Nancy Colbern Jones** who was born on 23 July 1937. She married **William MacFarlane Park** and they had two children, **Ewan Charles Park** who was born on 12 July 1967 and Andrew Culbreth Park who was born on 22 November 1970.

1249 iv. **Daisy Culbreth,** fourth child of Julius Culbreth and Vinie Bizzell, born 07 October 1907. She married (1) **Hazel Donalson.** She married (2) **Jack Berstein;** born 25 November 1898 in Poland; died 24 May 1976 in Goldsboro, North Carolina.

Daisy and Hazel had one son, **Donnie Donalson** on 23 May 1929.

Daisy's second husband, Jack, adopted Donnie Donalson and renamed him **Daniel Bernstein.** Daniel married **Mitzie Edmondson** who was born on the 9 September 1925 and they had four children. **Michael Julius Bernstein,** born on 13 August 1954; **Anita Rise Bernstein,** born 18 August 1959; **Celeste Zilphia Bernstein** was born 12 November 1963; **Vanessa Bernstein** was born 9 December 1969.

Daisy and Jack's second son, **William Maurice Bernstein** was born on 30 May 1940 and married **Nancy Weinstein** who was born on 5 May 1947. Williem Maurice and Nancy had two children. **Jonathan Bernstein** was born 16 August 1971 and **Jacob Richard Bernstein** who was born on 23 July 1976.

469. Virginia Isabell Culbreth (William[5], Daniel Maxwell[4], Mary[3] Holland, Thomas William[2], Unknown[1]) was born 08 October 1876, and died 19 January 1930. She married **Charles Henry Randall.** He was born 03 November 1878, and died 07 February 1943. he was the son of John Salles Randall and Virginia Hurley.

Virginia Isabell and Charles Henry were buried in Antioch Baptist Church Cemetery, Falcon, North Carolina.

Children of Virginia Culbreth and Charles Randall are:

1250 i. **Charles Culbreth Randall,** born 12 August 1904; died 27 September 1927 in Black River Township, Cumberland County, North Carolina.

Charles Culbreth was buried in Antioch Baptist Church Cemetery, Falcon, North Carolina

\+ 1251 ii. **William Hurley Randall, Sr.**, born 08 December 1906 in Falcon, North Carolina.

1252 iii. **Virginia Isabell Randall,** born 26 September 1909. She married **Hillary Tillette Cain** 04 October 1931; Hillary was born 05 August 1903 and died 10 March 1974 in Dunn, Harnett County, North Carolina.

Hillary Tillette was buried in Devotional Gardens, Dunn, Harnett County, North Carolina

No children.

1253 iv. **Eugene Ainsley Randall,** born 21 March 1912 in Lumberton; died 28 September 1954 in Durham. He married **Annie Laurie Hobbs** 30 July 1939 in Dillon, South Carolina. She was born 27 November 1916 in Johnston County, North Carolina.

Three Children.

Charles Clifford Randall, the first child of Eugene and Annie Laurie, was born on 26 June 1940 and married **Nancy Jane Boardman** on 21 April 1966. Nancy was born on 27 August 1940. Charles Clifford and Nancy Jane had one child, **Craig Joseph Randall** who was born 31 August 1970.

The second child of Eugene Ainsley and Annie Laurie was **Angela Randall** who was born 31 January 1942 and married on 21 December 1960 to **Marvin Edwin Bunce** who was born on 27 March 1938 and died on 15 June 1976. He was the son of **George Wesley Bunce** and **Eva Matthews.** Angela and Marvin Edwin had two children, **Sandra Ann Bunce** was born 20 February 1962 and **Pamela Dawn Bunce** was born on 16 December 1967.

The third child of Eugene Ainsley and Annie Laurie was **Nicholas Eugene Randall** who was born on 10 August 1944 and married on 13 April 1968 to **Linda Joyce Pearce** who was born on 22 October 1943. She was the daughter of **Carl Dems**

Pearce and **Nita Young**. Nicholas Eugene and Linda Joyce had two children, **Angela Marie Randall** was born on 25 June 1974 and **Stephanie Aneta Randall** was born 8 June 1976.

473. Minnie Nicholson Culbreth (William[5], Daniel Maxwell[4], Mary[3] Holland, Thomas William[2], Unknown[1]) was born 22 June 1883, and died 30 January 1939. She married **Vivian Lindley Bundy** 22 February 1911, son of Joseph Bundy and Junietta Winslow. He was born 20 January 1887, and died 15 July 1918.

In his book, Minnie's son, Dr. Vivian Mayo Bundy, wrote fondly of his mother and father, expressing their "humanity, humility and goodness." Minnie Nicholson was 11 when she lost her father, mother, and infant brother within ten days. It may have been the shock of this that resulted in her having what was known at the time as St. Vitus' Dance, a functional nervous disorder characterized by involuntary actions of the muscles. For a short time the condition"affected her schooling at Five Oaks and her status with the other members of the family." During this time and until 1903, most of Minnie's time was spent in the home, helping with her brother, Lattie, who was four at the time their parents died.

From "1903 until her marriage in 1911, she was a milliner at B. Fleishman's and Sons Department Store in Dunn, North Carolina," and was "known far and wide for her hats."

She and Vivian Lindley spent the first year of married life farming in Gates County, North Carolina. From 1912 until 1916, they farmed in Wayne County, near Mount Olive, North Carolina, and they then returned to Falcon where Vivian Lindley "started a lumber business near Fayetteville, North Carolina. The happiness they had shared for seven years was cut short on 14 July 1918 when Vivian Lindley was shot by one of his Black workers, Davis Evans; he died two days later. Minnie moved to her parents home and her son, William Joseph was born prematurely, six weeks later in Mount Olive. About a year later, after recovering from the shock of Vivian's death and other health problems, she discovered that most of his wealth had been used by some members of the family during her state of shock and illness. Some members of her family encouraged her to place her "children in the Falcon Orphanage which was started and operated by her older brother, Julius. Instead, she returned to Falcon, bought a house and continued her long, hard labor of love and dedication" to her family and friends. To survive, she sewed, "took in washing (even her brother's)" and farmed.

In the late 1920's, "North Carolina passed a law requiring all cows to be vaccinated against tuberculosis. Minnie's only cow tested positive and was destroyed". She and the children were also vacinated, but her eldest son, Lattie Ainsley, was found to have tuberculosis and died on 3 June 1931.

From 1920 to 1936, Minnie's sister, Hattie Culbreth, who had separated from her husband, spent many of her vacations and weekends with Minnie and the boys. Hattie worked at the North Carolina Laboratory as a secretary. Another tragedy struck this Culbreth family on "Mother's Day, 10 May 1936 when Hattie and her nephew, Laurice McLellan, a senior in the School of Pharmacy at the University of North Carolina, were killed in an automobile accident within site of his home, about two miles from Minnie's home."

Professor Bundy tells that his mother was never the same afterwards. She broke her hip and had surgery at Highsmith Hospital in Fayetteville; she died in that hospital on 30 January 1939.

By the standards of people in Falcon, North Carolina, Vivian Lindley Bundy "was a non-Christian because he and Minnie were not of the same religion as their neighbors. He was a chip off his Quaker ancestry, a Lincoln Republican, as were many of the early Bundy Quakers, and he was sensitive and concerned for humanity and its needs." One Sunday a "righteous" neighbor objected to his cutting wood on a Sunday. He responded with "My wife and children are cold and need wood. Would you like for me to bring some over to your place after I meet their needs.?"

Minnie "was an avid reader...she was often the last to be considered and was cast in the role of compromiser...In those days, many of her books, the contemporary novels of the time, were considered sinful and worldly by town standards. However, many of the so-called 'good' people would borrow her books with the request that no one was to know."

In spite of her many tragedies, Minnie was "known for her laughter, her hats, her good wit and her love of people. On the night Vivian was shot, "she pleaded with some friends and relatives who wanted to take the killer from the jail for a lynching party, to 'let the law take its course.'"

Children of Minnie Culbreth and Vivian Bundy are:

1254 i. **Lattie Ainsley Bundy**, born 12 February 1912; died 03 June 1931.

1255 ii. **Vivian Mayo Bundy**, born 08 June 1914; died 09 November 1996. He married **Norma Harrington Melvin** on 30 April 1940; she was born 21 September 1912. Vivian was buried in Antioch Baptist Church Cemetery, Falcon, North Carolina.

Dr. Bundy graduated from the University of North Carolina with an A.B. degree in 1935, his M.A. degree in 1941 and a D..Ed. in 1969. Other work was also completed at the University of Virginia.

" ...began his professional career as a teacher and coach at White Oak High School in Bladen County, North Carolina" Dr. Bundy speaks of the community where he lived in Bladen County as "isolated, backward, and clannish, but they respected and supported their schools and teachers."

He left White Oak High School when he was chosen "to be principal of Kelly High School in the same county. It was the county's smallest, most isolated high school, and had the worst reputation. Some of the stories of drownings, killings, beatings, etc., would be hard to match. Nevertheless, they were good to me and supported me in errors as well as in successes." In 1940, while at this school, he and Norma Melvin, an English teacher who had taught at Kelly for three years before he came, were married.

In 1941, he and Norma took "new jobs at Monticellin in Guilford County, North Carolina. He writes, "..it was like a new world, offering both a principal's home, and proximity to an urban center. Entertainment like dancing and card playing in public were accepted."

He, in 1944, accepted the Altamahaw-Ossipee school principalship in Alamance County, North Carolina, and remained there until 1953 when he was appointed Superintendent of the Madison City School in Madison, North Carolina. He was in this school system until 1971 and described the communities he served in this system as more complex, more self-serving, more materialistic and more divided as any he had ever served. While there he completed his doctoral degree. After his resignation was accepted, he taught at Bennett College in Greensboro, and at other colleges and worked part-time at North Carolina Agricultural and Technical State University and at the University of North Carolina-Greensboro.

Vivian Mayo and Norma had four children.

Their first child, **Vee Mayo Bundy**, was born on 17 November 1942. He married **Juliana Vaughn** who was born on 24 January 1945 and their daughter, **Gretchen Ann Bundy** was born on 7 January 1976.

Norma McKay Bundy, the second child of Vivian and Norma, was born on 7 November 1944 and on 23 June 1967, she married **Tommie Russell Bowman**; Tommie was born 21 March 1943. Norma and Tommie's daughter, **Karen Elizabeth Bowman** was born on 25 April 1974.

Deborah Herrington Bundy who was born 31 October 1950 was the third child of Vivian and Norma and on 27 May 1972, she married **John Charles Wilson** who was born on 2 May 1949. Their son, **Whitney Herrington Wilson** was born on 16 September 1974.

Linda Jo Bundy, born on 6 February 1954, was the fourth child of Vivian and Norma. On 27 May 1972 she married **Mickey Odell Johnson** who was born on 27 August 1950. Their son, **Brent Bundy Johnson** was born on 28 July 1975. Another son, **Nicholas Odell Johnson** was born 26 December 1977.

1256 iii. **James Autry Bundy, Sr.**, third child of Minnie Nicholson Culbreth and Vivian Lindley Bundy, was born 14 July 1916 in Mr. Olive, North Carolina; died 24 December 1987 in Goldsboro, North Carolina. He married (1) **Eloise Gwendolyn Simmons**; born 23 March 1918 in Goldsboro, North Carolina; died 24 March 1987 in Goldsboro, North Carolina. He married (2) **Mamie Gourley Hines**; born 12 May 1916.

James Autry had one child.

1257 iv. **William Joseph Bundy**, fourth child of Minnie and Vivian, was born 06 September 1918 in Mt. Olive, North Carolina; died 11 January 1985 in Fayetteville, Cumberland County, North Carolina.

William Joseph did not marry.

474. Clyde Cleveland Culbreth (William[5], Daniel Maxwell[4], Mary[3] Holland, Thomas William[2], Unknown[1]) was born 03 May 1885, and died 20 December 1959 in Black River Township, Cumberland County, North Carolina. She married **Wiley Rhodes McLellan** 07 March 1906 in Black River Township, Cumberland County, North Carolina. He was born 02 January 1885, and died 13 March 1945 in Fayetteville, Cumberland County, North Carolina.

Clyde Cleveland's father said "when a Decocrat was elected president he would name his next child for him." Hence, Clyde Cleveland, named for President Grover Cleveland.

Clyde was buried in Black's Chapel United Methodist Church Cemetery.

Children of Clyde Culbreth and Wiley McLellan are:

\+ 1258 i. **Earl Autry McLellan**, born 25 December 1906; died 25 October 1962.

1259 ii. **Laurice Rhodes McLellan**, born 17 October 1908; died 10 May 1936 in Black River Township, Cumberland County, North Carolina, in an automobile accident. He was buried in Black's Chapel United Methodist Church Cemetery.

\+ 1260 iii. **Margaret Elizabeth McLellan** was born 24 October 1911 in Rocky Mount, North Carolina, and died 27 March 1954 in Black River Township, Cumberland County, North Carolina.

1261 iv. **Clyde Culbreth McLellan**, born 09 December 1917. She married **EDWARD H. WOZELKA**; born 13 September 1917. Two children. Their first child **KATHRYN CLYDE WOZELKA** was born 7 January 1943. She married first **ROBERT EDWARD WHITE** and they had two children. Robert was born 11 August 1941, son of **BRUCE NORMAN WHITE** and **EDITH MAE GARRETT.**

Kathryn married second 91 January 1974 to **HOWARD EUGENE KIVETT** who was born 11 July 1927, son of **WILLIAM SEYMORE KIVETT** and **ALMA EURIDGE**. She and Howard had one child; he had three children by his first wife and Kathryn adopted two of these.

The second child of Clyde and Edward was **MARY JOSEPHINE WOZELKA** who was born 6 October 1949. She married **ROBERT DARDEN SWAIN, JR.**

475. Mamie Worth Culbreth (William[5], Daniel Maxwell[4], Mary[3] Holland, Thomas William[2], Unknown[1]) was born 14 February 1888, and died 17 March 1951. She married **Dr. Zeno Baker Spence, Sr.** 18 March 1909. He was born 16 July 1883, and died 13 March 1952.

Dr. Zeno Baker Spence, Sr. was buried in Goldsboro City Cemetery, Goldsboro, North Carolina.

Children of Mamie Culbreth and Zeno Spence are:

1262 i. **Wilma Gardner Spence**, born 11 April 1910; died 09 November 1976. She married Charles Thomson Gordon; born in Forfarshire, Scotland, Great Britain.

No Children.

1263 ii. **Mamie Louise Spence**, born 23 July 1925; died 26 July 1925.

1264 iii. **Zeno Baker Spence, Jr.**, born 13 February 1927.

He was married twice and had four children.

476. Lattie Alston Culbreth, Sr. (William[5], Daniel Maxwell[4], Mary[3] Holland, Thomas William[2], Unknown[1]) was born 14 October 1890, and died 29 May 1971 in Smithfield, North Carolina. He married **(1) Ada Helen Barnes** October 1912. She was born 31 July 1885, and died 29 November 1942 in Black River Township, Cumberland County, North Carolina. He married **(2) Helen Wallace Beasley** 14 October 1944.

Lattie Alston had six children by his first wife. No children by second wife.

Children of Lattie Culbreth and Ada Barnes are:

1265 i. **Lattie Alston Culbreth, Jr.**, born 04 July 1914; died 27 December 1968 in Sumter, South Carolina.

He had no children. A posting on Ancestry.com has 4 April 1913 for his date of birth.

1266 ii. **Hazel Elizabeth Culbreth**, born 07 September 1915 in Black River Township, Cumberland County, North Carolina. She married **Robert Wages**; born about 1922 in Denver, Colorado.

1st child: **PAMELA HELEN WAGES** was born 12 February 1948 in Dunn, North Carolina. She married 14 April 1970 as his second wife, **MAURICE THEODORE MCLAURIN** who was born 11 July 1946 in Dunn, son of EMPIE THEODORE MCLAURIN and BERA JOSEPHINE JONES. Maurice married first 17 September 1965 in Eastover Township, **MARY ALICE LOGAN**, daughter of ANSEL LOGAN and EUGENIA MCCALL. She was born about 1848 in Clarendon County, South Carolina. Two children.

2nd child: **GARY ROBERT WAGES** was born 17 November 1949.

3rd child: **TRAVIS WAGES** was born 15 July 1956 in Dunn, North Carolina. He married 30 July 1976 **SHEILA MAXWELL**, daughter of **DAVID MAXWELL** and **JOYCE HAIR**. One child.

1267 iii. **Blanche Culbreth**, born 12 July 1916 in Black River Township, Cumberland County, North Carolina. She married (1) **Charles Hicks Jackson** 01 November 1935 in Fayetteville, Cumberland County, North Carolina; born 26 June 1912; died 02 January 1958. She married (2) **Thomas I. Lucas** 24 September 1960; born 14 September 1927 in Averasboro Township, Harnett County, North Carolina.

Blanche Culbreth had no children by either husband. Charles Hicks Jackson was buried in the Wiley C. Jackson Family Cemetery in Dismal Township at corner of U.S. Route 13 and S. R. 1443, Sampson County, North Carolina.

1268 iv. **William Marshall Culbreth**, born 28 November 1917; died 14 November 1918.

1269 v. **Kathleen Dixon Culbreth**, born 17 August 1919 in Black River Township, Cumberland County, North Carolina.

She did not marry.

1270 vi. **Warren Briggs Culbreth**, born 16 March 1926. He married **Dolly Gray Morrison**.

Warren was adopted; he was the son of Thomas Briggs and Helen Grantham.

478. Matilda Jane Culbreth (Daniel L.[5], Daniel Maxwell[4], Mary[3] Holland, Thomas William[2], Unknown[1]) was born 19 April 1868 in Sampson County, North Carolina, and died 18 October 1897 in Sampson County, North Carolina. She married **William Thomas Hall, Jr.** before 1891, son of Thomas Hall and Margaret D. Howard. He was born 29 October 1862, and died 12 March 1921 in Dismal Township, Sampson County, North Carolina.

Matilda Jane and William Thomas were buried in the George Horne Cemetery near intersection of South River Road and Minnie Hall Road, Sampson County, North Carolina.

Children of Matilda Culbreth and William Hall are:

\+ 1271 i. **Victoria Hall**, born 10 August 1887; died 18 September 1971 in Falcon, Cumberland County, North Carolina.

\+ 1272 ii. **Julius D. Hall**, born 05 August 1891; died 06 November 1972.

1273 iii. **Mittie Lula Hall**, born 07 April 1894 in Sampson County, North Carolina; died 1898 in Sampson County, North Carolina. She was buried in the George Horne Cemetery near South River Road and Minnie Hall Road in Sampson County, North Carolina.

1274 iv. **Macy Mae Hall** who was born 28 September 1897 and died 09 November 1973 married **Seba Swendell Parker** who was born 28 May 1892 and died 06 September 1949 in Erwin, Harnett County, North Carolina. Both were buried in War Memorial Cemetery, Dunn, Harnett County, North Carolina.

1) **NENIA MAE PARKER,** the first child of Macy Mae and Seba was born 14 January 1916 and married **JOSEPH A. HONEYCUTT**, who was born 6 January 1916 and died 30 May 1959. Minnie and Joseph had one child, **MARY ALICE HONEYCUTT**, who was born 10 August 1940 and married a **Mr. Keen**. Nenia's name may be found as "Minnie Mae."

2) **WILLIAM SWENDELL PARKER,** second child of Macy Mae and Seba was born 12 November 1917, married **LUDELL G. PARKER** who was born 15 May 1916 and their son, **ROBERT SWINDELL PARKER** was born 22 September 1938.

3) **VIDA PARKER**, the third child, was born 9 January 1920 and married **SHERRILL WILLIAM AVERY** on 22 July 1938. Their children: **JACKY DARIUS AVERY**, born 22 October 1939; **WILLIAM PAUL AVERY**, born 7 February 1942; **JAMES MACK AVERY**, born 15 December 1944.

4) **JESSE JAMES PARKER**, Macy Mae and Seba Swendell Parker's fourth child was born 8 April 1922, died 25 December 1970. He married **ELIZABETH GOWER** who was born 5 December 1924 and their child, **LARRY JAMES PARKER** was born 25 April 1942 and married **ELIZABETH MOORE** who was born 8 August 1942. Their child, **LARRY JAMES PARKER, JR.**, was born 3 September 1968.

5) **EARL D. PARKER**, the fifth child was born 1 June 1924, died 21 March 1964. He married first to **BULAH BYRD** and they had one child, **PATSY PARKER**, on 2 February 1948. Earl married second to **BETTY JEAN RUSSELL** who was born 31 December 1938. Earl and Betty's children: **DONALD PARKER; DEBRA PARKER; DAVID PARKER.**

6) **LEDDIE JANE PARKER (Liddie)**, the sixth child of Macy Mae and Seba Swendell was born 13 November 1925, married **DANNY KERBLE MANNESS** who was born 3October 1924 and had six children: **JONATHAN MALANI MANNESS; SHAN MANNESS; JAYNE SHARMAYNE MANNESS; SHARON JEANETTE MANNESS; LYDIA KERBELIN MANNESS; THELMA VIDA LORAINNE MANNESS.**

7) **RUTH MILDRED PARKER,** seventh child of Macy May and Seba was born 10 November 1928 and married **BILLY RAY STEWART** who was born 20 October 1925. No children.

8) **NELL BARBARA PARKER**, the eighth child, was born 10 April 1933 and married first to **DONALD M. VALLEY** who was born 11 January 1930. They had two children: **RANDY MAREIS VALLEY** and **GARY MITCHELL VALLEY**. Nell married second, **JERRY POOLE POPE** who was born 20 January 1939 and they had one child, **JERRY KEITH POPE.**

9) **JOYCE GLENDON PARKER,** the ninth child of Macy Mae and Seba Swendell Parker was born 4 February 1936 and married **PAUL HURMAN JACKSON** who was born 7 June 1931. They had one child, **CONNIE T. JACKSON.**

479. Jannette Maxwell Culbreth (Daniel L.[5], Daniel Maxwell[4], Mary[3] Holland, Thomas William[2], Unknown[1]) was born 16 August 1870 in Sampson County, North Carolina, and died 17 March 1919. She married **Edward Lonza Hall**, son of Matthew Hall and Martha Daniel. He was born 08 January 1875 in Sampson County, North Carolina, and died 27 March 1934. Jannette's date of birth is also listed as 16 Aug 1872.

She and Edward were buried in Maxwell Cemetery near Clement in Sampson County, North Carolina.

Children of Jannette Culbreth and Edward Hall are:

1275 i. **Ivey Cleveland Culbreth**, born 10 August 1893. He married **Chellie Margaret Matthews**; born 07 June 1896 in Sampson County, North Carolina; died 02 May 1983, daughter of ALFRED IVERSON MATTHEWS, born 25 January 1866, died March 1950, and MARY ADELINE AUTRY, born 27 January 1874, died June 1958. Mary Adeline was the daughter of "Big" JOHN AUTRY and MARGARET MAXWELL Ivey and Chellie were buried in Maxwell Cemetery, southeast corner of Maxwell Road (SR 1006) and (SR 1427), Sampson County, North Carolina.

Ivy and Chellie had five children.

1) **MELVIA ADELAIDE CULBRETH,** first child of Ivey and Chellie was born 17 December 1917 and on 28 November 1935, married **ISAAC MARVIN WILLIAMS** who was born 15 January 1911. Melvia and Isaac's first child, **STANLEY DIXON WILLIAMS,** was born 30 September 1936 and

married on 18 October 1953 to **JOYCE ANN WILLIAMS** who was born 6 November 1940. Melvia and Isaac's second child was **MARVIN ELLIS WILLIAMS** who was born 19 February 1942 and married **BRENDA SUE AUTRY**.

2) **LILLIAN JEANETTE CULBRETH**, the second child of Ivey and Chellie, was born 25 October 1919 and married **ERNEST R. FRANCIS** who was born 26 September 1901.

3) **JAMES PITTMAN CULBRETH**, third child of Ivey and Chellie was born 3 September 1921 and deied 30 january 1977. He married **CLARA BELL FUTRELL** who was born 8 January 1927 and they had two children.

4) **PAUL CULBRETH**, the fourth child of Ivey and Chellie, was born 5 September 1923, married **MELBALINE WILLIAMS** who was born 20 July 1925. Two children.

5) **MARGARET CULBRETH**, fifth child, was born 20 February 1932 and married first to **MENDALL WARDELL HANCOCK** and they had two children. She married second to **JACK B. TROW** who was born 13 March 1927 and they had one daughter. Jack also adopted the two daughters of Margaret and Mendall.

1276 ii. **Empie Downing Hall**, second child of Jannette Maxwell Culbreth and Edward Lonza Hall was born 19 October 1897 in Sampson County, North Carolina; died 14 September 1960 in Dunn, Harnett County, North Carolina. He married (1) **Willard Hemmingway** before 1950; born 21 June 1903; died 26 June 1950 in Dunn, Harnett County, North Carolina. He married (2) **Ruby Mozelle Warren** after 1950; born 08 September 1911; died 04 June 1960 in Dunn, Harnett County, North Carolina. No children. Empie, Willard and Ruby were buried in Greenwood Cemetery, Dunn, North Carolina.

1277 iii. **Hughie Carson Hall**, third child of Jannette Maxwell Culbreth and Edward Lonza Hall was born 08 June 1899; died 30 August 1933. He married Allie M. West; born 29 May 1896; died 14 July 1957. Three children, **OVERTON HOMER HALL, JUNIUS BRAXTON HALL and HUGHIE LONGIE HALL**. Hughie Carson and Allie are buried in Maxwell Cemetery near Clement in Sampson County, North Carolina.

1278 iv. **Tera Blanche Hall,** born 31 December 1901. She married **John Hundley Douglas**; born 20 March 1887 in Florida. Six children.

1) **AUDREY MOZELLE DOUGLAS**, born 4 Septembr 1922 married **LEONIDAS LESLIE BOYD, JR.**, on 2 January 1924. Three children.

2) **JOHN HOMER DOUGLAS,** second child of Tera Blanche Hall and John Hundley Douglas was born 24 November 1923 and married **MARY JOYCE COBB** ; they had three children.

3) **WILLIAM CULBRETH DOUGLAS** was born 22 May 1928 and married **ANNE MCMILLAN,** daughter of ROBERT KNOX and IRIS MCMILLAN and they had three children.

4) **HAROLD FAXON DOUGLAS**, fourth child of Tera Blanche Hall and John Hundley Douglas was born 19 Novembr 1929 and married **GWENDOLYN BRACKEN** who was born 5 February 1933, daughter of ROBERT LYNDEL BRACKEN and MINNIE FINDLEY. Three children.

5) **HUEY CARSON DOUGLAS,** born 6 October 1933, married **NANCY THOMPSON** who was born 12 February 1938, daughter of ROBERT L. THOMPSON and LOUVEAN SMITH. Two children.

6) **DOROTHY ANELL DOUGLAS**, the sixth child of Tera Blanche Hall and John Hundley Douglas, was born 1 May 1939 and married **ROBERT LUMAN MADDOX** who was born 21 May 1936, son of LUMAN KIRKLAND MADDOX and LESSEE INEZ SIMS and they had two children.

1279 v. **James Casey Hall,** fifth child of Jannette Maxwell Culbreth and Edward Lonza Hall, was born 05 January 1904 and married **Addie Mae McLoud,** born 01 January 1908, daughter of JAMES COLUM MCLOUD and LAURETTA WEST.

Two children.

NELLIE MAE HALL was born 17 June 1927, married **ARTHUR THOMAS MOORE, JR.**, who was born 29 July 1927, son of ARTHUR THOMAS MOORE, SR., and CALLA WALLACE. They had two children.

JAMES EDWARD HALL born 17 September 1941, married **CAROLYN BROCK** who was born 14 March 1941, daughter of JAMES ALTON BROCK and BESSIE WHITE. They had three children.

\+ 1280 vi. **Iula Vern Hall** was the sixth child of Jannette Maxwell Culbreth and Edward Lonza Hall; he was born 20 April 1910; died 12 January 1984 in North Carolina.

481. William James Culbreth (Daniel L.[5], Daniel Maxwell[4], Mary[3] Holland, Thomas William[2], Unknown[1]) was born 01 November 1873 in Sampson County, North Carolina, and died 04 April 1916 in Dismal Township, Sampson County, North Carolina. He married **Theodocia Crumpler** 02 June 1907. "Docia" was born 13 January 1883, and died 20 May 1961. William James and Thodocia are buried in George Horne Cemetery on South River Road, one mile west of Minnie Hall Road, Sampson County, North Carolina. One source shows 29 May 1966 for her date of death.

Children of William Culbreth and Theodocia Crumpler are:

1281 i. **Kermit Taft Culbreth**, born 09 June 1908; died 28 April 1948. He married **Crayma Lee Autry** before 1932. She was born 25 April 1911 and was the daughter of JOHN HENRY AUTRY and CORDELIA BOWER. Crayma married second to **JOHNNIE FIELDS** who was born 12 August 1916, son of JOHN F. FIELDS and MINNIE VERDON.

Kermit Taft Culbreth was buried in George Horne Cemetery on South River Road, one mile west of Minnie Hall Road, Sampson County, North Carolina.

Kermit and Crayma had two children. **GLADYS JEWEL CULBRETH** was born 17 May 1932 and died 28 January 1935. **ALICE LEE CULBRETH** was born 15 August 1936 and married **RANDALL ALLEN HALL** who was born 4 September 1930, son of THEOPHILUS HALL and MALLISSIA FAIRCLOTH. Alice and Randall had two children.

\+ 1282 ii. **Mary Louise Culbreth**, born 08 February 1910.

1283 iii. **Grover Cleveland Culbreth**, born 26 March 1912; died 12 November 1984 in Chapel Hill, North Carolina. He married (1) **Vera Mc Williams Faircloth**; born about 1909 in Georgia. He married (2) **Rachel Parker**; born 16 December 1929, daughter of DAVID M. PARKER and ANNIE MAE HALES. He and Rachel had no children. Grover was buried in the George Horne Cemetery on South River Road one mile west of Minnie Hall Road, Sampson County, North Carolina.

Grover Cleveland and Vera had two children. **BETTY JEAN CULBRETH** was born 5 July 1941 and married **HUBERT BLAND**. They have three children.

WILLIE JAMES CULBRETH, the second child of Grover and Vera, was born 25 October 1945 and married **VERONICA MARIE (maiden name unknown.**) They had two children.

\+ 1284 iv. **Annie Ruth Culbreth**, born 27 October 1915; died 17 February 1999. She married **JAKE HERBERT SPELL** who was born 30 January 1912, son of GRADY SPELL and RACHEL AUTRY and they had one child, **JAMES HERBERT SPELL**.

482. Mary H. Culbreth (Daniel L.[5], Daniel Maxwell[4], Mary[3] Holland, Thomas William[2], Unknown[1]) was born 22 September 1875 in Sampson County, North Carolina, and died 15

January 1911. She married **Hardy Albert Spell** before 1898, son of Wiley Spell and Mary Faircloth. He was born 29 August 1879, and died 10 March 1952.

Mary and Hardy are buried in a Spell Family Cemetery on Dunn Road North of Roseboro, North Carolina.

Children of Mary Culbreth and Hardy Spell are:

1285 i. **Unidentified Spell,** born Before 1900.

1286 ii. **Alvin Dodd Spell,** born 25 October 1899; died 25 October 1958 in Taylors Bridge Township, Sampson County, North Carolina. He married **Mary Ellen Croom** before 1958; born 18 October 1910. Alvin Dodd and Mary Ellen had four children. He was buried at Mt. Gilead Baptist Church Cemetery, on 421 6.5 miles south of Clinton, North Carolina. Mary Ellen's year of birth is also listed as 1916 in one source.

Children of Alvin and Mary Ellen:

JUDITH ANN SPELL

LINDA FAYE SPELL

BRENDA GREY SPELL

ALVIN KENNETH SPELL

1287 iii. **Jesse Martin Spell,** born 12 September 1900; died 17 August 1973. He married **Estelle Jones;** born 22 August 1904.

Jesse Martin and Estelle had two children:

RICHARD SPELL was born 19 April 1931 and married **ANNIE PROCTOR** who was born 2 March 1933; they had two children.

FRANK SPELL second child of Jesse and Estelle was bor 18 Ocotber 1932. He first married **SARA HIGH** who was born 23 February 1934 and they had one child. Frank married 2nd **AMANDA IMES** who was born 24 March 1942 and they had four children.

1288 iv. **Lizzie Spell,** born 12 May 1902. She married **George Raeford Hall;** born 09 January 1898; died 28 May 1979 in Fayetteville, Cumberland County, North Carolina.

Lizzie andGeorge had one known child, **MARY SUE HALL** who was born in 1942 and married **CECIL DEVANE** who was born 7 June 1939, son of **JUNIE FRANKLIN DEVANE** and **DUEL STRICKLAND.**

1289 v. **Hurley Spell,** born 20 October 1903; died 04 June 1905.

1290 vi. **Lonnie Spell,** born 16 October 1905. He married **Alice Wade Faircloth;** born 20 December 1910.

Two known children.

MARY MARGARET SPELL, born 9 February 1934 married **WILLIAM C. PARSONS** and they had two known children.

JENNIE ELIZABETH SPELL, second chil of Lonnie and Alice was born 9 February 1934 and married first to **JOHN RAY OWENS;** they had one child. Jennie married second to **RAYMOND POORE.**

1291 vii. **Cecil Daniel Spell,** seventh child of Mary H. Culbreth and Hardy Albert Spell, was born 15 March 1908; died 09 January 1983. He married (1) **Lucille Spell;** born 14 August 1910, daughter of JACK SPELL and NANCY AUTRY. Lucille and her mother, Nancy Autry Spell, died on the same day, 19 January 1945 and both were buried on the same day. Cecil married (2) **Vivian Vinson;** born 23

July 1925, daughter of GROVER VINSON and NELLIE HUSS. Cecil and Lucill had two known children and he and Vivian had one known child.

He was buried in Sunrise Memorial Gardens, between Roseboro and Salemburg, Sampson County, North Carolina.

1292 viii. **Cladie Spell,** born 20 March 1909. She married (1) **Lonnie H. Williams**; died 31 August 1940. She married (2) **John D. Britt**; born 17 January 1914; died 1978. Cladie and Lonnie had one child.

Lonnie was a Corporal in the Quartermaster Corps. John Britt served in the U.S. Army in WW II.

483. John Thomas Culbreth, Sr. (Daniel L.[5], Daniel Maxwell[4], Mary[3] Holland, Thomas William[2], Unknown[1]) was born 06 September 1878 in Sampson County, North Carolina, and died 14 June 1963. He married **Adelaide Josephine Harrell**. She was born 14 September 1889, and died 14 October 1962. John Thomas and Adelaide were buried in Scott Hill Cemetery, Wilmington, North Carolina

Children of John Culbreth and Adelaide Harrell are:

1293 i. **John Thomas Culbreth, Jr.**, born 09 October 1913 in Scotts Hill and died 12 March 1932 in Wilmington, North Carolina. He was buried at Scotts Hill. Scotts Hill is in Pender County, North Carolina, near New Hanover County.

1294 ii. **Mary Dozier Culbreth**, born 29 August 1917. She married **Charles Roland Redmond, Jr.**; born 10 October 1915. Three chidlren. 1) **Charles Roland Redmond III** was born 11 March 1947 and first married **Mary Fredericka Feilke** on 10 April 171; she was born 20 October 1947. No children. Charles married second on 1 April 1976 to **Katherine Gowen Wilber** and they had one child, **Leif Charleson Redmond** who was born 9 January 1977. 2) **John Michael Redmond**, second child of Mary and Charles was born 7 October 1949. 3) Mary and Charles's third child, was **David Brian Redmon** who was born 28 July 1955.

1295 iii. **Emily Adelaide Culbreth**, born 12 September 1919. She married **Harold Bankston Marbut**; born 16 September 1917. Two children. **Stephen Harold Marbut** was born 3 February 1952. **Kathy Ann Marbut** was born 16 July 1956 and on 20 July 1974 married **Thomas Lanier Ramsey** who was born 7 August 1952, son of Jett and Dorcas Ramsey.

1296 iv. **Pamela Jeffords Culbreth**, born 18 August 1921 in Harnett Township in New **Hanover County, North Carolina, near Scotts Hill. She married on 12 April 1947 Carl** Eugene McBride. Two children. **Carl Eugene McBride, Jr.**, was born 4 November 1947 and **Robert Ora McBride** was born 10 November 1952.

1297 v. **Thomas Daniel Culbreth** was born 29 March 1932 married on 26 August 1956, **Helen E. DePonte** who was born 21 September 1933. Four children. **Susan Marie Culbreth**, born 3 May 1957; **Laura Ann Culbreth**, born 6 February 1959; **John Thomas Culbreth**, born 16 May 1960; **Pamela Jean Culbreth**, born 16 March 1966.

484. Susan Lee Culbreth (Daniel L.[5], Daniel Maxwell[4], Mary[3] Holland, Thomas William[2], Unknown[1]) was born 06 July 1881 in Sampson County, North Carolina, and died 31 January 1968 in Fayetteville, Cumberland County, North Carolina. She married **Ransom Barton Naylor** 17 January 1901 in Residence of Pheby Culbreth, son of Joseph Naylor and Nancy Spell. He was born 07 May 1879, and died 13 December 1943 in Little Coharie Township, Sampson County, North Carolina.

Susan Lee and Ransom were buried in a Spell Cemetery on Dunn Road (SR 1002) in Spell Town Community.

Children of Susan Culbreth and Ransom Naylor are:

1298 i. **Downey W. Naylor**, born 03 July 1901; died 25 July 1906.

He was buried in a Spell Cemetery on Dunn Road (SR 1002) in Spell Town Community in Sampson County, North Carolina.

1299 ii. **Lottie G. Naylor**, born 30 November 1903; died 31 January 1908.

She was buried in a Spell Cemetery on Dunn Road (SR 1002) in Spell Town Community in Sampson County, North Carolina.

\+ 1300 iii. **James Alton Naylor, Sr.**, born 14 July 1905 in Sampson County, North Carolina; died 03 April 1980 in Fayetteville, Cumberland County, North Carolina.

\+ 1301 iv. **Eunice Lee Naylor**, born 26 July 1908.

1302 v. **Jennie Ruth Naylor**, born 26 February 1912; died 22 March 1941 in Fayetteville, Cumberland County, North Carolina.

She did not marry and was buried in a Spell Cemetery on Dunn Road (SR 1002) in Spell Town Community in Sampson County, North Carolina.

\+ 1303 vi. **Jessie Wilson Naylor**, born 10 January 1914.

\+ 1304 vii. **Katie Jane Naylor**, born 06 June 1916 in Little Coharie Township, Sampson County, North Carolina; died 15 October 1989 in Richmond, Virginia. One source shows "Jewel" for Katie's middle name and her naming a daughter "Jewel" may indicate it is correct.

1305 viii. **Allie Irene Naylor**, born 19 November 1918 in Little Coharie Township, Sampson County, North Carolina. She married **Edward Schools**. No children.

487. William Perdie Williams (Martha Rebecca[5] Culbreth, Daniel Maxwell[4], Mary[3] Holland, Thomas William[2], Unknown[1]) was born 12 February 1876, and died 23 November 1961 in Dismal Township, Sampson County, North Carolina. He married **Oma Lessie Betts**. She was born 11 March 1892 in Harnett County, North Carolina, and died 17 January 1970. Both were buried in Maxwell Cemetery near Clement in Sampson County, North Carolina. Two other children of William Perdie and Oma died before 1922.

Children of William Perdie Williams and Oma Betts are:

1306 i. **J. FLOYD WILLIAMS** was born 21 September 1913 in Cumberland County, North Carolina, and married **VARA ISADELL BULLARD** in South Carolina. She was born 26 January 1914 in Sampson County, North Carolina, daughter of Alex Robinson Bullard and Betsy Rena Matthews. "Iredell" can also be found for Vara's middle name. Two children.

1) **Gloria Jean Williams** was born 3 February 1939 in Dismal Township and married 12 November **1954 David Earl Starling**, son of Wesley Elijah Starling and Annie Mae Davis. He was born 9 July 1935 in Cedar Creek Township in Cumberland County, North Carolina. Gloria and David have two children: **Gloria Christine Starling** who was born March 1956 in Clinton married on 4 December 1975, **Carmon Lee Faircloth**, son of Reason Haywood Faircloth and Eva Ruth Parker. He was born 3

June 1945 In Honeycutts Township. Gloria and Carmon have one child, **Terry Carmon Faircloth** who was born 6 September 1976.

2) **Betty Floyd Williams** was the second child of J. Floyd and Vara. She was born 17 May 1943 in Dismal Township in Sampson County, North Carolina and married **James Wayne Amos** on 4 September 1960; "Jimmy" was born about 1940 in Alabama. Betty and James have three children: **Jennifer Adele Amos**, born 5 March 1961 in Fayetteville; **James Wayne Amos**, born 10 August 1962 in Eureux, France; **Derrick Lee Amos**, born 25 August 1963 in Eureux, France.

ii. **ISADORE CARL WILLIAMS**, second child of William Perdie and Oma was born 16 August 1917 and died 30 November 1973. He married **CLADIE ESTELLE AUTRY**, daughter of WILLIAM HENRY BIZZELL AUTRY and ELLIE TAYLOR. She was born 8 January 1921 in Dismal Township, Sampson County, North Carolina. No children. Both were buried in Maxwell Cemetery.

iii. **MILDRED BERNICE WILLIAMS**, the third child was born 5 November 1918 and married **TONEY W. FITZGERALD** who was born about 1916 in Nash County, Virginia. They had three children.

1)**Peggy Catherine Fitzgerald** was born 7 December 1941 in Roseboro and on 8 April 1962, she married **Norman Wayne Adams** in Grace Baptist Church in Fayetteville, North Carolina, son of Preston W. Admas and Ruby T. Neely. He was born 23 July 1939 in Franklin County, Arkansas. One child: **Darrel Alan Adams** was born 28 March 1963 in Fayetteville.

2) **William Tony Fitzerald** was born 3 August 1946 in Roseboro.

3) **James Robert Fitzgerald** was born 23 July 1952 and on 12 September 1977, he married Debrah Elaine O'Barr, daughter of Denver O'Barr and Faye Hubbard.

iv. **HAZEL CHRISTINE WILLIAMS**, the fourth child of William Perdie and Oma, was born 25 March 1922 and in Dismal Township on 16 August 1953, she married **ARCHIE William OVERTON**, son of Archie Will Overton and Janie Roberts. Archie was born 25 February 1925 and died 2 June 1989 and was buried in Maxwell Cemetery in Sampson County. Hazel and Archiie had one known child: Patsy Barbara Overton was born 25 September 1963 and married James G. Laws as his second wife. Patsy and James have two children.

v. **HERMAN SHEARL WILLIAMS**, the fifth child of William Perdie and Oma was born 27 October 1924 and on 2 August 1952, married **CLESTA HALL**, daughter of REDDIN MCCOY HALL and ADA JEANIE HORNE. Four children.

1) **Mona Celesta Williams** was born 17 February 1957 in Fayetteville and married **Dewey Martin Williams III** on 20 August 1978 in Autryville, Sampson County, North Carolina. Dewey was born 8 October 1957 in Roseboro, North Carolina, son of Dewey M. Williams, Jr. and Mary Amalie Jackson. Mona and Dewey have one child.

2) **Lynn Frances Williams** was born 25 July 1958 near Fayetteville in Cumberland County, North Carolina. On 24 July 1977, she married **Wade Pittman Horne** in Long Branch Baptist Church. He was born 20 January 1956 in Fayetteville, son of Elree Pittman Horne and Sarah Elizabeth Faircloth.

3) **Herman Shearl Williams II** was born 6 February 1960 in fayetteville.

4) **Blackmon Stuart Williams** was born 25 September 1962 in Fayetteville.

489. Daniel Walter Williams (Martha Rebecca[5] Culbreth, Daniel Maxwell[4], Mary[3] Holland, Thomas William[2], Unknown[1]) was born 12 January 1880, and died 20 December 1959 in Near Autryville, Sampson County, North Carolina. He married **(1) Addie Belle Allen** 02 March 1923 in Fayetteville, Cumberland County, North Carolina. She was born 13 March 1894, and died 29 June 1924 in Dismal Township, Sampson County, North Carolina. He married **(2) Roberta A. Bain** 10 January 1929. She was born 21 August 1896, and died

08 August 1974 in Fayetteville, Cumberland County, North Carolina and was the daughter of SAMUEL ANGUS BAIN and LAURA ANN SESSOMS.

Addie Belle and Daniel had one child, a stillborn daughter on 27 June 1924, two days before Addie died. They were buried in Maxwell Cemetery near Clement in Sampson County, North Carolina.

Children of Daniel Williams and Roberta Bain are:

i. **CLARA ANN WILLIAMS**, their first child, was born 30 November 1930 in Dismal Township in Sampson County, North Carolina. She married on 27 February 1949 in Duplin County, North Carolina, **RALPH SIDNEY HIGHSMITH** who was born 18 January 1931 in Rockfish Township. Six children.

1) **Walter Thomas Highsmith** was born 24 October 1949 in Willard, North Carolina and died 21 August 1952 in Rockfish Township in Duplin County, North Carolina.

2) **Janice Ann Highsmith,** born 12 January 1954 in Clinton, married **Bruce Wayne Foggiano** of Bayville, New Jersey, at Harrells in Sampson County, North Carolina , on 22 December 1973. He was born 30 January 1952 in Somerville County, New Jersey, son of Charles Foggiano and Joan Van Fleet. Three children: **Neil Wayne Foggiano,** born 22 February 1975 in Clinton, North Carolina; **Patrick Heath Foggiano,** born 20 december 1976; **Briana Shannon Foggiano,** born 11 January 1978.

3) **Alma Annett Highsmith** was the third child of Clara Ann and Ralph Sidney. She was born 5 February 1955 in Clinton and on 18 April 1976 married **Gordon McDonald Coggins, Jr.** in Franklin Township in Sampson County. He was born 23 July 1949 in Princess Anne County, Virginia, son of Gordon McDonald Coggins and Hazel O'dell Manning.

4) **Sylvia Beryl Highsmith** was born 15 February 1957 in Clinton and on 20 August 1978, she married **James Perry Hall**, son of James Clyde Hall.

5) **Becky Cheryl Highsmith,** fifth child of Clara Ann and Ralph Sidney was born 24 April 1958 in Clinton and on 25 September 1976 in Franklin Township in Sampson County, married Samuel Filmore Burgess, Jr., son of Samuel Filmore Burgess and Angelyn Allen Maynard. Samuarl was born 29 April 1956 in Guilford County, North Carolina.

6) **Miriam Ralphine Highsmith** was born 4 October 1961 in Clinton, North Carolina.

\+ 1307 ii. **Rebecca Maxine Williams,** third child of Daniel Walter Williams and Roberta A. Bain, was born 03 June 1935 in Dismal Township, Sampson County, North Carolina.

493. Ida J. Autry (Tomzillia[5] Culbreth, Daniel Maxwell[4], Mary[3] Holland, Thomas William[2], Unknown[1]) was born 28 August 1871 in Sampson County, North Carolina, and died 21 May 1897 in Sampson County, North Carolina. She married **Clem Lane**. He was born About 1874 in Mt.Vernon Springs, North Carolina.

Ida was buried in Clement Missionary Baptist Church Cemetery on Maxwell Road in Sampson County, North Carolina. Her daughter, Irma, died in infancy and was buried near Ida.

Child of Ida Autry and Clem Lane is:

1308 i. **Irma Lane,** died 07 May 1897 in Sampson County, North Carolina.

496. William Mac Autry, Sr. (Tomzillia[5] Culbreth, Daniel Maxwell[4], Mary[3] Holland, Thomas William[2], Unknown[1]) was born 12 October 1878, and died 10 December 1966. He married **Janie Mariah Maxwell**, daughter of Hinton Maxwell and Anne Williams. She was born 30 March 1882, and died 11 March 1967.

His middle name also spelled "Mack." He and Janie were buried in Wauchula, Florida

Children of William Mac Autry and Janie Maxwell are:

They had a stillborn child on 10 February 1905 who was buried at Clement Baptist Church Cemetery.

1309 i. **H. Earl Autry**, born 18 May 1906. He married **Montrey Opel Lewis**; born 01 October 1904.

Twochildren.

1) **Joan Autry**, a twin, born 29 August 1934 married **H. Edward Terrell**,son of Hoyt and Ruth Terrell. Three children: **Hoyt Edward Terrell, Jr** was born 23 July 1957 and married **Teresa Henry**, daughter of John and Grace Henry; **Richard Earl Terrell** was born 12 May 1959; **Linda Ruth Terrell** was born 5 February 1961.

2) **Janie Autry**, a twin was born 29 August 1934 and married first, **Peter Allen Lambert** and they had one child. **Montry E. Labmert** who was born 17 February 1957. Janie married second 8 June 1973 **Cecil Kohn**.

1310 ii. **Annie Maria Autry**. She married (1) **Robert Roberts**. She married (2) **Louis Page**.

No children.

\+ 1311 iii. **James Hinton Autry**, child of William Mack Autry and Janie Mariah Maxwell, was born 11 November 1911; died 09 March 1993.

1312 iv. **William Mac Autry, Jr.**, fourth living child of William Mack and Janie Mariah, was born 22 January 1914. He married **Hazel Inez Long**; born 25 November 1918. They had three children

1) **William Mack Autry III** was born 20 August 1938 and married **Vinnie Fenton**, daughter of Carl and Catherine Fenton. Their son **William Kyle Autry** was born 13 December 1964.

2) **Horace Donnell Autry** was born 30 March 1940 and married **Anita Gail Wilson**. Three children: **Arthur Hoyt Autry**, born 19 october 1962; **Andrea Gail Autry**, born 25 November 1963; **Alan Donnell Autry**, born 5 March 1968.

3) **Arthur Spencer Autry** was born 10 November 1944 and married **Susan Shropshire**. Two children: **Shawn Michele Autry**, born 7 June 1967 and **Brennan Spence Autry**, born 8 August 1971.

1313 v. **Robert Laurence Autry**, born 10 November 1915. He married **Mildred Davis**.

Two children.

1) **Robert Michael Autry**, born 5 August 1948 married **Mary Carolyn Crews** and they had two children: **Catherine Mechele Autry**, born 26 August 1970 and **James Michael Autry**, born 10 June 1976.

2) **Susan Catherine Autry**, born 7 November 1951 married **Richard Laurence Dugger**.

1314 vi. **Edward Autry**, born 24 October 1917; died 16 September 1939.

Did not marry.

1315 vii. **Mary Virginia Autry**, seventh living child of William Mack and Janie Mariah, was born 05 September 1919. She married **J. Richard Henry**; born 12 September 1917. Two children.

1) **Myra Sue Henry** was born 6 November 1941 and married **Mr. Cannon**. Two children: **Debra Sue Cannon**, born 6 March 1964 and **Cynthia Lee Cannon**, born 30 December 1969.

2) **John William Henry** was born 7 March 1943 and married **Phyllis Hodges**. They had one child, **Suzanne Rynette Henry**, born 19 July 1971.

1316 viii. **Janie Kate Autry**, born 18 April 1922. She married **Dan James Cowart**; born 24 July 1922.

One child, **Dan James Cowart III** born 8 September 1946.

500. Armelia Bertha Autry (Tomzillia[5] Culbreth, Daniel Maxwell[4], Mary[3] Holland, Thomas William[2], Unknown[1]) was born 29 August 1887, and died 21 May 1983. She married **Hans Sivertsen**. He was born 05 June 1885 in Tonsberg, Norway, and died 25 September 1943.

Armelia Bertha was buried in Calvary Tabernacle PFB Church Cemetery, 1 mile from intersection of Hwy 242 and High House Road, Sampson County, North Carolina and also has a stone by her husband. Hans Sivertsen was buried in Clement Missionary Baptist Church Cemetery on Maxwell Road (SR1006) about 0.5 mile west of Sr 1425 in Sampson County, North Carolina.

Children of Armelia Autry and Hans Sivertsen are:

\+ 1317 i. **Olavia Tomzilia Sivertsen**, born 30 January 1914 in Dismal Township, Sampson County, North Carolina; died 01 February 1997.

1318 ii. **James Hansen Sivertsen**, born 11 December 1915; died 02 June 1973. He married **Cathrine Crouch.** No Children.

\+ 1319 iii. **Harold Lindsay Sivertsen**, born 16 August 1919.

\+ 1320 iv. **Mary Grace Sivertsen**, born 12 November 1921.

\+ 1321 v. **Louise Newcomb Sivertsen**, born 28 March 1926.

515. William Estel Hairr (Charles Henry[5], Daniel[4] Hairr, Orpah[3] Holland, Thomas William[2], Unknown[1]) was born 18 September 1892, and died 11 September 1948 in Fayetteville, North Carolina. He married **Sophia Elizabeth Tew** 07 January 1915 in Sampson County, North Carolina, daughter of **John Tew** and Jane Strickland. She was born 22 September 1897 in Sampson County, North Carolina, and died 25 June 1962 in Dismal Township, Sampson County, North Carolina.

"Wiley E." was entered for his name in a few census records; name also found as "William Eschol Hairr." Tombstone shows name as W. Estel."

William Estel and Sophia were buried in Union Grove Baptist Church Cemetery on Vander Road west of Rebel City, Sampson County, North Carolina.

Children of William Hairr and Sophia Tew are:

1322 i. **Lessie Hairr**, born 11 October 1917; died 22 October 1918.

1323 ii. **Charles Pitman Hairr**, born 18 October 1921 in Dismal Township, Sampson County, North Carolina; died 21 July 1992. He married **Bonnie Ozelle Williams** 16 May 1942; born 08 December 1923 in Dismal Township, Sampson County, North Carolina.

Charles was a Sergeant in the United States Air Force, and served in Africa and Italy in World War II. He was buried in Union Grove Baptist Church Cemetery on Vander Road one mile west of Rebel City, Sampson County, North Carolina.

One childL **Charles Eschol Hairr** was born 27 April 1955 in Roseboro, North Carolina, and married **Deborah Marie Doggett** on 1 December 1974, daughter of Thurman Clifton Doggett and Mary Francis Autry. Deborah was born 4 october 1955 in Goldsboro, North Carolina. Charles Eschol and Deborah had two children: **Heather Marie Hairr**, born 9 March 1977 in Fayetteville, North Carolina and **Stephanie Michelle Hairr**, born 26 August 1978 in Fayetteville.

520. Allen G. Hair (Charles Henry^5, Daniel^4 Hairr, Orpah^3 Holland, Thomas William^2, Unknown^1) was born 29 August 1906, and died 11 March 1970. He married **Rose B. Unknown**. She was born 17 September 1916, and died 09 January 1992.

Allen and Rose were buried in Beulah United Methodist Church Cemetery on Corinth Church Road (SR 1326), Sampson County, North Carolina.

Child of Allen Hair and Rose Unknown is:

1324 i. **Charlie Allen Hair**, born 07 June 1939.

531. Edward Redden Hare (Simon^5, Stephen^4, Orpah^3 Holland, Thomas William^2, Unknown^1) was born About 1868 in Sampson County, North Carolina, and died 02 December 1930 in Wilson County, North Carolina. He married **(1) Lovennia-Laura Ann Ginn** 09 November 1891 in North Carolina. She was born 03 November 1870 in Wayne County, North Carolina, died 27 July 1941 and was the daughter of **James Hiram Ginn** and **Mary E. Mattox**. Edward married **(2) Dolly Turner** about 1912 in Wilson County, North Carolina. She was born about 1884 in Wilson County, North Carolina.

Hare is also spelled "Hair" and "Hairr." One source notes in data on Ancestry.com that Redden died 2 December 1930. Another source on the site records 1918 for his death, but he and Dolly had at least one child after 1918.

It is said that he had red hair and his middle name was for his red hair, but his Spanish War record notes his hair was "brown." His Spanish War information records: "Muster-in Roll for 2 years. Raleigh, North Carolina, May 5, 1898. Age: 28. Height: 5 feet, 7 inches. Ruddy complexion. Eyes: blue. Hair: Brown. Born: Sampson County, North Carolina. Farmer.

"Camp Cuba Libre, Jacksonville, Florida. September 30th, 1898. The Adjutant General, Second Division 7th Army Corps Vol. Infantry.

"Sir:

"I have the honor to respectfully apply for a furlough of ten (10) days on or about October 8th to visit my family at Saulston, North Carolina. I have had no previous furlough. ... Respectfully, Redin (x) Hare. Private, Company B, 1st NC Vol. Infantry."

He was granted a furlough on 3 October 1898. Dr. John Spicer, MD, wrote on 10 October 1898 that he had visited "Mr. Reddin Hair at his home, and found him in bed with fever and unable to return to his...of duty at this time. ..."

Data on Ancestry.com states: "Redden Hare walked out on Laura Ginn-Hare in 1908 shortly after the birth of their last child, Hiram Hare. ... He settled in Wilson County, North Carolina, changed his name to **EDWARD HARRELL** and married for a second time." By 1920, Laura had married Adolph Antie Howell (Adolph Ante Howell) who was born about 1869 in North Carolina. One source notes that they married about 1905, but it was later than that; other sources tell that Redden did not leave his family until after the birth of Hiram about 1908 and Laura was head of household in Wayne County in 1910. Laura was Adolph Antie's first marriage; he had lived with his mother and 2 sisters and in 1930, his mother, Mary Ginn, was living with Adolph and Laura's family. Also in the household was a five year old niece whom Laura was raising and she is said to have been the daughter of Laura's sister.

On his deathbed, Redden called for Laura Ann (Louvennia). "Dolly asked who was Laura and was told that she was his first wife." Dolly did not know that he was married before and had changed his name.

Edward was buried in Helms Cemetery, Wayne County, North Carolina. Laura Ann was buried in a Family Cemetery in Greene County, North Carolina. A great-granddaughter of Redden is mentioned on the ancestry.com site as a source for Edward Redden Hare's family data.

Children of Edward Hairr and Laura Ginn are:

1327 i. **Durant Hairr**, born 31 August 1892 in Wayne County, North Carolina; died 29 March 1976 in Goldsboro, Wayne County, North Carolina. He married **Nancy Clyde West** about 1912; she was born about 1893 in Wayne County, North Carolina.

1328 ii. **Walter Hairr**, born 29 November 1894 in Wayne County, North Carolina; died 24 April 1969 in Pikeville, Wayne County, North Carolina. It is said that he was a 'mute." **WALTER HARE** is also found for his name. He was not married at time of death, but he may be the **Walter L. Hare** listed in the 1930 Federal census for Wake County, North Carolina, with wife, **IVA B. HARE**, who was born about 1902. One daughter, **Josephine L. Hare**, aged 4, was listed with them. He was buried in a Hill (?) Family Cemetery.

1329 iii. **Willie Horace Hairr,** born 31 July 1897 in Wayne County, North Carolina; died 09 April 1957 in Stony Creek, Wayne County, North Carolina. He married **BERTHA LILTON** who was born about 1902 in Wayne County, North Carolina and was a merchant (Grocery Store.) He died from a heart attack and was buried in a Family Cemetery in Stoney Creek Township.

Children of **Willie Hare and** Bertha all born in Stony Creek (?), Wayne County, North Carolina:

1) **LESTER H. HARE** born about 1921.

2) **SALLIE E. HARE,** born about 1923.

3) **NANNIE M. HARE**, born about 1925.

1330 iv. **Richard Lee Hairr**, fourth child of Edward and Laura, was born 13 February 1900 in Wayne County, North Carolina and died 17 January 1964. His Certificate of Death names Coronary Occlusion for cause of death and Deens Cemetery, in Stoney Creek Township in Wayne County for burial, but another source states he was buried in Evergreen Cemetery He was also listed as **RICHARD LEE HARE**, but most of the time, he is found as **RICHARD HARE** and he married **MATTIE LANGSTON;** born about 1901 in Wayne County, North Carolina. Mattie was also listed as **MATTIE WILLIAMS** with a birth date of 17 April 1907 in Wayne County; she died 5 April 1986 in a Nursing or Rest Home in Wayne County. Mattie may have been married prior to her marriage to Richard or Williams was possibly a middle name.

Richard and Mattie's daughter, **DOROTHY HARE** was born 5 November 1924 in Wayne County and married **LISKAR MCCULLEN** who was born 8 Spetmber 1922 in Wayne County.

Their daugher, **MARY V. HARE** was born 10 May 1926 in Wayne County and married a **"BRITT."**

1331 v. **Anne Lila Hairr**, daughter of Edward Hare and Laura Ginn, was born 01 April 1903 in Wayne County, North Carolina; died 21 September 1983 in Myrtle Beach, Horry County, South Carolina. She married **William Larry Jones** 20 September 1920 in Wayne County, North Carolina; born 21 October 1901 in Stoney Creek Township, Wayne County, North Carolina; died 16 June 1964 in Myrtle Beach, Horry County, South Carolina. An obituary from ? dated 22 September 1983 names three sons, **Carl Jones, Lynwood D. Jones**, and **W. Stewart Jones**. Six daughters: Mrs. **A. J. LETOURNEAU, (LAURA MAE JONES)**, Mrs. **GERTURDE J. BURRIS (ELIZABETH GERTRUDE JONES)**, Mrs. **C. B. TOMPKINS (HAZEL JONES)**, Mrs. BAILEY, Mrs. **V. R. MILLER (LENEELE JONES)**, Mrs. **P. D. HANDY (SUSAN JONES)**. One sister is named: Mrs. **DENVER DAVIS (NANNIE HARE)**, of Goldsboro. The daughter, **Laura Mae** Jones was born 27 January 1924 in Goldsboro, Wayne County and died 22 December 2003 in Horry County, South Carolina. She and Mr. Letourneau have three children. Anne Lila and William's daughter, **Elizabeth Gertrude Jones** was born 21 October 1930 in Goldsboro. Their daughter, **ALETHA JONES** was born 11 September 1935 in Wayne County and may be the "Mrs. Bailey" named in the obituary.

1332 vi. **Nannie Hairr**, daughter of Edward and Laura, was born 26 January 1906 in Goldsboro, Wayne County, North Carolina; died 05 October 1993 in Goldsboro, Wayne County, North Carolina. She married **WYLIE DAVIS** 23 December 1925 in Goldsboro, North Carolina; born About 1905 in North Carolina.

1333 vii. **Hiram Hairr**, (**HIRAM HARE**), son of Edward and Laura, was born 17 February 1908 in Wayne County, North Carolina; died 13 July 1961 in Myrtle Beach, Horry County, South Carolina. He married MARY (maiden name unknown) who was born about 1910 and they are listed in the 1930 Federal Census for Stantonsburg, Wilson, North Carolina, with a son, **EARL HARE**, aged 1.

Children of Edward Redden Hairr (Edward Harrell) and Dolly Turner are:

1334 i. **George Harrell**, born about 1912. Death records for **GEORGE WASHINGTON HARRELL** note a birth date of 7 November 1912 and date of death as 9 November 1988 in Wilson, North Carolina. This record may be for George, son of Edward Hairr and Dolly Turner.

1335 ii. **Orie Harrell**, born about 1915.

1336 iii. **Margaret Harrell**, born after 1920.

1337 iv. **Baby Girl Harrell**.

535. George William Hare, Sr. (Simon[5] Hairr, Stephen[4], Orpah[3] Holland, Thomas William[2], Unknown[1]) was born 02 May 1876 in Sampson County, North Carolina, and died 04 April 1955 in Pikeville, Wayne County, North Carolina. He married **(1) Mariah Sophie**

Futrell 17 August 1897 in Wayne County, North Carolina. She was born 07 August 1872 in Wayne County, North Carolina. He married **(2) Lillian Ginn** about 1907. She was born 02 November 1883 and died 27 January 1968 in Forest Hills Rest (Nursing?) Home in Goldsboro, Wayne County, North Carolina.

George and Mariah's son, George William, Jr., is not listed in the 1910 Federal Census indicating that perhaps he died at birth or between August 1906-1910.

Lillian was the daughter of Alfred J. Ginn and Julia Dickerson. Her cause of death is stated: Hypoistatic Pneumonia (2 weeks) due to Congestive Heart Failure (1 year). She had Arteriosclerotic Heart Discease and the doctor suspected(?) Cancer of the stomach.

The certificate of death for George incorrectly names his first spouse, "Mariar(sic) Futrell," for his mother. Cause of death: Apoplexy (16 years). Arteriosclerosis (5 years). Senility. Apoplexy: "A condition resulting from an apoplectic fit characterized by paralysis or limitation in the ability to control body movements, with or without loss of consciousness and often leaving the affected individual in a chronic state of debilitation." ***A Medical Miscellancy for Genealogists,"*** by Dr. Jeanette L. Jerger. Heritage Books, Inc. Copyright 1995.

George and Lillian were buried in Fremont Cemetery, Fremont, North Carolina.

Children of George Hare and Mariah Futrell are:

1338 i. Rossie Mae Hare, born 18 July 1898 in Pikeville, Wayne County, North Carolina and died 17 January 1939 in Pikeville, Wayne County, of Pulmonary Embolism. She had complications from a blood clot from a miscarriage. Rossie married on 17 December 1916 to **JOHN EXUM HOWELL** who was born 13 January 1892 in Pikeville and died 11 August 1955 in Stantonsburg, Wilson County, North Carolina. They had 10 children.

GEORGE DUDLEY HOWELL, the oldest son, was born 6 Novembr 1917 in Pikeville and died 23 September 1987 in Wilson, Wilson County, North Carolina of Ruptured Abdominal Aneurysm. He was an Engineer, with Imperial Tobacco Company. George married on 11 January 1946 **VERNA MAE CARRAWAY** who was born 28 August 1919 in Goldsboro, Wayne County. A daughter married **LARRY ROYAL NEWTON** who was 13 July 1949 and died 27 october 1989.

Second Child of Rossie Mae and John: no data.

EUGENE SILAS HOWELL, the third child was born 20 January 1922 and died 9 November 1986. He married a **"COOKE."**

Fourth Child of Rossie Mae and John married a **"SMITH."**

MARTHA MARIA HOWELL, the fifth child was born 16 November 1925 and died 9 September 1983; she married a Mr. **WATSON.**

Sixth Child of Rossie Mae and John married a Mr. **BROWN**.

Seventh Child, married first **HUGH DORTCH LEWIS** who died 12 February 1972. She then married a Mr. **PRICE.**

Eighth Child, married a **WOOTEN**.

Ninth Child, a son, was born and died in 1938.

TWINS, the tenth and eleventh children were born and died 1 January 1939.

1339 ii. **Harvey Hare,** born 27 October 1900 in Wayne County, North Carolina.

1340 iii. **Eli Craft Hare**, born 24 November 1901 in Wayne County, North Carolina and died 25 November 1967 in Wayne County. He first married **JACKIE LANCASTER** and his second spouse was **HILDA JONES** who died in Wayne County.

1341 iv. **Simeon Hare**, born 11 December 1904 in Wayne County, North Carolina. One source records that he was married to a **LIVING WEST, LIVING WISE, LIVING CRAWFORD** and **LIVING MILDRED!!**

1342 v. **George William Hare, Jr.**, born 03 August 1906 in Wayne County, North Carolina and died 25 August 1993 in Wilson Memorial Hospital in Wilson, North Carolina. He married **MAMIE SASSER.**

Children of George Hare and Lillian Ginn are:

1343 i. **Beulah Mae Hare**, born 19 March 1908 in Wayne County, North Carolina. She married **THURMAN LEWIS**.

1344 ii. **Jasper William Hare**, born 07 June 1909 in Wayne County, North Carolina. Jasper appears as Joseph in the 1910 Federal Census of Saulston Township, Wayne County, North Carolina. He married **LETHA SASSER** who was born about 1914 and died 19 November 1996 in Kinston, North Carolina. Jasper and Letha had a son, **WILLIAM BAYRON HARE.**

1345 iii. **Rolland Hare**, born 29 July 1910 in Wayne County, North Carolina and died in infancy.

1346 iv. **Living Hare**.

1347 v. **Julius Hare** (Julia Hare), born 18 February 1913 and died in infancy.

1348 vi. **Living Hare**.

1349 vii. **Living Hare**.

1350 viii. **Freddie Cooper Hare**, born 01 June 1917 in Wayne County, North Carolina, died in February 1978 in Wayne County. He married **PATSY STANCILL** who died in Pikeville, Wayne County.

1351 ix. **William Howard Hare**, born 30 June 1919 in Wayne County, North Carolina and died 18 September 1919 in Wayne County.

1352 x. **Quinton Rosevelt Hare**, born 03 February 1920 in Wayne County, North Carolina and died 23 December 1986 in Goldsoro, Wayne County.

538. Stephen Hardy Hairr (Blackman[5], Stephen[4], Orpah[3] Holland, Thomas William[2], Unknown[1]) was born 09 December 1873, and died 15 January 1944. He married **Susan Zula King**. She was born 09 February 1875, and died 27 March 1947.

Stephen Hardy and Susan Zula were buried in Piney Grove Baptist Church Cemetery on N. McCullen Road, (SR 1741), Sampson County, North Carolina.

Children of Stephen Hairr and Susan King are:

1353 i. **Josephine Hairr**, born about 1906.

1354 ii. **Florence Hairr**, born 18 June 1908; died 06 July 1908.

She was buried Piney Grove Baptist Church Cemetery on N. McCullen Road, (SR 1741), Sampson County, North Carolina.

539. Charlie E. Hairr (Blackman[5], Stephen[4], Orpah[3] Holland, Thomas William[2], Unknown[1]) was born March 1877, and died 11 August 1944 in Nash County, North Carolina. He married **Eva S. Friend**. She was born About 1878, and died 17 October 1944 in Nash County, North Carolina.

In 1920 and 1930, Charlie and Eva were living in Rocky Mount, Edgecombe County, North Carolina. Her father, I. J. Friend (?) was living with Eva and Charlie in 1920.

Child of Charlie Hairr and Eva Friend is:

1355 i. **Nellie E. Hairr,** born about 1916.

541. Giles Jasper Hairr (Blackman[5], Stephen[4], Orpah[3] Holland, Thomas William[2], Unknown[1]) was born 04 January 1880, and died 10 April 1926. He married **Sallie J. Unknown**. She was born 09 December 1882, and died 29 October 1949 in Newton Grove, North Carolina.

Children of Giles Hairr and Sallie Unknown are:

i. **Theana J. Hairr** was born about 1906 in Sampson County, North Carolina.

ii. **Elot J. Hairr** was born about 1912 in Sampson County.

1356 iii. **Leonard D. Hairr,** born 17 May 1921 in Sampson County, died 08 June 1922.

547. Elmond M. Hairr, (William H.[5], Stephen[4], Orpah[3] Holland, Thomas William[2], Unknown[1]) was born 29 March 1884, and died 31 October 1957. He is also found as **ELMON M. HAIRR**. He married **Vonnie Jane Bradshaw** 13 February 1916. She was the daughter of **MATTHEW BRADSHAW** and **LUCY JENE HOLLAND** and was born 01 January 1890, and died 16 August 1946.

See additional date for Lucy Jene Holland elsewhere in this book.Elmond and Vonnie were buried in Keener Methodist Church Cemetery on Keener Road West (SR 1746) in Sampson County, North Carolina.

Children of Elmond Hairr and Vonnie Bradshaw are:

\+ 1357 i. **Rossie Marie Hairr,** born 22 April 1917; died 07 April 1987.

\+ 1358 ii. **James Elmon Hairr,** born 05 April 1925 in North Carolina.

549. Laura Caroline Hairr (William H.[5], Stephen[4], Orpah[3] Holland, Thomas William[2], Unknown[1]) was born 31 August 1889, and died 06 July 1970. She married **Thomas C. Odom** 09 February 1909. He was born 26 January 1885, and died 10 June 1968.

Laura Caroline and Thomas were buried in Keener Methodist Church Cemetery on Keener Road West (SR 1746) in Sampson County, North Carolina.

Child of Laura Hairr and Thomas Odom is:

\+ 1359 i. **William Wright Odom**, born 14 June 1916.

550. Albert B. Hairr (William H.[5], Stephen[4], Orpah[3] Holland, Thomas William[2], Unknown[1]) was born 17 September 1893 in Sampson County, North Carolina, and died 16 November 1944. He married **Clara Barton Warren** 12 November 1916. She was born 11 August 1898, and died 09 January 1962. One source mentions that her tombstone shows "Clara B. Wilson Hairr."

Albert B. and Clara were buried in Keener Methodist Church Cemetery on Keener Road West (SR 1746) in Sampson County, North Carolina. Her gravestone shows "Clara B. WILSON Hairr."

Children of Albert Hairr and Clara Warren are:

1360 i. **Paul Hairr** was born 31 August 1917. He married **JOYCE HOBBS** on 14 August 1956 and they had two children:

1) **KENNETH HAIRR**, born 2 February 1963.

2) **STEPHANIE HAIRR**, born 6 December 1967.

. 1361 ii. **Albert Lennon Hairr** was born 15 February 1920 and died 09 November 1988. He never married and was buried in Keener Methodist Church Cemetery on Kenner Road West (SR 1746), Sampson County, North Carolina

1362 iii. **William Bluford Hairr** was born 20 December 1922 and never married.

William's middle name may have been "Bluford."

1363 iv. **Margaret Hairr** was born 21 December 1924 and she married **RALPH COLEMAN HODGES** on 26 May 1951. One known child, **ALBERT COLEMAN HODGES** was born 12 September 1952. Albert married **JOYCE CURRIE** on 15 August 1975 and they have one known child, **SCOTT COLEMAN HODGES** who was born 11 November 1977.

1364 v. **W. Hairr,** born about 1928.

1365 vi. **Juanita Hairr** was born 12 November 1927 and she married **WALTER TEACHY BATTS, SR.** Two known children:

1) **ALBERT FRANKLIN BATTS**, born 16 August 1952.

2) **WALTER TEACHY BATTS, JR.**, born 22 April 1954.

1366 vii. **Barton Lee Hairr** was born 14 May 1930 and he married **SHIRLEY B. ZACHARY** on 1 November 1953. Barton joined the United states Air Force in 1950 and made it his career. He and Shirley have two known children.

1) **DEBORAH LEE HAIRR.**

2) **MICHAEL SHELBY HAIRR.**

1367 viii. **Elwood Hairr**, born 14 May 1934 married **ROSIE LEWIS** who was born in Lumberton, North Carolina. They had one known child, **KENNETH HAIRR.**

1368 ix. **Llewellyn Hairr** was born 5 September 1936. She married **MARION ROBERT MCLAMB** on 3 March 1956 and they had two known children.

1) **KARREN ALICE MCLAMB**, born 10 October 1958, married **FREDDIE JONES** on 23 December 1974 and they have one known child, **CRYSTAL JONES** who was born 16 April 1977.

2) **MARY LYNN MCLAMB**, born 28 October 1966.

1369 x. **Bettie Alice Hairr**, born 4 April 1941, married **EARL BENNY KING** on 31 December 1957. They had two known children.

1) **BENJAMIN LEE KING**, born 18 May 1960.

2) **BRYON DOUGLAS KING**, born 14 October 1966.

551. John William Bradshaw (Eliza Jane^5 Hairr, Stephen^4, Orpah^3 Holland, Thomas William^2, Unknown^1) was born about 1866. He married **Emma Honeycutt.**

Children of John Bradshaw and Emma Honeycutt are:

1370 i. **Martha Bradshaw**. She married **James Simmons**.

1371 ii. **Mary Bradshaw**. She married **Jerry Powell**.

1372 iii. **Richard Bradshaw**. He married (1) **Lessie Viverette**. He married (2) **Luna Edwards**.

553. David L. Bradshaw (Eliza Jane^5 Hairr, Stephen^4, Orpah^3 Holland, Thomas William^2, Unknown^1) was born 05 September 1871 in Sampson County, North Carolina, and died 13 March 1955 in Sampson County, North Carolina. He married **Edith E. Royal** 01 January 1905 in Sampson County, North Carolina, daughter of Isham Royal and Laura West. She was born 18 February 1882 in Sampson County, North Carolina, and died 09 March 1927 in Sampson County, North Carolina.

David was called Date. He and Edith were buried in the David L. Bradshaw Family Cemetery.

On page 51 of the "Royal Family Legacy Addendum" is the following about Edith. "Edith E. Royal was always called 'Ince' and I have never found any records stating her full name. On her marriage records, her name is listed as 'Ainsey' and on her death certificate, it is 'Once." At the age of 45, a sore formed on her leg that wouldn't heal and from it, she developed blood poisoning. Her children developed diabetes, except James (Sark), who was killed in a car accident at age 37. She was said to love sweets, so we feel like she was probably diabetic also. My daddy (Gorman) always said his mother was a twin and that her twin brother died at birth. Her oldest sisters, Ella Jane and Georgiana were also twins. When my Grandpa David Bradshaw died in 1955, several of her relatives were at his funeral. I heard some of the older ones say that when Ince died in 1927, there were no flowers on her ..." Rest of sentence is missing.

Children of David Bradshaw and Edith Royal are:

1373 i. **Peyton Bradshaw**, born about 1906; died 1957.

\+ 1374 ii. **Leon Fulton Bradshaw** was born 31 August 1908 in Sampson County, North Carolina, and died 15 June 1963. He married **LUCILLE UNDERWOOD** on 2 August 1935. She was born 17 October 1915 and died 8 September 1997 in Rocky Mount, North Carolina. Two known children.

1) **ROTHAL VINSON BRADSHAW** was born 22 may 1936 in Sampson County.

2) **CHARLES ELLIOTT BRADSHAW** was born 18 May 1938 in Sampson County, and married YVONNE (maiden name unknown.) One child: **DAVID BRADSHAW**.

1375 iii. **Baby Girl Bradshaw**, born about 1910; died 1910.

1376 iv. **Graham Bradshaw**, born about 1910; died 1977.

\+ 1377 v. **Theodore Bradshaw**, born 09 April 1913 in Sampson County, North Carolina; died 03 July 1970 in Sampson County. He married **CLAUDIA VIVIAN MCCULLEN** on 3 July 1935. She was born in April 1920 and died 27 January 1986 in Sampson County. Theodore and Claudia were buried in the David L. Bradshaw Family Cemetery. They had a large family of nine children.

\+ 1378 vi. **Gorman Bradshaw**, born about 1915; died 1987.

1379 vii. **James Bradshaw**, born about 1917; died 1955.

554. Franklin Bradshaw (Eliza Jane[5] Hairr, Stephen[4], Orpah[3] Holland, Thomas William[2], Unknown[1]) was born 20 December 1873, Sampson County and died 05 August 1924 in Sampson County, North Carolina. He married **Minnie McCullen** 18 April 1905, daughter of John McCullen and Matilda Royal. She was born 01 May 1880, and died 11 July 1960.

Franklin was buried in the Frank Bradshaw Family Cemetery.

Children of Franklin Bradshaw and Minnie McCullen are:

\+ 1380 i. **Owen Bradshaw**, born 15 August 1906 in Sampson County, North Carolina; died 21 November 1961 in Sampson County, North Carolina.

1381 ii. **Jessie Bradshaw**, born 23 September 1908 in Sampson County; died 13 April 1915 in Sampson County. He was buried in the Frank Bradshaw Family Cemetery.

\+ 1382 iii. **Jasper Bradshaw**, born 17 February 1910 in Sampson County, North Carolina; died 17 May 1951 in Sampson County.

1383 iv. **Forrest Bradshaw**, born 18 October 1912 in Sampson County, North Carolina; died 22 November 1960 in Sampson County. Forrest was called "Mutt." He was buried in the Frank Bradshaw Family Cemetery.

\+ 1384 v. **Herbert Bradshaw**, born 06 October 1914 in Sampson County, North Carolina; died 10 February 1984 in Chapel Hill, North Carolina.

\+ 1385 vi. **Woodrow Bradshaw**, born 18 July 1916 in Sampson County, North Carolina; died 14 August 1978 in Columbia, South Carolina.

\+ 1386 vii. **Pearl Bradshaw**, born 27 May 1922 in Sampson County, North Carolina; died 05 July 1991.

571. Isaiah H. Hairr (James Thomas[5], John C.[4] Hair, Orpah[3] Holland, Thomas William[2], Unknown[1]) was born 26 May 1874, and died 01 January 1948. He married **Ella J. Tyndall**, daughter of Wiley Tyndall and Molsey Jackson. She was born 07 April 1880, and died 17 December 1966.

Ella is listed in one source as "Mary Ella;" other sources list her as "Ella J." Isaiah and Ella were buried in Piney Green Baptist Church Cemetery at intersection of Highway 242 and High House Road, Sampson County, North Carolina.

Children of Isaiah Hairr and Ella J.Tyndall are:

\+ 1387 i. **William Braxton Hairr,** born 19 October 1898 in North Carolina; died 07 February 1974 in Clinton, Sampson County, North Carolina.

\+ 1388 ii. **Spence B. Hairr,** born 29 July 1900 in Sampson County, North Carolina; died 23 November 1961 in Sampson County.

\+ 1389 iii. **Troy Addicus Hairr,** born 16 August 1902 in North Carolina; died 23 December 1989 in Cumberland County, North Carolina.

\+ 1390 iv. **Leona Hairr,** born 30 August 1905 in North Carolina; died 05 February 1998.

1391 v. **Annie Selma Hairr,** born 09 February 1908 in North Carolina; died 01 April 1993 in Sampson County, North Carolina. She married Ellie McDaniel who was born about 1908 and died 22 April 1973.

\+ 1392 vi. **Omie Tera Hairr,** born 12 August 1910; died 25 March 2000.

\+ 1393 vii. **Deames Elton Hairr,** born 31 March 1913; died 22 May 1972 in Sampson County, North Carolina.

1394 viii. **Ella May Hairr,** born 08 May 1917 in Sampson County, North Carolina; died 30 October 1919 in Sampson County, North Carolina.

Ella May is buried in Piney Green Baptist Church Cemetery at intersection of Hwy 242 and High House Road.

1395 ix. **Lattie Hairr,** born 27 July 1915 in Sampson County, North Carolina; died 06 August 1916 in Sampson County, North Carolina. He was buried in Burial: Piney Green Baptist Church Cemetery at intersection of Hwy 242 and High House Road.

572. Augustus Davis Hairr (James Thomas[5], John C.[4] Hair, Orpah[3] Holland, Thomas William[2], Unknown[1]) was born 06 August 1879, and died 08 March 1935 in Sampson County North Carolina. He can also be found as **Augusta David Hairr** and **Gus D. Hair.** He married **(1) Unknown Spouse** about 1900. He married **(2) Winnie Ann Honeycutt** about 1908. She was born 06 November 1890, and died 26 September 1932. "Vennie A." and Vennie Ann are found for Winnie's name and her certificate of death names her **VENIE A. HAIR.**"

His Certificate of Death states his name as "**Augustus Hair**" and **CHARLOTTE HAIR** is named for his wife. **Thomas Hair** and **Pacia Canady** are entered for his parents. Mrs. Richard Hair was the informant. It appears that Augustus married for a third time to Charlotte, (maiden name unknown.)

Augustus Davis and Winnie Ann are buried in Owens Grove Pentecostal FWB Church, on Mt. Moriah Church Road near Kitty Fork, Sampson County, North Carolina.

Child of Augustus Davis Hairr and Unknown Spouse is:

1396 i. **Ennis D. Hairr,** born about 1902.

Children of Augustus Hairr and Winnie Honeycutt are:

1397 i. **William Taft Hairr**, born 25 October 1908 in Sampson County, North Carolina, and died 2 August 1976 in Wilson, Wilson County, North Carolina. The North Carolina Birth Index, 1800-2000 listed him as **"William C. Taft Hair."** He may be the WILLIAM C. TAFT HAIRR listed in the 1930 Federal census for the Navel Base in Norfolk, Norfolk (Independent City), Virginia.

\+ 1398 ii. **Richard Howard Hair, Sr.**, born 19 January 1910; died 09 August 1989.

1399 iii. **Forest L. Hairr**, born about 1915.

1400 iv. **Vora D. Hairr**, born about 1916.

1401 v. **Gladys Clemmons Hairr**, born about 1918 is entered on a North Carolina Birth Index, but found as "**Gladys D. Hair** in other sources. **Gus D. Hair** is listed for her father.

1402 vi. **Lela D. Hairr,** born 15 August 1921 in Sampson County, North Carolina; died 15 August 1921.

She was buried in Owens Grove Pentecostal FWB Church Cemetery on Mt. Moriah Church Road (SR 1335) in Sampson County, North Carolina.

1403 vii. **Mexie E. Hairr**, born about 1923.

1404 viii. **James Davis Hairr**, born about 1925 in Sampson County, North Carolina.

1405 ix. **Roy E. Hairr**, born bout 1929.

573. George V. Hairr (James Thomas[5], John C.[4] Hair, Orpah[3] Holland, Thomas William[2], Unknown[1]) was born 1878. He married **(1) Lessie E. Unknown** before 1903. She was born 1880, and died 1915. He married **(2) Roena Unknown** about 1919. She was born about 1893. Lessie's maiden name may have been "Lellie Eldridge."

His middle initial is "G" in the 1920 Federal Census. The ages of some of his children and Roena listed as wife in 1920 and nearest relative on his WW I Draft Registration, indicates that he was probably married twice.

Children of George Hairr and Lessie Unknown are:

1406 i. **Clayton Hairr**, born about 1903.

1407 ii. **Carlye Hairr**, born about 1905.

1408 iii. **Ransom Hairr**, born about 1908. He may be the **WILLIAM RANSOM HAIRR**, who was born 14 May 1907 in North Carolina and died 1 December 1971 in Rural Sampson County, near Newton Grove, North Carolina, who has **GEORGE HAIRR** and **LELLIE ELDRIDGE** (sic) named for his parents on his certificate of death. **ALLIE THORNTON** is named for his wife on the certificate. North Carolina Death Collection show 8 November 1907 for her birth in Sampson County and 21 June 1999 for her death in Western Wake Medical Center in Wake County, North Carolina. The 1930 census for Dunn, Harnett County, North Carolina listed Ranson Hairr, aged 22, and Allie Hairr, aged 22, with one child, **FRANCIS HAIRR**, about 3 months and **FRANCIS THORNTON**, aged 61, was in the household.

1409 iv. **Pauline Hairr** was born 4 March 1909 and died 9 November 1987. She married **James Allen Fryar** who was born about 1908, son of **Stuart T. Fryar** and **Sarah E. Sutton**.

1410 v. **Bennie Hairr**, born about 1912.

1411 vi. **Harman Hairr,** born about 1914.

574. Claude Raste Hairr (James Thomas[5], John C.[4] Hair, Orpah[3] Holland, Thomas William[2], Unknown[1]) was born March 1881, and died 15 October 1935 in Turkey, Sampson County, North Carolina. He married **Hattie J. Haney** 23 October 1904 in Sampson County. She was born 1885, and died 1944.

Claude Raste and Hattie were buried in Owens Grove Pentecostal FWB Church Cemetery on Mt. Moriah Church Road (SR 1335) in Sampson County, North Carolina

Children of Claude Hairr and Hattie Haney are:

1412 i. **Ottis Cooper Hairr** was born 9 August 1906 and died 10 December 1961.

1413 ii. **Addie B. Hairr**, born about 1907.

1414 iii. **Etha D. Hairr**, born about 1909.

1415 iv. **Ray M. Hairr**, born 01 July 1921 in Sampson County, North Carolina; died 16 December 1927.

He was buried in Owens Grove Pentecostal FWB Church Cemetery on Mt. Moriah Church Road (SR 1335) in Sampson County, North Carolina.

591. Ida Dees Spell (Mariah Jetson[5] Autry, Starling[4], Millie[3] Holland, Thomas William[2], Unknown[1]) was born 27 May 1880 in North Carolina, and died 21 December 1952 in Salemburg, Sampson County, North Carolina. She married **(1) Duncan J. Bullard** 13 March 1898, son of Giles Bullard and Elizabeth Culbreth. He was born about 1860. She married **(2) Valentine T. Baggett** November 1902, son of William Baggett and Sallie Cooper. He was born 13 February 1867, and died 10 August 1942 in Fayetteville, Cumberland County, North Carolina.

Ida Dees and Valentine were buried in William A. Baggett Family Cemetery about 1-3/4 miles west of Salemburg at the south side of S.R. 1233 in Honeycutts Township, Sampson County, North Carolina.

Children of Ida Spell and Valentine Baggett are:

1416 i. **Ruth Baggett,** born about 1910 in Honeycutts Township, Sampson County, North Carolina.

\+ 1417 ii. **Marshall Fulton Baggett**, born 07 August 1912 in Honeycutts Township, Sampson County, North Carolina; died 25 February 2001.

1418 iii. **James William Baggett**, born 13 June 1914 in Honeycutts Township, Sampson County, North Carolina. James William Baggett is listed as "Milton Baggett" on a second birth certificate of the same date.

1419 iv. **Milton Baggett**, born About 1915 in Honeycutts Township, Sampson County, North Carolina.

592. Narena C. Spell (Mariah Jetson[5] Autry, Starling[4], Millie[3] Holland, Thomas William[2], Unknown[1]) was born 16 January 1883 in North Carolina, and died 24 May 1960 in Fayetteville, Cumberland County, North Carolina. She married **Alfred Lewis** 09 May 1901 in Residence of Lewis Carr Spell, son of David Lewis and Chelly Matthews. He was born

24 February 1874, and died 08 March 1942 in Dismal Township, Sampson County, North Carolina.

Her first name also listed as "Norena." Alfred's name also listed as "Alford." Narena and Alfred were buried in Hall's United Methodist Church Cemetery, 4 miles north of Autryville, North Carolina, on SR 1414.

Children of Narena Spell and Alfred Lewis are:

1420 i. **Craven Lewis**, born about 1902.

+ 1421 ii. **Hurley C. Lewis**, born about 1904.

+ 1422 iii. **Eva Clyde Lewis**, born 12 August 1905; died 19 January 1956 in Clinton, Sampson County, North Carolina.

593. Myrtle Irene Autry (Allen Merdeth[5], Starling[4], Millie[3] Holland, Thomas William[2], Unknown[1]) was born 20 November 1872 in Sampson County, North Carolina, and died 02 February 1952. She married **Holly Wright Hudson** 18 July 1895, son of Coleman Hudson and Mary Warrick. He was born 02 July 1871 in Sampson County, North Carolina, and died 01 July 1943.

Myrtle and Holly Wright were buried in The Clinton Cemetery, Clinton, Sampson County, North Carolina.

Children of Myrtle Autry and Holly Hudson are:

1423 i. **Flora Allen Hudson**, born 08 November 1896 in Duplin County, North Carolina; died 04 June 1957. She married **Walter J. Corbett**; born 10 November 1880; died 25 October 1964.

Flora Allen and Walter were buried in The Clinton Cemetery, Clinton, Sampson County, North Carolina.

1424 ii. **Bertous Holly Hudson**, born 07 August 1900; died 07 December 1976. He married **Lura E. Britt** 02 February 1922; born 11 February 1902; died 25 March 1990.

Bertous Holly and Lura were buried in The Clinton Cemetery, Clinton, Sampson County, North Carolina.

1425 iii. **Emma Kate Hudson**, born 05 May 1904.

1426 iv. **J. Charlie Hudson**, born 29 September 1906; died 09 December 1991.

Charlie was buried in The Clinton Cemetery, Clinton, Sampson County, North Carolina

594. Bettie Allen Autry (Allen Merdeth[5], Starling[4], Millie[3] Holland, Thomas William[2], Unknown[1]) was born 19 October 1875 in Near Beulah Church near Salemburg, Sampson County, North Carolina, and died 19 December 1939 in Sampson County, North Carolina. She and **Clarence Hubbard Butler** were married 18 March 1896 in Residence of Richard C. and Sudie Cobb Turlington by M. J. Newman, J.P. Clarence was the son of William Butler and Mariah Butler. He was born 07 October 1869 in Belvoir Township, Sampson County, North Carolina, and died 01 September 1942 in Sampson County.

Bettie Allen became a member of McGee United Methodist Church when she was a young girl and remained a member until she died. Clarence Hubbard was a member of Royal Chapel Missionary Baptist Church when he was young. He served as Sunday School Superintendent for a number of years. Royal Chapel was destroyed by a tornado and was not rebuilt. Clarence Hubbard then joined Corinth Baptist Church where he served as deacon.

Bettie Allen and Clarence Hubbard were buried in a Butler Cemetery on Five Bridge Road (SR 1311 in Sampson County, North Carolina.

Children of Bettie Autry and Clarence Butler are:

1427 i. **Stillborn Butler**, born 1897.

1428 ii. **William Prentis Butler**, born 02 April 1898; died 22 May 1931.

William Prentis did not marry. He attended Union Academy; Delway School, Delway, North Carolina; Campbell College, Buies Creek, North Carolina and Moody Bible Institute, Chicago, IL., and taught school. William Prentis was buried in a Butler Cemetery on Five Bridge Road (SR 1311 in Sampson County, North Carolina.

\+ 1429 iii. **Clarence Allen Butler**, born 14 May 1900; died 22 October 1970 in Duke Hospital, Wayne County, North Carolina.

1430 iv. **Bettie Pauline Butler**, born 16 July 1902; died 31 December 1987 in Sampson County, North Carolina. She married **Charlie Henry Vann** 04 January 1922; born 22 July 1897 in Sampson County, North Carolina; died 23 December 1983 in Sampson County, North Carolina.

She and Charlie Henry were buried in a Vann Cemetery on Mt. Mariah Church Road north of Reynolds Crossroads in Sampson County, North Carolina.

1431 v. **Caron Hubbard Butler**, born 11 September 1904; died 31 January 1924.

He did not marry and was buried in a Butler Cemetery on Five Bridge Road (SR 1311 in Sampson County, North Carolina.

\+ 1432 vi. **Lillie Nadine Butler**, born 12 July 1906; died 11 March 1990.

1433 vii. **Mamie Jane Butler**, born 07 September 1908; died 30 November 1999.

In June 1911, Mamie Jane has a severe attack of polio and was unable to walk after that. At that time, doctors did not know how to treat polio; her parents were told to take care of her the best they could. She started school at the age of eight and graduated at Salemburg High School as valedictorian of the class of 1929. She continued her education in business administration at Pineland College, Salemburg, North Carolina.

In 1952, Mamie bought an Oldsmobile with hand-controlled equipment.

In 1945, she presented a gift to be used to help natives in Africa build a church. The church located in southeast Africa was named "Butler Memorial" in memory of her parents.

Mamie Jane was buried in a Butler Cemetery on Five Bridge Road (SR 1311 in Sampson County, North Carolina.

\+ 1434 viii. **Eva Pearl Butler,** born 18 December 1910.

\+ 1435 ix. **Charles Marion Butler, Sr.**, born 14 July 1913.

\+ 1436 x. **Henry Bruce Butler**, born 29 November 1915.

1437 xi. **Sudie Elva Butler**, born 13 February 1919; died 27 November 2003.

Sudie Elva graduated from Pineland College, Salemburg, and East Carolina Teachers College, Greenville, North Carolina, in 1940 with a B.S. degree in Elementary Education.

She is buried in a: Butler Cemetery on Five Bridge Road (SR 1311 in Sampson County, North Carolina.

608. Lesley Faircloth (Miney L.[5] Lockerman, Olivia[4] Holland, Henry[3], Thomas William[2], Unknown[1]) was born about 1913.

Child of Lesley Faircloth is:

1438 i. **Lesley Faircloth.**

609. Henry Lee Holland (Jasper Lee[5], Stephen Senter[4], Henry[3], Thomas William[2], Unknown[1]) was born 28 October 1900 in Sampson County, North Carolina, and died 1978 in Yulee, Forida. He married **Maude Wilds**. She was born 17 May 1893, and died 31 March 1993 in Yulee, Florida.

A source on ancestry.com has Maude's date of birth as 17 May 1891 and date of death 31 March 1993. This would make her 19 years older than Henry (Coy) and 101 when she died. She was probably born later than 1893 as stated above.

His actual name was "**Coy Lee Holland**." When he moved to Florida, he either changed his name legally or just called himself Henry Lee Holland. His delayed certificate of birth in Sampson County, North Carolina was dated 25 February 1965 when he would have applied for Social Security. Apparently, he registered to vote in Precinct 5 in Florida on 26 July 1937.

Their infants were buried near Henry Lee and Maude in a Wilds Family Cemetery on Owens Road in Yulee, Florida.

Children of Henry Holland and Maude Wilds are:

1439 i. **Henry Lee Holland**, born 09 January 1930 in Yulee, Florida; died 09 January 1930 in Yulee, Florida.

He was buried in a Wilds Family Cemetery on Owens Road in Yulee, Florida.

1440 ii. **Esther Margaret Holland**, born 18 June 1933 in Yulee, Florida; died 19 June 1933 in Yulee, Florida.

She was buried in a Wilds Family Cemetery on Owens Road in Yulee, Florida.

610. Floy D. Holland (Jasper Lee[5], Stephen Senter[4], Henry[3], Thomas William[2], Unknown[1]) was born 28 June 1903 in Sampson County, North Carolina, and died 09 December 1927. She married **Raymond Badger Smith** 20 December 1923 in South Clinton Township in Sampson County, son of John Smith and Sophia Beard. He was born 02 August 1901, and died 16 February 1979.

Their date of marriage was taken from the marriage index in the courthouse in Sampson County, North Carolina. Witnesses were S. S. Holland, Wm Peterson and Clifton Haire.

Floy and Raymond Badger were buried in Windsor Methodist Church Cemetery on Highway 242, North of Turnbull Creek, Bladen County, North Carolina.

Children of Floy Holland and Raymond Smith are:

1441 i. **Pauline Smith**, born 01 February 1925. She married John Gray.

1442 ii. **Adel Smith**, born 15 September 1926. She married **Frankie West**; born 17 December 1929.

Known as "Bill" Smith.

611. Jimmy Minson Holland (Jasper Lee[5], Stephen Senter[4], Henry[3], Thomas William[2], Unknown[1]) was born 30 April 1906 in Sampson County, North Carolina, and died 01 March 1995 in Sampson County. He married **Mary Rachel Hollingsworth**. She was born 29 July 1912 in Sampson County and died 24 March 1996 in Clinton, Sampson County, North Carolina.

I also have the 3 April 1906 for Jimmy's birth. Jimmy Minson died in Sampson County Memorial Hospital, Clinton, North Carolina of Congestive Heart Failure and Artherosclerotic Heart Disease. He also had acute respiratory infection. Mary Rachel died in Mary-Gran Nursing Center in Clinton, North Carolina of pneumonia. She and Jimmy were buried in Zoar PFWB Church Cemetery in Salemburg, North Carolina. Informant was son, Jimmy Holland.

Children of Jimmy Holland and Mary Hollingsworth are:

\+ 1443 i. **Jimmy Huey Holland**, born 06 June 1936 in Honeycutts Township, Sampson County, North Carolina; died 20 July 2004.

1444 ii. **Carolyn Holland**, born 28 May 1940 in Sampson County, North Carolina.

612. Lonie Mae Holland (Jasper Lee[5], Stephen Senter[4], Henry[3], Thomas William[2], Unknown[1]) was born 20 March 1909 in Sampson County, North Carolina, and died 10 April 1993 in Highsmith Hospital, Fayetteville, Cumberland County, North Carolina. She married **Gaston Lucas Smith** 09 November 1924 in Dillon, South Carolina, son of John Smith and Sophia Beard. He was born 09 May 1906 in Bladen County, North Carolina, and died 05 December 1973 in Cumberland County, North Carolina.

Lonie Mae and Gaston were buried in Sunrise Memorial Gardens Cemetery, Salemburg, North Carolina

Children of Lonie Holland and Gaston Smith are:

1445 i. **Donnie Ray Smith**.

1446 ii. **Maude Elizabeth Smith**. She married ?? Graff.

1447 iii. **Mildred Lucille Smith**. She married Unknown Nance.

1448 iv. **Alice Berline Smith**, born August 1926 in Salemburg, North Carolina; died June 1989 in Tarheel, Bladen County, North Carolina. She married ?? Monroe.

Burial: Monroe Family Cemetery, Tarheel, Bladen County, North Carolina.

1449 v. **Jasper Washington Smith**, born 14 January 1930 in Ammon, Bladen County, North Carolina; died 08 January 1997 in Fayetteville, North Carolina.

Burial: Monroe Family Cemetery, Tarheel, Bladen County, North Carolina.

\+ 1450 vi. **Woodrow Smith**, born 21 July 1938 in Sampson County, North Carolina.

613. Ila Marie Holland (Jasper Lee[5], Stephen Senter[4], Henry[3], Thomas William[2], Unknown[1]) was born 27 March 1910 in Sampson County, North Carolina, and died 05 May 2003. She married **Murdie Oliver Hill, Sr.**, son of Claude Hill and Lula Faircloth. He was born 17 April 1904, and died 19 November 2000.

His name is also shown as "Merdie."

Ila Marie and Murdie Oliver Hill, Sr. were buried in Zoar Pentecostal FWB Church Cemetery on Zoar Church Rd, Sampson County, North Carolina

Children of Ila Holland and Murdie Hill are:

1451 i. **Alice Marie Hill.**

1452 ii. **Murdie Oliver Hill, Jr.**

614. Orlanda Lee Holland (Jasper Lee[5], Stephen Senter[4], Henry[3], Thomas William[2], Unknown[1]) was born 16 October 1912 in Sampson County, North Carolina, and died 24 December 1940 near Savannah, Georgia. He married **Mildred Westbrook**. She was born 26 September 1915, and died 24 December 1940 Near Savannah, Georgia.

Orlanda Lee, Mildred and their daughter, Dorothy, were killed along with four other family members in a tragic automobile accident near Savannah, Georgia, on 24 December 1940. He and his family were traveling from their home in Fernandina Beach, Florida, to Salemburg, North Carolina, for a Christmas visit with family. See notes for his sister, Geneva, listed below, who married Dewey Westbrook, brother of Mildred.

Orlanda's first name is spelled "Orlando" on his gravestone. Orlanda Lee Holland and Mildred were buried in Burial: Salemburg Cemetery, Bearskin Road, Salemburg, North Carolina.

Children of Orlanda Holland and Mildred Westbrook are:

1453 i. **Orlanda Lee Holland, Jr.**, born 24 September 1934; died 1968.

He was killed in an airplane crash.

1454 ii. **Bobby Brewer Holland**, born 21 October 1936.

1455 iii. **Dorothy Lucille Holland**, born 13 May 1938; died 24 December 1940.

She was buried in Salemburg Cemetery, Bearskin Road, Salemburg, North Carolina.

616. Geneva Holland (Jasper Lee[5], Stephen Senter[4], Henry[3], Thomas William[2], Unknown[1]) was born 23 June 1915 in Sampson County, North Carolina, and died 24 December 1940 in Near Savannah, Georgia. She married **Dewey Lee Westbrook**, He was born 17 June 1921 in Sampson County, North Carolina, and died 24 December 1940 near Savannah, Georgia. Dewey was the brother of Mildred Westbrook, who married Geneva's brother, Orlanda, listed above and their parents may have been William Westbrook and Sallie, Maiden Name Unknown.

Geneva, her husband, Dewey and their daughter, Margaret, were killed near Savannah, Georgia, along with 4 other family members on 24 Dec. 1940. All seven were traveling from their home in Fernandina Beach, Florida, to Salemburg, North Carolina, for a Christmas visit with family.

Geneva's Certificate of Birth may incorrectly register "Margaret Elizabeth Holland" for her name. She and Dewey were buried in Salemburg Cemetery, Bearskin Road, Salemburg, North Carolina.

Child of Geneva Holland and Dewey Westbrook is:

1456 i. **Margaret Westbrook**, born 14 August 1940; died 24 December 1940 near Savannah, Georgia.

Burial: Salemburg Cemetery, Bearskin Road, Salemburg, North Carolina.

617. Melissa Seawell Holland (Jasper Lee[5], Stephen Senter[4], Henry[3], Thomas William[2], Unknown[1]) was born 10 November 1917 in Sampson County, North Carolina, and died 18 January 1990 in Cumberland County, North Carolina. She married **Wilbur Kelly Roberts, Sr.**. He was born 02 October 1915, and died 27 April 1985.

On her Certificate of Birth, her name was written as Malissa Seawell Holland and Malissa has a line across it. Her mother's name is written as Allie May Della Lockerman with a line through Allie May Della and "Dallie" written above it. She was known as "Seawell."

Children of Melissa Holland and Wilbur Roberts are:

1457 i. **Rachael Ann Roberts** married Unknown Russell.

1458 ii. **Wilbur Kelly Roberts, Jr.**

1459 iii. **Janice Faye Roberts** married Unknown Jones.

1460 iv. **Patricia Roberts** married Unknown Tyner. Patricia appears to be the "Patricia Vestal " who posted several messages on genforum.genealogy.com , requesting information on Jasper Holland of Sampson County and his descendants. Her husband may be Larry Vestal

618. Elizabeth Ozell Holland (Jasper Lee[5], Stephen Senter[4], Henry[3], Thomas William[2], Unknown[1]) was born 23 August 1920 in Honeycutts Township, Sampson County, North Carolina. She married **Henry Elton Taylor**. He was born 26 December 1912, and died 16 January 1992.

She was called 'Ozella' by some family members. In March 2009 just before I am to publish this book, Ozell is still living. Henry Elton was buried in Salemburg Cemetery, Bearskin Road, Salemburg, North Carolina.

Children of Elizabeth Holland and Henry Taylor are:

1461 i. **Lamarie Taylor.**

1462 ii. **Dallie Faye Taylor**. She married **Max Truman Cooper**, son of Robbie Lee Cooper and Cora Glendon Butler. Max was born September 1945.

1463 iii. **Henry Pritchard Taylor** was born on 4 May 1947 in Sampson County, N orth Carolina.

On 6 March 1970, Henry married **Joan Wisch** in Chicago, Illinois. They have two children, **Carol Ann Taylor who** was born on 16 February 1972 **and David Henry Taylor** who was born on 5 December 1974. Carol Ann Taylor's daughter **Ashley Alyssa Taylor** was born on 27 December 1991 in Chicago, Illinois. Carol Ann married **Juan Robles** on 29 April 2006 in East Dundee, Illinois. Juan is called Tony;. he is a widower with two sons, **Nick Robles** born 1 November 1989 and **Phil Robles** who was born on 2 October 1991.

Henry and Joan Taylor's son, **David Henry Taylor** married **Ann Gonzales** (**Ana Margaret Mata**) (nee Gonzales) on 14 February 2004 in Rolling Meadows, Illinois.

1464 iv. **Shirley Ann Taylor**, born 07 November 1937 in Sampson County, North Carolina; died 07 November 1937.

619. Novella Olean Holland (Jasper Lee[5], Stephen Senter[4], Henry[3], Thomas William[2], Unknown[1]) was born 18 February 1922 in Sampson County, North Carolina, and died 11 December 1989 in Sampson County, North Carolina. She married **Venton Eugene Cannady**, son of Jonah Cannady and Cornelia Faircloth. He was born 16 August 1923, and died 01 October 2001 in Sampson County, North Carolina.

The source for Cannady family data gives 13 Dec 1989 for Novella's date of death. Her Certificate of Birth spells her middle name "Oleina" or "Olina." Novella and Venton were buried in Salemburg Baptist Church Cemetery, Salemburg, North Carolina

Children of Novella Holland and Venton Cannady are:

1465 i. **Jaspher Cannady.**

Jaspher is listed on the tombstone of her parents and no date is noted.

1466 ii. **Harry Gordon Cannady**, born 31 December 1942. He married Katie Parker; born August 1942.

1467 iii. **Lennie Ray Cannady**, born 02 May 1948.

1468 iv. **Margaret Ann Cannady**, born 26 March 1950. She married Terry Wensley.

1469 v. **Larry Glenn Cannady**, born 24 September 1956; died 10 October 1956.

He was buried in Salemburg Cemetery, Bearskin Road, Salemburg, North Carolina.

623. Leola Lockamy (Heman Cashwell[5], Orpah Caroline[4] Holland, Henry[3], Thomas William[2], Unknown[1]) was born 03 October 1907. She married **Albert Harrell.**

Her year of birth also listed as 1905.

Children of Leola Lockamy and Albert Harrell are:

1470 i. **Brenda Harrell.**

1471 ii. **Edna Harrell.** She married **John Parker.**

Four children.

639. James Senter Holland (Alger Rose[5], Stephen Senter[4], Henry[3], Thomas William[2], Unknown[1]) was born 09 December 1905 in Elizabethtown, Bladen County, North Carolina, and died 01 April 1988 in Garland, Sampson County, North Carolina. His certificate of death records Elizabethtown for his birth. He married **Vernita Simmons**, daughter of William Junius Simmons and Mary Miller Lockamy. William Simmons was known as "June." Vernita was born 07 October 1910 in Sampson County, North Carolina, and died 04 January 1989 in Sampson County, North Carolina.

The 'Certificate of Death' for James Senter names **Alger HOLLAND** and **Lorrane HOWARD** for his parents. Aunt Vernita (Varnita) is the informant listed on Uncle Senter's Certificate of Death. She may have had a family Bible or she had personal knowledge that Alger Rose Holland was married to a "Lorrane Howard" (Lorraine Howard). My mother, Roberta Holland Jackson, sister of James Senter, thought very highly of the Howards and this writer's memories indicate Roberta may have either known that Alger Rose was married to a Howard or there was another connection to the Howard family near Salemburg. Most family members believe that James Senter's mother was Ella Jane Howell and that is how I have listed him. Unless someone from the Howard families can clear up the mystery of "Lorrane Howard," it will always be an unknown link.

A sister says that Senter is really "SCENTER." Apparently, this name has been mispelled in each generation in all state and county records. I do not know what is written in the Alger Rose Holland Family Bible.

Uncle James Senter was six feet tall and his son is 6' 4" tall while Alger Rose Holland, his father, was short. Aunt Vernita (Lady) was also tall. Uncle John Westley, brother of James Senter, and two sisters were shorter.

James Senter died of Cardiac Arrest due to severe ASVB and severe atrial fibrillation at his rural home near Garland, Sampson County, North Carolina. He farmed most of his life and for several years before his death, was a machine operator at a Brick-tile Manufactoring plant.

He and his brother, John Wesley, married sisters. My research, indicates that Aunt Vernita and Aunt Vonita's family lived a short distance from Uncle James Senter and Uncle John Wesley's family. The families probably lived less than one mile apart and the Crumpler Mill on Crumpler Mill Road in Sampson County, North Carolina, was about mid-way between the farms.

Vernita's tombstone shows her name as 'Varnita Lady Sessoms.' 'Lady' was her nickname. Her first name is found as "Olita" and in the 1920 census it is "Lolela." On the 'Certificate of Death' for James Senter Holland and on her Certificate of Death, her first name is spelled Vernita. Her cause of death was congestive heart failure and acute respiratory failure. Both were buried in Zoar Pentecostal FWB Church Cemetery on Zoar Church Rd, Sampson County, North Carolina.

Aunt "Lady" had a small area of skin cancer on her face several years before she died; the surgeon didn't remove all of it and it eventually developed into a malignant tumor.

Children of James Holland and Vernita Simmons are:

+ 1472 i. **Alma Christine Holland,** born 04 August 1931 in Sampson County, North Carolina.

1473 ii. **Esterlene Holland,** born 02 November 1938 in Sampson County (or Cumberland County?), North Carolina; died 23 August 2004. The Cumberland County, North Carolina Birth Index lists her name as "Esther Holland." Never married.

She worked in hospital in Sanford for 13 years. Went on disability in 1991. She was buried in Zoar Pentecostal FWB Church Cemetery on Zoar Church Road in Sampson County.

+ 1474 iii. **William Gaddy Holland,** born 16 July 1935 in Sampson County, North Carolina.

+ 1475 iv. **Alice Faye Holland,** born 11 December 1951 in Sampson County, North Carolina.

640. John Wesley Holland (Alger Rose[5], Stephen Senter[4], Henry[3], Thomas William[2], Unknown[1]) was born 17 October 1907 possibly in Sampson County, North Carolina, and died 01 April 1998 in Sampson County, North Carolina. He married **Vonita Simmons** 20 October 1928 in Clinton, Sampson County, North Carolina, daughter of William Junius Simmons and Mary Miller Lockamy. William Simmons was known as "June." Vonita was born 20 September 1912 in Sampson County, North Carolina, and died 16 March 1950.

Uncle John Wesley's certificate of death shows he died of dilated cardiomyopathy, chronic obstructive lung disease, and anemia due(?) to myelodysphasia (this may be spelled incorrectly?). His sister, Roberta, was born in 1910 in Bladen County, North Carolina, and **most likely, he was also born in Bladen County**. Unfortunately, certificates of birth were not required until a few years later. The Voters' Registration for White Oak Township, Bladen County, North Carolina, records that his father, Alger, registered as "Algier Holland" on 26 October 1906. Alger's brother, John Wesley, registered in the same place on the same day.

Aunt Vonita often used "Lela" for her name and that was the name she listed when she and Uncle John Wesley were married. A date of 17 May 1912 has also been given for her birth.

Uncle John Wesley and Aunt Vonita were buried in Zoar Pentecostal FWB Church Cemetery on Zoar Church Rd, Sampson County, North Carolina.

Children of John Holland and Vonita Simmons are:

+ 1476 i. **Doris Gray Holland,** born 12 August 1930 in Sampson County, North Carolina; died 03 September 2006.

1477 ii. **Annie Clyde Holland**, born 27 May 1933 in Sampson County, North Carolina. She married **Albert Furman McLamb** 24 December 1952 in Dillon, South Carolina; born 20 August 1933 in Dismal Township, Sampson County, North Carolina; died 10 December 2004 in Sampson County, North Carolina. It is said he was a twin. No children.

Furman was buried in Union Grove Baptist Church Cemetery on Vander Road (SR 1438) Sampson County, North Carolina.

\+ 1478 iii. **Mary Leatrice Holland**, born 04 September 1935 in Sampson County, North Carolina.

\+ 1479 iv. **Brenda Sue Holland**, born After 1935.

\+ 1480 v. **John Wesley Holland, Jr.**, born 23 June 1947 in Roseboro, Sampson County, North Carolina.

641. Roberta Holland (Alger Rose[5], Stephen Senter[4], Henry[3], Thomas William[2], Unknown[1]) was born 01 September 1910 in Bladen County, North Carolina, and died 22 January 1985 in Sampson County Memorial Hospital, Clinton, North Carolina. She married **Oscar Davis Jackson** 29 May 1929 in Clinton, Sampson County, North Carolina, son of Haburn Jackson and Molsey Naylor. He was born 19 July 1909 in Honeycutts Township, Sampson County and died 02 September 1986 in Onslow County, Jacksonville, North Carolina.

Mother had beautiful auburn hair and looked stunning in green, but rarely wore any shade of green because my father did not like her to wear it. Her father had red hair, but he was practically bald when I was growing up and I can remember only a few red hairs on his head. Mother's sister, Aunt Dellar, also had red hair, but it was a lighter shade.

Mother, for some reason, especially noticed the color of the eyes of people she met. Once, when we were shopping for school clothes in Fayetteville, she turned to me after we passed an individual and asked, "Did you see those blue eyes?"

Mother died of Cardiac Arrest due to Ischemic Heart Disease for 2 years and diabetes mellitus for several years. A permanent pacemaker was placed in her chest a few years before her death.

In an "old" Family Bible that Mother had, "**Robertha**" is written in pencil on page 291. I believe this old Bible belonged to her mother, Ella Jane Howell, and a few notes in the Bible indicate that it may have belonged to Ella Jane's mother or father's family.

She listed "**Robertha**" for her name when she and Oscar Davis Jackson were married. This, most likely was her name, but she used "Roberta" more often and it is found on other records. Nickname was Robert (pronounced "Rowbert." Registration of birth was not a requirement when she was born, but when she applied for Social Security, she named Bladen County for her place of birth.

"Daniel P. Holland, born 10 September 1900" was also written in the old Howell (or Carter) Bible mentioned above. See notes for Lonnie Perry Holland, Alger's son by his first wife.

"GEORGE BEATTY SIKES born 07 October 1850" is a notation we also found in this old Carter or Howell Bible. I have not determined his relationship to the Carters, Howells or

Hollands? "George B. Sikes," aged 10 can be found in the 1860 census for Lisbon Township, Sampson County, North Carolina. He was the son of CHARLES M. SIKES who was born about 1825 and ANN M. HERRING, born about 1832. Ann was the daughter of WASHINGTON HERRING and MARGARET SPELL. Dr. GIBSON LEWIS SIKES (Sykes) practiced medicine in Salemburg, North Carolina. It appears that Sikes and Sykes were used interchangeably.

"***April 29 and 30 1860 cold, rainy and very stormy***," is another note in the Bible. This tells us that this "old Bible" was around in April 1860. Apparently, the Bible was passed down to Ella Jane Howell, Roberta's mother, and the notation about the weather in 1860 indicates it probably belonged to Ella Jane Howell's grandparents: either JOHN CARTER (1818) and his wife CHARLOTTE AVERITT (born about 1827) or DAVID HOWELL (born about 1809) and his wife, Rox A. (maiden name unknown), born about 1830. The cover and a few pages are missing from the Bible. The Bible is now in the care of Jackie, my sister.

Mother had birthmarks under her arm that looked like blueberries, and she believed they resulted from her mother's craving for blueberries during her pregnancy.

It is said that my father, Oscar Davis Jackson, left home when he was about 16. This would have been shortly after his mother died in 1925 when his mother's sister, Aunt Joanna Naylor, moved into the household to help care for the children. Apparently, Dad boarded with Clarence Hubbard Butler and Bettie Allen Autry. I never heard him mention this event of his life. A close relative told me that Mr. Butler financed a car for him and treated him like a son. It is unclear how long he stayed with them; on 29 May 1929, he and mother were married.

For a few years starting about 1942, my parents, Oscar Davis Jackson and Roberta Holland rented a farm from **James Crumpler**, brother of **Stacy Crumpler**. The small, unpainted three room, tenant house, still standing today, is now on land owned by a Strickland family and is across the road from Crumpler Grist Mill on the road that is today known as Crumpler Mill Road. The mill is known today as Stacy Crumpler Mill. My sister, Jackie, was born in 1943 in this house and although my parents were not living there in 1933, my older sister Betty Carolyn, who lived only about 24 hours after she was born in February 1933 was buried near the house in a small cemetery. This cemetery is at the edge of a field in an overgrown area on land now owned by either descendants of a sister of my mother or the Strickland Family. Joel Jackson and his wife, Hepsie, (see deed below) and their daughter, Sallie, were also buried there. Sallie was the only one who had a gravestone and about 1995 it was difficult to read the name and dates on it.

While we lived in the tenant house described above, my maternal grandparents lived a short distance from us and the shortest route to my paternal grandparents who lived on the road now known as "The Avenue," included paths through the woods, narrow roads at the edge of fields, and over what may have been the few old boards of the supporting structure for what I believed was an old mill and dam over Bearskin Swamp. However, these board may have been the remains of an old bridge, but I hated walking across them as it was necessary to look down in order to step safely from one board to another to avoid falling into the murky water which flowed swiftly at times. A sister of my mother tells that she and another sister walked this short route to visit James Senter Holland, their older brother and his wife, Vernita Simmons, who rented a house from Grandpa Haburn Rice Jackson, my father's father, and they walked on a bridge to cross over the water without fearing for their safety. The time they walked this bridge may have been around 1935 and I would have walked it about 8-10 later . I remember how the water frightened me each time I walked to my paternal grandparents with my dad.. This bridge was apparently over Bearskin and may have been on the dirt road I walked with my parents to a small field where they grew cotton one year while they rented this farm.

Today, this is a 65 year old memory, but the recollection of how I dreaded this walk over the water is vivid. To a child of six or seven who doesn't know how to swim, fast flowing water probably doesn't have to be very deep to create a frightful future memory. I recall my father trying to teach me to swim in the shallow water of Stacy Crumpler's Mill Pond; our movement in the clear water made the roots of a large tree that stood in the water appear to be snakes slithering around my feet and this intensified my fear of water.

After reading the deed below I apparently, incorrectly thought that the old Blewing Crumpler Mill and the mill William Stacy Crumpler's father, Macajah Thomas Crumpler, purchased in 1899, were different mills; I have been told that the Blewing Mill is known today as the Crumpler Mill that was owned by Stacy Crumpler on Crumpler Mill Road, but I had **incorrectly assumed** that the old boards mentioned above that my dad and I walked were probably the remains of the old Blewing Mill . Stacy told that when his father, Macajah, purchased this mill in 1899 it had already been in use for 133 years. William Stacy wrote a profile on his parents and his own family for ***The Heritage of Sampson County, North Carolina, 1784-1984***, Edited by Oscar M. Bizzell. In writing about the mill his father purchased in 1899, he never once referred to the mill as the Blewing Crumpler (or Blumin Crumpler) Mill. I don't know when my grandfather, Alger Rose Holland, started as the Miller at Stacy's Grist Mill or exactly when he retired. He was born in 1875 and died in 1968 and may have retired before 1962 when the last corn was ground in the mill. I can't be 100 percent positive, but I believe the picture I plan to place on the cover of this book is the old Crumpler Grist Mill as it appeared in the summer of 1994. Unfortunately, I failed to identifiy the photographs.

Tradition tells that when a Miller retires, he hangs his coat on the door of the Mill House and it is bad luck to remove it. When my sister and I visited with Stacy's daughter, Sabra, several years ago, she told us that our grandfather's tattered coat was still hanging behind a door in the mill house.

My grandfather or someone apparently picked me up on one occasion to show me the large stones in the millhouse. When I had my tonsils removed at about age 6, I dreamed I had fallen onto these stones while they were moving and it's one of the few, scary, old dreams I still remember. During my childhood, I had a recurring dream of a distant fire that was burning everything in its path and when it moved closer, I always tried to outrun it, waking up terrified just before it reached me. Perhaps the sermons of damnation and hellfire that were often preached at the time shaped that dream.

Water gushed from a pipe near the Crumpler Mill Race between the road and the dam.. When we lived near the mill, I remember my brother and I would walk down to the overflow with a large pail we filled with water from it and we carefully lugged it back up the hill to the house. Perhaps the well near the steps behind the house dried up or maybe my mother just liked the water from the overflow for her tea. Years later, water from a dug well that was piped into our home made a tea that was almost black and didn't taste very good. Mother would send us children over to a hand pump by another house on the property where we pumped water and carried it back to the house for our tea. The difference in taste and color of the tea made the trips for the water worthwhile.

Deed:

On the 23rd day of November 1905 **Joel Jackson** and wife, Hepsey Jackson (Hepsie) ...sold 40-1/2 acres of land to **M. J. Crumpler** for $70. This land "Beginning at a large sweet-gum on the west side of the old **Blewing Crumpler** mill pond at high water mark and runs S.23W.46 poles to an old field pine at the old cross way of the Juniper Branch on the south side, thence up the south side of said branch about 36 poles to a stake in the old line, thence with said old line S. 86 E.88 poles to the run of Bear Skin Swamp, thence up the run of said swamp 44 poles to the mouth of Crumpler's Mill race, thence up said mill race about 102 poles to the mill house sheets. Thence up the south side of mill dam S.46 w 4 poles to end of dam. Thence N. 40 W. 3 poles to a large sweet gum the beginning corner,..." Hepsey was examined on the same day to acknowledge she had voluntarily signed the deed. This deed was not recorded until 1912.

M. J. Crumpler was James Crumper, brother of Stacy and perhaps James' first name was Micajah.

My sparse research for Blewing Crumpler has turned up several spelling of the name and apparently, Blewing, was not correct. "Bluman H. Crumpler," son of John Crumpler (?) and Edith Gurley was born about 1815. It is a known fact that after John Crumpler died, John Honeycutt who lived nearby left his wife and moved in with Edith and they had several children. It appears that three of these male children had the middle initial "H" which possibly stood for "Honeycutt." Micajah B. Crumpler, Sr., was born about 1770 and died in 1860. Micajah B., Jr., (1809-1884), has a son named "Marshall B." who was born in 1837 and died in 1888. Did, at least one of these three "B" initials stand for Bluman? I also found "Bluin" for the spelling of this name.

It appears that the tributaries flowing into Bearskin Run were not always mentioned in old deeds which may refer to these areas as Bearskin Swamp. The deed below mentioning **"Little Bear Skin"** is interesting and it is the only written reference to Little Bear Skin I have found and I am told by my cousin that the stream feeding Crumpler Mill Pond is known as **"Bearskin Branch"**. Crumpler Mill Road crosses Little Bear Skin (Bearskin Branch). The land owned by my grandparents, Alger Rose Holland and Tomzil Holland, was on both sides of Crumpler Mill Road after turning right at Crumpler Mill and extended a short distance above the point where the road makes the next curve (maps show it as a sharp right). Crumpler Mill Road starts at Bearskin Road a short distance from Bearskin and makes what appears on maps as one curve to the right by the Stacy Crumpler Mill and a short distance later turns right (the sharp right) and continues to where it ends at Bearskin Road. Gerald Holland, a cousin, who with his wife, lives near his mother, and his sister and her family on part of what was the Alger Rose Holland farm, tells me that **Little Bear Skin** is today called **Little Bearskin Branch.** It is not named on any of the maps I have.

I remember the geese owned by my Holland grandparents would wander down to the water of **Little Bear Skin** and someone would be sent to bring them home. I don't remember who I was with or where we were going, but the group walked along the narrow dirt road known today as Crumpler Mill Road and we wanted to cross Little Bear Skin Branch, but the water was wider and flowing faster than usual; either someone must have picked me up and crossed the stream or we returned to my grandparents home. The deed below mentions a bridge at the Rachel overflow; it appears that the Rachels owned land adjoining the two acres recorded in the deed. I have no idea where the bridge and the overflow was, and if it was the place in the road where the geese gathered, the bridge was gone by the early 1940s. Today, the road is paved and a culvert probably is in the road. It is said that water rarely runs across the road today.

A deed of 23 September 1921 records that **Joel J. Jackson, Hepsie Jackson**, A. R. Holland and Thomsal (Tomzil) Holland sold to Augusta Rachels two acres of land for $100. This land began at "a stake on the run of "**Little Bear Skin**" in the Currie line just above the Bridge at the Rachel overflow and runs S. 25, W. 46 poles to a stake in the Rachel line, thence S. 65, E. 8 poles to a stake, thence N. 25, E. 46 poles to the run of said **Little Bear Skin,** thence up the run of of the said Bear Skin to the beginning corner." Both wives were examined on 26 September 1921 to determine whether they voluntarily signed the deed. Deed was filed January 25, 1923 and recorded 29 January 1923.

A North Carolina Gazetteer only shows Stacy's Pond. The area in Bearskin Swamp (Bearskin Run) where I apparently, erroneously believed an older mill stood, may have had very little running water at times. Mother worried that my brother and I would find our way to a deep hole where we might have an accident and I assume that it was the area around an old mill. Perhaps, the old boards on which my dad and I walked over the fast flowing water, were actualy what remained of an old bridge that crossed Bearskin Run and it could have been the old bridge my two aunts walked.

On the 24 October 1905, **J. A. Beaman** (John Allen Beaman) and wife, Elizabeth, in consideration of $135 sold to **Joel Jackson (Joseph Jackson)** two tracts of land. "First tract beginning at a stake in the edge of Juniper Branch on the Turlington Line and runs S.86 E.88 poles to the run of Bear Skin Swamp, thence up the run of said Bear Skin about 44 poles to the mouth of Crumpler's Mill race, thence up the mill race about 68 poles to the mouth of a small ditch, thence up the said ditch as it meanders about 31 poles to the crook of the ditch, thence up the south edge of branch 18 poles to the beginning containing about 31-1-2 acres. The second tract being lot # 4 in the division of the lands of **SARAH A. BRANCH** deceased and drawn by Betsy Simmons. Beginning at a black-gum at high water mark of the Crumpler Mill Pond and runs 88 poles to a stake on the ole line, thence S 85, E. 34-1/2 poles to a Juniper of **LUCIAN BRANCH**'s corner, thence his line down the **old ditch to the run of Bear Skin,** thence up **the run or mill race** about 34 poles to **mill house sheets**. Thence up the lower side of mill damS.46 W.4 poles to end of dam, thence (?) South Side of Mill pond at high water mark to the first station containing 33 acres more or less." Elizabeth was examined on the same day to determine whether she had voluntarily executed the deed. Deed was received by the Register of deeds on 19 October 1912 and recorded 21 October 1912.

Sarah A. Branch named above was Sallie Ann Hudson, 3rd wife of Jonas Branch and mother of Hepsie Branch and Elizabeth Branch. Joel (Joseph) Jackson married Hepsie Branch and John Allen Beaman married Elizabeth Branch who first married Charles B. Simmons. General Lucian C. Branch was half-brother to Hepsie and Elizabeth.

Bearskin Swamp covers a wide area as it meanders for several miles through Sampson County with small streams and other swampy areas feeding into it. Heavy rains caused "freshets" (overflowing water) in all these swamps, branches and streams and Bearskin Swamp was one of many perfect areas in the county to build mills and ponds. My paternal great-grandfather, Wiley Calvin Jackson, also had a small grist mill on his farm on a small stream that eventually flowed into Bearskin Swamp.

Between BearSkin Swamp and The Avenue were two farms that Dad and I passed each time we walked the short route to his parents. James Senter Holland and John Wesley Holland, older brothers of my mother, courted and married Simmons sisters who lived on the first farm. The second farm was owned, I believe by a Mr. Holden, a son of my father's great aunt, Elizabeth Royal, daughter of Gabriel Royal, Sr. and Sarah Crumpler, and a sister of Mary Jane Royal, my father's maternal grandmother.

Oscar David had diabetes and heart problems. After a stroke, he remained in a coma for a few months before his death in a nursing home in Jacksonville, North Carolina. He and mother were divorced and he married Betty, after my mother's death. Roberta, Oscar, and his second wife, Betty, were buried in Grandview Memorial Gardens, Clinton, North Carolina.

Children of Roberta Holland and Oscar Jackson are:

1481 i. **Betty Carolyn Jackson**, born February 1933 in Honeycutts Township, Sampson County, North Carolina; died February 1933 in Honeycutts Township, Sampson County, North Carolina.

She had webbed hands and feet, lived for about 24 hours, and was buried in an unmarked grave across from the Crumpler Mill owned by Stacy Crumpler now on Crumpler Mill Road near the boundary of the property owned, at that time, by Roberta's parents. The Cemetery may have been an old Branch, Hudson or Jackson Family Cemetery. Records show that Hepsie Branch, daughter of Sallie Ann Hudson and Jonas Branch may have inherited a portion of the property from her mother. Hepsie married Joseph E. Jackson who was known as Joel. Hepsie and Joel gave the property to Alger Rose Holland and his second wife, Tomzil Clyde Holland, for services Alger and Tomzil provided for them during their old age and for their daughter, Sallie, who died young.

\+ 1482 ii. **Nancy Eveline Jackson**, born 21 April 1936 in Honeycutts Township, Sampson County, North Carolina.

1483 iii. **Elon Adel Jackson**, born 08 May 1938 in Honeycutts Township, Sampson County, North Carolina; died 21 February 2002 in Rocky Mount Hospital, Nash County, North Carolina. He married Sudie Mae Pruitt 21 December 1960 in Sampson County, Clinton, North Carolina; born 14 August 1942 in Elkin, North Carolina.

After serving as a PFC in the Army from 27 November 1961 to 26 November 1963 (E-1), Adel work a a Machinist in a sock plant until he retired in 1999.

He liked gardening and old cars. In the spring of 2000 the doctors urged him to have an angiogram, but he was concerned about the deaths that occur with the procedure and refused. His health problems continued to get worse and he finally had the angiogram in early October 2000 and had open heart surgery on 19 October 2000. About two weeks later, he was rushed to the emergency room and one and 3/4 liters of fluid were removed from his lungs. He continued to have breathing problems and at times could not finish shaving.

For several years before his death, the pain in his legs and shortness of breath made it impossible for him to walk very far without resting. Apparently, the pain in his legs was caused by his diabetes, high blood pressure and other heart problems.

He was buried 24 February 2002, in Grandview Memorial Gardens, Clinton, North Carolina.

\+ 1484 iv. **Jackie Olene Jackson**, born 09 February 1943 in Honeycutts Township, Sampson County, North Carolina.

642. Dellar Jane Holland (Alger Rose[5], Stephen Senter[4], Henry[3], Thomas William[2], Unknown[1]) was born 15 October 1912 in Near Salemburg, Sampson County, North Carolina, and died 05 September 1979 in Clinton, Sampson County, North Carolina. She married **William Rafton Hairr** 07 October 1933 in Clinton, Sampson County, North Carolina, son of Wiley Cephas Hairr and Lou Gene Naylor. He was born 19 October 1911 in Sampson County, North Carolina, and died 23 December 1994.

Aunt Dellar had red hair. She and William Rafton were buried at Zoar Penecostal Free Will Baptist Church Cemetery, Salemburg, North Carolina.

Children of Dellar Holland and William Hairr are:

\+ 1485 i. **Alger Leevon Hairr**, born 29 May 1934 in Honeycutts Township, Sampson County, North Carolina.

\+ 1486 ii. **William Earl Hairr**, born 04 August 1935 in Honeycutts Township, Sampson County, North Carolina.

\+ 1487 iii. **Jean Elizabeth Hairr**, born 19 October 1937 in Sampson County, North Carolina.

647. Katie Dell Holland (Alger Rose[5], Stephen Senter[4], Henry[3], Thomas William[2], Unknown[1]) was born 20 April 1917 in Honeycutts Township, Sampson County, North Carolina, and died 02 March 1998. She married **John Davis Strickland, Jr.** 26 August 1939, son of John Davis Strickland, Sr. and Sudie Royal. He was born 09 August 1918 in Sampson County, North Carolina, and died 03 July 2006.

Aunt Katie Dell enjoyed cooking and sewing and she gave many home permanents to the women in her family and to friends. Uncle John Davis (J. D.) farmed and was a carpenter. He built many of the homes in the area.

She and Uncle J. D. were buried in Zoar Pentecostal FWB Church Cemetery on Zoar Church Rd, Sampson County, North Carolina.

Children of Katie Holland and John Strickland are:

\+ 1488 i. **Frankie Faye Strickland**, born 30 November 1940 in Honeycutts Township, Sampson County, north Carolina.

\+ 1489 ii. **Margaret Elaine Strickland**, born 01 September 1942 in Honeycutts Township, Sampson County, North Carolina.

648. George Bizzell Holland (Alger Rose[5], Stephen Senter[4], Henry[3], Thomas William[2], Unknown[1]) was born 30 April 1919, and died 10 August 1997 in Sampson Regional Medical Center, Clinton, Sampson County, North Carolina. He married **Cherry Idell Tyndall** 01 February 1947, daughter of Garley BraxtonTyndall and Annie Bell Hair. Idell was born 08 January 1931 in Honeycutts Township, Sampson County, North Carolina.

Uncle George served in the U.S Army from 05 Aug 1942 - 31 Jan 1946. He was a retired carpenter. Causes of death: Lobar pnemonia, Dementia, Alzheimers, multi infracts and coronary artery disease. He was buried at Zoar PFWB Church Cemetery, Salemburg, North Carolina.

Cherry Idell Tyndall Holland (Aunt Idell) is also my cousin through my father's line of Naylors. She and Ethel McDonald Naylor Honeycutt provided me with data on their grandparents, parents and their families that included full names, dates of birth and some dates of death. Their information was extremely helpful and I am grateful for their help.

Children of George Holland and Cherry Tyndall are:

1490 i. **Wayne Bizzell Holland**, born 07 December 1947 in Roseboro, Sampson County, North Carolina; died 26 October 1968 in Vietnam. He was a Sgt. CO3, 28th Inf. 1st inf. Division. Vietnam BSM-2PH. He was buried in Zoar Pentecostal FW Baptist Church Cemetery, Sampson County, North Carolina.

\+ 1491 ii. **Gerald Rogers Holland**, born 17 June 1950 in Roseboro, Sampson County, North Carolina.

\+ 1492 iii. **Evelyn Idell Holland**, born 07 December 1954 in Roseboro, Sampson County, North Carolina.

\+ 1493 iv. **Karen Darlene Holland**, born 06 June 1962 in Sampson County, North Carolina.

651. Freda Augustus Holland (Alger Rose[5], Stephen Senter[4], Henry[3], Thomas William[2], Unknown[1]) was born 25 July 1924 in Sampson County, North Carolina and died 2 April 2008. She married **John Thomas Strickland** 24 December 1938 in Sampson County, North Carolina, son of Rhonie Futrill Strickland and Annie Retha Baker. He was born 22 August 1918 in North Carolina, and died 23 October 1984 in Durham, North Carolina.

Grandma Tomzil Clide (Clyde) spelled Aunt Freda Augustus Holland's first name "Freeda." It has also been spelled "Freida." "Augusta" is also found for her middle name. Aunt Freda was quite helpful in providing information on the Hollands.

John Thomas Strickland served in the Marine Corps in WW II and later (in 1947) in the Army. He was buried at sea. Cause of death: Cancer. Aunt Freda was buried at Zoar Pentecostal FW Baptist Church Cemetery in Sampson County, near Salemburg.

Children of Freda Holland and John Strickland are:

\+ 1494 i. **Jeanette Strickland**, born 19 February 1940.

\+ 1495 ii. **Barbara Strickland**, born 18 December 1941.

\+ 1496 iii. **Anthony Strickland**, born 27 November 1946.

\+ 1497 iv. **Rodney Holland Strickland**, born 16 July 1949 in Salemburg, Honeycutts Township, Sampson County, North Carolina.

\+ 1498 v. **Audrey Augusta Strickland**, born 19 September 1952 in Sampson County, North Carolina.

652. Clyda Louise Holland (Henry[5], Stephen Senter[4], Henry[3], Thomas William[2], Unknown[1]) was born 11 January 1909 in Sampson County, North Carolina, and died 08 July 1997. She married **Dewitt Frost Simmons,** son of Franklin Pierce Simmons and Laura Cogdell. He was born 31 October 1895, and died 24 April 1964.

Dewitt served with the American Expeditionary Force during WWI. He and Clyda Louise were buried in Sunrise Memorial Gardens Cemetery on Highway 242 Between Roseboro and Salemburg, Sampson County, North Carolina. The name of their son was provided by a relative. Their daughter, Clarise (Clarice) Fay married Owen Fed Matthews, Jr.

Children of Clyda Holland and Dewitt Simmons are:

1499 i. **Matthew Simmons.**

\+ 1500 ii. **Clarise Fay Simmons**, born 30 April 1937 in McDaniels Township, Sampson County, North Carolina.

653. Laudie Mae Holland (Henry[5], Stephen Senter[4], Henry[3], Thomas William[2], Unknown[1]) was born 20 October 1912 in Sampson County, North Carolina, and died 22 August 1993 in Mary-Gran Nursing Center, Clinton, Sampson County, North Carolina. She married **Ransom Bluen Holland**, son of Rufus Holland and Della A.Lee. He was born 20 April 1910 in Sampson County, North Carolina, and died 19 October 1997 in Sampson Regional Medical Center, Clinton, Sampson County, North Carolina.

Laudie Mae died from Urosepsis. She and Ransom were buried in Zoar Pentecostal Free Will Baptist Church Cemetery, Salemburg, North Carolina.

Children of Laudie Holland and Ransom Holland are:

1501 i. **Geraldine Holland**. She married Unknown McGough.

1502 ii. **Anglo Dixon Holland**, born 05 May 1935 in Sampson County, North Carolina. He married **Barbara Faircloth**; born About 1936.

654. Letha Pearl Holland (Henry[5], Stephen Senter[4], Henry[3], Thomas William[2], Unknown[1]) was born 08 April 1915 in Honeycutts Township, Sampson County, North Carolina, and died April 2001. She married **Lambert Baggett** 15 September 1944 in Honeycutts Township, Sampson County, North Carolina, son of Worth Baggett and Ella Warren. He was born 03 July 1916 in Mingo Township, Sampson County, North Carolina, and died 08 July 1981 in Durham, North Carolina.

Letha Pearl and Lamber were buried in Salemburg Cemetery, Salemburg, Sampson County, North Carolina.

Children of Letha Holland and Lambert Baggett are:

1503 i. **Gwendolyn Sue Baggett**, born 04 September 1945 in Roseboro, North Carolina.

She married a "Perry" and lived in Mt. Airy.

1504 ii. **Tony Baggett**. He lived in Massachusetts.

665. Miles Clayton Holland (Miles[5], Stephen Senter[4], Henry[3], Thomas William[2], Unknown[1]) was born 30 September 1918 in Honeycutts Township, Sampson County, North Carolina, and died 22 August 1993 in Honeycutts Township, Sampson County, North Carolina. He married **Christine Tyndall** 13 February 1960.

He served in the Navy in WWII and later was a Produce Broker in Florida. It is thought that he died of a myocardial infarction. He was buried in Zoar Pentecostal Free Will Baptist Church Cemetery, Salemburg, North Carolina.

Children of Miles Holland and Christine Tyndall are:

1505 i. **Daughter Holland.**

1506 ii. **Ricky Clayton Holland**, born 10 February 1954.

1507 iii. **Timmy McLamb Holland**.

671. Eva D. Warren (Angolda[5] Holland, Stephen Senter[4], Henry[3], Thomas William[2], Unknown[1]) was born 20 May 1923 in Sampson County, North Carolina and died 3 November 2008. She married **(1) Earl Smith** who was born about 1920, and died about 1945. She married **(2) William Brady Johnson** who was born 5 June 1921 and died 7 June 1999. Eva and William Brady were buried in Sunrise Memorial Gardens on Highway 242 between Salemburg and Roseboro, North Carolina.

Children of Eva Warren and Earl Smith are:

1508 i. **Lanae Smith**, born about 1946. She married William Joseph Fowler; born 04 October 1945.

1509 ii. **Columbus Smith.**

Child of Eva Warren and Brady Johnson is:

1510 i. **Juan Johnson**.

676. Elizabeth Inez Holland (Stephen Senter[5], Stephen Senter[4], Henry[3], Thomas William[2], Unknown[1]) was born 21 October 1927. She married **Tommie Anderson Benson** 1944. He was born 29 December 1920, and died 27 July 2002.

Child of Elizabeth Holland and Tommie Benson is:

\+ 1511 i. **Sheilafaye Benson**, born 02 December 1952.

688. Addie Mae Holland (Malette[5], Joel[4], John[3], Thomas William[2], Unknown[1]) was born 20 October 1910 in Sampson County, North Carolina, and died 14 October 1982 in Fayetteville, North Carolina. She married **George Washington Bain, Sr.** 24 April 1926 in Flea Hill Township, Cumberland County, North Carolina, son of Daniel Bain and Nannie Bolton. He was born 19 May 1907.

Children of Addie Holland and **George Bain are:**

1512 **i.** **George** Washington Bain, Jr., born 22 March 1927 in Duke Township, Harnett County, North Carolina. He married Mattie Grace Cook; born 25 August 1933 in Coats, Harnett County, North Carolina.

Two children.

1513 ii. **Lila Mae Bain**, born 17 November 1930 in Averasboro Township, Harnett County, North Carolina.

1514 iii. **Loyd E. Bain**, born 29 October 1933; died 29 October 1933.

1515 iv. **James Arthur Bain**, born 15 July 1935 in Wade, Cumberland County, North Carolina.

1516 v. **Elma Mae Bain**, born 16 June 1937 in Wade, Cumberland County, North Carolina. She married Gene Allen Belflowers; born About 1939 in Florence County, South Carolina.

Four children.

1517 vi. **Lydia Carlene Bain**, born 18 May 1949 in Dunn, Harnett County, North Carolina.

Generation Number 6

699. Sabra Jane Holland (Calton Walker[6], William[5], James[4], Daniel[3], Thomas William[2], Unknown[1]) was born 16 September 1887 in Sampson County, North Carolina, and died 07 December 1961 in Sampson County, North Carolina. She married **Challie Cleveland Holland** 12 February 1908 in Residence of Bride's father, Sampson County, North Carolina, son of Jordan Holland and Mary Autry. He was born 17 October 1886 in Sampson County, North Carolina, and died 13 November 1957 in Clinton, Sampson County, North Carolina.

Her nickname was 'Janie.' Challie died of carcinoma. He and Sabra were buried in Salemburg Cemetery, Salemburg, Sampson County, North Carolina.

Children are listed above under (271) Challie Cleveland Holland.

704. Crayon Dewitt Holland (Calton Walker[6], William[5], James[4], Daniel[3], Thomas William[2], Unknown[1]) was born 30 July 1902 in Sampson County, North Carolina. She married **Hughie Lee Autry** before 1937, son of James Autry and Etta Faircloth. He was born 23 October 1898, and died 09 June 1972.

Crayon Dewitt and Hughie were buried in the George Horne Cemetery near intersection of South River Road and Minnie Hall Road, Sampson County, North Carolina

Children of Crayon Holland and Hughie Autry are:

1518 i. **Dora Dean Holland**, born 22 September 1924 in Honeycutts Township, Sampson County, North Carolina , married **Earl Gilbert Howard** who was born 07 June 1925 in Dismal Township, Sampson County, North Carolina.

Four children.

\+ 1519 ii. **Arthur Vance Autry**, born 23 April 1937.

\+ 1520 iii. **Lois Blanche Autry**, born 19 May 1939.

1521 iv. **Jeanette Autry**, born 19 November 1940.

\+ 1522 v. **Irland Lee Autry**, born 25 January 1944.

706. Shepard Rose Holland (William James[6], William[5], James[4], Daniel[3], Thomas William[2], Unknown[1]) was born 06 September 1888, and died 21 September 1966 in Sampson County, North Carolina. He married **(1) Bessie Clyde Holland** about 1913. She was born about 1896. He married **(2) Lillie Barbrey** before 1920. She was born about 1892.

Sheproe and Shep Rose are often found for his name. Barber and Barby are found for Lillie's maiden name.

Children of Shepard Holland and Bessie Holland are:

1523 i. **Clifton Holland**, born 03 September 1914; died 1936.

1524 ii. **Ruby Jackson Holland**, born 08 July 1915.

Children of Shepard Holland and Lillie Barbrey are:

1525 i. **Lovette Holland**, born about 1921.

1526 ii. **Stacy Holland**, born about 1923.

1527 iii. **Randale Holland**, born 10 May 1925; died 03 June 1975.

1528 iv. **Maggie Holland**, born 02 January 1929. She married Unknown Byrd.

1529 v. **William Owen Holland**, born 04 August 1932; died 16 September 1996.

716. Lydia Curl Holland (William James[6], William[5], James[4], Daniel[3], Thomas William[2], Unknown[1]) was born 15 August 1910 in Sampson County, North Carolina. She married **Grady Henderson.**

Child of Lydia Holland and Grady Henderson is:

1530 i. **Mary Sue Henderson**.

720. Percy Benson Holland (Lewis Benson[6], William[5], James[4], Daniel[3], Thomas William[2], Unknown[1]) was born 09 August 1912 in Sampson County, North Carolina, and died 28

October 1996 in Sampson County, North Carolina. He married **Alice Grey Daughtry**. She was born 17 May 1917, and died 06 November 1964.

"Percy Benton" and "Perry Benson" Holland are found for his name and the 9 August 1904 for his birth.

He and Alice were buried in The Clinton Cemetery, Clinton, Sampson County, North Carolina.

Children of Percy Holland and Alice Daughtry are:

+ 1531 i. **Michael Terrance Holland**, born 02 April 1942.

  1532 ii. **Jonathan Gregg Holland**, born 26 November 1956 in Clinton, North Carolina.

  1533 iii. **Percy Trent Holland.**

  1534 iv. **Kirk Walton Holland.**

726. Reba Mae Holland (Lewis Benson^6, William^5, James^4, Daniel^3, Thomas William^2, Unknown^1) was born 25 February 1921 in Honeycutts Township, Sampson County, North Carolina. She married **Amos Harrison Royal** Before 1945, son of Harrison Hanstein Royal and Lela Holland. He was born 16 January 1921 in Herrings Township, Sampson County, North Carolina, and died 28 October 1986 in Clinton, Sampson County, North Carolina.

The tombstone of Amos Harrison Royal shows October 29, 1986 for his date of death; he was buried in Hollywood Cemetery.

Child of Reba Holland and Amos Royal is:

+ 1535 i. **Mary Gail Royal**, born 17 July 1945 in Roseboro, Sampson County, North Carolina.

730. John William Holland (Bryant B.^{6}, Thomas James^5, James^4, Daniel^3, Thomas William^2, Unknown^1) was born 12 July 1897 in Sampson County, North Carolina, and died 01 September 1977 in Selma, Johnston County, North Carolina. He married **Bertie Victoria Vann** 28 May 1922 in Ingold Township, Sampson County, North Carolina, daughter of Moody Vann and Katie Carter. She was born about 1899 in Sampson County, North Carolina, and died November 1973 in Selma, Johnston County, North Carolina.

Berta is also found for Bertie's first name.

Children of John Holland and Bertie Vann are:

+ 1536 i. **William Radford Holland,** born 27 September 1923 in Smithfield, Johnston County, North Carolina.

+ 1537 ii. **Arthur Orell Holland**, born in Johnston County, North Carolina.

+ 1538 iii. **Marion Grady Holland**, born in Johnston County, North Carolina.

731. Lattie Rudesel Holland (Bryant B.[6], Thomas James[5], James[4], Daniel[3], Thomas William[2], Unknown[1]) was born 23 July 1900, and died 1965. He married **Marna Rose Blanchard** 24 May 1925 in North Clinton, Sampson County, North Carolina. She was born 1905, and died 1974.

Lattie Rudesel and Marna were buried in Clement Missionary Baptist Church Cemetery on Maxwell Road (SR1006) about 0.5 mile west of SR 1425 in Sampson County, North Carolina.

Children of Lattie Holland and Marna Blanchard are:

+ 1539 i. **Thurman A. Holland, born** about 1926.
+ 1540 ii. **Nelda Holland**, born about 1927.
+ 1541 iii. **Thelma Jane Holland**, born 21 September 1928 in Little Coharie Township, Sampson County, North Carolina.
+ 1542 iv. **Melba Eulane Holland**.

1543 v. **Donnie Holland**. He married **Kathy Weeks**.

No children. "B." may be his initial for his middle name.

1544 vi. **Shirley Rose Holland**. She married **Dale Lewis**.

No children.

732. Robert Elliott Holland (Bryant B.[6], Thomas James[5], James[4], Daniel[3], Thomas William[2], Unknown[1]) was born 08 September 1903, and died 15 December 1973 in Cumberland County, North Carolina. He married **Jennie Mae Hubbard**. She was born 03 April 1905, and died 23 March 1949 in Cumberland County, North Carolina.

His tombstone may have 1972 for his year of death and Jennie's tombstone may have 03 April 1908 for date of birth and 24 March 1950 for her date of death. They were buried in Magnolia Baptist Church Cemetery on Magnolia Baptist Church Road (SR 1843), Stedman, North carolina.

Children of Robert Holland and Jennie Hubbard are:

+ 1545 i. **Margaret Holland**, born 11 September 1925.
+ 1546 ii. **Audry Iretice Holland**, born 03 July 1931 in Cedar Creek Township, Cumberland County, North Carolina.
+ 1547 iii. **Betty Lee Holland**, born 07 February 1935.

735. Tabitha Hazel Holland (Bryant B.[6], Thomas James[5], James[4], Daniel[3], Thomas William[2], Unknown[1]) was born 21 November 1911. She married **Alfred Autry**.

Children of Tabitha Holland and Alfred Autry are:

1548 i. **Delane Autry**.

1549 ii. **Charles Autry.**

1550 iii. **Billie Autry.**

\+ 1551 iv. **Linda Hazel Autry.**

736. Mildred Holland (Bryant B.^{6}, Thomas James^{5}, James^{4}, Daniel^{3}, Thomas William^{2}, Unknown^{1}) was born 12 September 1914. She married **Thadeus Barefoot**. He was born 29 August 1907.

Children of Mildred Holland and Thadeus Barefoot are:

1552 i. **James Franklin Barefoot**, born 28 September 1937; died 06 June 1955.

\+ 1553 ii. **David Carmen Barefoot**, born 02 January 1942.

739. William Percy Holland (Richard Lee^{6}, Thomas James^{5}, James^{4}, Daniel^{3}, Thomas William^{2}, Unknown^{1}) was born 08 January 1899, and died 23 March 1965 in Hope Mills, Cumberland County, North Carolina. He married **Eulellan L. Beard** 26 December 1923 in Fayetteville, Cumberland County, North Carolina, daughter of James Beard and Margaret Bryant. She was born 18 September 1903, and died 30 June 1957 in Eastover Township, Cumberland County, North Carolina.

In the 1910 census, her name appears to be: "Eulellan L." Her tombstone may read "Bulla Beard Holland."

William Percy and Eulellan were buried in Magnolia Baptist Church Cemetery on Magnolia Baptist Church Road (SR 1843), Stedman, North carolina.

Children of William Holland and Eulellan Beard are:

1554 i. **Violet Nadine Holland**, born 17 September 1926 in Flea Hill Township, Cumberland County, North Carolina. She married **Thomas H. Hall**.

1555 ii. **William Ward Holland, Sr.**, born 02 February 1929 in Cedar Creek Township, Cumberland County, North Carolina. He married **Minnie Lea Farr** 16 April 1949 in Fayetteville, Cumberland County, North Carolina; born 17 April 1929 in Fayetteville, North Carolina.

One child: **William Ward Holland, Jr.** was born 7 July 1950 in Fayetteville. He married first **Susan Dudley** who was born about 1953 in Kentucky. He and Susan had one child, **Constance Renee Holland** who was born 9 April 1969 in Fayetteville. Divorced, William married second **Gwendolyn Sue Rogers** on 26 January 1975; she was born 13 May 1957 in Kershaw County, South Carolina, daughter of Raphu Rogers and Annie Mae Scott. William and Gwendolyn had one child, **Christina Nichole Holland** who was born 21 April 1978 in Fayetteville.

741. Lonnie Edward Holland (Richard Lee^{6}, Thomas James^{5}, James^{4}, Daniel^{3}, Thomas William^{2}, Unknown^{1}) was born 16 May 1902, and died 03 January 1977 in Fayetteville, Cumberland County, North Carolina. He married **Daisy Sealey**. She was born 10 July 1909, and died 10 October 1996.

Lonnie Edward and Daisy were buried in Maxwell Cemetery, Clement, Sampson County, North Carolina.

Children of Lonnie Holland and Daisy Sealey are:

1556 i. **Dorothy Maxine Holland**, born 03 August 1925 in Flea Hill Township, Cumberland County, North Carolina. She married first **Charles Fields Blair** and second, **William Chester Andrews** who was born about 1931.

Dorothy and Charles had three children:

1) **Larry Fields Blair**, born 8 October 1946 in Fayetteville, North Carolina.

2) **Cary Gray Glair** was born 1 January 1948 in Fayetteville.

3) **Terry Mitchell Blair** was born 27 November 1950 in Fayetteville.

Dorothy and William had two children:

1) **Marcia Jane Andrews**, born 17 March 1953 in Fayetteville.

2) **Mary Ann Andrews**, born 7 November 1962 in Fayetteville.

1557 ii. **Sabrina Denise Holland**, born 20 May 1927 in Flea Hill Township, Cumberland County, North Carolina. She married **Ernest Reece Smithman**.

One of her four children is known: **Sabrina Denise Smithman** who was born 14 December 1958 in Fayetteville.

1558 iii. **Edward Odell Holland**, born 11 January 1929 in Eastover Township, Cumberland County, North Carolina; died 09 October 1929 in Rockfish Township, Cumberland County, North Carolina.

He was buried in Maxwell Cemetery, southeast corner of Maxwell Road (SR 1006) and (SR 1427), Sampson County, North Carolina.

1559 iv. **Stillborn Daughter Holland,** born 23 May 1930 in Eastover Township, Cumberland County, North Carolina.

She was buried in Maxwell Cemetery, southeast corner of Maxwell Road (SR 1006) and (SR 1427), Sampson County, North Carolina.

746. Lottis Turner Holland (William Thomas[6], Thomas James[5], James[4], Daniel[3], Thomas William[2], Unknown[1]) was born 14 December 1902, and died 24 November 1988 in Clinton, Sampson County, North Carolina. He married **(1) Eva Clyde Lewis** 03 May 1924 in South Clinton, Sampson County, North Carolina, daughter of Alfred Lewis and Narena Spell. She was born 12 August 1905, and died 19 January 1956 in Clinton, Sampson County, North Carolina. He married **(2) Wilma Estelle Autry** After 1961, daughter of James Autry and Miranda Hall. She was born 28 October 1921 in Little Coharie Township, Sampson County, North Carolina, and died 13 March 1993.

Lottis Turner, Eve Clyde, and Wilma Estelle were buried in Hall's United Methodist Church Cemetery, 4 miles north of Autryville, North Carolina on SR 1414.

Child of Lottis Holland and Eva Lewis is:

\+ 1560 i. **Arrel Gipson Holland, Sr.**, born 25 April 1926 in Dismal Township, Sampson County, North Carolina.

747. Arizona T. Holland (William Thomas[6], Thomas James[5], James[4], Daniel[3], Thomas William[2], Unknown[1]) was born 01 July 1904, and died 07 May 1990. She married **William David Cannady** 16 September 1922 in Clinton, Sampson County, North Carolina, son of Randall Cannady and Doshie Tyndall. He was born 19 October 1902 in Dismal Township, Sampson County, North Carolina, and died 01 August 1927 in Dismal Township, Sampson County.

She is listed as "Ira J." in the 1910 Census. She and William David were buried in Union Grove Baptist Church Cemetery on SR 1438 one mile west of Rebel City, Sampson County, North Carolina.

Children of Arizona Holland and William Cannady are:

\+ 1561 i. **Aaron Cannady**, born 04 December 1923 in Dismal Township, Sampson County, North Carolina; died 26 November 1996 in Fayetteville, Cumberland County, North Carolina.

1562 ii. **William Crafton Cannady**, born 07 September 1926 in Dismal Township, Sampson County, North Carolina.

748. Ervin C. Holland (William Thomas[6], Thomas James[5], James[4], Daniel[3], Thomas William[2], Unknown[1]) was born About 1906. He married **Pauline A. Spell**. She was born About 1908.

Children of Ervin Holland and Pauline Spell are:

\+ 1563 i. **Irene Holland,** born 02 September 1926 in Dismal Township, Sampson County, North Carolina; died 15 October 1985.

1564 ii. **Polly Holland**. She married Unknown Kozma.

1565 iii. **Earl C. Holland**.

749. Angie Lee Holland (William Thomas[6], Thomas James[5], James[4], Daniel[3], Thomas William[2], Unknown[1]) was born 27 November 1907, and died 23 July 1979 in Clinton, Sampson County, North Carolina. She married **Rev. W. Oscar Honeycutt**. He was born 19 December 1904, and died 14 April 1991.

Angie Lee and Oscar are buried in the Old Mill Church of God Cemetery, 2 1/2 miles SE of Midway, Sampson County, North Carolina.

Children of Angie Holland and W. Honeycutt are:

1566 i. **Evelene Honeycutt**. She married Unknown Brinkley.

1567 ii. **Oscar Honeycutt**.

1568 iii. **Elmon Honeycutt**.

His full name may be **Elmon Keith Honeycutt** noted elsewhere in this database.

1569 iv. **Rev. John T. Honeycutt**, born 13 May 1934 in Honeycutts Township, Sampson County, North Carolina. He married Lillie Mae P. Unknown; born 26 September 1931; died 27 May 2000.

He was buried in The Old Mill Church of God Cemetery on Penny Tew Mill Road, Sampson County, North Carolina.

1570 v. **Unknown Child Honeycutt.**

1571 vi. **Mavis Louise Honeycutt**, born 15 May 1938 in Herrings Township, Sampson County, North Carolina. She married Unknown Knowles.

1572 vii. **Unknown Second Honeycutt.**

1573 viii. **Virginia Lee Honeycutt**, born 29 June 1941 in Herrings Township, Sampson County, North Carolina. She married **Lattie Earl Matthews**; born 27 May 1936 in Dismal Township, Sampson County, North Carolina.

750. Herman Crosby Holland (William Thomas[6], Thomas James[5], James[4], Daniel[3], Thomas William[2], Unknown[1]) was born 01 November 1909, and died 15 November 1992. He married **(1) Hepsey Trilma Honeycutt** About 1931, daughter of Richard Honeycutt and Stella Hayes. She was born 17 June 1914 in Dismal Township, Sampson County, North Carolina, and died 01 October 1963 in Near Salemburg, Sampson County, North Carolina. He married **(2) Issiebell Jackson** After 1963. She was born 09 April 1915, and died 14 September 1975.

"Hermon" is also found for his name. "Hepsia" is also found for Hepsey.

Herman Crosby, Hepsey and Issiebell were buried in Union Grove Baptist Church Cemetery on Vander Road (SR 1438) Sampson County, North Carolina.

Children of Herman Holland and Hepsey Honeycutt are:

\+ 1574 i. **Alice Freeman Holland**, born 10 July 1932 in Dismal Township, Sampson County, North Carolina.

1575 ii. **Martha M. Holland**, born 11 September 1934 in Dismal Township, Sampson County, North Carolina; died 14 November 1934 in Dismal Township, Sampson County.

She was buried in Union Grove Baptist Church Cemetery on Vander Road (SR 1438) Sampson County, North Carolina.

1576 iii. **Emma Jane Holland**, born 16 May 1936 in Roseboro, Sampson County, North Carolina; died 17 July 1936.

Her tombstone shows May 13, 1936 for her date of birth and "**Almeter Holland**" for her name.

Buried at Union Grove Baptist Church Cemetery on Vander Road (SR 1438) Sampson County, North Carolina.

Child of Herman Holland and Issiebell Jackson is:

1577 i. **Curtis Ray Jackson.**

751. Euland Randolph Holland (William Thomas[6], Thomas James[5], James[4], Daniel[3], Thomas William[2], Unknown[1]) was born 20 June 1912 in Clinton, Sampson County, North

Carolina, and died 22 July 1989. He married **Ida Marie Draughon** 29 October 1932 in Dillon, South Carolina, daughter of Wiley C. Draughon and Cornelia Naylor. She was born 13 September 1916 in Honeycutts Township, Sampson County, North Carolina, and died 24 October 2001 in Sampson County, North Carolina.

Euland Randolph and Ida Marie were buried in Calvary Tabernacle PFB Church Cemetery, 1 mile from intersection of Hwy 242 and High House Road, Sampson County, North Carolina.

Children of Euland Holland and Ida Draughon are:

+ 1578 i. **Vernon Holland**, born 14 April 1934 in Honeycutts Township, Sampson County, North Carolina.

+ 1579 ii. **Glenn Turner Holland**, born 28 August 1944 in Honeycutts Township, Sampson County, North Carolina; died 10 May 2007 in Sampson County, North Carolina.

754. Cleo Pearl Holland (William Thomas[6], Thomas James[5], James[4], Daniel[3], Thomas William[2], Unknown[1]) was born 15 October 1916 in Salemburg, Sampson County, North Carolina, and died 13 November 1985 in Route 1, Salemburg, Sampson County, North Carolina. She married **Quinton Butler** Before 1940, son of Miles Butler and Estella Honeycutt. He was born 06 August 1916, and died 19 August 1974 in Route 1, Salemburg, Sampson County, North Carolina.

Cleo Pearl and Quinton were buried in Union Grove Baptist Church Cemetery on Vander Road one mile west of Rebel City, Sampson County, North Carolina

Children of Cleo Holland and Quinton Butler are:

+ 1580 i. **Janice F. Butler**, born 25 June 1940 in Guilford County, North Carolina; died 28 August 1984 in Wake County, North Carolina.

1581 ii. **Patsy R. Butler**. She married Unknown Martin.

1582 iii. **Lynda Kay Butler**, born 02 November 1942; died 22 September 1943.

Lynda Lee Butler is the name on her gravestone. She was buried in Union Grove Baptist Church Cemetery on Vander Road one mile west of Rebel City, Sampson County, North Carolina.

+ 1583 iv. **Harold Tex Butler**, born 17 October 1945 in Greensboro, North Carolina.

+ 1584 v. **Brenda Marie Butler,** born 27 March 1948 in Roseboro, Sampson County, North Carolina.

1585 vi. **Edgar L. Butler**, born 24 June 1952 in Clinton, Sampson County, North Carolina.

1586 vii. **Quinton Travis Butler**, born 23 March 1955 in Clinton, Sampson County, North Carolina.

755. Eloise Holland (William Thomas[6], Thomas James[5], James[4], Daniel[3], Thomas William[2], Unknown[1]) was born 28 August 1918 in Dismal Township, Sampson County, North Carolina, and died 29 October 1978 in Route 1, Autryville, North Carolina. She married **James Clayton Howard** 20 July 1935 in Clinton, Sampson County, North Carolina, son of James Howard and Carrie Matthews. He was born 12 May 1914 in Dismal Township, Sampson County, North Carolina, and died 25 September 2000.

Eloise's tombstone shows August 29, 1918 for her birth. Louise is also found for her name in some records. She and James were buried in Union Grove Baptist Church Cemetery on Vander Road one mile west of Rebel City, Sampson County, North Carolina.

Children of Eloise Holland and James Howard are:

1587 i. **Leonard Gilbert Howard**, born 27 March 1936 in Dismal Township, Sampson County, North Carolina. He married **Naomi Bell Boyette**; born 14 February 1935 in Honeycutts Township, Sampson County, North Carolina.

In 1978, Leonard lived in Georgia. Three children.

\+ 1588 ii. **James Thomas Howard**, born 22 June 1942 in Roseboro, North Carolina.

757. Ella May Holland (William Thomas[6], Thomas James[5], James[4], Daniel[3], Thomas William[2], Unknown[1]) was born 22 August 1923 in Dismal Township, Sampson County, North Carolina. She married **Ollen Alton Tyndall**. He was born about 1920.

Ollen Alton may be the son of Ollen B. Tyndall and Nancy Elizabeth Edwards and was born 1919, died 2004 and was buried in the Tyndall Cemetery on SR 1329 in Sampson County, North Carolina.

Children of Ella Holland and Ollen Tyndall are:

1589 i. **Geronia Carolyn Tyndall**, born 19 March 1944 in Roseboro, Sampson County, North Carolina.

1590 ii. **David Alton Tyndall**, born 30 August 1946 in Honeycutts Township, Sampson County, North Carolina.

1591 iii. **Unknown Tyndall.**

1592 iv. **Maedean T. Tyndall**, born 02 December 1952 in Roseboro, Sampson County, North Carolina.

759. Viola Gertrude Page (Louetta J.[6] Holland, Thomas James[5], James[4], Daniel[3], Thomas William[2], Unknown[1]) was born 20 September 1905, and died 18 June 1988 in Sampson County, North Carolina. She married **Atticus Marvin Matthews** 16 October 1924 in Fayetteville, Cumberland County, North Carolina, son of Lewis Matthews and Lena Culbreth. He was born 16 October 1903, and died 09 August 1988 in Clinton, Sampson County, North Carolina.

Children of Viola Page and Atticus Matthews are:

1593 i. **Leona Marjorie Matthews**, born 23 January 1926. She married **D. C. Vinson**; born 08 August 1926 in Beaver Dam Township.

Three children.

1) **Marjorie Faye Vinson**, born 17 July 1948 in Fayetteville, married **Thomas E. Sherril** from Arkansas and they had one child, **James Clark Sherrill**, born 15 January 1975.

2) **Connie Lou Vinson**, born 15 June 1953 in Fayetteville, married **Tommy Hall.**

3) **Donovan Clark Vinson**, born 27 December 1954 in Fayetteville, married **Cathy Jane Tatum**, in Cedar Creek Township in Cumberland County, North Carolina on 21 May 1977. She was the daughter of **Harry Atwood Tatum** and **Catherine Emmett Denson**. Cathy was born 20 February 1955 in Fayetteville; she and Donovan had one known child, **Mary Catherine Vinson**, born 29 April 1981 in Fayetteville.

1594 ii. **Aletha Crystelle Matthews**, born 03 March 1928. She married **Drew Simon Smith**; born about 1924.

Seven children.

1) **Judy Annette Smith**, born 15 September 1947 in Roseboro, married in Beaver Dam Township, Cumberland County, North Carolina , **Gerald Haney** on 30 January 1971. He was the son of Lester Haney and Ennis Faircloth and was born 23 February 1947 in Little Coharie Township in Sampson County, North Carolina. Judy and Gerald had two children, **Donnie Gerald Haney II**, born 25 March 1973 in Fayetteville, and **Carrie Annette Haney**, born 28 October 1976 in Fayetteville.

2) **Harold Douglass Smith,** born 12 April 1949 in Roseboro, married **Merlyn Gail Riley**, daughter of Seavy Pershing Riley and Margaret Elizabeth Crescoe. Merlyn was born 9 August 1950 in Roseboro. Two children: **Harold Douglas Smith, Jr.**, born 13 April 1971 and **Christy Lane Smith**, born 21 January 1975; both born in Fayetteville.

3) **Franklin Atticus Smith,** born 15 January 1952 in Roseboro, married **Sandra Carol Serrano** on 25 November 1973 in Fayetteville. She was born 8 October 1953 at Fort Campbell, Kentucky, daughter of James D. Serrano and Roselynd G. O'Meara.

4) **Leonard James Smith,** born 19 January 1954 in Roseboro, North Carolina.

5) **Marion Earl Smith**, born 26 September 1956 in Roseboro married **Janet Elaine Melvin** in Beaver Dam Township on 25 September 1976 She was born 27 January 1959 near Fayetteville, daughter of Gaither Fulton Melvin and Evelyn Gladys Smith.

6) **Mary Alice Smith**, born 12 November 1958 in Roseboro, married 6 January 1980 in Beaver Dam Baptist Church, **Donald Ray Underwood**. He was born 17 June 1959 near Fayetteville, son of Raeford Wesley Underwood and Ruby Odell Williams.

7) **Arnold Drew Smith**, 11 October 1962 in Fayetteville.

1595 iii. **Etta Mae Matthews,** third child of Viola Gertrude Page and Atticus Marvin Matthews, was born 26 July 1929. She married **Prince Charles Bullard**; born 23 April 1927. Son of **Henry P. Bullard** and **Maggie G. Spell**.

Five children.

1) **Charles Richard Bullard**, born 5 October 1950 in Cumberland County, North Carolina, married **Marty Rose Bradshaw** on 6 June 1976 in Elizabeth Baptist Church. She was born 21 March 1955 in Clinton, North Carolina, daughter of Haywood Milton Bradshaw and Marguerite Pate.

2) **Johnnie Ray Bullard,** born 7 December 1951 in Fayetteville.

3) **Teresa Diane Bullard,** born 13 July 1954 in Fayetteville.

4) **Sharon Mae Bullard**, born 16 August 1956 in Fayetteville.

5) **Trudy Viola Bullard,** born 2 May 1960 in Fayetteville, married Clevin Toman, Jr. on 20 July 1980 in Beaver Dam Township. He was born 30 August 1958 in Fayetteville, son of William Clevin Toman and Elsie Maxine Alphin.

1596 iv. **Claris Gertrude Matthews**, born 10 March 1931 in Dismal Township, Sampson County, North Carolina; died 18 November 1947.

Buried in Clement Baptist Church Cemetery, Sampson County, North Carolina.

760. Ethel Elizabeth Autry (Frances Elizabeth[6] Holland, Thomas James[5], James[4], Daniel[3], Thomas William[2], Unknown[1]) was born 22 September 1900 in Sampson County, North Carolina, and died 14 December 1979. She married **Harvey G. Grantham** 23 December 1920, son of Needham Grantham and Nancy Cannady. He was born 16 June 1896 in Sampson County, North Carolina, and died 23 September 1960.

Ethel Elizabeth and Harvey were buried in John Autry Family Cemetery, Clement Community, Sampson County, North Carolina.

Children of Ethel Autry and Harvey Grantham are:

+ 1597 i. **Edith Lee Grantham**, born 29 November 1922.

1598 ii. **Stillborn Daughter Grantham**, born 19 May 1924; died 19 May 1924.

1599 iii. **Delbert Lennis Grantham**, born 26 July 1926; died 29 November 1929 in Sampson County, North Carolina.

Burial in the Autry Cemetery on Autry Mill Road (SR 1446) about one mile from Clement in Sampson County, North Carolina.

+ 1600 iv. **Lee Ronald Grantham**, born 07 August 1929.

+ 1601 v. **Mac Donald Grantham**, born 07 August 1929.

+ 1602 vi. **Eulas Gilbert Grantham**, born 04 August 1934.

762. Millard Filmore Holland (Bernice Culbreth[6], Thomas James[5], James[4], Daniel[3], Thomas William[2], Unknown[1]) was born 09 December 1910, and died 27 March 1987 in Clinton, Sampson County, North Carolina. He married **Livie Mae Tew** 28 April 1934 in Clinton, Sampson County, daughter of Lewis Tew and Martha Beasley. She was born 27 July 1908, and died 05 July 1969 in Clinton, North Carolina.

Millard "Fillmore" Holland is also found for his name. He and Livie were buried in Robert's Grove Baptist Church Cemetery near Spivey's Corner, Sampson County, North Carolina.

Children of Millard Holland and Livie Tew are:

1603 i. **Infant Son Holland**, born 25 February 1939 in Mingo Township, Sampson County, North Carolina; died 25 February 1939 and is buried in a Family Cemetery.

+ 1604 ii. **Brenda Frances Holland**, born 02 March 1942 in Mingo Township, Sampson County, North Carolina.

+ 1605 iii. **Judith Elaine Holland**, born 17 February 1945 in Mingo Township, Sampson County, North Carolina.

1606 iv. **Second Infant Son Holland**.

1607 v. **Third Infant Son Holland**.

763. James Adam Holland (Bernice Culbreth[6], Thomas James[5], James[4], Daniel[3], Thomas William[2], Unknown[1]) was born About 1911, and died before 1976. He married **Etta Autry** 09 January 1932 in Clinton, Sampson County, North Carolina, daughter of George Autry and Mary Daniel. She was born about 1914.

Children of James Holland and Etta Autry are:

1608 i. **Stillborn Daughter Holland**, born 17 November 1932 in Dismal Township, Sampson County, North Carolina.

1609 ii. **Joyce Christeen Holland**, born 07 September 1935 in Dismal Township, Sampson County.

1610 iii. **Mary Jo Holland**, born Before 01 April 1937 in Little Coharie Township, Sampson County, North Carolina.

1611 iv. **Helen Jean Holland**, born 26 September 1938 in Dismal Township, Sampson County; died 24 June 1941.

Buried in Williams Family Cemetery northeast of Clement in Dismal Township near Dunn Road (SR1002) at SR1441 in Sampson County, North Carolina.

1612 v. **Clara Patricia Holland**, born 26 September 1940 in Dismal Township, Sampson County, North Carolina.

1613 vi. **James Clyde Holland**, born 27 April 1942 in Dismal Township, Sampson County; died 11 May 1942.

Transcribed cemetery records shows April 17, 1942 for his birth and April 31, 1942 for his death.

Buried in Mingo Township, Sampson County, North Carolina.

764. Ruby Jane Holland (Bernice Culbreth[6], Thomas James[5], James[4], Daniel[3], Thomas William[2], Unknown[1]) was born 02 December 1913 in Dismal Township, Sampson County, North Carolina. She married **(1) Joseph Everette Edwards, Sr.** 25 June 1937 in Salemburg Sampson County, son of Joseph Edwards and Annie Jackson. He was born 15 October 1913, and died 10 July 1941 in Fayetteville, Cumberland County, North Carolina. She married **(2) Perry Donald Lyon** after 1941.

"Lynn" is also found for Perry's surname.

Joseph Everette was buried in the Sampson E. Jackson Family Cemetery.

Children of Ruby Holland and Joseph Edwards are:

1614 i. **Dorothy Ann Edwards**, born 29 March 1938 in Mingo Township, Sampson County, North Carolina.

1615 ii. **Joseph Everette Edwards, Jr.**, born 10 May 1941 in Dismal Township, Sampson County.

Child of Ruby Holland and Perry Lyon is:

1616 i. **Loretta Gray Lyon**. She married **Ronald Blake Warren.**

767. Nellie Holland (Bernice Culbreth[6], Thomas James[5], James[4], Daniel[3], Thomas William[2], Unknown[1]) was born 27 August 1920 in Dismal Township, Sampson

County, North Carolina. Nellie may have married **Henry Hubert Hairr**, son of **John Oliver Hairr** and **Annie Lee Horne.** Henry Hubert was born 18 July 1913 in Sampson County and died 9 July 1992 in Dunn, Harnett County, North Carolina.

Mr. Rosser's book, "Coharie to Cape Fear" records that **Hubert Hairr** who was born about 1910 married Nellie Holland and records appear to indicate that Mr. Rosser **incorrectly names Braston Hairr and Ressie Bass** for Hubert's parents. I have rarely found errors in Mr. Rosser's research, yet this one error built a nasty brick wall for me and by the time I found it and found sufficient data for the sparse information presented here for Nellie and Henry Hubert, I had a few doubts about my sanity.

The North Carolina Birth Index, 1800-2000, indicates that **Henry Hubert Hairr**, son of John Oliver Hairr, was born 18 July 1913 in Sampson County and a North Carolina Death Collection records that this Henry Hubert Hairr died 9 July 1992 at the age of 78 in Dunn, Harnett County, North Carolina. He was married at the time of death, but his actual certificate of death needs to be reviewed to determine the name of his wife at the time he died.

In another source, Mr. Rosser records that Hubert Bee Hairr, son of William Braston Hairr and Ressie Bass was born 16 October 1924 in Herrings Township, and died in June 1986 in Clinton, Sampson County, North Carolina; he names Margaret Lee Peterson who was born in November 1927 in Lisbon Township, daughter of Elliott Lee Peterson and Lillie Mae Bordeaux for Hubert's wife. When in doubt about what you find here, please follow up with your own research.

The 1930 census for Bernice Culbreth Holland and his wife, Lessie, does not list Nellie for a daughter. Yet, the North Carolina Birth Index, 1800-2000, does record the birth of Nellie Holland in 1919 or 1920(sic) in the Miscellaneous Volume, page 114, and names Bernice E. Holland for her parent. Was this Bernice E. the "Bernice C.," son of Thomas James or another Bernice? I have found no other record for Nellie and it appears that the data Mr. Rosser recorded for her children was probably told to him by someone who knew little about her and her husband. Nellie could have been visiting with grandparents in 1930.

Marriage records for Nellie and Margaret may support what I have entered here. In the event that my data for them is correct, Henry Hubert Hairr and Nellie Holland were very distant cousins through the descendants of three children of Thomas William Holland and his wife, Milley.

Margaret Lee Peterson was born in November 1927 and died 28 March 2005 at Wake Medical Center in Raleigh, North Carolina. Nellie Holland and her husband, Henry Hubert Hairr, were having their children in the same time period that Margaret Lee Peterson and her husband, Hubert Bee Hairr, were having their children. This strongly suggests that Henry Hubert Hairr and Hubert Bee Hairr were different men.

See Henry Hubert Hairr and also Margaret Lee Peterson and Hubert Bee Hairr elsewhere in this book.

Children of Nellie Holland and Henry Hubert Hairr are:

1617 i. **Billy Hairr.**

1618 ii. **Charles Hairr.**

1619 iii. **Patsy Hairr,** born about 1943.

Patsy married a doctor from Winston-Salem.

1620 iv. **Unknown Daughter Hairr.** She married **Edward Register.**

780. Leslie B. Holland (Lalister R.[6], Bluman[5], Harfrey[4], Daniel[3], Thomas William[2], Unknown[1]) was born 24 November 1907, and died 08 March 1993. He married **Thelma Inez Taylor** 16 February 1935. She was born 17 January 1912, and died 04 March 1997.

Leslie B. Pneumonia. Parkinson's disease. Thelma died from a Cerebrovascular accident (stroke) and Acute myocardial infarction. Both wee buried in Zoar PFW Baptist Church Cemetery near Salemburg, North Carolina.

Child of Leslie Holland and Thelma Taylor is:

\+ 1621 i. **Preston Pedro Holland,** born 20 December 1938.

784. Myrtle Holland (Rufus Addison[6], Bluman[5], Harfrey[4], Daniel[3], Thomas William[2], Unknown[1]) was born 13 September 1902, and died 18 June 1975. She married **Robbie Clifton Hairr,** son of Archie Hairr and Unknown Spouse. He was born 06 November 1904, and died 15 November 1990.

Also listed for her Date of Birth is 3 September 1902 and 15 November 1988 is also found for Robbie's death. Myrtle and Robbie were buried in Zoar FWBP Church Cemetery Near Salemburg, North Carolina.

Children of Myrtle and Robbie:

Bettie E. Hairr was born 1929.

Rufus Clifton Hairr was born 31 January 1932 and died 5 August 1991. He married Glenda C. (maiden name unknown) on 17 June 1956. She was born 1 February 1938. Rufus was buried in Zoar Pentecostal FW Baptist Church cemetery on Zoar Church Road (SR 1322) near Salemburg in Sampson county, North Carolina.

786. Ransom Bluen Holland (Rufus Addison[6], Bluman[5], Harfrey[4], Daniel[3], Thomas William[2], Unknown[1]) was born 20 April 1910 in Sampson County, North Carolina, and died 19 October 1997 in Sampson Regional Medical Center, Clinton, Sampson County, North Carolina. He married **Laudie Mae Holland,** daughter of Henry Holland and Rossie Royal. She was born 20 October 1912 in Sampson County, North Carolina, and died 22 August 1993 in Mary-Gran Nursing Center, Clinton, Sampson County, North Carolina.

Laudie Mae's cause of death was Urosepsis. Ransom and Laudie Mae are buried in Zoar Pentecostal Free Will Baptist Church Cemetery, Salemburg, North Carolina.

Children are listed above under (653) Laudie Mae Holland.

798. Lester Frank Spell (Janie Isabell[6] Hairr, Franklin[5] Holland, Harfrey[4], Daniel[3], Thomas William[2], Unknown[1]) was born 07 August 1912, and died 11 November 1987. He married **Iruthie Warren**, daughter of ADD WARREN. She was born 10 February 1918, and died 23 June 1979.

Lester Frank and Iruthie had four children. They both were buried in a Spell Family Cemetery on Dunn Road North of Roseboro, North Carolina.

Children of Lester Spell and Iruthie Warren are:

1622 i. **Janie Margaret Spell**, born 07 January 1935. She married **JEROME J. WALKER**, who was born 24 September 1930 and they had four known children.

1) **DIANNE WALKER** was born 30 December 1952 and married **CRAIG LOVICK** who was born 22 June 1954. Dianne and Craig had one child, **BRIAN CRAIG LOVICK**, born 9 April 1973.

2) **JEROME J. WALKER, JR.** was born 31 July 1956 and married **HILDA** KAY BULLARD.

3) **RONALD KEITH WALKER** was born 22 December 1957.

4) **RODNEY WALKER** was born 17 March 1962.

1623 ii. **James Bertice Spell**, born 12 June 1938. He married **Elizabeth Royal**; born 12 September 1935, daughter of IVEY D. ROYAL and REBECCA HOLLINGSWORTH. One source names Elizabeth's parents as Ivy D. Royal and Roberta Hollingsworth. Two known children.

1) **JAMES MICHAEL SPELL** was born 20 September 1958.

2) **SHARI ELIZABETH SPELL** was born 18 September 1868.

1624 iii. **Lonnie Wilbert Spell**, born 23 March 1942 married **NANCY KAY WYNN** who was born 23 April 1946. Two known children.

1) **LONNIE WILBERT SPELL, JR.** was born 5 May 1962.

2) **RHONDA LYNETTE SPELL** was born 19 November 1967.

\+ 1625 iv. **Brownie Catherine Spell**, born 12 January 1948 in Roseboro, North Carolina, marrried **DURWOOD KENNETH SPELL**, son of **D. C. SPELL**. Two known children.

800. David Peyton Spell (Janie Isabell[6] Hairr, Franklin[5] Holland, Harfrey[4], Daniel[3], Thomas William[2], Unknown[1]) was born 21 February 1924. He married **Elizabeth Autry**, daughter of Hughie Autry and Susan Spell. She was born 09 October 1929.

Children of David Spell and Elizabeth Autry are:

\+ 1626 i. **Susan Annette Spell**, born 07 September 1947.

1627 ii. **Joyce Ann Spell**, born 12 December 1958.

1628 iii. **Jill Kay Spell**, born 03 March 1963.

801. Rometta Spell (Janie Isabell[6] Hairr, Franklin[5] Holland, Harfrey[4], Daniel[3], Thomas William[2], Unknown[1]) was born 09 August 1917, and died 05 November 1989 in Goldsboro, North Carolina. She married **(1) Sidney Colon Sessoms, Sr.**, son of Ulysses Sessoms and Ida Autry. He was born 12 October 1908, and died 04 August 1973 in Autryville, North Carolina. She married **(2) Preston Williams**, son of Claude Williams and Julia Autry. He was born 26 November 1912, and died 01 September 1984 in Goldsboro, North Carolina.

The 14 of Aug 1917 is also listed for Rometta's date of birth. She and Sidney Colon had five children; four identified. Sidney Colon was buried in Autryville Baptist Church Cemetery, Autryville, North Carolina.

Children of Rometta Spell and Sidney Sessoms are:

1629 i. **Leo Sell Sessoms**, born 06 July 1937; died 21 July 1941. Leo's middle name was probably "Spell." He was buried in a Spell Cemetery in Spell Town Community on Dunn Road north of Roseboro, North Carolina.

ii. **BETTY CAROL ESSSOMS**, second child or Rometta and Sidney, was born 01 December 1939 and married **ROBERT REYNOLDS** who was born 1 August 1938. Two children.

1) **REUBEN REYNOLDS**, born 24 June 1963.

2) **DARAN REYNOLDS**, 24 June 1965.

1630 iii. **Sidney Colon Sessoms, Jr.**, born 06 November 1941; died 11 March 1989. He married **JANICE HALL** who was born 25 October 1942. Three children. He was buried in Autryville Baptist Church Cemetery, Autryville, North Carolina.

1) **DONNA ANGELA SESSOMS**, born 19 Auguts 1960.

2) **EDWARD ANTHONY SESSOMS**, born 12 March 1962.

3) **THEODORE GRANT SESSOMS**, born 23 February 1964.

iv. **THOMAS LEE SESSOMS**, the fourth child of Rometta Spell and Sidney Colon Sessoms, Jr., was born 19 July1952.

803. William Lloyd Holland I (Challie Cleveland[6], Jordan[5], Harfrey[4], Daniel[3], Thomas William[2], Unknown[1]) was born 16 October 1911, and died 11 September 1953. He married **Dorothy Jane Myers**.

Notes for William Lloyd Holland I:

William Lloyd Holland served with the U.S. Air Force in Ankara, Turkey.

Child of William Holland and Dorothy Myers is:

\+ 1631 i. **William Lloyd Holland II**, born 22 May 1950.

804. Mary Frances Holland (Challie Cleveland[6], Jordan[5], Harfrey[4], Daniel[3], Thomas William[2], Unknown[1]) was born 07 February 1914. She married **Kenneth MacDonald Raynor, Sr.**. He was born 22 September 1918, and died 03 February 1964.

Children of Mary Holland and Kenneth Raynor are:

+ 1632 i. **Sarah Frances Raynor**, born 16 September 1949.

1633 ii. **Kenneth MacDonald Raynor, Jr.**, born 04 November 1950. He married Deloris Marika; born 09 January 1957.

1634 iii. **Mary Ann Raynor,** born 05 November 1951. She married Joseph Latham Styons; born 02 August 1950.

1635 iv. **Gary Layne Raynor**, born 04 December 1954.

1636 v. **Dana Sue Raynor**, born 06 June 1956.

807. Oscar Calton Holland (Challie Cleveland[6], Jordan[5], Harfrey[4], Daniel[3], Thomas William[2], Unknown[1]) was born 09 August 1919, and died 06 August 1975. He married **Minnie West** before 1950. She was born 07 October 1923.

Oscar Calton's cause of death was Cerebral Thrombosis and coronary artery disease. He was buried on 07 August 1975, in Turkey Cemetery, Turkey, North Carolina.

Children of Oscar Holland and Minnie West are:

1637 i. **Oscar Glenn Holland**, born 22 November 1950. He married **Louise Boone**; born 18 September 1952.

1638 ii. **Jerry Dean Holland**, born 21 March 1958.

808. Jessie Mildridge Holland (Challie Cleveland[6], Jordan[5], Harfrey[4], Daniel[3], Thomas William[2], Unknown[1]) was born 30 August 1921, and died 12 July 1969. She married **William Paul King** Before 1939. He was born 12 July 1917 and died 29 September 1994.

Jessie Mildridge and William Paul were buried in The Clinton Cemetery, Clinton, Sampson County, North Carolina.

Children of Jessie Holland and William King are:

+ 1639 i. **Leonard Paul King**, born 21 April 1939.

+ 1640 ii. **Maurice Maxwell King**, born 19 July 1940; died 30 September 1965.

+ 1641 iii. **Mary Jane King**, born 22 August 1944.

+ 1642 iv. **Betty Susan King**, born 19 March 1952.

809. Jerutha Veve Holland (Challie Cleveland[6], Jordan[5], Harfrey[4], Daniel[3], Thomas William[2], Unknown[1]) was born 01 September 1922 in Honeycutts Township, Sampson

County, north Carolina. She married **Lewis Franklin Carter** About 1941. He was born 26 April 1920, and died 15 September 2004.

Children of Jerutha Holland and Lewis Carter are:

1643 i. **Judy Frances Carter,** born 01 February 1942.

\+ 1644 ii. **Bobby Franklin Carter,** born 12 September 1943.

812. Margaret Peace Holland (Challie Cleveland^{6}, Jordan^{5}, Harfrey^{4}, Daniel^{3}, Thomas William^{2}, Unknown^{1}) was born 28 December 1928. She married **Sampson Monroe Hudson** Before 1950, son of George Hudson and Mamie Dudley. He was born 10 June 1915 in Sampson County, North Carolina, and died 13 March 1989.

Sampson Monroe was buried in a Hudson Cemetery on Old Warsaw Road, Sampson County, North Carolina.

Children of Margaret Holland and Sampson Hudson are:

\+ 1645 i. **Peggy Joyce Hudson,** born 14 December 1951.

1646 ii. **Samuel Monroe Hudson,** born 24 December 1957.

\+ 1647 iii. **Jewel Margaret Hudson,** born 30 October 1950.

813. Zola Cannady (Annie Jane^{6} Holland, Jordan^{5}, Harfrey^{4}, Daniel^{3}, Thomas William^{2}, Unknown^{1}) was born 22 February 1910, and died 07 December 1991. She married **(1) Maurice Wrenn**. She married **(2) Cletus Odell Elam, Sr.**. He was born 17 March 1924, and died 07 November 1994.

Zola was buried in Fort Logan National Cemetery, Denver, Colorado. March 17, 1925 is also found for Cletus' death.

Child of Zola Cannady and Cletus Elam is:

1648 i. **Cletus Odell Elam, Jr.,** born 22 December 1953.

815. Lanty Pearl Cannady (Annie Jane^{6} Holland, Jordan^{5}, Harfrey^{4}, Daniel^{3}, Thomas William^{2}, Unknown^{1}) was born 27 September 1914, and died 14 August 2000. She married **Edwin Lowe Griffin, Sr.**. He was born 16 July 1911, and died 01 June 1966.

Edwin Lowe Griffin, Sr. is buried in Montlawn Memorial Park Cemetery near Raleigh, North Carolina.

Child of Lanty Cannady and Edwin Griffin is:

\+ 1649 i. **Edwin Lowe Griffin, Jr.,** born 17 April 1948.

817. Wilbert Cleveland Cannady (Annie Jane[6] Holland, Jordan[5], Harfrey[4], Daniel[3], Thomas William[2], Unknown[1]) was born 13 January 1919, and died 03 May 1994. He married **Brilla Unknown** before 1937. She was born 23 November 1919.

Children of Wilbert Cannady and Brilla Unknown are:

+ 1650 i. **Richard Harold Cannady**, born 05 June 1937.

1651 ii. **Fay Cannady**, born 28 April 1942. She married George Bruner; born 11 June 1944.

+ 1652 iii. **Ann Cannady**, born 25 August 1944.

818. Mable Cannady (Annie Jane[6] Holland, Jordan[5], Harfrey[4], Daniel[3], Thomas William[2], Unknown[1]) was born 26 April 1921, and died 21 August 1991. She married **Clarence Day**. He was born 26 July 1918.

Her tombstone may read "Mabel' Cannady Day." She was buried in Harrells Cemetery, Harrells, Sampson County, North Carolina.

Child of Mable Cannady and Clarence Day is:

+ 1653 i. **Ceanna Day**, born 10 March 1953; died 07 May 1979.

819. Elbert Alan Cannady (Annie Jane[6] Holland, Jordan[5], Harfrey[4], Daniel[3], Thomas William[2], Unknown[1]) was born 25 March 1923. He married **Gladys Maxine Flesher** who was born 07 November 1921.

Child of Elbert Cannady and Gladys Flesher is:

1654 i. **Charles Lee Cannady**, born 30 January 1949.

820. Julia Ann Cannady (Annie Jane[6] Holland, Jordan[5], Harfrey[4], Daniel[3], Thomas William[2], Unknown[1]) was born Bet. 08 - 29 January 1925, and died 23 May 1982. She married **Elmer Michael Grubbs** who was born 14 June 1920, and died 13 July 2000.

Julia Ann was buried in Hampton Cemetery, Hampton Township, Pittsburg, Pennsylvania.

Children of Julia Cannady and Elmer Grubbs are:

+ 1655 i. **Thomas E. Grubbs I**, born 11 May 1948.

1656 ii. **Aleta Joy Grubbs**, born 03 May 1955.

1657 iii. **Mary Ann Grubbs**, born 05 January 1962.

821. James Manly Cannady (Annie Jane[6] Holland, Jordan[5], Harfrey[4], Daniel[3], Thomas William[2], Unknown[1]) was born 05 May 1927, and died 21 March 1995. He married **Wilma Arlene Flesher** who was born 29 January 1927.

Children of James Cannady and Wilma Flesher are:

+ 1658 i. **Linda Arlene Cannady**, born 27 December 1947.

+ 1659 ii. **Shirley Lynette Cannady**, born 13 October 1949.

1660 iii. **Timothy James Cannady**, born 25 October 1953. He married **Jean Roth**.

822. Herbert Wayne Cannady I (Annie Jane[6] Holland, Jordan[5], Harfrey[4], Daniel[3], Thomas William[2], Unknown[1]) was born 07 August 1929. He married **Peggy Ann Cox** who was born 20 January 1934 in North Carolina, and died 22 March 1991 in Sampson County, North Carolina.

Peggy Ann was buried in Harrells Cemetery, Harrells, Sampson County, North Carolina.

Children of Herbert Cannady and Peggy Cox are:

+ 1661 i. **Robin Anne Cannady**, born 09 October 1959.

+ 1662 ii. **Herbert Wayne Cannady II**, born 27 August 1960.

1663 iii. **Alan Dale Cannady**, born 27 August 1962. He married Tammy Hair; born 11 August 1962.

1664 iv. **Pamela Killium Cannady**, born 27 December 1963.

823. Kenneth Neil Cannady (Annie Jane[6] Holland, Jordan[5], Harfrey[4], Daniel[3], Thomas William[2], Unknown[1]) was born 09 November 1932. He married **Drama Pauline Major** who was born 26 January 1934.

Children of Kenneth Canady and Drama Majors are:

+ 1665 i. **Lily Ann Cannady**, born 26 November 1961.

1666 ii. **Kendra Sue Cannady**, born 23 April 1966. She married **Ervin L. LeMand**; born 14 November 1966.

824. Frances Eliza Holland (Anderson[6], Jordan[5], Harfrey[4], Daniel[3], Thomas William[2], Unknown[1]) was born 06 May 1927. She married **Hubert Eugene Spell**, son of Clennie Spell and Maggie Tew. He was born 29 September 1924 in Sampson County, North Carolina, and died 17 September 1978.

May 06, 1927 is date of birth on Frances' tombstone; another source notes, May 06, 1922. Hubert Eugene was buried in Harmony Baptist Church Cemetery on Fleet Cooper Road in Sampson County, North Carolina. **Herbert Myron Spell** is also found for his name.

Children of Frances Holland and Hubert Spell are:

1667 i. **Frankie Gean Spell**, born 11 February 1950. She married Eugene Phillip Jackson 23 December 1973.

1668 ii. **Herbert Myron Spell,** (Hubert Myron Spell) was born 06 March 1960. He married **Sherry Eileen Williford** 25 September 1983 in Sampson County, North Carolina; born 17 March 1961 in Harnett County, North Carolina, and they have one child.

825. Hazelene Holland (Anderson[6], Jordan[5], Harfrey[4], Daniel[3], Thomas William[2], Unknown[1]) was born 02 October 1926. She married **Willie Clayton Bass, Jr.** 11 April 1945, son of Willie Bass and Annie Baggett. He was born 26 January 1924 in Lisbon Township in Sampson County, North Carolina, and died 28 July 1996.

Children of Hazelene Holland and Willie Bass are:

1669 i. **Rebecca Anne Bass,** born 17 October 1946. She married **James T. Blue, Jr.** 28 May 1977.

1670 ii. **Willie Clayton Bass III,** born 05 April 1952.

826. Lottie Mae Barker (Drucilla[6] Holland, Jordan[5], Harfrey[4], Daniel[3], Thomas William[2], Unknown[1]) was born 06 November 1922. She married **Lelon Rich** 10 September 1938.

Children of Lottie Barker and Lelon Rich are:

+ 1671 i. **W. C. Rich,** born 01 January 1942.

+ 1672 ii. **Alice Rich,** born 15 March 1945.

827. Janie Frances Barker (Drucilla[6] Holland, Jordan[5], Harfrey[4], Daniel[3], Thomas William[2], Unknown[1]) was born 1926. She married **Mack Self.**

Children of Janie Barker and Mack Self are:

+ 1673 i. **Billy Self,** born 1947.

+ 1674 ii. **Linda Self,** born 1949.

+ 1675 iii. **Barbara Self,** born 1951.

+ 1676 iv. **Connie Self,** born 1952.

828. Carl Barker (Drucilla[6] Holland, Jordan[5], Harfrey[4], Daniel[3], Thomas William[2], Unknown[1]) He married **Ethel Bryant** 1966.

Child of Carl Barker and Ethel Bryant is:

1677 i. **Randy Barker.**

829. Horace Barker (Drucilla[6] Holland, Jordan[5], Harfrey[4], Daniel[3], Thomas William[2], Unknown[1]) He married **Christine Bagley** 1956.

Child of Horace Barker and Christine Bagley is:

1678 i. **Randy Barker**, born 1958.

830. Louise Barker (Drucilla[6] Holland, Jordan[5], Harfrey[4], Daniel[3], Thomas William[2], Unknown[1])

Child of Louise Barker is:

1679 i. **Dale Barker**, born 1957.

831. Thelma Barker (Drucilla[6] Holland, Jordan[5], Harfrey[4], Daniel[3], Thomas William[2], Unknown[1]) She married **Weldon Shull** 1949. He died 01 January 1976.

Children of Thelma Barker and Weldon Shull are:

1680 i. **Ray Shull**, born 1950.

\+ 1681 ii. **Patricia Shull**, born 1953.

832. Elizabeth Grace Williams (Charlotte Elizabeth[6] Holland, Jordan[5], Harfrey[4], Daniel[3], Thomas William[2], Unknown[1]) was born 22 April 1933. She married **John Leonard Brock** who was born 21 February 1931.

Children of Elizabeth Williams and John Brock are:

\+ 1682 i. **Elizabeth Ann Brock**, born 14 October 1951.

\+ 1683 ii. **Elwood Glenn Brock**, born 19 January 1954.

\+ 1684 iii. **Deborah Elaine Brock**, born 13 December 1957.

1685 iv. **John Arnold Brock**, born 16 January 1962.

833. Olivia Ruth Williams (Charlotte Elizabeth[6] Holland, Jordan[5], Harfrey[4], Daniel[3], Thomas William[2], Unknown[1]) was born 11 November 1934. She married **Joseph Alton Lee**, son of Joseph Lee and Ida Dudley. He was born 24 December 1930.

Children of Olivia Williams and Joseph Lee are:

\+ 1686 i. **Brenda Ann Lee**, born 28 December 1951.

1687 ii. **Joseph Henry Lee**, born 12 March 1954. He married Marie Jackson; born 11 April 1957.

\+ 1688 iii. **Carolyn Sue Lee**, born 23 April 1955.

\+ 1689 iv. **Luby Mack Lee**, born 11 May 1956.

1690 v. **Gary Dean Lee**, born 18 February 1957; died 08 January 1959.

1691 vi. **Teresa Jean Lee**, born 18 February 1957. She married Donnie Franklyn Cain.

1692 vii. **Joyce Faye Lee**, born 06 November 1958. She married Charles Berry Lane; born 22 February 1957.

1693 viii. **Loyce Mae Lee**, born 06 November 1958.

1694 ix. **Ronald Wayne Lee**, born 07 November 1965.

1695 x. **Tena Michelle Lee**, born 12 January 1970.

834. Norma Jean Williams (Charlotte Elizabeth[6] Holland, Jordan[5], Harfrey[4], Daniel[3], Thomas William[2], Unknown[1]) was born 11 August 1937. She married **Benjamin Augustus Blagg** who was born 03 August 1926.

Children of Norma Williams and Benjamin Blagg are:

1696 i. **William Clifford Blagg**, born 15 August 1955.

1697 ii. **Charles Arthur Blagg**, born 18 February 1957.

1698 iii. **Deborah Jean Blagg**, born 06 July 1960.

1699 iv. **Roger Dale Blagg**, born 17 July 1964.

1700 v. **Robert Wayne Blagg**, born 19 December 1966.

1701 vi. **Sheila Louise Blagg**, born 11 October 1970.

1702 vii. **Helen Rena Blagg**, born 07 July 1974.

835. Joseph Jordan Williams, Sr. (Charlotte Elizabeth[6] Holland, Jordan[5], Harfrey[4], Daniel[3], Thomas William[2], Unknown[1]) was born 15 April 1940, and died 20 February 1965. He married **Sarah Jane Harris**.

Child of Joseph Williams and Sarah Harris is:

1703 i. **Joseph Jordan Williams, Jr.**.

837. Betty Ellen Williams (Charlotte Elizabeth[6] Holland, Jordan[5], Harfrey[4], Daniel[3], Thomas William[2], Unknown[1]) was born 12 May 1944. She married **Charles Asermely**.

Children of Betty Williams and Charles Asermely are:

1704 i. **James Joseph Asermely**, born 03 March 1965.

1705 ii. **Charles Lewis Asermely**, born 25 June 1968.

838. Jannie Bell Williams (Charlotte Elizabeth[6] Holland, Jordan[5], Harfrey[4], Daniel[3], Thomas William[2], Unknown[1]) was born 07 January 1946. She married **(1) Floyd Edmond Parker**. She married **(2) Arthur Clifton Yarborgh** who was born 28 March 1930.

Children of Jannie Williams and Floyd Parker are:

1706 i. **Thomas Edmond Parker**, born 24 November 1961.

1707 ii. **Linda Gail Parker**, born 24 November 1964; died 19 February 1965.

1708 iii. **Nancy Gail Parker**, born 18 April 1967.

1709 iv. **Mary Hellen Parker**, born 09 June 1968.

1710 v. **Michael Ray Parker**, born 02 September 1969.

Child of Jannie Williams and Arthur Yarborgh is:

1711 i. **Kristy Lynn Yarborgh**, born 25 May 1977.

839. Joseph Arthur Williams, Jr. (Charlotte Elizabeth[6] Holland, Jordan[5], Harfrey[4], Daniel[3], Thomas William[2], Unknown[1]) was born 03 March 1948. He married **Karen.**

Child of Joseph Williams and Karen is:

1712 i. **Jonathan Aaron Williams**, born 25 January 1974.

840. Edward Earl Williams (Charlotte Elizabeth[6] Holland, Jordan[5], Harfrey[4], Daniel[3], Thomas William[2], Unknown[1]) was born 03 July 1950. He married **(1) Rosey Bass.** He married **(2) Susie Gail Cox** who was born 11 April 1955.

Child of Edward Williams and Susie Cox is:

1713 i. **Christyl Gail Williams**, born 30 August 1975.

841. Albert Lewis Strickland (Katie Rebecca[6] Holland, Jordan[5], Harfrey[4], Daniel[3], Thomas William[2], Unknown[1]) was born 21 December 1936. He married **Betty Irene Coats.**

Children of Albert Strickland and Betty Coats are:

1714 i. **Ronnie Lewis Strickland**, born 18 November 1959.

1715 ii. **Nancy Rebecca Strickland**, born 01 October 1960.

1716 iii. **Betty Lee Ann Strickland**, born 21 March 1962; died 04 April 1962.

1717 iv. **Maxton Lee Strickland**, born 06 January 1964.

1718 v. **Jeffery Wayne Strickland**, born 17 December 1964.

1719 vi. **Albert Deleon Strickland**, born 30 June 1967.

842. Wadus Deleon Strickland (Katie Rebecca[6] Holland, Jordan[5], Harfrey[4], Daniel[3], Thomas William[2], Unknown[1]) was born 02 January 1938, and died 28 November 1963. He married **Josephine Stephens.**

Children of Wadus Strickland and Josephine Stephens are:

1720 i. **Kenneth Deleon Strickland,** born 24 May 1960.

1721 ii. **Wendell Wade Strickland,** born 29 December 1961.

844. Linda Faye Strickland (Katie Rebecca[6] Holland, Jordan[5], Harfrey[4], Daniel[3], Thomas William[2], Unknown[1]) was born 25 October 1942. She married **John Wayne Rackley.**

Child of Linda Strickland and John Rackley is:

1722 i. **Linda Louise Rackley,** born 21 February 1967.

845. Carol Rebecca Strickland (Katie Rebecca[6] Holland, Jordan[5], Harfrey[4], Daniel[3], Thomas William[2], Unknown[1]) was born 18 January 1945. She married **Richard Arlen Daughtry.**

Child of Carol Strickland and Richard Daughtry is:

1723 i. **Karen Denise Daughtry,** born 05 November 1967.

846. Mable Rose Strickland (Katie Rebecca[6] Holland, Jordan[5], Harfrey[4], Daniel[3], Thomas William[2], Unknown[1]) was born 03 June 1946. She married **George N. Butler.**

Child of Mable Strickland and George Butler is:

1724 i. **Gloria Butler,** born 22 November 1966.

848. Ellen Gail Strickland (Katie Rebecca[6] Holland, Jordan[5], Harfrey[4], Daniel[3], Thomas William[2], Unknown[1]) was born 27 August 1948. She married **Charles Ray Matthis.**

Child of Ellen Strickland and Charles Matthis is:

1725 i. **Nichole Matthis,** born 09 January 1971.

850. Jerry Holland Strickland (Katie Rebecca[6] Holland, Jordan[5], Harfrey[4], Daniel[3], Thomas William[2], Unknown[1]) was born 11 June 1951. He married **Arlene Marie Taylor.**

Children of Jerry Strickland and Arlene Taylor are:

1726 i. **Jason Woodrow Strickland,** born 27 February 1973.

1727 ii. **Cas Sandra Malissa Strickland,** born 04 December 1977.

851. Steven Craig Holland (David Jordan[6], Jordan[5], Harfrey[4], Daniel[3], Thomas William[2], Unknown[1]) was born 09 January 1941. He married **Barbara Bates** who was born 16 November 1941.

Children of Steven Holland and Barbara Bates are:

1728 i. **Pamela Jane Holland**, born 13 November 1962.

1729 ii. **Brian Craig Holland**, born 08 June 1972.

853. Lessie Jane Holland Williams (Repsie[6] Holland, Chester[5], Harfrey[4], Daniel[3], Thomas William[2], Unknown[1]) was born 04 August 1905. She married **Attie Giles** who was born 03 December 1899, and died 05 May 1974. Lessie was the informant named on Attie's certificate of death and she named John D. Giles and Sallie Hawley for his parents.

Lessie Jane Holland Williams and Attie were buried in Baptist Chapel Church Cemetery on Baptist Chapel Road, Sampson County, North Carolina.

Children of Lessie Williams and Attie Giles are:

\+ 1730 i. **Margaret Louvenia Giles**, born 29 January 1924 in Dismal Township, Sampson County, North Carolina.

1731 ii. **Annie Doris Giles**, born 03 October 1926; died 03 February 1929.

\+ 1732 iii. **Attie Edmon Giles**, born 01 September 1931.

\+ 1733 iv. **James Elton Giles**, born 13 November 1941.

854. Agnes Ruth Williams (Repsie[6] Holland, Chester[5], Harfrey[4], Daniel[3], Thomas William[2], Unknown[1]) was born 01 January 1918, and died 14 March 1972. She marred **(1) William Cleveland Hairr, Sr.** who was born about 1939, son of Reddin Hairr and Carrie Strickland. He was born about 1917. She married **(2) Earl Pope** about 1953. He was born 11 December 1925.

Children of Agnes Williams and William Hairr are:

\+ 1734 i. **Agnes Jane Hairr**, born 26 December 1939.

\+ 1735 ii. **William Cleveland Hairr, Jr.**, born 07 April 1943.

\+ 1736 iii. **Mary Ann Hairr**, born 14 December 1945.

Child of Agnes Williams and Earl Pope is:

\+ 1737 i. **Edna Ruth Pope**, born 29 October 1953.

855. Chellie Elizabeth Williams (Repsie[6] Holland, Chester[5], Harfrey[4], Daniel[3], Thomas William[2], Unknown[1]) was born 10 December 1919. She married **Henry Cleveland**

Bradshaw, Sr., son of Monroe Bradshaw and Della Tew. He was born 04 May 1917, and died 04 May 1983 in Fayetteville, North Carolina.

Henry Cleveland was a Cpl., United States Army in World War II. He was buried in Union Grove Baptist Church Cemetery on SR 1438 one mile west of Rebel City, Sampson County, North Carolina.

Children of Chellie Williams and Henry Bradshaw are:

1738 i. **Henry Cleveland Bradshaw, Jr.**, born 28 September 1942; died 12 March 1972.

He is buried in Union Grove Baptist Church Cemetery on Vander Road west of Rebel City, Sampson County, North Carolina.

1739 ii. **Charles Monroe Bradshaw**, born 24 September 1956.

856. Robert Chester Williams (Repsie[6] Holland, Chester[5], Harfrey[4], Daniel[3], Thomas William[2], Unknown[1]) was born 23 September 1923, and died 21 June 1998. He married **Virgie Mae Rozier**. She was born 29 October 1927.

Robert Chester served in the United States Army in World War II. He was buried in Union Grove Baptist Church Cemetery on Vander Road west of Rebel City, Sampson County, North Carolina.

Child of Robert Williams and Virgie Rozier is:

\+ 1740 i. **Emily Diann Williams**, born 16 July 1949.

857. Mattie Iona Holland (Columbus[6], Chester[5], Harfrey[4], Daniel[3], Thomas William[2], Unknown[1]) was born 21 July 1909, and died 06 August 1992. She married **Clayton Dekker McDonald** 31 October 1925. He was born 14 June 1901.

Mattie worked at Fleshman's Department Store. She and her husband, Clayton D. McDonald later moved to Fayetteville and they owned the 301 truck stop.

Children of Mattie Holland and Clayton McDonald are:

\+ 1741 i. **Eugene Dekker McDonald**, born 04 December 1926.

\+ 1742 ii. **Hubert Ellis McDonald**, born 24 December 1927.

858. James Albert Holland (Columbus[6], Chester[5], Harfrey[4], Daniel[3], Thomas William[2], Unknown[1]) was born 22 January 1911, and died 25 May 1982. He married **Alma Lonnie Warren** 05 June 1931, daughter of Junius Warren and Stella Royal. She was born 04 May 1912 in Sampson County, North Carolina.

James Albert was a painter and hunting racoons and foxes were his favorite hobbies. He was buried in Salemburg Cemetery, Salemburg, North Carolina.

The tombstone for Alma's mother, Stella Royal Warren, has May 09, 1890 for Stella's birth and December 14, 1917 for her death. She died in the Influenza Epidemic of 1918. Stella's husband and their infant daughter who was born on December 04, 1917 died on the same day in 1918. Another daughter, Alma, was born on May 04, 1918, but on page 126 in "Meet Our Ancestors, Culbreth, Autry, Maxwell-Bundy, Winslow, Henley and Allied Families, Second Edition," by V. Mayo Bundy, it states "Alma Lonnie" was born on May 04, 1912. Therefore, I have used this earlier date for Alma Lonnie and I have listed May 09, 1889 for Stella's date of birth and December 14, 1917 for her date of death.

Alma Lonnie was buried in Salemburg Cemetery, Salemburg, North Carolina.

Children of James Holland and Alma Warren are:

\+ 1743 i. **Peggy Florence Holland**, born 28 May 1932.

\+ 1744 ii. **Stella Royal Holland**, born 01 November 1934.

\+ 1745 iii. **Ann Holland**, born 25 February 1938.

\+ 1746 iv. **Alice Faye Holland**, born 17 June 1940.

\+ 1747 v. **Cathleen Holland**, born 20 June 1944.

\+ 1748 vi. **James Leon Holland**, born 25 January 1946.

\+ 1749 vii. **Ronald Nixon Holland**, born 07 January 1949.

\+ 1750 viii. **Joseph Wayne Holland**, born 28 June 1954.

1751 ix. **Alma Gail Holland**, born 27 August 1955. She married Leslie Martin Jerson 01 July 1990; born 25 March 1943.

860. Mabel Holland (Columbus[6], Chester[5], Harfrey[4], Daniel[3], Thomas William[2], Unknown[1]) was born 14 October 1917. She married **(1) Bryan Wilson Catlet** Before 1944, son of George Catlet and Bessie Nash. He was born 15 May 1915, and died 11 August 1966. She married **(2) William Harvey Pitman, Jr.** After 1944. He was born 21 July 1918.

Child of Mabel Holland and Bryan Catlet is:

1752 i. **David Catlet**, born 10 July 1944; died 10 July 1944.

861. Jessie Turlington Holland (Columbus[6], Chester[5], Harfrey[4], Daniel[3], Thomas William[2], Unknown[1]) was born 31 December 1921. He married **Bulah Mae Wilson** 11 April 1948. She was born 15 September 1922.

Notes for Jessie Turlington Holland:

Both their children were adopted and were brothers by birth.

Children of Jessie Holland and Bulah Wilson are:

1753 i. **Owen Gary Holland**, born 24 January 1946.

1754 ii. **Steven Ray Holland**, born 25 July 1952.

864. Chester Ausbon Holland (Erastus[6], Chester[5], Harfrey[4], Daniel[3], Thomas William[2], Unknown[1]) was born 12 February 1912 in Salemburg, Honeycutts Township, Sampson County, North Carolina, and died 11 February 1963 in Jacksonville, Florida. He married **Ethel Mae Best** Before 1931, daughter of George Best and Lizzie Best. She was born 20 November 1910.

Peggy Ann Tripp (Crouch, Workman) notes that Chester Ausbon Holland was born February 15, 1912.

Children of Chester Holland and Ethel Best are:

\+ 1755 i. **Emily Frances Holland**, born 23 October 1931.

1756 ii. **Ralph Lee Holland**, born 21 May 1933; died 11 August 1938.

He was buried in the Best Cemetery on Church Road (SR 1703), Sampson County, North Carolina

1757 iii. **Billy Mack Holland**, born 19 November 1939; died 19 November 1939.

He is buried in the Best Cemetery on Church Road (SR 1703), Sampson County, North Carolina

1758 iv. **Linda Lynette Holland**, born 09 January 1943. She married **Charles Wallace Tanner**; born 08 May 1941.

No children.

865. Aline Holland (Erastus[6], Chester[5], Harfrey[4], Daniel[3], Thomas William[2], Unknown[1]) was born 13 August 1914. She married **Vincent James Mezzacappa** 06 May 1936.

Child of Aline Holland and Vincent Mezzacappa is:

\+ 1759 i. **Joan Marie Mezzacappa**, born 05 May 1943.

866. Elma Holland (Erastus[6], Chester[5], Harfrey[4], Daniel[3], Thomas William[2], Unknown[1]) was born 11 July 1917 in Salemburg, Sampson County, North Carolina and died 30 October 2008 in Dunn Rehab Center in Dunn, Harnett County, North Carolina. She married **Rev. Merle Floyd Sollinger** 24 October 1937 in Salemburg, Sampson County, North Carolina. He was born 22 January 1909 in Emlenton, Venango, Pennsylvania, and died 17 March 1995 in Dunn, Harnett County, North Carolina.

My sister and her husband, Phillip, and I met Elma Sollinger in 2001. She loaned us a couple of books and was a delightful lady with many stories to tell about her research and family. She played the organ beautifully and entertained us by playing a few hymns.

Rev. Merle Floyd Sollinger and Elma were buried in Salemburg Cemetery, Salemburg, Sampson County, North Carolina.

Children of Elma Holland and Merle Sollinger are:

+ 1760 i. **Merle Floyd Sollinger, Jr.**, born 17 November 1938 in Salemburg, Sampson County, North Carolina; died 07 September 2005 in Dunn, Harnett County, North Carolina.

+ 1761 ii. **Thomas Franklin Sollinger**, born 25 June 1948.

867. Edna Louise Holland (John Love[6], Chester[5], Harfrey[4], Daniel[3], Thomas William[2], Unknown[1]) was born 12 September 1916 in Honeycutts Township, Sampson County, North Carolina, and died 29 February 1980 in Wake County, North Carolina. She married **Robert Edward Tripp, Jr.** 18 June 1940 in Salemburg, Sampson County, North Carolina. He was born 02 September 1915 in Bonnerton, Beaufort County, North Carolina, and died 13 August 1994 in Atlantic Beach, North Carolina.

Edna Louise and Robert were buried in Salemburg Cemetery, Salemburg, Sampson County, North Carolina.

Children of Edna Holland and Robert Tripp are:

+ 1762 i. **Peggy Ann Tripp**, born 30 June 1941 in Washington, North Carolina.

+ 1763 ii. **Robert Edward Tripp III**, born 16 June 1943 in Raleigh, North Carolina.

868. Ernest Ray Holland (John Love[6], Chester[5], Harfrey[4], Daniel[3], Thomas William[2], Unknown[1]) was born 10 December 1919 in Sampson County, North Carolina, and died 30 July 1972. He married **Hazel Dixon Lewis** Before 1948, daughter of Eddie Lewis and Mary Cooper. She was born 21 December 1924 in Honeycutts Township, Sampson County, North Carolina.

Hazel Dixon Lewis Holland married 2nd to Henry Maxwell Draughon who was born January 31, 1919.

Children of Ernest Holland and Hazel Lewis are:

+ 1764 i. **Celia Joyce Holland**, born 22 July 1948 in Roseboro, North Carolina.

1765 ii. **Hazel Kristina Holland**, born 16 September 1957.

870. Lester Floyd Holland (John Love[6], Chester[5], Harfrey[4], Daniel[3], Thomas William[2], Unknown[1]) was born 20 January 1924 in Sampson County, North Carolina, and died 13 July 1995 in Sampson County Memorial Hospital, Clinton, North Carolina. He married **Betty Jean Andrews** 28 June 1952 in Salemburg, Sampson County, North Carolina. She was born 01 May 1928.

Lester Floyd served in World War II and later owned and Operated a Tank Service business. Cause of death: Cerebrovascular Accident. He was buried in Salemburg Cemetery, Salemburg, North Carolina.

Children of Lester Holland and Betty Andrews are:

\+ 1766 i. **Linda Jo Holland**, born 08 October 1955 in Roseboro, North Carolina.

1767 ii. **Stephen Floyd Holland**, born 17 August 1959 in Clinton, Sampson County, North Carolina.

871. Alma Inez Holland (John Love[6], Chester[5], Harfrey[4], Daniel[3], Thomas William[2], Unknown[1]) was born 18 July 1929 in Salemburg, Honeycutts Township, Sampson County, North Carolina, and died 25 May 1984 in Fayetteville, Cumberland County, North Carolina. She married **Rev. Roger Aubigne White** 10 June 1956 in Honeycutts Township, Sampson County, North Carolina, son of Lyman White and Irene Tart. He was born 15 September 1929 in Honeycutts Township, Sampson County, North Carolina.

Alma Inez was buried in Salemburg Cemetery, Salemburg, Sampson County, North Carolina.

Children of Alma Holland and Roger White are:

1768 i. **Emily Rose White**, born 28 March 1957 in Roseboro, North Carolina.

1769 ii. **Bonnie Kate White**, born 14 February 1959 in Roseboro, North Carolina.

1770 iii. **Mary Love White**, born 15 July 1960 in Clinton, Sampson County, North Carolina.

1771 iv. **Timothy Roger White**, born 09 November 1961 in Clinton, Sampson County, North Carolina.

1772 v. **Edna Grace White**, born 19 January 1964.

1773 vi. **Ruth Ann White**, born 18 October 1966 in Clinton, Sampson County, North Carolina. She married Joel Keith Godwin 07 June 1986 in Magnolia Baptist Church, near Roseboro, North Carolina; born 02 July 1962 in Fayetteville, Cumberland County, North Carolina.

872. John Love Holland, Jr. (John Love[6], Chester[5], Harfrey[4], Daniel[3], Thomas William[2], Unknown[1]) was born 30 July 1932 in Sampson County, North Carolina. He married **Jean Carolyn Cooper** 11 January 1953 in Salemburg, Sampson County, North Carolina, daughter of Robbie Lee Cooper and Cora Glendon Butler. She was born 06 January 1932 in Honeycutts Township, Sampson County, North Carolina.

Children of John Holland and Jean Cooper are:

1774 i. **David Lynn Holland**, born 19 August 1953; died 12 April 1988.

He was buried in Salemburg Cemetery, Bearskin Road, Salemburg, North Carolina

1775 ii. **Brenda Carroll Holland**, born 19 February 1960 in Clinton, Sampson County, North Carolina.

874. Charles Hilliard Naylor (Lillie[6] Holland, Chester[5], Harfrey[4], Daniel[3], Thomas William[2], Unknown[1]) was born 09 November 1917 in Mingo Township, Sampson County, North Carolina. He married **(1) Annie Elizabeth Strickland** Before 1941, daughter of Neill Strickland and Lillian Taylor. She was born 12 March 1916 in Mingo Township, Sampson County, North Carolina, and died About 1946. He married **(2) Josephine Hayes** About 1948.

Charles Hilliard Naylor and Annie Elizabeth Strickland were divorced.

Child of Charles Naylor and Annie Strickland is:

+ 1776 i. **Barbara Elaine Naylor**, born 25 October 1941 in Dunn, Harrnett County, North Carolina.

Child of Charles Naylor and Josephine Hayes is:

1777 i. **Steve Van Naylor**, born 29 December 1948. He married Rosemary Privette.

875. Payton Thomas Naylor (Lillie[6] Holland, Chester[5], Harfrey[4], Daniel[3], Thomas William[2], Unknown[1]) was born 05 November 1919 in Mingo Township, Sampson County, North Carolina, and died 22 January 1985 in Wake County, North Carolina. He married **Helen Louise Eldridge** Before 1944. She was born 28 August 1917 in Meadow Township.

Children of Payton Naylor and Helen Eldridge are:

+ 1778 i. **Wanda Kaye Naylor**, born 07 August 1944 in Dunn, Harrnett County, North Carolina.
+ 1779 ii. **Diana Naylor**, born 28 August 1949 in Dunn, Harrnett County, North Carolina.

1780 iii. **Thomas Eldridge Naylor**, born 07 March 1955 in Dunn, Harrnett County, North Carolina.

876. Graham Willard Naylor (Lillie[6] Holland, Chester[5], Harfrey[4], Daniel[3], Thomas William[2], Unknown[1]) was born 06 May 1921 in Mingo Township, Sampson County, North Carolina. He married **Lollie Doris Barefoot** 1942, daughter of Junius Barefoot and Annie Herring. She was born 23 October 1921 in Mingo Township, Sampson County, North Carolina.

Children of Graham Naylor and Lollie Barefoot are:

+ 1781 i. **Doris Lynn Naylor**, born 26 January 1944 in New Hanover County, North Carolina.
+ 1782 ii. **Marinda Jean Naylor**, born 18 November 1946 in Dunn, Harrnett County, North Carolina.
+ 1783 iii. **Susan Ann Naylor**, born 16 September 1954 in Dunn, Harrnett County, North Carolina.

877. Irene Naylor (Lillie[6] Holland, Chester[5], Harfrey[4], Daniel[3], Thomas William[2], Unknown[1]) was born 26 August 1924 in Mingo Township, Sampson County, North Carolina. She married **Byron Grantham** Before 1949, son of Hezekiah Grantham and Armelia Barnes. He was born 27 January 1923 in Honeycutts Township, Sampson County, North Carolina, and died 31 December 2002 in Sampson County, North Carolina.

"Byran is also found for Byron's name and 19 January 1923 is also found for his date of birth. He is buried in Calvary Tabernacle PFWB Cemetery near Salemburg, North Carolina.

Children of Irene Naylor and Byron Grantham are:

\+ 1784 i. **Byron Wayne Grantham**, born 28 January 1949 in Roseboro, Sampson County, North Carolina.

\+ 1785 ii. **Cathy Lynette Grantham**, born 25 January 1952 in Roseboro, Sampson County, North Carolina.

878. Mary Maxine Naylor (Lillie[6] Holland, Chester[5], Harfrey[4], Daniel[3], Thomas William[2], Unknown[1]) was born 28 June 1926 in Mingo Township, Sampson County, North Carolina. She married **Carl Anderson Capps, Sr.** Before 1949. He was born 16 October 1917.

Children of Mary Naylor and Carl Capps are:

1786 i. **Carl Anderson Capps, Jr.**, born 28 January 1949.

1787 ii. **Betty Sue Capps**, born 05 December 1950. She married Richard Lee Rutledge.

880. Malissa Jane Naylor (Lillie[6] Holland, Chester[5], Harfrey[4], Daniel[3], Thomas William[2], Unknown[1]) was born 28 March 1933 in Mingo Township, Sampson County, North Carolina. She married **Elmond C. West** before 1957, son of Carson West and Betty Norris. He was born 15 September 1930 in Mingo Township, Sampson County, North Carolina.

Children of Malissa Naylor and Elmond West are:

1788 i. **Elmond Ray West**, born 06 October 1957 in Dunn, Harrnett County, North Carolina. He married **Mary Catherine Jackson**; born 26 August 1958 in Portsmouth, Virginia.

1789 ii. **Rebecca Lynn West**, born 23 July 1962 in Dunn, Harrnett County, North Carolina. She married **Jonathan Dwayne Beasley**; born 28 August 1968 in Dunn, Harrnett County, North Carolina.

881. Annie Bell Naylor (Lillie[6] Holland, Chester[5], Harfrey[4], Daniel[3], Thomas William[2], Unknown[1]) was born 17 October 1936 in Mingo Township, Sampson County, North Carolina. She married **Robin Adair Draughon** 08 November 1957 in Mingo Baptist Church, Mingo Township, Sampson County, North Carolina. He was born 29 September 1930 in Mingo Township, Sampson County, North Carolina.

Children of Annie Naylor and Robin Draughon are:

1790 i. **Michael Adair Draughon**, born 05 September 1962 in Dunn, Harrnett County, North Carolina.

1791 ii. **Rita Ann Draughon**, born 13 May 1965.

883. Lois Evelyn Grimes (Rosella[6] Holland, Chester[5], Harfrey[4], Daniel[3], Thomas William[2], Unknown[1]) was born 03 August 1922. She married **William Grant Trexler II**. He was born 15 May 1920.

Children of Lois Grimes and William Trexler are:

1792 i. **Elizabeth Grimes Trexler**, born 21 June 1952.

1793 ii. **William Grant Trexler III**, born 22 October 1955.

884. Joanne Grimes (Rosella[6] Holland, Chester[5], Harfrey[4], Daniel[3], Thomas William[2], Unknown[1]) was born 23 June 1930. She married **Henry Townes Maddux II**.

Children of Joanne Grimes and Henry Maddux are:

1794 i. **Emily Elizabeth Maddux**, born 18 December 1953.

1795 ii. **Gladys Maddux**, born 13 June 1961.

1796 iii. **Henry Townes Maddux III**, born 02 July 1962.

885. Cleveland DeVane Jackson, Sr. (Charlotte Ann[6] Holland, Chester[5], Harfrey[4], Daniel[3], Thomas William[2], Unknown[1]) was born 10 August 1920 in Honeycutts Township, Sampson County, North Carolina and died 13 February 2004 in Asheboro, Randolph County, North Carolina, USA. He married **Helen Frances Warren**. She was born 14 October 1923 and was still living in 2004.

He was known by relatives as "DeVon." It is thought that he added the name Cleveland because he like it. "**Cleveland Devone Jackson**" appears to be his name recorded at birth in the birth index. "Devane" was listed for his name in the 1930 census. His obituary below records "**Cleveland Devane Jackson, Sr.**, and **C.D. Jackson, Sr.** for his name.

His obituary appeared in the "*Sampson Independent Newspaper,*" Clinton, Sampson County, North Carolina, on 14 February 2004.

"Cleveland Devane "C.D." Jackson, Sr., 83.

"The funeral will be held at 3 p.m. Sunday, February 15, at First Baptist Church with the Rev. Dr. John Rogers and the Rev. Dr. J. B. Gibson officiating. Burial will be in Oaklawn Cemetery with military honors.

"Born August 10, 1920 in Salemburg, Mr. Jackson was the son of the late Robert A. "Bob" and Charlotte Holland Jackson. He is a United States Navy veteran having served in World War II.

"He is survived by his wife, Helen Warren Jackson; three sons, William Robet Jackson, Cleveland Devane Jackson, Jr. and Kent Jackson; and three grandchildren.

"The family will receive friends from 6 until 8 p.m. tonight at Pugh Funeral Home.

"In lieu of flowers, memorials may be made to First Baptist Church, 133 North Church St., Asheboro, N.C. 27204 or Christian's United Outreach Center, P. O. Box 784, Asheboro, N.C. 27204 or Hospice of Randolph, P. O. Box 9, Asheboro, N.C. 27204."

Children of Cleveland Jackson and Helen Warren are:

1797 i. **William Robert Jackson**, born 09 December 1950.

1798 ii. **Cleveland DeVane Jackson, Jr.**, born 27 May 1955.

1799 iii. **Allen Kent Jackson**, born 28 April 1959.

888. Thamer Lee Holland (James Monroe[6], Chester[5], Harfrey[4], Daniel[3], Thomas William[2], Unknown[1]) was born 02 April 1930 in Newton Grove, Westbrooks Township, Sampson County, North Carolina. She married **John Lenwood Butler** 04 April 1954. He was born 16 November 1927 in Clinton, North Carolina.

"Tharmer" is also found for the spelling of her first name.

Children of Thama Holland and John Butler are:

1800 i. **Kimbraugh Leigh Butler**, born 10 July 1957. In her early 20s Kim legally changed her name from Kimberly Teresa Butler to Kimbraugh Leigh Butler when she found that it was the name her mother had originally planned to give her. She married **Robert J. Martin, Jr.** on 8 August 1980. He was born 26 November 1955. No descendants.

1801 ii. **Thamer Denise Butler** was born 16 June 1958 and married **Charles Keith Lambert** who was born 7 October 1958. No descendants.

1802 iii. **Gary Lenwood Butler** was born 11 March 1960 and maried **Michelle Marie Ramberger** on 8 September 1984. She was born 9 August 1959. They have two children: **Glen Jefferson Butler** was born 21 July 1994 and **Graham Michael Butler** was born 11 July 1997.

1803 iv. **Melanie Holland Butler**, born 29 March 1977, married **Brian DeWitt Shank** on 10 July 1999. He was born 22 April 1974 and they have one child: **Alexander Mendenhall Shank** who was born 30 December 2006.

889. Lewis Alton Spell (Braxton[6], Romelia[5] Holland, Harfrey[4], Daniel[3], Thomas William[2], Unknown[1]) was born 25 July 1915 in Sampson County, North Carolina, and died 13 December 1978 in Cumberland County, North Carolina. He married **Eupha Mae Matthews** 04 March 1939 in Cumberland County, North Carolina, daughter of Lewis Martin Matthews and Lena Mae Culbreth. She was born 28 April 1917 in Sampson County, North Carolina, and died 21 October 1983 in Cumberland County, North Carolina.

July 25, 1913 is listed for his birth in one source. Lewis Alton and Eupha were buried in a Spell Family Cemetery.

Children of Lewis Spell and Eupha Matthews are:

\+ 1804 i. **Nixon Lewis Spell, Sr.**, born 07 October 1941 in Sampson County, North Carolina.

\+ 1805 ii. **Arthur Elwood Spell**, born 19 November 1951 in Sampson County, North Carolina.

891. Mae Olive Spell (Braxton[6], Romelia[5] Holland, Harfrey[4], Daniel[3], Thomas William[2], Unknown[1]) was born 01 January 1917 in Sampson County, North Carolina. She married **Daniel Crosby Matthews** 04 November 1939 in Sampson County, North Carolina, son of Lewis Matthews and Lena Culbreth. He was born 24 July 1911 in Cumberland County, North Carolina, and died 26 December 1987 in Cumberland County, North Carolina.

Daniel Crosby is buried in Autry-McAlphin Cemetery near Stedman, North Carolina.

Child of Mae Spell and Daniel Matthews is:

1806 i. **David Crosby Matthews**, born 20 November 1944 in Sampson County, North Carolina. He married **Patsy Ann Horne** 11 December 1964 in Cumberland County, North Carolina; born 09 November 1943 in Harnett County, North Carolina.

893. Pauline Spell (Braxton[6], Romelia[5] Holland, Harfrey[4], Daniel[3], Thomas William[2], Unknown[1]) was born 22 October 1922 in Sampson County, North Carolina. She married **Alfestus Faircloth, Sr.** He was born 01 October 1916 in Sampson County, North Carolina, and died 05 November 1989.

Alfestus Faircloth, Sr. was buried in a Spell Family Cemetery on Dunn Road North of Roseboro, North Carolina.

Children of Pauline Spell and Alfestus Faircloth are:

1807 i. **Alfestus Faircloth, Jr.**, born 14 October 1940 in Pasquotank County, North Carolina; died 27 February 1997 in Cumberland County, North Carolina. He married **Linda Faye Grantham** 11 January 1964 in Sampson County, North Carolina; born 24 March 1945 in Sampson County, North Carolina. See notes elsewhere in this book for Festus DeVone, his brother.

Alfestus Faircloth, Jr. was buried in a Spell Family Cemetery on Dunn Road, North of Roseboro, North Carolina

\+ 1808 ii. **Festus DeVone Faircloth**, born 23 December 1942 in Sampson County, North Carolina; died 27 February 1997.

\+ 1809 iii. **Henry Enoch Faircloth**, born 08 July 1946 in Sampson County, North Carolina.

\+ 1810 iv. **Robert Anthony Faircloth**, born 26 July 1951 in Sampson County, North Carolina.

\+ 1811 v. **Rebecca Dale Faircloth**, born 13 June 1955 in Sampson County, North Carolina.

\+ 1812 vi. **Martha Jane Faircloth**, born 28 May 1958 in Sampson County, North Carolina.

\+ 1813 vii. **Melody Ruth Faircloth**, born 25 November 1960 in Sampson County, North Carolina.

894. Ernie Minson Spell (Braxton[6], Romelia[5] Holland, Harfrey[4], Daniel[3], Thomas William[2], Unknown[1]) was born 22 September 1924 in Sampson County, North Carolina, and died 27 January 1966. He married **Mildred Spell.** She was born 13 November 1926, and died 03 December 1971.

Ernie Minson and Mildred were buried in a Spell Family Cemetery on Dunn Road North of Roseboro, North Carolina.

Children of Ernie Spell and Mildred Spell are:

1814 i. **Jimmy Spell.**

1815 ii. **Linda Spell.**

895. Almeta Spell (Braxton^6, Romelia^5 Holland, Harfrey^4, Daniel^3, Thomas William^2, Unknown^1) was born 29 August 1929 in Dismal Township, Sampson County, Noth Carolina. She married **Robert Layman Royal** Before 1946, son of Harrison Hanstein Royal and Lela Holland. He was born 19 January 1923 in Dismal Township, Sampson County, North Carolina.

Robert Layman Royal's middle name is also spelled "LEMAN."

Children of Almeta Spell and Robert Royal are:

1816 i. **Lela Faith Royal**, born 21 May 1946 in Roseboro, Sampson County, North Carolina; died 22 June 1946 in Roseboro, Sampson County, North Carolina.

She was buried in a Spell Cemetery

1817 ii. **Robert Ray Royal,** born 24 November 1947 in Roseboro, Sampson County, North Carolina; died 31 December 1948 in Dismal Township, Sampson County, Noth Carolina.

He is buried in a Spell Cemetery.

1818 iii. **Larry Colon Royal,** born 22 May 1950; died 1966.

He was buried in a Spell Cemetery.

1819 iv. **Stillborn Son Royal,** born 25 April 1953; died 25 April 1953.

Burial: Spell Cemetery.

896. James Oscar Spell (Braxton^6, Romelia^5 Holland, Harfrey^4, Daniel^3, Thomas William^2, Unknown^1) was born About 1930 in Sampson County, North Carolina. He married **Carolyn Osborne** who was born 09 January 1940.

Children of James Spell and Carolyn Osborne are:

1820 i. **Ray Spell.**

1821 ii. **Kathy Spell.**

\+ 1822 iii. **Janet Spell,** born 11 January 1960 in North Carolina.

897. Liston Spell (Braxton^6, Romelia^5 Holland, Harfrey^4, Daniel^3, Thomas William^2, Unknown^1) was born 17 April 1933 in Sampson County, North Carolina, and died 03 August 1981 in Sampson County, North Carolina. He married **Joyce Ann Faircloth.**

Liston was buried in a Spell Family Cemetery on Dunn Road North of Roseboro, North Carolina.

Children of Liston Spell and Joyce Faircloth are:

1823 i. **Elaine Spell.**

1824 ii. **Diane Spell.**

1825 iii. **Janet Spell.**

898. Leola Spell (Braxton[6], Romelia[5] Holland, Harfrey[4], Daniel[3], Thomas William[2], Unknown[1]) was born 28 July 1934 in Dismal Township, Sampson County, Noth Carolina. She married **Arman Onroe Royal** Before 1949, son of Harrison Hanstein Royal and Lela Holland. He was born 19 November 1929 in Dismal Township, Sampson County, North Carolina.

Children of Leola Spell and Arman Royal are:

1826 i. **Arman Roland Royal,** born 19 March 1949 in Roseboro, Sampson County, North Carolina.

1827 ii. **James Sherrill Royal,** born 03 November 1952 in Roseboro, Sampson County.

899. Margaret Doris Spell (Braxton[6], Romelia[5] Holland, Harfrey[4], Daniel[3], Thomas William[2], Unknown[1]) was born 09 December 1935 in Dismal Township, Sampson County, North Carolina. She married **Vernon Holland** 17 November 1951 in Dillon, South Carolina, son of Euland Randolph Holland and Ida Marie Draughon. He was born 14 April 1934 in Honeycutts Township, Sampson County, North Carolina.

Children of Margaret Spell and Vernon Holland are:

\+ 1828 i. **Euland Dwight Holland,** born 29 April 1953 in Clinton, Sampson County, North Carolina.

1829 ii. **Wanda Sue Holland,** born 18 May 1957 in Near Fayetteville, Cumberland County, North Carolina.

1830 iii. **Gary Holland,** born 31 August 1960 in Burlington, North Carolina.

1831 iv. **Danny Holland,** born 20 October 1962 in Hickory, North Carolina.

\+ 1832 v. **Sandra Kay Holland,** born 20 October 1962 in Hickory, North Carolina.

900. Muriel Grace Spell (Braxton[6], Romelia[5] Holland, Harfrey[4], Daniel[3], Thomas William[2], Unknown[1]) was born 11 November 1936 in Sampson County, North Carolina. She married **George William Willis, Jr.**. He was born 11 October 1926 in Sampson County, North Carolina.

Children of Muriel Spell and George Willis are:

\+ 1833 i. **George William Willis III,** born 04 July 1953 in Cumberland County, North Carolina.

1834 ii. **Kenneth H. Willis,** born 27 July 1977 in Cumberland County, North Carolina.

\+ 1835 iii. **Edward W. Willis,** born 10 June 1960 in Cumberland County, North Carolina.

904. Percy Blackman Spell (George Oliver[6], Romelia[5] Holland, Harfrey[4], Daniel[3], Thomas William[2], Unknown[1]) was born 26 October 1920, and died 02 June 1991. He married **Mallie Bullard,** daughter of Lambert Jones Bullard and Penny Autry. She was born 18 December 1925, and died 29 April 1997.

Percy Blackman and Mallie were buried in Union Grove Baptist Church Cemetery on Vander Road (SR 1438) Sampson County, North Carolina.

Child of Percy Spell and Mallie Bullard is:

\+ 1836 i. **Wanda Faye Spell**, born 24 February 1944 in Dismal Township, Sampson County, North Carolina.

907. Lona Marie Faircloth (Sophia[6] Horne, Laura Ann[5] Holland, Harfrey[4], Daniel[3], Thomas William[2], Unknown[1]) was born 02 July 1920. She married **Charlie Nixon**. He was born 20 March 1920.

Child of Lona Faircloth and Charlie Nixon is:

1837 i. **Carol Ann Nixon**, born 02 September 1960.

908. Eva Faircloth (Sophia[6] Horne, Laura Ann[5] Holland, Harfrey[4], Daniel[3], Thomas William[2], Unknown[1]) was born 09 October 1922. She married **William Henry Autry**, son of John Autry and Cordelia Bowers. He was born 30 November 1916, and died 21 July 1951.

His listed date of birth places his birth only eleven days before his sister; One of the dates of birth is incorrect

Child of Eva Faircloth and William Autry is:

\+ 1838 i. **Henry Arnold Autry**, born 14 February 1949 in Roseboro, North Carolina.

909. W. J. Faircloth (Sophia[6] Horne, Laura Ann[5] Holland, Harfrey[4], Daniel[3], Thomas William[2], Unknown[1]) was born 17 January 1924. He married **Frances Hall** who was born 03 November 1928.

Child of W. Faircloth and Frances Hall is:

1839 i. **Betty Faircloth,** born 06 December 1951. She married **Henry Riner, Jr.**; born 29 November 1949.

912. Sarah Elizabeth Faircloth (Sophia[6] Horne, Laura Ann[5] Holland, Harfrey[4], Daniel[3], Thomas William[2], Unknown[1]) was born 12 February 1933. She married **Elree Pittman Horne,** son of Joseph Horne and Ada Bullard. He was born 29 July 1926.

Children of Sarah Faircloth and Elree Horne are:

\+ 1840 i. **Joseph Elliott Horne**, born 03 June 1952.

1841 ii. **Dennis Gerald Horne**, born 11 November 1953. He married **Shellie Jane Horne**.

1842 iii. **Wade Pittman Horne**, born 20 January 1956. He married Lynn Frances Williams; born 25 July 1958.

1843 iv. **Jerry Wayne Horne**, born 11 July 1960.

917. Ruby Sykes Holland (Harvey[6], Henry Lee[5], Harfrey[4], Daniel[3], Thomas William[2], Unknown[1]) was born 08 August 1928 in Honeycutts Township, Sampson County, North Carolina. She married **Crafton Hudson,** son of Jonah Hudson and Hosie Crumpler. He was born 14 October 1928 in Sampson County, North Carolina.

Children of Ruby Holland and Crafton Hudson are:

\+ 1844 i. **Paula Sue Hudson,** born 06 October 1952.

\+ 1845 ii. **Stuart Hudson,** born 29 March 1957.

919. Doris M. Holland (Harvey[6], Henry Lee[5], Harfrey[4], Daniel[3], Thomas William[2], Unknown[1]) was born 19 May 1934, and died 08 May 1998. She married **Lyle Truett Warren, Sr.** 17 May 1953. He was born 05 August 1928, and died 23 September 1991.

It has been mentioned that she researched Holland records for her application for the DAR. Lyle served in the United State Army in Korea. Doris and Lyle are buried in the Salemburg Cemetery, Bearskin Road, Salemburg, North Carolina.

Child of Doris Holland and Lyle Warren is:

1846 i. **Unknown Daughter.**

ii. **Lyle Truett Warren, Jr.**

920. Isham O'Neal McLamb (Pauline[6] Holland, Henry Lee[5], Harfrey[4], Daniel[3], Thomas William[2], Unknown[1]) was born 02 September 1925 in Honeycutts Township, Sampson County, North Carolina, and died 24 May 1984 in Fayetteville, Cumberland County, North Carolina. He married **Lela Beatrice Warren** 24 October 1953 in Honeycutts Township, Sampson County, North Caorlina, daughter of Oscar Warren and Lela Honeycutt. She was born 02 July 1931 in Durham County, North Carolina, and died 17 January 1987 in Fayetteville, Cumberland County, North Carolina.

Child of Isham McLamb and Lela Warren is:

1847 i. **Living McLamb.**

921. William Lischer Lockamy (Onie Vendex[6] Holland, William Wright[5], Thomas James[4], Daniel[3], Thomas William[2], Unknown[1]) was born 17 February 1897 in Sampson County, North Carolina, and died 31 March 1961. He married **Dora Patience Pope** 18 June 1921 in Sampson County, North Carolina, daughter of Nathan Pope and Patience Dixon. She was born 01 May 1905, and died 03 June 1974.

William Lischer and Dora were buried in Owens Grove Pentecostal FWB Church Cemetery, Sampson County, North Carolina.

Children of William Lockamy and Dora Pope are:

+ 1848 i. **Thelma Mae Lockamy,** born 18 June 1922.

1849 ii. **Elma Lucille Lockamy,** born 08 February 1924. She married Jack Sublett; born 31 May 1922.

+ 1850 iii. **John Nathan Lockamy, Sr.,** born 31 August 1927 in Route 1, Clinton, Honeycutts Township, Sampson County, North Carolina; died 21 August 1986.

+ 1851 iv. **Lischer Maylon Lockamy,** born 13 March 1930; died 03 September 1979.

+ 1852 v. **Alton Rexford Lockamy,** born 14 June 1934.

+ 1853 vi. **Onie Evelyn Lockamy,** born 29 March 1937.

922. Annie Lockamy (Onie Vendex[6] Holland, William Wright[5], Thomas James[4], Daniel[3], Thomas William[2], Unknown[1]) was born 04 September 1898 in Sampson County, North Carolina, and died 23 July 1984 in Sampson County. She married **(1) Elger Muscoe C. Cannady**, son of George Cannady and Annie Tyndall. He was born 17 July 1899 in Honeycutts Township, Sampson County, and died 06 August 1948 in Sampson County, North Carolina. He is also found as **"Elder Muscoe Lockamy,"** son of Hanson Lockamy and Lizzie Tyndall.

This "Annie" is probably the daughter of John Robert Lockamy and his second wife, Onie Vendex Holland.

Elger "Muscoe" was the son of Hanson Lockamy and Lizzie Tyndall and Lizzie appears to have died during his birth or soon after. The 1900 census for Sampson County, North Carolina lists him as "Elder M. Lockerman, adopted." By family agreement he was raised by George Austine Cannady and Annie E. Tyndall, sister of Lizzie, his mother. He later changed his name to Cannady. His certificate of death names his "Muscoe C. Cannady," son of George Cannady and Annie E. Tyndell (sic).

The name on his tombstone is "Muscoe C. Cannady;" he was buried in Owens Grove Baptist Church Cemetery, 1085 Kitty Fork Rd, Clinton, North Carolina.

Children of Annie Lockamy and Elger Cannady are:

+ 1854 i. **Ethel L. Cannady,** born 23 September 1919 in North Carolina; died 03 August 2002 in Sampson County, North Carolina.

+ 1855 ii. **James Elder Cannady,** born 08 July 1926.

+ 1856 iii. **William John Cannady,** born 28 March 1930; died 08 July 1988 in Sampson County, North Carolina.

923. Ada Lockamy (Onie Vendex[6] Holland, William Wright[5], Thomas James[4], Daniel[3], Thomas William[2], Unknown[1]) was born 08 October 1901, and died 30 September 1964 in Sampson County, North Carolina. She married **William Adam Tyndall**, son of Solomon Tyndall and Ardella Spell. He was born 16 April 1888, and died 19 April 1980 in Sampson County, North Carolina.

Ada Lockamy and William were buried in Owens Grove PFWB Church Cemetery, Sampson County, North Carolina.

Children of Ada Lockamy and William Tyndall are:

1857 i. **William R. Tyndall,** born 25 March 1922; died 09 February 1973.

Served in the United States Army during World War II.

\+ 1858 ii. **Royce Wilton Tyndall,** born 17 September 1932; died 09 June 1980.

924. Robert Owen Lockamy (Onie Vendex[6] Holland, William Wright[5], Thomas James[4], Daniel[3], Thomas William[2], Unknown[1]) was born 02 September 1904 in Sampson County, North Carolina, and died 01 July 1966 in Sampson County, North Carolina. He married **Nina Metherbell Jackson** 26 September 1925 in Sampson County, Clinton, North Carolina, daughter of Elisha Moore Jackson and Levinnie Cannady. She was born 17 March 1904 in Sampson County, North Carolina, and died 24 September 2000 in Sampson County, North Carolina.

Robert Owen went by the nickname 'Buddy.' He and Nina were buried in Owens Grove Pentecostal FWB Church Cemetery, Sampson County, North Carolina.

Children of Robert Lockamy and Nina Jackson are:

\+ 1859 i. **Astraudia Brown Lockamy,** born 14 September 1926 in Sampson County, North Carolina; died 21 December 1995 in Sampson County, North Carolina.

1860 ii. **James Roland Lockamy,** born 28 March 1928; died October 2006. He married **Flora Jane Hall;** born About 1929 in Sampson County, North Carolina.

No children.

925. Janie Lou Lockamy (Onie Vendex[6] Holland, William Wright[5], Thomas James[4], Daniel[3], Thomas William[2], Unknown[1]) was born 22 July 1910, and died 30 March 1985. She married **Jefferson Franklin Ellis, Sr.,** son of Marion Ellis and Lou Stallings. He was born 31 July 1906, and died 01 May 1975.

Janie Lou and Jefferson were buried in Grandview Memorial Gardens, Clinton, North Carolina.

Children of Janie Lockamy and Jefferson Ellis are:

1861 i. **Jefferson Franklin Ellis, Jr.,** born 15 September 1928; died 15 September 1928.

\+ 1862 ii. **Doris Marie Ellis,** born 25 October 1930 in Honeycutts Township, Sampson County, North Carolina.

1863 iii. **Edna Vendex Ellis.** She married **William Howard Jordan;** born 21 January 1924; died 06 December 1989.

1864 iv. **William Rufus Ellis,** born 23 May 1934. He married **Evelyn Christine Smith;** born 15 July 1935.

One son.

1865 v. **Johnny Franklin Ellis**, born 27 June 1937; died 04 October 1998. He married (1) **Shirley Parish** **b**efore 1957. He married (2) Gloria Dean Cook Before 1966; born 03 August 1938.

Johnny had two children with each spouse. The two children with **Shirley Parish** were adopted by her second husband.

1866 vi. **Decosta Highsmith Ellis**, born 08 December 1939; died 11 January 1990. He married **Edna Marie Lane**; born 13 April 1940.

Two children.

1867 vii. **Mavis Lou Ellis**, born 22 November 1943. She married **Curtis Wesley Tyndall**; born 10 January 1938.

Three children.

1868 viii. **Tommy Jeffery Ellis**, born 24 December 1950. He married (1) **Donna Lynn Lewis** before 1974; born 04 September 1955. He married (2) **Julia Ann Ston**e after 1976; born 12 July 1945.

He and Donna were divorced. Two children.

944. Ivey Gilbert Harper (Vara Irene[6] Boyette, Catherine Grey[5] Holland, Thomas James[4], Daniel[3], Thomas William[2], Unknown[1]) was born 12 February 1922 in Kinston, Lenoir County, North Carolina. He married **Mary Elvera Rust** 09 May 1945 in Salt Lake City, Salt Lake, Utah. She was born 24 March 1927 in Belvedere Garden, Los Angeles, California.

Children of Ivey Harper and Mary Rust are:

1869 i. **Living Harper**.

1870 ii. Living Harper.

1871 iii. **David Wayne Harper**, born 28 February 1951 in Salt Lake City, Salt Lake, Utah.

953. Ivy D. Royal (Robertson[6] Royals, Agnes Matilda[5] Holland, Matthew[4], Daniel[3], Thomas William[2], Unknown[1]) was born 19 March 1910, and died 18 November 1966 in Fayetteville, Cumberland County, North Carolina. One source names him Ivey D. Royal. He married **Roberta Hollingsworth** 18 February 1933 in Clinton, Sampson County, North Carolina. She was born 17 July 1906 and one source names her Rebecca Hollingsworth.

Ivy is also spelled "Ivey."

Children of Ivy Royal and Roberta Hollingsworth are:

\+ 1872 i. **Truman D. Royal**, born 31 December 1933 in Honeycutts Township, Sampson County, North Carolina.

1873 ii. **Elizabeth Royal**, born 12 September 1935. She married **James Bertice Spell**; born 12 June 1938.

956. James Evelyn Royal (Robertson[6] Royals, Agnes Matilda[5] Holland, Matthew[4], Daniel[3], Thomas William[2], Unknown[1]) was born 27 August 1917, and died 13 February 2001. He married **(1) Grace Smith** who was born 28 June 1923, and died November 2002.

James Evelyn and Grace were buried in Sunrise Memorial Gardens, between Roseboro and Salemburg, Sampson County, North Carolina.

Child of James Royal and Grace Smith is:

+ 1874 i. **Evelyn Grace Royal**, born 12 March 1946 in Roseboro, Sampson County, North Carolina.

963. Blackman Dee Tew (Lessie[6] Royals, Agnes Matilda[5] Holland, Matthew[4], Daniel[3], Thomas William[2], Unknown[1]) was born 19 July 1914 in Little Coharie Township, Sampson County, North Carolina. He married **Thelma Hortense Williams** 13 October 1934 in Sampson County, North Carolina, daughter of John Williams and Alma Matthews. She was born 05 January 1917.

Children of Blackman Tew and Thelma Williams are:

1875 i. **John Dee Tew**, born 16 February 1937 in Dismal Township, Sampson County, North Carolina. He married **Annette Jackson** before 1977; born 30 April 1938 in Dunn, Harnett County, North Carolina.

1876 ii. **Jerry Tew**.

981. Julius David Holland, Jr. (Julius David[6], Marshall[5], Matthew[4], Daniel[3], Thomas William[2], Unknown[1]) was born 20 September 1942 in Newton Grove Township, Sampson County, North Carolina. He married **Johnny Faye King**, daughter of Johnny King and Mary Royal. She was born 01 October 1943 in Honeycutts Township, Salemburg, Sampson County, North Carolina.

Children of Julius Holland and Johnny King are:

1877 i. **Jenny Lou Holland**, born 04 January 1966 in Clinton, Sampson County, North Carolina.

1878 ii. **David Wayne Holland**, born 10 January 1970 in Clinton, Sampson County.

984. Roland Duvell Royal (Lela[6] Holland, Robert Mitchell[5], Matthew[4], Daniel[3], Thomas William[2], Unknown[1]) was born 08 December 1916 in Honeycutts Township, Sampson County, North Carolina, and died 29 November 1987 in Fayetteville, Cumberland County, North Carolina. He married **(1) Alma Inez Hall** before 1937, daughter of Charlie Hall and Ida Hall. She was born 03 January 1916 in Little Coharie Township, Sampson County, North Carolina. He married **(2) Mrytle Sessoms** about 1950.

Children of Roland Royal and Alma Hall are:

1879 i. **Betty Anne Royal**, born 18 May 1937 in Dismal Township, Sampson County, Noth Carolina.

She married a **Mr. Horne**.

1880 ii. **Margaret Royal**.

She married a **Mr. Collier**.

\+ 1881 iii. **Roger Ray Royal**, born 08 April 1940 in Roseboro, Sampson County, North Carolina.

1882 iv. **Carol Royal**.

She married **Mr. Stamp**.

1883 v. **Johnie Mack Royal**, born 22 June 1948 in Dismal Township, Sampson County, Noth Carolina.

1884 vi. **Kathy Royal**.

She married **Mr.Cluster**.

985. Coy Aaron Royal (Lela[6] Holland, Robert Mitchell[5], Matthew[4], Daniel[3], Thomas William[2], Unknown[1]) was born 08 August 1918 in Honeycutts Township, Sampson County, North Carolina. He married **Mary Evelyn Sessoms** 13 December 1947. She was born 31 October 1917 in Dismal Township, Sampson County, Noth Carolina, and died 20 January 1992.

Mary Evelyn was buried in the George Horne Cemetery near intersection of South River Road and Minnie Hall Road, Sampson County, North Carolina.

Children of Coy Royal and Mary Sessoms are:

1885 i. **Stillborn Son Royal**, born and died on 09 September 1954 in Roseboro, Sampson County, North Carolina.

He was buried in a Family Cemetery.

1886 ii. **Henry Allen Royal**, born 27 August 1955 in Roseboro, Sampson County, North Carolina.

\+ 1887 iii. **Polly Ann Royal**, born 14 October 1956 in Roseboro, Sampson County.

\+ 1888 iv. **Daniel Britt Royal**, born 15 December 1957 in Roseboro, Sampson County, North Carolina.

986. Amos Harrison Royal (Lela[6] Holland, Robert Mitchell[5], Matthew[4], Daniel[3], Thomas William[2], Unknown[1]) was born 16 January 1921 in Herrings Township, Sampson County, North Carolina, and died 28 October 1986 in Clinton, Sampson County. He married **Reba Mae Holland** before 1945, daughter of Lewis Holland and Carlessie Fann. She was born 25 February 1921 in Honeycutts Township, Sampson County, North Carolina.

The tombstone of Amos in Hollywood Cemetery, has October 29, 1986, for his date of death.

Child is listed above under (726) Reba Mae Holland.

987. Robert Layman Royal (Lela[6] Holland, Robert Mitchell[5], Matthew[4], Daniel[3], Thomas William[2], Unknown[1]) was born 19 January 1923 in Dismal Township, Sampson County, Noth Carolina. He married **Almeta Spell** before 1946, daughter of Braxton Spell and Lela Mae Royal. She was born 29 August 1929 in Dismal Township, Sampson County, Noth Carolina.

"Leman" is also found for his middle name.

Children are listed above under (895) Almeta Spell.

988. E.T. Royal (Lela[6] Holland, Robert Mitchell[5], Matthew[4], Daniel[3], Thomas William[2], Unknown[1]) was born 29 July 1925 in Dismal Township, Sampson County, Noth Carolina. He married **(1) Hazel Irene Johnson** before 1946. She was born about 1928. He married **(2) Jean Elizabeth Hairr** about 2003, daughter of William Rafton Hairr and Dellar Holland. She was born 19 October 1937 in Sampson County, North Carolina. Jean first married Wiley Dixon Knowles; see her elsewhere in this book.

Children of E. Royal and Hazel Johnson are:

1889 i. **Edward Tate Royal**, born 24 February 1946 in Roseboro, Sampson County, North Carolina. He married **Edna Pope**; born 22 November 1948; died 19 July 1994.

1890 ii. **Lela Jennette Royal**, born 19 April 1947 in Roseboro, Sampson County.

1891 iii. **Linda Joyce Royal**, born 16 May 1948 in Roseboro, Sampson County, North Carolina.

1892 iv. **Barbara Ellen Royal**, born 13 July 1950 in Roseboro, Sampson County.

\+ 1893 v. **Margie Helen Royal**, born 03 February 1952 in Roseboro, Sampson County, North Carolina.

1894 vi. **Hazel Lanelle Royal**, born 05 October 1953 in Roseboro, Sampson County.

1895 vii. **Sylvia Delores Royal**, born 17 January 1955 in Roseboro, Sampson County, North Carolina.

\+ 1896 viii. **Peggy Marilyn Royal**, born 08 November 1958 in Fayetteville, Cumberland County, North Carolina.

989. Arman Onroe Royal (Lela[6] Holland, Robert Mitchell[5], Matthew[4], Daniel[3], Thomas William[2], Unknown[1]) was born 19 November 1929 in Dismal Township, Sampson County, Noth Carolina. He married **Leola Spell** Before 1949, daughter of Braxton Spell and Lela Mae Royal. She was born 28 July 1934 in Dismal Township, Sampson County, Noth Carolina. Children are listed under (898) Leola Spell.

991. James William Barnes (Julia[6] Holland, Robert Mitchell[5], Matthew[4], Daniel[3], Thomas William[2], Unknown[1]) was born 05 November 1927 in Sampson County, North Carolina. He married **Elizabeth Gray Keene**, daughter of John Keene and Mamie Daughtry. She was born 20 June 1931.

"Keen" is also found for Elizabeth Gray's maiden name.

Children of James Barnes and Elizabeth Keene are:

\+ 1897 i. **Judy Katherine Barnes**, born 11 May 1948 in Clinton, Sampson County, North Carolina.

\+ 1898 ii. **Jennifer Gray Barnes**, born 16 June 1951.

\+ 1899 iii. **James Welton Barnes, Sr.**, born 19 April 1954.

\+ 1900 iv. **Jerry Trent Barnes**, born 26 November 1956.

\+ 1901 v. **Janet Marie Barnes**, born 20 March 1961.

992. Lester Lee Barnes (Julia[6] Holland, Robert Mitchell[5], Matthew[4], Daniel[3], Thomas William[2], Unknown[1]) was born 06 September 1931 in Sampson County, North Carolina. He married **Madeline Fann**, daughter of Lebron Fann and Olivia Spell. She was born 03 October 1930.

The 14 October 1930 is also found for Madeline's birth.

Children of Lester Barnes and Madeline Fann are:

\+ 1902 i. **Rebecca Sue Barnes**, born 18 November 1952.

1903 ii. **Gloria Ann Barnes**, born 09 June 1954. She married Elton Knowles.

\+ 1904 iii. **Leslie Kent Barnes**, born 24 November 1967.

994. James Rupert Holland, Sr. (Coy[6], Robert Mitchell[5], Matthew[4], Daniel[3], Thomas William[2], Unknown[1]) was born 24 October 1922 in Dismal Township, Sampson County, North Carolina, and died 22 January 1985 in Fayetteville, Cumberland County, North Carolina. He married **Claudette Elvira Pate** 16 October 1943 in Salemburg, North Carolina. She was born 16 March 1925 in Little Coharie Township, Sampson County, North Carolina, and died 03 May 1973 in Roseboro, Sampson County, North Carolina.

Six children. "Eloise" is found in transcribed cemetery records for Claudette's middle name. She and Jame Ruper were buried in Roseboro's Old Hollywood Cemetery on 242, Sampson County, North Carolina.

Child of James Holland and Claudette Pate is:

1905 i. **Claudia Mitchell Holland**, born 12 July 1954 in Roseboro.

Other children of James Rupert and Claudette:

1) **Cary James Holland**, born 30 September 1944 in Roseboro. He married **Della Ann Andrews** who was born 8 January 1946 in Roseboro, daughter of Charles Lee Andrews and Delphia Cathern Warren. One child< **Cary Ann Holland** was born 25 August 1964 in Clinton, North Carolina.

2) **Danny Pate Holland**, born 2 June 1946 in Roseboro.

3) **Larry Douglass Holland**, born 28 October 1947 in Roseboro, Sampson County, North Carolina.

4) **James Rupert Holland, Jr.** born 12 July 1963 in Clinton, Sampson County.

5) **John Winston Holland** was born 21 February 1966 in Clinton.

998. Matthew Mixton Knowles (Chellie[6] Holland, Robert Mitchell[5], Matthew[4], Daniel[3], Thomas William[2], Unknown[1]) was born 25 October 1923 in Honeycutts Township, Sampson County, North Carolina, and died 19 January 1987 in Clinton, Sampson County,

North Carolina. He married **Mallie Bass** 10 September 1944, daughter of Badie Bass and Lenna McLamb. She was born 17 January 1928 in Mingo Township, Sampson County, North Carolina.

Matthew Mixton was buried in Sunrise Memorial Gardens between Salemburg and Roseboro, North Carolina.

Children of Matthew Knowles and Mallie Bass are:

1906 i. **Sylvia Nadine Knowles**, born 17 December 1945 in Roseboro, North Carolina.

\+ 1907 ii. **Larry Mixton Knowles, Sr.**, born 19 October 1946 in Roseboro, Sampson County, North Carolina.

\+ 1908 iii. **Donald Nelson Knowles**, born 28 May 1950 in Roseboro, North Carolina.

1909 iv. **Unnamed Daughter Knowles**, born 11 November 1954 in Clinton, Sampson County, North Carolina.

1000. Wiley Dixon Knowles (Chellie[6] Holland, Robert Mitchell[5], Matthew[4], Daniel[3], Thomas William[2], Unknown[1]) was born 18 October 1928, and died 27 June 1984. He married **Jean Elizabeth Hairr**, daughter of William Rafton Hairr and Dellar Holland. She was born 19 October 1937 in Sampson County, North Carolina. Jean married second, E. T. Royal.

See entries for Jean Elizabeth Hairr and for E. T. Royal. Wiley Dixon was called "Doodle." He was buried in Sunrise Memorial Gardens Cemetery 3 miles north of Roseboro, North Carolina on 242.

Children of Wiley Knowles and Jean Hairr are:

\+ 1910 i. **Wiley Dwight Knowles**, born 01 November 1959.

1911 ii. **Russell Dickson Knowles**, born 11 January 1978.

1008. Daniel Robert Holland (Robert Minson[6], Robert Mitchell[5], Matthew[4], Daniel[3], Thomas William[2], Unknown[1]) was born 24 August 1934 in Honeycutts Township, Sampson County, North Carolina. He married **Betty Lou Smith**, daughter of Vander Smith and Brilla Williams. She was born 04 January 1935 in Dismal Township, Sampson County, North Carolina.

Children of Daniel Holland and Betty Smith are:

1912 i. **Daniel Mitchell Holland**, born 12 September 1956.

\+ 1913 ii. **Robert Mitchell Holland**, born 12 September 1956.

1914 iii. **Susan Michele Holland**, born 27 June 1963. She married Arthur Steven McPhail 14 February 1982; born 09 October 1961 in Germany.

1915 iv. **Daniel Mark Holland**, born 26 July 1971 in Clinton City Cemetery, Clinton, North Carolina. He married **June Michelle Lockamy**. See # 3330 elsewhere in this book for their family.

1009. Della Frances Holland (Robert Minson[6], Robert Mitchell[5], Matthew[4], Daniel[3], Thomas William[2], Unknown[1]) was born 22 October 1937 in Honeycutts Township, Sampson County, North Carolina. She married **Edward Blackman Hollingsworth, Jr.** 21 September 1957 in Dillon, South Carolina, son of Edward Hollingsworth and Eva Owens. He was born 15 July 1930 in Honeycutts Township, Sampson County, North Carolina.

Children of Della Holland and Edward Hollingsworth are:

1916 i. **Yolanda Gail Hollingsworth**, born 10 June 1958 in Suffolk County, New York.

1917 ii. **Sandra Kay Hollingsworth**, born 17 September 1962 in Clinton, Sampson County, North Carolina.

1010. Miles Oscar Simmons (Jathronia[6] Holland, Robert Mitchell[5], Matthew[4], Daniel[3], Thomas William[2], Unknown[1]) was born 23 October 1932 in Herrings Township, Sampson County, North Carolina. He married **Annie Reese Tyndall**, daughter of Garley BraxtonTyndall and Annie Hair. She was born 06 June 1935 in Honeycutts Township, Sampson County, North Carolina.

Annie Reese Tyndall was called Annie 'Recie.' Mr. Rosser, Jr. also refers to her as 'Annie Bell Tyndall.'

Children of Miles Simmons and Annie Tyndall are:

+ 1918 i. **Jewel Reese Simmons**.

+ 1919 ii. **Wade Simmons**, born 23 December 1953.

1012. Donald Ray Simmons (Jathronia[6] Holland, Robert Mitchell[5], Matthew[4], Daniel[3], Thomas William[2], Unknown[1]) was born 03 January 1937 in Herrings Township, Sampson County, North Carolina. He married **Judy Ann Hobbs** 17 August 1956, daughter of Otis Hobbs and Malvine Royal. She was born 02 May 1939 in Little Coharie Township, Sampson County, North Carolina.

Children of Donald Simmons and Judy Hobbs are:

+ 1920 i. **Donna Ann Simmons**, born 17 February 1960 in Clinton, Sampson County, North Carolina.

+ 1921 ii. **Kenneth Ray Simmons**, born 23 December 1972 in Clinton, Sampson County, North Carolina.

1017. Fleet Martin Hall (Mary J.[6] Williams, John E.[5], Tomzelle[4] Culbreth, Mary[3] Holland, Thomas William[2], Unknown[1]) was born 11 January 1885, and died 05 June 1950 in Fayetteville, Cumberland County, North Carolina. He married **Victoria Hall**, daughter of William Thomas Hall, Jr. and Matilda Jane Culbreth. She was born 10 August 1887, and died 18 September 1971 in Falcon, Cumberland County, North Carolina.

Fleet Martin and Victoria were buried in LaFayette Memorial Park, Fayetteville, Cumberland County, North Carolina.

Child of Fleet Hall and Victoria Hall is:

1922 i. **Allie F. Hall**, born about 1908 in Dismal Township, Sampson County, North Carolina.

1018. Thomas Iverson Hall (Mary J.[6] Williams, John E.[5], Tomzelle[4] Culbreth, Mary[3] Holland, Thomas William[2], Unknown[1]) was born 08 November 1886, and died 02 December 1923 in Dismal Township, Clement, Sampson County, North Carolina. He married **Mollie Matilda Autry** before 1923, daughter of John Slocumb Autry and Apsillie Honeycutt. She was born 10 September 1889, and died 29 October 1973 in Fayetteville, Cumberland County, North Carolina.

Thomas Iverson Hall was buried in an Autry Cemetery on Carrol Store Road, Sampson County, North Carolina. Mollie Matilda is buried in Halls United Methodist Church Cemetery on Minnie Hall Road, Sampson County, North Carolina.

Children of Thomas Hall and Mollie Autry are:

\+ 1923 i. **Fletcher Evans Hall**, born 25 January 1914 in Dismal Township, Sampson County, North Carolina.

ii. **William Arthur Hall** was the second child of Thomas and Mollie; he was born 7 March 1941 in Dismal Township, Sampson County, North Carolina.

1924 iii. **Pauline Hall**, born 26 August 1918 in Dismal Township, Sampson County, North Carolina. She married **Eulon Cosby Tyndall**; born 10 January 1915 in Dismal Township, Sampson County, North Carolina. He was the son of **MARTAIN TYNDALL** and **LOUETTA HUDSON.** Pauline and Eulon have four children; one is not identified. **GEORGE CLAYTON TYNDALL** was born 28 March 1943 in Little Choarie Township in Sampson County, North Carolina. **HARVEY LEE TYNDALL** was born 12 May 1945 in Dismal Township and **ORVILLE TRUITT TYNDALL** was born 10 June 1950 in Hope Mills and died either the 18 or 20 June 1950 in Hope Mills, North Carolina.

iv. **George Slocum Hall** was the fourth child or Thomas and Mollie Hall and was born 8 November 1920 in Dismal Township.

v. **Lillie Mae Hall** was born 6 December 1922 and was the fifth child of Thomas and Mollie. She married 17 September 1940 in Dismal Township, **WILBERT OLIVE AUTRY**, son of DANIEL JAMES AUTRY and ROMELIA ESTELLA PAGE Divorced, Lillie married second a **Mr. Hudson** and lived in other states.

Lillie and Wilbert had five children, all born in Roseboro, North Carolina: **MARY DORIS AUTRY,** born 12 March 1942. **GEORGE WILLIE AUTRY,** born 28 August 1943. **CAROLYN AUTRY,** born 18 August 1945. **IZETTA ELAINE AUTRY,** born 18 December 1946. **DANIEL WILBERT AUTRY,** born 10 June 1948.

1025. Jennette Lee Matthews (Susan L.[6] Williams, John E.[5], Tomzelle[4] Culbreth, Mary[3] Holland, Thomas William[2], Unknown[1]) was born 18 June 1900, and died 24 March 1989. She married **Minson Marion Williams** 22 January 1917, son of John D. Williams and Emma Alice McLamb. He was born 01 May 1892, and died 21 July 1966.

Jennette and Minson were buried in a Williams Family Cemetery northeast of Clement in Dismal Township near Dunn Road (SR1002) at SR1441 in Sampson County, North Carolina.

Children of Jennette Matthews and Minson Williams are:

1925 i. **Lawton Gilchrist Williams**, born 31 October 1917; died 26 September 1999.

1926 ii. **Newberry Williams**, born 29 May 1921; died March 1982.

1927 iii. **Nellie Von Williams**, born 23 March 1923; died 18 March 1993.

1928 iv. **Herbert Harrison Williams**, born 16 August 1924; died 05 December 1991.

See elsewhere in this book for other data and list of all known chilren of Jennette Lee Matthews and Minson Marion Williams.

1026. Alex Robinson Bullard (Isabelle[6] Williams, John E.[5], Tomzelle[4] Culbreth, Mary[3] Holland, Thomas William[2], Unknown[1]) was born 11 July 1886, and died 15 February 1958 in Dismal Township, Sampson County, North Carolina. He married **Betsy Rena Matthews,** daughter of Joel H. Mathews and Mary Delitha Hayes. She was born 03 May 1891 in Cumberland County, North Carolina, and died 28 June 1975.

Eight children.

Alex and Betsy Rena were buried in Maxwell Cemetery, Sampson County, North Carolina.

Children of Alex Bullard and Betsy Matthews are:

1929 i. **Mary Bell Bullard**, born 11 December 1911 in Cumberland County, North Carolina; died 29 September 1987 in Swansboro, North Carolina. She married **Howard Arthur Reeves**; born 11 March 1909 in Sampson County, North Carolina.

Mary Bell Bullard and Howard Arthur Reeves had nine children.

1) **HOWARD ASHLEY REEVES** was born 9 February 1934 in South Clinton Township, Sampson County, North Carolina. He married **ELAINE BEVERLY LAWSON** on 6 August 1955 in Arlington, Washington. She was the daughter of Orlon Lawson and Ida Borseth and was born 6 June 1936 in Seattle, Washington. Howard served in the United States Army for nine years. He and Elaine had six children: 1a) **JANICE KAYE REEVES** was born 12 April 1956. 1b) **SHARON FAYE REEVES** was born 1 August 1958. 1c) **BEVERLY JUNE REEVES** was born 23 June 1960. 1d) **WINDY SUE REEVES** was born 10 April 1962. 1e) **SHANDRA BELLE REEVES** was born 25 December 1964. 1f) **ROXANNE REEVES** was born 10 March 1962.

2) **BETSY JANICE REEVES** was born 23 July 1935 (or 20 July 1936) in Clinton, North Caorlina and died 17 July 1937. She was buried in Maxwell Cemetery near Clement in Dismal Township, Sampson County, North Carolina.

3) **SYLVIA ISABELLE REEVES,** third child of Mary Bell and Howard was born 24 October 1937 in South Clinton Township. In Dillon, South Carolina, on 5 September 1955, she married **WALTER WOODROW NORRIS, JR.**, son of Walter Woodrow Norris and Thelma Jones. Walter was born 26 September 1937 in Onslow County, North Carolina; he was a Chief Warrant Office in the United States Army. Three children: **SANDRA MARIE NORRIS**, born 3 March 1957; **DEBRA ANN NORRIS**, born 5 June 1958; **ANNETTE NORRIS**, born 16 July 1959.

4) **ALEX KERR REEVES** was born 11 November 1938 in Taylors Bridge Township in Sampson County, North Carolina. He married in Roanoke Rapids on 15 November 1966 to **FAYE MATTHEWS**, daughter of THELMA NATIONAL MATTHEWS and HATTIE ESTELLE WOODRUFF. Faye was born 25 March 1948 in Roanoke Rapids. One child.

5) **MARY ROBINSON REEVES**, the fifth child of Mary Bell and Howard was born 21 November 1940 in Dismal Township, Sampson County, North Carolina. She married **LARRY HINSON,** son of JOSEPH HOWARD HINSON and MYRTLE LOUISE GINN on 4 August 1959 in Piney Grove Baptist Church. He was born 22 January 1939 in Albemarle, Stanly County. Two children. **ANGELA DELOISE HINSON** was born 3 February 1959 and **LARRY C. HINSON** was born 5 October 1970.

6) **MARTHA BULLARD REEVES** was born 30 March 1942 in Dismal Township, Sampson County, North Carolina. On 25 November 1957 she married in the Grants Creek Parsonage, **ARTHUR BANKS**, son of Alfred Sills Banks and Ruby Estelle Riggs. He was born 10 June 1939 in Onslow County, North Carolina. Two children. **LEN WAYNE BANKS** was born 26 January 1958 and **HOWARD BRENT BANKS**, born 20 April 1966.

7) **LARRY ARTHUR REEVES** was born 19 September 1943 in Onslow County. He served in the United States Army in Vietnam.

8) **CAROLYN FAYE REEVES**, the eighth child of Mary Bell and Howard, was born 20 July 1945 in Jacksonville. She married 16 May 1963 in Swansboro, **RICHARD JOHN LAURINO**, son of Rarafino Laurino and Nicolina DeSimone. He was born 12 December 1942 in Providence, Rhode Island. Two children. **ROBIN ELIZABETH LAURINO** and **BRENDA SUE LAURINO.**

9) **ROBERT BERRY REEVES** was born 14 July 1949 in Onslow County, North Carolina.

1930 ii. **Vara Iredell Bullard**, born 26 January 1914 in Sampson County, North Carolina was the second child of Alex Robinson Bullard and Betsy Rena Matthews. She married **J. Floyd Williams**; born 21 September 1913 in Cumberland County, North Carolina.

1931 iii. **Joel Harding Bullard** who was born 19 August 1920 in Dismal Township, Sampson County, North Carolina was the third child of Alex Robinson Bullard and Betsy Ena Matthews. He died 27 January 1969 in Fayetteville, North Carolina. He married **Beatrice Black** 26 December 1950. She was born 10 November 1924 and died 16 October 1999 and was the daughter of John David Black and Mary Ann West.

Joel Harding and Beatrice were buried in the Maxwell Cemetery near intersectiion of Maxwell Road (SR 1006) and (SR 1427) in Sampson County, North Carolina.

Mrs. Bullard (Miss Black) taught me during my high school years in Salemburg High School, Salemburg, North Carolina. My fellow classmates and I dearly loved her. I'm not sure how many years she taught at Salemburg, but she was one of those dear teachers you always remember. Joel and Beatrice had four children.

1) **JOEL DOUGLAS BULLARD** was born 8 April 1952 in Fayetteville. He married **SUSAN CHRISTINE JOHNSON** who was born about 1955 in Virginia. Two children. **JASON BULLARD** and **CHRISTOPHER JOEL BULLARD**.

2) **DEBORAH ANN BULLARD**, the second child of Joel and Beatrice was born 16 June 1953 in Clinton, North Carolina. She married 17 December 1972 in clement Baptist Church, **KENNETH HAROLD HOUSE,** son of Arther Harold House and Margie Cathrine Page. He was born 8 May 1952 in Craven County. No children.

3) **BETSEY BEATRICE BULLARD** was born 23 January 1955 in Clinton.

4) **MARY BONITA BULLARD**, fourth child of Joel and Beatrice was born 23 September 1958 in Dunn, Harnett County, North Carolina. She married BRYAN WEST.

1932 iv. **Betsy Velva Bullard**, fourth child Alex Robinson Bullard and Betsy Rena Matthews, was born 23 July 1923 in Dismal Township, Sampson County, North Carolina; died 03 August 1923.

She is buried in the Maxwell Cemetery near intersectiion of Maxwell Road (SR 1006) and (SR 1427) in Sampson County, North Carolina.

1933 v. **Male Child Bullard**, fifth child, was born 15 February 1925 in Dismal Township, Sampson County, North Carolina; died 15 February 1925.

He was buried in the Maxwell Cemetery near intersectiion of Maxwell Road (SR 1006) and (SR 1427) in Sampson County, North Carolina.

1934 vi. **William Alex Bullard**, sixth child of Alex Robinson Bullard and Retsy Rena Matthews, was born 10 May 1926 in Dismal Township, Sampson County, North Carolina. He married **Katherine Lorraine Martin** 24 November 1949 in Gaffney, South Carolina; born 20 January 1930 in Black River Township, Cumberland County, North Carolina. Katherine was the daughter of WILLIAM CASPER MARTIN and LILA BELLE DRAUGHON. William served in the United States Marine Corps. He and Katherine had two children. **WILLIAM ALEX BULLARD, JR.**, was born 18 November 1950 in Fayetteville and on 8 June 1975 in Honeycutts Township in Sampson County, he married **SYLVIA PAULINE FANN** who was born 16 March 1953 in Clinton, daughter of RICHARD HILUARD FANN (middle name "Hiluard" may be mispelled) and MARY LOUISE WILLIAMSON. They had one son, **BLAKE ALEX BULLARD**.

William and Katherine's second child was **SUSAN LYNN BULLARD**, born 28 July 1957 in Clinton. She married **MICHAEL WILSON WILLIAMS** who was born 23 April 1958.

1935 vii. **Unknown Bullard**, born 13 May 1928; died 13 May 1928.

He was buried in the Maxwell Cemetery near intersectiion of Maxwell Road (SR 1006) and (SR 1427) in Sampson County, North Carolina.

1936 viii. **Estiline Bullard**, youngest child of Alex Robinson Bullard and Betsy Rena Matthews was born 09 September 1929 in Clinton, Sampson County, North Carolina; died 09 September 1929. Buried in the Maxwell Cemetery near intersectiion of Maxwell Road (SR 1006) and (SR 1427) in Sampson County, North Carolina.

1028. Annie Belle Bullard (Isabelle[6] Williams, John E.[5], Tomzelle[4] Culbreth, Mary[3] Holland, Thomas William[2], Unknown[1]) was born 15 July 1892, and died 14 February 1919 in Flea Hill Township, Cumberland County, North Carolina. She married **John Henry Faircloth** 23 April 1913, son of Raeford Faircloth and Martha Page. He was born 12 November 1892, and died 23 June 1968.

Annie Belle was buried in Bethabara United Methodist Church Cemetery near Clement in Dismal Township, Sampson County, North Carolina. John Henry is buried in the Hall Cemetery on dirt road off South River Road (SR 1424), Sampson County, North Carolina

Children of Annie Bullard and John Faircloth are:

1937 i. **Purvis Faircloth.**

1938 ii. **Janie P. Faircloth**, born 30 August 1917; died 28 February 1919.

1036. Nora Williams (Reason Raiford Robinson[6], John E.[5], Tomzelle[4] Culbreth, Mary[3] Holland, Thomas William[2], Unknown[1]) was born 27 November 1888, and died 13 December 1974 in Clinton, Sampson County, North Carolina. She married **Cleveland Williams** 06 January 1909 in Dismal Township, Sampson County, Nroth Carolina, son of James Williams and Chelly Tew. He was born 12 May 1888, and died 14 December 1910.

Nora and Cleveland were buried in the Union Grove Baptist Church Cemetery on Vander Road west of Rebel City, Sampson County, North Carolina.

Children of Nora Williams and Cleveland Williams are:

1939 i. **Demery C. Williams**, born 10 October 1909.

\+ 1940 ii. **Cleveland N. Williams**, born 20 August 1911; died 20 June 1975.

1039. George Robert Daughtry (George Thomas[6], Molcy[5] Williams, Tomzelle[4] Culbreth, Mary[3] Holland, Thomas William[2], Unknown[1]) was born 31 December 1886, and died 21 October 1938 in Fayetteville, Cumberland County, North Carolina. He married **(1) Nettie Maude Coats** 20 June 1926 in Cedar Creek Township, Cumberland County, North Carolina. She was born 20 February 1889, and died 04 October 1929 in Fayetteville, North Carolina. He married **(2) Elizabeth Jane Mintz** 20 September 1933 in Fayetteville, Cumberland County, North Carolina. She was born 22 November 1904, and died 16 January 1975 in Greenville, North Carolina.

Children of George Daughtry and Elizabeth Mintz are:

1941 i. **Elizabeth Mintz Daughtry**, born 11 July 1935; died 11 July 1935.

1942 ii. **Mary Frances Daughtry**, born 06 June 1937.

1042. Louida Williams (Nathan[6], Joel[5], Tomzelle[4] Culbreth, Mary[3] Holland, Thomas William[2], Unknown[1]) was born 03 July 1877, and died 27 June 1955 in Dunn, North Carolina. She married **Zachariah Collier** 07 October 1894 in Black River Township, Cumberland County, North Carolina. He was born 01 July 1873, and died 20 July 1947 in Black River Township, Cumberland County, North Carolina.

Twelve children. **The birth order of the children below is not correct**, and the format function of Microsoft Word can get downright nasty when I try to make a change and I'm not going to take time to correct the formatting problems here or in a few other places in the manuscript. Many readers of this history, probably understand the frustration of trying to revise a document that has been converted from one format in one software program to another one in a different software. The most problems occur when I try to add data. My age and health create an urgency to try to publish the data I have for several families without much further research. I confess that my patience runs thin when formatting problems occur, especially when in attempting to correct the formatting, I only make it worse.

Children of Louida Williams and Zachariah Collier are:

1943 i. **Lattie Marvin Collier**, born 07 April 1899; died 05 December 1982 in Raleigh, North Carolina. He married **Annie Newton Jernigan** 14 November 1920; born 29 June 1903; died 06 January 1985. Twelve children.

1) **Infant Collier** born 3 August 1921 and died 4 August 1921.

2) **Hannibal Hood Collier** married Thelma Owens.

3) **Burnice Odell Collier** was born 21 October 1924 in Rocky Mount, North Carolina and married Evelyn Ruth Owens on 27 November 1948 in Fayetteville, Cumberland County, North Carolina. She was born 11 March 1927 in Piedmont, South Carolina, daughter of Joseph Owens and Eva Callahan.

4) **William David Collier** was born 26 September 1926 in Meadow Township, Johnston County, North Carolina and died 4 January 1957 in Durham, North Carolina. He married **Bettie Jean Tutor** who was born 21 July 1935 in Erwin, Harnett County, North Carolina. One son, **William Ricky Collier.**

5) **Leroy Collier** was born 12 September 1929 in Meadow Township and married **Barbara Jacobs**. Six children. **Richard Collier**; **Adam Collier**; **Macom Collier**; **Jan Coillier**; **Mary W. Collier**; **Gordon Lee Collier** born 18 July 1956 and died 21 May 1977 in Sampson County, North Carolina.

6) **Ida Mae Collier** was born 26 October 1931 and died 13 October 1984. She married **Mac Donald Grantham** on 19 March 1951, son of **Harvey Grantham** and **Ethel Autry**. He was born 7 August 1929.

7) **Talmade Whitley Collier** was born 23 February 1934 in Eastover Township, Cumberland County, North Carolina and married Betty Jean Weeks on 7 August 1955 in Presbyterian Church in Godwin, Cumberland County, North Carolina. She was born 29 January 1935 in Piney Grove Township in Sampson County. Three children.

8) **Lula Pearl Collier**, born 28 October 1935 in Eastover Township married **William Anthony McLaurin** who was born 25 February 1936 in Eastover Township.

9) **Child Collier** born and died 22 August 1937.

10) **Daughter Collier** born and died 22 August 1937.

11) **Clarence Lloyd Collier** was born 2 November 1940 in Cumberland County, North Carolina and married **Anita Joy McLaurin** 28 March 1964 in Cumberland County, daughter of Leighton McLaurin and Georgia Matthews. She was born 1 June 1946 in Sampson County.

12) **Son Collier** was born and died 21 August 1943 in Wade, Cumberland County.

1944 ii. **Clara Roger Collier**, second child of Louida Williams and Zachariah Collier, was born 06 April 1910. He married **Bernice Inez Jackson** 28 November 1935 in Fayetteville, Cumberland County, North Carolina. She was born 03 November 1918; died 14 August 1978 in Fayetteville, North Carolina and was the daughter of **Gilliam Lester Jackson** and **Loucinda Royals**. Gilliam was the son of Josiah Jackson and Ardella Parker; Loucinda Royals, was the daughter of **Thomas Jefferson Royal** and **Mary Eliza Glover**. Roger married second **Linda Clyde McLellan** on 7 June 1981 in Black's Chapel. She was born 25 December 1936 in Black River Township. Two children.

1) **Clara Louise Collier** was born 28 February 1942 in Grove Township, Harnett County, North Carolina and married **Jack Sherrill Wise** 1 August 1959 in Dillon, South Carolina. He was born 4 March 1937 in Black River Township, Cumberland County.

2) **Sybil Evelyn Collier** was born 25 October 1944 in Grove Township.

\+ 1945 iii. **Blake Oliver Collier**, was born 25 August 1895; died 01 August 1973 in Fayetteville, Cumberland County, North Carolina. Blake married 27 July 1927 in Fayetteville, **Lela Vira Williams**. They are buried in Minson M. Williams Memorail Cemetery. One child, **Mary Maxine Collier**.

iv. **Nora Ophelia Collier**, fourth child of Louida Williams and Zachariah Collier was born 25 March.

1897 and died 29 December 1944 in Dunn, North Carolina. She married 26 November 1916 in Flea Hill Township, **Junious Festus Royal**, son of **Thomas Jefferson Royal** and Mary Eliza Glover who was born 15 May 1887 and died 31 October 1972 in Dunn. No Children. June married second **Selma Gladys Barefoot**, daughter of Jesse Allen Barefoot and Cara Pope. Selma was born 5 October 1904 and died 16 August 1981 in Chapel Hill. No children. Nora, Junious and Selma were buried in Black's Chapel United Methodist Church Cemetery.

v. **James Carlton Collier**, fifth child of Louida Williams and Zachariah Collier, was born 11 April 1901 at Linden and died 29 October 1963 in Fayetteville. He married first 15 may 1921 in Wade, North Carolina, his first cousin **Daisy Maxine Bass,** daughter of **James M. Bass** and **Mackie Collier**. She was born about 1906. One child. Divorced, James married second **Bertha Lemae Taylor** who was born 22 February 1927 in Flea Hill Township. James and Bertha had four children.

I) **Gwendolyn Collier** was born 8 July 1944 in Fayetteville, North Carolina and married **James Frederick Langston** on 29 December 1965 in Fayetteville. He was born 29 October 1944 in Brooklyn New York.

II) **Jessica Colleen Collier** was born 20 February 1948 in Fayetteville and married **James Leon White** 25 July 1965 in Salemburg, North Carolina. He was born 9 April 1947 in Columbia, South Carolina. Jessie married second **Jeff Coutu** before 1983.

III) **Donald James Collier** was born 29 August 1951 in Fayetteville and married **Gail Pruitt** on 7 October 1973 in Wade, Cumberland County, North Carolina. She was born 27 February 1955 in Cobb County, Georgia.

IV) Thomas Gregory Collier was born 22 November 1952 in Fayetteville.

vi. **Roberson Lelland Collier**, child of Louida and Zachariah, was born 1 November 1903 and died 29 August 1979. He married 8 November 1924 in Fayetteville, **Nellie Victoria McMillan**, daughter of **Samuel James McMillan** and **Margie M. Williams**. Nellie was born about 1906.

Eleven children.

1) **Nellie Frances Collier** was born 26 July 1926 in Flea Hill Township, Cumberland County, North Carolina and married Broadus Coolidge Bunce 29 December 1946 in Florence, South Carolina, son of Walter Bunce and Molsey Matthews. He was born 2 September 1924 in Flea Hill Township, Cumberland County. Six children.

2) **Jarvis Talmadge Collier** was born 11 August 1928 in Flea Hill Township and married Polly Ann Kirby, daughter of Arthur Kirby and Dora Tew. She was born 1 March 1939. Three children.

3) **Doris McQueen Collier** was born 13 July 1930 in Eastover Township, Cumberland County.

4) **Lellan Macress Collier** was born 12 October 1931 in Eastover Township and married Ernestine Johnson, daughter of Ernest Johnson and Mary Tew. She was born 6 November 1938. Two children.

5) **Ettrice Louida Collier** was born 26 March 1934 in Eastover Township and married **George Lee Sutherland, Jr.,** who was born 8 June 1931.

6) **Melba Joyce Collier** was born 26 March 1936 in Eastover Township and married Ottis Arthur Thames, Jr., who was born 7 September 1933 in Eastover Township. Two children.

7) **Helen Gray Collier** was born about 1938 and married Floyd Leon Autry on 30 June 1957 in Eastover Township, Cumberland County, North Carolina. He was born 31 January 1936 in Cumberland County.

8) **Jearl Uriah Collier** was born 30 December 1940 and died 17 January 1941 in Eastover Township.

9) **Marjory Anne Collier** was born 11 July 1942 in Eastover Township and married Charles Hester Autry on 24 December 1959 in Dillon, South Carolina. He was born 10 December 1941 in Cedar Creek Township, Cumberland County. Two children.

10) **Gary Bryson Collier** was born 4 December 1945 in Eastover Township.

11) **Jerry Samuel Collier** was born 31 May 1951 in Eastover Toiwnship and married Lois Rouse who was born 8 August 1951 in Fort Bragg, North Carolina. Two children.

vii. **Lonnie Francis Collier,** sevemth child of Louida williams and Zachariah Collier, was born 18 November 1905 and died 11 September 1965 in Eastover Township. He first married 24 December 1928 in Fayetteville, **Nellie Florence Lee**, daughter of **James Robert Lee** and **Virginia Florence Matthews**. Nellie was born 21 March 1906 and died 11 June 1965 in Fayetteville. Both were buried at McMillan Presbyterian Church Cemetery. Four children. Lonnie married second **Ruth Bass**, daughter of **James M. Bass** and **Mackie Collier.**

Children of Lonnie and Nellie:

1) **Lonnie Francis Collier, Jr.** was born 2 October 1929 in Raleigh, North Carolina and died 20 March 1989 in Suffolk, Virginia.

2) **Neuland Craig Collier** was born 30 March 1931 in Dunn, Harnett County, North Carolina.

3) **Robert Riah Collier** married Margaret Mustin. Three children.

4) **Bernard Collier** was born 25 June 1936 in Eatover Township, Cumberland County, North Carolina.

viii. **Sallie Payton Collier**, child of Louida and Zachariah, was born 16 March 1908 and married **Clayton Horace Collier**, son of **James McKenny Collier** and **Kitty Bright Wilkins**. Clayton was born 1 April 1911 in Linden, North Carolina and died 14 July 1981 in Erwin, Harnett County. He is buried at Parker's Grove United Methodist Church Cemetery near Linden. Six children.

1) **Clayton Horace Collier, Jr.,** was born 13 September 1930 in Black River Township, Cumberland County, North Carolina and married **Ruth Ellen Fowler** in October 1950. She was born 29 October 1933 in Erwin, Harnett County, North Carolina. Three children.

2) **Dixie Earlene Collier** was born 15 July 1932 in Carvers Creek Township, Cumberland County and married Bobby Bowman Godwin 31 August 1950. He was born about 1932 in Alamance County, North Carolina. Two children.

3) **Dewey Earl Collier** was born 11 March 1934 in Carvers Creek Township.

4) **Sherrill Allen Collier** was born 29 June 1936 and married Panthia Helen Buie who was born on 10 September 1938 in Carvers Creek Township.

5) **Katie Lue Collier** was born 30 April 1942 in carvers Creek Township.

6) **Brenda Faye Collier** was born 16 February 1945 in Erwin, Harnett County, North Carolina. She first married a Mr. Wood before 1970 and married second to **Robert Lewis Andrews** on 29 May 1971 in Fort Bragg, North Carolina. He was born 28 March 1945 in Washington, D. C. One child with Mr. Wood and they were divorced.

ix. **Zachariah Collier, Jr.** was born 9 August 1912 in Black River Township, Cumberland County and married 22 December 1934 in Wade, **Della Mabel Thornton** of Godwin, daughter of **Luther Washington Thornton** and **Lena Jackson.** Della was born 3 April 1917 in Black River Township. Two children. Lena Jackson was the daughter of **Josiah Jackson** and **Ardella Parker.**

x. Zylphia Lou Collier, tenth child of Louida and Zachariah was born 28 August 1915 in Flea Hill Township and married **Robert Bruce Godwin,** son of **Olin Godwin** and **Millie Bowers**. Bruce was born 14 April 1910. Four children.

xi. **Nathan Penrose Collier** was born 26 January 1918 in Flean Hill Township and married **Edna Florence Stevens** who was born 31 January 1925. Four children.

xii. **William Robert Collier** was born 21 August 1920 in Flea Hill Township and married **Veda Geraldine Smith** on 8 June 1943 in McClenny, Florida. Four children.

1043. John Lewis Williams (Nathan[6], Joel[5], Tomzelle[4] Culbreth, Mary[3] Holland, Thomas William[2], Unknown[1]) was born 25 September 1879, and died 25 September 1959 in Fayetteville, Cumberland County, North Carolina. He married **Julia Catherine Starling,** daughter of George Starling and Mary Williams. She was born 21 November 1882, and died 25 December 1951 in Black River Township, Cumberland County, North Carolina.

Children of John Williams and Julia Starling are:

1946 i. **Dora Mae Williams,** born about 1904. She married **George Lee Sutherland**; born 26 April 1883; died 10 December 1944. Three children.

1) **Annie Virginia Sutherland** was born about 1927 in North Carolina.

2) **Fronnie Berline Sutherland** was born 16 December 1929 in North Carolina.

3) **George Lee Sutherland** was born 8 June 1931 and married **Ettrice Louida Collier** who was born 26 March 1934 in Eastover Township in Cumberland County.

1947 ii. **Ada Pearl Williams,** born 22 October 1905. She married **Hiram Godwin**; born 16 July 1904.

Two children.

1) **Hiram Lewis Godwin** was born about 1926 in Sampson County, North Carolina.

2) **Peggy Godwin** was born about 1928 in Sampson County.

1948 iii. **Lester Clifton Williams,** born 17 May 1907; died 11 September 1979. He married **Belle Wilkinson**; born About 1910.

1949 iv. **Margaret Catherine Williams,** born 12 February 1909. She married **Phillip Benjamin Skillman;** born About 1902.

1950 v. **Berline Frances Williams,** born 13 April 1911.

1951 vi. **Lillian Lewise Williams,** born 13 June 1913; died 12 November 1915.

\+ 1952 vii. **Bonnie Kaye Williams,** born 09 August 1915 in Black River Township, Cumberland County, North Carolina.

1953 viii. **Vergie Irene Williams,** born 07 September 1917, married **Clarence Gilbert Andrews** who was born about 1916. Five children.

1) **Julia Marie Andrews** was born 3 March 1937 in Wilmington.

2) **Teddy Gray Andrews** was born 12 September 1941 in Wilmington.

3) **Robert Lewis Andrews** was born 28 March 1945 in Washington, D.C. and married Brenda Faye Collier on 29 May 1971 in Fort Bragg, North Carolina. She was born 16 February 1945 in Erwin, Harnett County, North Carolina.

4) **David Andrews**

5) **Janet Andrews**

1954 ix. **Ellis Washington Williams,** born 22 October 1919; died 13 January 1934.

1955 x. **Ethel Ruby Williams,** born 22 October 1919 and married Joseph Dewey Smith 22 December 1937 in Westbrooks Township in Sampson County, North Carolina. He was born 25 June 1917 in Mingo Township in Sampson County.

1956 xi. **Julia Melbalene Williams,** born 02 September 1925, married Leo Cecil Strickland on 25 March 1943 in Black River Townahip, Cumberland County, North Carolina, son of William Stricland and Minnie

Tew. He was born 5 March 1918 in Sampson County, North Carolina and died 24 November 1967 in Fayetteville, North Carolina. Two children.

1) **John William Strickland** was born 12 June 1944 in Roseboro, Sampson County and married **Dorothy Louise Markham** who was born 8 June 1945 in Durham County, North CArolina. One child.

2) **Karran Cecilia Strickland** was born 18 July 1949 in Dunn, Harnett County, North Carolina and married **Bruce Harold Cain** who was born 7 January 1949 in Hope Mills, Cumberland County, North Carolina.

1044. Mary Frances Williams (Nathan[6], Joel[5], Tomzelle[4] Culbreth, Mary[3] Holland, Thomas William[2], Unknown[1]) was born 19 October 1881, and died 27 February 1919 in Black River Township, Cumberland County, North Carolina. She married **Charles Herman Starling** 24 April 1909 in Godwin, Cumberland County, North Carolina, son of Murdock Starling and Adeline Autry. He was born 08 January 1888, and died 03 July 1958 near Fayetteville, Cumberland County, North Carolina.

Children of Mary Williams and Charles Starling are:

1957 i. **Alma Starling**, born 23 July 1909.

1958 ii. **Henry Alton Starling**, born 05 October 1910; died 26 August 1977. He married Nettie Clara Williams 01 December 1934 in Wade, Cumberland County, North Carolina; born 02 July 1904; died 25 September 1981 in Fayetteville, Cumberland County, North Carolina.

He and Nettie had one known child, **Herbert Eldon Starling** who was born 6 November 1937 in Dismal Township. Herbert married **Patricia Lester Taylor** who was born 31 January 1941 in Little Coharie Township, Patricia was the daughter of Thomas Lee Taylor and Dorothy Florence Butler. He and Nettie were buried in the Williams Family Cemetery northeast of Clement in Dismal Township near Dunn Road (SR1002) at SR1441 in Sampson County, North Carolina

1959 iii. **Claudia Starling**, born 16 February 1912.

1960 iv. **John C. Starling**, born 08 October 1914 (monument reads 8 November 1913) in Black River Township and died 18 December 1970 in Fayetteville. He married **Mamie Adams** who was born 24 April 1908. Two children, **Shelby Jean Starling** who was born 24 April 1908 and **Arnold Gray Starling.** John was buried in LaFayette Memorial Park in Fayetteville.

1961 v. **Myra Merle Starling**, born 21 November 1916 and died 19 January 1984 in Fayetteville, She married **Winston Larkins** of Florida. She was buried at the Bluff Presbyterian Church Cemetery. Two sons: **Richard Larkins** and **Carl Larkins.**

1962 vi. **Vira Pearl Starling**, born 21 November 1916, a twin, was born 21 November 1916 in Dunn, Harnett County. She married first **Donald Billman**, second **Victor Malone**, third **to Frank Stansbury** and fourth, and fifth **Kenneth C. Patterson.**

1963 vii. **Child Starling**, born and died on 18 February 1919.

1048. Janie Williams (Joel E.[6], Joel[5], Tomzelle[4] Culbreth, Mary[3] Holland, Thomas William[2], Unknown[1]) was born 20 June 1890, and died 01 April 1940 in Fayetteville, North Carolina. She married **Joseph Palmer Riddle** 11 April 1918 in Cross Creek Township, Cumberland County, North Carolina. He was born 19 May 1899 in Moon City, Moore County, North Carolina, and died 04 November 1948 in Fayetteville, North Carolina.

Child of Janie Williams and Joseph Riddle is:

1964 i. **Sherrill Hampton Riddle**, born 18 November 1925 in Fayetteville, North Carolina. He married **Bronnie Jean Kinsauls**; born 11 November 1933 in Fayetteville, Cumberland County, North Carolina.

1052. Alexander Williams, Jr. (Alexander[6], Joel[5], Tomzelle[4] Culbreth, Mary[3] Holland, Thomas William[2], Unknown[1]) died 1947. He married **Leola Steward**. She was born 21 October 1906, and died 1987.

Alexander and Leola were buried in Greenwood Cemetery, Dunn, Harnett County, North Carolina.

Children of Alexander Williams and Leola Steward are:

1965 i. **Willie Rudolph Williams**, born 1924.

1966 ii. **Beatrice W. Williams**, born 1927.

1967 iii. **Bobby Shelton Williams**, born 1931.

1968 iv. **Stanley Parker Williams**, born 1933.

1056. Myrtle Williams (Alexander[6], Joel[5], Tomzelle[4] Culbreth, Mary[3] Holland, Thomas William[2], Unknown[1]) was born 19 May 1903 in Sampson County, North Carolina, and died 14 September 1981 in Erwin, North Carolina. She married **Matthew Royals** 30 June 1927, son of Henry H. Royals, Sr. and Agnes Matilda Holland. He was born 04 November 1895 in Sampson County North Carolina, and died 05 December 1976 in Erwin, North Carolina.

Myrtle and Matthew were buried in Erwin Memorial Park, Harnett County, North Carolina.

Children are listed above under (337) Matthew Royals.

1065. Pinkie Williams (John Robert[6], Joel[5], Tomzelle[4] Culbreth, Mary[3] Holland, Thomas William[2], Unknown[1]) was born 01 November 1899 in Hayne, Samspon County, North Carolina. She married **(1) Albert W. Bolton** 10 March 1917 in Grays Creek Township, Cumberland County, North Carolina. He was born about 1896. She married **(2) D. C. Ackerman** before 1920. He was born in about 1893. She married **(3) Unknown Cannon** before 1957.

Child of Pinkie Williams and D. Ackerman is:

1969 i. **Ruth Devere Ackerman**, born 27 September 1920 in Cumberland County, North Carolina.

1070. Julia Catherine Starling (Mary Catherine[6] Williams, Isaac[5], Tomzelle[4] Culbreth, Mary[3] Holland, Thomas William[2], Unknown[1]) was born 21 November 1882, and died 25 December 1951 in Black River Township, Cumberland County, North Carolina. She married **John Lewis Williams**, son of Nathan Williams and Mary Strickland. He was born 25 September 1879, and died 25 September 1959 in Fayetteville, Cumberland County, North Carolina.

Children are listed above under (1043) John Lewis Williams.

1071. Emily Jane Starling (Mary Catherine[6] Williams, Isaac[5], Tomzelle[4] Culbreth, Mary[3] Holland, Thomas William[2], Unknown[1]) was born 21 June 1885 in Cumberland County, North Carolina, and died 19 July 1969 in Fayetteville, Cumberland County, North Carolina. She married **John Julian Autry** 16 November 1919 in Black River Township, Cumberland County, North Carolina, son of Daniel Autry and Rebecca Honeycutt. He was born 16 April 1881 in Sampson County, North Carolina, and died 29 January 1943 in Dismal Township, Sampson County, North Carolina.

Children of Emily Starling and John Autry are:

1970 i. **Dixie Alease Autry**, born 30 December 1920. She married **WILLIAM SESSOMS CULBRETH** 31 July 1939 in Fayetteville, Cumberland County, North Carolina; born 22 October 1918 in Flea Hill Township, Cumberland County, North Carolina; died 03 October 1974 in Fayetteville, North Carolina.

Three children.

William was buried in Salem United Methodist Church Cemetery on SR 1003, three miles west of Delway, Sampson County, North Carolina.

1971 ii. **Child Autry**, born 21 June 1922; died 21 June 1922.

1972 iii. **Jessie Autry**, born 20 August 1923.

1973 iv. **Mary Magdalene Autry**, born 30 April 1925.

1974 v. **James Julian Autry**, born 25 April 1927.

1073. Arthur Leon Starling, Sr. (Mary Catherine[6] Williams, Isaac[5], Tomzelle[4] Culbreth, Mary[3] Holland, Thomas William[2], Unknown[1]) was born 14 January 1890, and died 21 June 1974 in Rocky Mount, North Carolina. He married **Sarah Elizabeth Dorman** 28 June 1914 in Godwin, Cumberland County, North Carolina. She was born 08 May 1886, and died 04 December 1954.

Children of Arthur Starling and Sarah Dorman are:

1975 i. **Arthur Leon Starling, Jr.**, born 22 September 1915.

1976 ii. **Mabel Elizabeth Starling**, born 10 November 1917; died 18 October 1918.

1074. Luther Washington Starling (Mary Catherine[6] Williams, Isaac[5], Tomzelle[4] Culbreth, Mary[3] Holland, Thomas William[2], Unknown[1]) was born 06 November 1891, and died 16 January 1982 in Dunn, Harnett County, North Carolina. He married **Myrtle**

Matilda Baggett 08 February 1914, daughter of William Baggett and Delia Godwin. She was born 10 March 1897 in Sampson County, North Carolina, and died 05 December 1992 in Dunn, Harnett County, North Carolina.

Luther was a retired school teacher. He taught for 45 years at Mary Stewart, Plain View, Union Academy, Five Oaks, South River, and Mingo schools. He and Myrtle were buried in Antioch Baptist Church Cemetery, Falcon, Cumberland County, North Carolina.

Children of Luther Starling and Myrtle Baggett are:

+ 1977 i. **Ruth Starling**, born 16 November 1915 in Mingo Township, Sampson County, North Carolina.

+ 1978 ii. **Avis Starling**, born 26 November 1919 in Mingo Township, Sampson County, North Carolina.

1979 iii. **Burnice Starling**, born 14 May 1920 in Black River Township, Cumberland County, North Carolina. She married Glenn Stewart.

+ 1980 iv. **Don Ella Starling**, born 16 September 1922 in Black River Township, Cumberland County, North Carolina.

+ 1981 v. **Doris Elaine Starling**, born about 1926.

1075. Mary Eliza Starling (Mary Catherine[6] Williams, Isaac[5], Tomzelle[4] Culbreth, Mary[3] Holland, Thomas William[2], Unknown[1]) was born 19 August 1893, and died 12 August 1934 in Newton Grove Township, Sampson County, North Carolina. She married **James Thomas Hayes** 24 December 1911 in Black River Township, Cumberland County, North Carolina, son of Dempsey Hayes and Emily Jackson. He was born 12 October 1889 in Sampson County, North Carolina, and died 27 March 1963 in Eastover Township, Cumberland County, North Carolina.

Children of Mary Starling and James Hayes are:

1982 i. **Agnes Marie Hayes**, born 09 January 1914.

1983 ii. **James Willard Hayes**, born 13 May 1916.

1984 iii. **Jessamine Estaline Hayes**, born 28 September 1918.

1985 iv. **Thomas Wilbur Hayes**, born 18 December 1920.

1986 v. **Doris Eloise Hayes**, born 25 July 1924.

1076. Martha Ann Starling (Mary Catherine[6] Williams, Isaac[5], Tomzelle[4] Culbreth, Mary[3] Holland, Thomas William[2], Unknown[1]) was born 19 August 1893, and died 04 November 1987 in Eastover Township, Cumberland County, North Carolina. She married **John Hinton Matthews, Sr.** 23 October 1910 in Black River Township, Cumberland County, North Carolina. He was born 08 July 1888, and died 11 February 1971 in Fayetteville, Cumberland County, North Carolina.

Children of Martha Starling and John Matthews are:

1987 i. **Percy Olive Matthews**, born 24 March 1912; died 30 December 1914.

1988 ii. **Bessie Mae Matthews**, born 18 August 1914.

1989 iii. **Nellie Inez Matthews**, born 24 December 1916.

1990 iv. **Eunice Marie Matthews**, born 26 August 1919.

1991 v. **Anne Christine Matthews**, born 25 February 1924.

1992 vi. **Elizabeth Starling Matthews**, born 24 April 1927.

1993 vii. **John Hinton Matthews, Jr.**, born 26 September 1929.

1077. Leonard Bryan Starling (Mary Catherine[6] Williams, Isaac[5], Tomzelle[4] Culbreth, Mary[3] Holland, Thomas William[2], Unknown[1]) was born 14 October 1896 in Sampson County, North Carolina, and died 31 December 1978 in Rocky Mount, North Carolina. He married **(1) Meta Ellen Jernigan** 24 March 1920 in Falcon, Cumberland County, North Carolina. She was born About 1903. He married **(2) Blanche Quincy** After 1922. She was born about 1900.

Meta's name is also shown as "Mattie Ellen."

Child of Leonard Starling and Meta Jernigan is:

1994 i. **Evelyn L. Starling**, born 09 October 1922.

1078. Rev. Hiram Roberson Starling (Mary Catherine[6] Williams, Isaac[5], Tomzelle[4] Culbreth, Mary[3] Holland, Thomas William[2], Unknown[1]) was born 12 May 1898 in Godwin, Sampson County, North Carolina, and died 29 May 1983. He married **Denative Irene Hawley**, daughter of Jonathan Hawley and Louise Naylor. She was born 06 September 1902 in Sampson County, North Carolina, and died 25 November 1979 in Near Lillington, North Carolina, Harnett County, North Carolina.

Rev. Hiram Starling was buried in Antioch Baptist Church Cemetery.

Children of Hiram Starling and Denative Hawley are:

+ 1995 i. **Hiram Roberson Starling, Jr.**, born 23 April 1923 in Nash County, North Carolina; died 18 July 1980 in Erwin, Harnett County, North Carolina.

1996 ii. **Edna Starling**, born 07 August 1929; died 12 August 1929.

She was buried in Antioch Baptist Church Cemetery.

+ 1997 iii. **George Washington Starling**, born 07 March 1931 in Rocky Mount Township, Nash County, North Carolina; died 06 November 1977.

1080. Fletcher E. Wrench (Lovdie Ann[6] Williams, Isaac[5], Tomzelle[4] Culbreth, Mary[3] Holland, Thomas William[2], Unknown[1]) was born 01 January 1882, and died 22 March 1968 near Autryville, North Carolina. He married **Anna Belle Williams** 10 July 1910 in Dismal Township, Sampson County, Nroth Carolina, daughter of James Williams and Elizabeth

Williams. She was born 01 July 1892 in Sampson County, North Carolina, and died 08 August 1940 in Dismal Township in Sampson County.

Fletcher and Anna Bell were buried in the Minson M. Williams Family Cemetery at the northeast corner of Dunn Road (SR 1002 and SR 1441. Dismal Township, Sampson County, North Carolina.

Children of Fletcher Wrench and Anna Williams are:

\+ 1998 i. **Straudia Almeta Wrench**, born 07 March 1912; died 11 October 1995.

\+ 1999 ii. **Quinton Randall Wrench**, born 11 March 1914; died 25 August 1994.

2000 iii. **Winnie Marguerite Wrench**, born 17 November 1916.

1081. Cornelia Wrench (Lovdie Ann[6] Williams, Isaac[5], Tomzelle[4] Culbreth, Mary[3] Holland, Thomas William[2], Unknown[1]) was born 05 September 1884, and died 15 July 1969. She married **Theophilus Beaufort Tew, Sr.** 09 February 1902 in Sampson County, North Carolina, son of James Jackson and Sylvania Tew. He was born 25 September 1872 in Sampson County, North Carolina, and died 29 October 1949 in Dismal Township, Sampson County, North Carolina.

Theophilus was called "Offe." He and Cornelia were buried in Baptist Chapel Church Cemetery on Baptist Chapel Road (SR 1455), Sampson County, North Carolina.

Children of Cornelia Wrench and Theophilus Tew are:

2001 i. **Juanita Tew**, born 31 December 1902 in Sampson County, North Carolina; died 30 May 1983 in Fayetteville, Cumberland County, North Carolina. She married **Harold Worth Heath**; born 23 August 1903; died 11 November 1968 in Dismal Township, Sampson County, North Carolina.

No children.

Juanita and Harold were buried in Baptist Chapel Church Cemetery on Baptist Chapel Road, Sampson County, North Carolina.

2002 ii. **James C. Tew**, born 14 June 1904; died 19 May 1907.

He was buried in Baptist Chapel Church Cemetery on Baptist Chapel Road, Sampson County, North Carolina.

\+ 2003 iii. **Roy Vernon Tew, Sr.**, born 14 June 1904; died 15 October 1953.

2004 iv. **Hazel Tew**, born 06 June 1905; died 18 February 1906.

She was buried in Baptist Chapel Church Cemetery on Baptist Chapel Road, Sampson County, North Carolina.

\+ 2005 v. **Earl Gladstone Tew**, born 25 November 1907 in Sampson County, North Carolina; died 10 September 1940 in Dismal Township, Sampson County, North Carolina.

2006 vi. **Berkie Carwin Tew**, born 26 July 1909; died 23 October 1909.

He was buried in Baptist Chapel Church Cemetery on Baptist Chapel Road, Sampson County, North Carolina.

2007 vii. **Wallace Linwood Tew**, born 30 July 1910 in Sampson County, North Carolina. He married **Shellie A. Wood**; born 03 April 1913 in Columbia, South Carolina; died 04 August 1997.

Shellie was buried in Baptist Chapel Church Cemetery on Baptist Chapel Road (SR 1455), Sampson County, North Carolina.

\+ 2008 viii. **May Dee Tew**, born 12 May 1912 in Sampson County, North Carolina.

2009 ix. **Wilma Tew**, born 02 January 1914; died 08 February 1915.

She was buried in Baptist Chapel Church Cemetery on Baptist Chapel Road, Sampson County, North Carolina.

\+ 2010 x. **Wyman A. Tew**, born 02 January 1914; died 12 December 1980.

\+ 2011 xi. **Desmon Shelton Tew**, born 21 August 1915 in Dismal Township, Sampson County, North Carolina.

2012 xii. **Infant Tew**, born 20 October 1917; died 20 October 1917.

\+ 2013 xiii. **Theophilus Beaufort Tew, Jr.**, born 13 September 1919 in Dismal Township, Sampson County, North Carolina; died 13 March 1992.

2014 xiv. **Wallace Tew**, born 26 April 1921; died 26 September 1921.

He was buried in Baptist Chapel Church Cemetery on Baptist Chapel Road, Sampson County, North Carolina.

\+ 2015 xv. **Sylvia Ann Tew**, born 02 October 1923 in Dismal Township, Sampson County, North Carolina.

1083. Viola Beatrice Williams (Daniel[6], Isaac[5], Tomzelle[4] Culbreth, Mary[3] Holland, Thomas William[2], Unknown[1]) was born 16 May 1891, and died 16 July 1964. She married **William Ferdinand Matthews** 10 June 1914 in Sampson County, North Carolina, son of Frederick Matthews and Amanda Hayes. He was born 28 October 1873 in Dismal Township, Sampson County, North Carolina, and died 15 January 1948 in Dismal Township, Sampson County, North Carolina.

Viola Beatrice and William were buried in the Minson M. Williams Family Cemetery at the northeast corner of Dunn Road (SR 1002 and SR 1441. Dismal Township, Sampson County, North Carolina.

Child of Viola Williams and William Matthews is:

\+ 2016 i. **Trixy Hilda Matthews**, born 16 August 1919 in Dismal Township, Clement, Sampson County, North Carolina; died 19 November 1983 in Durham, North Carolina.

1085. Mary V. Williams (Daniel[6], Isaac[5], Tomzelle[4] Culbreth, Mary[3] Holland, Thomas William[2], Unknown[1]) was born 03 December 1893, and died 06 April 1964 in Grays Creek Township, Cumberland County, North Carolina. She married **Ivey D. Tyndall** 07 April 1920 in Dismal Township, Sampson County, Nroth Carolina, son of Peter Tyndall and Spicey Tew. He was born 21 March 1894, and died 26 March 1940 in Dismal Township, Sampson County, North Carolina.

Mary and Ivey were buried in Baptist Chapel Church Cemetery on Baptist Chapel Road, Sampson County, North Carolina.

Children of Mary Williams and Ivey Tyndall are:

2017 i. **Virginia Marilyn Tyndall**, born 18 February 1921; died in Lorrianne.

2018 ii. **Lorrianne Tyndall**, born 24 August 1923.

2019 iii. **Margie Azalie Tyndall**, born 29 June 1925.

2020 iv. **Wynona Adaline Tyndall**, born 02 June 1927.

1087. Lela Vira Williams (Daniel[6], Isaac[5], Tomzelle[4] Culbreth, Mary[3] Holland, Thomas William[2], Unknown[1]) was born 16 June 1897, and died 16 March 1978 in Fayetteville, Cumberland County, North Carolina. She married **Blake Oliver Collier** 27 July 1927 in Fayetteville, Cumberland County, North Carolina, son of Zachariah Collier and Louida Williams. He was born 25 August 1895, and died 01 August 1973 in Fayetteville, Cumberland County, North Carolina.

Child of Lela Williams and Blake Collier is:

2021 i. **Mary Maxine Collier.**

1088. Joel Judson Williams (Daniel[6], Isaac[5], Tomzelle[4] Culbreth, Mary[3] Holland, Thomas William[2], Unknown[1]) was born 21 January 1899 in Sampson County, North Carolina, and died 25 August 1980 in Clinton, Sampson County, North Carolina. He married **Lula Pearl Tyndall**, daughter of Ollen Tyndall and Nancy Edwards. She was born 18 October 1906 in Sampson County, North Carolina, and died 24 November 1988 in Orlando, Florida.

August 1, 1973, is also found for Lula's date of death. Joel Judson and Lula Pearl were buried in the Williams Family Cemetery northeast of Clement in Dismal Township near Dunn Road (SR1002) at SR1441 in Sampson County, North Carolina

Children of Joel Williams and Lula Tyndall are:

2022 i. **Hubert McCoy Williams**, born 16 November 1923 in Honeycutts Township, Sampson County, North Carolina.

He lived in Orlando, Florida.

2023 ii. **China Belle Williams**, born 17 October 1925 in Dismal Township, Sampson County.

She married a "**Wilson**" and lived Maryland.

2024 iii. **Judson McCantol Williams**, born 15 June 1927 in Honeycutts Township, Sampson County, North Carolina; died 01 August 1927.

He was buried in Minson M. Williams Memorial Cemetery.

\+ 2025 iv. **Lubie Egbert Williams**, born 29 August 1928 in Fayetteville, Cumberland County, North Carolina; died 02 December 1984 in Durham, North Carolina.

\+ 2026 v. **Bonnie Dell Williams**, born 26 November 1930 in Herrings Township, Sampson County, North Carolina.

2027 vi. **Herbert Preston Williams**, born 25 April 1932 in Dismal Township, Sampson County.

At one time, Herbert lived in Detroit, Michigan.

1090. Daniel Webster Williams (Daniel[6], Isaac[5], Tomzelle[4] Culbreth, Mary[3] Holland, Thomas William[2], Unknown[1]) was born 09 November 1901, and died 08 August 1982. He married **Lossie Mae Tew**, daughter of William Tew and Malissa Honeycutt. She was born 24 October 1906 in Sampson County, North Carolina, and died 09 January 2000.

Daniel Webster and Lossie Mae were buried in the Williams Family Cemetery northeast of Clement in Dismal Township near Dunn Road (SR1002) at SR1441 in Sampson County, North Carolina.

Children of Daniel Williams and Lossie Tew are:

2028 i. **First Stillborn Williams**, born 28 February 1924.

2029 ii. **Second Stillborn Williams**, born 28 February 1924.

2030 iii. **William Norwood Williams**, born 01 March 1925.

2031 iv. **Glenwood Lee Williams**, born 25 September 1926.

2032 v. **Maxton Parker Williams**, born 26 May 1928.

2033 vi. **Claxton Webster Williams**, born 13 September 1929.

2034 vii. **Raxton Ray Williams**, born 10 May 1931; died 14 April 1949.

He was buried in the Williams Family Cemetery northeast of Clement in Dismal Township near Dunn Road (SR1002) at SR1441 in Sampson County, North Carolina

2035 viii. **Malisha L. Williams**, born 16 July 1932; died 20 July 1933.

2036 ix. **Vanita Ann Williams**, born 14 January 1934.

2037 x. **Luther R. Williams**, born 26 October 1935; died 09 February 1936.

2038 xi. **Patricia Mae Williams**, born 17 December 1936.

1093. Olive Earl Williams (Daniel[6], Isaac[5], Tomzelle[4] Culbreth, Mary[3] Holland, Thomas William[2], Unknown[1]) was born 23 February 1910, and died 23 October 1984. He married **Katy Pearl Mathis** 30 January 1932 in South Carolina. She was born 12 January 1916 in Cedar Creek Township, Cumberland County, North Carolina.

Olive Earl and Katy Pearl were buried in Clement Missionary Baptist Church Cemetery on Maxwell Road (SR1006) about 0.5 mile west of Sr 1425 in Sampson County, North Carolina.

Child of Olive Williams and Katy Mathis is:

2039 i. **Havens Williams,** born 30 October 1939. She married Donald Strickland.

1094. Oleta Gladys Williams (Daniel[6], Isaac[5], Tomzelle[4] Culbreth, Mary[3] Holland, Thomas William[2], Unknown[1]) was born 02 November 1913 in Dismal Township, Sampson County, North Carolina, and died 17 September 1981 in Clinton, Sampson County, North Carolina. She married **Alec Martin Parker**. He was born 22 October 1908, and died 23 April 1966 in Clinton, Sampson County, North Carolina.

Children of Oleta Williams and Alec Parker are:

2040 i. **Stillborn Parker.**

2041 ii. **Susan Elaine Parker,** born 28 November 1940.

Stillborn.

2042 iii. **Martain Stephen Parker,** born 28 October 1945.

2043 iv. **Stillborn Daughter Parker,** born 01 September 1947.

2044 v. **Lexie Dale Parker,** born about 1953.

1095. Elizabeth Jane Williams (Sarah Eliza[6], Isaac[5], Tomzelle[4] Culbreth, Mary[3] Holland, Thomas William[2], Unknown[1]) was born 17 November 1886 in Sampson County, North Carolina, and died 09 November 1935. She married **John Ed Page** 24 October 1909 in Dismal Township, Sampson County, North Carolina, son of Alexander Page and Elizabeth Bain. He was born 13 June 1887, and died 01 June 1968 near Clinton, Sampson County, North Carolina.

Elizabeth Jane and John were buried in Baptist Chapel Church Cemetery on Baptist Chapel Road, Sampson County, North Carolina.

Child of Elizabeth Williams and John Page is:

2045 i. **Cladie Verle Page,** born 08 October 1912; died 25 February 2000. She married **James Stacy Hairr** 27 February 1932; born 07 August 1909; died 27 July 1970 in Dunn, North Carolina.

She and James were buried in Baptist Chapel Church Cemetery on Baptist Chapel Road, Sampson County, North Carolina.

1097. Molcy Jo Williams (Sarah Eliza[6], Isaac[5], Tomzelle[4] Culbreth, Mary[3] Holland, Thomas William[2], Unknown[1]) was born 01 September 1890 in Sampson County, North Carolina, and died 24 November 1976. She married **Troy Spell** 10 May 1928 in Sampson County, North Carolina, son of Wiley Spell and Narcissa Royal. He was born 06 May 1875 in Sampson County, North Carolina, and died 04 December 1943 in Dismal Township, Sampson County, North Carolina.

Eight children. Molcy Jo and Troy were buried in Union Grove Baptist Church Cemetery on Vander Road (SR 1438) Sampson County, North Carolina.

Child of Molcy Williams and Troy Spell is:

2046 i. **Vera Spell.** She married **Harmon L. Baucom**.

1098. Lillie Mae Williams (Sarah Eliza[6], Isaac[5], Tomzelle[4] Culbreth, Mary[3] Holland, Thomas William[2], Unknown[1]) was born 03 May 1893 in Sampson County, North Carolina, and died 27 January 1976. She married **Algie Matthews** 02 August 1914 in Sampson County, North Carolina. He was born 16 September 1894, and died 21 August 1971 in Clinton, Sampson County, North Carolina.

Lillie Mae and Algie were buried in Bethabara United Methodist Church Cemetery in Sampson County on SR1006 about 3 miles east of the Cumberland County line.

Children of Lillie Williams and Algie Matthews are:

2047 i. **Dorothy Elmo Matthews,** born 25 April 1915.

2048 ii. **Myrtle L. Matthews,** born 26 June 1919; died 21 April 1920.

2049 iii. **William Love Matthews.**

2050 iv. **Waylon Matthews.**

2051 v. **Susan Matthews.**

2052 vi. **Sarah Matthews.**

2053 vii. **Naomi Matthews.**

2054 viii. **Robert Matthews.**

2055 ix. **Lillian Matthews.**

2056 x. **Reba Matthews.**

2057 xi. **Shelby Matthews,** born 24 May 1937; died 30 October 1937.

1099. King Sanford Williams, Sr. (Sarah Eliza[6], Isaac[5], Tomzelle[4] Culbreth, Mary[3] Holland, Thomas William[2], Unknown[1]) was born April 1895 in Sampson County, North Carolina. He married **Annie Mae Hall**. She was born September 1899.

Children of King Williams and Annie Hall are:

2058 i. **King Sanford Williams, Jr.**

2059 ii. **Howard Williams.**

2060 iii. **Zinnia Williams.**

2061 iv. **Leslie Williams.**

2062 v. **Helen Williams.**

1100. Samuel Tilden Williams (Sarah Eliza[6], Isaac[5], Tomzelle[4] Culbreth, Mary[3] Holland, Thomas William[2], Unknown[1]) was born 25 May 1898 in Sampson County, North Carolina, and died 28 December 1977 in Clinton, Sampson County, North Carolina. He married **Mae Zula Lewis**. She was born 18 July 1909, and died 15 November 1981.

Samuel Tilden and Mae Zula were buried in the Minson M. Williams Memorial Cemetery near Clement, Dismal Township, Sampson County, North Carolina, at the northeast corner of Dunn Road (SR1002) at (SR1441).

Child of Samuel Williams and Mae Lewis is:

2063 i. **Billy Samuel Williams**, born 13 February 1933 in Dismal Township, Sampson County, North Carolina. He married **Mary Cathrine Vann**; born 17 April 1934 in Clinton, Sampson County, North Carolina.

1101. Raeford James Williams (Sarah Eliza[6], Isaac[5], Tomzelle[4] Culbreth, Mary[3] Holland, Thomas William[2], Unknown[1]) was born 19 June 1901 in Sampson County, North Carolina, and died 26 December 1979 in Dunn, Harnett County, North Carolina. He married **Eutha Lillian Page**. She was born 15 October 1907, and died 08 December 1961 in Dismal Township, Sampson County, North Carolina.

Raeford James and Eutha were buried in the Williams Family Cemetery northeast of Clement in Dismal Township near Dunn Road (SR1002) at SR1441 in Sampson County, North Carolina.

Children of Raeford Williams and Eutha Page are:

2064 i. **Stillborn Son Williams**, born 05 November 1933.

\+ 2065 ii. **Jacqueline Williams**, born 06 October 1937.

1102. Kate Ann Williams (Sarah Eliza[6], Isaac[5], Tomzelle[4] Culbreth, Mary[3] Holland, Thomas William[2], Unknown[1]) was born 19 June 1901 in Sampson County, North Carolina, and died 16 January 1982 in Fayetteville, Cumberland County, North Carolina. She married **Ernest Dewey Page** 28 March 1921 in North Clinton Township, Sampson County, North Carolina. He was born 10 February 1898, and died 12 July 1960 in Cedar Creek Township, Cumberland County, North Carolina.

Kate Ann and Ernest were buried in the Williams Family Cemetery northeast of Clement in Dismal Township near Dunn Road (SR1002) at SR1441 in Sampson County, North Carolina.

Children of Kate Williams and Ernest Page are:

2066 i. **Sulia Elva Page**, born 29 April 1921; died 06 January 1942.

She was buried in the Williams Family Cemetery northeast of Clement in Dismal Township near Dunn Road (SR1002) at SR1441 in Sampson County, North Carolina.

2067 ii. **Merle Oma Page**, born 11 October 1922.

2068 iii. **Elta Christine Page**, born 01 December 1923; died 01 December 1923.

Stillborn. Buried in the Williams Family Cemetery northeast of Clement in Dismal Township near Dunn Road (SR1002) at SR1441 in Sampson County, North Carolina.

2069 iv. **Arnold Delton Page**, born 24 March 1925.

2070 v. **Prennis Harold Page**, born 28 June 1926.

2071 vi. **Joyce Velerie Page**, born 27 January 1928.

2072 vii. **Dewey Vernon Page**, born 24 November 1929.

2073 viii. **Rupert Gleeon Page**, born 07 January 1932.

1104. Thera Wesley Williams (Sarah Eliza[6], Isaac[5], Tomzelle[4] Culbreth, Mary[3] Holland, Thomas William[2], Unknown[1]) was born 20 January 1907 in Sampson County, North Carolina, and died 13 March 1986 in Clinton, Sampson County, North Carolina. He married **Macie Tew** 23 April 1927 in North Clinton Township, Sampson County, North Carolina, daughter of Carey Tew and Annie Culbreth. She was born 13 October 1907.

Thera Wesley was buried in Baptist Chapel Cemetery near Autryville, North Carolina

Children of Thera Williams and Macie Tew are:

2074 i. **James Elwood Williams**, born 29 March 1928 in Dismal Township, Sampson County, North Carolina; died 01 June 1929.

He was buried in Baptist Chapel Cemetery near Autryville, North Carolina.

2075 ii. **Lalon Iradell Williams**, born 22 June 1930 in Dismal Township, Sampson County, North Carolina. She married **Arthur Brady Jackson**.

No children.

\+ 2076 iii. **Dicie Catherine Williams**, born 17 October 1932 in Dismal Township, Sampson County, North Carolina.

\+ 2077 iv. **Donald Elvin Williams**, born 13 March 1936 in Dismal Township, Sampson County, North Carolina; died 14 February 1986 in Fayetteville, Cumberland County, North Carolina.

2078 v. **Unnamed Williams.**

\+ 2079 vi. **Thomas Elva Williams**, born 06 April 1943.

1106. Edgar Leonidas Bain (John C.[6], Susan Ann[5] Williams, Tomzelle[4] Culbreth, Mary[3] Holland, Thomas William[2], Unknown[1]) was born 01 February 1892, and died 03 June 1981 in Lumberton, North Carolina. He married **Allie Letha Downing** 28 September 1921 in Fayetteville, Cumberland County, North Carolina. She was born 13 August 1896, and died 11 November 1981 in Near Lumberton, North Carolina.

Child of Edgar Bain and Allie Downing is:

2080 i. **Allie Maxine Bain**, born 03 November 1922 in Flea Hill Township, Cumberland County, North Carolina; died 10 December 1941 in Fayetteville, North Carolina.

1107. Alma May Bain (John C.[6], Susan Ann[5] Williams, Tomzelle[4] Culbreth, Mary[3] Holland, Thomas William[2], Unknown[1]) was born 28 February 1896, and died 08 July 1968 in Raleigh, North Carolina. She married **(1) Alzona Albert McLaurin** 23 March 1918, son of Daniel McLaurin and Aredella Royal. He was born 24 January 1887 in Cumberland County, North Carolina, and died 23 April 1966 in Cumberland County, North Carolina. His name is also spelled **"Alonza Albert McLaurin."**

Alma May and Alzona were buried in Bluff Presbyterian Church Cemetery in Cumberland County, North Carolina.

Child of Alma Bain and Alzona McLaurin is:

+ 2081 i. **Augustus Merrill McLaurin, Sr.**, born 08 January 1919 in Cumberland County, North Carolina.

1109. Anna Lillian Bain (Hugh Alexander[6], Susan Ann[5] Williams, Tomzelle[4] Culbreth, Mary[3] Holland, Thomas William[2], Unknown[1]) was born 05 October 1900, and died 03 August 1955 in Fayetteville, North Carolina. She married **David McNeill** 05 March 1925 in Fayetteville, Cumberland County, North Carolina. He was born 27 April 1892, and died 17 November 1966 in Fayetteville, North Carolina.

Child of Anna Bain and David McNeill is:

2082 i. **Robert Edward McNeill**, born 01 August 1927 in Flea Hill Township, Cumberland County, North Carolina. He married **Doris Ann Bain**; born 04 October 1928 in Flea Hill Township, Cumberland County, North Carolina. Two children: 1) **Libby Lynn McNeill** married **James Craig Seymore** who was born in New Jersey. 2) **Robert Edward McNeill, Jr.**

1120. Julia Elizabeth Faircloth (Edna[6] Autry, Daniel[5], Millzy Adelme[4] Culbreth, Mary[3] Holland, Thomas William[2], Unknown[1]) was born 04 October 1896, and died 27 June 1971. She married **Henry Grady Autry** 04 December 1913, son of Wiley Autry and Romelia Sessoms. He was born 21 June 1890, and died 09 November 1979.

Julia Elizabeth and Henry Grady were buried in Autry Cemetery 3.5 miles east of Autryville on Autryville Road (SR 1233), Sampson County, North Carolina.

Children of Julia Faircloth and Henry Autry are:

2083 i. **Jordan Autry**, born about 1916.

2084 ii. **Lillian Autry**, born about 1918.

2085 iii. **Ruth Autry**, born about 1921.

2086 iv. **Vilona Autry**, born about 1923.

2087 v. **Kemit W. Autry**, born about 1927.

1126. Flossie Autry (William Ashford[6], Daniel[5], Millzy Adelme[4] Culbreth, Mary[3] Holland, Thomas William[2], Unknown[1]) was born 09 February 1901, and died 01 August

1986. She married **Marion Devotion Faircloth, Sr.**, son of Latimus Faircloth and Estella Matthews. He was born 03 March 1893, and died 09 May 1985 in Fayetteville, Cumberland County, North Carolina.

Marion Devotion was a pilot in U.S. Army in World War I. He and Flossie were buried in Old Hollywood Cemetery, Roseboro, North Carolina

Children of Flossie Autry and Marion Faircloth are:

2088 i. **Marion Devotion Faircloth, Jr.**, born 03 July 1928 in Little Coharie Township, Sampson County, North Carolina. He married **Ethel Ann Newberry**; born 21 April 1927; died 12 July 1992 in Sampson County, North Carolina. Ethel was buried in Old Hollywood Cemetery, Roseboro, North Carolina.

Two children. **NANCY ANN FAIRCLOTH** was born 3 April 1961 in Alexandria, Viginia, and died 8 December 1979 in Turkey Township in Sampson County in an automobile accident.

JAMES MARION FAIRCLOTH is the second child.

2089 ii. **Worth Hampton Faircloth**, born 26 January 1930 in Little Coharie Township, Sampson County, North Carolina. He married **Willie Joyce Sessoms**.

Four children.

2090 iii. **Peggy Joyce Faircloth**, born 20 November 1931 in Little Coharie Township, Sampson County, North Carolina. She married **Douglas McNeil**.

\+ 2091 iv. **Fred Allen Faircloth**, born 30 November 1937 in Little Coharie Township, Sampson County, North Carolina.

2092 v. **Oscar Landon Faircloth**, born 06 December 1938 in Little Coharie Township, Sampson County, North Carolina. He married **Almer Jeane Spell**; born 21 July 1939 in Dismal Township, Sampson County, North Carolina.

Two children.

1135. Maggie Pearl Autry (James Love[6], Daniel[5], Millzy Adelme[4] Culbreth, Mary[3] Holland, Thomas William[2], Unknown[1]) was born 05 October 1908, and died 01 June 1990. She married **Ballard Bee Autry**, son of Wiley Autry and Romelia Sessoms. He was born 25 June 1896, and died 28 August 1984.

Maggie Pearl and Ballard were buried in the Autry Cemetery on Autryville Road about 3.5 miles east of Autryville, North Carolina.

Children of Maggie Autry and Ballard Autry are:

2093 i. **Romelia Autry**, born 25 August 1933 in Little Coharie Township, Sampson County, North Carolina. She married **Oliver Grover Hall**; born 17 March 1926 in Sampson County, North Carolina; died 13 January 1990.

Four children. Oliver was buried in the Salemburg Cemetery, Bearskin Road, Salemburg, North Carolina

2094 ii. **Daughter Autry**, born about 1924.

Her name is unclear as written in the 1930 census.

2095 iii. **Honesta Autry,** born 19 December 1926. She married Odell Faircloth 21 July 1945; born 17 September 1924; died 14 October 1993.

Name is unclear as written in the 1930 census, but it looks like "**Romeata.**" Odell Faircloth is buried in the Autry Cemetery on Autryville Road about 3.5 miles east of Autryville, North Carolina.

2096 iv. **Bertie M. Autry,** born about 1928.

2097 v. **Earl C. Autry,** born about 1929.

1137. Myrtle Lois Autry (James Love[6], Daniel[5], Millzy Adelme[4] Culbreth, Mary[3] Holland, Thomas William[2], Unknown[1]) was born 14 November 1912, and died 26 February 1982. She married **W. Dewey Nunnery**. He was born 01 May 1912, and died 28 February 1981.

Myrtle Lois and Dewey were buried in the Macedonia Baptist Church Cemetery on Macedonia Church Road (SR 2014), Cumberland County, North Carolina.

Child of Myrtle Autry and W. Nunnery is:

2098 i. **Howard Nunnery,** born 03 June 1932; died 03 June 1932.

He was buried in Macedonia Baptist Church Cemetery on Macedonia Church Road (SR 2014), Cumberland County, North Carolina.

1141. Lula Mae Autry (James Love[6], Daniel[5], Millzy Adelme[4] Culbreth, Mary[3] Holland, Thomas William[2], Unknown[1]) was born 04 January 1920. She married **Edwin Festus Tyndall** 21 December 1940 in Roseboro, Sampson County, North Carolina, son of Ollen Tyndall and Nancy Edwards. He was born 25 January 1914 in Roseboro, Sampson County, North Carolina, and died 23 April 1995.

"Fustus" is also found for Edwin's middle name. He was buried in Sunrise Memorial Gardens, between Roseboro and Salemburg, Sampson County, North Carolina.

Children of Lula Autry and Edwin Tyndall are:

\+ 2099 i. **Charles Edwin Tyndall,** born 25 October 1944 in Sampson County, North Carolina.

2100 ii. Prentice Austin Tyndall, born 09 September 1946 in Honeycutts Township, Sampson County, North Carolina. He married **Nancy Andree Taylor** 02 July 1967 in Fayetteville, Cumberland County, North Carolina; born 08 May 1950 in Fayetteville, Cumberland County, North Carolina.

2101 iii. **Johnny Robert Tyndall,** born 30 October 1948 in Honeycutts Township, Sampson County, North Carolina.

1143. Mildred Autry (James Love[6], Daniel[5], Millzy Adelme[4] Culbreth, Mary[3] Holland, Thomas William[2], Unknown[1]) was born 12 August 1923 in Little Coharie Township, Sampson County, North Carolina, and died 15 December 1998. She married **Lattie Draughon, Sr.** 08 July 1939 in Clinton, North Carolina, son of Wiley C. Draughon and Cornelia Naylor.

He was born 01 January 1919 in Sampson County, North Carolina, and died 04 December 1979.

Mildred and Lattie Draughon, Sr. were buried in Calvary Tabernacle PFB Church Cemetery, 1 mile from intersection of Hwy 242 and High House Road, Sampson County, North Carolian.

Children of Mildred Autry and Lattie Draughon are:

+ 2102 i. **Billy Carrol Draughon**, born 06 May 1940 in Honeycutts Township, Sampson County, North Carolina.

+ 2103 ii. **Lattie Draughon, Jr.**, born 07 May 1942 in Pearces Mill Township, Cumberland County, North Carolina.

2104 iii. **Lois Fay Draughon**, born 23 November 1943 in Fayetteville, Cumberland County, North Carolina. She married Harry Daino; born 04 June 1941.

+ 2105 iv. **Judy Ann Draughon**, born 09 March 1946 in Fayetteville, Cumberland County, North Carolina.

1144. Leroy Autry (James Love[6], Daniel[5], Millzy Adelme[4] Culbreth, Mary[3] Holland, Thomas William[2], Unknown[1]) was born 21 October 1925 in Little Coharie Township, Sampson County, North Carolina. He married **Cherrie Carnell Tyndall** 15 July 1944, daughter of Ollen Tyndall and Nancy Edwards. She was born 27 September 1925 in Honeycutts Township, Sampson County, North Carolina.

Children of Leroy Autry and Cherrie Tyndall are:

2106 i. **Ray Coleman Autry**, born 05 November 1945 in Roseboro, Sampson County, North Carolina.

+ 2107 ii. **Jannie Dorcas Autry**, born 11 August 1949 in Roseboro, Sampson County.

2108 iii. **Rhonda Lynette Autry**, born 03 March 1968 in Clinton, Sampson County, North Carolina.

1145. William Redin Williams (Susan Anner[6], Rebecca Elizabeth[5] Autry, Millzy Adelme[4] Culbreth, Mary[3] Holland, Thomas William[2], Unknown[1]) was born 18 May 1880, and died 26 October 1930 in Little Coharie Township, Sampson County, North Carolina. He married **Willie Earnie Hall** 20 April 1907, daughter of John Hall and Jeanette Autry. She was born 18 September 1883, and died 03 March 1962 in Little Coharie Township, Sampson County, North Carolina.

Children are listed above under (408) Willie Earnie Hall.

1146. Repsie Williams (Susan Anner[6], Rebecca Elizabeth[5] Autry, Millzy Adelme[4] Culbreth, Mary[3] Holland, Thomas William[2], Unknown[1]) was born 09 December 1881, and died 07 August 1952 in Little Coharie Township, Sampson County, North Carolina. She married **George W. Faircloth** 20 December 1902, son of Sylvania Faircloth. He was born 10 September 1867, and died 14 July 1907. Two children.

George first married **LUCY R. WILLIAMS,** daughter of REDDEN WILLIAMS and NANCY FAIRCLOTH. Lucy was born 17 April 1867 and died 19 July 1902. No children. George and Lucy were buried in the Raeford Faircloth Family Cemetery on SR 1411 and SR 1233 in Little Coharie Township, Sampson County, North Carolina.

Repsie was buried in the Charles A. William's Family Cemetery off SR 1418 in Little Coharie Township in Sampson County, North Carolina, more recently called the Jesse Williams Family Cemetery.

Children of Repsie Williams and George Faircloth are:

2109 i. **Beulah Faircloth,** born 1903; died 1991 in Sampson County, North Carolina. She married **Thomas Mason Sessoms** 07 December 1919; born 1895; died 1966 in Sampson County, North Carolina.

Twelve children.

1st child: **AGNES SESSOMS** was born 10 September 1920 in Little Coharie Township and died 22 September1980 in Fayetteville. She married 23 February 1946 in Fayetteville's Hay Street Methodist Church, **Roy Cecil Nunnery**, son of G. E. Nunnery and Lizzie Hinson. He was born 23 May 1919 in Seventy-First Township. Agnes was buried at Elizabeth Baptist Church. She and Roy have three children.

2nd child: **DAISY MAY SESSOMS** was born 24 June 1922. She married a "Riley" and they had one child.

3rd child: **LILLIE MARIE SESSOMS** was born 19 March 1924 in Little Coharie Township. She married a "Warren."

4th child: **JAMES ALBERT SESSOMS** was born 7 May 1926 in Little Coharie Township.

5th child: **SUSIE BLANCHARD SESSOMS** was born 29 June 1929 in Little Coharie Township. She married a "Godwin."

6th child**: RANEY ELIZABETH SESSOMS** was born 3 May 1931 in Little Coharie Township. She married a "Lamb."

7th child: **KATIE LULA SESSOMS** was born 1 September 1933 in Little Coharie Township and died 13 April 1986 in Fayetteville. She married **GEORGE EVERETTE BOSWELL, JR**. who was born about 1933 in Ohio. She was buried in Sunrise Memorial Gardens between Roseboro and Salemburg, Sampson County, North Carolina. Four children.

8th child: **EDWARD THOMAS SESSOMS** was born 22 June 1935 in Little Coharie Township.

9th child: **BEULAH VIRGINIA SESSOMS** was born 17 March 1937 in Little Coharie Township. She married **BILLY GENE SEGER** who was born about 1936 in Mississippi. He served in the United States Air Force. Three children.

10th child: **HIRAM DIXON SESSOMS** was born 22 July 1940 in Little Coharie Township. He married 15 September 1961 in Little Coharie Township, **LOTTIE JANE NEW**, daughter of **WILLIE CLEVELAND NEW** and **KATIE MAE SESSOMS**. She was born 25 November 1943 in Little Coharie Township. Two children.

11th child: **BETTY JANE SESSOMS** was born and died 8 September 1941 in Honeycutts Township, Sampson County, and was buried in the Mary Ann Sessoms Family Cemetery on S.R. 1406 in Little Coharie Township.

12th child: **CECIL NELSON SESSOMS** was born 11 July 1944 in Little Coharie Township.

\+ 2110 ii. **Marion Faircloth,** born 28 May 1905; died 30 December 1980 in Clinton, North Carolina. He married 21 October 1922 in Clinton, **CALLIE MAE HALL**, daughter of **JOHN O. HALL** and

MARGARET JANE WILLIS. She was born 24 September 1904 and died 15 May 1974 on Rural Route, Autryville, North Carolina. They are buried in the Charles A. Williams Family Cemetery. Seven children.

1st child: **GEORGE VERNON FAIRCLOTH** was born 30 June 1924 in Sampson County and died 11 September 1984 in Fayetteville, North Carolina. Vernon married 5 April 1947 **CHRISTELLE STRICKLAND** from Harnett County who was born 7 April 1927. He served as a private in the United States Army in World War II and is buried in the Charles A. Williams Family Cemetery. Six children.

2nd child: **NOVA KERMIT FAIRCLOTH** was born 24 October 1926 in Little Coharie Township, died 25 May 1928 and is buried in the Charles A. Williams Family Cemetery.

3rd child: **GARLAND NARION FAIRCLOTH** was born 15 June 1929 in Roseboro and died 1 December 1987 in Clinton as **GARLAND MARION FAIRCLOTH.** He married **VELMA LEWIS** who was born 28 August 1927. "Junior" was buried in the Mt. Carmel Church of God of Prophecy Cemetery (sic). Two children.

4th child: **ESTER MALY FAIRCLOTH** was born 8 March 1933 in Little Coharies township. She married **JAMES RODELL HALL**, son of **LONNIE JAMES HALL** and **MARY CATHERINE SESSOMS.** He was born 21 July 1929 in Little Coharie Township. Six children.

5th child: **DAVID ASHLEY FAIRCLOTH** was born 22 September 1936 in Little Coharies Township.

6th child: **BENNIE ROSE FAIRCLOTH**

7th child: **JOHNNY CARSON FAIRCLOTH** was born about 1946. He married **JUDY MAE MARTIN** who was born about 1948 in South Carolina. Two children.

1149. Mollie Williams (Susan Anner6, Rebecca Elizabeth5 Autry, Millzy Adelme4 Culbreth, Mary3 Holland, Thomas William2, Unknown1) was born 24 November 1887, and died 22 December 1960 in Little Coharie Township, Sampson County, North Carolina. She married **Eddie Lee Sessoms** 21 March 1914. He was born 19 October 1886, and died 23 January 1967.

Mollie and Eddie were buried in Mt. Carmel Church of God of Prophecy Cemetery on SR 1418, Sampson County, North Carolina.

Children of Mollie Williams and Eddie Sessoms are:

+ 2111 i. **Roland Sessoms,** born 23 April 1915; died 16 September 1978.

+ 2112 ii. **Nina Sessoms,** born 13 September 1918; died 21 October 1982 in Sampson County, North Carolina.

1150. John Frank Williams (Susan Anner6, Rebecca Elizabeth5 Autry, Millzy Adelme4 Culbreth, Mary3 Holland, Thomas William2, Unknown1) was born 28 January 1890, and died 15 November 1962 in Little Coharie Township, Sampson County, North Carolina. He married **Viola Mae Edge** 03 January 1925 in Fayetteville, Cumberland County, North Carolina. She was born 18 March 1906 in Cumberland County, North Carolina, and died 09 May 1959 in Fayetteville, North Carolina.

John Frank and Viola were buried in the Williams Family Cemetery off SR 1418 in Little Coharie Township in Sampson County, North Carolina.

Child of John Williams and Viola Edge is:

i. **RUBY ODELL WILLIAMS.** born 5 November 1925 in Little Coharied Township, married **RAEFORD WESLEY UNDERWOOD** who was born 5 July 1922 in Beaver Dam Township, Sampson County, North Carolina. Three children.

ii. **OBIE ALVIN WILLIAMS** was born 19 December 1927 in Little Coharied Township and died 25 July 1980 in Clinton. Alvin married **SALLIE EVELYN HERRING**, daughter of HERMAN HERRING and NANCY MATHIS. She was born 25 October 1929 in Franklin Township. He served as a PFC in the United States Army in World War II and was buried in the Charles A. Williams Family Cemetery. Five children.

1) **Glenda Jane Williams** was born 18 November 1950 in Roseboro, North Carolina and married **Mr. Lynch**.

2) **John Leo Williams**, born 11 February 1952 in Clinton, North Carolina, married **Nancy Teresa Faircloth** on 20 October 1974 in Roseboro. She was born 17 September 1957 in Roseboro, daughter of Roy Cosby Faircloth and Christine Elizabeth Faircloth. Two children, **Missy Renee Williams** and **LaRoy Alvin Williams.**

3) **Nancy Mae Williams**, born 20 January 1954 in Clinton, married **Alex Dwight Hobson** on 29 July 1972 in Roseboro, son of Alexander Hobson and Olice Faircloth. He was born 12 December 1952 in Roseboro.

4) **Pamela Evelyn Williams** was born 13 March 1957 in Clinton and married **Donnie Martin Williams**, son of Milton Dewey Williams and Kathleen Black. One child.

5) **Teresa Fay Williams** was the fifth child of Obie Alvin Williams and Sallie Evelyn Herring. She married **Mr. Williams.**

2113 iii. **Carl Brink Williams,** third child of John Frank Williams and Viola Mae Edge, was born 30 June 1929 in Little Coharie Township, Sampson County, North Carolina; died 28 September 1973 in Autryville, North Carolina. He married **Bobbie Deane Honeycutt**; born 17 March 1933 in Sampson County, North Carolina; died 03 April 1958 in Clinton, North Carolina.

He and Bobbie Deane were buried in the Charles A. Williams Family Cemetery (now Jesse Williams Family Cemetery) near SR 1418 and SR 1233, Sampson County, North Carolina

iv. **ANNIE BELL WILLIAMS,** fourth child of John Frank and Viola Mae was born 2 November 1936 in Little Coharie Township. She married **MARTIN LEVI HALL** who was born 30 April 1934 in Little Coharie Township, son of LONNIE JAMES HALL and MARY CATHERINE SESSOMS. Two children.

1) **Jerry Martin Hall**, born 24 January 1955 in Clinton, North Carolina married first **Sylvia Diane Branch**, daughter of Paul Wilson Branch and Clara Mae Brisson. Sylvia was born 23 December 1955 in Roseboro. She and Jerry have two children: **Christopher Martin Hall** born 6 January 1975 in Clinton and **Tabitha Diane Hall,** born 20 July 1978 in Clinton. Jerry married second **Erbia Dianne Faircloth** weho was born 10 June 1958 in Dunn, Harnett County, North Carolina., daughter of John Kelly Faircloth and Mary Mildred House. Jerry and Erbia have one child, **John Nicholas Hall** who was born 29 July 1981 in Clinton.

v. **ORA PAULINE WILLIAMS** was born 1 May 1939 in Little Coharie Township. She married a **"Faircloth."**

1151. George W. Williams (Susan Anner[6], Rebecca Elizabeth[5] Autry, Millzy Adelme[4] Culbreth, Mary[3] Holland, Thomas William[2], Unknown[1]) was born 21 June 1893, and died 08

September 1958 in Little Coharie Township, Sampson County, North Carolina. He married **Vinnie Ezzell**. She was born 15 August 1895, and died 12 March 1970 in Clinton, North Carolina.

George and Vinnie were buried in the Charles A. Williams Family Cemetery (now Jesse Williams Family Cemetery) near SR 1418 and SR 1233, Sampson County, North Carolina.

Children of George Williams and Vinnie Ezzell are:

\+ 2114 i. **Ira Gladys Williams,** born 22 May 1915; died 02 February 1940 in Little Coharie Township, Sampson County, North Carolina.

2115 ii. **Emily Eliabeth Williams,** born 22 November 1919 in Little Coharie Township, Sampson County, North Carolina. She married **Voyd Faircloth**; born 03 March 1920 in Little Coharie Township, Sampson County, North Carolina, son of TONY FAIRCLOTH and GERTIE LEE FAIRCLOTH.

Six children.

1) **Jimmie Void Faircloth,** born 23 May 1949 in Roseboro, North Carolina, died 21 January 1948 in Fayetteville, North Carolina, and wass buried in the Charles A. Williams Family Cemetery.

2) **Elmer Gail Faircloth,** born 23 May 1949, married 23 May 1982 in Dillon, South Carolina, **Edna J. Collins** of Chesapeake, Virginia, who was born 11 November 1949.

3) **Nannie Carolyn Faircloth,** born 14 September 1952 in Roseboro, married **James Franklin Pope, Jr.** He was born 19 July 1952, son of James Franklin Pope and Gladys Josephine Rich. Three children, all born in Clinton: **Melissa Dawn Pope**, born 31 July 1975; **James Kevin Pope,** born September 1977; **Jonathan Ryan Pope**, born 18 March 1981.

4) **George Wayne Faircloth,** born 5 December 1953 in Roseboro.

5) **Tony Lawrence Faircloth,** born 25 July 1959 in Roseboro, North Carolina, **married Sheila Darlene Bullard** on 24 August 1978. She was born 15 April 1961 in fayetteville, Cumberland County, North Carolina, daughter of Billy Fred Bullard and Edith Smith.

6) **Gladys Frances Faircloth,** was born 23 May 1960 and married 1 September 1979 **Billy Joseph Tucker** who was born 24 July 1959, son of Joseph Clifton Tucker and Mattie Viola Smith.

2116 iii. **Harvey Andrew Williams,** born 12 June 1922 in Little Coharie Township, Sampson County, North Carolina; died 28 December 1978. He married **Margaret Catherine Butler** who was born 22 January 1938, daughter of JOSEPH CLEVELAND BUTLER and BESSIE JEAN SHERMAN. Margaret first married a "Bostic" and they had three children. She and Harvey had no children. Harvey was buried in the Charles A. Williams Family Cemetery (now Jesse Williams Family Cemetery) near SR 1418 and SR 1233, Sampson County, North Carolina.

1161. Henry Grady Autry (Wiley C.[6], Molsey[5], Millzy Adelme[4] Culbreth, Mary[3] Holland, Thomas William[2], Unknown[1]) was born 21 June 1890, and died 09 November 1979. He married **Julia Elizabeth Faircloth** 04 December 1913, daughter of Thomas Faircloth and Edna Autry. She was born 04 October 1896, and died 27 June 1971.

Henry and Julia were buried in the Autry Cemetery 3.5 miles east of Autryville on Autryville Road (SR 1233), Sampson County, North Carolina.

Children are listed above under (1120) Julia Elizabeth Faircloth.

1164. Ballard Bee Autry (Wiley C.[6], Molsey[5], Millzy Adelme[4] Culbreth, Mary[3] Holland, Thomas William[2], Unknown[1]) was born 25 June 1896, and died 28 August 1984. He married **Maggie Pearl Autry**, daughter of James Autry and Bertha Bullard. She was born 05 October 1908, and died 01 June 1990.

Ballard Bee and Maggie were buried in the Autry Cemetery on Autryville Road about 3.5 miles east of Autryville, North Carolina.

Children are listed above under (1135) Maggie Pearl Autry.

1177. Mattie Kate Autry (Fountain[6], Miles Costin[5], Millzy Adelme[4] Culbreth, Mary[3] Holland, Thomas William[2], Unknown[1]) was born 27 October 1923 in Little Coharie Township, Sampson County, North Carolina, and died 22 March 1966 in Clinton, North Carolina. She married **Leon Williams, Sr.** 05 June 1937 in Little Coharie Township, Sampson County, North Carolina, son of William Williams and Willie Hall. He was born 12 July 1909, and died 25 May 1975 in Fayetteville, North Carolina.

Child of Mattie Autry and Leon Williams is:

2117 i. **Leon Williams, Jr.**, born 26 February 1938 in Little Coharie Township, Sampson County, North Carolina. He married **Geneva Pearl Faircloth**; born 31 May 1946 in Roseboro, North Carolina.

Three children.

1179. Eulie Marvin Sessoms (Cordelia[6] Autry, Miles Costin[5], Millzy Adelme[4] Culbreth, Mary[3] Holland, Thomas William[2], Unknown[1]) was born 05 April 1928 in Little Coharie Township, Sampson County, North Carolina, and died 18 September 1998 in North Carolina. He married **Alice Jane Lockamy**, daughter of Mack Lockamy and Magdalene Bass. She was born 11 April 1931 in Mingo Township, Sampson County, North Carolina.

Eulie was buried in the Penial Pentecostal Holiness Church Cemetery on Dunn Road, Sampson County, North Caorlina.

Children of Eulie Sessoms and Alice Lockamy are:

2118 i. **Alice Faye Sessoms**, born 10 November 1950 in Roseboro, Sampson County, North Carolina.

2119 ii. **Unnamed Sessoms.**

\+ 2120 iii. **Marvin Keith Sessoms**, born 01 October 1957 in Clinton, Sampson County.

2121 iv. **Daughter Sessoms**, born 22 October 1960 in Clinton, Sampson County, North Carolina.

2122 v. **Unnamed Son Sessoms**, born 16 September 1969 in Clinton, Sampson County.

1180. Lonnie Oliver Hall (Francenia Jane[6], Jeanette[5] Autry, Millzy Adelme[4] Culbreth, Mary[3] Holland, Thomas William[2], Unknown[1]) was born 14 November 1886, and died 27

April 1967. He married **Roe Vennie Faircloth**, daughter of Wright Faircloth and Eliza Sessoms. She was born 16 September 1894, and died 13 March 1959.

Known children of Lonnie Hall and Roe Faircloth are:

2123 i. **Fannie Hazel Hall**, born 22 December 1912 in Sampson County, North Carolina; died 01 March 1990. She married **Alphonzo Butler.** Fannie Hazel was buried in the Autry Cemetery on Autryville Road about 3.5 miles east of Autryville, North Carolina.

2124 ii. **Lonnie Raymond Hall**, born 20 December 1914; died 16 March 1944.

Killed in action during World War II

2125 iii. **Elsie Jane Hall,** born 24 January 1929. She married **Vonnie Edgar Autry**; born 18 September 1921; died 18 February 1987.

2126 iv. **R. F. Hall**, born 14 September 1931; died 20 April 1941.

He was buried in the Autry Cemetery on Autryville Road about 3.5 miles east of Autryville, North Carolina.

2127 v. **Sharon Ann Hall**, born 06 July 1939; died 22 March 1972. She married **Unknown Faircloth.**

She was buried in the Autry Cemetery on Autryville Road about 3.5 miles east of Autryville, North Carolina.

1188. Leon Williams, Sr. (William Redin[7], Susan Anner[6], Rebecca Elizabeth[5] Autry, Millzy Adelme[4] Culbreth, Mary[3] Holland, Thomas William[2], Unknown[1]) was born 12 July 1909, and died 25 May 1975 in Fayetteville, North Carolina. He married **(1) Mattie Kate Autry** 05 June 1937 in Little Coharie Township, Sampson County, North Carolina, daughter of Fountain Autry and Mamie Peterson. She was born 27 October 1923 in Little Coharie Township, Sampson County, North Carolina, and died 22 March 1966 in Clinton, North Carolina. He married **(2) Elsie Lee Wise** before 1954, daughter of James Noah Wise and Alice Jane Jackson. She was born 26 January 1911, and died 13 August 1971 in Clinton, North Carolina. He married **(3) Lucille Garner** after 1971.

Elsie Wise's nickname was 'Nini."

Child is listed above under (1177) Mattie Kate Autry.

Child of Leon Williams and Elsie Wise is:

2128 i. **Ernestine Williams**, born 06 February 1954 in Roseboro, North Carolina.

Stillborn. She was buried in the William Redin Williams Family Cemetery, Sampson County, North Carolina.

1194. Lessie Dolan Autry (William Isaac[6], Martha Jane[5] Culbreth, Isaac[4], Mary[3] Holland, Thomas William[2], Unknown[1]) was born 10 August 1899 in Sampson County, North Carolina, and died 22 May 1979 in Fayetteville, North Carolina. She married **Bond English Faircloth** 06 May 1917 in Moors (sic) Bridge, North Carolina, son of William Faircloth and Sarah Autry. He was born 20 September 1895, and died 08 May 1964.

The 22 May 1970 is also found for Lessie's date of death. She and Bond English were buried in the Bethabara United Methodist Church Cemetery near Clement in Dismal Township, Sampson County, North Carolina.

Children of Lessie Autry and Bond Faircloth are:

\+ 2129 i. **Sarah Catherine Faircloth**, born 15 March 1918 in Dismal Township, Sampson County, North Carolina; died 02 April 1999.

\+ 2130 ii. **Cladie May Faircloth**, born 06 September 1920 in Dismal Township, Sampson County; died 22 May 1992.

2131 iii. **Fred English Faircloth**, born 29 June 1923 in Dismal Township, Sampson County, North Carolina; died 14 March 1924 in Dismal Township, Sampson County, North Carolina.

He was buried in Bethabara United Methodist Church Cemetery near SR 1006 and SR 1442, Sampson County, North Carolina.

\+ 2132 iv. **William Raeford Faircloth**, born 19 April 1925 in Dismal Township, Sampson County, North Carolina; died 30 August 1969 in Near Autryville, North Carolina.

\+ 2133 v. **Lena Earline Faircloth**, born 27 October 1927 in Dismal Township, Sampson County.

1195. McKinley Blackmon Autry (William Isaac[6], Martha Jane[5] Culbreth, Isaac[4], Mary[3] Holland, Thomas William[2], Unknown[1]) was born 28 August 1900 in Sampson County, North Carolina, and died 23 March 1969 in Clinton. He married **Hosie Myrtle Autry**, daughter of Wesley Autry and Lucy Hall. She was born 13 May 1904.

McKinley Blackmon was buried in Bethabara United Methodist Church, Dismal Township, Sampson County, North Carolina.

Child of McKinley Autry and Hosie Autry is:

\+ 2134 i. **Letha Ethelyne Autry**, born 21 November 1923; died 22 September 1991 in Chapel Hill, Orange County, North Carolina.

1203. William Wellington McLaurin (Mary Ellen[6] Culbreth, Sabra[5], Isaac[4], Mary[3] Holland, Thomas William[2], Unknown[1]) was born 31 March 1894, and died 27 October 1957 in Fayetteville, Cumberland County, North Carolina. He married **Nancy Jane Averitt** 04 January 1914 in Cedar Creek Township, Cumberland County, North Carolina, daughter of Devotion Averitt and Lucinda Howell. She was born 18 July 1896, and died 15 November 1980 in Fayetteville, Cumberland County, North Carolina.

William and Nancy Jane were buried in Salem United Methodist Church.

Children of William McLaurin and Nancy Averitt are:

2135 i. **James Vance McLaurin**, born 30 November 1914 in Flea Hill Township, Cumberland County, North Carolina; died 08 March 1983 in Dunn, North Carolina. He married **Bonnie Elizabeth Culbreth;** born 04 August 1914, daughter of Walter Marcellus Culbreth and Laura Elizabeth Geddie.

Three children.

1) **Julius Vance McLaurin**, born 26 June 1939 in Eastover Township, Cumberland County, North Carolina, died 7 December 1983 in Fayetteville in Cumberland County. He married **Patricia Elizabeth Walker**, born 14 July 1940 in Eastover Township, daughter of Richard Alexander Walker and Edith Veronica House. Julius was buried at Salem United Methodist Church Cemetery.. Three children: **Bryan Douglas McLaurin** was born 12 March 1961 in Fayetteville and married 17 October 1987 in Salem United Methodist Church, **Tina Marcia Melvin** on 17 October 1987.. She was born 23 February 1961 in Lee County, daughter of Tolar James Melvin, Jr. and Faye Preddy.. **Veronica Elizabeth McLaurin**, second child of Julius and Patricia was born 6 December 1962 in Fayetteville and married **Jeffrey Daniel Hedges** on 1 July 1984 in Salem United Methodist Church. Jeffrey was born 18 April 1961 in Cumberland County, son of George Lavern Hedges and Deloris Rae McLaurin. **Julia Denise McLaurin**, born 21 April 1964 in Fayetteville, was the third child of Julius and Patricia.

2) **Charles Douglas McLaurin** was the second child of William Wellington McLaurin and Nancy Jane Averitt and was born 17 November 1941 in Fayetteville.. He married **Mary Joyce Horne** who was born 22 February 1949 in Autryville, daughter of Paul Horne and Mary Lee Doris Autry. One child, **Carl Julius McLaurin** was born 8 November 1971 in Fayetteville.

3) **Nancy Janette McLaurin**, thrid child of William Wellington and Nancy Jane, was born 11 December 1943 in fayetteville. She married **Johnnie Page Draughon**, son of George Compton Draughon and Lila Edney Page. Johnnie was born 12 December 1944 in Falcon, Cumberland County, North Carolina. Four children: **Lisa Jeanine Draughon**, the first child was born 4 August 1965 in Lumberton and married in Falcon on 8 December 1985, **Alan Johnson Parker**, son of Joseph Thompson Parker and Melrose Johnson. Alan was born 20 July 1965 in Clinton, North Carolina. **Jason Compton Draughon**, the second child was born 13 January 1971 in Lumberton and **Janna Michelle Draughon**, third child was a twin born 16 July 1975 in Lumberton. **Julia Marie Draughon**, fourth child, was a twin and was born 16 July 1975 in Lumberton.

2136 ii. **William Aaron McLaurin**, born 18 June 1916 in Flea Hill Township, Cumberland County, North Carolina. He married **Ruby Alice Fitchett**; born 03 April 1924; died 15 December 1983 in Fayetteville, Cumberland County, North Carolina. Three children.

Ruby Alice is buried in Salem United Methodist Church Cemetery.

2137 iii. **Stillborn Son McLaurin**, born 11 November 1917.

Burial: John A. McLaurin Family Cemetery.

1207. Pauline Royal (Jennette Ida[6] Culbreth, John[5], Daniel Maxwell[4], Mary[3] Holland, Thomas William[2], Unknown[1]) was born 10 May 1895 in Salemburg, Sampson County, North Carolina, and died 09 February 1924 in Salemburg, Sampson County, North Carolina. She married **John Stewart Howard** 27 June 1915 in Salemburg, Sampson County, North Carolina, son of Henry Howard and Elizabeth Cooper. He was born 20 November 1893 in Salemburg, Sampson County, North Carolina, and died 22 November 1978 in Clinton, Sampson County, North Carolina. After Pauline died, John married **MARY COX** who was born 3 March 1899 in Wayne County and died 10 January 1979.

Pauline died at the birth of her third child, who also died. John Stewart Howard and his second wife, **Mary Cox** were teachers and they established Laurel Lake Gardens and Nursery in 1950 on the farm where John was born; it was later destroyed by a tornado.

Pauline, John, and Mary are buried in Salemburg Cemetery, Salemburg, Sampson County, North Carolina.

Children of Pauline Royal and John Howard are:

\+ 2138 i. **Ida Elizabeth Howard**, born 12 September 1916 in Salemburg, Sampson County, North Carolina; died 05 December 1989.

2139 ii. **Son Howard**, born and died 29 September 1922.

2140 iii. **Son Howard**, born and died 09 February 1924.

1209. Viola Royal (Jennette Ida[6] Culbreth, John[5], Daniel Maxwell[4], Mary[3] Holland, Thomas William[2], Unknown[1]) was born 29 November 1899 in Salemburg, Sampson County, North Carolina, and died 03 January 1990 in Salemburg, Sampson County, North Carolina. She married **Lonney Randolph McCall** 29 September 1925 in Honeycutts Township, Sampson County, North Carolina. He was born 17 July 1892 in Honeycutts Township, Salemburg, Sampson County, North Carolina, and died 22 March 1980 in Salemburg, Sampson County, North Carolina.

Viola and Lonney were buried in Salemburg Cemetery, Salemburg, Sampson County, North Carolina.

Children of Viola Royal and Lonney McCall are:

\+ 2141 i. **Ernest Vance McCall,** born 11 June 1927 in Lisbon Township, Bladen County, North Carolina.

2142 ii. **Thomas Culbreth McCall**, born 28 June 1932 in Lisbon Township, Bladen County, North Carolina. He married **Emma Estell Maxwell**; born 21 May 1932 in Cedar Creek Township, Cumberland County, North Carolina.

Thomas Culbreth taught English at the University of North Carolina at Wilmington and later moved to Mt. Olive, North Carolina, where he operated a furniture store.

\+ 2143 iii. **Mary Ida McCall,** born 05 September 1937 in Lenoir County, North Carolina.

1212. John Robert Royal (Jennette Ida[6] Culbreth, John[5], Daniel Maxwell[4], Mary[3] Holland, Thomas William[2], Unknown[1]) was born 04 March 1904 in Salemburg, Sampson County, North Carolina, and died 04 October 1984 in Pittsboro, Chatham County, North Carolina. He married **Eleanor Hale Tipton**. She was born 24 November 1903 in Tennessee, and died 02 December 1985 in Siler City, Chatham County, North Carolina.

The 4 October 1981 in Pttsboro can also be found for his death. He and Eleanor were buried in Pittsboro Mt. Gilead Baptist Church Cemetery.

Children of John Royal and Eleanor Tipton are:

2144 i. **John Tipton Royal,** born 07 May 1928 in Honeycutts Township, Salemburg, Sampson County, North Carolina. He married **Shirley Ball.**

John Tipton worked as a truck driver. Shirley graduated from Highsmith Hospital School of Nursing and worked as a nurse until retirement. John is buried in Orange County, North Carolina

\+ 2145 ii. **Eleanor Catherine Royal**, born 30 April 1931 in Honeycutts Township, Sampson County, North Carolina.

1213. James Molton Royal (Jennette Ida[6] Culbreth, John[5], Daniel Maxwell[4], Mary[3] Holland, Thomas William[2], Unknown[1]) was born 13 June 1906 in Salemburg, Sampson County, North Carolina, and died 03 February 1988 in Clinton, Sampson County, North Carolina. He married **Charlotte Pope**. She was born 07 May 1912 in Pender County, North Carolina, and died 13 September 1998 in Salemburg, Sampson County, North Carolina.

James and Charlotte were buried in Salemburg Cemetery, Salemburg, Sampson County, North Carolina.

Child of James Royal and Charlotte Pope is:

2146 i. **Carol Pope Royal**, born 13 August 1953 in Clinton, Sampson County, North Carolina; died 13 August 1953 in Clinton, Sampson County, North Carolina.

1215. Percy Maxwell Tew (Roberta[6] Culbreth, John[5], Daniel Maxwell[4], Mary[3] Holland, Thomas William[2], Unknown[1]) was born 16 January 1901 in North Carolina, and died 09 February 1980 in Clinton, Sampson County, North Carolina. He married **Irutha Fann** 19 January 1922 in South Clinton Township, Sampson County, North Carolina, daughter of William Fann and Georgianna Knowles. She was born 03 September 1903, and died 23 August 1983 in Clinton, Sampson County, North Carolina.

Percy Maxwell and Irutha were buried in Baptist Chapel Cemetery, Clement Community near Autryville, North Carolina.

Children of Percy Tew and Irutha Fann are:

\+ 2147 i. **Vertile Estelle Tew**, born 20 October 1922 in Honeycutts Township, Sampson County, North Carolina.

\+ 2148 ii. **Lambert Dixon Tew,** born 08 August 1924 in Sampson County, North Carolina; died 14 October 1961 in Fayetteville, Cumberland County, North Carolina.

\+ 2149 iii. **Loren Maxwell Tew**, born 08 September 1926 in Honeycutts Township, Sampson County, North Carolina; died 20 November 1956 in Charlotte, North Carolina.

\+ 2150 iv. **Leland Elmo Tew**, born 13 March 1930 in Sampson County, North Carolina.

\+ 2151 v. **Ruthey Faydene Tew**, born 22 October 1936 in Sampson County, North Carolina.

\+ 2152 vi. **Judy Ann Tew**, born 15 March 1942 in Sampson County, North Carolina.

1216. Ernest Blackman Tew (Roberta[6] Culbreth, John[5], Daniel Maxwell[4], Mary[3] Holland, Thomas William[2], Unknown[1]) was born 22 August 1903 in North Carolina, and died 31 March 1979 in Cumberland County, North Carolina. He married **Minnie Charlotte Batton**, daughter of Grover Batton and Daisy Cashwell. She was born 09 September 1915, and died 09 April 1999.

The 19 September 1915 is also found for her date of birth. Ernest Blackman was buried in Cumberland Memorial Cemetery, Fayetteville, North Carolina.

Children of Ernest Tew and Minnie Batton are:

+ 2153 i. **Doris Lee Tew**, born 21 September 1932.

+ 2154 ii. **James Blackman Tew**, born 12 October 1933; died 19 June 1976 in Fayetteville, Cumberland County, North Carolina.

+ 2155 iii. **Robert Glenn Tew**, born 13 March 1936 in North Carolina; died 24 March 1992 in Hope Mills, Cumberland County.

+ 2156 iv. **Laura Ernestine Tew**, born 08 August 1937.

+ 2157 v. **Hardy Gaine Tew**, born 22 September 1939 in North Carolina; died 14 December 1991 in Fayetteville, Cumberland County, North Carolina.

+ 2158 vi. **William Gibson Tew**, born 26 June 1945.

1218. John Tew (Roberta[6] Culbreth, John[5], Daniel Maxwell[4], Mary[3] Holland, Thomas William[2], Unknown[1]) was born 14 November 1909 in North Carolina, and died 16 January 1985 in Cumberland County, North Carolina. He married **Maude William Dean**. She was born 16 December 1910 in Cumberland County, North Carolina, and died 19 August 1997.

Children of John Tew and Maude Dean are:

+ 2159 i. **William Blackman Tew**, born 13 October 1929.

+ 2160 ii. **Joyce Grey Tew**, born 25 September 1935.

+ 2161 iii. **John Maxie Tew**, born 10 April 1940.

1219. Sudie Viola Tew (Roberta[6] Culbreth, John[5], Daniel Maxwell[4], Mary[3] Holland, Thomas William[2], Unknown[1]) was born 03 March 1912 in Sampson County, North Carolina. She married **Rev. Thomas Lee Cashwell**. He was born 04 July 1910 in Cumberland County, North Carolina, and died 08 November 1977 in Fayetteville, Cumberland County, North Carolina.

Rev. Thomas was called 'Tommie' and was buried in Cumberland Memorial Cemetery, Fayetteville, North Carolina.

Children of Sudie Tew and Thomas Cashwell are:

2162 i. **Margaret Hazel Cashwell**, born 16 July 1928; died 29 January 2001 in Cowpens, South Carolina. She married Unknown Patty.

+ 2163 ii. **Marcie Roberta Cashwell**, born 26 July 1934.

2164 iii. **Shirley Lee Cashwell**, born 05 April 1937. She married Unknown Simpson.

2165 iv. **Ellen Florence Cashwell**, born 24 September 1939. She married Unknown Baker.

+ 2166 v. **Erline Cashwell,** born 10 February 1942 in Cumberland County, North Carolina.

2167 vi. **Juanita Cashwell**, born 25 January 1945. She married Unknown Ferguson.

\+ 2168 vii. **Thomas Andrew Cashwell**, born 02 December 1953 in Fayetteville, Cumberland County, North Carolina.

1220. Arthur Gibson Tew (Roberta[6] Culbreth, John[5], Daniel Maxwell[4], Mary[3] Holland, Thomas William[2], Unknown[1]) was born 14 February 1914 in Dismal Township, Clement, Sampson County, North Carolina, and died 09 May 1963 in Fayetteville, Cumberland County, North Carolina. He married **Margaret Lucille Batton**. She was born 10 December 1918 in Rockfish Township, Cumberland County, North Carolina.

The 11 February 1914 is also found for his birth. He served as a Seaman Second Class in the United States Navy Reserves in World War II and was buried in Cumberland Cemetery, Fayetteville, North Carolina.

Children of Arthur Tew and Margaret Batton are:

2169 i. **Donnie Gibson Tew**, born 09 June 1937; died 09 June 1937.

Burial: Cumberland Cemetery, Fayetteville, North Carolina

2170 ii. **Tonie Lee Tew**, born 06 October 1938.

1221. E. Hardy Blackman Tew (Roberta[6] Culbreth, John[5], Daniel Maxwell[4], Mary[3] Holland, Thomas William[2], Unknown[1]) was born 24 October 1917 in Honeycutts Township, Sampson County, North Carolina, and died 02 May 1982 in Cumberland County, North Carolina. He married **(1) Viola Jewett Frye** Before 1940, daughter of Joseph Weldon Fry and Callie Cameron. She was born 01 February 1916 in Rockfish Township, Cumberland County, North Carolina, and died 13 September 1975 in Fayetteville, Cumberland County, North Carolina. He married **(2) L. Jones** after 1975 and they were divorced.

For some reason, it appears that E. Hardy Blackman Tew became "Albert Erdmon Tew. E. Hardy Blackman Tew, son of Hardy B. Tew is listed in the birth index for Sampson County, North Carolina. Albert E. Tew is listed in the 1920 Census records for Little Coharie Township in Sampson County, North Carolina, for a son of H. B. and Roberta Tew; Albert E. is listed in the 1930 Census for Rockfish Township in Cumberland County, North Carolina, for a son of Hardy B. and Roberta Tew. "E. Hardy Blackman" is not listed in these two census records for a son.

Albert Erdman Tew (husband) was the informant on the Certificate of Death for Viola Jewett Tew and gives the names of Joseph Weldon Fry and Callie Cameron for her parents. I find a death collection record for Albert Erdman Tew on ancestry.com, but a copy of his death certificate is not available on the site. Further research may be needed.

E. Hardy Blackman Tew was buried in Cumberland Memorial Cemetery, Fayetteville, North Carolina.

Children of E. Tew and Viola Frye are:

2171 i. **Erdmon Bruce Tew**, born 30 January 1940.

+ 2172 ii. **Nancy Delores Tew**, born 17 January 1944 in Cumberland County, North Carolina.

2173 iii. **Earl Cedric Tew**, born 28 May 1947.

His date of birth is also given as 23 May 1947 in a source for Cannady Family data.

+ 2174 iv. **Candace Ann Tew**, born 15 April 1950 in Cumberland County, North Carolina.

1222. Lela Pearl Matthews (Virginia^6 Culbreth, John^5, Daniel Maxwell^4, Mary^3 Holland, Thomas William^2, Unknown^1) was born 10 July 1897 in Cumberland County, North Carolina, and died 13 May 1978 in Harnett County, North Carolina. She married **James Rosker Royal, Sr.**, son of Enoch Royal and Henrietta Hollingsworth. He was born 26 September 1893 in Sampson County, North Carolina, and died 02 September .1964 in Harnett County, North Carolina.

Roscoe is also listed for James' middle name. He and Lela were buried in the Erwin Memorial Park Cemetery, Harnett County, North Carolina.

Children of Lela Matthews and James Royal are:

+ 2175 i. **Virginia Alice Royal**, born 09 April 1914 in Dismal Township, Sampson County, North Carolina; died About 1978 in Harnett County, North Carolina.

+ 2176 ii. **Mary Evelyn Royal**, born 14 October 1917 in Dismal Township, Sampson County, North Carolina.

+ 2177 iii. **Etta Marie Royal**, born 23 February 1924 in Orange County, North Carolina.

+ 2178 iv. **Eva Dale Royal**, born 27 February 1926 in Harnett County, North Carolina.

+ 2179 v. **James Rosker Royal, Jr.**, born 04 May 1932 in Sampson County, North Carolina.

+ 2180 vi. **Donald Gray Royal**, born 29 May 1934 in Harnett County, North Carolina.

+ 2181 vii. **Donnie Ray Royal**, born 29 May 1934 in Harnett County, North Carolina.

1223. Radford Carl Matthews (Virginia^6 Culbreth, John^5, Daniel Maxwell^4, Mary^3 Holland, Thomas William^2, Unknown^1) was born 06 June 1899, and died 04 January 1985 in Raeford, North Carolina. He married **Gladys Holmes Williams**. She was born 08 October 1914 in Clinton, Sampson County, North Carolina.

Children of Radford Matthews and Gladys Williams are:

2182 i. **Carl Grayson Matthews**, born 05 October 1935. He married Carol Mae Welch; born 08 May 1940. Two sons.

2183 ii. **Carolyn Holmes Matthews**, born 02 March 1938. She married Lawrence Ervin Wilkes; born 24 March 1936. Two children.

1224. Irma G. Matthews (Virginia^6 Culbreth, John^5, Daniel Maxwell^4, Mary^3 Holland, Thomas William^2, Unknown^1) was born 24 August 1901, and died 31 October 1990. She married **Lonnie Aaron Matthews** 20 February 1926 in South Carolina, son of Ollen Matthews and Sarah Autry. He was born 16 November 1903, and died 23 July 1962.

Irma and Lonnie were buried in the Williams Family Cemetery northeast of Clement in Dismal Township near Dunn Road (SR1002) at SR1441 in Sampson County, North Carolina.

Children of Irma Matthews and Lonnie Matthews are:

+ 2184 i. **Edna Louise Matthews**, born 15 December 1926 in Dismal Township, Sampson County, North Carolina.

2185 ii. **Aaron Max Matthews**, born 11 May 1933. He married **Sudie Maxine Matthis** 21 January 1967 in Ingold Baptist Church, Ingold, North Carolina; born 23 March 1931 in Taylors Bridge Township, Sampson County, North Carolina.

Sudie Maxine was not expected to live. After birth, she would not accept her mother's breast milk. Finally, they decided to try buttermilk. She apparently liked it and came through, even after having diptheria.

1226. William Garland Matthews (Virginia[6] Culbreth, John[5], Daniel Maxwell[4], Mary[3] Holland, Thomas William[2], Unknown[1]) was born 09 September 1905. He married **Ara Ana Barnes**, daughter of Rufus Barnes and Effie Peele. She was born 27 November 1910.

Children of William Matthews and Ara Barnes are:

2186 i. **Minerva Lee Matthews**, born 02 June 1935.

2187 ii. **Catherine Lynette Matthews**, born 09 February 1938.

2188 iii. **William Dale Matthews**, born 24 October 1942. He married Julie Clyde Carter.

2189 iv. **Kenneth Fate Matthews**, born 06 April 1948.

1227. Ola Ann Matthews (Virginia[6] Culbreth, John[5], Daniel Maxwell[4], Mary[3] Holland, Thomas William[2], Unknown[1]) was born 21 October 1908. She married **Henry Paul Hales** 19 August 1933 in Clinton, North Carolina. He was born 21 April 1905.

Children of Ola Matthews and Henry Hales are:

+ 2190 i. **Lucy Frances Hales**, born 17 October 1934.

+ 2191 ii. **Julius Augustus Hales**, born 17 April 1936 in Little Coharie Township, Sampson County, North Caorlina.

1228. Lula Jane Matthews (Virginia[6] Culbreth, John[5], Daniel Maxwell[4], Mary[3] Holland, Thomas William[2], Unknown[1]) was born 14 September 1911 in Dismal Township, Sampson County, North Carolina, and died 28 August 2002. She married **Ottis Ofield Vann** 20 February 1932 in Clinton, North Carolina, son of Wellie Vann and Bessie Herring. He was born 28 April 1913 in Clinton, Sampson County, North Carolina.

Children of Lula Matthews and Ottis Vann are:

+ 2192 i. **Dorothy Jean Vann**, born 02 July 1933.

2193 ii. **Billy Vann**. He married **Glenda Gainey**.

1233. Atticus Marvin Matthews (Lena Mae[6] Culbreth, John[5], Daniel Maxwell[4], Mary[3] Holland, Thomas William[2], Unknown[1]) was born 16 October 1903, and died 09 August 1988 in Clinton, Sampson County, North Carolina. He married **Viola Gertrude Page** 16 October 1924 in Fayetteville, Cumberland County, North Carolina, daughter of John Page and Louetta Holland. She was born 20 September 1905, and died 18 June 1988 in Sampson County, North Carolina.

Children are listed above under (759) Viola Gertrude Page.

1235. Mabel Inez Matthews (Lena Mae[6] Culbreth, John[5], Daniel Maxwell[4], Mary[3] Holland, Thomas William[2], Unknown[1]) was born 25 November 1908, and died 24 June 1995. She married **Roby Wrench** 20 October 1926 in Dillon, South Carolina, son of Golallus Wrench and Celestial Carroll. He was born 01 September 1907, and died 22 February 1974 in Dunn, North Carolina.

"Mabel" is also spelled "Mable" and Roby found as "Robie." Four children.

Mabel Inez and Roby were buried in Baptist Chapel Church Cemetery on Baptist Chapel Road, Sampson County, North Carolina.

Children of Mabel Matthews and Roby Wrench are:

+ 2194 i. **Reba Nadene Wrench,** born 17 October 1927 in Dismal Township, Sampson County, North Carolina.

2195 ii. **Hazel Eveline Wrench,** born 05 May 1930 in Erwin, Harnett County, North Carolina. She married **Carnell Elton House;** born 15 December 1929 in Godwin, Sampson County, North Carolina and they had seven children. Their first child, **HAZEL JOYCE HOUSE,** born 18 July 1953 first married **LARRY ARNOLD FAIRCLOTH,** son of WILLIAM RAEFORD FAIRCLOTH and RUTH ELAINE HAIR and they had one child. Hazel "Joyce" married second as his second wife, **DENIS CLAY HALL** son of CORNELIUS W. HALL and WILMA ALLEN.

JUDY GAIL HOUSE was the second child of Hazel Eveline and Carnell Elton House. She was born 9 November 1957 and married **LARRY DON TYNDALL**, son of DONNIE PITTMAN TYNDALL and MAVIS MATTHEWS.

ELTON LEWIS HOUSE, the third child, was born in 1959 and married **CHERYL LYNN MORAN.** Divorced, he married second, **CYNTHIA ANN GODWIN,** daughter of MARVIN THOMAS GODWIN and DOROTHY JOHNSON.

DONNIE HOUSE , a twin, was the fourth child.

RONNIE HOUSE, a twin, ws the fifth child.

DWAYNE EDDIE HOUSE, the sixth child, married **LISA ANN BRANCH,** daughter of LINWOOD WAYNE BRANCH and JO ANN JOHNSON.

CATHERINE DENISE HOUSE, is the seventh and youngest child of Hazel Eveline Wrench and Carnell Elton House.

iii. **THOMAS EARL WRENCH,** the third child of Mabel Inez Matthews and Roby (Robie) Wrench was born 10 November 1938 in Dismal Township, Sampson County, North Carolina and married **ADA MAE BASS,** daughter of MARTIN BASS, JR. and LENA WEST. Ada was born 6 January 1940 in Mingo Township in Sampson County. Ada and Thomas Earl have four children: 1) **EARL GLENN WRENCH** their oldest child married **SANDRA JOYCE HUGHES** and they have one child. 2) **RONALD WAYNE WRENCH** married **JOYCE ANNETTE WADE.** 3) **DANNIE KEITH WRENCH.** 4) **KELLY WADE WRENCH.**

iv. **WILLIE GERALD WRENCH,** fourth child of Mabel Inez Matthews and Roby was born 14 December 1942 in Dismal Township and married **DOROTHY HAWLEY.**

1236. Daniel Crosby Matthews (Lena Mae[6] Culbreth, John[5], Daniel Maxwell[4], Mary[3] Holland, Thomas William[2], Unknown[1]) was born 24 July 1911 in Cumberland County, North Carolina, and died 26 December 1987 in Cumberland County, North Carolina. He married **Mae Olive Spell** 04 November 1939 in Sampson County, North Carolina, daughter of Braxton Spell and Lela Mae Royal. She was born 01 January 1917 in Sampson County, North Carolina.

Daniel Crosby is buried in the Autry-McAlphin Cemetery near Stedman, North Carolina.

Child is listed above under (891) Mae Olive Spell.

1238. Eupha Mae Matthews (Lena Mae[6] Culbreth, John[5], Daniel Maxwell[4], Mary[3] Holland, Thomas William[2], Unknown[1]) was born 28 April 1917 in Sampson County, North Carolina, and died 21 October 1983 in Cumberland County, North Carolina. She married **Lewis Alton Spell** 04 March 1939 in Cumberland County, North Carolina, son of Braxton Spell and Lela Mae Royal. He was born 25 July 1915 in Sampson County, North Carolina, and died 13 December 1978 in Cumberland County, North Carolina.

The 25 July 1913 is also found for Lewis' date of birth. He and Eupha Mae are buried in a Spell Family Cemetery.

Children are listed above under (889) Lewis Alton Spell.

1239. Maggie Nessie Matthews (Lena Mae[6] Culbreth, John[5], Daniel Maxwell[4], Mary[3] Holland, Thomas William[2], Unknown[1]) was born 15 August 1918 in Dismal Township, Sampson County, North Carolina. She married **Roscoe James Carter**. He was born about 1917.

Children of Maggie Matthews and Roscoe Carter are:

2196 i. **Treva Carter.**

2197 ii. **James Attis Carter.**

1241. Adrian Huston Matthews (Lena Mae[6] Culbreth, John[5], Daniel Maxwell[4], Mary[3] Holland, Thomas William[2], Unknown[1]) was born 15 January 1924. He married **(1) Lena Cannady** 07 July 1945 in Fayetteville, Cumberland County, North Carolina, daughter of Randall Cannady and Betty Tyndall. She was born 28 July 1929. He married **(2) Geneva Cooper** After 1971. She was born 19 May 1920.

Children of Adrian Matthews and Lena Cannady are:

+ 2198 i. **James Huston Matthews**, born 20 May 1946 in Cumberland County, North Carolina.

+ 2199 ii. **Peggy Diane Matthews**, born 07 May 1947.

+ 2200 iii. **Tommy Leroy Matthews**, born 23 December 1949 in Cumberland County, North Carolina.

1242. Macie Tew (Annie Vara[6] Culbreth, John[5], Daniel Maxwell[4], Mary[3] Holland, Thomas William[2], Unknown[1]) was born 13 October 1907. She married **Thera Wesley Williams** 23 April 1927 in North Clinton Township, Sampson County, North Carolina, son of William Williams and Sarah Williams. He was born 20 January 1907 in Sampson County, North Carolina, and died 13 March 1986 in Clinton, Sampson County, North Carolina.

Thera Wesley is buried in Baptist Chapel Cemetery near Autryville, North Carolina.

Children are listed above under (1104) Thera Wesley Williams.

1243. Glaspy Elwood Tew (Annie Vara[6] Culbreth, John[5], Daniel Maxwell[4], Mary[3] Holland, Thomas William[2], Unknown[1]) was born 08 October 1916 in Dismal Township, Sampson County, North Carolina. He married **Lerotha Peterson** 10 October 1936, daughter of Eddie Peterson and Emma Naylor. She was born 01 December 1918 in Honeycutts Township, Sampson County, North Carolina.

Children of Glaspy Tew and Lerotha Peterson are:

+ 2201 i. **Reba Gray Tew**, born 23 June 1938 in Little Coharie Township, Sampson County, North Carolina.

+ 2202 ii. **William Elwood Tew**, born 09 March 1945 in Roseboro, North Carolina.

1245. Willa Grey Honeycutt (Rebeckah Olivia[6] Culbreth, John[5], Daniel Maxwell[4], Mary[3] Holland, Thomas William[2], Unknown[1]) was born 21 January 1929 in Sampson County, North Carolina. She married **Leland Elmo Tew**, son of Percy Tew and Irutha Fann. He was born 13 March 1930 in Sampson County, North Carolina.

'Lelon' is also found for "Leland."

Children of Willa Honeycutt and Leland Tew are:

+ 2203 i. **Ida Grey Tew**, born 23 April 1948 in Sampson County, North Carolina.

+ 2204 ii. **Ruthie Rebeckah Tew**, born 02 May 1956 in Sampson County, North Carolina.

1251. William Hurley Randall, Sr. (Virginia Isabell[6] Culbreth, William[5], Daniel Maxwell[4], Mary[3] Holland, Thomas William[2], Unknown[1]) was born 08 December 1906 in Falcon, North Carolina. He married **Verna Evangeline Maxwell**. She was born 24 December 1909 and was the daughter of Percy Sherrel Maxwell and Hattie Estelle Godwin

William Hurley Randall, Sr. was an organ and piano salesman for 40 years. Verna Evangeline taught in the Cumberland County schools for 43 years.

Children of William Randall and Verna Maxwell are:

2205 i. **William Hurley Randall, Jr.**, born 07 December 1929 in Black River Township, Cumberland County, North Carolina. He married Margaret Ray 07 August 1955.

William Hurley and Margaret had two children; **Margaret Diane Randall** was born 29 July 1956 and **Patricia Ruth Randall** was born on 7 June 1959.

2206 ii. **Virginia Estelle Randall**, born 17 September 1931 in Black River Township, Cumberland County, North Carolina. She married **Archie Brigman** who was born about 1925. Virginia and Robert Elvin had four children. **Linda Fay Brigman** was born on 23 December 1949; was born 22 March 1952; **David Eugene Brigman** was born on 27 September 1955 and died on 28 October 1955; **Verna Sue Brigman** was born on 26 August 1956 and married on 31 August 1974 **Ray Curtis Hughes, Jr.**, who was born on 26 August 1955. Verna Sue and Ray Curtis had one child, **Jennifer Cain Hughes** who was bon on 26 October 1976.

1258. Earl Autry McLellan (Clyde Cleveland[6] Culbreth, William[5], Daniel Maxwell[4], Mary[3] Holland, Thomas William[2], Unknown[1]) was born 25 December 1906, and died 25 October 1962. He married **Madge Lee.**

Children of Earl McLellan and Madge Lee are:

2207 i. **Linda Clyde McLellan**, born 25 December 1936.

Linda did not marry.

\+ 2208 ii. **Shirley Joy McLellan**, born 19 December 1939.

1260. Margaret Elizabeth McLellan (Clyde Cleveland[6] Culbreth, William[5], Daniel Maxwell[4], Mary[3] Holland, Thomas William[2], Unknown[1]) was born 24 October 1911 in Rocky Mount, and died 27 March 1954 in Black River Township, Cumberland County, North Carolina. She married **James Edgar Lucas** 30 December 1928 in Dillon, South Carolina. He was born 11 September 1908, and died 11 July 1988 in Near Lillington, North Carolina.

Child of Margaret McLellan and James Lucas is:

2209 i. **Evelyn McLellan Lucas**, born 25 June 1929 in Black River Township, Cumberland County, North Carolina. She married **Lester Carl Langston, Jr.**; born 06 November 1925 in Dunn, Harnett County, North Carolina.

Middle name was "Clyde." She changed it to "McLellan" in 1973. Three children.

2nd child of Margaret and James is **JAMES OWEN LUCAS** who was born 24 January 1933 in Black River Township in Cumberland County, North Carolina. "Jimmy" married 30 january 1952 to **SYLVIA COATES TAYLOR** of Wade, who was born 9 April 1934 in Eastover Township, daughter of GROVER CLEVELAND TAYLOR and BERTHA VIRGINIA COATS. One child.

3rd child of Margaret and James is **WILLIAM RHODES LUCAS** who was born 18 September 1937. He married 1 May 1960 **CHARLOTTE MARIE GLOVER** who was born 21 April 1942 in Black River Township, daughter of ESTHER VANEY GLOVER. Four children.

4th child was **NANCY CAROLYN LUCAS** who was born 10 Augsut 1942 in Godwin and married 19 November 1960 in Dillon, South Carolina, to **RAY ALLEN REEP** of Iredell County, North Carolina. Two children.

5th child was **LAURICE MCLELLAN LUCAS** was born 18 August 1944 in Godwin. He married **BRENDA GAIL STRICKLAND** and they divorced. No children.

6th child of Margaret and James was **LABERT EARL LUCAS** who was born 22 January 1947 in Black River Township. He married 31 May 1968 in Cumberland County, **EDNA EARL WILLIAMS** who was born 5 March 1948 in Roseboro, daughter of PAUL WILLIAMS and LOURETTA MAE STRICKLAND **(Louretta Mae Lee)**. Four children.

1271. Victoria Hall (Matilda Jane[6] Culbreth, Daniel L.[5], Daniel Maxwell[4], Mary[3] Holland, Thomas William[2], Unknown[1]) was born 10 August 1887, and died 18 September 1971 in Falcon, Cumberland County, North Carolina. She married **Fleet Martin Hall**, son of George Lofton Hall and Mary J. Williams. He was born 11 January 1885, and died 05 June 1950 in Fayetteville, Cumberland County, North Carolina.

Victoria and Fleet Martin were buried in LaFayette Memorial Park, Fayetteville, Cumberland County, North Carolina.

Child is listed above under (1017) Fleet Martin Hall.

1272. Julius D. Hall (Matilda Jane[6] Culbreth, Daniel L.[5], Daniel Maxwell[4], Mary[3] Holland, Thomas William[2], Unknown[1]) was born 05 August 1891, and died 06 November 1972. He married **Vivia Jane Lewis**. She was born 28 September 1891, and died 28 June 1971.

Julius and Vivia Jane were buried in Halls United Methodist Church Cemetery on Minnie Hall Road north of Autryville, North Carolina.

Child of Julius Hall and Vivia Lewis is:

2210 i. **Herman Harold Hall,** born 14 December 1914. He married **Elizabeth Autry**; born 11 December 1916. Three children. 1st child: **HERMAN HAROLD HALL, JR.**, was born 10 March 1937. He married **MARTHA ANN REDFERN**. They have one child and one grandchild.

2nd child: **PEYTON WELDON HALL** was born 7 November 1938. He married **Joyce Smith** who was born 28 February 1940, daughter of JOSEPH E. Smith and MABEL RUTH SMITH. Two children. 3rd child. **CHARLES HENRY HALL** was born 24 April 1944. He married **CAROLYN WILLIAMSON** who was born 22 October 1944, daughter of Earl Williamson and Ruby Williamson. Two children.

The second child of Julius Hall and Vivia Lewis: **JULIUS PATON HALL** who was born 22 September 1917 in Dismal Township and died 3 July 1918.

The third child of Julius and Vivia, **WILLIAM JAMES HALL** who was born 8 May 1921 in Dismal Township, married 11 June 1949 **LAURA NOVELLA CRUMPLER** who was born 11 March 1931 in Little Coharie Township, daughter of DAVID DEE CRUMPLER and LAURA BULLOCK. Two children. 1) **BRENDA ELMIRA HALL** who married **JAMES EDWARD WILLIAMS, JR.**, son of JAMES EDWARD WILLIAMS, SR. and MERIENE WILLIAMS. 2) **PHYLLIS KAY HALL** who married **EDWARD TILLMAN WILLIAMS**, son of LEROY OSCAR WILLIAMS and HATTIE FLORENCE MCLAMB.

The fourth child: **THELDA ELIZABETH HALL** was born 6 November 1925 in White Oak Township and died 8 July 1968 in Fayetteville. She married 25 December 1949 in Autryville, **WILLIAM ALEXANDER COOK** who was born 15 May 1923 in Seventy-First Township and died 27 August 1974 in Fayetteville, son of Ernest Lester Cook and Ida Mae Lindsay. They were buried in Galatia Presbyterian Church Cemetery. No children.

The fifth child of Julius and Vivia: **JOSEPH ELWIN HALL** was born 14 July 1928 in Dismal Township in Sampson County. Elwin married 21 December 1958 in Hall's United Methodist Church, **SYLVIA JEAN JOLLY** who was born 24 April 1939 in Little Coharie Township, daughter of AARON JOLLY and WILMA ESTELLE AUTRY. Three children: **DIANA LYNNE**

HALL, stillborn. **MICHAEL ELWIN HALL**, and **SANDRA JEAN HALL.**

1280. Iula Vern Hall (Jannette Maxwell[6] Culbreth, Daniel L.[5], Daniel Maxwell[4], Mary[3] Holland, Thomas William[2], Unknown[1]) was born 20 April 1910, and died 12 January 1984 in North Carolina. She married **Earl Gibson Spell**, son of Bernice Blair Spell and Mary Russell Autry. He was born 21 April 1906, and died 26 January 1974 near Roseboro, North Carolina. Iula Vern and Earl Gibson are buried in Spell Family Cemetery on Dunn Road (SR 1002) about 5.5 miles north of Roseboro, North Carolina.

It appears that Iula Vern Hall was listed as Ida Vera Hall on at least one record for her daughter, Margaret.

Children of Iula Hall and Earl Spell are:

2211 i. **Susan Janet Spell**, born 29 October 1931 in Little Coharie Township, Sampson County, North Carolina. She married **Ronald Norman Thompson**; born about 1929 in Illinois.

Three children.

\+ 2212 ii. **Alma Doris Spell**, born 08 June 1933 in Little Coharie Township, Sampson County, North Carolina.

2213 iii. **Avis Jean Spell,** born 07 August 1934 in Little Coharie Township, Sampson County, North Carolina; died 07 August 1934 and is buried in a Spell Family Cemetery on Dunn Road (SR 1002) about 5.5 miles north of Roseboro, North Carolina. Her name is also found as "Alvis Jean."

2214 iv. **Earl Delano Spell**, born 30 December 1936 in Little Coharie Twnsp, Sampson County, North Carolina. He married **Betty Merle Cashwell**, daughter of **BRAFFORD G.ARNER CASHWELL** and **ETHEL BULLARD.** They had three children.

v. **ALTA BLANCHE SPELL**, fifth child of Iula and Earl, was born 20 July 1940 and married **WILLIAM NATHAN MCLAMB** who was born 26 December 1939, son of **JAMES L. MCLAMB** and **ELOUISE STRICKLAND**. One child.

vi. **MARGARET GENEVIEVE SPELL**, sixth child of Iula and Earl was born 31 January 1942 and married **ROBERT LEE HUMBERT.** Three children.

vii. **PATSY HALL SPELL,** born 30 October 1944, married **GEORGE O. MARKHAM** and they had three children.

viii. **SELBY CARSON SPELL** was the eighth child of Iula and Earl and he married **ROSE ANN HESTER** and had two children.

ix. **CATHY DARNELLE SPELL,** ninth child was born 8 March 1950, married **JAMES LARRY TAYLOR** who was born 8 January 1949, son of JAMES HAROLD TAYLOR and EVA MAE NAYLOR.

x. **DAVID WOODROW SPELL** the tenth and youngest child of Iula and Earl, was born 31 January 1952 and married **JUDY KAY FAIRCLOTH.**

1282. Mary Louise Culbreth (William James[6], Daniel L.[5], Daniel Maxwell[4], Mary[3] Holland, Thomas William[2], Unknown[1]) was born 08 February 1910. She married **(1) Evolyn Neal Lewis, Sr.** before 1930. He was born 27 December 1903, and died 06 February 1942. She married **(2) Henry Guilford Hall** After 1942. He was born 17 December 1920, and died 19 June 1979.

Children of Mary Culbreth and Evolyn Lewis are:

\+ 2215 i. **Willie Gibson Lewis**, born 23 April 1930; died 27 June 1972.

\+ 2216 ii. **James Evolyn Lewis, Sr.**, born 18 February 1932 in Honeycutt Township, Sampson County, North Carolina.

2217 iii. **Lillie Culbreth Lewis**, born 10 March 1935. She married **George Clayton Carroll**; born 22 August 1931.

Two children.

Children of Mary Culbreth and Henry Hall are:

\+ 2218 i. **Mary Etta Hall**, born 30 March 1947 in Roseboro, North Carolina.

2219 ii. **Henry Gerald Hall** was born 03 August 1948, died 14 October 1965 and is buried in Hollywood Cemetery, Roseboro, North Carolina.

1284. Annie Ruth Culbreth (William James[6], Daniel L.[5], Daniel Maxwell[4], Mary[3] Holland, Thomas William[2], Unknown[1]) was born 27 October 1915, and died 17 February 1999. She married **Jake Herbert Spell.** He was born 30 January 1912, and died 15 December 1983 in Clinton, Sampson County, North Carolina.

Annie Ruth and Jake were buried in a Spell Cemetery in Spell Town Community on Dunn Road north of Roseboro, North Carolina.

Child of Annie Culbreth and Jake Spell is:

2220 i. **James Herbert Spell**, born 28 January 1944.

1300. James Alton Naylor, Sr. (Susan Lee[6] Culbreth, Daniel L.[5], Daniel Maxwell[4], Mary[3] Holland, Thomas William[2], Unknown[1]) was born 14 July 1905 in Sampson County, North

Carolina, and died 03 April 1980 in Fayetteville, Cumberland County, North Carolina. He married **Clara Hazel Ezzell** 15 July 1945. She was born 08 July 1922 in Autryville, North Carolina, and died 28 February 1991 in Clinton, Sampson County, North Carolina.

James Alton and Clara were buried at Pleasant Union Baptist Church Cemetery on Pleasant Union Road (SR 1405), Sampson County, North Carolina.

Children of James Naylor and Clara Ezzell are:

+ 2221 i. **Betty Ruth Naylor**, born 18 March 1946 in Fayetteville, Cumberland County, North Carolina.

+ 2222 ii. **James Alton Naylor, Jr.**, born 27 September 1956.

1301. Eunice Lee Naylor (Susan Lee[6] Culbreth, Daniel L.[5], Daniel Maxwell[4], Mary[3] Holland, Thomas William[2], Unknown[1]) was born 26 July 1908. She married **Otto Sylvester James Lucas** before 1926 who was the son of Jasper Herring Lucas and Theodocia L. Ezzell. He was born 21 February 1902, died 22 November 1940 in Roseboro, Sampson County, North Carolina, and was buried at Pleasant Union Baptist Church Cemetery on Pleasant Union Road (SR 1405), Sampson County, North Carolina.

Children of Eunice Naylor and Otto Lucas are:

2223 i. **Floyd Herring Lucas**, born 20 September 1926 in Little Coharie Township, Sampson County, North Carolina; died 19 May 1931 in Little Coharie Township, Sampson County, North Carolina.

Floyd Herring Lucas was first buried at Lucas Family Cemetery and later moved to Pleasant Union Baptist Church Cemetery on Pleasant Union Road (SR 1405), Sampson County, North Carolina.

2224 ii. **James Lucas**, born 05 February 1928, died 06 February 1928 in Little Coharie Township, Sampson County, North Carolina, and was buried at Pleasant Union Baptist Church Cemetery on Pleasant Union Road (SR 1405), Sampson County, North Carolina.

+ 2225 iii. **Gladys Elease Lucas**, born 17 February 1929 in Little Coharie Township, Sampson County, North Carolina.

2226 iv. **Gadys Lucas**, born 17 February 1929 in Little Coharie Township, Sampson County, North Carolina; died 17 February 1929 in Little Coharie Township, Sampson County, North Carolina.

Gadys Lucas was a stillborn twin and was buried at Pleasant Union Baptist Church Cemetery on Pleasant Union Road (SR 1405), Sampson County, North Carolina.

+ 2227 v. **Sadie Geneva Lucas**, born 22 December 1930 in Little Coharie Township, Sampson County.

+ 2228 vi. **Janie Mae Lucas**, born 21 December 1932.

2229 vii. **Thomas Weldon Lucas**, born 09 October 1934 in Roseboro, Sampson County, North Carolina. He married first **Nancy Buckwell** and second **Carol Hilditch** and had no children by either wife.

+ 2230 viii. **Helen Grey Lucas**, born 14 March 1936 in Little Coharie Township, Sampson County.

+ 2231 ix. **James Landon Lucas**, born 31 January 1938 in Little Coharie Township, Sampson County, North Carolina; died 05 August 1976.

2232 x. **Charles Lucas**, born 11 December 1939 in Little Coharie Township, Sampson County, North Carolina. He married Annie Deloris Hall; born 15 December 1942 in Little Coharie Township, Sampson County, North Carolina. No children.

+ 2233 xi. **Wendell Otto Lucas**, born 04 August 1941 in Little Coharie Township, Sampson County.

1303. Jessie Wilson Naylor (Susan Lee[6] Culbreth, Daniel L.[5], Daniel Maxwell[4], Mary[3] Holland, Thomas William[2], Unknown[1]) was born 10 January 1914. She married **Willie J. Christmas**. He was born 28 April 1910, and died 04 March 1977.

Children of Jessie Naylor and Willie Christmas are:

2234 i. **William Christmas.**

+ 2235 ii. **Susan Annette Christmas**, born 20 July 1944.

1304. Katie Jane Naylor (Susan Lee[6] Culbreth, Daniel L.[5], Daniel Maxwell[4], Mary[3] Holland, Thomas William[2], Unknown[1]) was born 06 June 1916 in Little Coharie Township, Sampson County, North Carolina, and died 15 October 1989 in Richmond, Virginia. She married **(1) James Grady Capps** 09 June 1934 in Clinton, North Carolina. He was born 17 December 1914 in Wilson County, and died 19 September 1938 in Little Coharie Township, Sampson County, North Carolina. She married **(2) Horace Wendell Spell** After 1939, son of Noah Spell and Mattie Autry. He was born 10 April 1918, and died 24 June 1974 in Fayetteville, Cumberland County, North Carolina.

"Jewel" is listed for Katie's middle name by one source. Her naming a daughter "Jewel" may indicate that it is her middle name. Katie Jane and Horace were buried in Horne Family Cemetery on Minnie Hall Road about 1.5 miles north of Autryville, North Carolina.

James Grady Capps was buried Old Swamp Church Cemetery?

Children of Katie Naylor and James Capps are:

+ 2236 i. **Jewel Ray Capps**, born 26 March 1936 in Little Coharie Township, Sampson County, North Carolina.

+ 2237 ii. **Jean Allyson Capps**, born 03 February 1939.

1307. Rebecca Maxine Williams (Daniel Walter[6], Martha Rebecca[5] Culbreth, Daniel Maxwell[4], Mary[3] Holland, Thomas William[2], Unknown[1]) was born 03 June 1935 in Dismal Township, Sampson County, North Carolina. She married **Robert Bruce McPhail** 08 January 1956, son of James McPhail and Stella Lewis. He was born 31 March 1930 in Black River Township, Cumberland County, North Carolin.

Children of Rebecca Williams and Robert McPhail are:

2238 i. **James Walter McPhail**, born 14 September 1956.

2239 ii. **Robert Douglas McPhail**, born 04 March 1958 in Clinton, Sampson County, North Carolina.

2240 iii. **Michael Thomas McPhail**, born 27 December 1959.

2241 iv. **Arthur Steven McPhail**, born 09 October 1961 in Germany. He married **Susan Michele Holland** 14 February 1982; born 27 June 1963.

1311. James Hinton Autry (William[6] Mac Autry, Sr., Tomzillia[5] Culbreth, Daniel Maxwell[4], Mary[3] Holland, Thomas William[2], Unknown[1]) was born 11 November 1911, and died 09 March 1993. He married **Straudia Almeta Wrench** 25 August 1937, daughter of Fletcher E. Wrench and Anna Belle Williams. She was born 07 March 1912, and died 11 October 1995.

James Hinton and Straudia were buried in the Minson M. Williams Family Cemetery at the northeast corner of Dunn Road (SR 1002 and SR 1441. Dismal Township, Sampson County, North Carolina.

Children of James Autry and Straudia Wrench are:

+ 2242 i. **Lynell Hinton Autry**, born 11 November 1938.

+ 2243 ii. **James Reid Autry**, born 03 August 1953 in Fayetteville, Cumberland County, North Carolina.

1317. Olavia Tomzilia Sivertsen (Armelia Bertha[6] Autry, Tomzillia[5] Culbreth, Daniel Maxwell[4], Mary[3] Holland, Thomas William[2], Unknown[1]) was born 30 January 1914 in Dismal Township, Sampson County, North Carolina, and died 01 February 1997. She married **Clifford Carlton Jackson** 22 August 1931, son of John Jackson and Mittie Tew. He was born 20 March 1909 in Sampson County, North Carolina, and died 17 December 1996.

Olavia Tomzilia and Clifford were buried in Clement Missionary Baptist Church Cemetery on Maxwell Road (SR1006) about 0.5 mile west of Sr 1425 in Sampson County, North Carolina.

Children of Olavia Sivertsen and Clifford Jackson are:

+ 2244 i. **Mary Amalie Jackson**, born 01 July 1934 in Dismal Township, Sampson County, North Carolina.

+ 2245 ii. **Olavia Faye Jackson**, born 29 August 1936 in Dismal Township, Sampson County.

+ 2246 iii. **Donna Jean Jackson**, born 07 August 1941 in Dismal Township, Sampson County, North Carolina.

2247 iv. **Magda Elaine Jackson**, born 24 August 1944 in Roseboro, North Carolina. She married **James Merle Bass**; born 19 September 1947 in Roseboro, Sampson County, North Carolina.

1319. Harold Lindsay Sivertsen (Armelia Bertha[6] Autry, Tomzillia[5] Culbreth, Daniel Maxwell[4], Mary[3] Holland, Thomas William[2], Unknown[1]) was born 16 August 1919. He married **(1) Sue Kennedy**. He married **(2) Lenora Wilson**.

No children by either wife. "Neal Grady" is by Sue's name and it's unclear whether this was the name of a first husband. Lenora was first married to a "**Porter**."

Children of Harold Sivertsen and Lenora Wilson are:

2248 i. **Ray Porter**, died January 1976 in an automobile accident.

2249 ii. **Jeff Porter.**

1320. Mary Grace Sivertsen (Armelia Bertha[6] Autry, Tomzillia[5] Culbreth, Daniel Maxwell[4], Mary[3] Holland, Thomas William[2], Unknown[1]) was born 12 November 1921. She married **John Stacey Hair, Sr.**. He was born 21 December 1921 in Fayetteville, Cumberland County, North Carolina.

Children of Mary Sivertsen and John Hair are:

2250 i. **Sarah Catherine Hair**. She married **John Thomas Shipman III**.

\+ 2251 ii. **John Stacey Hair, Jr**.

1321. Louise Newcomb Sivertsen (Armelia Bertha[6] Autry, Tomzillia[5] Culbreth, Daniel Maxwell[4], Mary[3] Holland, Thomas William[2], Unknown[1]) was born 28 March 1926. She married **Terrell Randolph Smith**. He was born 15 January 1924 in Dismal Township, Sampson County, North Carolina.

Children of Louise Sivertsen and Terrell Smith are:

2252 i. **Cecelia Louise Smith**. She married **Hugh Marks**.

2253 ii. **Terrell Bronzie Smith**. He married **Connie Besse**.

1357. Rossie Marie Hairr (Elmond[6], William H.[5], Stephen[4], Orpah[3] Holland, Thomas William[2], Unknown[1]) was born 22 April 1917, and died 07 April 1987. She married **James Ervin Floyd** 30 November 1939. He was born 13 December 1914 in Columbus County, North Carolina, and died 08 October 1966.

Rossie Marie and James Ervin were buried in Keener Methodist Church Cemetery on Kenner Road West (SR 1746), Sampson County, North Carolina.

Rossie and her brother, James Elmon, listed below, provided a profile on the "Hare Family" of Sampson County in the first Sampson County, North Carolina, Heritage book.

Children of Rossie Hairr and James Floyd are:

2254 i. **Jimmy Edward Floyd**, born 21 September 1940, he married **LINDA GRAY SUTTON** who was born 14 June 1941. Two known children.

1) **PHYLLIS RENEE FLOYD** was born 1 October 1960 and married **ANTHONY NORRIS** on 30 September 1979. He was born 16 July 1957. They have one known child, **DUSTIN EDWARD NORRIS** who was born 10 September 1980.

2) **TONI LYNN FLOYD** was born 12 October 1962.

2255 ii. Jane Marie Floyd, born 03 March 1945. She married **David C. Sagel** on 3 July 1970; born 26 May 1945 in New Jersey. Two known children:

1) **CARRIE ANNE SAGEL** was born 3 November 1974 and

2) ANNA LEE SAGEL was born 20 April 1977.

1358. James Elmon Hairr (Elmond[6], William H.[5], Stephen[4], Orpah[3] Holland, Thomas William[2], Unknown[1]) was born 05 April 1925 in North Carolina. He married **Rachel Phillips** on 4 October 1963. She was born in Siler City, North Carolina.

During World War II, James served in the United States Army from 25 October 1950 until 29 September 1952. He was stationed on Okinawa Island.

Child of James Hairr and Rachel Phillips is:

2256 i. **Joe Elmon Hairr.**

1359. William Wright Odom (Laura Caroline[6] Hairr, William H.[5], Stephen[4], Orpah[3] Holland, Thomas William[2], Unknown[1]) was born 14 June 1916. He married **Helen June Horne** 17 March 1945. She was born in Burgaw, North Carolina.

Child of William Odom and Helen Horne is:

2257 i. **Laura Helen Odom**, born 17 August 1947; she married **TOMMY C. DAUGHTRY** on 17 August 1970. He was born 14 February 1947 in Sampson County.

Two known children were born in Sampson County.

1) TODD DAUGHTRY, born 11 October 1972.

2) TONYA DAUGHTRY, born 13 February 1977.

1374. Leon Fulton Bradshaw (David L.[6], Eliza Jane[5] Hairr, Stephen[4], Orpah[3] Holland, Thomas William[2], Unknown[1]) was born 31 August 1908 in Sampson County, North Carolina, and died 15 June 1963. He married **Lucille Underwood** 02 August 1935. She was born 17 October 1915, and died 08 September 1997 in Rocky Mount, North Carolina.

Children of Leon Bradshaw and Lucille Underwood are:

2258 i. **Rothal Vinson Bradshaw**, born 22 May 1936 in Sampson County, North Carolina.

\+ 2259 ii. **Charles Elliott Bradshaw**, born 18 May 1938 in Sampson County, North Carolina, married **YVONNE** (maiden name unknown) and they had one child: **DAVID BRADSHAW**.

1377. Theodore Bradshaw (David L.[6], Eliza Jane[5] Hairr, Stephen[4], Orpah[3] Holland, Thomas William[2], Unknown[1]) was born 09 April 1913 in Sampson County, North Carolina, and died 03 July 1970 in Sampson County. He married **Claudia Vivian McCullen** 03 July 1935. She was born April 1920, and died 27 January 1986 in Sampson County, North Carolina.

Theodore and Claudia Vivian were buried in the David L. Bradshaw Family Cemetery.

Children of Theodore Bradshaw and Claudia McCullen are:

\+ 2260 i. **Edith Juanita Bradshaw**, born 26 August 1936.

\+ 2261 ii. **Leon Sherrill Bradshaw**, born 06 September 1938 in Sampson County, North Carolina; died 14 October 1999 in Sampson County, North Carolina.

\+ 2262 iii. **Theodore Leslie Bradshaw, Sr.**, born 02 July 1940 in Sampson County, North Carolina.

2263 iv. **Peggy Faye Bradshaw**, born 22 March 1942 in Sampson County, North Carolina.

\+ 2264 v. **Jo Ann Bradshaw**, born 15 April 1944 in Sampson County, North Carolina.

\+ 2265 vi. **Roy Rogers Bradshaw**, born 22 July 1945 in Sampson County, North Carolina.

2266 vii. **Lillian Kay Bradshaw**, born 24 November 1946 in Sampson County, North Carolina; died 22 February 1992. She married **Harold Wise**.

Lillian Kay and Harold were buried in the David L. Bradshaw Family Cemetery/

\+ 2267 viii. **Ted Larry Bradshaw, Sr.**, born 23 April 1948 in Sampson County, North Carolina; died 04 May 2000 in Nashville, Tennessee.

\+ 2268 ix. **Danny Ray Bradshaw**, born 10 December 1950 in Sampson County, North Carolina.

1378. Gorman Bradshaw (David L.[6], Eliza Jane[5] Hairr, Stephen[4], Orpah[3] Holland, Thomas William[2], Unknown[1]) was born about 1915, and died 1987. He married **Flora Mae Bradley** who was born 1920 in Cherokee County, Alabama.

Children of Gorman Bradshaw and Flora Bradley are:

2269 i. **Nadine Bradshaw.**

2270 ii. **David Ray Bradshaw.**

2271 iii. **Judy Ann Bradshaw.**

2272 iv. **Connie Bradshaw.**

2273 v. **Gary Bradshaw.**

2274 vi. **Virginia Bradshaw.**

1380. Owen Bradshaw (Franklin[6], Eliza Jane[5] Hairr, Stephen[4], Orpah[3] Holland, Thomas William[2], Unknown[1]) was born 15 August 1906 in Sampson County, North Carolina, and died 21 November 1961 in Sampson County, North Carolina. He married **Betty Autry**. She was born 10 September 1912, and died 20 May 1995 in Sampson County, North Carolina.

Owen Bradshaw and Betty were buried in the Frank Bradshaw Family Cemetery.

Children of Owen Bradshaw and Betty Autry are:

\+ 2275 i. **Hilda Elizabeth Bradshaw**, born 15 October 1930.

\+ 2276 ii. **Janet Romona Bradshaw**, born 12 January 1933 in Sampson County, North Carolina.

\+ 2277 iii. **Della Gray Bradshaw**, born 31 January 1934 in Sampson County, North Carolina; died 25 May 1995 in Cumberland County, North Carolina.

\+ 2278 iv. **Elsie Mae Bradshaw**, born 21 May 1936 in Sampson County.

2279 v. **Franklin Bradshaw**, born 09 February 1939 in Sampson County, North Carolina.

\+ 2280 vi. **Betty Davis Bradshaw**, born 21 October 1945 in Sampson County.

1382. Jasper Bradshaw (Franklin[6], Eliza Jane[5] Hairr, Stephen[4], Orpah[3] Holland, Thomas William[2], Unknown[1]) was born 17 February 1910 in Sampson County, North Carolina, and died 17 May 1951 in Sampson County, North Carolina. He married **Olive Mae Howell** 25 April 1947. She was born 28 February 1930.

Jasper was called "Jap." He was buried in the Frank Bradshaw Family Cemetery.

Children of Jasper Bradshaw and Olive Howell are:

2281 i. **Brenda Kay Bradshaw**, born 19 March 1948 in Sampson County, North Carolina.

2282 ii. **Gary Nelson Bradshaw**, born 07 July 1949 in Sampson County; died 26 February 1952 in Sampson County, North Carolina and is buried in the Frank Bradshaw Family Cemetery.

2283 iii. **Jewel Mae Bradshaw**, born 26 October 1950 in Sampson County.

1384. Herbert Bradshaw (Franklin[6], Eliza Jane[5] Hairr, Stephen[4], Orpah[3] Holland, Thomas William[2], Unknown[1]) was born 06 October 1914 in Sampson County, North Carolina, and died 10 February 1984 in Chapel Hill, North Carolina. He married **Pauline Fleming** 12 October 1939. She was born 25 January 1923 in Sampson County, North Carolina.

Herbert was called "Hub." He was buried in the Frank Bradshaw Family Cemetery.

Children of Herbert Bradshaw and Pauline Fleming are:

\+ 2284 i. **Jackie Ray Bradshaw**, born 12 December 1941 in Sampson County, North Carolina.

2285 ii. **Violet Ann Bradshaw**, born 17 April 1945 in Sampson County; died 04 February 1996. Buried in the Frank Bradshaw Family Cemetery.

\+ 2286 iii. **Ronnie Gene Bradshaw**, born 24 May 1947 in Sampson County, North Carolina.

\+ 2287 iv. **Herbert Wayne Bradshaw**, born 27 December 1951 in Sampson County.

2288 v. **Susan Marie Bradshaw**, born 06 July 1967 in Sampson County, North Carolina.

2289 vi. **Jeffrey Scott Bradshaw**, born 23 July 1969 in Sampson County. He married **Beverly Darlene Gainey** 13 August 1994.

2290 vii. **Stephen Clark Bradshaw**, born 23 July 1969 in Sampson County, North Carolina. He married **Melanie Renee Byrd** 18 May 1996.

1385. Woodrow Bradshaw (Franklin[6], Eliza Jane[5] Hairr, Stephen[4], Orpah[3] Holland, Thomas William[2], Unknown[1]) was born 18 July 1916 in Sampson County, North Carolina, and died 14 August 1978 in Columbia, South Carolina. He married **Margaret Rush** 07 July 1949 in Lexington, South Carolina. She was born 07 May 1921 and died 05 January 1991 in Columbia, South Carolina.

Woodrow and Margaret were buried in Crescent Hill Memorial Gardens, Columbia, South Carolina.

Children of Woodrow Bradshaw and Margaret Rush are:

\+ 2291 i. **Claudia Ann Bradshaw**, born 04 February 1951.

\+ 2292 ii. **Susan Faye Bradshaw**, born 15 March 1953.

\+ 2293 iii. **Woodrow Michael Bradshaw, Sr.**, born 01 January 1956; died 22 May 2001.

1386. Pearl Bradshaw (Franklin[6], Eliza Jane[5] Hairr, Stephen[4], Orpah[3] Holland, Thomas William[2], Unknown[1]) was born 27 May 1922 in Sampson County, North Carolina, and died 05 July 1991. She married **Cluster Honrine** 20 April 1940. He was born 07 September 1913 in Sampson County, North Carolina, and died 06 July 1969 in Sampson County.

Cluster was called "Duck."

Children of Pearl Bradshaw and Cluster Honrine are:

2294 i. **Sadie Mae Honrine**, born 09 April 1941 in Sampson County, North Carolina. She married **Ronald Jackson** 26 April 1987. He was born 10 April 1943.

\+ 2295 ii. **Carolyn Gray Honrine**, born 17 August 1942 in Sampson County, North Carolina.

1387. William Braxton Hairr (Isaiah H.[6], James Thomas[5], John C.[4] Hair, Orpah[3] Holland, Thomas William[2], Unknown[1]) was born 18 October 1898 in North Carolina, and died 07 February 1974 in Clinton, Sampson County, North Carolina. He married **Ressie Bass** 05 October 1918 in Clinton, North Carolina, daughter of **William Bass** and **Penelope Jackson**. She was born 12 June 1901, and died 10 January 1971 in Clinton, Sampson County, North Carolina.

He and Ressie were divorced. He was buried in Piney Green Baptist Church Cemetery at intersection of Highway 242 and High House Road, Sampson County, North Carolina. She was buried in Owens Grove PFW Baptist Church, Kitty Fork, Sampson County, North Carolina.

Children of William Hairr and Ressie Bass are:

2296 i. **Glenda Ruth Hairr,** born 12 March 1920 in Herrings Township, Sampson County, North Carolina.

Her first name is also spelled 'Glinda.'

2297 ii. **Rubert Hairr**, born 26 September 1922 in Herrings Township, Sampson County, North Carolina; died 09 January 1923 in Herrings Township, Sampson County, North Carolina.

Transcribed cemetery records state hie tombstone reads June 15, 1927 for birth and December 12, 1928 for death? Another source notes 26 October 1923 for his birth. He was buried in the Alvin Bass Family Cemetery, Plain View Township, Sampson County, North Carolina.

+ 2298 iii. **Hubert Bee Hairr**, born 16 October 1924 in Herrings Township, Sampson County, North Carolina; died 25 June 1986.

2299 iv. **Lemon D. Hairr**, born 25 June 1927 in Herrings Township, Sampson County, North Carolina; died 12 February 1929 in North Clinton Township, Sampson County, North Carolina.

One source states Lemon's tombstone shows a birth date of October 12, 1925 and a death date of February 15, 1926. The other dates are county vital records.

He was buried in the Alvin Bass Family Cemetery, Plain View Township, Sampson County, North Carolina.

2300 v. **Louise Hairr**, born 14 July 1929 in Herrings Township, Sampson County, North Carolina; died 18 July 1929. One source gives 15 June 1933 for her birth and about 24 October 1933. for her death.

She was buried in the Alvin Bass Family Cemetery, Plain View Township, Sampson County, North Carolina.

1388. Spence B. Hairr (Isaiah[6], James Thomas[5], John C.[4] Hair, Orpah[3] Holland, Thomas William[2], Unknown[1]) was born 29 July 1900 in Sampson County, North Carolina, and died 23 November 1961 in Sampson County, North Carolina. He married **Lula Bee Lockamy**, daughter of James Thomas Lockamy and Jemima Jewel Jackson. She was born 25 September 1903 in Honeycutts Township, Sampson County, North Carolina, and died 16 May 1993 in Sampson County, North Carolina.

Lula Bee sang in a group with her sisters, Flora Della and Martha Ann and brother, Robert C.; Martha Ann played guitar.

Spence and Lula Bee were buried in the Owens Grove Pentecostal FWB Church Cemetery, Sampson County, North Carolina.

Children of Spence Hairr and Lula Lockamy are:

2301 i. **Bruce Hairr**, born about 1924. He married (1) **Edith Unknown** and married (2) **Geneva Hall**.

He is deceased.

+ 2302 ii. **Floyd Lutrell Hairr**, born 01 November 1928 in Sampson County, North Carolina.

1389. Troy Addicus Hairr (Isaiah[6], James Thomas[5], John C.[4] Hair, Orpah[3] Holland, Thomas William[2], Unknown[1]) was born 16 August 1902 in North Carolina, and died 23 December 1989 in Cumberland County, North Carolina. He married **Pauline E. Bass**, daughter of Bythal Bass and Hepsie Godwin. She was born 29 November 1908, and died 28 July 1998.

Troy Addicus and Pauline were buried in Shady Grove FW Baptist Church Cemetery on Hudsontown Road (SR 1634) in Sampson County, North Carolina.

Children of Troy Hairr and Pauline Bass are:

+ 2303 i. **Christine Hairr,** born 25 October 1928 in Mingo Township, Sampson County, North Carolina.

+ 2304 ii. **Bobby Ray Hairr,** born 14 February 1936.

1390. Leona Hairr (Isaiah[6], James Thomas[5], John C.[4] Hair, Orpah[3] Holland, Thomas William[2], Unknown[1]) was born 30 August 1905 in North Carolina, and died 05 February 1998. She married **James Lee Lockamy,** son of James Thomas Lockamy and Jemima Jewel Jackson. He was born 29 August 1901, and died 07 December 1985 in Sampson County, North Carolina.

Leona and James Lee were buried in Owens Grove Pentecostal FWB Church Cemetery, Sampson County, North Carolina.

Child of Leona Hairr and James Lockamy is:

+ 2305 i. **James Houston Lockamy,** born 12 February 1924; died 30 December 1997 in Sampson County, North Carolina.

1392. Omie Tera Hairr (Isaiah[6], James Thomas[5], John C.[4] Hair, Orpah[3] Holland, Thomas William[2], Unknown[1]) was born 12 August 1910, and died 25 March 2000. She married **William Arthur Weeks.** He was born 16 September 1907 in North Carolina, and died 01 March 1991 in Sampson County, North Carolina.

Children of Omie Hairr and William Weeks are:

+ 2306 i. **Paul Graham Weeks,** born About 1926.

2307 ii. **Fulton Weeks,** born about 1929.

1393. Deames Elton Hairr (Isaiah[6], James Thomas[5], John C.[4] Hair, Orpah[3] Holland, Thomas William[2], Unknown[1]) was born 31 March 1913, and died 22 May 1972 in Sampson County, North Carolina. He married **Macey Lewis.** She was born 25 June 1917, and died 30 August 1974 in Sampson County, North Carolina.

Deames Elton and Macey were buried in Rowan Baptist Church Cemetery on Rowan Road (SR 1924), Sampson County, North Carolina.

Children of Deames Hairr and Macey Lewis are:

2308 i. **Deames Glenwood Hairr,** born 03 April 1940 in North Carolina; died 28 September 1993 in Fayetteville, Cumberland County, North Carolina. He married Judy Puryear; born 19 February 1941. Deames Glenwood is buried in Rowan Baptist Church Cemetery on Rowan Road (SR 1924), Sampson County, North Carolina.

+ 2309 ii. **Sudie Hairr,** born 10 May 1944 in Sampson County, North Carolina.

1398. Richard Howard Hairr, Sr. (Augustus Davis[6] Hairr, James Thomas[5], John C.[4] Hair, Orpah[3] Holland, Thomas William[2], Unknown[1]) was born 19 January 1910, and died

09 August 1989. He married **Josephine Cooper Tew** 25 December 1929, daughter of John Tew and Della Daniel. She was born 18 December 1912. "Hairr" is found for Richard's surname.

Richard Howard and Josephine were buried in the Rowan Baptist Church Cemetery on Rowan Road (SR 1924), Sampson County, North Carolina.

Children of Richard Hair and Josephine Tew are:

2310 i. **Richard Howard Hairr, Jr.** was born 1938. He married **Helen Sinclair** after 1966. She was born 03 February 1939 in Herrings Township, Sampson County, North Carolina. Richard and Helen have no children. Helen first married **PRESTON CARR POPE**, son of AMY LEE JACKSON and WILLIAM HARVEY POPE, who was born 16 February 1935. Helen and Preston have two children: **TERRY PRESTON POPE** who was born 19 August 1959 in sampson County and died 02 February 1976 in Sampson County. **TAMMY LYNETTE POPE** was born 12 June 1964 in Clinton, Sampson County, North Carolina, and married **CHARLES DAVIS SMITH** who was born 22 June 1982 in Clinton, son of Charles Phillip Smith and Jackie Olene Jackson.

See **Jackie Olene Jackson.**

2311 ii. J. D. Hairr.

2312 iii. **Melva Ray Hairr**, born 07 March 1933; died 14 August 1941 in Sampson County, North Carolina.

She was buried in Rowan Baptist Church Cemetery on Rowan Road (SR 1924), Sampson County, North Carolina. Her name may be found as Melva Ray Hair.

1417. Marshall Fulton Baggett (Ida Dees[6] Spell, Mariah Jetson[5] Autry, Starling[4], Millie[3] Holland, Thomas William[2], Unknown[1]) was born 07 August 1912 in Honeycutts Township, Sampson County, North Carolina, and died 25 February 2001. He married **Victoria Hinson** before 1936. She was born 19 May 1911, and died 22 November 1948 in Honeycutts Township, Sampson County, North Carolina.

Marshall Fulton remarried and lived in Florida. He and Victoria were buried in the William A. Baggett Family Cemetery two miles west of Salemburg, North Carolina, on Autryville Road.

Child of Marshall Baggett and Victoria Hinson is:

2313 i. **Dorothy Annette Baggett**, born about 1936. She married **Robert Douglas Norton** 26 December 1956 in Salemburg, Sampson County, North Carolina; born 14 November 1934 in Honeycutts Township, Sampson County, North Carolina.

ii. **Connie Baggett**. She married **Mr. Januesheske**.

1421. Hurley C. Lewis (Narena C.[6] Spell, Mariah Jetson[5] Autry, Starling[4], Millie[3] Holland, Thomas William[2], Unknown[1]) was born About 1904. He married **Lou Anna Tew** 06 November 1937 in Fayetteville, Cumberland County, North Carolina, daughter of Hinton Tew and Arhillon Spell. She was born 02 September 1903 in Sampson County, North Carolina. Her name is also shown as "Luana" Tew.

Child of Hurley Lewis and Lou Tew is:

2314 i. **Donald Lewis.**

1422. Eva Clyde Lewis (Narena C.[6] Spell, Mariah Jetson[5] Autry, Starling[4], Millie[3] Holland, Thomas William[2], Unknown[1]) was born 12 August 1905, and died 19 January 1956 in Clinton, Sampson County, North Carolina. She married **Lottis Turner Holland** 03 May 1924 in South Clinton, Sampson County, North Carolina, son of William Thomas Holland and Jeronia Harriett Williams. He was born 14 December 1902, and died 24 November 1988 in Clinton, Sampson County, North Carolina.

Eva Clyde and Lottis are buried in Hall's United Methodist Church Cemetery, 4 miles north of Autryville, North Carolina on SR 1414.

Child is listed above under (746) Lottis Turner Holland.

1429. Clarence Allen Butler (Bettie Allen[6] Autry, Allen Merdeth[5], Starling[4], Millie[3] Holland, Thomas William[2], Unknown[1]) was born 14 May 1900, and died 22 October 1970 in Duke Hospital, Wayne County, North Carolina. He married **Agnes Elizabeth Vann** 01 December 1918. She was born 29 January 1900, and died 12 February 1967 in Sampson County, North Carolina.

Clarence Allen and Agnes were buried in a Butler Cemetery near the C. A. Butler homeplace.

Children of Clarence Butler and Agnes Vann are:

2315 i. **Chevis Allen Butler**, born 02 October 1919.

Chevis Allen went to Washington, D.C. about the age of 17, married, and made his home there.

2316 ii. **Agnes Marie Butler**, born 16 March 1921. She married **James Robert Blackmon** in 1944.

2317 iii. **Bonnie Lee Butler**, born 20 August 1922; died 19 July 1985. She married **William Otis Michie** in 1955.

She was buried in a Butler Cemetery on Five Bridge Road (SR 1311 in Sampson County, North Carolina.

2318 iv. **Howard Hubbard Butler**, born 21 December 1925. He married Betty Jean Adams 1951.

1432. Lillie Nadine Butler (Bettie Allen[6] Autry, Allen Merdeth[5], Starling[4], Millie[3] Holland, Thomas William[2], Unknown[1]) was born 12 July 1906, and died 11 March 1990. She married **Langdon Demanister Warren** 27 March 1927, son of DeManister Warren and Martha Jane Crumpler. He was born 28 August 1904, and died 15 July 1967.

"Lillie" is also spelled "Lily." The Langdon Demanister Warren home place is located near Mt. Elam Baptist Church, Sampson County, North Carolina. Lillie and Langdon Demanister were buried in Mt. Elam Baptist Church Cemetery on Mt. Elam Church Road in Sampson County, North Carolina.

Children of Lillie Butler and Langdon Warren are:

+ 2319 i. **Samuel Ernestine Warren,** born 23 November 1931 in Mingo Township, Sampson County, North Carolina.

+ 2320 ii. **Elsie Jane Warren**, born 31 March 1951 in Clinton, Sampson County, North Carolina.

+ 2321 iii. **Houston Warren**.

+ 2322 iv. **Alice Dean Warren**.

+ 2323 v. **Betty Allen Warren**.

1434. Eva Pearl Butler (Bettie Allen[6] Autry, Allen Merdeth[5], Starling[4], Millie[3] Holland, Thomas William[2], Unknown[1]) was born 18 December 1910. She married **Braston Packer** 24 December 1938.

She graduated from East Carolina Teachers' College at Greenville, North Carolina in 1932. She was a teacher and supervisor of schools.

Child of Eva Butler and Braston Packer is:

2324 i. **Dr. John Wesley Packer**.

1435. Charles Marion Butler, Sr. (Bettie Allen[6] Autry, Allen Merdeth[5], Starling[4], Millie[3] Holland, Thomas William[2], Unknown[1]) was born 14 July 1913. He married **Eulalia Simmons** 06 August 1938 in Route 1, Clinton, North Carolina, daughter of James Simmons and Lula Honeycutt. She was born 09 October 1912.

Charles Marion Butler served as Chairman of the Sampson County Board of Commissioners for many years. He graduated from North Carolina State College in 1937 with a B.S. degree in agricultur and was a teacher, businessman, and Sampson County Commissioner.

Children of Charles Butler and Eulalia Simmons are:

+ 2325 i. **Charles Marion Butler, Jr.**, born 09 September 1939 in Dunn, Harrnett County, North Carolina; died 30 December 1966.

+ 2326 ii. **James Hubbard Butler**, born 22 July 1942 in Mingo Township, Sampson County, North Carolina.

1436. Henry Bruce Butler (Bettie Allen[6] Autry, Allen Merdeth[5], Starling[4], Millie[3] Holland, Thomas William[2], Unknown[1]) was born 29 November 1915. He married **Honoree Pierce** 1940. She was born 25 February 1917 in Near Apex, North Carolina.

Henry Bruce graduated from North Carolina State College in 1938 with a B.S. degree in Vocational Agriculture. Honoree graduated from North Carolina State University (Magna Cum laude) in 1938 with a B.S. Degree in Education (Language Arts - Social Studies).

Children of Henry Butler and Honoree Pierce are:

2327 i. **George Bruce Butler.**

2328 ii. **David Carlton Butler.**

1443. Jimmy Huey Holland (Jimmy Minson[6], Jasper Lee[5], Stephen Senter[4], Henry[3], Thomas William[2], Unknown[1]) was born 06 June 1936 in Honeycutts Township, Sampson County, North Carolina, and died 20 July 2004. He married **Bettie Lois Spell** 05 June 1954 in Roseboro, Sampson County, North Carolina, daughter of Lawrence Spell and Havens Williams. She was born 01 January 1937 in Dismal Township.

Jimmy Huey is buried in Zoar FWBP Church Cemetery Near Salemburg, North Carolina.

Children of Jimmy Holland and Bettie Spell are:

2329 i. **Lois Faye Holland,** born 10 April 1955 in Roseboro.

2330 ii. **Jimmie Keith Holland,** born 18 December 1957 in Roseboro.

1450. Woodrow Smith (Lonie Mae[6] Holland, Jasper Lee[5], Stephen Senter[4], Henry[3], Thomas William[2], Unknown[1]) was born 21 July 1938 in Sampson County, North Carolina. He married **Joyce Faye Matthews** 01 June 1958 in Oak Grove PFWB Church, daughter of Charlie Wade Matthews and Jessie Oleta Strickland. She was born 18 January 1939 in Eastover Township, Cumberland County, North Carolina.

Children of Woodrow Smith and Joyce Matthews are:

\+ 2331 i. **Cynthia Mae Smith,** born 06 March 1959 in Fayetteville.

\+ 2332 ii. **Tamela Joyce Smith,** born 21 February 1962 in Fayetteville.

\+ 2333 iii. **Oleta Michelle Smith,** born 23 July 1966.

1472. Alma Christine Holland (James Senter[6], Alger Rose[5], Stephen Senter[4], Henry[3], Thomas William[2], Unknown[1]) was born 04 August 1931 in Sampson County, North Carolina. She married **(2) ?? Eastwood** after 1947 and owned a cafe or restaurant in Oklahoma.

Child of Alma Christine Holland is:

\+ 2334 i. **Houstus Bennie Holland,** born 14 February 1947; died 17 October 2002.

Children of Alma Holland and ?? Eastwood are:

2335 i. **Larry Eastwood,** born in Paoli, Oklahoma. He married Debbie ??.

2336 ii. **Gary Eastwood.** He married Jamie ??.

2337 iii. **Timmy Eastwood.**

2338 iv. **James Eastwood.**

2339 v. **Unknown Son Eastwood.**

1474. William Gaddy Holland (James Senter[6], Alger Rose[5], Stephen Senter[4], Henry[3], Thomas William[2], Unknown[1]) was born 16 July 1935 in Sampson County, North Carolina. He married **(1) Annie Enola Jones**. He married **(2) Bernice ??**.

William Geddy is also listed for his name. Open heart surgery in 1983 and had an Aneurism in his abdomen on 10 March 1994. He has arthritis. Bill is 6 feet 4 inches tall; his dad, Uncle Senter (Scenter) was 6 feet tall. See notes for his father.

Children of William Holland and Annie Jones are:

2340 i. **James Leon Holland**, born 10 October 1958 in Clinton, Sampson County, North Carolina; died 27 August 2001 in Turkey, Sampson County, North Carolina. He married **Betty Sue Tyndall** who was born 24 January 1962 in Fayetteville, North Carolina, daughter of James Elliott Tyndall and Susan Jane Neal. James Leon died from bone cancer. He and Betty Sue had two children.

1) **CHERYL DENISE HOLLAND**, born 5 December 1982, in Clinton, North Carolina.

2) **JAMES WILLIAM HOLLAND**, born 22 August 1984 in Clinton, North Carolina.

2341 ii. **Charles David Holland**, born 28 December 1961 in Sampson County, North Carolina.

Child of William Holland and Bernice ?? is:

2342 i. **Terry Holland**.

1475. Alice Faye Holland (James Senter[6], Alger Rose[5], Stephen Senter[4], Henry[3], Thomas William[2], Unknown[1]) was born 11 December 1951 in Sampson County, North Carolina. She married **(1) Glen Thomas Bullard**. He was born 22 June 1950. She married **(2) Bobby Wayne Norris**. He was born 20 May 1948. She married **(3) Robert Allen Thornton**. He was born 20 June 1952.

Children of Alice Holland and Bobby Norris are:

\+ 2343 i. **Lori Ann Norris**, born 10 May 1969 in Sampson County, North Carolina.

\+ 2344 ii. **Carrie Nicole Norris**, born 21 September 1976 in Sampson County, North Carolina.

2345 iii. **Whitney Norris**, born in Sampson County, North Carolina.

1476. Doris Gray Holland (John Wesley[6], Alger Rose[5], Stephen Senter[4], Henry[3], Thomas William[2], Unknown[1]) was born 12 August 1930 in Sampson County, North Carolina, and died 03 September 2006. She married **William Earl Tew**, son of Rassie Tew and Bertha Williams. He was born 16 November 1924 in Autryville, North Carolina and died 29 March 2009 in Wake Hospital, Wake County, North Carolina.

William Earl served in the World War II from March 1943 to 1946.

Children of Doris Holland and William Tew are:

\+ 2346 i. **Linda Dianne Tew**, born 14 March 1948 in Roseboro, Sampson County, North Carolina.

\+ 2347 ii. **James Brewer Tew, Sr.**, born 25 January 1949 in Sampson County, North Carolina.

2348 iii. **Barbara Jean Tew**, born 25 February 1951.

1478. Mary Leatrice Holland (John Wesley[6], Alger Rose[5], Stephen Senter[4], Henry[3], Thomas William[2], Unknown[1]) was born 04 September 1935 in Sampson County, North Carolina. She married **Rhudon Butler** 04 April 1953. He was born 14 November 1930.

Children of Mary Holland and Rhudon Butler are:

2349 i. **Gary Rheudon Butler**, born **30 March 1954 in Roseboro, Sampson County, North Carolina.** He married (1) **Phoebe Denise Honeycutt**; born 16 December 1954. He married (2) **Margaret LeAnn Barefoot** 21 December 1981 in Clinton, Sampson County, North Carolina; born 25 April 1960 in Erwin, Harnett County, North Carolina.

Gary Rheudon Butler and Phoebe Denise Honeycutt were divorced in February 1981.

2350 ii. **Larry Leon Butler**, born 06 December 1955. He married Debra Sue Hope 06 October 1979; born 26 August 1960.

1479. Brenda Sue Holland (John Wesley[6], Alger Rose[5], Stephen Senter[4], Henry[3], Thomas William[2], Unknown[1]) was born After 1935. She married **William Colon Marley**, son of William Marley and Hattie Tew.

Child of Brenda Holland and William Marley is:

\+ 2351 i. **Wanda Sue Marley**, born 21 August 1962 in Washington, D.C..

1480. John Wesley Holland, Jr. (John Wesley[6], Alger Rose[5], Stephen Senter[4], Henry[3], Thomas William[2], Unknown[1]) was born 23 June 1947 in Roseboro, Sampson County, North Carolina. He married **Glenda Gail Faircloth.**

Children of John Holland and Glenda Faircloth are:

2352 i. **Velma LeAnn Holland**, born 12 December 1972.

2353 ii. **Johna Marion Holland**, born 24 April 1975.

2354 iii. **John Wesley Holland III**, born 02 August 1977; died 20 February 1978 in Sampson County Memorial Hospital, Clinton, North Carolina.

He died of Congenital Heart Disease. Possible Aspiration. Viral lower respiratory tract infection.

Buried at Union Grove Baptist Church Cemetery on Vander Road (SR 1438) Sampson County, North Carolina.

1482. Nancy Eveline Jackson (Roberta[6] Holland, Alger Rose[5], Stephen Senter[4], Henry[3], Thomas William[2], Unknown[1]) was born 21 April 1936 in Honeycutts Township, Sampson County, North Carolina. She married **(1) Richard Joseph Pleitt**18 September 1954 in St. Bonaventure Church, 1615 Diversey Avenue, Cook County, Chicago, IL. He was the son of Joseph Edward Pleitt and Margaret Francis Waclawek and was born 19 May 1933 in Chicago, Cook County, Illinois, and died 29 June 1981 in Mt. Sinai Medical Center, Milwaukee, Wisconsin. She married **(2) Robert Collins** in January1983 in Waukegan, Lake County, Illinois, and divorced him in December 1983. She married **(3) Edwin John Fenner** 09 June 1988 in Waukesha County Courthouse, Waukesha, Wisconsin. He was born 25 March 1925 in Eau Claire, Wisconsin, and died 05 July 2001 in Clearview Nursing Home, Juneau, Dodge County, Wisconsin.

See notes for Roberta Holland.

I was born prematurely at seven months; the certificate of birth signed by the midwife, Steller Butler records I was born at 10 p.m. and the one signed by Dr. W. H. Nelson records 10:45 p.m. for my birth. Dr. Nelson, who apparently arrived 45 minutes after I was born, told my parents that I probably would not live long, but advised them to keep a large steel hot water container on one side of me while I would have the heat from my mother's body on the other side. This was my incubator for a few weeks! Considering Dr. Nelson's prediction, I thank God for the 72+ years he has given me.

With the exception of a short time my family lived in the town of Fayetteville, North Carolina, I lived the first 12 years of my life on various tenant farms in Sampson County, North Carolina. In 1948, my paternal Grandfather, Haburn Rice Jackson, gave each of his three boys one third of his small farm. My parents grew tobacco, cotton and what was known at the time in Sampson County as truck crops, which for us included corn, tomatoes, cucumbers, peppers, summer squash, lima beans and field peas. At times my dad also worked off the farm in the cotton mills and at other odd jobs to supplement his income. For several weeks before the end of each school year, we started school earlier each day and classes were shortened to allow us to go home earlier to help during the planting season. For several weeks at the start of the school year we had the same short scheduled day to give us time to help with the harvest.

I never knew that the field pea is classified as forage. Therefore, I chuckled when I found it defined as a strain of the common pea (Pisum sativum var. arventse) with mottled leaves and purplish flowers, grown for forage for domestic animals. This definition prompted me to search the internet for "field pea" and there I found more evidence that many university web sites of the Northern States in America present information on how to grow several varieties of field peas for hogs. However, I also found limited interesting information about the field pea grown for humankind!

One web site states that the Field Pea (Pisum sativum L.) originated in India and was among the oldest of cultivated crops and in prehistoric times, seeds were carried to Europe and in the 1600s introduced to the New World.

On the web site of Clemson University Cooperative Extension Service, I found: **"Southern peas, black-eyed peas** and **field peas** are all names for the crop known worldwide as cowpeas (Vigna unguiculata ssp. unguiculata). Cowpeas probably originated in Africa and were introduced to the United States during early colonial times. They quickly became a staple crop in the Southeast ...

“There are four types of peas---Field pea: Robust, viny type usually with small seeds that produce a dark liquid when cooked. Crowder pea: Starchy seeded types “crowded” into the pods, normally cooking up dark. Cream pea: Smaller plant type with light colored seeds that cook up light. ‘Black-eyed’ pea: Intermediate in its plant type and seed cooking characteristics.

“Cultivars. Field-’Iron/Clay,’ various heirlooms. Crowder-’Carolina,’‘Colussus 80’. Cream-’Zipper Cream,’‘Carolina Cream.’ Black-eye type-’Pinkeye Purple Hull,’‘Dixielee,’‘Santee Early Pinkeye.’

Other web sites mention additional cultivars (varities) and note that the field peas became a staple food among poor people in the southern United States! Interesting! My family was poor and we enjoyed eating the peas in season; freezers made it possible to enjoy a “mess” of peas year round. I’d like to inform those of you who believe field peas to be the staple food among poor people, that the families of landlords and other well-to-do families also find that they like this staple food of the poor.

Today, my relatives in Sampson County, North Carolina, grow or buy the Dixielee (Dixie Lee) pea when possible. During my childhood, I looked forward to each summer and those servings of peas seasoned with salt pork, cured ham or bacon. The light sandy soil of eastern North Carolina is ideal for growing the field peas. During the 1970s, my dad shipped me a pint of the field pea seed and I attempted to grow it in the short growing season of northen Illinois; I had a beautiful row of tall pea bushes with few pea pods that reached maturity. The cows and hogs would probably have had a feast on the bushes!

Many years ago in a neighborhood grocery store in Chicago, Illinois, I found fresh field peas and couldn’t wait to shell and cook them. I was the only one in the family who ate them and since then I have never found either the fresh or frozen field peas in a grocery store in the northern states.

Most of my childhood was before mechanical cotton pickers were invented. I remember how my body ached after that first day of picking cotton each fall. I had difficulty walking upright for a few days and the sharp pointed burr tips of the cotton boll would prick and scratch my fingers, hands and arms and at least a few minutes during lunch time and in the evening of each day I had to spend time removing the burrs that were embedded in my fingers, hands and arms.

On page 553 in “The Heritage of Sampson County, North Carolina, 1784-1984,” edited by Oscar M. Bizzell, **Mary John Parker** gives a good description of how the cotton was weighed at the end of each day and she probably remembers more than I do:

“Somehow a cotton picker could always tell when weighing-up time came. The sun told them when to start picking in the morning and when to quit picking at night. And of course Daddy always showed up about weighing-up time...He would pull the weigh horse that stayed with us so long. Now the weigh horse was a homemade contraption made with a long pole tilted up at one end and fastened in the middle to two wooden legs which held one end up while the other rested on the ground until you were ready to weigh cotton. To do this you lifted up the end off the ground and the other end would go down and pick up a cotton sheet by the long slender iron scales that dangled with a hook used for catching the sheets. Then with a lift upward of the end that was down, the other end went down and the cotton sheet was hooked to the scales and then pulled back up again with the bursting open cotton sheet rising and swaying back and forth. Somehow I always liked to watch Daddy's eyes squint in the sunset and his hand run along those black scales -- tapping and pushing the weights (called "peas') along that told you how much cotton each picker had. Each one had an account page that was added at the end of each week when paying-up time came around. That was when the biggest and loudest part of the humming and singing came, a sign of real 'old-time satisfaction from a hard weeks' work. That was when it was time to stop and rest. it was a known fact that Daddy had about the best cotton pickers around. It was nothing for one to pick several hundred pounds in a single day. In fact, Daddy had such good cotton pickers that he was about the last one to convert over to the mechanical way of picking cotton."

Apparently, Mary John Parker's parents owned a large farm compared to the acreage owned by my parents. Only on rare occasions did my father, Oscar Jackson, hire cotton pickers. This was a time when we three children sometimes stayed home from school on nice days to pick cotton.

A "cotton sheet" most of the time was a sheet made from several large burlap bags sewed together. The pickers would empty their bags of cotton onto these sheets during the day. The corners of the sheets were tied together and the hooks on the scales with your help would slip under the knot at weighing-up time. The cotton pickers also used a large burlap bag to stuff the cotton into as they worked along the rows; the bag had a strap that you wore around your shoulder to enable you to pull it along as you picked cotton. Children generally had smaller bags.

Mary John Parker says this: "A cotton sheet had character. ... Not only did it hold the cotton -- it held the babies, too. It was hardly any job at all to convert a cotton sheet into a playpen. You had only to stretch it out between two rows of cotton, tie the corners to cotton stalks, empty a sack or two of cotton in it and there it was, a perfect playpen. Stretch another sheet high up over it and you have a sun-proof job."

The cotton stalks were a lot larger when I (Nancy Jackson Pleitt Fenner) was a child and probably even larger when Mary John Parker was a child. Today, It would be almost impossible to find cotton stalks large enough to serve as corners of a playpen.

My first husband, Richard Joseph Pleitt, at the age of nine, made his first Holy Communion on May 30, 1942 at St. Bonaventure Catholic Church, Diversey Parkway and North Marshfield Ave., Chicago, Illinois. The Priest was Rev O. (V.?) J. Moran.

At the age of 17, Richard had been told not to take the family car out while his parents worked. Hisfather drove semi-trucks for large Chicago companies and one day, while driving through the city, he was surprised to see Richard driving the family car with several friends for passengers. Later that day, after an argument with his father about the car, he left home, lied about his age and enlisted for three years in the United States Marine Corp. His friends promised to also enlist, but never did. Most of his service was in Korea and after he returned to the States, he was stationed in North Carolina.

Wanting to stir up some action with the servicemen from Fort Bragg, Richard and a couple of fellow Marines started to Fayetteville, North Carolina, one Saturday in August, 1953. They made a stop in Clinton, where they shopped for a few items in Rose's Dime Store where he met me (Nancy.) They never made it to Fayetteville and Richard and sometimes a friend, found their way to my childhood home almost every weekend until his discharge in May 1954.

Witnesses for our marriage in Chicago in September 1954 were a Pleitt family friend, Earl R. McClaughry and Richard's Aunt, Rose Seiler, his mother's sister. A reception was held in the evening at the home of Richard's parents, **Margaret Frances Waclawek** and **Joseph Edward Pleitt** in Chicago.

Richard attended college after we were married and he graduated in 1960 with a B. S. in Physics from Roosevelt University in Chicago and while working for A B Dick Company and Bruning Corporation, he continued his education at DePaul University in Chicago and Illinois Institute of Technology in Chicago for a Doctorate in the field of Physics. His education was interrupted when he accepted a position with another company in Lewistown, Pennsylvania, and we moved there from Rockford, Illinois. One year later, after the company announced it was moving to California, we moved to Orangeburg, South Carolina, where he had accepted a position with SCM Corporation. One year later, SCM closed the plant in Orangeburg and moved that operation to California. SCM transferred him to the Chicago area from South Carolina, and he decided not to resume his education. After several years, SCM decided to move the Chicago suburban operation to California! This was the third time Richard had been offered a transfer to California and for the third time he refused. SCM produced the Smith Corona Typewriter. We later heard of problems the company had in California and several managers who had moved there lost their positions a couple of years later.

After open heart surgery in late June 1981, Richard's heart would not resume beating on its own. He was buried on 03 July 1981, in Resurrection Cemetery, Justice, Illinois.

Edwin John Fenner, my second husband was buried near his first wife in Flora Cemetery, Flora, near Belvidere, Illinois.

Children of Nancy Jackson and Richard Pleitt are:

2355 i. **Margaret Roberta Pleitt**, born 21 April 1956 in Illinois Masonic Hospital, Cook County, Chicago, Illinois. She married **Keith Allen Clark** 18 August 1978 in Church of the Holy Apostles, Wauconda, Lake County, Illinois; born 28 August 1953 in Battle Creek, Michigan.

Both Margaret and Keith graduated from Indiana University, Bloomington, Indiana, and Keith has taught in the Monroe County Schools since he graduated. Margaret has a B. S. in Communication and works at Indiana University.

2356 ii. **Baby Girl Pleitt**, born 27 December 1959 in Chicago, Cook County, Illinois; died 27 December 1959. Burial: 28 December 1959, Resurrection Cemetery, Justice, Illinois.

+ 2357 iii. **Joseph Richard Pleitt**, born 05 December 1961 in Lutheran General Hospital, Park Ridge, Cook County, Illinois.

+ 2358 iv. **Anna Bernadette Pleitt**, born 13 January 1965 in Holy Family Hospital, Cook County, Illinois.

1484. Jackie Olene Jackson (Roberta[6] Holland, Alger Rose[5], Stephen Senter[4], Henry[3], Thomas William[2], Unknown[1]) was born 09 February 1943 in Honeycutts Township, Sampson County, North Carolina. She married **Charles Phillip Smith** 15 August 1959 in Dillon, South Carolina, son of Jacob Smith and Fannie Waters. He was born 23 August 1939 in Benton County, Tennessee.

One fall day while my mother and others were in the field picking cotton I was charged with watching Jackie, my sister, who was an infant. She was born in February 1943 and this day had to be later that fall. Cotton was packed pretty high on a sheet at the edge of the field and for some reason, I placed Jackie on top of the cotton. I can't remember all the playful details now, but she rolled down and hurt herself and I well remember the punishment from my mother when she quickly arrived after hearing the screams of Jackie.

When Charles Davis and Michael Edward, Jackie and Phillip's two older sons were young, they were playing in a mudhole during a storm when lightning struck nearby and they saw a hand and stars come down into the mudhole. The boys didn't understand what happened, but Jackie, Phillip and others understand the Lord kept those boys safe that day.

Children of Jackie Jackson and Charles Smith are:

+ 2359 i. **Charles Davis Smith**, born 03 April 1961 in Clinton, Sampson County, North Carolina.

+ 2360 ii. **Michael Edward Smith**, born 29 May 1962 in Bethel, Pitt County, North Carolina.

+ 2361 iii. **Jackie Gregory Smith**, born 22 April 1966 in Tarboro, North Carolina.

1485. Alger Leevon Hairr (Dellar Jane[6] Holland, Alger Rose[5], Stephen Senter[4], Henry[3], Thomas William[2], Unknown[1]) was born 29 May 1934 in Honeycutts Township, Sampson County, North Carolina. He married **Magdalene Taylor** 31 October 1954 in Clinton, Sampson County, North Carolina, daughter of Floyd Taylor and Atha Peacock. She was born 03 June 1936 in Mingo Township, Sampson County, North Carolina.

Leevon is a contractor. He has diverticulosis.

Children of Alger Leevon Hairr and Magdalene Taylor are:

+ 2362 i. **Kenneth Lee Hairr**, born 28 February 1958 in Clinton, Sampson County, North Carolina.

2363 ii. **Melissa Lea Hairr**, born 29 April 1963 in Clinton, Sampson County, North Carolina. She married (1) **Curtis Allen McLamb** 02 June 1984 in Salemburg, Sampson County, North Carolina; born 19 March 1961 in Clinton, Sampson County, North Carolina. She married (2) **Gregory Keith Baker** 04 April 1992 in Salemburg, Sampson County, North Carolina; born 21 April 1963 in Oklahoma County, Oklahoma.

Curtis Allen and Melissa Lea Hairr were divorced in March 1990. She and Gregory Keith Baker have children; names are unknown.

1486. William Earl Hairr (Dellar Jane[6] Holland, Alger Rose[5], Stephen Senter[4], Henry[3], Thomas William[2], Unknown[1]) was born 04 August 1935 in Honeycutts Township, Sampson County, North Carolina. He married **Sara Madalene McLamb**, daughter of Felton McLamb and Annie Honeycutt. She was born 13 December 1936 in Dismal Townsip, Sampson County, North Carolina.

William Earl was a carpenter and worked at Burlington Mill in Fayetteville for almost 10 years. "Earl," over the years, also has had problems that may be related to diverticulosis. One of his daughters and her son have similar problems. It appears that diverticulosis may be hereditary in the Alger Rose Holland family. I have had it for years and Aunt Freda also had it.

Children of William Hairr and Sara McLamb are:

+ 2364 i. **Thomas Earl Hairr**, born 10 September 1957 in Clinton, Sampson County, North Carolina.

+ 2365 ii. **Sarah Denise Hairr**, born 14 April 1962 in Clinton, Sampson County.

2366 iii. **Kathy Lynn Hairr,** born 02 September 1964 in Clinton, Sampson County, North Carolina. She married (1) **Lexie Edward Tyndall** 04 September 1983 in First Baptist Church, Clinton, Sampson County, North Carolina; born 09 November 1962 in Fayetteville, Cumberland County, North Carolina. She married (2) **Troy Faircloth** after 1984. She and Lexie Edward were divorced.

1487. Jean Elizabeth Hairr (Dellar Jane[6] Holland, Alger Rose[5], Stephen Senter[4], Henry[3], Thomas William[2], Unknown[1]) was born 19 October 1937 in Sampson County, North Carolina. She married **(1) Wiley Dixon Knowles**, son of Wiley C.Knowles and Chellie Holland. He was born 18 October 1928, and died 27 June 1984. She married **(2) E. T. Royal** About 2003, son of Harrison Hanstein Royal and Lela Holland. He was born 29 July 1925 in Dismal Township, Sampson County, North Carolina and E. T. first married Hazel Irene Johnson; he and Hazel and their children can be found elsewhere in this book.

Wiley Dixon was called "Doodle." He was buried in Sunrise Memorial Gardens Cemetery three miles north of Roseboro, North Carolina, on 242.

Children of Jean and Wiley Dixon are listed above under (1000) Wiley Dixon Knowles.

1488. Frankie Faye Strickland (Katie Dell[6] Holland, Alger Rose[5], Stephen Senter[4], Henry[3], Thomas William[2], Unknown[1]) was born 30 November 1940 in Honeycutts Township, Sampson County, north Carolina. She married **Max Brewer Tew**, son of Rassie Tew and Bertha Williams. He was born 23 January 1938.

Children of Frankie Strickland and Max Tew are:

2367 i. **John Daryl Tew**, born 07 June 1963.

2368 ii. **Robert Alan Tew**, born 06 December 1964 in Clinton, Sampson County, North Carolina. He married **Penny Madonna Williams** 24 August 1991 in Baptist Chapel Church near Autryville, Sampson County, North Carolina; born 07 November 1968 in Clinton, Sampson County, North Carolina.

1489. Margaret Elaine Strickland (Katie Dell[6] Holland, Alger Rose[5], Stephen Senter[4], Henry[3], Thomas William[2], Unknown[1]) was born 01 September 1942 in Honeycutts Township, Sampson County, North Carolina. She married **Harold Tex Butler,** son of Quinton Butler and Cleo Pearl Holland. He was born 17 October 1945 in Greensboro, North Carolina.

Children of Margaret Strickland and Harold Butler are:

2369 i. **Harold Lamar Butler**, born 20 October 1965 in Clinton, Sampson County, North Carolina.

2370 ii. **Jonathan Tex Butler**, born 20 March 1971 in Clinton, Sampson County.

1491. Gerald Rogers Holland (George Bizzell[6], Alger Rose[5], Stephen Senter[4], Henry[3], Thomas William[2], Unknown[1]) was born 17 June 1950 in Roseboro, Sampson County, North Carolina. He married **Carrie Ann Fann** 11 March 1973 in Salemburg, North Carolina, daughter of Henry Fann and Helen Howard. She was born 14 June 1951 in Roseboro, Sampson County, North Carolina.

Child of Gerald Holland and Carrie Fann is:

2371 i. **Brandon Holland**, born 14 March 1982.

1492. Evelyn Idell Holland (George Bizzell[6], Alger Rose[5], Stephen Senter[4], Henry[3], Thomas William[2], Unknown[1]) was born 07 December 1954 in Roseboro, Sampson County, North Carolina. She married **(1) Oscar Thomas Fann** 11 December 1971 in Honeycutts Township, Sampson County, North Carolina, son of Royce Fann and Anna Strickland. He was born 12 November 1953 in Clinton, Sampson County, North Carolina. She married **(2) Leon Michael Chesnutt** 18 August 1979 in Dillon, South Carolina. He was born 22 July 1951 in Fayetteville, Cumberland County, North Carolina.

Oscar Thomas and Evelyn Idell Holland divorced in June 1978 and she and Leon were divorced and she has remarried.

Children of Evelyn Holland and Oscar Fann are:

\+ 2372 i. **Lathan Thomas Fann**, born 19 June 1972 in Clinton, Sampson County, North Carolina.

2373 ii. **Justin Heath Fann**, born 29 November 1973 in Clinton, Sampson County, North Carolina.

Children of Evelyn Holland and Leon Chesnutt are:

2374 i. **Darby LeNae Chesnutt**, born 26 September 1981.

2375 ii. **Terran Michael Chesnutt**, born 11 August 1983.

1493. Karen Darlene Holland (George Bizzell[6], Alger Rose[5], Stephen Senter[4], Henry[3], Thomas William[2], Unknown[1]) was born 06 June 1962 in Sampson County, North Carolina. She married **Paul John Wolf** 28 August 1982 in Salemburg, North Carolina. He was born

08 September 1952 in Albemarle, Stanley County, North Carolina. Karen Darlene and Paul John Wolf are divorced.

Children of Karen Holland and Paul Wolf are:

2376 i. **Nathan Wayne Wolf**, born 17 October 1983.

2377 ii. **Jessica Rose Wolf**, born 03 January 1986.

2378 iii. **Hannah Evelyn Wolf**, born 11 February 1990.

1494. Jeanette Strickland (Freda Augustus[6] Holland, Alger Rose[5], Stephen Senter[4], Henry[3], Thomas William[2], Unknown[1]) was born 19 February 1940. She married **Preston Pedro Holland** 05 July 1959 in Dillon, South Carolina, son of Leslie B. Holland and Thelma Inez Taylor. He was born 20 December 1938.

Children of Jeanette Strickland and Preston Holland are:

\+ 2379 i. **Lynn Renae Holland**, born 07 March 1967.

2380 ii. **Jason Keith Holland**, born 31 January 1973. He married **Courtney Paige Franklin** 19 June 1999 in Wallace Chapel, Christ Church, Nashville, Tennessee.

1495. Barbara Strickland (Freda Augustus[6] Holland, Alger Rose[5], Stephen Senter[4], Henry[3], Thomas William[2], Unknown[1]) was born 18 December 1941. She married **(1) Hersey Carl Williams** Before 1962, son of William Wiliams and Lillie Williams. He was born 27 November 1939. She married **(2) Corrie Edward Waeldin** Before 1970. He was born 20 September 1941.

Child of Barbara Strickland and Hersey Williams is:

2381 i. **Tina Lori Williams**, born 06 October 1962.

Child of Barbara Strickland and Corrie Waeldin is:

2382 i. **Corrie Fredrika Waeldin**, born 20 June 1970.

1496. Anthony Strickland (Freda Augustus[6] Holland, Alger Rose[5], Stephen Senter[4], Henry[3], Thomas William[2], Unknown[1]) was born 27 November 1946. He married **Susan Diane Briley** before 1971. She was born 01 June 1950.

Children of Anthony Strickland and Susan Briley are:

2383 i. **Monique Tomsel Strickland**, born 21 February 1971.

2384 ii. **Daniel Alois Strickland**, born 01 February 1974.

1497. Rodney Holland Strickland (Freda Augustus[6] Holland, Alger Rose[5], Stephen Senter[4], Henry[3], Thomas William[2], Unknown[1]) was born 16 July 1949 in Salemburg,

Honeycutts Township, Sampson County, North Carolina. He married **Linda Gail Smith** Before 1967. She was born 13 September 1950 in Clinton, Sampson County, North Carolina.

Children of Rodney Strickland and Linda Smith are:

2385 i. **Sheila Faye Strickland**, born 25 October 1967.

2386 ii. **Michael Holland Strickland**, born 21 December 1969. He married Lisa Karen Norris.

2387 iii. **Jennifer Dolores Strickland**, born 21 November 1973.

\+ 2388 iv. **Kevin Wayne Strickland** I, born 31 October 1974 in Wake County, North Carolina; died 22 July 1995 in Orange County, North Carolina.

1498. Audrey Augusta Strickland (Freda Augustus[6] Holland, Alger Rose[5], Stephen Senter[4], Henry[3], Thomas William[2], Unknown[1]) was born 19 September 1952 in Sampson County, North Carolina. She married **Thomas Worth Tew**, son of Grover Tew and Kathleen Smith. He was born 19 March 1952.

After she and Thomas Worth divorced, she assumed her maiden name of Strickland.

Child of Audrey Strickland is:

2389 i. **Brian Strickland.**

1500. Clarise Fay Simmons (Clyda Louise[6] Holland, Henry[5], Stephen Senter[4], Henry[3], Thomas William[2], Unknown[1]) was born 30 April 1937 in McDaniels Township, Sampson County, North Carolina. She married **Owen Fed Matthews, Jr.** 28 October 1956 in Mintz Baptist Church, Sampson County, North Carolina, son of Owen Fed Matthews, Sr. and Addie Vann. He was born 04 March 1929 in Roseboro, North Carolina.

Her first name is also noted as "Clarke" which may be incorrect since it is stated as "Clarise" on her mother's delayed certificate of birth.

Children of Clarise Simmons and Owen Matthews are:

\+ 2390 i. **Jerry Craig Matthews**, born 18 December 1957 in Wayne County.

2391 ii. **Edward Dewitt Matthews**, born 16 November 1967 in Clinton, North Carolina.

1511. Sheilafaye Benson (Elizabeth Inez[6] Holland, Stephen Senter[5], Stephen Senter[4], Henry[3], Thomas William[2], Unknown[1]) was born 02 December 1952. She married **Baxter Smith.**

Child of Sheilafaye Benson and Baxter Smith is:

2392 i. **Bryan Smith**..

Generation Number 7

1519. Arthur Vance Autry (Crayon Dewitt[7] Holland, Calton Walker[6], William[5], James[4], Daniel[3], Thomas William[2], Unknown[1]) was born 23 April 1937. He married **Hilda Mae Autry**, daughter of Lester Autry and Lutie Tew. She was born 31 January 1941.

Children of Arthur Autry and Hilda Autry are:

+ 2393 i. **Dianne Autry**, born 08 August 1958.

2394 ii. **Donna Faye Autry,** born 13 November 1960. She married **Johnnie Carter** 20 January 1978.

1520. Lois Blanche Autry (Crayon Dewitt[7] Holland, Calton Walker[6], William[5], James[4], Daniel[3], Thomas William[2], Unknown[1]) was born 19 May 1939. She married **(1) Willie Gibson Lewis** before 1964, son of Evolyn Neal Lewis and Mary Louise Culbreth. He was born 23 April 1930, and died 27 June 1972. She married **(2) Billie Martin** after June 1972. He was born 15 November 1950, son of WILLIE JOSEPH MARTIN and JESSIE KING.. Lois and Billie had no children. Willie Gibson Lewis was buried in Salemburg Cemetery, Salemburg, North Carolina.

Child of Lois Autry and Willie Lewis is:

2395 i. **Robert Lance Lewis,** born 23 August 1964.

1522. Irland Lee Autry (Crayon Dewitt[7] Holland, Calton Walker[6], William[5], James[4], Daniel[3], Thomas William[2], Unknown[1]) was born 25 January 1944. He married **Becky Thorpe.**

Child of Irland Autry and Becky Thorpe is:

2396 i. **Natalie Autry,** born 14 August 1969.

1531. Michael Terrance Holland (Percy Benson[7], Lewis Benson[6], William[5], James[4], Daniel[3], Thomas William[2], Unknown[1]) was born 02 April 1942. He married **Nancy Ann Johnson.**

He was called "Terry." Apparently, he made quite a name for himself. He was a three-sport standout at Clinton, North Carolina, High School. He attended Davidson College, and under head coach Lefty Driesell, he helped the Widlcats build a worthy program that held national attention before his graduation. In 1974, he took over Virginia's basketball program and projected the Cavaliers into national championship contention.

Professor V. Mayo Bundy wrote the profile on Michael Terrance Holland on page 435 in *The Heritage of Sampson County, North Carolina, 1784-1984*, Oscar M. Bizzell, Editor. The profile provides the above information and more about Michael's career and states the following about him.

"Michael Terrance Holland, one of the four children of **Perry Holland** and **Alice Grey Daughtry,** is the grandson of **Lewis Benson Holland** and **Carlessie Fann**. He is the great-grandson of **William Holland** and **Laura E. Gautier**; and the great-great-grandson of **William Holland** who married **Ann Eliza Daniel**. William Holland was the son of **James Holland** and **Sabra Holland**. Ann Eliza Daniel was the daughter of Civil Hall and John Daniel, and Civil was the oldest child of Sabrina (Sabra" Culbreth and Allen Hall. Sabrina "Sabra" Culbreth was the daughter of Neil Culbreth and Martha Autry."

The certificate of death for William J. Holland names William Holland and "**Anna Elizabeth Daniel** for his parents. Prof. Bundy spells Civil as "Civel" and may have not been aware that James Holland married Sabra Culbreth.

My research revealed a different descendancy:

Perry was "**Percy Benson Holland**," son of Lewis Benson Holland and Carlessie E. Fann.

Ann Eliza Daniel, who Prof. Bundy mentioned as Michael's great-great-grandmother, was listed "Eliza Holland," and head of household in the 1880 Federal Census for Dismal Township, Sampson County, North Carolina. Listed with her were four sons, Calton, William, Dennis and Benson Holland. Various sources indicate that the full names of the sons were: Calton Walker, William James, Dennis P. and Lewis Benson Holland. This indicates that **Lewis Benson Holland was the brother of William James, not his son.** It appears to show that William James Holland and Laura Ellen Gautier were Michael's Great Uncle and Great Aunt, respectively, not his Great-Grandparents.

Lewis Benson was living in the household of his brother, James, and Laura, in 1900 and that is probably what leads some to believe that William was his father. William James was listed as "William B. Holland in transcribed 1900 census records. William James and Laura did name a son, Lewis Guilford.

However, the certificate of death for Lewis Benson Holland names Annie E. Daniel for his mother and "Unknown" for his father; Percy Holland, his son, was the informant. Ann or "Anna" is named Annie Eliza Holland on her own certificate of death. I have been unable to find William Holland or Ann Eliza in the 1870 census records and only she was listed with the four sons in 1880.

Children of Michael Holland and Nancy Johnson are:

2397 i. **Katie Gray Holland**, born 08 July 1973.

2398 ii. **Ann Michael Holland**, born 08 March 1976.

1535. Mary Gail Royal (Amos Harrison[7], Lela[6] Holland, Robert Mitchell[5], Matthew[4], Daniel[3], Thomas William[2], Unknown[1]) was born 17 July 1945 in Roseboro, Sampson County, North Carolina. She married **Joseph Franklin Parker, Sr.** 04 January 1970.

Children of Mary Royal and Joseph Parker are:

2399 i. **Joseph Franklin Parker, Jr.**, born 04 January 1971 in Clinton, Sampson County, North Carolina.

2400 ii. **Nelson Lee Parker**, born 09 April 1973 in Clinton, Sampson County, North Carolina.

1536. William Radford Holland (John William[7], Bryant B.[6], Thomas James[5], James[4], Daniel[3], Thomas William[2], Unknown[1]) was born 27 September 1923 in Smithfield, Johnston County, North Carolina. He married **Doris Wilson Adams** 23 June 1946 in Johnston County, North Carolina. She was born 21 April 1928 in Smithfield, Johnston County, North Carolina.

Children of William Holland and Doris Adams are:

2401 i. **Lorea Holland.**

2402 ii. **William Radford Holland, Jr..**

1537. Arthur Orell Holland (John William[7], Bryant B.[6], Thomas James[5], James[4], Daniel[3], Thomas William[2], Unknown[1]) was born in Johnston County, North Carolina. He married **Margaret (Maiden Name Unknown.)**

Children of Arthur Holland and Margaret Unknown are:

2403 i. **Bertha Sue Holland.**

2404 ii. **Ricky Holland.**

1538. Marion Grady Holland (John William[7], Bryant B.[6], Thomas James[5], James[4], Daniel[3], Thomas William[2], Unknown[1]) was born in Johnston County, North Carolina. He married **Allie.**

Children of Marion Holland and Allie are:

2405 i. **Johnnie Holland.**

2406 ii. **Bertha Sue Holland.**

2407 iii. **Joanne Holland.**

2408 iv. **David Holland.**

2409 v. **Linda Holland.**

1539. Thurman A. Holland (Lattie Rudesel[7], Bryant B.[6], Thomas James[5], James[4], Daniel[3], Thomas William[2], Unknown[1]) was born about 1926. He married **Jessie Bell Strickland.**

Child of Thurman Holland and Jessie Strickland is:

2410 i. **Dwight Holland.**

1540. Nelda Holland (Lattie Rudesel[7], Bryant B.[6], Thomas James[5], James[4], Daniel[3], Thomas William[2], Unknown[1]) was born about 1927. She married **Frank Hollingsworth.**

Children of Nelda Holland and Frank Hollingsworth are:

2411 i. **Steve Hollingsworth.**

2412 ii. **Stacie Hollingsworth.**

2413 iii. **Jimmie Hollingsworth.**

1541. Thelma Jane Holland (Lattie Rudesel[7], Bryant B.[6], Thomas James[5], James[4], Daniel[3], Thomas William[2], Unknown[1]) was born 21 September 1928 in Little Coharie Township, Sampson County, North Carolina. She married **(1) Lemuel Odell Autry,** son of Willie Autry and Maude Barefoot. He was born 12 January 1927 in Flea Hill Township, Cumberland County, North Carolina. She married **(2) Delane Autry.**

Three children with Lemuel; one unidentified. No children with second husband.

Children of Thelma Holland and Lemuel Autry are:

2414 i. **Beaver Autry.**

2415 ii. **Donna Autry.**

1542. Melba Eulane Holland (Lattie Rudesel[7], Bryant B.[6], Thomas James[5], James[4], Daniel[3], Thomas William[2], Unknown[1]) She married **Herschel Smith.**

Children of Melba Holland and Herschel Smith are:

2416 i. **Michael Smith.**

2417 ii. **Marlane Smith.**

2418 iii. **Linda Smith.**

1545. Margaret Holland (Robert Elliott[7], Bryant B.[6], Thomas James[5], James[4], Daniel[3], Thomas William[2], Unknown[1]) was born 11 September 1925. She married **George Vernon Strickland.** He was born 05 February 1922.

Child of Margaret Holland and George Strickland is:

\+ 2419 i. **John Wayne Strickland,** born 21 October 1949.

1546. Audry Iretice Holland (Robert Elliott[7], Bryant B.[6], Thomas James[5], James[4], Daniel[3], Thomas William[2], Unknown[1]) was born 03 July 1931 in Cedar Creek Township, Cumberland County, North Carolina. She married **Albert Joe Williford** 02 July 1950 in Eastover Township, Cumberland County, North Carolina. He was born 23 June 1930.

Children of Audry Holland and Albert Williford are:

2420 i. **Audrey Gail Williford**, born 24 June 1954.

2421 ii. **Tammy Jo Williford**, born 23 March 1960.

1547. Betty Lee Holland (Robert Elliott[7], Bryant B.[6], Thomas James[5], James[4], Daniel[3], Thomas William[2], Unknown[1]) was born 07 February 1935. She married **William Raeford Beard**.

Children of Betty Holland and William Beard are:

2422 i. **Robin Lynn Beard**, born 09 October 1955.

2423 ii. **Anna Rae Beard**, born 05 January 1963.

1551. Linda Hazel Autry (Tabitha Hazel[7] Holland, Bryant B.[6], Thomas James[5], James[4], Daniel[3], Thomas William[2], Unknown[1]) She married **John Atkins**.

Child of Linda Autry and John Atkins is:

2424 i. **Amanda Atkins**.

1553. David Carmen Barefoot (Mildred[7] Holland, Bryant B.[6], Thomas James[5], James[4], Daniel[3], Thomas William[2], Unknown[1]) was born 02 January 1942. He married **Carolyn Agee**.

Child of David Barefoot and Carolyn Agee is:

2425 i. **Timberly Barefoot**, born 06 May 1966.

1560. Arrel Gipson Holland, Sr. (Lottis Turner[7], William Thomas[6], Thomas James[5], James[4], Daniel[3], Thomas William[2], Unknown[1]) was born 25 April 1926 in Dismal Township, Sampson County, North Carolina. He married **Margaret Loriane Collier**. She was born 01 July 1927 in Flea Hill Township, Cumberland County, North Carolina.

He was also known as "Arval Gipson" Holland."

Children of Arrel Holland and Margaret Collier are:

\+ 2426 i. **Arval Gipson Holland, Jr.**, born 02 June 1951 in Fayetteville, Cumberland County, North Carolina.

\+ 2427 ii. **Robert Turner Holland**, born 25 June 1952 in Fayetteville, North Carolina.

2428 iii. **Shari Jan Holland**, born 05 September 1958 in Fayetteville, Cumberland County, North Carolina.

1561. Aaron Cannady (Arizona T.[7] Holland, William Thomas[6], Thomas James[5], James[4], Daniel[3], Thomas William[2], Unknown[1]) was born 04 December 1923 in Dismal Township, Sampson County, North Carolina, and died 26 November 1996 in Fayetteville, Cumberland County, North Carolina. He married **Letha Ethelyne Autry** 26 January 1952, daughter of McKinley Blackmon Autry and Hosie Myrtle Autry. She was born 21 November 1923, and died 22 September 1991 in Chapel Hill, Orange County, North Carolina.

Her certificate of death records 21 November 1924 for her birth and 29 September 1991 for her death. Aaron and Letha Ethelyne were buried in Union Grove Baptist Church Cemetery on SR 1438 one mile west of Rebel City, Sampson County, North Carolina.

Child of Aaron Cannady and Letha Autry is:

\+ 2429 i. **Sandra Dale Cannady**, born 19 October 1952 in Roseboro, Sampson County, North Carolina.

1563. Irene Holland (Ervin C.[7], William Thomas[6], Thomas James[5], James[4], Daniel[3], Thomas William[2], Unknown[1]) was born 02 September 1926 in Dismal Township, Sampson County, North Carolina, and died 15 October 1985. She married **Kermit Payton Sessoms,** son of William Sessoms and Ida Hall. He was born 03 November 1921 in Duke (now Erwin), Harnett County, North Carolina, and died 29 November 1982 in Erwin, Harnett County, North Carolina.

Kermit served as Staff Sergeant in the United States Air Force in World War II and served in Korea. Irene and Kermit Payton were buried in Erwin Memorial Park, Erwin, North Carolina.

Children of Irene Holland and Kermit Sessoms are:

2430 i. **Carol Lee Sessoms**, born 13 March 1946 in Erwin, Harnett County, North Carolina. She married Unknown Clearman.

2431 ii. **Kenneth Peyton Sessoms**, born 22 December 1949 in Erwin, Harnett County, North Carolina.

Kenneth lived in Georgia at one time.

1574. Alice Freeman Holland (Herman Crosby[7], William Thomas[6], Thomas James[5], James[4], Daniel[3], Thomas William[2], Unknown[1]) was born 10 July 1932 in Dismal Township, Sampson County, North Carolina. She married **Ray Randolph Naylor**, son of Tilghman Naylor and Gertrude Daughtry. He was born 22 March 1933 in Herrings Township, Sampson County, North Carolina.

Children of Alice Holland and Ray Naylor are:

2432 i. **Wanda Sue Naylor**, born 21 July 1960 in Clinton, Sampson County, North Carolina.

2433 ii. **Trilma Ann Naylor**, born 16 August 1965 in Clinton, Sampson County, North Carolina.

1578. Vernon Holland (Euland Randolph[7], William Thomas[6], Thomas James[5], James[4], Daniel[3], Thomas William[2], Unknown[1]) was born 14 April 1934 in Honeycutts Township, Sampson County, North Carolina. He married **Margaret Doris Spell** 17 November 1951 in Dillon, South Carolina, daughter of Braxton Spell and Lela Mae Royal. She was born 09 December 1935 in Dismal Township, Sampson County, North Carolina.

Children are listed above under (899) Margaret Doris Spell.

1579. Glenn Turner Holland (Euland Randolph[7], William Thomas[6], Thomas James[5], James[4], Daniel[3], Thomas William[2], Unknown[1]) was born 28 August 1944 in Honeycutts Township, Sampson County, North Carolina, and died 10 May 2007 in Sampson County, North Carolina. He married **Beatrice Faircloth** 17 June 1962 in Mt. Carmel Church of God, Autryville, Sampson County, North Carolina, daughter of Ralph Faircloth and Molly Autry. She was born 18 September 1942 in Little Coharie Township, Sampson County, North Carolina.

Children of Glenn Holland and Beatrice Faircloth are:

2434 i. **Douglas Glenn Holland**, born 26 May 1963 in Clinton, Sampson County, North Carolina; died 26 May 1963 in Clinton, Sampson County, North Carolina.

Burial: Mt. Carmel Church of God of Prophecy Cemetery

\+ 2435 ii. **Donna Marie Holland**, born 26 October 1965 in Clinton, Sampson County, North Carolina.

\+ 2436 iii. **Linda Jo Holland**, born 21 October 1967 in Clinton, Sampson County, North Carolina.

1580. Janice F. Butler (Cleo Pearl[7] Holland, William Thomas[6], Thomas James[5], James[4], Daniel[3], Thomas William[2], Unknown[1]) was born 25 June 1940 in Guilford County, North Carolina, and died 28 August 1984 in Wake County, North Carolina. She married **Miles Joel Parker** before 1960, son of Miles Simpson Parker and Mattie Ruth Jackson. He was born 30 July 1939 in Honeycutts Township, Sampson County, North Carolina.

Janice died in an automobile accident and was buried in Corinth Baptist Church Cemetery near Bearskin, Sampson County, North Carolina.

Children of Janice Butler and Miles Parker are:

\+ 2437 i. **Melanie Joy Parker**, born 10 September 1960 in Honeycutts Township, Sampson County, North Carolina.

\+ 2438 ii. **Melina Jill Parker**, born 26 December 1964 in Sampson County.

2439 iii. **Millette Jana Parker**, born 27 December 1967 in Sampson County, North Carolina. She married **Freddie West.**

1583. Harold Tex Butler (Cleo Pearl[7] Holland, William Thomas[6], Thomas James[5], James[4], Daniel[3], Thomas William[2], Unknown[1]) was born 17 October 1945 in Greensboro, North

Carolina. He married **Margaret Elaine Strickland**, daughter of John Davis Strickland and Katie Dell Holland. She was born 01 September 1942 in Honeycutts Township, Sampson County, North Carolina.

Children are listed above under (1489) Margaret Elaine Strickland.

1584. Brenda Marie Butler (Cleo Pearl[7] Holland, William Thomas[6], Thomas James[5], James[4], Daniel[3], Thomas William[2], Unknown[1]) was born 27 March 1948 in Roseboro, Sampson County, North Carolina. She married **Junie Mack Hairr** 18 June 1966 in Salemburg, Sampson County, North Carolina, son of Stephen Hairr and Edna Edwards. He was born 08 February 1947 in Roseboro, Sampson County, North Carolina.

Children of Brenda Butler and Junie Hairr are:

\+ 2440 i. **Steven Mack Hairr**, born 07 March 1968 in Clinton, Sampson County, North Carolina.

\+ 2441 ii. **Brent Allen Hairr**, born 01 February 1971 in Clinton, Sampson County, North Carolina.

1588. James Thomas Howard (Eloise[7] Holland, William Thomas[6], Thomas James[5], James[4], Daniel[3], Thomas William[2], Unknown[1]) was born 22 June 1942 in Roseboro, North Carolina. He married **Norma Page**, daughter of Preston Page and Elizabeth Faircloth. She was born 17 July 1946.

Children of James Howard and Norma Page are:

2442 i. **Darryll Thomas Howard**, born 16 March 1966.

2443 ii. **James Kevin Howard**, born 14 February 1969.

1597. Edith Lee Grantham (Ethel Elizabeth[7] Autry, Frances Elizabeth[6] Holland, Thomas James[5], James[4], Daniel[3], Thomas William[2], Unknown[1]) was born 29 November 1922. She married **(1) Rev. Johnny Charles Hoard, Sr.** Before 1943. He was born 31 March 1916, and died 31 December 1973. She married **(2) Jimmie Cartrette** after 1952. He was born 03 February 1936.

Children of Edith Grantham and Johnny Hoard are:

\+ 2444 i. **Johnny Charles Hoard, Jr.**, born 26 February 1943.

\+ 2445 ii. **Janice Lee Hoard**, born 15 November 1945.

\+ 2446 iii. **Larry Glenn Hoard**, born 04 November 1952.

1600. Lee Ronald Grantham (Ethel Elizabeth[7] Autry, Frances Elizabeth[6] Holland, Thomas James[5], James[4], Daniel[3], Thomas William[2], Unknown[1]) was born 07 August 1929. He married **Jewel Hudson**. She was born 06 November 1931.

Children of Lee Grantham and Jewel Hudson are:

\+ 2447 i. **Garry Lee Grantham**, born 20 December 1952.

2448 ii. **Mitchell Guyton Grantham**, born 17 September 1955. He married Betty Moore; born 23 May 1958.

2449 iii. **Mark Allen Grantham**, born 27 January 1962.

1601. Mac Donald Grantham (Ethel Elizabeth[7] Autry, Frances Elizabeth[6] Holland, Thomas James[5], James[4], Daniel[3], Thomas William[2], Unknown[1]) was born 07 August 1929. He married **(1) Brenda Faye Autry**. She was born 24 September 1943. He married **(2) Ida Mae Collier** 19 March 1951. She was born 26 October 1931, and died 13 October 1984.

Mr. Rosser, Jr., records that Brenda Fay(e) Autry married Eugene Roger Hall on 24 October 1967; he was born 04 June 1937 in Halifax County, North Carolina, and died 10 April 1980 in Fayetteville.

Ida Mae was buried in Minson M. Williams Family Cemetery at the northeast corner of Dunn Road (SR 1002 and SR 1441, Dismal Township, Sampson County, North Carolina.

Children of Mac Grantham and Ida Collier are:

2450 i. **Donald Keith Grantham**, born 07 October 1953. He married Cynthia Diane Godwin; born 05 February 1960.

2451 ii. **Douglas Marvin Grantham**, born 28 August 1955 in Fayetteville, Cumberland County, North Carolina; died 25 March 1975 in Route 1, Autryville, North Carolina. He married **Wanda Jane Honeycutt** 02 March 1974 in Wade, North Carolina; born 13 July 1956 in Clinton, Sampson County, North Carolina.

Douglas Marvin was buried in Baptist Chapel Cemetery near Autryville, North Carolina.

2452 iii. **Karen Elizabeth Grantham**, born 15 February 1958. She married **Frederick Paul Schubert III**; born 14 April 1953.

2453 iv. **Martha Lou Grantham**, born 23 September 1961.

1602. Eulas Gilbert Grantham (Ethel Elizabeth[7] Autry, Frances Elizabeth[6] Holland, Thomas James[5], James[4], Daniel[3], Thomas William[2], Unknown[1]) was born 04 August 1934. He married **(1) Shirley Barbour**. She was born 15 November 1934. He married **(2) Joyce Maurice Klein**. She was born 10 May 1945.

Children of Eulas Grantham and Shirley Barbour are:

2454 i. **Johnny Ray Grantham**, born 08 December 1952. He married **Nancy Louise Drerig**; born 02 February 1948.

2455 ii. **Jolyn Grantham**, born 17 March 1959. She married **Phillip Alan Reinbolt**; born 03 October 1949.

2456 iii. **Michael Dean Grantham**, born 17 December 1960.

2457 iv. **Michelle Grantham**, born 18 January 1963.

1604. Brenda Frances Holland (Millard Filmore[7], Bernice Culbreth[6], Thomas James[5], James[4], Daniel[3], Thomas William[2], Unknown[1]) was born 02 March 1942 in Mingo Township, Sampson County, North Carolina. She married **Aaron Thomas Tyndall** 03 July 1960 in Robert's Grove Baptist Church, Spivey's Corner, Sampson County, North Carolina, son of Aaron Tyndall and Suzanna Wrench. He was born 08 September 1939 in Dismal Township, Sampson County, North Carolina.

Mr. Rosser's book spells her name "Brinda Fay Holland."

Children of Brenda Holland and Aaron Tyndall are:

2458 i. **Anthony Thomas Tyndall**, born 06 October 1961 in Clinton, Sampson County, North Carolina.

2459 ii. **Gregory Scott Tyndall**, born 10 June 1981.

1605. Judith Elaine Holland (Millard Filmore[7], Bernice Culbreth[6], Thomas James[5], James[4], Daniel[3], Thomas William[2], Unknown[1]) was born 17 February 1945 in Mingo Township, Sampson County, North Carolina. She married **Donald Sherill Register** 27 October 1963 in Roberts Grove Parsonage near Spivey's Corner, Sampson County, North Carolina, son of William Register and Mary Naylor. He was born 26 December 1941 in Mingo Township, Sampson County, North Carolina.

February 02, 1945 is also found for her birth.

Children of Judith Holland and Donald Register are:

2460 i. **Kimberly Sue Register**, born 23 April 1965.

2461 ii. **Donald Kevin Register**, born 05 November 1966; died 05 November 1966.

Donald Kevin was buried in Robert's Grove Baptist Church Cemetery near Spivey's Corner, Sampson County, North Carolina.

2462 iii. **Infant Son Register**, born 29 February 1968; died 29 February 1968.

Infant Son is buried in Robert's Grove Baptist Church Cemetery near Spivey's Corner, Sampson County, North Carolina.

2463 iv. **Donald Lynn Register**, born 01 February 1971.

1621. Preston Pedro Holland (Leslie B.[7], Lalister R.[6], Bluman[5], Harfrey[4], Daniel[3], Thomas William[2], Unknown[1]) was born 20 December 1938. He married **Jeanette Strickland** 05 July 1959 in Dillon, South Carolina, daughter of John Thomas Strickland and Freda Augustus Holland. She was born 19 February 1940.

Children are listed above under (1494) Jeanette Strickland.

1625. Brownie Catherine Spell (Lester Frank[7], Janie Isabell[6] Hairr, Franklin[5] Holland, Harfrey[4], Daniel[3], Thomas William[2], Unknown[1]) was born 12 January 1948 in Roseboro, North Carolina. She married **Durwood Kenneth Spell**, son of Durwood Spell and Elzora Jackson. He was born 22 July 1941 in Honeycutts Township, Sampson County, North Carolina.

Children of Brownie Spell and Durwood Spell are:

\+ 2464 i. **Durwood Kenneth Spell, Jr.**, born 08 August 1970.

\+ 2465 ii. Bryan Christopher Spell, born 21 March 1973.

1626. Susan Annette Spell (David Peyton[7], Janie Isabell[6] Hairr, Franklin[5] Holland, Harfrey[4], Daniel[3], Thomas William[2], Unknown[1]) was born 07 September 1947. She married **Richard Patrick Glancy, Jr.**. He was born 14 October 1941.

Child of Susan Spell and Richard Glancy is:

2466 i. **Richard Patrick Glancy III**, born 25 January 1969.

1631. William Lloyd Holland II (William Lloyd[7], Challie Cleveland[6], Jordan[5], Harfrey[4], Daniel[3], Thomas William[2], Unknown[1]) was born 22 May 1950. He married **Debbie Jane Armstrong.**

Child of William Holland and Debbie Armstrong is:

2467 i. **Rebecca Jane Holland**, born 04 August 1977.

1632. Sarah Frances Raynor (Mary Frances[7] Holland, Challie Cleveland[6], Jordan[5], Harfrey[4], Daniel[3], Thomas William[2], Unknown[1]) was born 16 September 1949. She married **Roger Lee Blue**. He was born 11 April 1946.

Children of Sarah Raynor and Roger Blue are:

2468 i. **Anthony Dwayne Blue**, born 07 April 1971.

2469 ii. **Craig Lee Blue**, born 11 April 1973.

2470 iii. **Kenneth Duncan Blue**, born 28 April 1977.

1639. Leonard Paul King (Jessie Mildridge[7] Holland, Challie Cleveland[6], Jordan[5], Harfrey[4], Daniel[3], Thomas William[2], Unknown[1]) was born 21 April 1939. He married **(1) Rena Florence Parker** about 1964, daughter of Miles Simpson Parker and Mattie Ruth Jackson. She was born 09 January 1941. He married **(2) Paulette Welch** Before 1978. She was born 02 November 1946.

Rena Florence's first husband is deceased. Rena and Ronnie Bradshaw either separated or divorced. See Rena elsewhere in this book.

Children of Leonard King and Rena Parker are:

+ 2471 i. **Leonard Scott King,** born 06 March 1965.

+ 2472 ii. **Timmy Maxwell King,** born 26 January 1968.

Child of Leonard King and Paulette Welch is:

2473 i. **Michael Paul King,** born 05 February 1978.

1640. Maurice Maxwell King (Jessie Mildridge[7] Holland, Challie Cleveland[6], Jordan[5], Harfrey[4], Daniel[3], Thomas William[2], Unknown[1]) was born 19 July 1940, and died 30 September 1965. He married **Janet Honeycutt**. She was born 12 January 1940.

Maurice Maxwell was buried in The Clinton Cemetery, Clinton, Sampson County, North Carolina.

Children of Maurice King and Janet Honeycutt are:

2474 i. **Jeffrey Wilson King,** born 27 March 1960.

2475 ii. **Kara Lynn King,** born 30 July 1961.

1641. Mary Jane King (Jessie Mildridge[7] Holland, Challie Cleveland[6], Jordan[5], Harfrey[4], Daniel[3], Thomas William[2], Unknown[1]) was born 22 August 1944. She married **David Edward Carter I**. He was born 08 November 1940.

Children of Mary King and David Carter are:

2476 i. **Kimberly Ann Carter,** born 23 March 1969.

2477 ii. **David Edward Carter II,** born 01 June 1971.

1642. Betty Susan King (Jessie Mildridge[7] Holland, Challie Cleveland[6], Jordan[5], Harfrey[4], Daniel[3], Thomas William[2], Unknown[1]) was born 19 March 1952. She married **(1) Kenneth Anders** Before 1972. He was born 27 August 1952, and died 18 October 1975. She married **(2) Frank Oliver Puryear** After 1972. He was born 04 April 1953.

Child of Betty King and Kenneth Anders is:

2478 i. **Jessica Leigh Anders,** born 12 March 1972.

1644. Bobby Franklin Carter (Jerutha Veve[7] Holland, Challie Cleveland[6], Jordan[5], Harfrey[4], Daniel[3], Thomas William[2], Unknown[1]) was born 12 September 1943. He married **Ester Louise Ezzell**. She was born 10 April 1949.

Child of Bobby Carter and Ester Ezzell is:

2479 i. **Richard Wayne Carter**, born 29 July 1969.

1645. Peggy Joyce Hudson (Margaret Peace[7] Holland, Challie Cleveland[6], Jordan[5], Harfrey[4], Daniel[3], Thomas William[2], Unknown[1]) was born 14 December 1951. She married **Leslie Everett Spell, Sr.**. He was born 08 October 1956.

Child of Peggy Hudson and Leslie Spell is:

2480 i. **Leslie Everett Spell, Jr.**, born 18 October 1976.

1647. Jewel Margaret Hudson (Margaret Peace[7] Holland, Challie Cleveland[6], Jordan[5], Harfrey[4], Daniel[3], Thomas William[2], Unknown[1]) was born 30 October 1950. She married **Roy Glenn Cannady** Before 1972, son of Franklin Cannady and Ozelle Porter. He was born 01 March 1949.

Her name has also been listed as "Margaret Jewel Hudson."

Children of Jewel Hudson and Roy Cannady are:

2481 i. **Nathan Scott Cannady**, born 30 April 1972.

2482 ii. **Kelly Jewel Cannady**, born 14 April 1977 in Sampson County, North Carolina.

1649. Edwin Lowe Griffin, Jr. (Lanty Pearl[7] Cannady, Annie Jane[6] Holland, Jordan[5], Harfrey[4], Daniel[3], Thomas William[2], Unknown[1]) was born 17 April 1948. He married **(1) Terry Suzanne Beam** About 1973. She was born 08 February 1949, and died 31 December 1978. He married **(2) Cynthia Louise Brown** Before 1981. She was born 26 April 1956.

Edwin Lowe, Jr., was buried in Montlawn Memorial Park Cemetery near Raleigh, North Carolina.

Children of Edwin Griffin and Terry Beam are:

2483 i. **Edwin Lowe Griffin III**, born 01 December 1974.

2484 ii. **Ashley Michelle Griffin**, born 18 January 1977.

Child of Edwin Griffin and Cynthia Brown is:

2485 i. **Caroline Allyson Griffin**, born 01 July 1981.

1650. Richard Harold Cannady (Wilbert Cleveland[7], Annie Jane[6] Holland, Jordan[5], Harfrey[4], Daniel[3], Thomas William[2], Unknown[1]) was born 05 June 1937. He married **Sandy Lee** Before 1965. She was born 01 July 1940.

Child of Richard Cannady and Sandy Lee is:

\+ 2486 i. **Paula Kay Cannady**, born 31 March 1965.

1652. Ann Cannady (Wilbert Cleveland[7], Annie Jane[6] Holland, Jordan[5], Harfrey[4], Daniel[3], Thomas William[2], Unknown[1]) was born 25 August 1944. She married **Phil Taylor**. He was born 26 May 1944.

Children of Ann Cannady and Phil Taylor are:

2487 i. **Michael Taylor**, born 02 January 1971.

2488 ii. **Michelle Taylor**, born 26 December 1974.

1653. Ceanna Day (Mable[7] Cannady, Annie Jane[6] Holland, Jordan[5], Harfrey[4], Daniel[3], Thomas William[2], Unknown[1]) was born 10 March 1953, and died 07 May 1979. She married **Paul Hilton Davis, Sr.**. He was born about 1950.

Ceanna Day was buried in Harrells Cemetery, Harrells, Sampson County, North Carolina

Child of Ceanna Day and Paul Davis is:

2489 i. **Paul Hilton Davis, Jr.**, born October 1973.

1655. Thomas E. Grubbs I (Julia Ann[7] Cannady, Annie Jane[6] Holland, Jordan[5], Harfrey[4], Daniel[3], Thomas William[2], Unknown[1]) was born 11 May 1948. He married **Sally Unknown**. She was born 31 May 1954.

Children of Thomas Grubbs and Sally Unknown are:

2490 i. **Thomas E. Grubbs II**, born 12 October 1983.

2491 ii. **Wade Cannady Grubbs**, born 26 January 1989.

1658. Linda Arlene Cannady (James Manly[7], Annie Jane[6] Holland, Jordan[5], Harfrey[4], Daniel[3], Thomas William[2], Unknown[1]) was born 27 December 1947. She married **Roger Winford Robinson**. He was born between 13 September 1947 - 1949, and died 06 December 1983.

Children of Linda Cannady and Roger Robinson are:

2492 i. **Zachariah Winford Robinson**, born 19 August 1976.

2493 ii. **Cassia Carrie Robinson**, born 04 September 1979.

2494 iii. **Andrea Lynn Robinson**, born 04 September 1979.

2495 iv. **Rodger Jeremiah Frederich Robinson**, born 13 May 1983.

1659. Shirley Lynette Cannady (James Manly[7], Annie Jane[6] Holland, Jordan[5], Harfrey[4], Daniel[3], Thomas William[2], Unknown[1]) was born 13 October 1949. She married **Ronald Pate** who was born 15 October 1942.

Children of Shirley Cannady and Ronald Pate are:

2496 i. **Shawn Ronald Pate**, born 28 June 1971.

2497 ii. **Heather Lynette Pate**, born 27 March 1973.

1661. Robin Anne Cannady (Herbert Wayne[7], Annie Jane[6] Holland, Jordan[5], Harfrey[4], Daniel[3], Thomas William[2], Unknown[1]) was born 09 October 1959. She married **Robert Vann Little** who was born 12 January 1957.

Children of Robin Cannady and Robert Little are:

2498 i. **Michael Vann Little**, born 12 December 1984.

2499 ii. **David Alan Little**, born 17 July 1987.

1662. Herbert Wayne Cannady II (Herbert Wayne[7], Annie Jane[6] Holland, Jordan[5], Harfrey[4], Daniel[3], Thomas William[2], Unknown[1]) was born 27 August 1960. He married **Angela Dee Edge** who was born 20 February 1960.

Child of Herbert Cannady and Angela Edge is:

2500 i. **Anna Caitlin Cannady**, born 12 July 1991.

1665. Lily Ann Canady (Kenneth Neil[7], Annie Jane[6] Holland, Jordan[5], Harfrey[4], Daniel[3], Thomas William[2], Unknown[1]) was born 26 November 1961. She married **Stewart Roe Crowell**. He was born 13 February 1957.

Children of Lily Canady and Stewart Crowell are:

2501 i. **Braden Roe Crowell**, born 05 January 1989.

2502 ii. **Colbey Whitney Crowell**, born 08 March 1991.

1671. W. C. Rich (Lottie Mae[7] Barker, Drucilla[6] Holland, Jordan[5], Harfrey[4], Daniel[3], Thomas William[2], Unknown[1]) was born 01 January 1942. He married **Judy Bass** 20 March 1963.

Children of W. Rich and Judy Bass are:

2503 i. **Leisa Rich.**

2504 ii. **Teresa Rich.**

2505 iii. **Steve Rich.**

1672. Alice Rich (Lottie Mae[7] Barker, Drucilla[6] Holland, Jordan[5], Harfrey[4], Daniel[3], Thomas William[2], Unknown[1]) was born 15 March 1945. She married **Clayton Straughn** 20 March 1963.

Children of Alice Rich and Clayton Straughn are:

2506 i. **Katrinia Straughn.**

2507 ii. **Carolyn Straughn.**

2508 iii. **Gary Straughn.**

1673. Billy Self (Janie Frances[7] Barker, Drucilla[6] Holland, Jordan[5], Harfrey[4], Daniel[3], Thomas William[2], Unknown[1]) was born 1947. He married **Ann McLeary.**

Child of Billy Self and Ann McLeary is:

2509 i. **Gleen McLeary Self.**

1674. Linda Self (Janie Frances[7] Barker, Drucilla[6] Holland, Jordan[5], Harfrey[4], Daniel[3], Thomas William[2], Unknown[1]) was born 1949. She married **Dennis Mann.**

Child of Linda Self and Dennis Mann is:

2510 i. **Robert Mann.**

1675. Barbara Self (Janie Frances[7] Barker, Drucilla[6] Holland, Jordan[5], Harfrey[4], Daniel[3], Thomas William[2], Unknown[1]) was born 1951. She married **Gary Freeman.**

Child of Barbara Self and Gary Freeman is:

2511 i. **Kimberly Freeman.**

1676. Connie Self (Janie Frances[7] Barker, Drucilla[6] Holland, Jordan[5], Harfrey[4], Daniel[3], Thomas William[2], Unknown[1]) was born 1952. She married **Leland Bailey.**

Child of Connie Self and Leland Bailey is:

2512 i. **Clifton Bailey.**

1681. Patricia Shull (Thelma[7] Barker, Drucilla[6] Holland, Jordan[5], Harfrey[4], Daniel[3], Thomas William[2], Unknown[1]) was born 1953. She married **Steven Jenkins** 1972.

Child of Patricia Shull and Steven Jenkins is:

2513 i. **Steve Jenkins.**

1682. Elizabeth Ann Brock (Elizabeth Grace[7] Williams, Charlotte Elizabeth[6] Holland, Jordan[5], Harfrey[4], Daniel[3], Thomas William[2], Unknown[1]) was born 14 October 1951. She married **James David Stocks.**

Child of Elizabeth Brock and James Stocks is:

2514 i. **James David Stocks, Jr.**, born 23 August 1971.

1683. Elwood Glenn Brock (Elizabeth Grace[7] Williams, Charlotte Elizabeth[6] Holland, Jordan[5], Harfrey[4], Daniel[3], Thomas William[2], Unknown[1]) was born 19 January 1954. He married **Mollie Fisher.**

Child of Elwood Brock and Mollie Fisher is:

2515 i. **Olivia Ann Brock**, born 27 December 1977.

1684. Deborah Elaine Brock (Elizabeth Grace[7] Williams, Charlotte Elizabeth[6] Holland, Jordan[5], Harfrey[4], Daniel[3], Thomas William[2], Unknown[1]) was born 13 December 1957. She married **Randall Marvin Hyde.** He was born 25 August 1948.

Child of Deborah Brock and Randall Hyde is:

2516 i. **Timothy Dan Hyde**, born 02 April 1974.

1686. Brenda Ann Lee (Olivia Ruth[7] Williams, Charlotte Elizabeth[6] Holland, Jordan[5], Harfrey[4], Daniel[3], Thomas William[2], Unknown[1]) was born 28 December 1951. She married **Daniel Murphy McLoud.** He was born 14 March 1947, and died 03 November 1976.

Children of Brenda Lee and Daniel McLoud are:

2517 i. **Sheila McLoud**, born 04 February 1970.

2518 ii. **Daniel Murphy McLoud**, born 27 July 1972; died 27 July 1972.

2519 iii. **Kelly Mendall McLoud**, born 08 April 1973.

1688. Carolyn Sue Lee (Olivia Ruth[7] Williams, Charlotte Elizabeth[6] Holland, Jordan[5], Harfrey[4], Daniel[3], Thomas William[2], Unknown[1]) was born 23 April 1955. She married **Thomas Franklyn Pope.** He was born 05 February 1953.

Child of Carolyn Lee and Thomas Pope is:

2520 i. **Victor Glenn Pope**, born 26 September 1972.

1689. Luby Mack Lee (Olivia Ruth[7] Williams, Charlotte Elizabeth[6] Holland, Jordan[5], Harfrey[4], Daniel[3], Thomas William[2], Unknown[1]) was born 11 May 1956. He married **Kilema Jean West**. She was born 04 November 1958.

Child of Luby Lee and Kilema West is:

2521 i. **Shyannen Louise Lee,** born 09 May 1975.

1730. Margaret Louvenia Giles (Lessie Jane Holland[7] Williams, Repsie[6] Holland, Chester[5], Harfrey[4], Daniel[3], Thomas William[2], Unknown[1]) was born 29 January 1924 in Dismal Township, Sampson County, North Carolina. She married **Eddie Rose Aman** before 1944, son of Eddie Aman and Vida Naylor. He was born 03 December 1920 in Mingo Township, Sampson County, North Carolina.

The date of birth for Eddie is also found as December 31, 1920.

Children of Margaret Giles and Eddie Aman are:

+ 2522 i. **Margarette Rose Aman,** born 06 October 1944 in Roseboro, Sampson County, North Carolina.

+ 2523 ii. **Anna Jeanette Aman, born** 28 November 1947.

+ 2524 iii. **Iris Marlene Aman,** born 09 April 1952 in Dunn, Harrnett County, North Carolina.

+ 2525 iv. **Donna Sue Aman,** born 07 October 1953 in Dunn, Harrnett County, North Carolina.

2526 v. **Terry Eddie Aman,** born 05 June 1959 in Dunn, Harrnett County, North Carolina.

1732. Attie Edmon Giles (Lessie Jane Holland[7] Williams, Repsie[6] Holland, Chester[5], Harfrey[4], Daniel[3], Thomas William[2], Unknown[1]) was born 01 September 1931. He married **Sue Hughes**.

Children of Attie Giles and Sue Hughes are:

2527 i. **Michael Edmon Giles,** born 10 February 1964.

2528 ii. **Mark Dwayne Giles,** born 30 March 1965.

2529 iii. **John Matthew Giles,** born 26 June 1971.

1733. James Elton Giles (Lessie Jane Holland[7] Williams, Repsie[6] Holland, Chester[5], Harfrey[4], Daniel[3], Thomas William[2], Unknown[1]) was born 13 November 1941. He married **Rose Cox**. She was born 06 November 1941.

Children of James Giles and Rose Cox are:

2530 i. **Richard Elton Giles,** born 18 June 1968.

2531 ii. **Rondal Scott Giles,** born 28 October 1969.

1734. Agnes Jane Hairr (Agnes Ruth[7] Williams, Repsie[6] Holland, Chester[5], Harfrey[4], Daniel[3], Thomas William[2], Unknown[1]) was born 26 December 1939. She married **Billie Ray Tart**. He was born 19 August 1938.

Children of Agnes Hairr and Billie Tart are:

2532 i. **Deborah Ann Tart**, born 15 November 1959.

2533 ii. **Lisa Dianne Tart**, born 15 January 1962.

2534 iii. **Johnnie R. Tart**, born 21 September 1963.

1735. William Cleveland Hairr, Jr. (Agnes Ruth[7] Williams, Repsie[6] Holland, Chester[5], Harfrey[4], Daniel[3], Thomas William[2], Unknown[1]) was born 07 April 1943. He married **Carolyn Lois Free**. She was born 09 November 1946.

Children of William Hairr and Carolyn Free are:

2535 i. **William Cleveland Hairr III**, born 09 August 1966.

2536 ii. **Robert Allen Hairr**, born 22 November 1968.

2537 iii. **Meddin Monroe Hairr,** born 18 July 1970.

1736. Mary Ann Hairr (Agnes Ruth[7] Williams, Repsie[6] Holland, Chester[5], Harfrey[4], Daniel[3], Thomas William[2], Unknown[1]) was born 14 December 1945. She married **David Earl Weeks** who was born 20 April 1941.

Children of Mary Hairr and David Weeks are:

2538 i. **David Wayne Weeks**, born 20 August 1966.

2539 ii. **Paula Annette Weeks**, born 01 April 1972.

1737. Edna Ruth Pope (Agnes Ruth[7] Williams, Repsie[6] Holland, Chester[5], Harfrey[4], Daniel[3], Thomas William[2], Unknown[1]) was born 29 October 1953. She married **Charles Kennedy**.

Child of Edna Pope and Charles Kennedy is:

2540 i. **Karol Elizabeth Kennedy**, born 07 October 1972.

1740. Emily Diann Williams (Robert Chester[7], Repsie[6] Holland, Chester[5], Harfrey[4], Daniel[3], Thomas William[2], Unknown[1]) was born 16 July 1949. She married **Malcom Currie Williams, Jr.**, son of Malcom Currie Williams, Sr. and Gertrude Cannady. He was born 23 December 1947.

Child of Emily Williams and Malcom Williams is:

2541 i. **Jamie Denise Williams,** born 30 September 1976.

1741. Eugene Dekker McDonald (Mattie Iona[7] Holland, Columbus[6], Chester[5], Harfrey[4], Daniel[3], Thomas William[2], Unknown[1]) was born 04 December 1926. He married **Frances Elizabeth Black.**

Children of Eugene McDonald and Frances Black are:

2542 i. Clayton Bryon McDonald, born 29 March 1960.

2543 ii. **Wade Hampton McDonald,** born 28 April 1962.

1742. Hubert Ellis McDonald (Mattie Iona[7] Holland, Columbus[6], Chester[5], Harfrey[4], Daniel[3], Thomas William[2], Unknown[1]) was born 24 December 1927. He married **Ruth Olive.**

Child of Hubert McDonald and Ruth Olive is:

2544 i. **Debra Demond McDonald,** born 16 July 1953. She married Marvin Eugene Waters III.

1743. Peggy Florence Holland (James Albert[7], Columbus[6], Chester[5], Harfrey[4], Daniel[3], Thomas William[2], Unknown[1]) was born 28 May 1932. She married **Norwood Gene Lee** 25 June 1948. He was born 24 January 1929.

May 23, 1932 is also listed for her date of birth.

Children of Peggy Holland and Norwood Lee are:

\+ 2545 i. **Norwood Brent Lee,** born 27 August 1954.

\+ 2546 ii. **Peggy Joy Lee,** born 31 August 1956.

\+ 2547 iii. **Charlotte Ginny Lee,** born 07 April 1961.

\+ 2548 iv. **Nancy Catherine Lee,** born 25 February 1967.

1744. Stella Royal Holland (James Albert[7], Columbus[6], Chester[5], Harfrey[4], Daniel[3], Thomas William[2], Unknown[1]) was born 01 November 1934. She married **Ralph McDonald** 16 August 1951. He was born 11 December 1929.

On page 424 in "Royal Family Legacy" by Wanda Royal, Stella Royal's date of birth is stated as November 01, 1933.

Children of Stella Holland and Ralph McDonald are:

2549 i. **Yvonne McDonald,** born 18 November 1955. She married Eric Anderson 04 August 1995; born 07 October 1968.

\+ 2550 ii. **Jeanne McDonald,** born 01 October 1963.

1745. Ann Holland (James Albert[7], Columbus[6], Chester[5], Harfrey[4], Daniel[3], Thomas William[2], Unknown[1]) was born 25 February 1938. She married **(1) Alvin J. Jones** 01 June 1952. He was born 08 May 1932. She married **(2) Bennie Bacret** 11 September 1971. He was born 12 November 1931.

Bacret is correct spelling of name. Corrected on page 44 in "Royal Family Legacy Addendum."

Children of Ann Holland and Alvin Jones are:

+ 2551 i. **Brenda Ann Jones**, born 19 August 1956.

+ 2552 ii. **Alvin Keith Jones**, born 21 February 1959.

Children of Ann Holland and Bennie Bacret are:

2553 i. **Terry Dwayne Bacret**, born 11 May 1972.

Bacret is correct spelling of name.

2554 ii. **Larry Wayne Bacret**, born 11 May 1972.

1746. Alice Faye Holland (James Albert[7], Columbus[6], Chester[5], Harfrey[4], Daniel[3], Thomas William[2], Unknown[1]) was born 17 June 1940. She married **Ellis Ray Howell** 19 July 1959. He was born 05 March 1936.

Children of Alice Holland and Ellis Howell are:

+ 2555 i. **Gloria Faye Howell**, born 12 December 1962.

+ 2556 ii. **Selina Raye Howell**, born 26 October 1965.

1747. Cathleen Holland (James Albert[7], Columbus[6], Chester[5], Harfrey[4], Daniel[3], Thomas William[2], Unknown[1]) was born 20 June 1944. She married **(1) Jerry Lee Parker** 02 June 1962. He was born 24 June 1941, and died 26 September 1976. She married **(2) Nelson West** after 1967. She married **(3) James Buchanan** after September 1976. He was born 31 March 1941.

"Cathleen" is correct, but "Kathleen" is also found.

Children of Cathleen Holland and Jerry Parker are:

2557 i. **Jeffrey Lee Parker**, born 24 September 1963; died 17 July 1981.

+ 2558 ii. **Deborah Ann Parker**, born 19 October 1965.

+ 2559 iii. **George Michael Parker**, born 20 March 1967.

1748. James Leon Holland (James Albert[7], Columbus[6], Chester[5], Harfrey[4], Daniel[3], Thomas William[2], Unknown[1]) was born 25 January 1946. He married **(1) Deborah Koonce**

Before 1980. He married **(2) Diane Jackson** 09 October 1982. She was born 10 May 1956.

Pages 424, 448 in "Royal Family Legacy" by Wanda Royal state that James Leon was born January 27, 1946.

Child of James Holland and Deborah Koonce is:

2560 i. **Gina Michelle Holland.**

Children of James Holland and Diane Jackson are:

\+ 2561 i. **Bobbie Jo Jackson**, born 04 September 1973.

\+ 2562 ii. **Tonya Jackson**, born 19 July 1976.

2563 iii. **Sonya Kay Jackson**, born 19 July 1976.

1749. Ronald Nixon Holland (James Albert[7], Columbus[6], Chester[5], Harfrey[4], Daniel[3], Thomas William[2], Unknown[1]) was born 07 January 1949. He married **(1) Elizabeth Taylor** Before 1973. She was born 01 June 1948. He married **(2) Carolyn Cain** 31 August 1986. She was born 27 November 1942.

Elizabeth is listed as "Lil" on page 448 in "Royal Family Legacy" by Wanda Royal.

Children of Ronald Holland and Elizabeth Taylor are:

\+ 2564 i. **Angela Kaye Holland**, born 15 August 1973.

\+ 2565 ii. **Ronnie Tyson Holland**, born 22 August 1975.

1750. Joseph Wayne Holland (James Albert[7], Columbus[6], Chester[5], Harfrey[4], Daniel[3], Thomas William[2], Unknown[1]) was born 28 June 1954. He married **Cindy Bennett** 28 May 1993. She was born 08 March 1951.

"Royal Family Legacy" on page 448 had Joseph Wayne's spouse as Carolyn West. Her name was corrected to Cindy Bennett in "Royal Family Legacy Addendum."

Child of Joseph Holland and Cindy Bennett is:

2566 i. **Amy Bennett**, born 07 May 1980.

1755. Emily Frances Holland (Chester Ausbon[7], Erastus[6], Chester[5], Harfrey[4], Daniel[3], Thomas William[2], Unknown[1]) was born 23 October 1931. She married **Jack Maurice Holton, Sr.** 24 August 1951.

Children of Emily Holland and Jack Holton are:

\+ 2567 i. **Jack Maurice Holton, Jr.**, born 02 December 1953.

2568 ii. **Julie Catherine Holton**, born 13 January 1970.

1759. Joan Marie Mezzacappa (Aline[7] Holland, Erastus[6], Chester[5], Harfrey[4], Daniel[3], Thomas William[2], Unknown[1]) was born 05 May 1943. She married **Kenneth Allen Payne** 16 November 1961.

Children of Joan Mezzacappa and Kenneth Payne are:

2569 i. **Kelvin Warren Payne**, born 14 August 1964. He married Cindy Ann Capitelle 24 November 1991 in Deer Park, New York; born 22 September 1962.

2570 ii. **Jeffrey Allen Payne**, born 10 June 1970.

1760. Merle Floyd Sollinger, Jr. (Elma[7] Holland, Erastus[6], Chester[5], Harfrey[4], Daniel[3], Thomas William[2], Unknown[1]) was born 17 November 1938 in Salemburg, Sampson County, North Carolina, and died 07 September 2005 in Dunn, Harnett County, North Carolina. He married **Barbara Mae Strum** 27 November 1960.

Barbara Mae's parents were from Nova Scotia, Canada.

Children of Merle Sollinger and Barbara Strum are:

\+ 2571 i. **Linda Louise Sollinger**, born 31 May 1963.

2572 ii. **Robert Bruce Sollinger**, born 02 May 1966.

2573 iii. **Jean Marie Sollinger**, born 10 August 1967.

1761. Thomas Franklin Sollinger (Elma[7] Holland, Erastus[6], Chester[5], Harfrey[4], Daniel[3], Thomas William[2], Unknown[1]) was born 25 June 1948. He married **Judy Lynn Harrell** 29 June 1974. She was born 11 January 1951.

Children of Thomas Sollinger and Judy Harrell are:

2574 i. **Regina Lynn Sollinger**, born 16 April 1976.

2575 ii. **Jennifer Lynn Sollinger**, born 09 May 1977.

1762. Peggy Ann Tripp (Edna Louise[7] Holland, John Love[6], Chester[5], Harfrey[4], Daniel[3], Thomas William[2], Unknown[1]) was born 30 June 1941 in Washington, North Carolina. She married **(1) Richard Earl Crouch** 26 August 1961 in Raleigh, North Carolina. He was born 23 August 1938. She married **(2) Robert Franklin Workman** 05 December 1992 in Wilmington, New Hanover County, North Carolina. He was born 04 April 1939 in Newport News, Virginia.

Children of Peggy Tripp and Richard Crouch are:

2576 i. **Cassandra Anne Crouch**, born 05 November 1962 in Watts General Hospital, Durham, North Carolina. She married **Scott Alan Meckes** 20 April 1985 in Wilmington, New Hanover County, North Carolina; born 01 March 1961 in Lehighton, Carbon, Pennsylvania.

\+ 2577 ii. **Catherine Louise Crouch**, born 06 June 1970 in Wilmington, North Carolina.

2578 iii. **Christina Love Crouch**, born 16 December 1973.

1763. Robert Edward Tripp III (Edna Louise[7] Holland, John Love[6], Chester[5], Harfrey[4], Daniel[3], Thomas William[2], Unknown[1]) was born 16 June 1943 in Raleigh, North Carolina. He married **Mary Emma Peele** 18 November 1968. She was born 28 December 1942.

Child of Robert Tripp and Mary Peele is:

2579 i. **Robert Edward Tripp IV**, born 23 June 1970. He married Elizabeth King.

1764. Celia Joyce Holland (Ernest Ray[7], John Love[6], Chester[5], Harfrey[4], Daniel[3], Thomas William[2], Unknown[1]) was born 22 July 1948 in Roseboro, North Carolina. She married **Allen Wayne Smith**. He was born 06 June 1944.

Child of Celia Holland and Allen Smith is:

2580 ✓ i. **Jennifer Leigh Smith**, born 25 August 1976.

1766. Linda Jo Holland (Lester Floyd[7], John Love[6], Chester[5], Harfrey[4], Daniel[3], Thomas William[2], Unknown[1]) was born 08 October 1955 in Roseboro, North Carolina. She married **Philbert Steve Lewis** 05 October 1973 in Salemburg, Sampson County, North Carolina. He was born 21 May 1948 in Elizabethtown Township, Bladen County, North Carolina.

Child of Linda Holland and Philbert Lewis is:

2581 ✓ i. **Eric Michael Lewis**, born 07 March 1974 in Clinton, Sampson County, North Carolina.

1776. Barbara Elaine Naylor (Charles Hilliard[7], Lillie[6] Holland, Chester[5], Harfrey[4], Daniel[3], Thomas William[2], Unknown[1]) was born 25 October 1941 in Dunn, Harrnett County, North Carolina. She married **William H. Dodson, Jr.**. He was born 11 July 1940.

Children of Barbara Naylor and William Dodson are:

2582 i. **Tray Dodson**.

2583 ii. **Travis Dodson**.

2584 iii. **Daniel Dodson**.

2585 iv. **Amanda Dodson**.

1778. Wanda Kaye Naylor (Payton Thomas[7], Lillie[6] Holland, Chester[5], Harfrey[4], Daniel[3], Thomas William[2], Unknown[1]) was born 07 August 1944 in Dunn, Harrnett County, North Carolina. She married **Johnny Ray Gardner** 22 May 1966 in Trinity Baptist Church, Meadow Township. He was born 20 November 1939 in Martin County, North Carolina.

Child of Wanda Naylor and Johnny Gardner is:

2586 i. **Scarlette Kay Gardner**, born 06 October 1974.

1779. Diana Naylor (Payton Thomas[7], Lillie[6] Holland, Chester[5], Harfrey[4], Daniel[3], Thomas William[2], Unknown[1]) was born 28 August 1949 in Dunn, Harrnett County, North Carolina. She married **Graham Dwight Turner** 29 August 1969, son of Merwin Turner and Linda Williams. He was born 19 August 1950 in Erwin, Harnett County, North Carolina.

Date or 19 August 1950 is also found for his birth.

Children of Diana Naylor and Graham Turner are:

2587 i. **Lisa Ann Turner**, born 28 April 1970.

2588 ii. **Andrea Renee Turner**, born 27 June 1974.

1781. Doris Lynn Naylor (Graham Willard[7], Lillie[6] Holland, Chester[5], Harfrey[4], Daniel[3], Thomas William[2], Unknown[1]) was born 26 January 1944 in New Hanover County, North Carolina. She married **Earl Dalton Pope** 27 December 1964 in Mingo Baptist Church, Mingo Township, Sampson County, North Carolina, son of Martin Pope and Magdalene Wade. He was born 07 September 1945 in Dunn, Harrnett County, North Carolina.

Children of Doris Naylor and Earl Pope are:

2589 i. **Earl Scott Pope**, born 09 June 1967 in Fayetteville, Cumberland County, North Carolina. He married **Margaret Adeline Royal** 27 April 1990 in Piney Green Baptist Church, Sampson County, North Carolina; born 06 July 1967.

2590 ii. **Amy Lynn Pope,** born 21 December 1970 in Fayetteville, Cumberland County, North Carolina.

1782. Marinda Jean Naylor (Graham Willard[7], Lillie[6] Holland, Chester[5], Harfrey[4], Daniel[3], Thomas William[2], Unknown[1]) was born 18 November 1946 in Dunn, Harrnett County, North Carolina. She married **Bobby Howell Earp, Sr.** Before 1969, son of Ruth Earp.

Children of Marinda Naylor and Bobby Earp are:

2591 i. **Bobby Howell Earp, Jr.**, born 25 August 1969.

2592 ii. **Marinda Dee Ann Earp**, born 03 February 1971.

1783. Susan Ann Naylor (Graham Willard[7], Lillie[6] Holland, Chester[5], Harfrey[4], Daniel[3], Thomas William[2], Unknown[1]) was born 16 September 1954 in Dunn, Harrnett County, North Carolina. She married **Gary Wayne Faircloth** November 1975 in Mingo Township, Sampson County, North Carolina, son of James Faircloth and Elgree Daniels. He was born 21 October 1954 in Richmond County, South Carolina.

Child of Susan Naylor and Gary Faircloth is:

2593 i. **Anna Garrett Faircloth**, born 02 September 1988 in Fayetteville, Cumberland County, North Carolina.

1784. Byron Wayne Grantham (Irene[7] Naylor, Lillie[6] Holland, Chester[5], Harfrey[4], Daniel[3], Thomas William[2], Unknown[1]) was born 28 January 1949 in Roseboro, Sampson County, North Carolina. He married **(1) Polly Ann Callette** before 1972.

In one source I found 'Polly Collet" for her name.

Children of Byron Grantham and Polly Callette are:

\+ 2595 i. **Ginger Marie Grantham**, born 15 November 1972.

2596 ii. **David Wayne Grantham**, born 02 April 1975.

I also found 2 April 1976 for his birth.

1785. Cathy Lynette Grantham (Irene[7] Naylor, Lillie[6] Holland, Chester[5], Harfrey[4], Daniel[3], Thomas William[2], Unknown[1]) was born 25 January 1952 in Roseboro, Sampson County, North Carolina. She married **Wyman Edward McDaniel** 06 August 1972 in Roseboro, Sampson County, North Carolina. He was born 26 February 1947 in Roseboro.

Children of Cathy Grantham and Wyman McDaniel are:

2597 i. **Jennifer Lynette McDaniel**, born 22 March 1977 in Clinton, Sampson County, North Carolina.

2598 ii. **Melissa McDaniel**, born 31 August 1980.

1804. Nixon Lewis Spell, Sr. (Lewis Alton[7], Braxton[6], Romelia[5] Holland, Harfrey[4], Daniel[3], Thomas William[2], Unknown[1]) was born 07 October 1941 in Sampson County, North Carolina. He married **Mary Alice Nunnery**. She was born 15 May 1944 in Cumberland County, North Carolina.

Children of Nixon Spell and Mary Nunnery are:

2599 i. **Nixon Lewis Spell, Jr.**, born 25 February 1964 in Cumberland County, North Carolina.

2600 ii. **Sue Ellen Spell**, born 15 May 1967 in Cumberland County, North Carolina.

1805. Arthur Elwood Spell (Lewis Alton[7], Braxton[6], Romelia[5] Holland, Harfrey[4], Daniel[3], Thomas William[2], Unknown[1]) was born 19 November 1951 in Sampson County, North Carolina. He married **Connie Sue Faircloth** 15 July 1972 in Cumberland County, North Carolina. She was born 06 February 1954 in Sampson County, North Carolina.

Children of Arthur Spell and Connie Faircloth are:

2601 i. **Christy Lane Spell**, born 21 June 1975 in Cumberland County, North Carolina.

2602 ii. **Regina Suzanne Spell**, born 25 October 1976 in Cumberland County, North Carolina.

1808. Festus DeVone Faircloth (Pauline[7] Spell, Braxton[6], Romelia[5] Holland, Harfrey[4], Daniel[3], Thomas William[2], Unknown[1]) was born 23 December 1942 in Sampson County, North Carolina, and died 27 February 1997. He married **Linda Faye Grantham** 11 January 1964 in Little Coharie Township, Sampson County, North Carolina, daughter of Almond Grantham and Ina Williams. She was born 04 March 1945 in Dismal Township, Sampson County, North Carolina.

One source shows February 27, 1997 for date of death for Festus, and same date of death for Alfestus, Jr. his brother. Different dates are shown for their birth. Accident? Linda Grantham is found for the wife of Alfestus and for the wife of Festus Devone Faircloth which certainly indicates they are the same person.

Children of Festus Faircloth and Linda Grantham are:

\+ 2603 i. **Eric Napoleon Faircloth**, born 15 April 1965 in Clinton, Sampson County, North Carolina.

2604 ii. **Nena Charleen Faircloth**, born 03 November 1966 in Clinton, Sampson County, North Carolina. She married **Chad Thompson** 11 February 1989; born 17 May 1968 in Wayne County, North Carolina.

2605 iii. **Unnamed Faircloth.**

1809. Henry Enoch Faircloth (Pauline[7] Spell, Braxton[6], Romelia[5] Holland, Harfrey[4], Daniel[3], Thomas William[2], Unknown[1]) was born 08 July 1946 in Sampson County, North Carolina. He married **Molly Faye Hill** September 1965, daughter of Arthur Hill and Mollie Ellis. She was born 05 March 1945 in Sampson County.

Children of Henry Faircloth and Molly Hill are:

\+ 2606 i. **Ryan Arthur Faircloth**, born 30 June 1972 in Sampson County, North Carolina; died 31 August 1996 in Sampson County, North Carolina.

2607 ii. **Henry Ashley Faircloth**, born September 1975.

2608 iii. **Heath Evan Faircloth**, born 28 September 1977.

1810. Robert Anthony Faircloth (Pauline[7] Spell, Braxton[6], Romelia[5] Holland, Harfrey[4], Daniel[3], Thomas William[2], Unknown[1]) was born 26 July 1951 in Sampson County, North Carolina. He married **Doris Eloine Faircloth.**

Children of Robert Faircloth and Doris Faircloth are:

2609 i. **Monica Jewel Faircloth**, born 25 July 1975 in Sampson County, North Carolina. She married **John Patrick Crolle**.

2610 ii. **Brandon Anthony Faircloth**, born 06 June 1983 in Sampson County, North Carolina.

1811. Rebecca Dale Faircloth (Pauline[7] Spell, Braxton[6], Romelia[5] Holland, Harfrey[4], Daniel[3], Thomas William[2], Unknown[1]) was born 13 June 1955 in Sampson County, North Carolina. She married **William Arthur Warren**. He was born 25 January 1954.

Children of Rebecca Faircloth and William Warren are:

2611 i. **Marie Dale Warren,** born 07 August 1979.

2612 ii. **Martha Allison Warren,** born 25 October 1981.

2613 iii. **Novelle Rebecca Warren,** born 04 November 1987.

1812. Martha Jane Faircloth (Pauline[7] Spell, Braxton[6], Romelia[5] Holland, Harfrey[4], Daniel[3], Thomas William[2], Unknown[1]) was born 28 May 1958 in Sampson County, North Carolina. She married **John David Shelton.** He was born 08 February 1957 in Virginia, and died 26 January 1988 in Sampson County, North Carolina.

Children of Martha Faircloth and John Shelton are:

2614 i. **David Michael Shelton,** born 10 November 1979.

2615 ii. **Joshua Paul Shelton,** born 06 March 1982.

2616 iii. **Nathan Israel Shelton,** born 20 December 1983.

2617 iv. **James Isaac Shelton,** born 05 March 1987.

1813. Melody Ruth Faircloth (Pauline[7] Spell, Braxton[6], Romelia[5] Holland, Harfrey[4], Daniel[3], Thomas William[2], Unknown[1]) was born 25 November 1960 in Sampson County, North Carolina. She married **Randy Austin Tyndall** 09 March 1980, son of Archie Tyndall and Lois Ellis. He was born 07 July 1957 in Sampson County, North Carolina.

Children of Melody Faircloth and Randy Tyndall are:

2618 i. **Lois Paulette Tyndall,** born 26 October 1981 in Sampson County, North Carolina; died December 1982.

2619 ii. **Pamela Denise Tyndall,** born 11 November 1984 in Sampson County, North Carolina.

2620 iii. **Casey Melody Tyndall,** born 13 June 1988 in Sampson County, North Carolina.

1822. Janet Spell (James Oscar[7], Braxton[6], Romelia[5] Holland, Harfrey[4], Daniel[3], Thomas William[2], Unknown[1]) was born 11 January 1960 in North Carolina. She married **Bobby Hall.** He was born 24 September 1956 in Sampson County, North Carolina, and died 09 November 1996.

Children of Janet Spell and Bobby Hall are:

2621 i. **Stephanie Hall,** born 01 September 1978.

2622 ii. **Bobbie Lynn Hall,** born 20 July 1980.

1828. Euland Dwight Holland (Vernon[8], Euland Randolph[7], William Thomas[6], Thomas James[5], James[4], Daniel[3], Thomas William[2], Unknown[1]) was born 29 April 1953 in Clinton, Sampson County, North Carolina. He married **(1) Sylvia Jean Preddy** 17 July 1971 in Dillon, South Carolina, daughter of Henry Preddy and Ethel Spell. She was born 22 May 1953 in Clinton, Sampson County, North Carolina. He married **(2) Karen Dawn Jackson** 08 December 1984 in Route 2, Dunn, Harnett County, North Carolina, daughter of Randolph Jackson and Brenda Hudson. She was born 17 July 1961 in Dunn, Harnett County, North Carolina.

Syllvia Jean Preddy married second a Mr. Wilson.

Child of Euland Holland and Sylvia Preddy is:

2623 i. **Ashley Euland Holland**, born about 1974.

1832. Sandra Kay Holland (Vernon[8], Euland Randolph[7], William Thomas[6], Thomas James[5], James[4], Daniel[3], Thomas William[2], Unknown[1]) was born 20 October 1962 in Hickory, North Carolina. She married **Brewer Christopher Matthews** 27 September 1996 in Tennessee, son of Rupert Matthews and Linda Spell. He was born 12 October 1972.

Children of Sandra Holland and Brewer Matthews are:

2624 i. **Cortney Rogers Matthews.**

2625 ii. **Tiffany Rogers Matthews.**

1833. George William Willis III (Muriel Grace[7] Spell, Braxton[6], Romelia[5] Holland, Harfrey[4], Daniel[3], Thomas William[2], Unknown[1]) was born 04 July 1953 in Cumberland County, North Carolina. He married **Kathy McNelly.**

Child of George Willis and Kathy McNelly is:

2626 i. **George William Willis IV.**

1835. Edward W. Willis (Muriel Grace[7] Spell, Braxton[6], Romelia[5] Holland, Harfrey[4], Daniel[3], Thomas William[2], Unknown[1]) was born 10 June 1960 in Cumberland County, North Carolina. He married **Maria Lute.**

Children of Edward Willis and Maria Lute are:

2627 i. **Christopher Willis.**

2628 ii. **Aaron Willis.**

1836. Wanda Faye Spell (Percy Blackman[7], George Oliver[6], Romelia[5] Holland, Harfrey[4], Daniel[3], Thomas William[2], Unknown[1]) was born 24 February 1944 in Dismal Township, Sampson County, North Carolina. She married **George Rosdan Beal, Jr.** 24 July 1963 in Little Coharie Township, Sampson County, North Carolina, son of George Rosdan Beal and Olita Williams. He was born 14 April 1942 in Roseboro, Sampson County.

Children of Wanda Spell and George Beal are:

2629 i. **Lana Kay Beal**, born 18 March 1964 in Clinton, Sampson County, North Carolina. She married **James Timothy Williams** 28 July 1985 in Herrings Township, Sampson County; born 05 October 1961 in Clinton, Sampson County, North Carolina.

2630 ii. **Karen Yvonne Beal**, born 02 February 1965 in Clinton, Sampson County, North Carolina.

1838. Henry Arnold Autry (Eva[7] Faircloth, Sophia[6] Horne, Laura Ann[5] Holland, Harfrey[4], Daniel[3], Thomas William[2], Unknown[1]) was born 14 February 1949 in Roseboro, North Carolina. He married **Carrie Jean Honeycutt** 23 March 1968 in Autryville, North Carolina, daughter of Eazary Honeycutt and Eutha McLamb. She was born 13 July 1949 in Roseboro, North Carolina.

Child of Henry Autry and Carrie Honeycutt is:

2631 i. **William Henry Autry**, born 21 July 1969 in Clinton, Sampson County, North Carolina.

1840. Joseph Elliott Horne (Sarah Elizabeth[7] Faircloth, Sophia[6] Horne, Laura Ann[5] Holland, Harfrey[4], Daniel[3], Thomas William[2], Unknown[1]) was born 03 June 1952. He married **Linda Arnette.**

Child of Joseph Horne and Linda Arnette is:

2632 i. **Sarah Renee Horne**, born 17 September 1973.

1844. Paula Sue Hudson (Ruby Sykes[7] Holland, Harvey[6], Henry Lee[5], Harfrey[4], Daniel[3], Thomas William[2], Unknown[1]) was born 06 October 1952. She married **(1) Leo Jon Hildebrand** before 1986. He was born 30 April 1950. She married **(2) Michael Collins** after 1986. He was born 12 April 1952.

Children of Paula Hudson and Leo Hildebrand are:

2633 i. **Jonathan Hildebrand**, born 10 April 1983.

2634 ii. **Joseph Hildebrand**, born 10 October 1986.

1845. Stuart Hudson (Ruby Sykes[7] Holland, Harvey[6], Henry Lee[5], Harfrey[4], Daniel[3], Thomas William[2], Unknown[1]) was born 29 March 1957. He married **Becky McGee**. She was born 03 October 1958.

Child of Stuart Hudson and Becky McGee is:

2635 i. **Abbey McGee Hudson**, born 07 April 1992.

1848. Thelma Mae Lockamy (William Lischer[7], Onie Vendex[6] Holland, William Wright[5], Thomas James[4], Daniel[3], Thomas William[2], Unknown[1]) was born 18 June 1922. She married **Willie Fowler.** He was born 1920.

Children of Thelma Lockamy and Willie Fowler are:

\+ 2636 i. **Helen Fowler**, born 11 June 1944.

2637 ii. **William Joseph Fowler**, born 04 October 1945. He married **Lanae Smith**; born about 1946.

\+ 2638 iii. **Ronald Wayne Fowler**, born 07 November 1947; died 01 March 1983.

2639 iv. **Phil Asber Fowler**, born 07 December 1950. He married **Janet Parker.**

One son.

\+ 2640 v. **Jimmy Ray Fowler**, born 29 May 1952.

\+ 2641 vi. **Glenda Kaye Fowler**, born 26 January 1954 in Clinton, Sampson County, North Carolina.

\+ 2642 vii. **Brenda Faye Fowler**, born 26 January 1954.

1850. John Nathan Lockamy, Sr. (William Lischer[7], Onie Vendex[6] Holland, William Wright[5], Thomas James[4], Daniel[3], Thomas William[2], Unknown[1]) was born 31 August 1927 in Route 1, Clinton, Honeycutts Township, Sampson County, North Carolina, and died 21 August 1986. He married **Jean Evelyn Strickland.** She was born 21 March 1928.

John Nathan, Sr. was buried in Grandview Memorial Gardens, three miles north of Clinton, North Carolina.

Child of John Lockamy and Jean Strickland is:

2643 i. **Dr. John Nathan Lockamy, Jr.**, born 04 February 1955. He married **Julie Lane Troy** 17 July 1982; born in Birmingham, Alabama.

Dr. Lockamy began his practice of Veterinary Medicine in July 1982 in El Reno, Oklahoma.

1851. Lischer Maylon Lockamy (William Lischer[7], Onie Vendex[6] Holland, William Wright[5], Thomas James[4], Daniel[3], Thomas William[2], Unknown[1]) was born 13 March 1930, and died 03 September 1979. He married **(1) Jean Brown** before 1955. She was born in Morrisville, Vermont. He married **(2) Bonnie Holder Ingram** after 1955.

Lischer Maylon is buried in Owens Grove PFWB Church Cemetery, Sampson County, North Carolina.

Child of Lischer Lockamy and Jean Brown is:

2644 i. **Clayton Ernest Lockamy**, born 05 February 1955.

Child of Lischer Lockamy and Bonnie Ingram is:

2645 i. **William Lockamy**, born after 1955.

1852. Alton Rexford Lockamy (William Lischer[7], Onie Vendex[6] Holland, William Wright[5], Thomas James[4], Daniel[3], Thomas William[2], Unknown[1]) was born 14 June 1934. He married **Nancy Ann Moore**. She was born 22 June 1935.

Child of Alton Lockamy and Nancy Moore is:

2646 i. **Mark Lockamy**, born 10 January 1955. He married **Robn Intrican.**

Two children.

1853. Onie Evelyn Lockamy (William Lischer[7], Onie Vendex[6] Holland, William Wright[5], Thomas James[4], Daniel[3], Thomas William[2], Unknown[1]) was born 29 March 1937. She married **David Porter Williams**, son of Harvey Williams and Vennie Porter. He was born 24 April 1935.

Child of Onie Lockamy and David Williams is:

2647 i. **Robert Wade Williams**, born 19 April 1964. He married **Jeannie Unknown.**

One son.

1854. Ethel L. Cannady (Annie[7] Lockamy, Onie Vendex[6] Holland, William Wright[5], Thomas James[4], Daniel[3], Thomas William[2], Unknown[1]) was born 23 September 1919 in North Carolina, and died 03 August 2002 in Sampson County, North Carolina. She married **Zebulon Vance Satterfield, Jr.**. He was born 12 August 1920 in North Carolina, and died 14 December 1996 in Sampson County, North Carolina.

Ethel and Zebulon are buried in Grandview Gardens, Clinton, North Carolina

Children of Ethel Cannady and Zebulon Satterfield are:

\+ 2648 i. **Billy Satterfield**, born 06 April 1943.

\+ 2649 ii. **Barbara Jean Satterfield**, born 28 October 1945.

1855. James Elder Cannady (Annie[7] Lockamy, Onie Vendex[6] Holland, William Wright[5], Thomas James[4], Daniel[3], Thomas William[2], Unknown[1]) was born 08 July 1926. He married **Kathleen Parsons**. She was born 14 March 1927.

James E. enlisted on 18 August 1944 in Fort Bragg, North Carolina, to serve in World War II. A transcribed enlistment records shows 100 lbs for his weight and 80 inches for his height. His height may be entered incorrectly.

Children of James Cannady and Kathleen Parsons are:

2650 i. **Mavis Cannady**, born 29 November 1944. She married Jackie Hobbs.

\+ 2651 ii. **James Harold Cannady**, born 07 December 1946.

\+ 2652 iii. **Jewell Denise Cannady**, born 23 October 1955.

1856. William John Cannady (Annie[7] Lockamy, Onie Vendex[6] Holland, William Wright[5], Thomas James[4], Daniel[3], Thomas William[2], Unknown[1]) was born 28 March 1930, and died 08 July 1988 in Sampson County, North Carolina. He married **Edna Unknown**. She was born 1933. One source provides "Willie John Cannady" for his name and it appears that he may have been known as "Jay."

William John was buried in Grandview Gardens, Clinton, North Carolina.

Child of William Cannady and Edna Unknown is:

\+ 2653 i. **Chris Cannady**.

1858. Royce Wilton Tyndall (Ada[7] Lockamy, Onie Vendex[6] Holland, William Wright[5], Thomas James[4], Daniel[3], Thomas William[2], Unknown[1]) was born 17 September 1932, and died 09 June 1980. He married **Sarah Inez Spell** 1954, daughter of James Spell and Almeta Warren. She was born 28 November 1934.

Royce Wilton was buried in Owens Grove Pentecostal FWB Church Cemetery, Kitty Fork, Sampson County, North Carolina.

Children of Royce Tyndall and Sarah Spell are:

2654 i. **Royce Dwayne Tyndall**, born 1955. He married Lisa Turlington; born about 1955.

2655 ii. **Robert Wilton Tyndall**, born 1961.

1859. Astraudia Brown Lockamy (Robert Owen[7], Onie Vendex[6] Holland, William Wright[5], Thomas James[4], Daniel[3], Thomas William[2], Unknown[1]) was born 14 September 1926 in Sampson County, North Carolina, and died 21 December 1995 in Sampson County, North Carolina. She married **Wyatt Allen Adams** 21 January 1949 in Owens Grove Pentecostal FWB Church, Sampson County, North Carolina. He was born 22 January 1924 in Angier, Harnett County, North Carolina, and died 23 November 1972 in Angier, Harnett County, North Carolina.

Astraudia and Wyatt Allen were buried in Owens Grove Pentecostal FWB Church Cemetery, Sampson County, North Carolina. He served in World War II. NC SGT COM 1 Inf. is found on his monument.

Children of Astraudia Lockamy and Wyatt Adams are:

\+ 2656 i. **Robert Wayne Adams was** born 28 February 1950 in Dunn Hospital, North Carolina.

2657 ii. **Margie Joanne Adams**, born 21 October 1952 in Sampson Memorial Hospital, Clinton, Sampson County, North Carolina. She married (1) **Maxwell Ivey Minnich** 10 June 1972. She married (2) **Michael Ramsey** after 1972.

Margie Joanne and Maxwell Ivey Minnich separated in 1974 and she assumed her maiden name.

1862. Doris Marie Ellis (Janie Lou[7] Lockamy, Onie Vendex[6] Holland, William Wright[5], Thomas James[4], Daniel[3], Thomas William[2], Unknown[1]) was born 25 October 1930 in Honeycutts Township, Sampson County, North Carolina. She married **William Alton Tyndall**, son of William Tyndall and Nannie Tyndall. He was born 17 December 1927 in Herrings Township, Sampson County, North Carolina, and died 12 September 1996.

William Alton was buried in Grandview Memorial Gardens, three miles north of Clinton, North Carolina.

Children of Doris Ellis and William Tyndall are:

\+ 2658 i. **William Albert Tyndall**, born 30 June 1947 in Honeycutts Township, Sampson County, North Carolina.

\+ 2659 ii. **Diane Marie Tyndall**, born 01 October 1950 in Herrings Township, Sampson County, North Carolina.

2660 iii. **Stephanie Gail Tyndall**, born 10 July 1954 in Clinton, Sampson County, North Carolina. She married (1) **Alton Howard Pope**; born 21 February 1951; died 13 May 1990. She married (2) **Travis Butler**.

Divorced. One daughter.

2661 iv. **Jeff Michael Tyndall**, born 15 June 1957 in Clinton, Sampson County, North Carolina. He married **Wanda Melody Barker**; born 30 November 1956.

One daughter.

1872. Truman D. Royal (Ivy D.[7], Robertson[6] Royals, Agnes Matilda[5] Holland, Matthew[4], Daniel[3], Thomas William[2], Unknown[1]) was born 31 December 1933 in Honeycutts Township, Sampson County, North Carolina. He married **Deloris Jane McLamb** 05 September 1953 in Dillon, South Carolina, daughter of Thedie McLamb and Annie Tew. She was born 22 June 1936 in Honeycutts Township, Sampson County, North Carolina.

Children of Truman Royal and Deloris McLamb are:

\+ 2662 i. **Bronzell Truman Royal**, born 28 February 1955 in Roseboro, North Carolina; died 17 August 1993.

2663 ii. **Darrell Wayne Royal**, born 07 April 1960 in Clinton, Sampson County. He married **Donna Lisa Dudley** 11 February 1979 in Salemburg, Sampson County, North Carolina; born 17 October 1959 in Dunn, Harnett County, North Carolina.

1874. Evelyn Grace Royal (James Evelyn[7], Robertson[6] Royals, Agnes Matilda[5] Holland, Matthew[4], Daniel[3], Thomas William[2], Unknown[1]) was born 12 March 1946 in Roseboro, Sampson County, North Carolina. She married **Ellis Wayne McLamb** 10 February 1968 in Honeycutts Township, Sampson County, North Carolina, son of Orsen McLamb and Lillian

Lockerman. He was born 21 September 1945 in Honeycutts Township, Sampson County, North Carolina.

Children of Evelyn Royal and Ellis McLamb are:

2664 i. **Windy Michelle McLamb**, born 29 October 1968 in Clinton, Sampson County, North Carolina.

2665 ii. **Cindy LaJune McLamb**, born 29 October 1968 in Clinton, Sampson County, North Carolina.

1881. Roger Ray Royal (Roland Duvell[7], Lela[6] Holland, Robert Mitchell[5], Matthew[4], Daniel[3], Thomas William[2], Unknown[1]) was born 08 April 1940 in Roseboro, Sampson County, North Carolina. He married **Annette Rose Poserina.** She was born about 1924 in New York.

Children of Roger Royal and Annette Poserina are:

2666 i. **Unnamed Royal.**

2667 ii. **Second Unnamed Royal**, born 02 April 1971.

2668 iii. **Judy Ann Royal**, born 23 February 1974 in Fayetteville, Cumberland County, North Carolina.

1887. Polly Ann Royal (Coy Aaron[7], Lela[6] Holland, Robert Mitchell[5], Matthew[4], Daniel[3], Thomas William[2], Unknown[1]) was born 14 October 1956 in Roseboro, Sampson County, North Carolina. She married **Danny Martin Matthews** 01 July 1974 in Clinton, North Carolina. He was born 30 October 1954 in Clinton, Sampson County, North Carolina.

Child of Polly Royal and Danny Matthews is:

2669 i. **Kimberly Carol Matthews**, born 30 October 1974 in Clinton, Sampson County, North Carolina.

1888. Daniel Britt Royal (Coy Aaron[7], Lela[6] Holland, Robert Mitchell[5], Matthew[4], Daniel[3], Thomas William[2], Unknown[1]) was born 15 December 1957 in Roseboro, Sampson County, North Carolina. He married **Lydia Ruth Collier** 04 May 1978. She was born 17 December 1961 in Clinton, Sampson County, North Carolina.

Children of Daniel Royal and Lydia Collier are:

2670 i. **Lillian Ruth Royal**, born 28 October 1978 in Clinton, Sampson County, North Carolina.

2671 ii. **Mandy Lynn Royal**, born 01 August 1980 in Clinton, Sampson County.

1893. Margie Helen Royal (E. T.[7], Lela[6] Holland, Robert Mitchell[5], Matthew[4], Daniel[3], Thomas William[2], Unknown[1]) was born 03 February 1952 in Roseboro, Sampson County, North Carolina. She married **James William Haire** before 1976, son of Melvin Haire and Susan Daniel. He was born 01 June 1950 in Roseboro, Sampson County, North Carolina.

Children of Margie Royal and James Haire are:

2672 i. **Amanda Helen Haire**, born 02 November 1976 in Fayetteville, Cumberland County, North Carolina.

2673 ii. **James Andrew Haire**, born 11 November 1979 in Fayetteville, Cumberland County, North Carolina; died 16 November 1979 in Chapel Hill.

Burial: Autryville Church of God, Autryville, North Carolina.

2674 iii. **Veronica Jane Haire**, born 21 April 1982.

1896. Peggy Marilyn Royal (E. T.[7], Lela[6] Holland, Robert Mitchell[5], Matthew[4], Daniel[3], Thomas William[2], Unknown[1]) was born 08 November 1958 in Fayetteville, Cumberland County, North Carolina. She married **Thomas Gardner Honeycutt** 06 March 1976, son of Buck Honeycutt and Florence Hubbard. He was born 09 October 1957 in Dunn, Harrnett County, North Carolina.

Children of Peggy Royal and Thomas Honeycutt are:

2675 i. **Peggy Susanne Honeycutt**, born 28 September 1976 in Fayetteville, Cumberland County, North Carolina.

2676 ii. **Brian Thomas Honeycutt**, born 09 April 1979 in Fayetteville, Cumberland County.

1897. Judy Katherine Barnes (James William[7], Julia[6] Holland, Robert Mitchell[5], Matthew[4], Daniel[3], Thomas William[2], Unknown[1]) was born 11 May 1948 in Clinton, Sampson County, North Carolina. She married **James Elvin Jackson, Sr.** 12 June 1966 in Roseboro, Sampson County, North Carolina, son of Elvin Sykes Jackson and Virginia Lee Horne. He was born 02 January 1946 in Roseboro, Sampson County, North Carolina.

Judy Katherine graduated with a B.S. from Campbell University, North Carolina. James Elvin is known as "Jimmy" and he attended Fayetteville Techical Institute, Fayetteville, North Carolina.

Children of Judy Barnes and James Jackson are:

\+ 2677 i. **James Elvin Jackson, Jr.**, born 21 January 1968 in Raleigh, North Carolina.

\+ 2678 ii. **John Trent Jackson**, born 15 December 1974.

\+ 2679 iii. **Joseph Wayne Jackson**, born 15 December 1974.

1898. Jennifer Gray Barnes (James William[7], Julia[6] Holland, Robert Mitchell[5], Matthew[4], Daniel[3], Thomas William[2], Unknown[1]) was born 16 June 1951 in Clinton, Sampson County, North Carolina. She married **David Farrell Fann** 23 August 1970, son of William Fann and Elizabeth Strickland. He was born 26 June 1949 in Honeycutts Township, Sampson County, North Carolina.

Children of Jennifer Barnes and David Fann are:

+ 2680 i. **Jennifer Lynn Fann**, born 02 January 1975 in Clinton, Sampson County, North Carolina.

2681 ii. **Jeffrey Farrell Fann**, born 06 March 1978 in Clinton, Sampson County. He married **Melodie Brooke Hall**; born 06 September 1982.

1899. James Welton Barnes, Sr. (James William[7], Julia[6] Holland, Robert Mitchell[5], Matthew[4], Daniel[3], Thomas William[2], Unknown[1]) was born 19 April 1954. He married **Pamela Annette Johnson.** She was born 13 May 1956.

Children of James Barnes and Pamela Johnson are:

2682 i. **James Welton Barnes, Jr.**, born 10 October 1979. He married **Laura Floyd**; born 24 September 1982.

2683 ii. **Jonathan Bradley Barnes**, born 24 August 1981.

2684 iii. **Christian Annette Barnes**, born 02 February 1984. She married **Ilya Vladimirovich Shlyapnikov;** born 22 February 1982 in Russia.

1900. Jerry Trent Barnes (James William[7], Julia[6] Holland, Robert Mitchell[5], Matthew[4], Daniel[3], Thomas William[2], Unknown[1]) was born 26 November 1956. He married **Doris Teresa Beal**. She was born 26 February 1960.

Children of Jerry Barnes and Doris Beal are:

2685 i. **Jana Lee Barnes**, born 17 May 1987.

2686 ii. **Dylan James Barnes**, born 30 June 1993.

1901. Janet Marie Barnes (James William[7], Julia[6] Holland, Robert Mitchell[5], Matthew[4], Daniel[3], Thomas William[2], Unknown[1]) was born 20 March 1961. She married **(1) Unknown Daughtry** About 1985. She married **(2) Kenneth Dewayne Burchette** Before 1996. He was born 04 February 1963.

Child of Janet Barnes and Unknown Daughtry is:

2687 i. **Jillian Gray Daughtry**, born 16 January 1989.

Child of Janet Barnes and Kenneth Burchette is:

2688 i. **Jared Wayne Burchette**, born 09 October 1996.

1902. Rebecca Sue Barnes (Lester Lee[7], Julia[6] Holland, Robert Mitchell[5], Matthew[4], Daniel[3], Thomas William[2], Unknown[1]) was born 18 November 1952. She married **Samuel Butler Holden**, son of Joshua Holden and Christine Crumpler.

Child of Rebecca Barnes and Samuel Holden is:

2689 i. **Candace Holden**, born 25 April 1989.

1904. Leslie Kent Barnes (Lester Lee[7], Julia[6] Holland, Robert Mitchell[5], Matthew[4], Daniel[3], Thomas William[2], Unknown[1]) was born 24 November 1967. He married **Vivian Katrina Wozniak**. She was born 22 July 1969.

Children of Leslie Barnes and Vivian Wozniak are:

2690 i. **Dillon Austin Barnes**, born 16 March 1994.

2691 ii. **Lynsey Morgan Barnes**, born 21 August 1996.

1907. Larry Mixton Knowles, Sr. (Matthew Mixton[7], Chellie[6] Holland, Robert Mitchell[5], Matthew[4], Daniel[3], Thomas William[2], Unknown[1]) was born 19 October 1946 in Roseboro, Sampson County, North Carolina. He married **Georgia Faye Hobbs**. She was born about 1950.

Children of Larry Knowles and Georgia Hobbs are:

2692 i. **Larry Mixton Knowles, Jr.**, born 26 April 1970 in Clinton, Sampson County, North Carolina.

2693 ii. **Sheila Faye Knowles**, born 13 March 1975 in Clinton, Sampson County.

1908. Donald Nelson Knowles (Matthew Mixton[7], Chellie[6] Holland, Robert Mitchell[5], Matthew[4], Daniel[3], Thomas William[2], Unknown[1]) was born 28 May 1950 in Roseboro, North Carolina. He married **Clara Faye Cannady** 13 July 1969, daughter of Franklin Cannady and Clara Crumpler. She was born 16 November 1950 in Fayetteville, Cumberland County, North Carolina.

Children of Donald Knowles and Clara Cannady are:

2694 i. **Kimberly Faye Knowles**, born 08 October 1972 in Clinton, Sampson County, North Carolina.

2695 ii. **Donald Dewayne Knowles**, born 30 June 1976 in Clinton, Sampson County.

1910. Wiley Dwight Knowles (Wiley Dixon[7], Chellie[6] Holland, Robert Mitchell[5], Matthew[4], Daniel[3], Thomas William[2], Unknown[1]) was born 01 November 1959. He married **(1) Marshall Annette Lee**. He married **(2) Joyce Estes**.

Child of Wiley Knowles and Marshall Lee is:

2696 i. **Shanna Annette Knowles**, born 19 December 1984.

1913. Robert Mitchell Holland (Daniel Robert[7], Robert Minson[6], Robert Mitchell[5], Matthew[4], Daniel[3], Thomas William[2], Unknown[1]) was born 12 September 1956. He married **Marilyn Stewart**, daughter of Lattie Stewart and Ida Faircloth. She was born 15 March 1957.

Child of Robert Holland and Marilyn Stewart is:

2697 i. **Monica Gail Holland**, born 05 January 1975.

1918. Jewel Reese Simmons (Miles Oscar[7], Jathronia[6] Holland, Robert Mitchell[5], Matthew[4], Daniel[3], Thomas William[2], Unknown[1]) She married **Jimmy Mathias.**

Jewel Simmons married twice. The name of the first husband is unknown. Jimmy Mathias was her second husband and they are divorced.

Children of Jewel Simmons and Jimmy Mathias are:

2698 i. **Walter Mathias**, born 22 February 1971.

2699 ii. **Reane Mathias**, born 26 September 1973.

2700 iii. **Travis Mathias**, born 09 August 1976.

1919. Wade Simmons (Miles Oscar[7], Jathronia[6] Holland, Robert Mitchell[5], Matthew[4], Daniel[3], Thomas William[2], Unknown[1]) was born 23 December 1953. He married **Teresa Brewington.**

It is unclear whether Brewington is Teresa's maiden name.

Children of Wade Simmons and Teresa Brewington are:

2701 i. **Lisa Simmons.** She **married Jeff Unknown.**

Her year of birth is found as 1987 and 13 October 1975.

2702 ii. **Austin Simmons**, born 19 January 1985.

1920. Donna Ann Simmons (Donald Ray[7], Jathronia[6] Holland, Robert Mitchell[5], Matthew[4], Daniel[3], Thomas William[2], Unknown[1]) was born 17 February 1960 in Clinton, Sampson County, North Carolina. She married **Mike Boone** 01 July 1979 in Sampson County, North Carolina. He was born 27 January 1958 in Sampson County.

Child of Donna Simmons and Mike Boone is:

2703 i. **Dawn Michelle Boone**, born 14 March 1982 in Sampson County, North Carolina.

1921. Kenneth Ray Simmons (Donald Ray[7], Jathronia[6] Holland, Robert Mitchell[5], Matthew[4], Daniel[3], Thomas William[2], Unknown[1]) was born 23 December 1972 in

Clinton, Sampson County, North Carolina. He married **Jaime Kelly.**

Child of Kenneth Simmons and Jaime Kelly is:

2704 i. **Dylan Ray Simmons**, born 08 July 2000 in Cape Fear Valley Hospital, Fayetteville, Cumberland County, North Carolina.

1923. Fletcher Evans Hall (Thomas Iverson[7], Mary J.[6] Williams, John E.[5], Tomzelle[4] Culbreth, Mary[3] Holland, Thomas William[2], Unknown[1]) was born 25 January 1914 in Dismal Township, Sampson County, North Carolina. He married **Hermie Maggie Hall**, daughter of Marshall Hall and Ennis Sessoms. She was born 30 March 1919 in Little Coharie Township in Sampson County.

Children of Fletcher Hall and Hermie Hall are:

1) **Berline Hall** was born 17 December 1935 in Little Coharie Township, Sampson County, North Carolina.

2) **Arthur David Hall** was born 28 July 1937 in Dismal Township, Sampson County, North Carolina.

3) **Nellie Marie Hall** was born 22 December 1938 in Dismal Township.

4) **Bonnie Catherine Hall** was born 18 January 1941 in Dismal Township. She married **John L. Matthews** who was born 21 June 1940 in Dismal Township, son of Murphy Nelson Matthews and Roden Elberta Page and they have two children.

\+ 2705 5) **Janice Faye Hall**, born 07 March 1942 in Dismal Township, Sampson County, North Carolina was the fifth child of Fletcher Hall and Hermie Hall.

1940. Cleveland N. Williams (Nora[7], Reason Raiford Robinson[6], John E.[5], Tomzelle[4] Culbreth, Mary[3] Holland, Thomas William[2], Unknown[1]) was born 20 August 1911, and died 20 June 1975 in Clinton, North Carolina. He married **Stella Mae Hair**. She was born 15 September 1909 in Cumberland County, North Carolina, and died 19 July 1993.

Cleveland and Stella were buried in Union Grove Baptist Church Cemetery on Vander Road west of Rebel City, Sampson County, North Carolina.

Child of Cleveland Williams and Stella Hair is:

2706 i. **Nancy Laverne Williams**, born 07 June 1940 in Erwin, Harnett County, North Carolina. She married **Donnie Freeman Barefoot** 18 June 1961 in Union Grove Baptist Church, Sampson County, North Carolina; born 23 March 1940 in Mingo Township, Sampson County, North Carolina.

1945. Blake Oliver Collier (Louida[7] Williams, Nathan[6], Joel[5], Tomzelle[4] Culbreth, Mary[3] Holland, Thomas William[2], Unknown[1]) was born 25 August 1895, and died 01 August 1973 in Fayetteville, Cumberland County, North Carolina. He married **Lela Vira Williams** 27 July 1927 in Fayetteville, Cumberland County, North Carolina, daughter of Daniel Williams and Susan Page. She was born 16 June 1897, and died 16 March 1978 in Fayetteville in Cumberland County.

Child is listed above under (1087) Lela Vira Williams.

1952. Bonnie Kaye Williams (John Lewis[7], Nathan[6], Joel[5], Tomzelle[4] Culbreth, Mary[3] Holland, Thomas William[2], Unknown[1]) was born 09 August 1915 in Black River Township, Cumberland County, North Carolina. She married **Allen Ray Naylor** 19 October 1938 in Buies Creek, Harnett County, North Carolina, son of Rassie R. Naylor and Lula Jackson (Lula Jane Jackson). He was born 18 August 1915 in Herrings Township, Sampson County, North Carolina, and died 25 October 1993 in Conyers, Georgia.

Children of Bonnie Williams and Allen Naylor are:

2707 i. **Rev. Larry Gray Naylor,** born 08 July 1942 in Dunn, Harnett County, North Carolina.

He lived at one time, in Conyers, Georgia.

2708 ii. **Robert Naylor,** born 11 April 1949 in Dunn, Harnett County, North Carolina.

1977. Ruth Starling (Luther Washington[7], Mary Catherine[6] Williams, Isaac[5], Tomzelle[4] Culbreth, Mary[3] Holland, Thomas William[2], Unknown[1]) was born 16 November 1915 in Mingo Township, Sampson County, North Carolina. She married **Herman Warren** 02 November 1935. He was born 10 July 1915 in Mingo Township, Sampson County, North Carolina.

Children of Ruth Starling and Herman Warren are:

\+ 2709 i. **Janet Rose Warren,** born 07 December 1938 in Mingo Township, Sampson County, North Carolina.

\+ 2710 ii. **Dixie Ruth Warren,** born 23 May 1945 in Dunn, Harnett County, North Carolina.

\+ 2711 iii. **Herman Denning Warren,** born 07 January 1950 in Dunn, Harnett County.

1978. Avis Starling (Luther Washington[7], Mary Catherine[6] Williams, Isaac[5], Tomzelle[4] Culbreth, Mary[3] Holland, Thomas William[2], Unknown[1]) was born 26 November 1919 in Mingo Township, Sampson County, North Carolina. She married **Wilton Ezzell Jackson** Before 1941, son of Simpson Jackson and Malissie Porter. He was born 03 April 1916 in Mingo Township, Sampson County, North Carolina.

Children of Avis Starling and Wilton Jackson are:

\+ 2712 i. **Luther Simpson Jackson,** born 24 September 1941 in Dunn, Harnett County, North Carolina.

2713 ii. **Diane Jackson,** born 24 January 1946 in Dunn, Harnett County; died 18 October 1948 in Mingo Township, Sampson County, North Carolina.

Burial: Mt. Elam Baptist Church, Sampson County, North Carolina.

\+ 2714 iii. **Wanda Baggett Jackson,** born 14 January 1953 in Dunn, Harnett County, North Carolina.

1980. Don Ella Starling (Luther Washington[7], Mary Catherine[6] Williams, Isaac[5], Tomzelle[4] Culbreth, Mary[3] Holland, Thomas William[2], Unknown[1]) was born 16 September 1922 in Black River Township, Cumberland County, North Carolina. She married **Paul Bernard Drew, Sr.** About 1943. He was born 02 August 1920 in Harrellson County, Georgia, and died 05 January 1987 in Chapel Hill, Orange County, North Carolina.

Don Ella and Paul Bernard were divorced. He was buried in Greenwood Cemetery, Dunn, Harnett County, North Carolina.

Children of Don Starling and Paul Drew are:

2715 i. **Paul Bernard Drew, Jr.,** born 11 December 1943 in Dunn, Harnett County, North Carolina; died 22 December 1943.

Burial: Greenwood Cemetery, Dunn, Harnett County.

2716 ii. **Paulette Drew,** born 10 December 1945. She married Donald Thero Barefoot 17 August 1968 in Harnett County, North Carolina; born 25 June 1942 in Dunn, Harnett County, North Carolina.

1981. Doris Elaine Starling (Luther Washington[7], Mary Catherine[6] Williams, Isaac[5], Tomzelle[4] Culbreth, Mary[3] Holland, Thomas William[2], Unknown[1]) was born about 1926. She married **Richard Jackson Carr** 20 December 1947 in Falcon, Cumberland County, North Carolina, son of Hubert Carr and Annie Jackson. He was born about 1927.

Children of Doris Starling and Richard Carr are:

2717 i. **Unidentified Carr.**

2718 ii. **Unidentified Daughter Carr.**

It is said that this daughter married a "White" who was the son of Paul White, Jr.

1995. Hiram Roberson Starling, Jr. (Hiram Roberson[7], Mary Catherine[6] Williams, Isaac[5], Tomzelle[4] Culbreth, Mary[3] Holland, Thomas William[2], Unknown[1]) was born 23 April 1923 in Nash County, North Carolina, and died 18 July 1980 in Erwin, Harnett County, North Carolina. He married **Dorothy Louise Morris.**

Hiram Roberson and Dorothy Louise were divorced. He was buried in Antioch Baptist Church Cemetery.

Children of Hiram Starling and Dorothy Morris are:

\+ 2719 i. **Sidney Jo Starling,** born 21 May 1951.

\+ 2720 ii. **Tracy Ann Starling,** born 09 February 1954.

1997. George Washington Starling (Hiram Roberson[7], Mary Catherine[6] Williams, Isaac[5], Tomzelle[4] Culbreth, Mary[3] Holland, Thomas William[2], Unknown[1]) was born 07 March 1931 in Rocky Mount Township, Nash County, North Carolina, and died 06 November 1977. He married **Opal Lee Hackler.** She was born 28 December 1936, and died 19 September 1975.

George Washington and Opal were buried in Scotland Neck Cemetery, Scotland Neck, Halifax County, North Carolina

Children of George Starling and Opal Hackler are:

2721 i. **George Wesley Starling,** born 06 May 1958. He married Teresa Dale Powell; born 21 July 1960.

2722 ii. **Michelle Starling,** born 08 March 1961; died 10 March 1961.

2723 iii. **Andrew Roberson Starling,** born 14 December 1970.

1998. Straudia Almeta Wrench (Fletcher E.[7], Lovdie Ann[6] Williams, Isaac[5], Tomzelle[4] Culbreth, Mary[3] Holland, Thomas William[2], Unknown[1]) was born 07 March 1912, and died 11 October 1995. She married **James Hinton Autry** 25 August 1937, son of William Mac Autry and Janie Maxwell. He was born 11 November 1911, and died 09 March 1993.

Straudia Almeta and James Hinton were buried in Minson M. Williams Family Cemetery at the northeast corner of Dunn Road (SR 1002 and SR 1441. Dismal Township, Sampson County, North Carolina

Children are listed above under (1311) James Hinton Autry.

1999. Quinton Randall Wrench (Fletcher E.[7], Lovdie Ann[6] Williams, Isaac[5], Tomzelle[4] Culbreth, Mary[3] Holland, Thomas William[2], Unknown[1]) was born 11 March 1914, in Dismal Township, Sampson County, and died 25 August 1994. He married **Rochelle Naylor**, daughter of Miles Aaron Naylor, Jr. and Florida Butler. She was born 28 October 1921 in Herrings Township, Sampson County, North Carolina.

Burial: Minson M. Williams Family Cemetery at the northeast corner of Dunn Road (SR 1002 and SR 1441. Dismal Township, Sampson County, North Carolina.

Children of Quinton Wrench and Rochelle Naylor are:

\+ 2724 i. **Patricia Ann Wrench**, born 12 October 1940.

\+ 2725 ii. **James Philip Wrench**, born 13 September 1942 in Roseboro, North Carolina.

2726 iii. **Bettie Jo Wrench**, born 28 February 1945 in Roseboro, North Carolina. She married **Larry Jonathan Barnhill**; born about 1947.

Betty Jo and her husband have one adopted son.

2003. Roy Vernon Tew, Sr. (Cornelia[7] Wrench, Lovdie Ann[6] Williams, Isaac[5], Tomzelle[4] Culbreth, Mary[3] Holland, Thomas William[2], Unknown[1]) was born 14 June 1904, and died 15 October 1953. He married **Nannie Kathryn Ennis**. She was born about 1902.

Roy Tew may have died in Windsor, Bertie County, North Carolina. He was buried in Baptist Chapel Church Cemetery on Baptist Chapel Road, Sampson County, North Carolina.

Children of Roy Tew and Nannie Ennis are:

2727 i. **Roy Vernon Tew, Jr.**, born 10 September 1927.

2728 ii. **Beulah Kathryn Tew**, born 10 October 1928.

2729 iii. **Nancy Cornelia Tew** was born 30 June 1933 in Dismal Township and died 12 December 1973 in Jacksonville, Florida. In Dillon, South Carolina on 29 December 1954, she married **Arthur Carlyle McPhail** who was born 11 October 1934 in Dismal Township, Sampson County, North Carolina, son of **LORENZO CURTIS MCPHAIL** and **LETTIE LEE MATTHEWS**. He served in the United States Coast Guard. Nancy was buried at Baptist Chapel Cemetery. She and Arthur had four children.

1) **DEBRA SUSAN MCPHAIL**, the first child was born 28 May 1955 in Fayetteville and married **HOWARD HOUSE** , a gruduate of the University of North Carolina at Chapel Hill School of Pharmacy.

2) **A daughter, a twin**, was born 12 May 1956, died 13 May 1956 and was buried in Baptist Chapel Cemetery.

3) **A son, a twin, was** born 12 May 1956, died 13 May 1956 and was buried in Baptist Chapel Cemetery.

4) **KATHRYN LEE MCPHAIL**, the youngest child of Nancy Cornelia Tew and Arthur Carlyle McPhail was born 3 May 1959.

2730 iv. **Lynn C. Tew.**

2005. Earl GladstoneTew (Cornelia[7] Wrench, Lovdie Ann[6] Williams, Isaac[5], Tomzelle[4] Culbreth, Mary[3] Holland, Thomas William[2], Unknown[1]) was born 25 November 1907 in Sampson County, North Carolina, and died 10 September 1940 in Dismal Township, Sampson County, North Carolina. He married **Minnie Ellen Tew** 04 July 1932, daughter of Lewis Tew and Julia Jernigan. She was born 05 September 1910 in Sampson County, North Carolina, and died 03 October 1983.

Earl Gladstone and Minnie were buried in Baptist Chapel Church Cemetery on Baptist Chapel Road (SR 1455), Sampson County, North Carolina.

Children of Earl Tew and Minnie Tew are:

2731 i. **Edna EarleTew**, born 07 March 1934.

2732 ii. **Jackie Cooper Tew**, born 01 September 1938. He married Annette Audry Smith; born 26 September 1938 in Little Coharie Township, Sampson County, North Carolina.

2733 iii. **Jerry Grandon Tew**, born 28 April 1940.

2008. May Dee Tew (Cornelia[7] Wrench, Lovdie Ann[6] Williams, Isaac[5], Tomzelle[4] Culbreth, Mary[3] Holland, Thomas William[2], Unknown[1]) was born 12 May 1912 in Sampson County, North Carolina. She married **James Earl Draughon** 19 May 1934 in Dillon, Dillon County, South Carolina. He was born 30 October 1912 in Sampson County, North Carolina, and died 18 July 1986 in Fayetteville, Cumberland County, North Carolina.

James Earl was buried in Baptist Chapel Church Cemetery on Baptist Chapel Road, Sampson County, North Carolina.

Child of May Tew and James Draughon is:

\+ 2734 i. **Mildred Joyce Draughon,** born 24 December 1934 in Fayetteville, Cumberland County, North Carolina.

2010. Wyman A. Tew (Cornelia[7] Wrench, Lovdie Ann[6] Williams, Isaac[5], Tomzelle[4] Culbreth, Mary[3] Holland, Thomas William[2], Unknown[1]) was born 02 January 1914, and died 12 December 1980. He married **Eunice Gainey** 15 August 1935, daughter of Gillead Gainey and Emma Starling. She was born 09 August 1913.

Wyman was buried in Baptist Chapel Church Cemetery on Baptist Chapel Road (SR 1455), Sampson County, North Carolina.

Children of Wyman Tew and Eunice Gainey are:

+ 2735 i. **Mary Ann Tew,** born 10 June 1936.

+ 2736 ii. **Wilma Gainey Tew,** born 16 August 1938.

+ 2737 iii. **Billie Frances Tew,** born 30 October 1940.

+ 2738 iv. **Sarah Lou Tew,** born 12 October 1951.

2011. Desmon Shelton Tew (Cornelia[7] Wrench, Lovdie Ann[6] Williams, Isaac[5], Tomzelle[4] Culbreth, Mary[3] Holland, Thomas William[2], Unknown[1]) was born 21 August 1915 in Dismal Township, Sampson County, North Carolina. He married **Louise Warren,** daughter of Walter Warren and Claudia Warren. She was born 23 July 1919 in Mingo Township in Sampson County.

Children of Desmon Tew and Louise Warren are:

2739 i. **Linda Louise Tew.**

+ 2740 ii. **James Shelton Tew,** born 10 January 1950.

2741 iii. **Daughter Tew.**

2013. Theophilus Beaufort Tew, Jr. (Cornelia[7] Wrench, Lovdie Ann[6] Williams, Isaac[5], Tomzelle[4] Culbreth, Mary[3] Holland, Thomas William[2], Unknown[1]) was born 13 September 1919 in Dismal Township, Sampson County, North Carolina, and died 13 March 1992. He married **Alma Edwards Butler** 07 July 1940 in Salemburg, Sampson County, North Carolina, daughter of Giddie Butler and Sallie Sinclair. She was born 06 June 1922 in Honeycutts Township in Sampson County.

Theophilus was called "Offie, Jr." He was buried in Salemburg Cemetery, Salemburg, Sampson County, North Carolina.

Children of Theophilus Tew and Alma Butler are:

2742 i. **Jean Butler Tew,** born 02 October 1941 in Roseboro, North Carolina.

+ 2743 ii. **Offie B. Tew III,** born 26 July 1947 in Honeycutts Township, Sampson County, North Carolina. Theophilus Beaufort Tew II was known as "Offie."

2744 iii. **Unnamed Son Tew.**

2015. Sylvia Ann Tew (Cornelia[7] Wrench, Lovdie Ann[6] Williams, Isaac[5], Tomzelle[4] Culbreth, Mary[3] Holland, Thomas William[2], Unknown[1]) was born 02 October 1923 in Dismal Township, Sampson County, North Carolina. She married **David Preston Gainey** 04 October 1947 in Sampson County, son of Gillead Gainey and Emma Starling. He was born 06 March 1920 in Flea Hill Township, Cumberland County, North Carolina.

Children of Sylvia Tew and David Gainey are:

2745 i. **Denise Gainey**.

2746 ii. **Dwight David Gainey** was born 07 August 1953 and married **Rhonda Strickland** on 20 November 1977.

2016. Trixy Hilda Matthews (Viola Beatrice[7] Williams, Daniel[6], Isaac[5], Tomzelle[4] Culbreth, Mary[3] Holland, Thomas William[2], Unknown[1]) was born 16 August 1919 in Dismal Township, Clement, Sampson County, North Carolina, and died 19 November 1983 in Durham, North Carolina. She married **Lorian Vaden Carroll, Sr.** 29 June 1942 in Sampson County, North Carolina, son of John Carroll and Flora Tew. He was born 08 September 1913 in Sampson County, North Carolina, and died 24 April 1976.

Children of Trixy Matthews and Lorian Carroll are:

2749 i. **Lorian Vaden Carroll, Jr.**, born 02 April 1943.

2750 ii. **John Williams Carroll**, born 10 August 1945.

2025. Lubie Egbert Williams (Joel Judson[7], Daniel[6], Isaac[5], Tomzelle[4] Culbreth, Mary[3] Holland, Thomas William[2], Unknown[1]) was born 29 August 1928 in Fayetteville, Cumberland County, North Carolina, and died 02 December 1984 in Durham, North Carolina. He married **Annie Marie Smith** 21 December 1946 in South Carolina.

Lubie Egbert was buried in Williams Family Cemetery northeast of Clement in Dismal Township near Dunn Road (SR1002) at SR1441 in Sampson County, North Carolina.

Children of Lubie Williams and Annie Smith are:

2751 i. **Virgie Marie Williams**, born 14 October 1952 in Durham, North Carolina.

2752 ii. **Lana Jeanette Williams**, born 02 August 1956 in Orange County, Florida. She married Unknown Kepler.

2753 iii. **Larry Williams**.

2754 iv. **Connie Williams**.

2026. Bonnie Dell Williams (Joel Judson[7], Daniel[6], Isaac[5], Tomzelle[4] Culbreth, Mary[3] Holland, Thomas William[2], Unknown[1]) was born 26 November 1930 in Herrings Township, Sampson County, North Carolina. She married **David J. Pope** 24 June 1950 in Clinton, Sampson County, North Carolina. He was born about 1929.

Children of Bonnie Williams and David Pope are:

2755 i. **Bonnie Faye Pope,** born 21 July 1953 in Turkey, North Carolina.

2756 ii. **Janet Gray Pope,** born 21 July 1954 in Turkey, North Carolina.

2065. Jacqueline Williams (Raeford James^{7}, Sarah Eliza^{6}, Isaac^{5}, Tomzelle^{4} Culbreth, Mary^{3} Holland, Thomas William^{2}, Unknown^{1}) was born 06 October 1937. She married **James Curtis Haire,** son of James Hair and Flonnie Carter. He was born 30 March 1935 in Cedar Creek Township, Cumberland County, North Carolina, and died 23 July 1980 in Fayetteville in Cumberland County.

James Curtis was buried in Stedman Church of God Prophecy Cemetery, Stedman, North Carolina.

Children of Jacqueline Williams and James Haire are:

2757 i. **Anthony Curtis Haire,** born 20 November 1960 in Fayetteville, Cumberland County, North Carolina. He married **Linda Ann McLeod** 16 May 1982; she was born 02 May 1963 in Fayetteville, Cumberland County, North Carolina.

2758 ii. **Sandra Gail Haire,** born 28 November 1963 in Fayetteville, Cumberland County, North Carolina, married **Robert Joseph Nelson, Jr.** 16 July 1982; he was born 18 February 1964 in Fayetteville, Cumberland County, North Carolina.

2076. Dicie Catherine Williams (Thera Wesley^{7}, Sarah Eliza^{6}, Isaac^{5}, Tomzelle^{4} Culbreth, Mary^{3} Holland, Thomas William^{2}, Unknown^{1}) was born 17 October 1932 in Dismal Township, Sampson County, North Carolina. She married **Guthrie Odell Ivey.** He was born 19 September 1930 in Mingo Township, Sampson County, North Carolina.

Children of Dicie Williams and Guthrie Ivey are:

\+ 2759 i. **Joan Marie Ivey,** born 10 November 1959 in Fayetteville, Cumberland County, North Carolina.

2760 ii. **Melinda Faye Ivey,** born 04 December 1961 in Clinton, Sampson County, North Carolina.

\+ 2761 iii. **Kathryn Ann Ivey,** born 07 May 1965 in Clinton, Sampson County.

2077. Donald Elvin Williams (Thera Wesley^{7}, Sarah Eliza^{6}, Isaac^{5}, Tomzelle^{4} Culbreth, Mary^{3} Holland, Thomas William^{2}, Unknown^{1}) was born 13 March 1936 in Dismal Township, Sampson County, North Carolina, and died 14 February 1986 in Fayetteville, Cumberland County, North Carolina. He married **(1) Pennie Winkle Wrench** 26 January 1957 in Stedman, North Carolina. She was born 19 September 1938 in Dismal Township, Sampson County, North Carolina. He married **(2) Della Gertrude** after 1970.

Donald Elvin was buried in Baptist Chapel Cemetery near Autryville, North Carolina.

Children of Donald Williams and Pennie Wrench are:

2762 i. **Debra Lea Williams**, born 07 July 1957 in Roseboro, North Carolina. She married **Maynard Martin Brock**.

2763 ii. **Vivian Sue Williams**, born 15 July 1959 married **Cullen Gatlin**.

2764 iii. **Penny Madonna Williams**, born 07 November 1968 in Clinton, Sampson County, North Carolina. She married **Robert Alan Tew** 24 August 1991 in Baptist Chapel Church near Autryville, Sampson County, North Carolina; he was born 06 December 1964 in Clinton, Sampson County, North Carolina.

2765 iv. **Pamela Denise Williams**, born 29 October 1970 in Fayetteville, Cumberland County, North Carolina.

2079. Thomas Elva Williams (Thera Wesley[7], Sarah Eliza[6], Isaac[5], Tomzelle[4] Culbreth, Mary[3] Holland, Thomas William[2], Unknown[1]) was born 06 April 1943. He married **Jo Ann Strickland** 16 January 1965 in Baptist Chapel Church near Autryville, Sampson County, North Carolina. She was born 21 June 1948.

Children of Thomas Williams and Jo Strickland are:

\+ 2766 i. **Tammy Ann Williams**, born 12 February 1966 in Dunn, Harnett County, North Carolina.

\+ 2767 ii. **Kimberly Ruth Williams**, born 27 March 1974 in Clinton Cemetery, Clinton, Sampson County, North Carolina.

2081. Augustus Merrill McLaurin, Sr. (Alma May[7] Bain, John C.[6], Susan Ann[5] Williams, Tomzelle[4] Culbreth, Mary[3] Holland, Thomas William[2], Unknown[1]) was born 08 January 1919 in Cumberland County, North Carolina. He married **Thelma Kathryn Melson**. She was born 1920 in Hartsville, South Carolina.

Children of Augustus McLaurin and Thelma Melson are:

2768 i. **Melton Alonza McLaurin**, born 11 July 1941 in Cumberland County, North Carolina.

2769 ii. **Sarah Juanita McLaurin**, born 09 April 1943 in Cumberland County, married **Walter Bennett Parrish, Jr.** 25 August 1968 in Cumberland County, North Carolina; he was born 24 May 1945 in Rocky Mount, North Carolina.

\+ 2770 iii. **Norman Timothy McLaurin**, born 13 March 1945 in Cumberland County.

2771 iv. **Kathryn Maxine McLaurin**, born 08 April 1947 married **Thomas Wade Anders** 14 July 1968; he was born 26 September 1940 in Cumberland County, North Carolina.

2772 v. **Augustus Merrill McLaurin, Jr.**, born 25 August 1951 in Cumberland County.

2773 vi. **Angela Renee McLaurin**, born 31 August 1956 in Cumberland County, North Carolina, married **Charles Adam Giles** 21 August 1977 who was born 24 August 1955.

2091. Fred Allen Faircloth (Flossie[7] Autry, William Ashford[6], Daniel[5], Millzy Adelme[4] Culbreth, Mary[3] Holland, Thomas William[2], Unknown[1]) was born 30 November 1937 in Little Coharie Township, Sampson County, North Carolina. He married **Mary Cherl**

Vinson, daughter of Rufus Vinson and Bettie Hair. She was born 18 June 1940 in Beaver Dam Township, Cumberland County, North Carolina.

Cherl Vinson may have been called "Cherry." A date of 18 June 1942 is also shown for her birth.

Child of Fred Faircloth and Mary Vinson is:

2774 i. **Charles Allen Faircloth**, born 18 September 1959 in Clinton, Sampson County, North Carolina.

2099. Charles Edwin Tyndall (Lula Mae[7] Autry, James Love[6], Daniel[5], Millzy Adelme[4] Culbreth, Mary[3] Holland, Thomas William[2], Unknown[1]) was born 25 October 1944 in Sampson County, North Carolina. He married **Heidi Jane Jackson** 04 July 1965 in Dillon, South Carolina, daughter of Elvin Sikes Jackson and Virginia Lee Horne. She was born 18 September 1948 in Sampson County, North Carolina.

Child of Charles Tyndall and Heidi Jackson is:

\+ 2775 i. **Cheryl Elaine Tyndall**, born 13 April 1968 in Clinton, Sampson County, North Carolina.

2102. Billy Carrol Draughon (Mildred[7] Autry, James Love[6], Daniel[5], Millzy Adelme[4] Culbreth, Mary[3] Holland, Thomas William[2], Unknown[1]) was born 06 May 1940 in Honeycutts Township, Sampson County, North Carolina. He married **Jeanetta Carroll Young** 30 August 1958 in Dillon, South Carolina, daughter of James Young and Trecia Carroll. She was born 29 February 1940 in Honeycutts Township, Sampson County, North Carolina.

Children of Billy Draughon and Jeanetta Young are:

2776 i. **Rhonda Carole Draughon**, born 04 November 1960 in Raleigh, North Carolina.

\+ 2777 ii. **James Randall Draughon**, born 07 June 1962 in Raleigh, North Carolina.

2778 iii. **Gina Renee Draughon**, born 09 January 1974 in Monroe, North Carolina. She married **John Michael Carroll**; born 03 March 1969.

2103. Lattie Draughon, Jr. (Mildred[7] Autry, James Love[6], Daniel[5], Millzy Adelme[4] Culbreth, Mary[3] Holland, Thomas William[2], Unknown[1]) was born 07 May 1942 in Pearces Mill Township, Cumberland County, North Carolina. He married **(1) Marylynn Maraupt** 06 April 1963 in Omak, Washington. She was born About 1945. He married **(2) Carol J. Penton** 30 August 1966. She was born 16 July 1946.

Child of Lattie Draughon and Marylynn Maraupt is:

2779 i. **Delmus Ray Draughon**, born 13 May 1964 in Omak, Washington.

Children of Lattie Draughon and Carol Penton are:

\+ 2780 i. **Brenda Jean Draughon**, born 23 December 1967 in Aurora, Colorado.

2781 ii. **Dwayne Lance Draughon**, born 30 December 1970 in Aurora, Colorado.

2105. Judy Ann Draughon (Mildred^7 Autry, James Love^6, Daniel^5, Millzy Adelme^4 Culbreth, Mary^3 Holland, Thomas William^2, Unknown^1) was born 09 March 1946 in Fayetteville, Cumberland County, North Carolina. She married **Samuel Franklin Parker** 30 September 1962 in South Carolina, son of Sam Parker and Eva Jackson. He was born 21 October 1942 in Roseboro, Sampson County, North Carolina.

Children of Judy Draughon and Samuel Parker are:

2782 i. **Judy Michelle Parker**, born 13 June 1963 in Clinton, Sampson County, North Carolina. She married **David Muse**; born 25 July 1969.

2783 ii. **Havene Parker**, born 24 February 1966 in Clinton, Sampson County, North Carolina. She married **Scott Chaisson**; born 13 March 1971.

\+ 2784 iii. **Karen Faye Parker**, born 04 June 1967 in Monroe, North Carolina.

2107. Jannie Dorcas Autry (Leroy^7, James Love^6, Daniel^5, Millzy Adelme^4 Culbreth, Mary^3 Holland, Thomas William^2, Unknown^1) was born 11 August 1949 in Roseboro, Sampson County, North Carolina. She married **Aaron Ellis Fisher** June 1970 in Sampson County, North Carolina, son of Charlie Fisher and Grace Williams. He was born 02 January 1948 in Little Coharie Township, Sampson County, North Carolina, and died 06 May 1990 in Chapel Hill, North Carolina.

Aaron Ellis was buried in Sunrise Memorial Gardens Cemetery, between Salemburg and Roseboro, North Carolina.

Children of Jannie Autry and Aaron Fisher are:

2785 i. **Julie Dorcas Fisher**, born 03 December 1973 in Fayetteville, Cumberland County, North Carolina.

2786 ii. **Derek Aaron Fisher**, born 08 August 1976 in Fayetteville, Cumberland County.

2787 iii. **Daryl Alan Fisher**, born 08 August 1976 in Fayetteville, Cumberland County, North Carolina.

2110. Marion Faircloth (Repsie^7 Williams, Susan Anner^6, Rebecca Elizabeth^5 Autry, Millzy Adelme^4 Culbreth, Mary^3 Holland, Thomas William^2, Unknown^1) was born 28 May 1905, and died 30 December 1980 in Clinton, North Carolina. He married **Callie Mae Hall,** daughter of JOHN O. HALL and MARGARET JANE WILLIS. She was born 24 September 1904, and died 15 May 1974 in Route 2, Autryville, North Carolina. Seven children

Marion Faircloth and Callie Mae Hall were buried in the Charles A. Williams Family Cemetery (now Jesse Williams Family Cemetery) near SR 1418 and SR 1233, Sampson County, North Carolina.

Children of Marion Faircloth and Callie Hall are:

i. **GEORGE VERNON FAIRCLOTH**, the first child of Marion Faircloth and Callie Hall was born 20 June 1924 in Sampson County and died 11 September 1984 in Fayetteville, Cumberland County, North Carolina. He married 5 April 1947 **CHRISTELLE STRICKLAND** who was born 7 April 1927 in Harnett County, North Carolina. George served as a private in the United states Army in World War II. He was buried in the Charles A. Williams Family Cemetery.

George and Christelle have six children.

1) **GEORGE VERNON FAIRCLOTH, JR.**, was born 5 May 1948 in Roseboro and married **WILMA LEE JACKSON** who was born about 1951. She was the daughter **of HERMAN JACKSON** and **LOIS MCLEOD**. George, Jr., and Wilma have four children: **SIRENA JEAN FAIRCLOTH, VIRGINIA CHRISTELLE FAIRCLOTH, JENNIFER LEE FAIRCLOTH** and **CALLIE VERONICA FAIRCLOTH**.

2) **SYVAL JEAN FAIRCLOTH** was the second child and was born 15 May 1950.

3) **a STILLBORN SON**.

4) **TOMMY D. FAIRCLOTH.**

5) **MIKE FAIRCLOTH**.

6) **ALDA MAE FAIRCLOTH** was the sixth and youngest known child of George Vernon Faircloth and Christelle Strickland.

2788 ii. **Nova Kermit Faircloth**, the second child of Marion Faircloth and Callie Hall, was born 24 October 1926 in Sampson County, North Carolina, and died 25 May 1928 in Sampson County, North Carolina. He was buried in the Charles A. Williams Family Cemetery on a dirt road through field off SR 1418 about 1.1 mile from SR 1233 in Sampson County, North Carolina

iii. **GARLAND NARION FAIRCLOTH**, the third child was born 15 June 1929 in Roseboro and died 1 December 1987 in Clinton as GARLAND MARION FAIRCLOTH. He married **VELMA LEWIS** who was born 28 August 1927 and they had two children: **GLENDA GAIL FAIRCLOTH** who is probably the Glenda Gail who married **John Wesley Holland, Jr.**; see them elsewhere in this book. **GARLAND DUANE FAIRCLOTH** was the second child of Garland and Velma.

iv. **ESTER MALY FAIRCLOTH**, the fourth child of Marion Faircloth and Callie Hall was born 8 March 1933 in Little Coharie Township in Sampson County. She married **JAMES RODELL HALL**, son of LONNIE JAMES HALL and MARY CATHERINE SESSOMS. He was born 21 July 1929 in Little Coharies Township. They have six children.

1) **SHIRLEY ANN HALL** was born 21 February 1954 in Clinton and married **EULIE ALLEN AUTRY** who was born 21 January 1951 in Roseboro, son of ORIS AUTRY and ERNESTINE WEST. Two children: **JASON ALLEN AUTRY** and **GRETCHIN ANN AUTRY.**

2) **RONALD JAMES HALL** was born 19 July 1956 in Clinton and married **SHIRLEY ELAINE WILLIAMS** who was born 5 September 1959 in Clinton, daughter of JEAN DAVID WILLIAMS and MYRTICE MARIE GOODRICH. One child: **MALISSA ANN HALL.**

3) **TONY HALL** was born 12 January 1959 in Clinton.

4) A STILLBORN SON on 15 April 1961.

5) **MARTY HALL** was born 28 July 1965 in Clinton.

6) **REBECCA KAY HALL** was born 7 October 1966 in Clinton.

v. **DAVID ASHLEY FAIRCLOTH**, the fifth child was born 22 September 1936 in Little Coharie Township, Sampson County.

vi. **BENNIE ROSE FAIRCLOTH** was the sixth child of Marion and Callie and may not have married.

vii. **JOHNNY CARSON FAIRCLOTH** was the seventh and youngest known child of Marion Faircloth and Callie Hall. He was born about 1946 and married **JUDY MAE MARTIN** who was born about 1948 in South Carolina. They have two children. **JODI PATRICIA FAIRCLOTH** and **CONNIE FAYE FAIRCLOTH**.

2111. Roland Sessoms (Mollie[7] Williams, Susan Anner[6], Rebecca Elizabeth[5] Autry, Millzy Adelme[4] Culbreth, Mary[3] Holland, Thomas William[2], Unknown[1]) was born 23 April 1915, and died 16 September 1978. He married **Celester Wise**, daughter of James Noah Wise and Alice Jackson. She was born 02 January 1916, and died 28 October 1990.

Roland and Celester were buried in the Mt. Carmel Church of God Cemetery near Autryville, North Carolina.

Children of Roland Sessoms and Celester Wise are:

+ 2789 i. **Bobby Lee Sessoms**, born 01 August 1939; died 02 April 2001.

+ 2790 ii. **Billy Roland Sessoms**, born 14 May 1942 in Roseboro, North Carolina.

+ 2791 iii. **Jackie Lester Sessoms**, born 27 October 1944 in Roseboro, North Carolina.

+ 2792 iv. **Brenda Sessoms**, born 16 November 1946.

2112. Nina Sessoms (Mollie[7] Williams, Susan Anner[6], Rebecca Elizabeth[5] Autry, Millzy Adelme[4] Culbreth, Mary[3] Holland, Thomas William[2], Unknown[1]) was born 13 September 1918, and died 21 October 1982 in Sampson County, North Carolina. She married **(1) Willie Cornelius Faircloth, Sr.**, son of William Faircloth and Sarah Autry. He was born 01 June 1902, and died 11 May 1972. She married **(2) W. Friday Faircloth**. He was born 03 September 1926, and died 05 February 1993 in Sampson County, North Carolina.

Nina, Willie and W. Friday were buried in the Autry Cemetery about 0.8 mile from Halls Crossroads on dirt path called Calico Lane in Sampson County, North Carolina.

Children of Nina Sessoms and Willie Faircloth are:

+ 2793 i. **Cyrus James Faircloth I**, born 27 March 1936 in Little Coharie Township, Sampson County, North Carolina.

+ 2794 ii. **Resson Oliver Faircloth, Sr.**, born 10 August 1937.

2795 iii. **Minnie Frances Faircloth**, born 07 November 1939; died 07 August 1955 in Dismal Township, Sampson County, North Carolina.

She drowned and was buried in the Raiford Autry Family Cemetery about 0.8 mile from Halls Crossroads on dirt path called Calico Lane in Sampson County, North Carolina.

2796 iv. **Joel Layton Faircloth**, born 26 August 1943; died 04 October 1996. He married (1) **Betty Carol Hall**; born 06 June 1943. He married (2) **Marilyn Pope**; born 30 October 1941.

He was buried in the Autry Cemetery on Calico Lane (dirt path about 0.8 mile from Halls Crossroads. Sampson County, North Carolina.

+ 2797 v. **Rosa Faye Faircloth**, born 07 August 1947.

2798 vi. **Willie Cornelius Faircloth, Jr.**, born 12 February 1954. He married Sandra Jean Pope; born 06 April 1955. Two children.

2114. Ira Gladys Williams (George W.[7], Susan Anner[6], Rebecca Elizabeth[5] Autry, Millzy Adelme[4] Culbreth, Mary[3] Holland, Thomas William[2], Unknown[1]) was born 22 May 1915, and died 02 February 1940 in Little Coharie Township, Sampson County, North Carolina. She married **Fleet Lee Sessoms**, son of McCager Sessoms and Margaret Hall. He was born 02 July 1904, and died 02 December 1961 in Fayetteville, North Carolina.

Ira Gladys was buried in the Charles A. Williams Family Cemetery (now Jesse Williams Family Cemetery) near SR 1418 and SR 1233, Sampson County, North Carolina. Fleet Lee was buried in Saunders Fisher Cemetery about three miles sw of Roseboro, North Carolina.

Children of Ira Gladys Williams and Fleet Sessoms are:

\+ 2799 i. **Sallie Fleet Sessoms,** born 17 November 1934 in Little Coharie Township, Sampson County, North Carolina; died 09 May 1968 in Near Autryville, North Carolina. She married **EARL FRANKLIN SESSOMS**, son of LEONARD JASPER SESSOMS and DOLLY MARGARET FAIRCLOTH. He was born 20 August 1931 and died 13 January 1975 in Clinton, North Carolina. Sallie was buried in the Charles A. Williams Family Cemetery (now Jesse Williams Family Cemetery) near SR 1418 and SR 1233 in Sampson County, North Carolina. Earl was buried in the LEMUEL SESSOMS Family Cemetery located east of Peniel Pentecostal Holiness Church. Sallie and Earl have one child, **DONNIE FLEET SESSOMS** who was born 10 September 1952 and married **KAREN SESSOMS**, daughter of BILLY ROLAND SESSOMS and ELIZABETH ARMEALLIA FAIRCLOTH.

ii. **GEORGE RUDOLPH SESSOMS**, the second child of Gladys and Fleet, was born 16 January 1937 in Little Coharie Township and married on 18 August 1963 in Autryville, **HELEN GREY SESSOMS**, daughter of PAUL SESSOMS and MILDRED ADELL SMITH. She was born 14 April 1944 in Sampson County. One child, **RUDOLPH LEE SESSOMS**.

iii. **SHERMAN MCCAGER SESSOMS**, the third child of Ira Gladys Williams and Fleet Sessoms was born 2 February 1940 in Little Coharie Township. He married 19 February 1961 in Sampson County, **JOYCE JEAN BAREFOOT** who was born 24 July 1941 in Mingo Township, daughter of LOFTON BAREFOOT and ELSIE HODGES. Two children: **SHIRLEY DENISE SESSOMS** and **MELANIE DARLENE SESSOMS**.

2120. Marvin Keith Sessoms (Eulie Marvin[7], Cordelia[6] Autry, Miles Costin[5], Millzy Adelme[4] Culbreth, Mary[3] Holland, Thomas William[2], Unknown[1]) was born 01 October 1957 in Clinton, Sampson County, North Carolina. He married **Rhonda Sue Malpass**, daughter of Norris Malpass and Alice Lockamy. She was born 10 December 1957 in Clinton, Sampson County, North Carolina.

Child of Marvin Sessoms and Ronda Malpass is:

2800 i. **Shannon Leigh Sessoms**, born 06 February 1978 in Clinton, Sampson County, North Carolina.

2129. Sarah Catherine Faircloth (Lessie Dolan[7] Autry, William Isaac[6], Martha Jane[5] Culbreth, Isaac[4], Mary[3] Holland, Thomas William[2], Unknown[1]) was born 15 March 1918 in Dismal Township, Sampson County, North Carolina, and died 02 April 1999. She married

Corvie Peterson, son of Eddie Peterson and Emma Naylor. He was born 04 September 1915, and died 18 March 1999.

The date of March 16, 1918 is also found for Sarah's birth. She and Corvie were buried in Baptist Chapel Church Cemetery on Baptist Chapel Road (SR 1455), Sampson County, North Carolina.

Children of Sarah Faircloth and Corvie Peterson are:

\+ 2801 i. **Billy Gerald Peterson,** born 08 March 1943 in Dismal Township, Sampson Caounty, North Carolina.

2802 ii. **Janet Faye Peterson,** born 18 January 1945 in Dismal Township, Sampson Caounty, North Carolina.

Janet's first name is given as "Janice" on page 154 of Professor Bundy's book.

2130. Cladie May Faircloth (Lessie Dolan[7] Autry, William Isaac[6], Martha Jane[5] Culbreth, Isaac[4], Mary[3] Holland, Thomas William[2], Unknown[1]) was born 06 September 1920 in Dismal Township, Sampson County, North Carolina, and died 22 May 1992. She married **Ernest Stanley Carter** 28 September 1945 in Dillon, South Carolina, son of Benjamin Carter and Joanna Carter. He was born 16 October 1921.

Child of Cladie Faircloth and Ernest Carter is:

2803 i. **Robert Stanley Carter,** born 15 July 1946. He married **Shirley Gail Long**; born 13 May 1949.

2132. William Raeford Faircloth (Lessie Dolan[7] Autry, William Isaac[6], Martha Jane[5] Culbreth, Isaac[4], Mary[3] Holland, Thomas William[2], Unknown[1]) was born 19 April 1925 in Dismal Township, Sampson County, North Carolina, and died 30 August 1969 near Autryville, North Carolina. He married **Ruth Elaine Hair,** daughter of George Washington Hairr and Ida Florence Beasley. She was born 21 June 1929 in Dismal Township, Sampson County, North Carolina.

William Raeford served as a PFC in the 407th Infantry. 102nd Division in World War II. He was buried in Bethabara United Methodist Church Cemetery in Dismal Township, Sampson County, North Catolina.

Children of William Faircloth and Ruth Hair are:

\+ 2804 i. **William Keith Faircloth,** born 17 January 1950 in Roseboro, North Carolina.

\+ 2805 ii. **Larry Arnold Faircloth,** born 05 November 1951.

\+ 2806 iii. **James Wyman Faircloth,** born 06 June 1955.

2133. Lena Earline Faircloth (Lessie Dolan[7] Autry, William Isaac[6], Martha Jane[5] Culbreth, Isaac[4], Mary[3] Holland, Thomas William[2], Unknown[1]) was born 27 October 1927 in Dismal Township, Sampson County, North Carolina. She married **Herbert Thornley**

Buck, Jr. 14 June 1950 in Dillon, South Carolina. He was born 26 December 1926, and died 26 February 1977 in Fayetteville, North Carolina.

Child of Lena Faircloth and Herbert Buck is:

2807 i. **Lisa Ann Buck,** born 01 September 1963 in Fayetteville, North Carolina. She married **Harrell Corbett Sessoms, Jr.** 20 September 1986 in Salem United Methodist Church, Cumberland County, North Carolina; born 26 June 1963.

2134. Letha Ethelyne Autry (McKinley Blackmon[7], William Isaac[6], Martha Jane[5] Culbreth, Isaac[4], Mary[3] Holland, Thomas William[2], Unknown[1]) was born 21 November 1923, and died 22 September 1991 in Chapel Hill, Orange County, North Carolina. She married **Aaron Cannady** 26 January 1952, son of William David Cannady and Arizona T. Holland. He was born 04 December 1923 in Dismal Township, Sampson County, North Carolina, and died 26 November 1996 in Fayetteville, Cumberland County, North Carolina.

Her certificate of death gives 21 November 1924 for her date of birth and 29 September 1991 for her death.

Letha Ethelyne and Aaron were buried in Union Grove Baptist Church Cemetery on SR 1438 one mile west of Rebel City, Sampson County, North Carolina.

Child is listed above under (1561) Aaron Cannady.

2138. Ida Elizabeth Howard (Pauline[7] Royal, Jennette Ida[6] Culbreth, John[5], Daniel Maxwell[4], Mary[3] Holland, Thomas William[2], Unknown[1]) was born 12 September 1916 in Salemburg, Sampson County, North Carolina, and died 05 December 1989. She married **William James Freeman, Jr.** 03 August 1934. He was born 23 September 1912, and died 31 July 1986.

Ida Elizabeth and William James were buried in Salemburg Cemetery, Bearskin Road, Salemburg, North Carolina.

Children of Ida Howard and William Freeman are:

\+ 2808 i. **Pauline Roberta Freeman,** born 06 July 1935.

2809 ii. **James Stewart Freeman,** born 22 September 1954. He married **Janet Norton.**

Professor Bundy notes that James Stewart Freeman married **Elaine Silver** who was born September 05, 1956. She was the daughter of Maria Silver, born 8 September 1930 and David Silver, born 19 October 1935.

2141. Ernest Vance McCall (Viola[7] Royal, Jennette Ida[6] Culbreth, John[5], Daniel Maxwell[4], Mary[3] Holland, Thomas William[2], Unknown[1]) was born 11 June 1927 in Lisbon Township, Bladen County, North Carolina. He married **Annie Lee Kinney**. She was born 15 February 1931 in Dunn, Harnett County, North Carolina.

Annie Lee was called "Dunn." Page 25 in the source for the Culbreth and Autry data notes that Annie's maiden name was "DUNN." "Kinney" may have been the name from a prior marriage.

Children of Ernest McCall and Annie Kinney are:

2810 i. **Beth Ann McCall,** born 09 November 1955.

2811 ii. **Dale Lee McCall,** born 08 February 1957. She married **Mark Stuart Middleton.**

2812 iii. **Todd Ernest McCall,** born 24 November 1960 in Fayetteville, Cumberland County, North Carolina.

2143. Mary Ida McCall (Viola[7] Royal, Jennette Ida[6] Culbreth, John[5], Daniel Maxwell[4], Mary[3] Holland, Thomas William[2], Unknown[1]) was born 05 September 1937 in Lenoir County, North Caroline. She married **Walter Richard Spell** 06 October 1956. He was born 24 June 1933 in Little Coharie Township, Sampson County, North Carolina.

Children of Mary McCall and Walter Spell are:

\+ 2813 i. **Mary Mac Spell,** born 30 July 1957.

\+ 2814 ii. **Vara Leigh Spell,** born 15 February 1960 in Clinton, Sampson County, North Carolina.

\+ 2815 iii. **Paige Elizabeth Spell,** born 12 October 1963.

2145. Eleanor Catherine Royal (John Robert[7], Jennette Ida[6] Culbreth, John[5], Daniel Maxwell[4], Mary[3] Holland, Thomas William[2], Unknown[1]) was born 30 April 1931 in Honeycutts Township, Sampson County, North Carolina. She married **John Paul Brazell.** He was born 26 December 1929 in Richland County, South Carolina, and died 07 March 1984 in Clinton, Sampson County, North Carolina.

Children of Eleanor Royal and John Brazell are:

2816 i. **Eleanor Victoria Brazell,** born 25 June 1954 in Fort Bragg, Cumberland County, North Carolina. She married **Walter Clark Howard.**

2817 ii. **John Robert Brazell,** born 08 January 1957.

2818 iii. **Elizabeth Marie Brazell,** born 19 November 1958.

\+ 2819 iv. **Mary Elaine Brazell,** born 19 November 1958.

2820 v. **David Wayne Brazell,** born 08 April 1960.

2821 vi. **Glenda Kay Brazell,** born 04 July 1962 in Clinton, Sampson County, North Carolina.

2147. Vertile Estelle Tew (Percy Maxwell[7], Roberta[6] Culbreth, John[5], Daniel Maxwell[4], Mary[3] Holland, Thomas William[2], Unknown[1]) was born 20 October 1922 in Honeycutts Township, Sampson County, North Carolina. She married **Charlie Delwin Autry,** son of Tom Autry and Levonia Honeycutt. He was born 28 July 1925 in Dismal Township,

Sampson County, North Carolina, and died 28 February 1984 in Route 1, Autryville, North Carolina.

Charlie Delwin was buried in Baptist Chapel Cemetery near Autryville, North Carolina.

Children of Vertile Tew and Charlie Autry are:

2822 i. **Charles Linwood Autry**, born 03 March 1944 in Dismal Township, Sampson County, North Carolina; died 13 December 1945.

He was buried in Baptist Chapel Cemetery near Autryville, North Carolina.

\+ 2823 ii. **Earthy Delwin Autry**, born 01 December 1946 in Dismal Township, Sampson County, North Carolina; died 05 October 1996.

2824 iii. **Winfred Eric Autry**, born 12 December 1954 in Roseboro, North Carolina.

\+ 2825 iv. **Ray Lynn Autry**, born 11 December 1955 in Roseboro, North Carolina.

2148. Lambert Dixon Tew (Percy Maxwell[7], Roberta[6] Culbreth, John[5], Daniel Maxwell[4], Mary[3] Holland, Thomas William[2], Unknown[1]) was born 08 August 1924 in Sampson County, North Carolina, and died 14 October 1961 in Fayetteville, Cumberland County, North Carolina. He married **Geraldine Vann.**

Lambert served as a private in the United States Army in World War II. He was buried in Baptist Chapel Cemetery, Clement Community near Autryville, North Carolina.

Children of Lambert Tew and Geraldine Vann are:

2826 i. **Graham Tew**, born 14 October 1945; died 24 January 1946 in Dismal Township, Sampson County, North Carolina. He is buried in Baptist Chapel Cemetery, Clement Community near Autryville, North Carolina.

2827 ii. **Dianne Tew**, born about 1943.

2149. Loren Maxwell Tew (Percy Maxwell[7], Roberta[6] Culbreth, John[5], Daniel Maxwell[4], Mary[3] Holland, Thomas William[2], Unknown[1]) was born 08 September 1926 in Honeycutts Township, Sampson County, North Carolina, and died 20 November 1956 in Charlotte, North Carolina. He married **May Ernestine Tew** Before 1947, daughter of Ernest Tew and Vinnie Jackson. She was born 03 February 1930.

He served as a PFC in Company E, 17th Infantry in WW II. He died in Charlotte after an automobile accident near Crouse, North Carolina, and was buried in Baptist Chapel Cemetery, Clement Community near Autryville, North Carolina.

One source provides 21 October 1927 for May's birth.

Children of Loren Tew and May Tew are:

2828 i. **Loren Wayne Tew**, born 28 March 1947 in Dunn, Harnett County, North Carolina.

\+ 2829 ii. **Hilbert Gordon Tew**, born about 1953.

2150. Leland Elmo Tew (Percy Maxwell[7], Roberta[6] Culbreth, John[5], Daniel Maxwell[4], Mary[3] Holland, Thomas William[2], Unknown[1]) was born 13 March 1930 in Sampson County, North Carolina. He married **Willa Grey Honeycutt**, daughter of Roscus Honeycutt and Rebeckah Olivia Culbreth. She was born 21 January 1929 in Sampson County, North Carolina.

One source shows "Leland Elmo Tew" for his first name; Mr. Bundy's book provides 'Lelon.'

Children are listed above under (1245) Willa Grey Honeycutt.

2151. Ruthey Faydene Tew (Percy Maxwell[7], Roberta[6] Culbreth, John[5], Daniel Maxwell[4], Mary[3] Holland, Thomas William[2], Unknown[1]) was born 22 October 1936 in Sampson County, North Carolina. She married **Joe Robert Matthews, Sr.**, son of John Matthews and Mary Faircloth. He was born 10 February 1929 in Dismal Township, Sampson County, North Carolina.

'Ruthy' is also found for her first name.

Child of Ruthey Tew and Joe Matthews is:

2830 i. **Joe Robert Matthews, Jr.**, born 15 October 1954 in Sampson County, North Carolina. He married **Debbie McLemore**; born 26 November 1954.

2152. Judy Ann Tew (Percy Maxwell[7], Roberta[6] Culbreth, John[5], Daniel Maxwell[4], Mary[3] Holland, Thomas William[2], Unknown[1]) was born 15 March 1942 in Sampson County, North Carolina. She married **George Washington Hairr, Jr.** before 1960, son of George Washington Hairr, Sr., and Sarah Hall. He was born 04 July 1937 in Sampson County, North Carolina.

Child of Judy Tew and George Hairr is:

2831 i. **Felicia Ann Hairr**, born 21 April 1960.

2153. Doris Lee Tew (Ernest Blackman[7], Roberta[6] Culbreth, John[5], Daniel Maxwell[4], Mary[3] Holland, Thomas William[2], Unknown[1]) was born 21 September 1932. She married **(1) Nash Samuel Thornton** about 1947. He was born 26 October 1927, and died November 1965. She married **(2) William McLeod** about 1949. He was born about 1930. She married **(3) Lee Daniel McLeod** about 1950. He was born about 1923. She married **(4) Unknown Godwin** about 1960.

Child of Doris Tew and Nash Thornton is:

\+ 2832 i. **Shirley Ann Thornton**, born 30 September 1948.

Child of Doris Tew and Lee Daniel McLeod:

2833 i. **Larry Wayne McLeod, Jr.**, born 06 December 1950.

Children of Doris Tew and Unknown Godwin:

2837 i. **Charlotte Lee McLeod Godwin**, born 04 February 1953.

2838 ii. **Lee Daniel McLeod Godwin**, born 06 March 1956.

2154. James Blackman Tew (Ernest Blackman[7], Roberta[6] Culbreth, John[5], Daniel Maxwell[4], Mary[3] Holland, Thomas William[2], Unknown[1]) was born 12 October 1933, and died 19 June 1976 in Fayetteville, Cumberland County, North Carolina. He married **(1) Kathlene Sloan** About 1951. She was born About 1934. He married **(2) Jodie Maxine Gardner McLaurin** About 1956. She was born 05 December 1937 in Eastover Township, Cumberland County, North Carolina.

James Blackman Tew was buried in Cumberland Memorial Cemetery, Fayetteville, North Carolina.

Child of James Tew and Kathlene Sloan is:

2839 i. **Stanley Mitchell Tew**, born 26 April 1952.

Children of James Tew and Jodie McLaurin are:

2840 i. **David Tew**, born About 1957.

2841 ii. **Patricia Jane Tew**, born 27 August 1959.

2842 iii. **Deborah Kay Tew**, born 05 March 1961.

The 3 February 1961 is also found for her birth.

2843 iv. **Samuel Wayne Tew**, born 13 October 1966.

2155. Robert Glenn Tew (Ernest Blackman[7], Roberta[6] Culbreth, John[5], Daniel Maxwell[4], Mary[3] Holland, Thomas William[2], Unknown[1]) was born 13 March 1936 in North Carolina, and died 24 March 1992 in Hope Mills, Cumberland. He married **Janie Marie Benner** who was born about 1937.

Children of Robert Tew and Janie Benner are:

2844 i. **Joyce Ann Tew**, born 22 June 1958 in Fayetteville, Cumberland County, North Carolina; died 14 January 1959 in Fayetteville, Cumberland County.

She was buried in Cumberland Cemetery, Fayetteville, North Carolina.

2845 ii. **Michael Glenn Tew**, born 08 August 1959 in Fayetteville, North Carolina.

2846 iii. **Claudia Jeanette Tew**, born 16 October 1963 in Fayetteville, Cumberland County, North Carolina.

2847 iv. **Betty Ruth Tew**, born 23 June 1965.

2156. Laura Ernestine Tew (Ernest Blackman[7], Roberta[6] Culbreth, John[5], Daniel Maxwell[4], Mary[3] Holland, Thomas William[2], Unknown[1]) was born 08 August 1937. She married **(1) George Knox Pomeroy**. He was born 14 January 1933 in Tennessee, and died 10 December 1991. She married **(2) E. J. Griffin** who was born about 1935.

Children of Laura Tew and George Pomeroy are:

2848 i. **Rhonda Gail Pomeroy,** born 09 August 1953.

2849 ii. **Kenneth Knox Pomeroy,** born 20 October 1954.

\+ 2850 iii. **Patricia Dean Pomeroy,** born 12 April 1956 in Hope Mills, Cumberland.

2157. Hardy Gaine Tew (Ernest Blackman[7], Roberta[6] Culbreth, John[5], Daniel Maxwell[4], Mary[3] Holland, Thomas William[2], Unknown[1]) was born 22 September 1939 in North Carolina, and died 14 December 1991 in Fayetteville, Cumberland County, North Carolina. He married **Peggy Vonne Love,** daughter of Herman Love and Levon Unknown who was born about 1944.

Professor Bundy shows 'Caine' for his middle name.

Child of Hardy Tew and Peggy Love is:

2851 i. **Sandra Vonne Tew,** born 09 March 1962.

2158. William Gibson Tew (Ernest Blackman[7], Roberta[6] Culbreth, John[5], Daniel Maxwell[4], Mary[3] Holland, Thomas William[2], Unknown[1]) was born 26 June 1945. He married **Brenda Karen Jones**. She was born about 1949.

Children of William Tew and Brenda Jones are:

2852 i. **Unknown Tew,** born 22 July 1965.

2853 ii. **Karen Michelle Tew,** born 28 June 1973.

2159. William Blackman Tew (John[7], Roberta[6] Culbreth, John[5], Daniel Maxwell[4], Mary[3] Holland, Thomas William[2], Unknown[1]) was born 13 October 1929. He married **Mavis Lancaster.**

Child of William Tew and Mavis Lancaster is:

\+ 2854 i. **Anthony Clark Tew,** born 03 July 1948 in Cumberland County, North Carolina.

2160. Joyce Grey Tew (John[7], Roberta[6] Culbreth, John[5], Daniel Maxwell[4], Mary[3] Holland, Thomas William[2], Unknown[1]) was born 25 September 1935. She married **(1) William Edward Pate**. He was born 13 December 1933. She married **(2) William N. Smith** After 1963. It isn't clear whether William N. Smith is her first or second husband.

Children of Joyce Tew and William Pate are:

2855 i. **Dianna Pate,** born about 1959. She is deceased.

2856 ii. **William Michael Pate,** born 03 February 1963.

2161. John Maxie Tew (John[7], Roberta[6] Culbreth, John[5], Daniel Maxwell[4], Mary[3] Holland, Thomas William[2], Unknown[1]) was born 10 April 1940. He married **(1) Paquita Ann Fowler** About 1959. She was born 26 April 1941. He married **(2) Shirley Ann Russ** After 1961. She was born 01 December 1942.

Children of John Tew and Paquita Fowler are:

2857 i. **Mark Steven Tew,** born 06 April 1960.

2858 ii. **Pamela Grace Tew,** born 02 November 1961.

2163. Marcie Roberta Cashwell (Sudie Viola[7] Tew, Roberta[6] Culbreth, John[5], Daniel Maxwell[4], Mary[3] Holland, Thomas William[2], Unknown[1]) was born 26 July 1934. She married **Allen Leon Grimes** 25 June 1959 in Stedman, Cumberland County, North Carolina. He was born between 18 August 1924 - 1929, and died 26 July 1987.

Children of Marcie Cashwell and Allen Grimes are:

2859 i. **Unknown Child Grimes,** born About 1960.

2860 ii. **Sharon Dale Grimes,** born 14 August 1964 in Fayetteville, Cumberland County, North Carolina.

2166. Erline Cashwell (Sudie Viola[7] Tew, Roberta[6] Culbreth, John[5], Daniel Maxwell[4], Mary[3] Holland, Thomas William[2], Unknown[1]) was born 10 February 1942 in Cumberland County, North Carolina. She married **Joseph Lindsey Arrant, Sr.** He was born about 1944.

Children of Erline Cashwell and Joseph Arrant are:

2861 i. **Rebecca Lynn Arrant,** born 13 February 1962.

2862 ii. **Joseph Lindsey Arrant, Jr.,** born 14 November 1963.

2168. Thomas Andrew Cashwell (Sudie Viola[7] Tew, Roberta[6] Culbreth, John[5], Daniel Maxwell[4], Mary[3] Holland, Thomas William[2], Unknown[1]) was born 02 December 1953 in Fayetteville, Cumberland County, North Carolina. He married **Kathy Lynn Autry** who was born 07 October 1956.

Children of Thomas Cashwell and Kathy Autry are:

2863 i. **Crystal Alison Cashwell,** born 09 December 1981.

2864 ii. **Ryan Thomas Cashwell,** born 20 March 1986.

2172. Nancy Delores Tew (E. Hardy Blackman[7], Roberta[6] Culbreth, John[5], Daniel Maxwell[4], Mary[3] Holland, Thomas William[2], Unknown[1]) was born 17 January 1944 in Cumberland County, North Carolina. She married **Robert Ebson Madison** 18 November 1977 in Fayetteville, Cumberland County, North Carolina. He was born 27 May 1929.

Children of Nancy Tew and Robert Madison are:

2865 i. **Daniel Robert Madison,** born 10 October 1979 in Cumberland County, North Carolina.

2866 ii. **Michael Anthony Madison,** born 12 December 1980 in Cumberland County, North Carolina.

2174. Candace Ann Tew (E. Hardy Blackman[7], Roberta[6] Culbreth, John[5], Daniel Maxwell[4], Mary[3] Holland, Thomas William[2], Unknown[1]) was born 15 April 1950 in Cumberland County, North Carolina. She married **(1) L. Jones.** She married **(2) Edward Earl Britt** 24 June 1973 in Cumberland County, North Carolina. He was born 15 January 1953 in Robeson County, North Carolina.

Child of Candace Tew and Edward Britt is:

2867 i. **Mackenie Leigh Britt,** born 14 January 1978.

2175. Virginia Alice Royal (Lela Pearl[7] Matthews, Virginia[6] Culbreth, John[5], Daniel Maxwell[4], Mary[3] Holland, Thomas William[2], Unknown[1]) was born 09 April 1914 in Dismal Township, Sampson County, North Carolina, and died about 1978 in Harnett County, North Carolina. She married **Daniel Winton Byrd.** He was born about 1913 in Harnett County, North Carolina.

Professor Bundy has her born in March 1914. Another source names her "Alice Virginia Royal."

Child of Virginia Royal and Daniel Byrd is:

\+ 2868 i. **Betty Hope Byrd,** born 04 April 1935.

2176. Mary Evelyn Royal (Lela Pearl[7] Matthews, Virginia[6] Culbreth, John[5], Daniel Maxwell[4], Mary[3] Holland, Thomas William[2], Unknown[1]) was born 14 October 1917 in Dismal Township, Sampson County, North Carolina. She married **Ernest Clayton Tart,** son of Lewis Tart and Hepsey Taylor. He was born 10 November 1905 in Harnett County, North Carolina, and died 26 August 1973 in Harnett County, North Carolina.

Ernest Clayton was buried in Devotional Gardens in Dunn.

Children of Mary Royal and Ernest Tart are:

\+ 2869 i. **Janet Faye Tart,** born 28 January 1938.

\+ 2870 ii. **Phyllis Renthia Tart,** born 20 September 1943.

2177. Etta Marie Royal (Lela Pearl[7] Matthews, Virginia[6] Culbreth, John[5], Daniel Maxwell[4], Mary[3] Holland, Thomas William[2], Unknown[1]) was born 23 February 1924 in Orange County, North Carolina. She married **James Otto Lambert I**. He was born 31 August 1915 in Orange County, North Carolina.

Etta may have been born in Sampson County, North Carolina.

Children of Etta Royal and James Lambert are:

2871 i. **Laura Gaye Lambert**, born 13 April 1954 in Harnett County, North Carolina. She married **James Ruffin Stanley;** born 25 November 1949.

No Children.

2872 ii. **James Otto Lambert II**, born 18 July 1956 in Harnett County, North Carolina married **Jeanette Mary Hoffman**; born 23 November 1956.

No Children.

2178. Eva Dale Royal (Lela Pearl[7] Matthews, Virginia[6] Culbreth, John[5], Daniel Maxwell[4], Mary[3] Holland, Thomas William[2], Unknown[1]) was born 27 February 1926 in Harnett County, North Carolina. She married **Carl Robinson Jernigan, Jr.** who was born 07 February 1924.

Eva's middle name is also spelled "Dell".

Child of Eva Royal and Carl Jernigan is:

2873 i. **Jeffery Steven Jernigan**, born 26 November 1955. He married **Jo Beth Vaughn**; born 29 May 1955.

2179. James Rosker Royal, Jr. (Lela Pearl[7] Matthews, Virginia[6] Culbreth, John[5], Daniel Maxwell[4], Mary[3] Holland, Thomas William[2], Unknown[1]) was born 04 May 1932 in Sampson County, North Carolina. He married **Betty Jean Sutton** who was born 12 October 1938 in Johnston County, North Carolina.

Children of James Royal and Betty Sutton are:

2874 i. **James Rosker Royal III**, born 01 June 1957. He married Danna Montanez.

2875 ii. **Donna Marie Royal**, born 13 January 1967.

2876 iii. **David Sutton Royal**, born 23 September 1969.

2180. Donald Gray Royal (Lela Pearl[7] Matthews, Virginia[6] Culbreth, John[5], Daniel Maxwell[4], Mary[3] Holland, Thomas William[2], Unknown[1]) was born 29 May 1934 in Harnett County, North Carolina. He married **Gerleen Hester** who was born 09 November 1935.

Donald's middle name is also spelled "Grey."

Children of Donald Royal and Gerleen Hester are:

2877 i. **Kathryn Gaye Royal**, born 01 September 1959.

2878 ii. **Karen Renee Royal**, born 19 October 1961.

2879 iii. **Angela Sheree Royal**, born 25 December 1962.

2880 iv. **Marsha Ann Royal**, born 14 November 1966.

2181. Donnie Ray Royal (Lela Pearl[7] Matthews, Virginia[6] Culbreth, John[5], Daniel Maxwell[4], Mary[3] Holland, Thomas William[2], Unknown[1]) was born 29 May 1934 in Harnett County, North Carolina. He married **Janet Joan Walker** who was born 27 March 1935.

Children of Donnie Royal and Janet Walker are:

2881 i. **Rebecca Gwyn Royal**, born 18 November 1959.

2882 ii. **Shannon Donn Royal**, born 07 October 1964.

2883 iii. **Marcus Jack Royal**, born 25 April 1966.

2184. Edna Louise Matthews (Irma G.[7], Virginia[6] Culbreth, John[5], Daniel Maxwell[4], Mary[3] Holland, Thomas William[2], Unknown[1]) was born 15 December 1926 in Dismal Township, Sampson County, North Carolina. She married **Jesse Heron Tew** 21 September 1946 in South Carolina, son of Lewis Tew and Mamie Williams. He was born 16 December 1919 in Dismal Township, Sampson County, North Carolina, and died 12 July 1977.

His name is sometimes shown as "Jessie Herom Tew." Burial: Union Grove Baptist Church Cemetery on Vander Road west of Rebel City, Sampson County, North Carolina.

Child of Edna Matthews and Jesse Tew are:

\+ 2885 ii. **Susan Gail Tew**, born 16 July 1947 in Roseboro, North Carolina, married **Gary Dale Harris** who was born 19 May 1950 in Arkansas.

2190. Lucy Frances Hales (Ola Ann[7] Matthews, Virginia[6] Culbreth, John[5], Daniel Maxwell[4], Mary[3] Holland, Thomas William[2], Unknown[1]) was born 17 October 1934. She married **James Evolyn Lewis**, Sr. son of Evolyn Neal Lewis and Mary Louise Culbreth. He was born 18 February 1932 in Honeycutt Township, Sampson County, North Carolina.

Children of Lucy Hales and James Lewis are:

2886 i. **Melody Kim Lewis**, born 11 June 1960 in Clinton, Sampson County, North Carolina. She married **Edward Wayne Honeycutt** 06 October 1984 in Hall's United Methodist Church; He was born 16 July 1961 in Clinton, Sampson County, North Carolina.

JAMES EVOLYN LEWIS, JR. was the second child of Lucy annd James.

PAULA LEWIS was the third child of Lucy and James.

2191. Julius Augustus Hales (Ola Ann[7] Matthews, Virginia[6] Culbreth, John[5], Daniel Maxwell[4], Mary[3] Holland, Thomas William[2], Unknown[1]) was born 17 April 1936 in Little Coharie Township, Sampson County, North Caorlina. He married **Retha Mae Carter**, daughter of David Carter and Lona Carter. She was born about 1938.

Child of Julius Hales and Retha Carter is:

2887 i. **Rose Marie Hales**, born 26 June 1960.

2192. Dorothy Jean Vann (Lula Jane[7] Matthews, Virginia[6] Culbreth, John[5], Daniel Maxwell[4], Mary[3] Holland, Thomas William[2], Unknown[1]) was born 02 July 1933. She married **(1) Jessie Thomas Cox, Sr.** She married **(2) Arnold Smith**. He died 1999.

Children of Dorothy Vann and Jessie Cox are:

2888 i. **Mary Ann Cox**.

2889 ii. **Jessie Thomas Cox, Jr.**

2194. Reba Nadene Wrench (Mabel Inez[7] Matthews, Lena Mae[6] Culbreth, John[5], Daniel Maxwell[4], Mary[3] Holland, Thomas William[2], Unknown[1]) was born 17 October 1927 in Dismal Township, Sampson County, North Carolina. She married **Arnold Kirby Lockamy** before 1949, son of Jesse Lockamy and Rosie Daniels. He was born 10 September 1930 in Erwin, Harnett County, North Carolina.

'Nadene' is also spelled "Nadine.

Children of Reba Wrench and Arnold Lockamy are:

\+ 2890 i. **Edith Karen Lockamy**, born 09 August 1949.

\+ 2891 ii. **Reaber Doris Lockamy**, born 23 December 1950 in Erwin, Harnett County, North Carolina.

\+ 2892 iii. **Wilma Leigh Lockamy**, born 07 May 1955 in Erwin, Harnett County, North Carolina.

2893 iv. **Arnold Ray Lockamy**, born 07 October 1959 in Erwin, Harnett County, North Carolina.

2198. James Huston Matthews (Adrian Huston[7], Lena Mae[6] Culbreth, John[5], Daniel Maxwell[4], Mary[3] Holland, Thomas William[2], Unknown[1]) was born 20 May 1946 in Cumberland County, North Carolina. He married **Mary Nelms**. She was born About 1946.

Children of James Matthews and Mary Nelms are:

2894 i. **Janet Lynn Matthews**, born 09 September 1964.

2895 ii. **James Kelly Matthews**, born 17 May 1970.

2199. Peggy Diane Matthews (Adrian Huston[7], Lena Mae[6] Culbreth, John[5], Daniel Maxwell[4], Mary[3] Holland, Thomas William[2], Unknown[1]) was born 07 May 1947. She married **James H. Etheridge** 08 January 1966 in Cumberland County, North Carolina. He was born 22 October 1942 in Halifax County, North Carolina.

Children of Peggy Matthews and James Etheridge are:

2896 i. **Michelle Etheridge**, born 07 May 1969.

2897 ii. **Stephanie Etheridge**, born 07 May 1971.

2898 iii. **Randolph Etheridge**, born 25 May 1974 in Cumberland County, North Carolina.

2200. Tommy Leroy Matthews (Adrian Huston[7], Lena Mae[6] Culbreth, John[5], Daniel Maxwell[4], Mary[3] Holland, Thomas William[2], Unknown[1]) was born 23 December 1949 in Cumberland County, North Carolina. He married **Judy Diana Godwin** who was born 17 June 1952 in Cumberland County, North Carolina.

Child of Tommy Matthews and Judy Godwin is:

2899 i. **Tammy Diane Matthews**, born 13 April 1971 in Cumberland County, North Carolina.

2201. Reba Gray Tew (Glaspy Elwood[7], Annie Vara[6] Culbreth, John[5], Daniel Maxwell[4], Mary[3] Holland, Thomas William[2], Unknown[1]) was born 23 June 1938 in Little Coharie Township, Sampson County, North Carolina. She married **Larry Ray Godwin, Sr.** 30 June 1956 in Baptist Chapel Church near Autryville, Sampson County, North Carolina. He was born 16 April 1936.

Children of Reba Tew and Larry Godwin are:

\+ 2900 i. **Larry Ray Godwin, Jr.**, born 24 July 1957 in Fayetteville, Cumberland County, North Carolina.

2901 ii. **Sheila Kathryn Godwin**, born 28 March 1963 in Fayetteville, Cumberland County.

2902 iii. **Valerie Sue Godwin**, born 27 July 1964 in Fayetteville, Cumberland County.

2903 iv. **Curtis Martin Godwin**, born 09 July 1966 in Fayetteville, Cumberland County, North Carolina.

2202. William Elwood Tew (Glaspy Elwood[7], Annie Vara[6] Culbreth, John[5], Daniel Maxwell[4], Mary[3] Holland, Thomas William[2], Unknown[1]) was born 09 March 1945 in Roseboro, North Carolina. He married **Dixie Faye Fann** 01 September 1963 in Dismal Township, Sampson County, North Carolina. She was born 09 November 1945 in Sampson County, North Carolina.

Child of William Tew and Dixie Fann is:

2904 i. **William Cary Tew**, born 22 April 1966 in Clinton, Sampson County, North Carolina. He married **Doris Michelle Warren** 19 November 1988 in Lee's Chapel, Plain View Township, Sampson County, North Carolina; born 09 April 1969 in Clinton, Sampson County, North Carolina.

2203. Ida Grey Tew (Leland Elmo[8], Percy Maxwell[7], Roberta[6] Culbreth, John[5], Daniel Maxwell[4], Mary[3] Holland, Thomas William[2], Unknown[1]) was born 23 April 1948 in Sampson County, North Carolina. She married **James Wayne Autry** 06 January 1968 in Dismal Township, Sampson County, North Carolina, son of James Autry and Ella Hairr. He was born 06 October 1947.

Other sources show 06 Sep 1946 for his date of birth.

Child of Ida Tew and James Autry is:

2905 i. **Kevin Wayne Autry**, born 29 May 1971; died 06 April 1977.

Burial: Joe Moore Hill Cemetery, Sampson County, North Carolina

2204. Ruthie Rebeckah Tew (Leland Elmo[8], Percy Maxwell[7], Roberta[6] Culbreth, John[5], Daniel Maxwell[4], Mary[3] Holland, Thomas William[2], Unknown[1]) was born 02 May 1956 in Sampson County, North Carolina. She married **John Woodrow Spell, Jr.** Before 1976, son of John Woodrow Spell, Sr. and Ellen Dudley. He was born 12 March 1952 in Dunn, North Carolina.

The source for Cannady family data spells her middle name 'Rebecca.'

Child of Ruthie Tew and John Spell is:

2906 i. **Tina Michele Spell**, born 18 October 1976 in Sampson County, North Carolina.

2208. Shirley Joy McLellan (Earl Autry[7], Clyde Cleveland[6] Culbreth, William[5], Daniel Maxwell[4], Mary[3] Holland, Thomas William[2], Unknown[1]) was born 19 December 1939. She married **Robert Saunders Tew, Sr.** 23 October 1956.

Children of Shirley McLellan and Robert Tew are:

2907 i. **Robert Saunders Tew, Jr.**, born 08 October 1957.

2908 ii. **Darrin Earl Tew**, born 23 March 1964.

2909 iii. **Steven Bart Tew**, born 09 September 1966.

2212. Alma Doris Spell (Iula Vern[7] Hall, Jannette Maxwell[6] Culbreth, Daniel L.[5], Daniel Maxwell[4], Mary[3] Holland, Thomas William[2], Unknown[1]) was born 08 June 1933 in Little Coharie Township, Sampson County, North Carolina. She married **(1) John Newton Honeycutt** 02 May 1953, son of George Honeycutt and Meta Honeycutt. He was born 30 November 1929 in Honeycutts Township in Sampson County and died 19 May 1975 near Roseboro, North Carolina. She married **(2) Talford Lofton Autry** 10 November 1978 in Dismal Township, Sampson County, North Carolina, son of Tom Autry and Levonia Honeycutt. He was born 13 November 1930 in Dismal Township in Sampson County.

John Newton Honeycutt was buried in the Honeycutt Cemetery on Huntley School Road, Sampson County, North Carolina.

Child of Alma Spell and John Honeycutt is:

2910 i. **Phoebe Denise Honeycutt**, born 16 December 1954. She married **Gary Rheudon Butler**; born 30 March 1954 in Roseboro, Sampson County, North Carolina.

Gary Rheudon Butler and Phoebe Denise Honeycutt were divorced in February 1981.

2215. Willie Gibson Lewis (Mary Louise^7 Culbreth, William James^6, Daniel L.^{5}, Daniel Maxwell^4, Mary^3 Holland, Thomas William^2, Unknown^1) was born 23 April 1930, and died 27 June 1972. He married **Lois Blanche Autry** Before 1964, daughter of Hughie Lee Autry and Crayon Dewitt Holland. Lois was born 19 May 1939.

Willie is buried in Salemburg Cemetery, Salemburg, North Carolina.

Child is listed above under (1520) Lois Blanche Autry.

2216. James Evolyn Lewis (Mary Louise^7 Culbreth, William James^6, Daniel L.^{5}, Daniel Maxwell^4, Mary^3 Holland, Thomas William^2, Unknown^1) was born 18 February 1932 in Honeycutt Township, Sampson County, North Carolina. He married **Lucy Frances Hales**, daughter of Henry Paul Hales and Ola Ann Matthews. She was born 17 October 1934.

Children are listed above under (2190) Lucy Frances Hales.

2218. Mary Etta Hall (Mary Louise^7 Culbreth, William James^6, Daniel L.^{5}, Daniel Maxwell^4, Mary^3 Holland, Thomas William^2, Unknown^1) was born 30 March 1947 in Roseboro, North Carolina. She married **Jerry Wayne Tew** 14 December 1966, son of John Tew and Betty Turlington. He was born 15 January 1947 in Roseboro, North Carolina.

Children of Mary Hall and Jerry Tew are:

2911 i. **Jada Kim Tew**, born 28 March 1970 in Clinton, Sampson County, North Carolina.

2912 ii. **Joshua Wayne Tew**, born 22 March 1974.

2221. Betty Ruth Naylor (James Alton^7, Susan Lee^6 Culbreth, Daniel L.^{5}, Daniel Maxwell^4, Mary^3 Holland, Thomas William^2, Unknown^1) was born 18 March 1946 in Fayetteville, Cumberland County, North Carolina. She married **Furney Soles, Jr.** before 1967. He was born 04 May 1941.

Children of Betty Naylor and Furney Soles are:

2913 i. **Michael Soles**, born 18 July 1967.

2914 ii. **Tracy Soles**, born 25 February 1970.

2915 iii. **Jon Christopher Soles**, born 17 January 1976 in Clinton, Sampson County, North Carolina.

2916 iv. **Phillip Soles**, born 30 April 1977.

2222. James Alton Naylor, Jr. (James Alton[7], Susan Lee[6] Culbreth, Daniel L.[5], Daniel Maxwell[4], Mary[3] Holland, Thomas William[2], Unknown[1]) was born 27 September 1956. He married **Donna Susan Staley Mulvaney** 28 December 1985 in Calvary United Methodist Church, Fayetteville, North Carolina. She was born 11 January 1949 in Fayetteville, Cumberland County, North Carolina.

Child of James Naylor and Donna Mulvaney is:

2917 i. **Lindsay Allison Naylor**, born 02 July 1986 in Fayetteville, Cumberland County, North Carolina.

2225. Gladys Elese Lucas (Eunice Lee[7] Naylor, Susan Lee[6] Culbreth, Daniel L.[5], Daniel Maxwell[4], Mary[3] Holland, Thomas William[2], Unknown[1]) was born 17 February 1929 in Little Coharie Township, Sampson County, North Carolina. She married **Max Marson Batchelor**. He was born 17 April 1920 in Little Coharie Township, Sampson County, North Carolina, and died 07 April 1991 in Fayetteville, Cumberland County, North Carolina.

Max Marson Batchelor was buried in Pleasant Union Baptist Church Cemetery.

Children of Gladys Lucas and Max Batchelor are:

2918 i. **Gary Wayne Batchelor**, born 18 February 1958 in Near Fayetteville, North Carolina; died 31 May 1958 in Fayetteville, Cumberland County, North Carolina and was buried in Pleasant Union Baptist Church Cemetery.

2919 ii. **Effie Jeanette Batchelor**, born 01 January 1960 in Fayetteville, Cumberland County, North Carolina.

2227. Sadie Geneva Lucas (Eunice Lee[7] Naylor, Susan Lee[6] Culbreth, Daniel L.[5], Daniel Maxwell[4], Mary[3] Holland, Thomas William[2], Unknown[1]) was born 22 December 1930 in Little Coharie Township, Sampson County, North Carolina. She married **(1) Robert David Johnson** 04 November 1950. He was born 12 August 1918 in North Clinton Township, Sampson County, North Carolina, and died 07 August 1958 in Roseboro, Sampson County, North Carolina. She married **(2) Bob Kunkel** before 1970.

Sadie Geneva Lucas was the second wife of Robert David Johnson. He was buried in Pleasant Union Baptist Church Cemetery.

Child of Sadie Lucas and Robert Johnson is:

2920 i. **Randal Keith Johnson**, born 22 August 1953 in Clinton, Sampson County, North Carolina; died 14 August 1987 near Philadelphia, Pennsylvania.

Burial: Pleasant Union Baptist Church Cemetery.

Child of Sadie Lucas and Bob Kunkel is:

2921 i. **Ann Kunkel**, born 09 January 1970.

2228. Janie Mae Lucas (Eunice Lee[7] Naylor, Susan Lee[6] Culbreth, Daniel L.[5], Daniel Maxwell[4], Mary[3] Holland, Thomas William[2], Unknown[1]) was born 21 December 1932. She married **Tony Lee Spell** Before 1954, son of Clarence Spell and Jessie Royal. He was born 05 March 1931 in Erwin, Harnett County, North Carolina, and died 18 June 1985 in Fayetteville, Cumberland County, North Carolina.

Tony Lee Spell was buried in Hollywood Cemetery, Roseboro, North Carolina.

Children of Janie Lucas and Tony Spell are:

\+ 2922 i. **Sandra Kaye Spell,** born 17 December 1954 in Clinton, Sampson County, North Carolina.

\+ 2923 ii. **Audrey Lynn Spell,** born 03 May 1956 in Hope Mills, North Carolina.

2230. Helen Grey Lucas (Eunice Lee[7] Naylor, Susan Lee[6] Culbreth, Daniel L.[5], Daniel Maxwell[4], Mary[3] Holland, Thomas William[2], Unknown[1]) was born 14 March 1936 in Little Coharie Township, Sampson County, North Carolina. She married **Charles Gesino** Before 1959.

Child of Helen Lucas and Charles Gesino is:

2924 i. **Linda Gesino,** born 18 May 1959.

2231. James Landon Lucas (Eunice Lee[7] Naylor, Susan Lee[6] Culbreth, Daniel L.[5], Daniel Maxwell[4], Mary[3] Holland, Thomas William[2], Unknown[1]) was born 31 January 1938 in Little Coharie Township, Sampson County, North Carolina, and died 05 August 1976. He married **Dorothy Luisi** Before 1963.

Apparently one record in Sampson County, North Carolina, has his date of birth as February 31, 1938.

Children of James Lucas and Dorothy Luisi are:

2925 i. **David Lucas,** born 08 March 1963.

2926 ii. **Lisa Lucas,** born 25 March 1966.

2927 iii. **Gary Lucas,** born 14 May 1967.

2928 iv. **Michael Lucas,** born 13 August 1969.

2233. Wendell Otto Lucas (Eunice Lee[7] Naylor, Susan Lee[6] Culbreth, Daniel L.[5], Daniel Maxwell[4], Mary[3] Holland, Thomas William[2], Unknown[1]) was born 04 August 1941 in Little Coharie Township, Sampson County, North Carolina. He married **Aurene Sabo** before 1963.

Children of Wendell Lucas and Aurene Sabo are:

2929 i. **Donna Lucas,** born 09 October 1963.

2930 ii. **Susan Lucas**, born 01 February 1967.

2931 iii. **Stephen Lucas**, born 25 September 1970.

2235. Susan Annette Christmas (Jessie Wilson[7] Naylor, Susan Lee[6] Culbreth, Daniel L.[5], Daniel Maxwell[4], Mary[3] Holland, Thomas William[2], Unknown[1]) was born 20 July 1944. She married **James Vernon Robinson** who was born 03 August 1944.

Children of Susan Christmas and James Robinson are:

2932 i. **James Stephen Robinson**, born 05 February 1969.

2933 ii. **Jason Vaughn Robinson**, born 06 February 1971.

2236. Jewel Ray Capps (Katie Jane[7] Naylor, Susan Lee[6] Culbreth, Daniel L.[5], Daniel Maxwell[4], Mary[3] Holland, Thomas William[2], Unknown[1]) was born 26 March 1936 in Little Coharie Township, Sampson County, North Carolina. She married **Frank Trent, Jr.** before 1971.

Children of Jewel Capps and Frank Trent are:

2934 i. **Anthony Trent**, born 19 December 1971.

2935 ii. **Casey Trent**, born 06 November 1973.

2237. Jean Allyson Capps (Katie Jane[7] Naylor, Susan Lee[6] Culbreth, Daniel L.[5], Daniel Maxwell[4], Mary[3] Holland, Thomas William[2], Unknown[1]) was born 03 February 1939. She married **Wayne Stinett** before 1971.

Children of Jean Capps and Wayne Stinett are:

2936 i. **Angie Allyson Stinett**, born 18 May 1971.

2937 ii. **Cavell Wayne Stinett**, born 15 February 1976.

2242. Lynell Hinton Autry (James Hinton[7], William[6] Mac Autry, Sr., Tomzillia[5] Culbreth, Daniel Maxwell[4], Mary[3] Holland, Thomas William[2], Unknown[1]) was born 11 November 1938. She married **Carlton Cleveland Martin**. He was born 29 April 1935.

Children of Lynell Autry and Carlton Martin are:

2938 i. **Jeffery Carlton Martin**, born 13 July 1958 in Clinton, Sampson County, North Carolina. He married **Carla Yvette Tew** 14 June 1981 in Dismal Township, Sampson County, North Carolina; born 01 September 1962 in Dunn, Harnett County, North Carolina.

Carla's first name is spelled "Yevette" and her date of birth is given as September 01, 1961 in one source.

2939 ii. **Jennifer Lynn Martin**, born 07 August 1961.

2940 iii. **Christopher Edward Martin**, born 12 June 1966.

2243. James Reid Autry (James Hinton[7], William[6] Mac Autry, Sr., Tomzillia[5] Culbreth, Daniel Maxwell[4], Mary[3] Holland, Thomas William[2], Unknown[1]) was born 03 August 1953 in Fayetteville, Cumberland County, North Carolina. He married **Sandra Dale Cannady**, daughter of Aaron Cannady and Letha Autry who was born 19 October 1952 in Roseboro, Sampson County, North Carolina.

Page 145 in the source for the data on the Culbreth and Autry families, Sandra's date of birth is given as May 10, 1952. Page 169 of the same source gives it as October 19, 1952, the same date given on page 9 of the source for data Cannadys.

Children of James Autry and Sandra Cannady are:

2941 i. **James Dale Autry**, born 14 April 1977 in Sampson County, North Carolina.

2942 ii. **Sandy Michelle Autry**, born 17 March 1980 in Sampson County, North Carolina.

2244. Mary Amalie Jackson (Olavia Tomzilia[7] Sivertsen, Armelia Bertha[6] Autry, Tomzillia[5] Culbreth, Daniel Maxwell[4], Mary[3] Holland, Thomas William[2], Unknown[1]) was born 01 July 1934 in Dismal Township, Sampson County, North Carolina. She married **Dewey Martin Williams, Jr.** 01 July 1952 in Clement Baptist Church, Sampson County, North Carolina, son of Dewey Martin Williams, Sr. and Arie Spell. He was born 27 December 1931 in Dismal Township, Sampson County, North Carolina, and died 29 October 2002.

Children of Mary Jackson and Dewey Williams are:

2943 i. **Dennis Keith Williams**, born 03 October 1953 in Roseboro, North Carolina.

\+ 2944 ii. **Dewey Martin Williams III**, born 08 October 1957 in Roseboro, North Carolina.

2945 iii. **Mary Beth Williams**, born 24 May 1966 in Clinton, Sampson County, North Carolina.

Mary Beth was attending North Carolina State University in 1985.

2245. Olavia Faye Jackson (Olavia Tomzilia[7] Sivertsen, Armelia Bertha[6] Autry, Tomzillia[5] Culbreth, Daniel Maxwell[4], Mary[3] Holland, Thomas William[2], Unknown[1]) was born 29 August 1936 in Dismal Township, Sampson County, North Carolina. She married **William Keith Faulkner** 27 December 1959 in Dismal Township, Sampson County, North Carolina. He was from Burlington.

Children of Olavia Jackson and William Faulkner are:

2946 i. **William Keith Faulkner**, Jr., born 24 December 1960.

2947 ii. **Lisa Olavia Faulkner**, born 03 August 1965.

2246. Donna Jean Jackson (Olavia Tomzilia^{7} Sivertsen, Armelia Bertha^{6} Autry, Tomzillia^{5} Culbreth, Daniel Maxwell^{4}, Mary^{3} Holland, Thomas William^{2}, Unknown^{1}) was born 07 August 1941 in Dismal Township, Sampson County, North Carolina. She married **Richard Cornelius Williford** 06 August 1967 in Dismal Township. He was born 17 January 1938 in Fayetteville, Cumberland County, North Carolina, and died 03 September 1993.

Child of Donna Jackson and Richard Williford is:

2948 i. **Amy Leigh Williford,** born 03 September 1968.

2251. John Stacey Hair, Jr. (Mary Grace^{7} Sivertsen, Armelia Bertha^{6} Autry, Tomzillia^{5} Culbreth, Daniel Maxwell^{4}, Mary^{3} Holland, Thomas William^{2}, Unknown^{1}) He married **Barbara Kuykendall.**

Child of John Hair and Barbara Kuykendall is:

2949 i. **Sarah Elizabeth-Ann Hair.**

2259. Charles Elliott Bradshaw (Leon Fulton^{7}, David L.^{6}, Eliza Jane^{5} Hairr, Stephen^{4}, Orpah^{3} Holland, Thomas William^{2}, Unknown^{1}) was born 18 May 1938 in Sampson County, North Carolina. He married **Yvonne (Maiden Name Unknown).**

Child of Charles Bradshaw and Yvonne is:

2950 i. **David Bradshaw.**

2260. Edith Juanita Bradshaw (Theodore^{7}, David L.^{6}, Eliza Jane^{5} Hairr, Stephen^{4}, Orpah^{3} Holland, Thomas William^{2}, Unknown^{1}) was born 26 August 1936. She married **Billy Graham Mozingo**. He was born 24 October 1931 in Wayne County, North Carolina, and died in Wayne County, North Carolina.

Children of Edith Bradshaw and Billy Mozingo are:

\+ 2951 i. **William Travis Mozingo**, born 28 October 1956.

\+ 2952 ii. **Steve Dirk Mozingo, Sr.**, born 23 September 1957.

2953 iii. **Michael Theodore Mozingo**, born 24 January 1959.

\+ 2954 iv. **Sandra Maria Mozingo**, born 15 December 1959.

2261. Leon Sherrill Bradshaw (Theodore^{7}, David L.^{6}, Eliza Jane^{5} Hairr, Stephen^{4}, Orpah^{3} Holland, Thomas William^{2}, Unknown^{1}) was born 06 September 1938 in Sampson County, North Carolina, and died 14 October 1999 in Sampson County. He married **Lillie Faye Dodson** who was born 17 September 1949.

Leon Sherrill was buried in the David L. Bradshaw Family Cemetery.

Children of Leon Bradshaw and Lillie Dodson are:

2955 i. **Janet Lynn Bradshaw**, born 11 October 1973 in Sampson County, North Carolina. She married **David Ryan Clark** 27 December 1997.

2956 ii. **Chryl Jean Bradshaw**, born 16 January 1975 in Sampson County, North Carolina.

2262. Theodore Leslie Bradshaw, Sr. (Theodore[7], David L.[6], Eliza Jane[5] Hairr, Stephen[4], Orpah[3] Holland, Thomas William[2], Unknown[1]) was born 02 July 1940 in Sampson County, North Carolina. He married **(1) Mary Cook** who was born in New York. He married **(2) Barbara Ann Kozlowski.**

Child of Theodore Bradshaw and Mary Cook is:

2957 i. **Kelly Bradshaw.**

Children of Theodore Bradshaw and Barbara Kozlowski are:

2958 i. **Theodore Leslie Bradshaw, Jr.**, born 20 March 1974 in Sampson County, North Carolina.

2959 ii. **David Graham Bradshaw**, born 01 March 1976 in Sampson County, North Carolina.

2960 iii. **Dawn Marie Bradshaw**, born 11 March 1977 in Sampson County, North Carolina.

2961 iv. **Bradford Lee Bradshaw**, born 12 July 1978 in Sampson County, North Carolina.

2264. Jo Ann Bradshaw (Theodore[7], David L.[6], Eliza Jane[5] Hairr, Stephen[4], Orpah[3] Holland, Thomas William[2], Unknown[1]) was born 15 April 1944 in Sampson County, North Carolina. She married **Willie Lee Thornton** and they are divorced.

Children of Jo Bradshaw and Willie Thornton are:

2962 i. **Melissa Ann Thornton**, born 27 July 1962 married Mark Herndon.

2963 ii. **Rodney Lee Thornton** married Lari Ann Weeks.

2265. Roy Rogers Bradshaw (Theodore[7], David L.[6], Eliza Jane[5] Hairr, Stephen[4], Orpah[3] Holland, Thomas William[2], Unknown[1]) was born 22 July 1945 in Sampson County, North Carolina. He married **(1) Shirley Fueller**. He married **(2) Holly Unknown.**

Children of Roy Bradshaw and Shirley Fueller are:

2964 i. **Amanda Bradshaw.**

2965 ii. **Sheila Vivian Bradshaw.**

2966 iii. **Wesley Bradshaw.**

Children of Roy Bradshaw and Holly Unknown are:

2967 i. **Victoria Claudia Bradshaw.**

2968 ii. **Susanne Bradshaw.**

2267. Ted Larry Bradshaw, Sr. (Theodore[7], David L.[6], Eliza Jane[5] Hairr, Stephen[4], Orpah[3] Holland, Thomas William[2], Unknown[1]) was born 23 April 1948 in Sampson County, North Carolina, and died 04 May 2000 in Nashville, Tennessee. He married **Mae Bellard.** She was born 19 January 1953 in Enterprise, Alabama.

Ted was buried in the David L. Bradshaw Family Cemetery.

Children of Ted Bradshaw and Mae Bellard are:

2969 i. **Ted Larry Bradshaw, Jr.**, born 05 August 1973 in Charleston, South Carolina.

2970 ii. **Kristin Vivian Bradshaw**, born 11 September 1980 in Enterprise, Alabama.

2268. Danny Ray Bradshaw (Theodore[7], David L.[6], Eliza Jane[5] Hairr, Stephen[4], Orpah[3] Holland, Thomas William[2], Unknown[1]) was born 10 December 1950 in Sampson County, North Carolina. He married **(1) Terra Lynn McLamb.** He married **(2) Deborah Jewel Porter** February 2001.

Child of Danny Bradshaw and Terra McLamb is:

2971 i. **Courtner Blaire Bradshaw**, born 07 November 1979.

2275. Hilda Elizabeth Bradshaw (Owen[7], Franklin[6], Eliza Jane[5] Hairr, Stephen[4], Orpah[3] Holland, Thomas William[2], Unknown[1]) was born 15 October 1930. She married **James Bradshaw.**

Child of Hilda Bradshaw and James Bradshaw is:

2972 i. **Dorothy Bradshaw.**

2276. Janet Romona Bradshaw (Owen[7], Franklin[6], Eliza Jane[5] Hairr, Stephen[4], Orpah[3] Holland, Thomas William[2], Unknown[1]) was born 12 January 1933 in Sampson County, North Carolina. She married **Paul Jordan.** He died 25 February 1990.

Child of Janet Bradshaw and Paul Jordan is:

2973 i. **Janet Lynn Jordan**, born 06 July 1954 in Sampson County, North Carolina.

2277. Della Gray Bradshaw (Owen[7], Franklin[6], Eliza Jane[5] Hairr, Stephen[4], Orpah[3] Holland, Thomas William[2], Unknown[1]) was born 31 January 1934 in Sampson County, North Carolina, and died 25 May 1995 in Cumberland County, North Carolina. She married **(1) Robert Odell Travis, Jr.** before 1954. She married **(2) William Jackson** after 1956.

Della Gray was buried in the Frank Bradshaw Family Cemetery.

Children of Della Bradshaw and Robert Travis are:

\+ 2974 i. **Deborah Ann Travis**, born 12 June 1954.

\+ 2975 ii. **Donna Jean Travis**, born 10 October 1956.

Child of Della Bradshaw and William Jackson is:

\+ 2976 i. **Mary Jennifer Jackson.**

2278. Elsie Mae Bradshaw (Owen[7], Franklin[6], Eliza Jane[5] Hairr, Stephen[4], Orpah[3] Holland, Thomas William[2], Unknown[1]) was born 21 May 1936 in Sampson County, North Carolina. She married **John Marshall Thornton, Sr.,** who was born 12 April 1932 in Sampson County, North Carolina, and died 29 July 1976.

John Marshall is buried in the Frank Bradshaw Family Cemetery.

Children of Elsie Bradshaw and John Thornton are:

2977 i. **John Marshall Thornton,** Jr., born 28 March 1956.

\+ 2978 ii. **Romona Diane Thornton,** born 10 March 1957 in Sampson County, North Carolina.

2979 iii. **Alice Mae Thornton,** born 24 August 1958.

2280. Betty Davis Bradshaw (Owen[7], Franklin[6], Eliza Jane[5] Hairr, Stephen[4], Orpah[3] Holland, Thomas William[2], Unknown[1]) was born 21 October 1945 in Sampson County, North Carolina. She married **(1) Henry Thornton.** She married **(2) Johnny Autry.**

Children of Betty Bradshaw and Henry Thornton are:

2980 i. **Owen Thornton.**

2981 ii. **David Thornton.**

2982 iii. **Christy Thornton.**

2284. Jackie Ray Bradshaw (Herbert[7], Franklin[6], Eliza Jane[5] Hairr, Stephen[4], Orpah[3] Holland, Thomas William[2], Unknown[1]) was born 12 December 1941 in Sampson County, North Carolina. He married **Sylvia Corbett.**

Child of Jackie Bradshaw and Sylvia Corbett is:

2983 i. **Patrick Neal Bradshaw,** born 23 May 1973.

2286. Ronnie Gene Bradshaw (Herbert[7], Franklin[6], Eliza Jane[5] Hairr, Stephen[4], Orpah[3] Holland, Thomas William[2], Unknown[1]) was born 24 May 1947 in Sampson County, North Carolina. He married **Rena Florence Parker,** daughter of Miles Simpson Parker, and Mattie Ruth Jackson; Rena was born 9 January 1941 and they were divorced.

Child of Ronnie Bradshaw and Rena is:

2984 i. **Breezy Farah Bradshaw** was born 17 July 1977 and she has one child, **TAKODA SEAN-MAXWELL BRADSHAW** who was born 7 February 2000.

2287. Herbert Wayne Bradshaw (Herbert[7], Franklin[6], Eliza Jane[5] Hairr, Stephen[4], Orpah[3] Holland, Thomas William[2], Unknown[1]) was born 27 December 1951 in Sampson County, North Carolina. He married **Gladys Raynor.**

Child of Herbert Bradshaw and Gladys Raynor is:

2985 i. **Kimberly Bradshaw.**

2291. Claudia Ann Bradshaw (Woodrow[7], Franklin[6], Eliza Jane[5] Hairr, Stephen[4], Orpah[3] Holland, Thomas William[2], Unknown[1]) was born 04 February 1951. She married **Donald Baldwin** 07 October 1969 and they divorced 30 November 1982.

Children of Claudia Bradshaw and Donald Baldwin are:

2986 i. **Heather Renee Baldwin**, born 21 December 1972.

2987 ii. **Crystal Dawn Baldwin**, born 15 June 1974.

2292. Susan Faye Bradshaw (Woodrow[7], Franklin[6], Eliza Jane[5] Hairr, Stephen[4], Orpah[3] Holland, Thomas William[2], Unknown[1]) was born 15 March 1953. She married **William Michael Vinson** 03 May 1972.

Child of Susan Bradshaw and William Vinson is:

2988 i. **Jo Marie Vinson**, born 25 November 1972.

2293. Woodrow Michael Bradshaw, Sr. (Woodrow[7], Franklin[6], Eliza Jane[5] Hairr, Stephen[4], Orpah[3] Holland, Thomas William[2], Unknown[1]) was born 01 January 1956, and died 22 May 2001.

Child of Woodrow Michael Bradshaw, Sr. is:

2989 i. **Woodrow Michael Bradshaw, Jr.**, born 15 March 1985.

2295. Carolyn Gray Honrine (Pearl[7] Bradshaw, Franklin[6], Eliza Jane[5] Hairr, Stephen[4], Orpah[3] Holland, Thomas William[2], Unknown[1]) was born 17 August 1942 in Sampson County, North Carolina. She married **William Honeycutt, Sr.** 23 December 1961.

Children of Carolyn Honrine and William Honeycutt are:

2990 i. **William Honeycutt, Jr.**, born 25 January 1966.

2991 ii. **Michael Honeycutt**, born 18 December 1969.

2298. Hubert Bee Hairr (William Braxton[7], Isaiah[6], James Thomas[5], John C.[4] Hair, Orpah[3] Holland, Thomas William[2], Unknown[1]) was born 16 October 1924 in Herrings Township, Sampson County, North Carolina, and died 25 June 1986. He married **Margaret Lee Peterson**, daughter of Elliott Peterson and Lillian Bordeaux. She was born 03 November 1927 in Lisbon Township, Sampson County, North Carolina.

Margaret Lee Peterson was born in November 1927 and died 28 March 2005 at Wake Medical Center in Raleigh, North Carolina.

Three surviving children are named in obituary of Margaret Hairr: William Hairr of Rose Hill, Wesley Hairr of Clinton and Jeannette McGee of Four Oaks. The six children of Hubert and Margaret were: **Jeanette Rose Hairr** who was born 15 December 1942 in Clinton; **Luther Columbus Hairr** was born 3 November 1945 in Halls Township and died 29 September 1988 in Smithfield; **Lemon B. Hairr** was born 9 January 1948 in Halls Township and died 19 September 1951; **William James Hairr** was born 5 December 1949 in Halls Township; **Emmet Lee Hairr** was born 8 May 1953 in Halls Township and died 9 November 1955; **Kenneth Wesley Hairr** was born 13 September 1958 in Clinton.

Hubert Bee and Margaret were buried in the McGee United Methodist Church Cemetery, Sampson County, North Carolina, about three miles west of church on McGee Church Road (SR 1319), Sampson County, North Carolina.

Children of Hubert Hairr and Margaret Peterson are:

2992 i. **Jeanette Rose Hairr**, born 15 December 1942 in Clinton, Sampson County, North Carolina. She married a **Mr. McGee.**

\+ 2993 ii. **Luther Columbus Hairr**, born 03 November 1945 in Halls Township in Sampson County; died 29 September 1988 in Smithfield, Johnston County, North Carolina.

2994 iii. **Lemon B. Hairr**, born 09 January 1948 in Halls Township, Sampson County, North Carolina; died 19 September 1951.

Mr. Rosser, Jr., notes in his book that the tombstone for Lemon B. Hairr has different dates: Birth was December 03, 1945 and date of death was September 19, 1952. He was buried in the Alvin Bass Family Cemetery, Plain View Township, Sampson County, North Carolina.

\+ 2995 iv. **William James Hairr**, born 05 December 1949 in Halls Township in Sampson County.

2996 v. **Emmet Lee Hairr**, born 08 May 1953 in Halls Township, Sampson County, North Carolina; died 09 November 1955 in Route 3, Clinton, North Carolina. Emmet Lee was buried in Alvin Bass Family Cemetery in Sampson County.

2997 vi. **Kenneth Wesley Hairr**, born 13 September 1958 in Clinton, Sampson County, North Carolina. He married Robin Gail McLamb 28 June 1981 in Clinton, North Carolina; born 18 November 1964 in Clinton, Sampson County, North Carolina.

2302. Floyd Lutrell Hairr (Spence B.[7], Isaiah[6], James Thomas[5], John C.[4] Hair, Orpah[3] Holland, Thomas William[2], Unknown[1]) was born 01 November 1928 in Sampson County, North Carolina. He married **Barbara Jean Jordan** 10 November 1957, daughter of

Oscar Jordan and Armathia Tew. She was born 04 June 1938 in Sampson County, North Carolina.

Children of Floyd Hairr and Barbara Jordan are:

+ 2998 i. **Ronald Keith Hairr,** born 08 June 1959.

+ 2999 ii. **Shelia Rose Hairr,** born 11 April 1965.

2303. Christine Hairr (Troy Addicus[7], Isaiah[6], James Thomas[5], John C.[4] Hair, Orpah[3] Holland, Thomas William[2], Unknown[1]) was born 25 October 1928 in Mingo Township, Sampson County, North Carolina. She married **Ermon Honeycutt Godwin** 03 July 1947 in Shady Grove FWB Church, Spivey's Corner, Sampson County, North Carolina, son of Ermon Godwin and Ruby Honeycutt. He was born 30 November 1927 in Erwin, Duke Twnshp., Harnett County, North Carolina.

Children of Christine Hairr and Ermon Honeycutt Godwin are:

+ 3000 i. **David Patrick Godwin,** born 03 June 1950.

+ 3001 ii. **Michael Ray Godwin,** born 24 April 1957 in Dunn, Harrnett County, North Carolina.

2304. Bobby Ray Hairr (Troy Addicus[7], Isaiah[6], James Thomas[5], John C.[4] Hair, Orpah[3] Holland, Thomas William[2], Unknown[1]) was born 14 February 1936. He married **Patricia Ann Ferrell** 27 September 1958 in Raleigh, Wake County, North Carolina. She was born 30 September 1937.

Child of Bobby Hairr and Patricia Ferrell is:

3002 i. **Dianna Louise Hairr,** born 25 September 1961. She married **Michael Boyce** 31 May 1989.

2305. James Houston Lockamy (Leona[7] Hairr, Isaiah[6], James Thomas[5], John C.[4] Hair, Orpah[3] Holland, Thomas William[2], Unknown[1]) was born 12 February 1924, and died 30 December 1997 in Sampson County, North Carolina. He married **Revah Spell** 25 May 1942 in Dillon, South Carolina, daughter of **John Spell** and **Clennie McKenzie**. She was born 21 July 1923, and died 03 July 2005.

James Houston and Revah are buried in Grandview Memorial Gardens, Clinton, Sampson County, North Carolina.

Children of James Lockamy and Revah Spell are:

+ 3003 i. **Houston Lee Lockamy,** born 25 February 1944.

3004 ii. **Brenda Faye Lockamy,** born 03 January 1946. She married Darious Woodrow Wilson.

+ 3005 iii. **Omie Kaye Lockamy,** born 09 February 1948.

+ 3006 iv. **Jimmy McThomas Lockamy,** born 27 March 1950.

+ 3007 v. **Jackie Lou Lockamy**, born 26 September 1953.

2306. Paul Graham Weeks (Omie Tera[7] Hairr, Isaiah[6], James Thomas[5], John C.[4] Hair, Orpah[3] Holland, Thomas William[2], Unknown[1]) was born About 1926. He married **Mary Unknown.**

Children of Paul Weeks and Mary Unknown are:

+ 3008 i. **Stephen Anthony Weeks**, born about 1950.

3009 ii. **Denise Weeks**.

2309. Sudie Hairr (Deames Elton[7], Isaiah[6], James Thomas[5], John C.[4] Hair, Orpah[3] Holland, Thomas William[2], Unknown[1]) was born 10 May 1944 in Sampson County, North Carolina. She married **Anthony Darrow Cannady**, son of Erastus Cannady and Betty Johnson. He was born 18 November 1943 in Sampson County, North Carolina, and died 30 September 1999.

Anthony Darrow was buried in Rowan Baptist Church Cemetery, Rowan Road, Clinton, North Carolina.

Children of Sudie Hairr and Anthony Cannady are:

+ 3010 i. **Nelson Cannady**, born 22 March 1972.

+ 3011 ii. **Kimberly Dawn Cannady**, born 26 January 1976.

2319. Samuel Ernestine Warren (Lillie Nadine[7] Butler, Bettie Allen[6] Autry, Allen Merdeth[5], Starling[4], Millie[3] Holland, Thomas William[2], Unknown[1]) was born 23 November 1931 in Mingo Township, Sampson County, North Carolina. He married **Elma Mae Naylor** 09 April 1955, daughter of Earlie Naylor and Lillian Wilkes. She was born 11 October 1934 in Herrings Township, Sampson County, North Carolina.

Children of Samuel Warren and Elma Naylor are:

+ 3012 i. **Wanda Ernestine Warren**, born 10 October 1957 in Clinton, Sampson County, North Carolina.

3013 ii. **Samuel Keith Warren**, born 26 April 1964 in Clinton, Sampson County, North Carolina. He married **Vicky Jo Pittman** 23 May 1992 in First Baptist Church of Scotland Neck, Halifax County, North Carolina.

2320. Elsie Jane Warren (Lillie Nadine[7] Butler, Bettie Allen[6] Autry, Allen Merdeth[5], Starling[4], Millie[3] Holland, Thomas William[2], Unknown[1]) was born 31 March 1951 in Clinton, Sampson County, North Carolina. She married **Robie Brooks McLamb** 21 May 1972 in Mingo Township, Sampson County, North Carolina, son of Ralph McLamb and Reva Naylor. He was born 10 September 1949 in Roseboro, North Carolina.

Children of Elsie Warren and Robie McLamb are:

3014 i. **Nicholas Warren McLamb**, born 14 January 1979 in Durham, North Carolina.

3015 ii. **Jeffrey Brooke McLamb**, born 12 July 1983 in Durham, North Carolina.

2321. Houston Warren (Lillie Nadine[7] Butler, Bettie Allen[6] Autry, Allen Merdeth[5], Starling[4], Millie[3] Holland, Thomas William[2], Unknown[1]) He married **(1) Louise O'Tuel** 02 July 1955. She was from Nichols, South Carolina. He married **(2) Doris June Lambeth** after October 1968.

Children of Houston Warren and Louise O'Tuel are:

\+ 3016 i. **William Houston Warren**, born 02 August 1956 in Loris, South Carolina.

3017 ii. **James O'Tuel Warren**. He attended the Citadel at Charleston, South Carolina and graduated in Biology.

3018 iii. **Louis Langdon Warren**. He attended the University of North Carolina at Chapel Hill and majored in Industrial Relations.

2322. Alice Dean Warren (Lillie Nadine[7] Butler, Bettie Allen[6] Autry, Allen Merdeth[5], Starling[4], Millie[3] Holland, Thomas William[2], Unknown[1]) She married **Dan McBane.**

Children of Alice Warren and Dan McBane are:

3019 i. **Debra McBane**. She attended Guilford College in Greensboro, North Carolina.

3020 ii. **Everette McBane**.

3021 iii. **Don McBane**.

2323. Betty Allen Warren (Lillie Nadine[7] Butler, Bettie Allen[6] Autry, Allen Merdeth[5], Starling[4], Millie[3] Holland, Thomas William[2], Unknown[1]) She married **Roy Clifton Jackson**.

Betty Allen and her husband may have lived in Louisiana.

Children of Betty Warren and Roy Jackson are:

3022 i. **Allan Jackson.**

3023 ii. **Scott Jackson.**

2325. Charles Marion Butler, Jr. (Charles Marion[7], Bettie Allen[6] Autry, Allen Merdeth[5], Starling[4], Millie[3] Holland, Thomas William[2], Unknown[1]) was born 09 September 1939 in Dunn, Harrnett County, North Carolina, and died 30 December 1966. He married **Bonnie Lee Davis** Before 1963, daughter of Arthur Davis and Luna Jackson. She was born 29 December 1945 in Herrings Township, Sampson County, North Carolina.

Charles Marion Butler, Jr, died as a result of an automobile accident and was buried in Grandview Memorial Gardens, near Clinton, Sampson County, North Carolina.

Children of Charles Butler and Bonnie Davis are:

3024 i. **Bonnie Lisa Butler**, born 20 March 1963 in Clinton, Sampson County, North Carolina.

3025 ii. **Charles Marion Butler III**, born 15 July 1964 in Clinton, North Carolina.

3026 iii. **Brenda Catherine Butler**, born 21 December 1966 in Clinton, Sampson County, North Carolina.

2326. James Hubbard Butler (Charles Marion[7], Bettie Allen[6] Autry, Allen Merdeth[5], Starling[4], Millie[3] Holland, Thomas William[2], Unknown[1]) was born 22 July 1942 in Mingo Township, Sampson County, North Carolina. He married **Eddie Sue Weeks** before 1964. She was born 07 February 1946 in Herrings Township, Sampson County, North Carolina.

Children of James Butler and Eddie Weeks are:

\+ 3027 i. **Cynthia Sue Butler,** born 24 May 1964 in Clinton, Sampson County, North Carolina.

3028 ii. **Tammy James Butler**, born 19 November 1966 in Clinton, Sampson County, North Carolina. She married **Wade Graham Warren** 19 May 1991 in Hickory Grove Baptist Church; born 16 February 1966 in Dunn, Harrnett County, North Carolina.

3029 iii. **Crissie Weeks Butler**, was born 19 December 1972 in Clinton, North Carolina, died 19 December 1972 in Clinton, Sampson County, North Carolina, and was buried in the Grandview Memorial Gardens, Clinton, Sampson County, North Carolina

2331. Cynthia Mae Smith (Woodrow[7], Lonie Mae[6] Holland, Jasper Lee[5], Stephen Senter[4], Henry[3], Thomas William[2], Unknown[1]) was born 06 March 1959 in Fayetteville. She married **John Bearden Willard, Jr.** who was born 06 March 1959.

Children of Cynthia Smith and John Willard are:

3030 i. **Joshua Lane Willard,** born 06 March 1981.

3031 ii. **Adam Jared Willard,** born 23 March 1983.

2332. Tamela Joyce Smith (Woodrow[7], Lonie Mae[6] Holland, Jasper Lee[5], Stephen Senter[4], Henry[3], Thomas William[2], Unknown[1]) was born 21 February 1962 in Fayetteville. She married **Henry Jay Norris** who was born 21 February 1962.

Children of Tamela Smith and Henry Norris are:

3032 i. **Spencer Smith Norris,** born 09 September 1995.

3033 ii. **Parker Scott Norris,** born 28 June 2001.

2333. Oleta Michelle Smith (Woodrow[7], Lonie Mae[6] Holland, Jasper Lee[5], Stephen Senter[4], Henry[3], Thomas William[2], Unknown[1]) was born 23 July 1966. She married **Robert Warren Wells** who was born 23 July 1966.

Children of Oleta Smith and Robert Wells are:

3034 i. **Ashley Holland Wells**, born 13 June 1984.

3035 ii. **Caitlin Michelle Wells**, born 14 September 1991.

2334. Houstus Bennie Holland (Alma Christine[7], James Senter[6], Alger Rose[5], Stephen Senter[4], Henry[3], Thomas William[2], Unknown[1]) was born 14 February 1947, and died 17 October 2002. He married **Unknown Spouse.**

One step-daughter, Melissa Perry. Houstus was buried in Zoar FWBP Church Cemetery near Salemburg, North Carolina.

Child of Houstus Holland and Unknown Spouse is:

3036 i. **Sophia Dawn Holland**, born 21 September 1973. She married Unknown Lee.

2343. Lori Ann Norris (Alice Faye[7] Holland, James Senter[6], Alger Rose[5], Stephen Senter[4], Henry[3], Thomas William[2], Unknown[1]) was born 10 May 1969 in Sampson County, North Carolina. She married **Christopher Sutton.**

Children of Lori Norris and Christopher Sutton are:

3037 i. **Emily Hope Sutton**, born 15 November 2006.

3038 ii. **Aaron Sutton**, born 14 May 2007.

2344. Carrie Nicole Norris (Alice Faye[7] Holland, James Senter[6], Alger Rose[5], Stephen Senter[4], Henry[3], Thomas William[2], Unknown[1]) was born 21 September 1976 in Sampson County, North Carolina. She married **Jeffrey Spell.**

Child of Carrie Norris and Jeffrey Spell is:

3039 i. **Brittany Nicole Spell**, born 05 March 2001.

2346. Linda Dianne Tew (Doris Gray[7] Holland, John Wesley[6], Alger Rose[5], Stephen Senter[4], Henry[3], Thomas William[2], Unknown[1]) was born 14 March 1948 in Roseboro, Sampson County, North Carolina. She married **Carl Braston Tyndall** 20 January 1969 in Honeycutts Township, Sampson County, North Carolina, son of Garley Braxton Tyndall and Annie Hair. He was born 11 October 1948 in Roseboro, Sampson County, North Carolina.

Children of Linda Tew and Carl Tyndall are:

3040 i. **William Christopher Tyndall**, born 23 August 1971 in Clinton, Sampson County, North Carolina. He married **Beth Unknown.**

3041 ii. **Carla Diane Tyndall**, born 21 April 1975.

3042 iii. **Braston Wayne Tyndall**, born 24 July 1983.

2347. James Brewer Tew, Sr. (Doris Gray[7] Holland, John Wesley[6], Alger Rose[5], Stephen Senter[4], Henry[3], Thomas William[2], Unknown[1]) was born 25 January 1949 in Sampson County, North Carolina. He married **(1) Henrietta Fann** 31 March 1966 in Salemburg, Sampson County, North Carolina, daughter of Henry Fann and Helen Howard. She was born 11 May 1950 in Roseboro, North Carolina. He married **(2) Joan Vann** 18 August 1979. She was born 05 April 1943.

Children of James Tew and Henrietta Fann are:

+ 3043 i. **Sherry Ann Tew**, born 27 July 1966 in Clinton, Sampson County, North Carolina.

3044 ii. **Tammy Victoria Tew**, born 17 October 1971 in Clinton, Sampson County, North Carolina.

Child of James Tew and Joan Vann is:

3045 i. **James Brewer Tew, Jr.**, born 03 July 1980.

2351. Wanda Sue Marley (Brenda Sue[7] Holland, John Wesley[6], Alger Rose[5], Stephen Senter[4], Henry[3], Thomas William[2], Unknown[1]) was born 21 August 1962 in Washington, D.C.. She married **Johnny Nelson McLamb**, son of Harvey McLamb and Laura Pope. He was born 08 April 1961 in Clinton, Sampson County, North Carolina, and died 16 February 2005 in Sampson County, North Carolina.

Children of Wanda Marley and Johnny McLamb are:

3046 i. **Joshua McLamb**, born in Sampson County, North Carolina.

3047 ii. **Tiffany McLamb**. She married Unknown Johnson.

2357. Joseph Richard Pleitt (Nancy Eveline[7] Jackson, Roberta[6] Holland, Alger Rose[5], Stephen Senter[4], Henry[3], Thomas William[2], Unknown[1]) was born 05 December 1961 in Lutheran General Hospital, Park Ridge, Cook County, Illinois. He married **Denise Rose Dion** 09 August 1986 in Sacred Heart Catholic Church, Lombard, Du Page County, Illinois, daughter of Edward Dion and Marcella Stoffel. She was born 19 April 1961 in Oak Lawn, Cook County, Illinois.

Joseph Richard has a B.S. in Chemical Engineering from the University of Missouri, Columbia. He was in ROTC 1981-1982. Confirmation name for Denise Rose Dion is 'Denise Rose Ann Dion.' She has an Associate Degree in Applied Science and for several years has worked with elementary school aged children who have special needs.

Children of Joseph Pleitt and Denise Dion are:

3048 i. **Jason Joseph Pleitt,** born 26 August 1987 in Lombard, Du Page County, Illinois. He is a Junior at Missouri University of Science and Technology in Rolla, Missouri, and majoring Mechanical and Nuclear Engineering.

3049 ii. **Kristina Rose Pleitt,** born 06 February 1990 in Lombard, Du Page, Illinois. She is attending Missouri University of Science and Technology in Rolla, Missouri, and majoring in Bio-Medical Engineering.

3050 iii. **Nicholas Richard Pleitt** was born 11 July 1995 in Lombard, Du Page, Illinois, died 19 July 1995 in Loyola University Medical Center, Maywood, Cook County, Illinois and was buried on 21 July 1995, Assumption Cemetery, Winfield, Du Page County, Illinois. It was known before he was born that Nicholas would have severe heart problems and would require surgery soon after birth. He survived his surgery, but developed problems about eight hours later and soon passed away.

3051 iv. **Nathan Alexander Pleitt,** born 03 September 1998 in Lombard, Du Page, Illinois.

2358. Anna Bernadette Pleitt (Nancy Eveline[7] Jackson, Roberta[6] Holland, Alger Rose[5], Stephen Senter[4], Henry[3], Thomas William[2], Unknown[1]) was born 13 January 1965 in Holy Family Hospital, Cook County, Illinois. She married **William Peter Kootstra** 05 November 1992 in Island Lake, Lake County, Illinois, son of Peiter Kootstra and Alida Trijntje Wesselink. William (Willie) was born 26 June 1964 in Canada when his parents stayed there for a short time before they settled in Illinois. He is now a United States Citizen and Director of Public Works in Island Lake, Illinois.

Peiter (Peter) Kootstra was born 29 December 1929 in Fries, Stroobos, Netherlands to Willem Kootstra and Anna Ferwerda; Alida was born 25 October 1939 in Harlingen, Netherlands to Hendrik Fokke Wesselink and Alberdiena Aaltiena Koster who was born in Holland.

William (Willie) Peter Kootstra first married Donna Korous who was born in 1955; no children. Donna first married a Mr. Kessler and with him she had two children. Pieter Kootstra and Alida were divorced and he married second as her second husband, Ruby (Maiden name unknown) Nellis who was born 29 August 1920 and she first married a Mr. Nellis. Alida Wesselink married second, Frank Bellastar; married third to Brooks Leigh and fourth to Vern Risley. Records show that Alida, her parents and family were sponsored on arrival in America on 16 of January 1957, by the First Presbyterian Church in Downers Grover, Illinois, USA.

Anna Bernadette Pleitt Kootstra graduated from Northeastern Illinois University, Chicago, Illinois, with a B.S. in Biology.

Children of Anna Pleitt and William Kootstra are:

3052 i. Peter Willem Kootstra, born 12 June 1993 in Good Shepherd Hospital, Barrington, Lake County, Illinois.

3053 ii. **Haley Marie Kootstra,** born 10 May 1995 in Good Shepherd Hospital, Barrington, Lake County, Illinois.

2359. Charles Davis Smith (Jackie Olene[7] Jackson, Roberta[6] Holland, Alger Rose[5], Stephen Senter[4], Henry[3], Thomas William[2], Unknown[1]) was born 03 April 1961 in Clinton, Sampson County, North Carolina. He married **Tammy Lynnette Pope** 22 June 1982 in

Clinton, North Carolina, daughter of Preston Carr Pope and Helen Sinclair. She was born 12 June 1964 in Clinton, Sampson County, North Carolina.

Children of Charles Smith and Tammy Pope are:

+ 3054 i. **Charles Terry Smith**, born 17 September 1983.

+ 3055 ii. **Amanda Dawn Smith**, born 09 October 1984.

2360. Michael Edward Smith (Jackie Olene[7] Jackson, Roberta[6] Holland, Alger Rose[5], Stephen Senter[4], Henry[3], Thomas William[2], Unknown[1]) was born 29 May 1962 in Bethel, Pitt County, North Carolina. He married **Lecia Allen Boyd** 06 May 1983 in Dillon, South Carolina, daughter of William Boyd and Rachel Thornton. She was born 20 September 1966 in Sampson County, North Carolina.

Michael Edward had problems with mitral valve prolapse as a child starting about 1972. His and Lecia's son, Jonah Phillip, was born with Atrial Septal Defect and had surgery to correct it at about age two.

Jonah's doctors first told Lecia and Mike that they suspected Jonah's problem was genetic and when they were told that Michael had problems as a child the doctors explained that there has been an association between A.S.D. and Mitral Valve Prolapse and they believed there was a connection between Mike and Jonah's problem. At least two other descendants of Oscar Davis Jackson and Roberta Holland had or have similar heart problems; my grandson died after surgery when only eight days old and I am now aged 72 and was told when I was 18 that I had Mitral Valve Prolapse. A son of a cousin from the Jackson and Holland lines was born with similar severe problem as Jonah, had surgery at about age two. He is now a teenager.

Children of Michael Smith and Lecia Boyd are:

+ 3056 i. **Michael Allen Smith**, born 26 January 1986 in Sampson County, North Carolina.

3057 ii. **Brittany Faith Smith**, born 17 March 1989 in Sampson County, North Carolina.

3058 iii. **Jonah Phillip Smith**, born 28 September 1991 in Sampson County, North Carolina.

Jonah was born with Atrial Septal Defect. Surgery was performed to correct the problem and he is in very good health today.

3059 iv. **Rachel Courtney Smith**, born 04 April 1993 in Sampson County, North Carolina.

3060 v. **Destiny Hope Smith**, born 29 May 1995 in Sampson County, North Carolina.

3061 vi. **Gage Ransom Smith**, born 07 June 2005 in Sampson County, North Carolina.

3062 vii. **Jaden Reid Smith**, born 08 November 2006 in Sampson County, North Carolina.

2361. Jackie Gregory Smith (Jackie Olene[7] Jackson, Roberta[6] Holland, Alger Rose[5], Stephen Senter[4], Henry[3], Thomas William[2], Unknown[1]) was born 22 April 1966 in Tarboro, North Carolina. He married **Linda Ann McClenny** 28 July 1984 in Dillon, South Carolina, daughter of Joseph McClenny and Carrie Unknown. She was born 13 March 1965 in Clinton, Sampson County, North Carolina.

Children of Jackie Smith and Linda McClenny are:

+ 3063 i. **Erica Nicole Smith**, born 18 December 1985 in Clinton, Sampson County, North Carolina.

3064 ii. **Heather Nicole Smith**, born 15 April 1992 in Clinton, North Carolina.

3065 iii. **Savannah Lynn Smith**, born 31 July 1998 in Clinton, Sampson County, North Carolina.

2362. Kenneth Lee Hairr (Alger Leevon[7], Dellar Jane[6] Holland, Alger Rose[5], Stephen Senter[4], Henry[3], Thomas William[2], Unknown[1]) was born 28 February 1958 in Clinton, Sampson County, North Carolina. He married **Judith Lea Wells**.

Child of Kenneth Hairr and Judith Wells is:

3066 i. **Evan Wells Hairr**, born 14 October 1992 in Cape Fear Valley Hospital, Fayetteville, Cumberland County, North Carolina.

2364. Thomas Earl Hairr (William Earl[7], Dellar Jane[6] Holland, Alger Rose[5], Stephen Senter[4], Henry[3], Thomas William[2], Unknown[1]) was born 10 September 1957 in Clinton, Sampson County, North Carolina. He married **(1) Laura Ann Dale** 11 September 1982 in Godwin, North Carolina. She was born 12 September 1962 in Dunn, Harnett County, North Carolina. He married **(2) Shari Ann Britt** Before 1985, daughter of Billy Britt and Dorothy Dean. She was born 07 June 1964 in Erwin, Harnett County, North Carolina.

Child of Thomas Hairr and Laura Dale is:

3067 i. **Franklin Dale Hairr**, born 16 January 1984 in Clinton, Sampson County, North Carolina.

Children of Thomas Hairr and Shari Britt are:

3068 i. **Jamie Lynn Hairr**, born 06 June 1985 in Clinton, Sampson County, North Carolina.

3069 ii. **Travis Lee Hairr** was born prematurely on 18 April 1987 and has asthma.

3070 iii. **Cody Britt Hairr**, born 24 October 1994.

Cody Britt was born with several heart defects: a double outlet from the right ventricle, ASD (hole in the heart) and pulmonary stenois and VSD between left and right ventricle. The major problem was the double outlet which is the VSD between Left and Right ventricle. The ASD was between atrium in top of heart. Pulmonary stenois in left right ventricle along the aorta. There was an inlet to left ventricle but no outlet from pulmonary valve. He has had several surgeries. When this writer saw him in 1996 (?), Cody was quite lively when playing with his siblings.

2365. Sarah Denise Hairr (William Earl[7], Dellar Jane[6] Holland, Alger Rose[5], Stephen Senter[4], Henry[3], Thomas William[2], Unknown[1]) was born 14 April 1962 in Clinton, Sampson County, North Carolina. She married **James Michael Williams** 12 April 1981 in Roseboro, Sampson County, North Carolina. He was born 12 October 1962 in Clinton, Sampson County.

Child of Sarah Hairr and James Williams is:

3071 i. **Michael Allen Williams**, born 04 June 1983 in Clinton, Sampson County, North Carolina.

2372. Lathan Thomas Fann (Evelyn Idell[7] Holland, George Bizzell[6], Alger Rose[5], Stephen Senter[4], Henry[3], Thomas William[2], Unknown[1]) was born 19 June 1972 in Clinton, Sampson County, North Carolina. He married **Talissa Register** who was born 06 April 1971.

Children of Lathan Fann and Talissa Register are:

3072 i. **Lathan Tate Fann**, born 29 January 1993.

3073 ii. **Walker Thomas Fann**, born 17 February 1995.

2379. Lynn Renae Holland (Preston Pedro[8], Leslie B.[7], Lalister R.[6], Bluman[5], Harfrey[4], Daniel[3], Thomas William[2], Unknown[1]) was born 07 March 1967. She married **Michael Herndon**.

Child of Lynn Holland and Michael Herndon is:

3074 i. **Challie Marie Herndon**, born 03 September 1990.

2388. Kevin Wayne Strickland I (Rodney Holland[7], Freda Augustus[6] Holland, Alger Rose[5], Stephen Senter[4], Henry[3], Thomas William[2], Unknown[1]) was born 31 October 1974 in Wake County, North Carolina, and died 22 July 1995 in Orange County, North Carolina. He married **Holly Marie Herring** 22 January 1995 in Dillon, South Carolina. She was born 17 August 1978 in Clinton, Sampson County, North Carolina.

Kevin Wayne I, died in an automobile accident on a very foggy night and is buried in The Clinton Cemetery, Clinton, Sampson County, North Carolina.

Child of Kevin Strickland and Holly Herring is:

3075 i. **Kevin Wayne Strickland II**, born 19 August 1995.

2390. Jerry Craig Matthews (Clarise Fay[7] Simmons, Clyda Louise[6] Holland, Henry[5], Stephen Senter[4], Henry[3], Thomas William[2], Unknown[1]) was born 18 December 1957 in Wayne County. He married **Pamela Mae Jackson**, daughter of Almoye Jackson and Bonnie Gilchrist. She was born 03 December 1958 in Clinton, North Carolina.

Child of Jerry Matthews and Pamela Jackson is:

3076 i. **Alexander Craig Matthews**, born 07 March 1993.

Generation Number 8

2393. Dianne Autry (Arthur Vance[8], Crayon Dewitt[7] Holland, Calton Walker[6], William[5], James[4], Daniel[3], Thomas William[2], Unknown[1]) was born 08 August 1958. She married **Stanley Faircloth**. He was born 30 December 1954.

Child of Dianne Autry and Stanley Faircloth is:

3077 i. **Audrey Dianne Faircloth**, born 14 August 1975.

2419. John Wayne Strickland (Margaret[8] Holland, Robert Elliott[7], Bryant B.[6], Thomas James[5], James[4], Daniel[3], Thomas William[2], Unknown[1]) was born 21 October 1949. He married **Agnes Pendergrass** June 1967.

Child of John Strickland and Agnes Pendergrass is:

3078 i. **Timothy Wayne Strickland**, born 21 August 1969.

2426. Arval Gipson Holland, Jr. (Arrel Gipson[8], Lottis Turner[7], William Thomas[6], Thomas James[5], James[4], Daniel[3], Thomas William[2], Unknown[1]) was born 02 June 1951 in Fayetteville, Cumberland County, North Carolina. He married **Barbara Jean Spell** 15 July 1974 in Roseboro, Sampson County, North Carolina. She was born 03 August 1961 in Clinton, Sampson County, North Carolina.

Children of Arval Holland and Barbara Spell are:

3079 i. **Craig Gipson Holland**, born 15 December 1979 in Fayetteville, Cumberland County, North Carolina.

3080 ii. **Charles Clint Holland**, born 26 July 1984 in Fayetteville, Cumberland County, North Carolina.

2427. Robert Turner Holland (Arrel Gipson[8], Lottis Turner[7], William Thomas[6], Thomas James[5], James[4], Daniel[3], Thomas William[2], Unknown[1]) was born 25 June 1952 in Fayetteville, Cumberland County, North Carolina. He married **Judy Faye Honeycutt**. She was born about 1956 in Sampson County, North Carolina.

Children of Robert Holland and Judy Honeycutt are:

3081 i. **Lisa Marie Holland**, born 25 March 1975 in Fayetteville, Cumberland County, North Carolina.

3082 ii. **Cary Jeanette Holland**, born 30 October 1977 in Fayetteville, Cumberland County, North Carolina.

3083 iii. **Johnnie Robert Holland**, born 16 December 1980 in Fayetteville, Cumberland County, North Carolina.

2429. Sandra Dale Cannady (Aaron[8], Arizona T.[7] Holland, William Thomas[6], Thomas James[5], James[4], Daniel[3], Thomas William[2], Unknown[1]) was born 19 October 1952 in Roseboro, Sampson County, North Carolina. She married **James Reid Autry**, son of James

Hinton Autry and Straudia Almeta Wrench. He was born 03 August 1953 in Fayetteville, Cumberland County, North Carolina.

Sandra's date of birth is given as May 10, 1952 on one page in Prof. Bundy's family history and on another page, October 19, 1952, is listed. The Cannady Family History by Sue Cannady Barefoot provides the October date.

Children are listed above under (2243) James Reid Autry.

2435. Donna Marie Holland (Glenn Turner[8], Euland Randolph[7], William Thomas[6], Thomas James[5], James[4], Daniel[3], Thomas William[2], Unknown[1]) was born 26 October 1965 in Clinton, Sampson County, North Carolina. She married **Clarence Lee Cannady** 29 August 1987 in Mt. Moriah United Methodist Church, Sampson County, North Carolina, son of Joseph Cannady and Carol Parker. He was born 06 January 1966 in Clinton, Sampson County, North Carolina.

Children of Donna Holland and Clarence Cannady are:

3084 i. **Cody Lee Cannady**, born 25 August 1989.

3085 ii. **Josie Abagail Cannady** was born 21 May 1994, died 21 May 1994 and was buried in Sunrise Memorial Gardens Cemetery on Highway 242 Between Roseboro and Salemburg, Sampson County, North Carolina.

3086 iii. **Jada Holland Cannady**, born 14 August 1995.

2436. Linda Jo Holland (Glenn Turner[8], Euland Randolph[7], William Thomas[6], Thomas James[5], James[4], Daniel[3], Thomas William[2], Unknown[1]) was born 21 October 1967 in Clinton, Sampson County, North Carolina. She married **Erick O'Neal McLamb**. He was born 05 June 1960.

Children of Linda Holland and Erick McLamb are:

3087 i. **Shannon O'Neal McLamb**, born 29 June 1995.

3088 ii. **Adam Taylor McLamb**, born 16 October 1996.

2437. Melanie Joy Parker (Janice F.[8] Butler, Cleo Pearl[7] Holland, William Thomas[6], Thomas James[5], James[4], Daniel[3], Thomas William[2], Unknown[1]) was born 10 September 1960 in Honeycutts Township, Sampson County, North Carolina. She married **(1) Joseph Devane Capps, Jr.**, son of Joseph Devane Capps, Sr., and Sonja Williams. He was born 03 February 1960 in Clinton, Sampson County, North Carolina. She married **(2) Derold Cannady** who was born about 1960.

Child of Melanie Parker and Joseph Capps is:

3089 i. **Jennifer Dawn Capps**, born 19 May 1981.

Child of Melanie Parker and Derold Cannady is:

3090 i. **Miles Cannady**, born about 1982.

2438. Melina Jill Parker (Janice F.[8] Butler, Cleo Pearl[7] Holland, William Thomas[6], Thomas James[5], James[4], Daniel[3], Thomas William[2], Unknown[1]) was born 26 December 1964 in Sampson County, North Carolina. She married **David Lynn Horner** who was born 05 December 1961 in Bluefield, West Virginia.

Jill has been diabetic since 17 year of age.

Children of Melina Parker and David Horner are:

3091 i. **Dustin Frank Horner**, born about 1987.

3092 ii. **Parker Horner,** born about 1992.

2440. Steven Mack Hairr (Brenda Marie[8] Butler, Cleo Pearl[7] Holland, William Thomas[6], Thomas James[5], James[4], Daniel[3], Thomas William[2], Unknown[1]) was born 07 March 1968 in Clinton, Sampson County, North Carolina. He married **Angela Dawn Carter**. She was born 10 April 1969.

Children of Steven Hairr and Angela Carter are:

3093 i. **Jordan Mack Hairr**, born 08 November 1991.

3094 ii. **Megan Marie Hairr**, born 13 November 1994.

2441. Brent Allen Hairr (Brenda Marie[8] Butler, Cleo Pearl[7] Holland, William Thomas[6], Thomas James[5], James[4], Daniel[3], Thomas William[2], Unknown[1]) was born 01 February 1971 in Clinton, Sampson County, North Carolina. He married **Rhonda Claudette Barwick**. She was born 11 January 1971.

Children of Brent Hairr and Rhonda Barwick are:

3095 i. **Allison Dawn Hairr,** born 17 August 1993.

3096 ii. **Hannah Elizabeth Hairr**, born 21 August 1995.

3097 iii. **Emily Caroline Hairr**, born 11 September 1998.

2444. Johnny Charles Hoard, Jr. (Edith Lee[8] Grantham, Ethel Elizabeth[7] Autry, Frances Elizabeth[6] Holland, Thomas James[5], James[4], Daniel[3], Thomas William[2], Unknown[1]) was born 26 February 1943. He married **(1) Judith Hall** About 1965. She was born 27 February 1946. He married **(2) Brenda Edge** About 1979. She was born 28 December 1946.

Children of Johnny Hoard and Judith Hall are:

3098 i. **Robin Ann Hoard**, born 28 May 1966.

3099 ii. **Charles Alex Hoard**, born 18 February 1968.

Child of Johnny Hoard and Brenda Edge is:

3100 i. **Myranda Renee Hoard**, born 26 July 1980.

2445. Janice Lee Hoard (Edith Lee[8] Grantham, Ethel Elizabeth[7] Autry, Frances Elizabeth[6] Holland, Thomas James[5], James[4], Daniel[3], Thomas William[2], Unknown[1]) was born 15 November 1945. She married **James Simpson** who was born 26 March 1943.

Children of Janice Hoard and James Simpson are:

3101 i. **Suzette Simpson**, born 23 May 1965.

3102 ii. **Jamie Lynn Simpson**, born 24 August 1967.

2446. Larry Glenn Hoard (Edith Lee[8] Grantham, Ethel Elizabeth[7] Autry, Frances Elizabeth[6] Holland, Thomas James[5], James[4], Daniel[3], Thomas William[2], Unknown[1]) was born 04 November 1952. He married **Cynthia Powell.** She was born 20 December 1954.

Children of Larry Hoard and Cynthia Powell are:

3103 i. **Stephanie Hoard**, born 20 September 1977.

3104 ii. **Jennifer Lynn Hoard**, born 04 December 1981.

2447. Garry Lee Grantham (Lee Ronald[8], Ethel Elizabeth[7] Autry, Frances Elizabeth[6] Holland, Thomas James[5], James[4], Daniel[3], Thomas William[2], Unknown[1]) was born 20 December 1952. He married **Darlene Brock.** She was born 04 January 1952.

Child of Garry Grantham and Darlene Brock is:

3105 i. **Kellie Darlen Grantham**, born 19 October 1977.

2464. Durwood Kenneth Spell, Jr. (Brownie Catherine[8], Lester Frank[7], Janie Isabell[6] Hairr, Franklin[5] Holland, Harfrey[4], Daniel[3], Thomas William[2], Unknown[1]) was born 08 August 1970. He married **Cynthia Dawn Jackson.** She was born 16 April 1969.

Children of Derwood Spell and Cynthia Jackson are:

3106 i. **Kenneth Blake Spell**, born 23 May 1996.

3107 ii. **Bryce Jackson Spell**, born 30 April 1999.

3108 iii. **Mallory Catherine Spell**, born 10 January 2004.

2465. Bryan Christopher Spell (Brownie Catherine[8], Lester Frank[7], Janie Isabell[6] Hairr, Franklin[5] Holland, Harfrey[4], Daniel[3], Thomas William[2], Unknown[1]) was born 21 March 1973. He married **Susan Gail Zucker**. She was born 09 September 1974.

Child of Bryan Spell and Susan Zucker is:

3109 i. **Hallie Caroline Spell**, born 29 June 2004.

2471. Leonard Scott King (Leonard Paul[8], Jessie Mildridge[7] Holland, Challie Cleveland[6], Jordan[5], Harfrey[4], Daniel[3], Thomas William[2], Unknown[1]) was born 06 March 1965. He married **Billie Jo Butler**. She was born 11 June 1967.

Child of Leonard King and Billie Butler is:

3110 i. **Dalton Scott King**, born 08 March 1995.

2472. Timmy Maxwell King (Leonard Paul[8], Jessie Mildridge[7] Holland, Challie Cleveland[6], Jordan[5], Harfrey[4], Daniel[3], Thomas William[2], Unknown[1]) was born 26 January 1968. He married **Lesa Thigpin**. She was born 18 September 1965.

Child of Timmy King and Lesa Thigpin is:

3111 i. **Payson Trot King**, born 22 December 2002.

2486. Paula Kay Cannady (Richard Harold[8], Wilbert Cleveland[7], Annie Jane[6] Holland, Jordan[5], Harfrey[4], Daniel[3], Thomas William[2], Unknown[1]) was born 31 March 1965. She married **Emilio Alcaraz** who was born 24 May 1965.

Child of Paula Cannady and Emilio Alcaraz is:

3112 i. **Daniel Richard Alcaraz**, born 04 October 1990.

2522. Margarette Rose Aman (Margaret Louvenia[8] Giles, Lessie Jane Holland[7] Williams, Repsie[6] Holland, Chester[5], Harfrey[4], Daniel[3], Thomas William[2], Unknown[1]) was born 06 October 1944 in Roseboro, Sampson County, North Carolina. She married **William Howard Strickland, Jr.** 28 November 1963 in Mingo Baptist Church, Mingo Township, Sampson County, North Carolina. He was born 30 October 1942 in Durham County, North Carolina.

Children of Margarette Aman and William Strickland are:

3113 i. **Paula Michelle Strickland**, born 28 March 1968.

3114 ii. **Dena Renea Strickland**, born 07 May 1970.

2523. Anna Jeanette Aman (Margaret Louvenia[8] Giles, Lessie Jane Holland[7] Williams, Repsie[6] Holland, Chester[5], Harfrey[4], Daniel[3], Thomas William[2], Unknown[1]) was born 28 November 1947. She married **Robert Franklin Youngblood II** 06 October 1968. He was born 19 April 1941 and was from Clayton (probably the Clayton in Johnston County, North Carolina).

Children of Anna Aman and Robert Youngblood are:

3115 i. **Robert Franklin Youngblood III**, born 28 April 1968.

3116 ii. **Cynthia Jeanette Youngblood**, born 26 May 1973.

2524. Iris Marlene Aman (Margaret Louvenia[8] Giles, Lessie Jane Holland[7] Williams, Repsie[6] Holland, Chester[5], Harfrey[4], Daniel[3], Thomas William[2], Unknown[1]) was born 09 April 1952 in Dunn, Harrnett County, North Carolina. She married **Michael Allen O'Neal, Sr.** 21 July 1974 in Mingo Township, Sampson County, North Carolina. He was born 19 September 1952 in Wilson County, North Carolina.

Children of Iris Aman and Michael O'Neal are:

3117 i. **Michael Allen O'Neal, Jr.**, born 18 March 1980.

3118 ii. **Joseph Giles O'Neal**, born 19 April 1983.

2525. Donna Sue Aman (Margaret Louvenia[8] Giles, Lessie Jane Holland[7] Williams, Repsie[6] Holland, Chester[5], Harfrey[4], Daniel[3], Thomas William[2], Unknown[1]) was born 07 October 1953 in Dunn, Harrnett County, North Carolina. She married **Robert Eugene Rupert** 09 September 1973 in Mingo Township, Sampson County, North Carolina. He was born 09 July 1953 in Fort Bragg, North Carolina.

Children of Donna Aman and Robert Rupert are:

3119 i. **Hollie Suzanne Rupert**, born 11 October 1977 in Fayetteville, Cumberland County, North Carolina.

3120 ii. **Laura Rochelle Rupert**, born 10 May 1979.

3121 iii. **Robert Palmer Rupert**, born 21 October 1980.

2545. Norwood Brent Lee (Peggy Florence[8] Holland, James Albert[7], Columbus[6], Chester[5], Harfrey[4], Daniel[3], Thomas William[2], Unknown[1]) was born 27 August 1954. He married **Deborah Susan Roberson** 18 October 1980. She was born 29 May 1958.

Children of Norwood Lee and Deborah Roberson are:

3122 i. **Regan Alexis Lee**, born 19 April 1984.

3123 ii. **Jordan Brent Lee**, born 23 July 1986.

3124 iii. **Kenton Alexander Lee**, born 26 February 1989.

2546. Peggy Joy Lee (Peggy Florence[8] Holland, James Albert[7], Columbus[6], Chester[5], Harfrey[4], Daniel[3], Thomas William[2], Unknown[1]) was born 31 August 1956. She married **Charles Brown** 12 April 1985. He was born 06 January 1945.

Child of Peggy Lee and Charles Brown is:

3125 i. **Natalie Elyse Brown**, born 29 September 1996.

2547. Charlotte Ginny Lee (Peggy Florence[8] Holland, James Albert[7], Columbus[6], Chester[5], Harfrey[4], Daniel[3], Thomas William[2], Unknown[1]) was born 07 April 1961. She married **Michael Sledge** 30 January 1993. He was born 03 May 1964.

Children of Charlotte Lee and Michael Sledge are:

3126 i. **Kerri Michael Sledge**, born 10 June 1994.

3127 ii. **Haley Rebecca Sledge**, born 28 March 1996.

2548. Nancy Catherine Lee (Peggy Florence[8] Holland, James Albert[7], Columbus[6], Chester[5], Harfrey[4], Daniel[3], Thomas William[2], Unknown[1]) was born 25 February 1967. She married **Ray McDonald, Jr.** 03 November 1990. He was born 28 August 1966.

Children of Nancy Lee and Ray McDonald are:

3128 i. **Molly Catherine McDonald**, born 19 December 1995.

3129 ii. **Clayton Lee McDonald**, born 11 August 1998.

2550. Jeanne McDonald (Stella Royal[8] Holland, James Albert[7], Columbus[6], Chester[5], Harfrey[4], Daniel[3], Thomas William[2], Unknown[1]) was born 01 October 1963. She married **Timothy Paul Keene** 22 September 1988. He was born 05 April 1966.

Children of Jeanne McDonald and Timothy Keene are:

3130 i. **Seneca Royal Keene**, born 16 September 1983.

3131 ii. **Cameron Paul Keene**, born 15 March 1989.

2551. Brenda Ann Jones (Ann[8] Holland, James Albert[7], Columbus[6], Chester[5], Harfrey[4], Daniel[3], Thomas William[2], Unknown[1]) was born 19 August 1956. She married **Michael James Harrison** 27 March 1985. He was born 23 December 1944.

Child of Brenda Jones and Michael Harrison is:

3132 i. **Heather Ann Harrison**, born 30 November 1986.

2552. Alvin Keith Jones (Ann^8 Holland, James Albert^7, Columbus^6, Chester^5, Harfrey^4, Daniel^3, Thomas William^2, Unknown^1) was born 21 February 1959. He married **Mary Ann Rames** 13 April 1996.

Child of Alvin Jones and Mary Rames is:

3133 i. **Brandon Keith Jones**, born 17 February 1999.

2555. Gloria Faye Howell (Alice Faye^8 Holland, James Albert^7, Columbus^6, Chester^5, Harfrey^4, Daniel^3, Thomas William^2, Unknown^1) was born 12 December 1962. She married **David Neal Swinson** 01 May 1982. He was born 08 August 1962.

Child of Gloria Howell and David Swinson is:

3134 i. **Gregory Scott Swinson**, born 07 November 1986.

2556. Selina Raye Howell (Alice Faye^8 Holland, James Albert^7, Columbus^6, Chester^5, Harfrey^4, Daniel^3, Thomas William^2, Unknown^1) was born 26 October 1965. She married **William Powell Puryear** 26 October 1985. He was born 26 June 1950.

“Selina Raye’s middle name is also spelled “Rae.”

Child of Selina Howell and William Puryear is:

3135 i. **William Tyler Puryear**, born 21 October 1990.

2558. Deborah Ann Parker (Cathleen^8 Holland, James Albert^7, Columbus^6, Chester^5, Harfrey^4, Daniel^3, Thomas William^2, Unknown^1) was born 19 October 1965. She married **Jimmy Wayne Smith** 28 August 1988. He was born 22 November 1968.

Child of Deborah Parker and Jimmy Smith is:

3136 i. **Carlton Wayne Smith**, born 13 April 1989.

2559. George Michael Parker (Cathleen^8 Holland, James Albert^7, Columbus^6, Chester^5, Harfrey^4, Daniel^3, Thomas William^2, Unknown^1) was born 20 March 1967. He married **Sandra Marie Carlisle** 04 October 1986. She was born 02 October 1968.

On source states Michael’s date of birth is March 29, 1967.

Children of George Parker and Sandra Carlisle are:

3137 i. **Kayla Marie Parker**, born 11 August 1988.

3138 ii. **Kelly Maria Parker**, born 17 January 1994.

2561. Bobbie Jo Jackson (James Leon[8] Holland, James Albert[7], Columbus[6], Chester[5], Harfrey[4], Daniel[3], Thomas William[2], Unknown[1]) was born 04 September 1973. She married **Michael Robert Walter** 01 July 1995. He was born 14 November 1972.

Children of Bobbie Jackson and Michael Walter are:

3139 i. **Savannah Jo Walter**, born 04 October 1996.

3140 ii. **Justin Michael Walter**, born 29 November 1998.

2562. Tonya Jackson (James Leon[8] Holland, James Albert[7], Columbus[6], Chester[5], Harfrey[4], Daniel[3], Thomas William[2], Unknown[1]) was born 19 July 1976. She married **Michael Harold Melton I** 16 September 1995. He was born 03 August 1968.

Children of Tonya Jackson and Michael Melton are:

3141 i. **Samatha Pearl Melton**, born 11 May 1998.

3142 ii. **Michael Harold Melton II**, born 10 May 1999.

2564. Angela Kaye Holland (Ronald Nixon[8], James Albert[7], Columbus[6], Chester[5], Harfrey[4], Daniel[3], Thomas William[2], Unknown[1]) was born 15 August 1973. She married **(1) David Malpas** 19 October 1990. He was born 15 July 1969. She married **(2) Stanley Williams** 19 November 1994.

"Kay" is also found for her middle name.

Child of Angela Holland and David Malpas is:

3143 i. **Michael Malpas**, born 09 September 1992.

2565. Ronnie Tyson Holland (Ronald Nixon[8], James Albert[7], Columbus[6], Chester[5], Harfrey[4], Daniel[3], Thomas William[2], Unknown[1]) was born 22 August 1975. He married **Carolyn Yolanda Worley** 09 November 1998.

Child of Ronnie Holland and Carolyn Worley is:

3144 i. **Mya Elon Holland**, born 12 May 1999.

2567. Jack Maurice Holton, Jr. (Emily Frances[8] Holland, Chester Ausbon[7], Erastus[6], Chester[5], Harfrey[4], Daniel[3], Thomas William[2], Unknown[1]) was born 02 December 1953. He married **(1) Kathryn Marie Smith** 28 May 1977. He married **(2) Virginia Elkin Phillips** 20 April 1985. She was born in Richmond, Virginia.

Children of Jack Holton and Virginia Phillips are:

3145 i. **Ben Wiley Holton**, born 21 July 1986.

3146 ii. **Rebecca Jean Holton,** born 11 April 1989.

2571. Linda Louise Sollinger (Merle Floyd[8], Elma[7] Holland, Erastus[6], Chester[5], Harfrey[4], Daniel[3], Thomas William[2], Unknown[1]) was born 31 May 1963. She married **Aubry Lee Toler, Jr.** 23 October 1984. He was born 02 June 1963.

Child of Linda Sollinger and Aubry Toler is:

3147 i. **Christopher Scott Toler,** born 11 November 1987.

2577. Catherine Louise Crouch (Peggy Ann[8] Tripp, Edna Louise[7] Holland, John Love[6], Chester[5], Harfrey[4], Daniel[3], Thomas William[2], Unknown[1]) was born 06 June 1970 in Wilmington, North Carolina. She married **Kenneth Gerald Baker** October 1990 in Wilmington, New Hanover County, North Carolina.

Child of Catherine Crouch and Kenneth Baker is:

3148 i. **Kenneth Michael Zackary Baker,** born 29 April 1990.

2595. Ginger Marie Grantham (Byron Wayne[8], Irene[7] Naylor, Lillie[6] Holland, Chester[5], Harfrey[4], Daniel[3], Thomas William[2], Unknown[1]) was born 15 November 1972. She married **Hank Hossell.** The year1973 is found for her birth.

Children of Ginger Grantham and Hank Hossell are:

3149 i. **Brent Hossell.**

3150 ii. **Jay Michael Hossell.**

2603. Eric Napoleon Faircloth (Festus DeVone[8], Pauline[7] Spell, Braxton[6], Romelia[5] Holland, Harfrey[4], Daniel[3], Thomas William[2], Unknown[1]) was born 15 April 1965 in Clinton, Sampson County, North Carolina. He married **Jenifer Mae Naylor** 08 December 1985 in Corinth Missionary Baptist Church near Salemburg, North Carolina, daughter of James Naylor and Gracy Barefoot. She was born 08 March 1965 in Dunn, Harnett County, North Carolina.

"Erick" is found for his first name. and "Jennifer" for the spelling of her first name.

Children of Eric Faircloth and Jenifer Naylor are:

3151 i. **Jonathan Eric Faircloth,** born 03 February 1990 in Dunn, Harnett County, North Carolina.

3152 ii. **Erica Brooke Faircloth,** born May 1993 in Harnett County, North Carolina.

3153 iii. **Ethan Alexander Faircloth,** born February 1995 in Harnett County, North Carolina.

2606. Ryan Arthur Faircloth (Henry Enoch[8], Pauline[7] Spell, Braxton[6], Romelia[5] Holland, Harfrey[4], Daniel[3], Thomas William[2], Unknown[1]) was born 30 June 1972 in Sampson County, North Carolina, and died 31 August 1996 in Sampson County, North Carolina. He married **Rachel Marie Oliver**.

Child of Ryan Faircloth and Rachel Oliver is:

3154 i. **Ryan Lanier Oliver Faircloth**, born 26 December 1996 in Sampson County, North Carolina.

2636. Helen Fowler (Thelma Mae[8] Lockamy, William Lischer[7], Onie Vendex[6] Holland, William Wright[5], Thomas James[4], Daniel[3], Thomas William[2], Unknown[1]) was born 11 June 1944. She married **William J. Carr**.

Children of Helen Fowler and William Carr are:

3155 i. **Jennifer Carr.**

3156 ii. **Allison Carr.**

2638. Ronald Wayne Fowler (Thelma Mae[8] Lockamy, William Lischer[7], Onie Vendex[6] Holland, William Wright[5], Thomas James[4], Daniel[3], Thomas William[2], Unknown[1]) was born 07 November 1947, and died 01 March 1983. He married **Brenda Faye Jackson**, daughter of Andrew Davis Jackson and Georgia Long. She was born 27 May 1951.

Ronald and Brenda were divorced. He was buried in Grandview Memorial Gardens, Clinton, North Carolina.

Child of Ronald Fowler and Brenda Jackson is:

3157 i. **Cristal Gail Fowler.** She married **Unknown Smith.**

2640. Jimmy Ray Fowler (Thelma Mae[8] Lockamy, William Lischer[7], Onie Vendex[6] Holland, William Wright[5], Thomas James[4], Daniel[3], Thomas William[2], Unknown[1]) was born 29 May 1952. He married **Brenda Mitchell.**

Children of Jimmy Fowler and Brenda Mitchell are:

3158 i. **Allen Fowler.**

3159 ii. **Neil Fowler.**

2641. Glenda Kaye Fowler (Thelma Mae[8] Lockamy, William Lischer[7], Onie Vendex[6] Holland, William Wright[5], Thomas James[4], Daniel[3], Thomas William[2], Unknown[1]) was born 26 January 1954 in Clinton, Sampson County, North Carolina. She married **Gary Bertrand Jackson** 11 January 1975 in Belvoir Township, Sampson County, North Carolina, son of Calvin Jackson and Lula Godbold. He was born 24 September 1950 in Roseboro, Sampson County, North Carolina.

Children of Glenda Fowler and Gary Jackson are:

3160 i. **Gary Bradley Jackson**, born 21 July 1978 in Clinton, Sampson County, North Carolina.

3161 ii. **William Martin Jackson**, born 10 August 1980 in Clinton, Sampson County, North Carolina.

2642. Brenda Faye Fowler (Thelma Mae[8] Lockamy, William Lischer[7], Onie Vendex[6] Holland, William Wright[5], Thomas James[4], Daniel[3], Thomas William[2], Unknown[1]) was born 26 January 1954. She married **Steve Coats**.

Children of Brenda Fowler and Steve Coats are:

3162 i. **Stephen Coats.**

3163 ii. **Stephanie Coats.**

3164 iii. **Joseph Coats.**

2648. Billy Satterfield (Ethel L.[8] Cannady, Annie[7] Lockamy, Onie Vendex[6] Holland, William Wright[5], Thomas James[4], Daniel[3], Thomas William[2], Unknown[1]) was born 06 April 1943. He married **Donna Sumner**.

Children of Billy Satterfield and Donna Sumner are:

3165 i. **Kelly Satterfield**, born 06 March 1971. She married **Scott Jones**.

\+ 3166 ii. **Brent Satterfield**, born 10 August 1973.

2649. Barbara Jean Satterfield (Ethel L.[8] Cannady, Annie[7] Lockamy, Onie Vendex[6] Holland, William Wright[5], Thomas James[4], Daniel[3], Thomas William[2], Unknown[1]) was born 28 October 1945. She married **Dennis Raynor**.

Children of Barbara Satterfield and Dennis Raynor are:

3167 i. **Glenwood Carroll Raynor.**

\+ 3168 ii. **Karen Denise Raynor.**

2651. James Harold Cannady (James E.[8], Annie[7] Lockamy, Onie Vendex[6] Holland, William Wright[5], Thomas James[4], Daniel[3], Thomas William[2], Unknown[1]) was born 07 December 1946. He married **Linda (Maiden Name Unknown)**.

Child of James Cannady and Linda Unknown is:

3169 i. **Jamie Cannady.**

2652. Jewell Denise Cannady (James E.[8], Annie[7] Lockamy, Onie Vendex[6] Holland, William Wright[5], Thomas James[4], Daniel[3], Thomas William[2], Unknown[1]) was born 23 October 1955. She married **(1) Robert Wayne Shatterly**. She married **(2) Mike Bass.**

Child of Jewell Cannady and Wayne Shatterly is:

3170 i. **Bobby Shatterly.**

2653. Chris Cannady (William John[8], Annie[7] Lockamy, Onie Vendex[6] Holland, William Wright[5], Thomas James[4], Daniel[3], Thomas William[2], Unknown[1]) He married **Lee Ann Unknown.**

Child of Chris Cannady and Lee Unknown is:

3171 i. **Cameron Cannady.**

2656. Robert Wayne Adams, Sr., (Astraudia Brown[8] Lockamy, Robert Owen[7], Onie Vendex[6] Holland, William Wright[5], Thomas James[4], Daniel[3], Thomas William[2], Unknown[1]) was born 28 February 1950 in Dunn Hospital, North Carolina. He married **Christie Leigh Shaw** 01 June 1973, daughter of Clifford Shaw and Dorothy Pepin. She was born 26 July 1952 in Galena Park, Texas.

Children of Robert Adams and Christie Shaw are:

3172 i. **Amy Charriene LaVal Adams,** born 13 August 1974.

3173 ii. **Angelyn Marie Stellaundine Adams,** born 18 March 1977.

3174 iii. **Robert Wayne Adams, Jr.,** born Between 1977 - 1981.

3175 iv. **Amber Christine Hennritta Adams,** born 27 December 1979.

2658. William Albert Tyndall (Doris Marie[8] Ellis, Janie Lou[7] Lockamy, Onie Vendex[6] Holland, William Wright[5], Thomas James[4], Daniel[3], Thomas William[2], Unknown[1]) was born 30 June 1947 in Honeycutts Township, Sampson County, North Carolina. He married **Peggy Irene Thornton** who was born 15 January 1946.

His middle name is also given as Alfred.

Children of William Tyndall and Peggy Thornton are:

3176 i. **William Allen Tyndall.**

Living wife and two daughters.

3177 ii. **Valeria Rose Tyndall.**

She married twice and has one child with each spouse.

2659. Diane Marie Tyndall (Doris Marie[8] Ellis, Janie Lou[7] Lockamy, Onie Vendex[6] Holland, William Wright[5], Thomas James[4], Daniel[3], Thomas William[2], Unknown[1]) was born 01 October 1950 in Herrings Township, Sampson County, North Carolina. She married **Samuel Lee Cannady**, son of Samuel Cannady and Eva Gallagher. He was born 02 December 1948.

Child of Diane Tyndall and Samuel Cannady is:

\+ 3178 i. **Donnie Lee Cannady**, born 12 December 1967.

2662. Bronzell Truman Royal (Truman D.[8], Ivy D.[7], Robertson[6] Royals, Agnes Matilda[5] Holland, Matthew[4], Daniel[3], Thomas William[2], Unknown[1]) was born 28 February 1955 in Roseboro, North Carolina, and died 17 August 1993. He married **(1) Vickie Ann Guinn** Before 1974. She was born About 1957. He married **(2) Feebee B. Unknown** After 1974.

Bronzell Truman is buried in Union Grove Baptist Church Cemetery, Sampson County, North Carolina.

Child of Bronzell Royal and Vickie Guinn is:

3179 i. **Bridget Ann Royal**, born 18 January 1974 in Clinton, Sampson County, North Carolina.

Children of Bronzell Royal and Feebee Unknown are:

3180 i. **Margaret Rose Royal.**

3181 ii. **Marsha Royal.**

3182 iii. **James Carl Brehm.**

2677. James Elvin Jackson, Jr. (Judy Katherine[8] Barnes, James William[7], Julia[6] Holland, Robert Mitchell[5], Matthew[4], Daniel[3], Thomas William[2], Unknown[1]) was born

21 January 1968 in Raleigh, North Carolina. He married **(1) Rebecca Rivers**. He married **(2) Sharon Jacquline Umstead** 28 July 1995 in Garner, North Carolina, daughter of Alexander Umstead and Jacquline Thigpen. She was born 16 January 1968 in Raleigh, North Carolina.

James Elvin is known as "Jimmy." Sharon Jacquline has a B.S. from UNCW and is in Health Care.

Child of James Jackson and Rebecca Rivers is:

3183 i. **Joshua Arthur Jackson**, born 08 February 1994.

Children of James Jackson and Sharon Umstead are:

3184 i. **James Alexander Jackson**, born 24 September 1996.

3185 ii. **Jenna Marie Jackson**, born 12 May 2000.

2678. John Trent Jackson (Judy Katherine[8] Barnes, James William[7], Julia[6] Holland, Robert Mitchell[5], Matthew[4], Daniel[3], Thomas William[2], Unknown[1]) was born 15 December 1974. He married **Michele Angelique Garceau** 27 July 1996 in Highland Baptist Church, Raleigh, North Carolina. She was born 26 June 1974.

John Trent is called "Johnny." He and Michele Angelique are divorced.

Child of John Jackson and Michele Garceau is:

3186 i. **JoAnn Nicole Jackson**, born 07 January 1999.

2679. Joseph Wayne Jackson (Judy Katherine[8] Barnes, James William[7], Julia[6] Holland, Robert Mitchell[5], Matthew[4], Daniel[3], Thomas William[2], Unknown[1]) was born 15 December 1974. He married **Misty Jo Allen**. She was born 12 July 1975.

Joseph Wayne is called "Jody."

Child of Joseph Jackson and Misty Allen is:

3187 i. **Joseph Allen Jackson**, born 15 February 2003.

2680. Jennifer Lynn Fann (Jennifer Gray[8] Barnes, James William[7], Julia[6] Holland, Robert Mitchell[5], Matthew[4], Daniel[3], Thomas William[2], Unknown[1]) was born 02 January 1975 in Clinton, Sampson County, North Carolina. She married **(1) Dean Wilson** about 1998. She married **(2) Donnie Osborne** about 2002.

Child of Jennifer Fann and Dean Wilson is:

3188 i. **Jordan Brianne Wilson**, born 29 January 1999.

Child of Jennifer Fann and Donnie Osborne is:

3189 i. **Jennifer Paige Osborne**, born 11 November 2003.

2705. Janice Faye Hall (Fletcher Evans[8], Thomas Iverson[7], Mary J.[6] Williams, John E.[5], Tomzelle[4] Culbreth, Mary[3] Holland, Thomas William[2], Unknown[1]) was born 07 March 1942 in Dismal Township, Sampson County, North Carolina. She married **Joseph Preston Naylor,** son of Earphy Naylor and Jennette Naylor. He was born 01 July 1938 in Herrings Township, Sampson County, North Carolina.

Children of Janice Hall and Joseph Naylor are:

3190 i. **Susan Paulette Naylor**, born 17 November 1960 in Clinton, Sampson County, North Carolina.

3191 ii. **Jeffrey Preston Naylor**, born 19 February 1963 in Clinton, Sampson County, North Carolina.

2709. Janet Rose Warren (Ruth[8] Starling, Luther Washington[7], Mary Catherine[6] Williams, Isaac[5], Tomzelle[4] Culbreth, Mary[3] Holland, Thomas William[2], Unknown[1]) was born 07 December 1938 in Mingo Township, Sampson County, North Carolina. She married **Worth Wingate Collier** 30 December 1962 in Mt. Elam Baptist Church near Piney Green, Sampson County, North Carolina. He was born 09 January 1938 on a Rural Route of Wade, Cumberland County, North Carolina.

Child of Janet Warren and Worth Collier is:

3192 i. **David Allen Collier**, born 20 June 1973.

2710. Dixie Ruth Warren (Ruth[8] Starling, Luther Washington[7], Mary Catherine[6] Williams, Isaac[5], Tomzelle[4] Culbreth, Mary[3] Holland, Thomas William[2], Unknown[1]) was born 23 May 1945 in Dunn, Harnett County, North Carolina. She married **Jerry Lee Honeycutt I** 28 June 1964 in Mt. Elam Baptist Church near Piney Green, Sampson County, North Carolina. He was born 02 July 1944 in Mingo Township, Sampson County, North Carolina.

Dixie Ruth and Jerry Lee were divorced.

Children of Dixie Warren and Jerry Honeycutt are:

3193 i. **Angela Rose Honeycutt**, born 20 November 1969 in Clinton, Sampson County, North Carolina.

3194 ii. **Ginger Warren Honeycutt**, born 27 October 1971 in Clinton, Sampson County, North Carolina.

3195 iii. Jerry Lee Honeycutt II, born 12 August 1976 in Clinton, Sampson County, North Carolina.

2711. Herman Denning Warren (Ruth[8] Starling, Luther Washington[7], Mary Catherine[6] Williams, Isaac[5], Tomzelle[4] Culbreth, Mary[3] Holland, Thomas William[2], Unknown[1]) was born 07 January 1950 in Dunn, Harnett County, North Carolina. He married **Darlene Jane Howell**, daughter of Marvis E. Howell.

Herman may live in Texas. Darlene Jane married first Jimmy L. Jackson of Duplin County. The had two children who are listed as Warrens here. The year of Darlene Jane's birth, about 1961 listed by Mr. Rosser, Jr., may be incorrect since he gives the birth date of her daughter as April 30, 1961. Darlene lives in North Carolina.

Children of Herman Warren and Darlene Howell are:

\+ 3196 i. **Deborah Kathryn Jackson Warren**, died 24 August 1993 in Raleigh, Wake County, North Carolina.

3197 ii. **Jimmy Lee Jackson Warren**, born 24 June 1964.

2712. Luther Simpson Jackson (Avis[8] Starling, Luther Washington[7], Mary Catherine[6] Williams, Isaac[5], Tomzelle[4] Culbreth, Mary[3] Holland, Thomas William[2], Unknown[1]) was born 24 September 1941 in Dunn, Harnett County, North Carolina. He married **Florence Annette Autry** 09 September 1961 in Clement Baptist Church, Sampson County, North

Carolina, daughter of James Autry and Ella Hairr. She was born 02 June 1942 in Dismal Township, Sampson County, North Carolina.

Luther Simpson and Florence Annette are divorced.

Children of Luther Jackson and Florence Autry are:

3198 i. **Scott Jackson.**

3199 ii. **Lisa Ann Jackson,** born 24 October 1963 in Fayetteville, Cumberland County, North Carolina.

3200 iii. Christopher Todd Jackson, born 21 August 1967 in Fayetteville, Cumberland County, North Carolina.

3201 iv. **Michael Lynn Jackson**, born 01 December 1968 in Fayetteville, Cumberland County, North Carolina.

2714. Wanda Baggett Jackson (Avis[8] Starling, Luther Washington[7], Mary Catherine[6] Williams, Isaac[5], Tomzelle[4] Culbreth, Mary[3] Holland, Thomas William[2], Unknown[1]) was born 14 January 1953 in Dunn, Harnett County, North Carolina. She married **Alton William Hardison, Jr.** in October 1975 in Mt. Elam Baptist Church, Sampson County, North Carolina. He was born 23 February 1953 in Dunn, Harnett County, North Carolina.

Children of Wanda Jackson and Alton Hardison are:

3202 i. **Sarah Ines Hardison,** born 19 January 1981 in Raleigh, North Carolina.

3203 ii. **Mary Kathryn Hardison,** born 06 November 1988 in Raleigh, North Carolina.

2719. Sidney Jo Starling (Hiram Roberson[8], Hiram Roberson[7], Mary Catherine[6] Williams, Isaac[5], Tomzelle[4] Culbreth, Mary[3] Holland, Thomas William[2], Unknown[1]) was born 21 May 1951. She married **John Francis Davis**. He was born 25 February 1948.

Sidney Jo Starling and her husband, John Francis Davis, lived in Dallas, Texas, at one time.

Child of Sidney Starling and John Davis is:

3204 i. **Cari Ann Davis,** born 11 February 1970.

2720. Tracy Ann Starling (Hiram Roberson[8], Hiram Roberson[7], Mary Catherine[6] Williams, Isaac[5], Tomzelle[4] Culbreth, Mary[3] Holland, Thomas William[2], Unknown[1]) was born 09 February 1954. She married **James Carl Hensarling**. He was born 10 December 1949.

Tracy Ann Starling and her husband, James Carl Hensarling, lived at one time in Dallas, Texas.

Child of Tracy Starling and James Hensarling is:

3205 i. **Jake Lee Hensarling,** born 21 May 1980.

2724. Patricia Ann Wrench (Quinton Randall[8], Fletcher E.[7], Lovdie Ann[6] Williams, Isaac[5], Tomzelle[4] Culbreth, Mary[3] Holland, Thomas William[2], Unknown[1]) was born 12 October 1940. She married **Elliott Lee Spell, Jr.** He was born 11 December 1939 in Little Coharie Township, Sampson County, North Carolina.

Children of Patricia Wrench and Elliott Spell are:

3206 i. **Eric Dale Spell,** born 17 February 1967 in Clinton, Sampson County, North Carolina.

\+ 3207 ii. **Lee Ann Spell,** born 12 January 1972.

2725. James Philip Wrench (Quinton Randall[8], Fletcher E.[7], Lovdie Ann[6] Williams, Isaac[5], Tomzelle[4] Culbreth, Mary[3] Holland, Thomas William[2], Unknown[1]) was born 13 September 1942 in Roseboro, North Carolina. He married **(1) Ondra Elizabeth Honeycutt** Before 1964. She was born About 1943 in Sampson County, North Carolina. He married **(2) Georgia Bell Williams** after 1964. She was born 06 April 1945 in Dismal Township, Sampson County, North Carolina.

Georgia Bell Williams first married Denning Ray Breedlove and they had two children who are not noted in the source.

Child of James Wrench and Ondra Honeycutt is:

3208 i. **James Gregory Wrench,** born 26 September 1964 in Clinton, Sampson County, North Carolina. He married **Tracy Jeannette Register** 03 October 1987 in Lee's Chapel Free Will Baptist Church; born 14 December 1964 in Dunn, Harnett County, North Carolina.

2734. Mildred Joyce Draughon (May Dee[8] Tew, Cornelia[7] Wrench, Lovdie Ann[6] Williams, Isaac[5], Tomzelle[4] Culbreth, Mary[3] Holland, Thomas William[2], Unknown[1]) was born 24 December 1934 in Fayetteville, Cumberland County, North Carolina. She married **Howard Odell Baggett** 13 June 1953 in Baptist Chapel Church near Autryville, Sampson County, North Carolina, son of Aldon Baggett and Verta Lee. He was born 07 July 1931 in Erwin, Harnett County, North Carolina.

Howard Odell was called "Billy."

Children of Mildred Draughon and Howard Baggett are:

3209 i. **Billy Dwayne Baggett,** born 04 July 1954 in Fayetteville, Cumberland County, North Carolina.

3210 ii. **Joyce Elaine Baggett,** born 02 October 1956; died 05 October 1956.

She is buried in Baptist Chapel near Autryville, Sampson County, North Carolina.

\+ 3211 iii. **Wendy Sue Baggett,** born 11 May 1961 in Mt. View, California.

2735. Mary Ann Tew (Wyman A.[8], Cornelia[7] Wrench, Lovdie Ann[6] Williams, Isaac[5], Tomzelle[4] Culbreth, Mary[3] Holland, Thomas William[2], Unknown[1]) was born 10 June 1936. She married **Miguel Rodrigues.**

Children of Mary Tew and Miguel Rodrigues are:

3212 i. **Michael Rodrigues.**

3213 ii. **Male Child Rodrigues.**

2736. Wilma Gainey Tew (Wyman A.[8], Cornelia[7] Wrench, Lovdie Ann[6] Williams, Isaac[5], Tomzelle[4] Culbreth, Mary[3] Holland, Thomas William[2], Unknown[1]) was born 16 August 1938. She married **Bobby J. Bailey**.

Children of Wilma Tew and Bobby Bailey are:

3214 i. **Lex Bailey.**

3215 ii. **Bobbi Ann Bailey.**

3216 iii. **Becky Bailey.**

2737. Billie Frances Tew (Wyman A.[8], Cornelia[7] Wrench, Lovdie Ann[6] Williams, Isaac[5], Tomzelle[4] Culbreth, Mary[3] Holland, Thomas William[2], Unknown[1]) was born 30 October 1940. She married **William P. Jackson**.

Children of Billie Tew and William Jackson are:

3217 i. **Chet Jackson.**

3218 ii. **Marla Rai Jackson.**

3219 iii. **Ashley Jackson.**

2738. Sarah Lou Tew (Wyman A.[8], Cornelia[7] Wrench, Lovdie Ann[6] Williams, Isaac[5], Tomzelle[4] Culbreth, Mary[3] Holland, Thomas William[2], Unknown[1]) was born 12 October 1951. She married **Bud Kuchman**.

Child of Sarah Tew and Bud Kuchman is:

3220 i. **Carrie Kelly Kuchman.**

2740. James Shelton Tew (Desmon Shelton[8], Cornelia[7] Wrench, Lovdie Ann[6] Williams, Isaac[5], Tomzelle[4] Culbreth, Mary[3] Holland, Thomas William[2], Unknown[1]) was born 10 January 1950. He married **Sandra Hope House**. She was born 24 June 1949.

Child of James Tew and Sandra House is:

3221 i. **Angela Hope Tew**, born 15 November 1969 in Fayetteville, Cumberland County, North Carolina. She married **James Timothy Naylor** 22 August 1992 in Baptist Chapel Church near Autryville, Sampson County, North Carolina; born 21 June 1970 in Cumberland County, North Carolina.

2743. Offie B. Tew III (Theophilus Beaufort[8], Cornelia[7] Wrench, Lovdie Ann[6] Williams, Isaac[5], Tomzelle[4] Culbreth, Mary[3] Holland, Thomas William[2], Unknown[1]) was born 26 July 1947 in Honeycutts Township, Sampson County, North Carolina. His name may have been Theophilus Beaufort III and he was known by Offie. He married **Junette Vaughn Butler**. She was born 19 November 1947 in Roseboro, North Carolina.

Offie B. was called "Benny."

Child of Offie Tew and Junette Butler is:

3222 i. **Kimberly Vaughn Tew**, born 17 May 1969 in Clinton, Sampson County, North Carolina. She married **Stephen Lee Mallard**; born 02 November 1966 in Craven County, North Carolina.

2759. Joan Marie Ivey (Dicie Catherine[8] Williams, Thera Wesley[7], Sarah Eliza[6], Isaac[5], Tomzelle[4] Culbreth, Mary[3] Holland, Thomas William[2], Unknown[1]) was born 10 November 1959 in Fayetteville, Cumberland County, North Carolina. She married **Larry Thomas Lee** 17 April 1976 in Baptist Chapel Church near Autryville, Sampson County, North Carolina, son of Charles Lee and Lois Page. He was born 29 December 1958 in Dunn, Harnett County, North Carolina, and died 19 March 1978 on Route 1, Dunn, Harnett County, North Carolina in an automobile accident.

Child of Joan Ivey and Larry Lee is:

3223 i. **Marsha Gail Lee**, born 22 October 1976 in Dunn, Harnett County, North Carolina.

2761. Kathryn Ann Ivey (Dicie Catherine[8] Williams, Thera Wesley[7], Sarah Eliza[6], Isaac[5], Tomzelle[4] Culbreth, Mary[3] Holland, Thomas William[2], Unknown[1]) was born 07 May 1965 in Clinton, Sampson County, North Carolina. She married **(1) Unknown Blount** Before 1988. She married **(2) Robert Wayne Moore** 17 August 1992 in Baptist Chapel Church near Autryville, Sampson County, North Carolina. He was born 15 July 1966.

Child of Kathryn Ivey and Unknown Blount is:

3224 i. **Wesley Blount**.

2766. Tammy Ann Williams (Thomas Elva[8], Thera Wesley[7], Sarah Eliza[6], Isaac[5], Tomzelle[4] Culbreth, Mary[3] Holland, Thomas William[2], Unknown[1]) was born 12 February 1966 in Dunn, Harnett County, North Carolina. She married **Arthur Lee Naylor** 27 January 1985 in Baptist Chapel, near Autryville, North Carolina, son of Leatrice Naylor and Merlin Crumpler. He was born 14 September 1961 in Clinton Cemetery, Clinton, North Carolina.

Children of Tammy Williams and Arthur Naylor are:

3225 i. **Leslie Marie Naylor**, born 04 May 1989 in Clinton, Sampson County, North Carolina.

3226 ii. **Daniel Lee Naylor**, born 06 April 1992 in Clinton, Sampson County, North Carolina.

2767. Kimberly Ruth Williams (Thomas Elva[8], Thera Wesley[7], Sarah Eliza[6], Isaac[5], Tomzelle[4] Culbreth, Mary[3] Holland, Thomas William[2], Unknown[1]) was born 27 March 1974 in Clinton Cemetery, Clinton, Sampson County, North Carolina. She married **Darrell Scott Naylor**, son of Vernon Naylor and Leta Jackson. He was born 07 June 1965 in Clinton, Sampson County, North Carolina.

Child of Kimberly Williams and Darrell Naylor is:

3227 i. **Johnathan Scott Naylor**, born 16 December 1991 in Clinton, Sampson County, North Carolina.

2770. Norman Timothy McLaurin (Augustus Merrill[8], Alma May[7] Bain, John C.[6], Susan Ann[5] Williams, Tomzelle[4] Culbreth, Mary[3] Holland, Thomas William[2], Unknown[1]) was born 13 March 1945 in Cumberland County, North Carolina. He married **Jennie Sylvia Culbreth**. She was born 11 December 1944 in Cumberland County, North Carolina.

Children of Norman McLaurin and Jennie Culbreth are:

3228 i. **Tammy Jenneane McLaurin**, born 04 January 1964.

3229 ii. **Darrell Timothy McLaurin**, born 30 December 1965 in Cumberland County, North Carolina. He married **Patricia Louise Pate** 24 May 1986; born 27 February 1965.

2775. Cheryl Elaine Tyndall (Charles Edwin[8], Lula Mae[7] Autry, James Love[6], Daniel[5], Millzy Adelme[4] Culbreth, Mary[3] Holland, Thomas William[2], Unknown[1]) was born 13 April 1968 in Clinton, Sampson County, North Carolina. She married **Thomas Worth Smith** 01 September 1990 in Salemburg, North Carolina. He was born 19 September 1967 in Statesville, North Carolina.

Children of Cheryl Tyndall and Thomas Smith are:

3230 i. **Hunter Worth Smith**, born 18 October 1993.

3231 ii. **Jennie Gayle Smith**, born 21 November 1996.

3232 iii. **Thomas Edwin Smith**, born 03 May 2002.

2777. James Randall Draughon (Billy Carrol[8], Mildred[7] Autry, James Love[6], Daniel[5], Millzy Adelme[4] Culbreth, Mary[3] Holland, Thomas William[2], Unknown[1]) was born 07 June 1962 in Raleigh, North Carolina. He married **Cindy Hansen**. She was born 27 October 1954.

Children of James Draughon and Cindy Hansen are:

3233 i. **Andrew James Draughon**, born 03 January 1985.

3234 ii. **Christopher Carroll Draughon**, born 06 May 1987.

3235 iii. **Steven Randall Draughon**, born 14 April 1989.

3236 iv. **Michael Grant Draughon**, born 14 April 1989.

2780. Brenda Jean Draughon (Lattie[8], Mildred[7] Autry, James Love[6], Daniel[5], Millzy Adelme[4] Culbreth, Mary[3] Holland, Thomas William[2], Unknown[1]) was born 23 December 1967 in Aurora, Colorado. She married **Unknown Haire**.

Children of Brenda Draughon and Unknown Haire are:

3237 i. **Ryan Haire**, born 04 October 1998.

3238 ii. **Chadwick Haire**, born 03 August 2000; died 03 April 2002.

2784. Karen Faye Parker (Judy Ann[8] Draughon, Mildred[7] Autry, James Love[6], Daniel[5], Millzy Adelme[4] Culbreth, Mary[3] Holland, Thomas William[2], Unknown[1]) was born 04 June 1967 in Monroe, North Carolina. She married **Aaron Griffin**. He was born 02 October 1972.

Child of Karen Parker and Aaron Griffin is:

3239 i. **Samuel Aaron Griffin**, born 23 March 2002.

2789. Bobby Lee Sessoms (Roland[8], Mollie[7] Williams, Susan Anner[6], Rebecca Elizabeth[5] Autry, Millzy Adelme[4] Culbreth, Mary[3] Holland, Thomas William[2], Unknown[1]) was born 01 August 1939, and died 02 April 2001. He married **Oloby May McPhail** 29 June 1961, daughter of James McPhail and Lessie Honeycutt. She was born 13 May 1942.

Apparently, county records show 2 August 1940 for his date of birth. He is buried in Union Grove Baptist Church Cemetery on Vander Road one mile west of Rebel City, Sampson County, North Carolina.

Child of Bobby Sessoms and Oloby McPhail is:

3240 i. **Jane Michelle Sessoms**, born About 1965.

2790. Billy Roland Sessoms (Roland[8], Mollie[7] Williams, Susan Anner[6], Rebecca Elizabeth[5] Autry, Millzy Adelme[4] Culbreth, Mary[3] Holland, Thomas William[2], Unknown[1]) was born 14 May 1942 in Roseboro, North Carolina. He married **(1) Elizabeth Armeallia Faircloth**. She was born 24 November 1942 in Little Coharie Township, Sampson County, North Carolina. He married **(2) Jeanette Cook**. She was born Unknown.

Children of Billy Sessoms and Elizabeth Faircloth are:

\+ 3241 i. **James Roland Sessoms**, born 23 June 1965.

\+ 3242 ii. **Karen Celester Sessoms**, born About 1968.

\+ 3243 iii. **Deana LeeAnn Sessoms**, born About 1972.

2791. Jackie Lester Sessoms (Roland[8], Mollie[7] Williams, Susan Anner[6], Rebecca Elizabeth[5] Autry, Millzy Adelme[4] Culbreth, Mary[3] Holland, Thomas William[2], Unknown[1]) was born 27 October 1944 in Roseboro, North Carolina. He married **Margaret Ann Smith**. She was born 04 September 1947.

Children of Jackie Sessoms and Margaret Smith are:

+ 3244 i. **Kimberly Ann Sessoms**, born 01 August 1967.
+ 3245 ii. **Melonie Denice Sessoms**, born 03 August 1971.

2792. Brenda Sessoms (Roland[8], Mollie[7] Williams, Susan Anner[6], Rebecca Elizabeth[5] Autry, Millzy Adelme[4] Culbreth, Mary[3] Holland, Thomas William[2], Unknown[1]) was born 16 November 1946. She married **Earl Clayton Tanner**. He was born 19 February 1947.

Children of Brenda Sessoms and Earl Tanner are:

+ 3246 i. **Kevin Earl Tanner**, born 11 April 1972.
3247 ii. **Shannon Noah Tanner**, born 24 April 1974.
3248 iii. **Brian Clay Tanner**, born 14 February 1984.

2793. Cyrus James Faircloth I (Nina[8] Sessoms, Mollie[7] Williams, Susan Anner[6], Rebecca Elizabeth[5] Autry, Millzy Adelme[4] Culbreth, Mary[3] Holland, Thomas William[2], Unknown[1]) was born 27 March 1936 in Little Coharie Township, Sampson County, North Carolina. He married **(1) Emma Ernestine Baggett** 05 November 1960 in Dismal Township, Sampson County, North Carolina, daughter of Ernie Baggett and Oleta Peterson. She was born 01 January 1942 in Dismal Township, Sampson Caounty, North Carolina. He married **(2) Betty Josephine Honeycutt** 14 July 1984 in North Clinton Township, Sampson County, North Carolina, daughter of Samuel Honeycutt and Levonnie Chestnutt. She was born 09 August 1936 in Honeycutts Township, Sampson County, North Carolina.

Emma "Tina" and Cyrus divorced in November 1982.

Children of Cyrus Faircloth and Emma Baggett are:

+ 3249 i. **Marilyn Lynette Faircloth**, born 24 March 1963 in Fayetteville, Cumberland County, North Carolina.
3250 ii. **Cyrus James Faircloth II**, born 24 May 1965 in Fayetteville, Cumberland County, North Carolina. He married Ashlea Brenner.

2794. Resson Oliver Faircloth, Sr. (Nina[8] Sessoms, Mollie[7] Williams, Susan Anner[6], Rebecca Elizabeth[5] Autry, Millzy Adelme[4] Culbreth, Mary[3] Holland, Thomas William[2], Unknown[1]) was born 10 August 1937. He married **Hilda Mae Hobbs**. She was born 30 July 1937 in Little Coharie Township, Sampson County, North Carolina.

Children of Resson Faircloth and Hilda Hobbs are:

3251 i. **Hilda Frances Faircloth**, born 30 July 1959; died 31 July 1959 in Clinton, North Carolina.

3252 ii. **Resson Oliver Faircloth, Jr.**, born 01 February 1962.

3253 iii. **John Norwood Faircloth**, born 08 December 1963.

3254 iv. **Frankie Mae Faircloth**, born 09 December 1964.

2797. Rosa Faye Faircloth (Nina[8] Sessoms, Mollie[7] Williams, Susan Anner[6], Rebecca Elizabeth[5] Autry, Millzy Adelme[4] Culbreth, Mary[3] Holland, Thomas William[2], Unknown[1]) was born 07 August 1947. She married **David Mitchell Hall, Sr.** 05 August 1968 in South Carolina, son of Wilbert Hall and Melva Faircloth. He was born 12 December 1945.

Her first name also listed as "Rosie."

Children of Rosa Faircloth and David Hall are:

3255 i. **David Mitchell Hall, Jr.**, born 27 November 1967 in Clinton, North Carolina.

3256 ii. **Pamela Rose Hall**, born 08 December 1968 in Clinton, North Carolina.

2799. Sallie Fleet Sessoms (Ira Gladys[8] Williams, George W.[7], Susan Anner[6], Rebecca Elizabeth[5] Autry, Millzy Adelme[4] Culbreth, Mary[3] Holland, Thomas William[2], Unknown[1]) was born 17 November 1934 in Little Coharie Township, Sampson County, North Carolina, and died 09 May 1968 in Near Autryville, North Carolina. She married **Earl Franklin Sessoms** Before 1952, son of Leonard Jasper Sessoms and Dolly Margaret Faircloth. He was born 20 August 1931, and died 13 January 1975 in Clinton, North Carolina.

Sallie Fleet and Earl are buried in the Charles A. Williams Family Cemetery (now Jesse Williams Family Cemetery) near SR 1418 and SR 1233, Sampson County, North Carolina.

Child of Sallie Sessoms and Earl Sessoms is:

3257 i. **Donnie Fleet Sessoms**, born 10 September 1952. He married **Karen Celester Sessoms**; born About 1968.

2801. Billy Gerald Peterson (Sarah Catherine[8] Faircloth, Lessie Dolan[7] Autry, William Isaac[6], Martha Jane[5] Culbreth, Isaac[4], Mary[3] Holland, Thomas William[2], Unknown[1]) was born 08 March 1943 in Dismal Township, Sampson Caounty, North Carolina. He married **Susan Gail Ezzell** 08 August 1963 in Hall United Methodist Church. She was born 27 March 1945 in Roseboro, North Carolina.

Children of Billy Peterson and Susan Ezzell are:

3258 i. **Michael Gerald Peterson**, born 02 July 1965 in Fayetteville, Cumberland County, North Carolina.

3259 ii. **Marcus Edgar Peterson**, born 02 June 1968 in Fayetteville, Cumberland County, North Carolina.

3260 iii. **Marjorie Peterson**, born 13 July 1970 in Fayetteville, Cumberland County, North Carolina.

2804. William Keith Faircloth (William Raeford[8], Lessie Dolan[7] Autry, William Isaac[6], Martha Jane[5] Culbreth, Isaac[4], Mary[3] Holland, Thomas William[2], Unknown[1]) was born 17 January 1950 in Roseboro, North Carolina. He married **Gailya Lynn Rich** 05 September 1971 in Salemburg, Sampson County, North Carolina, daughter of Norman Rich and Edna McLamb. She was born 16 August 1952 in Roseboro, North Carolina.

Children of William Faircloth and Gailya Rich are:

3261 i. **Brian Keith Faircloth**, born 19 January 1973 in Fayetteville, North Carolina.

3262 ii. **Charis Lynn Faircloth**, born 20 November 1976 in Fayetteville, Cumberland County, North Carolina.

2805. Larry Arnold Faircloth (William Raeford[8], Lessie Dolan[7] Autry, William Isaac[6], Martha Jane[5] Culbreth, Isaac[4], Mary[3] Holland, Thomas William[2], Unknown[1]) was born 05 November 1951. He married **Hazel Joyce House**. She was born 18 July 1953.

Child of Larry Faircloth and Hazel House is:

3263 i. **Carnella Joyce Faircloth**, born 07 October 1972.

2806. James Wyman Faircloth (William Raeford[8], Lessie Dolan[7] Autry, William Isaac[6], Martha Jane[5] Culbreth, Isaac[4], Mary[3] Holland, Thomas William[2], Unknown[1]) was born 06 June 1955. He married **(1) Glenda Hariss** About 1976. He married **(2) Elizabeth Alice Evans** About 1990 in Dillon, South Carolina. She was born 31 January 1962.

Child of James Faircloth and Glenda Hariss is:

3264 i. **Michele Lynn Faircloth**, born 18 October 1976.

Child of James Faircloth and Elizabeth Evans is:

3265 i. **Rebekah Faye Faircloth**, born 27 May 1991.

2808. Pauline Roberta Freeman (Ida Elizabeth[8] Howard, Pauline[7] Royal, Jennette Ida[6] Culbreth, John[5], Daniel Maxwell[4], Mary[3] Holland, Thomas William[2], Unknown[1]) was born 06 July 1935. She married **Clarence Brady Darden, Sr.** 07 July 1956. He was born 16 February 1931.

Children of Pauline Freeman and Clarence Darden are:

3266 i. **Clarence Brady Darden, Jr.**, born 17 January 1958.

3267 ii. **William Allen Darden**, born 16 September 1961.

2813. Mary Mac Spell (Mary Ida[8] McCall, Viola[7] Royal, Jennette Ida[6] Culbreth, John[5], Daniel Maxwell[4], Mary[3] Holland, Thomas William[2], Unknown[1]) was born 30 July 1957. She married **Howard Thomas Brock** 28 February 1981. He was born 31 January 1957.

Children of Mary Mac Spell and Howard Brock are:

3268 i. **Katherine Brock**, born 11 March 1983.

3269 ii. **Zachary Brock**, born 24 September 1987.

2814. Vara Leigh Spell (Mary Ida[8] McCall, Viola[7] Royal, Jennette Ida[6] Culbreth, John[5], Daniel Maxwell[4], Mary[3] Holland, Thomas William[2], Unknown[1]) was born 15 February 1960 in Clinton, Sampson County, North Carolina. She married **Archie Rueben Welch, Jr.** 02 March 1985 in First Presbyterian Church, Raleigh, Wake County, North Carolina. He was born 28 October 1955 in Atlanta, Fulton County, Georgia.

Children of Vara Spell and Archie Welch are:

3270 i. **Lindsey Welch**, born 06 May 1986.

3271 ii. **Blair Welch**, born 29 August 1988.

2815. Paige Elizabeth Spell (Mary Ida[8] McCall, Viola[7] Royal, Jennette Ida[6] Culbreth, John[5], Daniel Maxwell[4], Mary[3] Holland, Thomas William[2], Unknown[1]) was born 12 October 1963. She married **Kevin Hyman.**

Children of Paige Spell and Kevin Hyman are:

3272 i. **Andrew Hyman**, born 04 November 1993.

3273 ii. **Alexander Hyman**, born 06 November 1996.

2819. Mary Elaine Brazell (Eleanor Catherine[8] Royal, John Robert[7], Jennette Ida[6] Culbreth, John[5], Daniel Maxwell[4], Mary[3] Holland, Thomas William[2], Unknown[1]) was born 19 November 1958. She married **Stephen Charles Harrell.**

Children of Mary Brazell and Stephen Harrell are:

3274 i. **Alana Brooke Harrell.**

3275 ii. **Lauren Harrell.**

2823. Earthy Delwin Autry (Vertile Estelle[8] Tew, Percy Maxwell[7], Roberta[6] Culbreth, John[5], Daniel Maxwell[4], Mary[3] Holland, Thomas William[2], Unknown[1]) was born 01 December 1946 in Dismal Township, Sampson County, North Carolina, and died 05 October 1996. He married **Prudence Lavonne Jones** 01 August 1964 in Newton Grove, Sampson County, North Carolina. She was born 12 April 1947 in Dunn, Harnett County, North Carolina.

Earthy Delwin was buried in Baptist Chapel Church Cemetery on Baptist Chapel Road, Sampson County, North Carolina.

Children of Earthy Autry and Prudence Jones are:

3276 i. **Charlie Dean Autry,** born 11 March 1965 in Dunn, Harnett County, North Carolina.

3277 ii. **Amanda Lavonne Autry,** born 11 May 1967 in Dunn, Harnett County, North Carolina.

3278 iii. **Anthony Dale Autry,** born 17 March 1976 in Dunn, Harnett County, North Carolina.

2825. Ray Lynn Autry (Vertile Estelle[8] Tew, Percy Maxwell[7], Roberta[6] Culbreth, John[5], Daniel Maxwell[4], Mary[3] Holland, Thomas William[2], Unknown[1]) was born 11 December 1955 in Roseboro, North Carolina. He married **Karen Gail Stewart** 22 August 1976 in Bethabara United Methodist Church, Dismal Township, Sampson County, 3 miles east of the Cumberland County line, North Carolina, daughter of Reginald Stewart and Sannie Hairr. She was born 26 August 1958 in Elizabethtown, Bladen County, North Carolina.

Child of Ray Autry and Karen Stewart is:

3279 i. **Jeanie Lynn Autry,** born 27 September 1981.

2829. Hilbert Gordon Tew (Loren Maxwell[8], Percy Maxwell[7], Roberta[6] Culbreth, John[5], Daniel Maxwell[4], Mary[3] Holland, Thomas William[2], Unknown[1]) was born about 1953. He married **Brenda Kay Pearsall.** She was born about 1953.

Child of Hilbert Tew and Brenda Pearsall is:

3280 i. **Gordon Maxton Tew,** born 07 September 1972 in Clinton, Sampson County, North Carolina.

2832. Shirley Ann Thornton (Doris Lee[8] Tew, Ernest Blackman[7], Roberta[6] Culbreth, John[5], Daniel Maxwell[4], Mary[3] Holland, Thomas William[2], Unknown[1]) was born 30 September 1948. She married **Clifford Manley Jordan,** who was born 13 March 1944.

Child of Shirley Thornton and Clifford Jordan is:

3281 i. **Kevin Manley Jordan,** born 04 May 1968 in Fayetteville, Cumberland County, North Carolina.

2850. Patricia Dean Pomeroy (Laura Ernestine[8] Tew, Ernest Blackman[7], Roberta[6] Culbreth, John[5], Daniel Maxwell[4], Mary[3] Holland, Thomas William[2], Unknown[1]) was born 12 April 1956 in Hope Mills, Cumberland. She married **(1) Bobby Ray Hancock, Sr.,** son of Robert Hancock and Roberta Williams. He was born 21 May 1950. She married **(2) E. J. Griffin.**

Children of Patricia Pomeroy and Bobby Hancock are:

3282 i. **Edward Blackmon Hancock**, born 28 November 1972 in Fayetteville, Cumberland County, North Carolina.

3283 ii. **Bobby Ray Hancock, Jr.**, born 17 December 1973 in Fayetteville, Cumberland County, North Carolina.

2854. Anthony Clark Tew (William Blackman[8], John[7], Roberta[6] Culbreth, John[5], Daniel Maxwell[4], Mary[3] Holland, Thomas William[2], Unknown[1]) was born 03 July 1948 in Cumberland County, North Carolina. He married **(1) Barbara Irene Scroggins**. She was born 24 September 1948 in Tennessee. He married **(2) Teresa Faye Brady**. She was born 02 November 1959.

Child of Anthony Tew and Teresa Brady is:

3284 i. **Andrea Nicole Tew**, born 28 September 1979.

2868. Betty Hope Byrd (Virginia Alice[8] Royal, Lela Pearl[7] Matthews, Virginia[6] Culbreth, John[5], Daniel Maxwell[4], Mary[3] Holland, Thomas William[2], Unknown[1]) was born 04 April 1935. She married **(1) Lowel Thomas**. She married **(2) John Dixon**.

John Dixon adopted Gwen Hope and Lowel Thomas.

Children of Betty Byrd and Lowel Thomas are:

3285 i. **Gwen Hope Thomas Dixon,** born 15 July 1955.

3286 ii. **Lowel Thomas Dixon,** born 07 August 1959.

2869. Janet Faye Tart (Mary Evelyn[8] Royal, Lela Pearl[7] Matthews, Virginia[6] Culbreth, John[5], Daniel Maxwell[4], Mary[3] Holland, Thomas William[2], Unknown[1]) was born 28 January 1938. She married **Robert Lorman Hodges I**. He was born 16 May 1935 in Harnett County, North Carolina.

Janet's name is also found as "Janice Page Tart."

Children of Janet Tart and Robert Hodges are:

3287 i. **Cynthia Faye Hodges**, born 29 March 1956 in Harnett County, North Carolina.

3288 ii. **Rebecca Lynn Hodges**, born 30 January 1958 in Harnett County, North Carolina.

3289 iii. **Robert Lorman Hodges II**, born 01 July 1959 in Harnett County, North Carolina.

His date of birth is also found as 07 January1959.

2870. Phyllis Renthia Tart (Mary Evelyn[8] Royal, Lela Pearl[7] Matthews, Virginia[6] Culbreth, John[5], Daniel Maxwell[4], Mary[3] Holland, Thomas William[2], Unknown[1]) was born

20 September 1943. She married **William Howard Godwin**. He was born 07 February 1940.

Phyllis's middle name is also spelled "Renthea."

Child of Phyllis Tart and William Godwin is:

3290 i. **Melanie Faye Godwin**, born 02 January 1963.

2885. Susan Gail Tew (Edna Louise[8] Matthews, Irma G.[7], Virginia[6] Culbreth, John[5], Daniel Maxwell[4], Mary[3] Holland, Thomas William[2], Unknown[1]) was born 16 July 1947. She married **Gary Dale Harris**. He was born 19 May 1950.

Child of Gail Tew and Gary Harris is:

3291 i. **Jennifer Harris**, born 17 July 1976.

2890. Edith Karen Lockamy (Reba Nadene[8] Wrench, Mabel Inez[7] Matthews, Lena Mae[6] Culbreth, John[5], Daniel Maxwell[4], Mary[3] Holland, Thomas William[2], Unknown[1]) was born 09 August 1949. She married **Gerry Wade Cook** Before 1970, son of Lanier Cooke and Bertha Norris. He was born 13 October 1950 in Erwin, Harnett County, North Carolina.

Children of Edith Lockamy and Gerry Cook are:

3292 i. **Hayley Michelle Cook**, born 25 May 1970 in Dunn, North Carolina.

3293 ii. **Gary Mark Cooke**, born 07 May 1973 in Dunn, North Carolina.

3294 iii. **Michael Anthony Cooke**, born 08 July 1974 in Fayetteville, North Carolina.

2891. Reaber Doris Lockamy (Reba Nadene[8] Wrench, Mabel Inez[7] Matthews, Lena Mae[6] Culbreth, John[5], Daniel Maxwell[4], Mary[3] Holland, Thomas William[2], Unknown[1]) was born 23 December 1950 in Erwin, Harnett County, North Carolina. She married **John Mack Overby** About 1969. He was born 12 February 1949 in Erwin, Harnett County, North Carolina.

"Reba Doris" is also found for her name.

Children of Reaber Lockamy and John Overby are:

3295 i. **Timothy Troy Overby**, born 06 October 1969 in Dunn, North Carolina.

3296 ii. **Christopher Clint Overby**, born 08 October 1970 in Dunn.

3297 iii. **Tami Nicole Overby**, born 22 November 1973 in Dunn, North Carolina.

2892. Wilma Leigh Lockamy (Reba Nadene[8] Wrench, Mabel Inez[7] Matthews, Lena Mae[6] Culbreth, John[5], Daniel Maxwell[4], Mary[3] Holland, Thomas William[2], Unknown[1]) was born 07 May 1955 in Erwin, Harnett County, North Carolina. She married **Marvin Roy Miller** 17 June 1973 in Erwin's Antioch Pentecostal Free Will Baptist Church, son of Marvin Miller and Rachel McLamb. He was born 20 May 1951 in Erwin, Harnett County, North Carolina.

Children of Wilma Lockamy and Marvin Miller are:

3298 i. **Kevin Ray Miller**, born 04 August 1975 in Fayetteville, North Carolina.

3299 ii. **Jason Lee Miller**, born 22 February 1978 in Fayetteville, North Carolina.

2900. Larry Ray Godwin, Jr. (Reba Gray[8] Tew, Glaspy Elwood[7], Annie Vara[6] Culbreth, John[5], Daniel Maxwell[4], Mary[3] Holland, Thomas William[2], Unknown[1]) was born 24 July 1957 in Fayetteville, Cumberland County, North Carolina. He married **Cynthia Joy Strickland** 10 July 1977 in Fayetteville, Cumberland County, North Carolina. She was born 04 December 1955 in Fayetteville, Cumberland County, North Carolina.

Child of Larry Godwin and Cynthia Strickland is:

3300 i. **Jennifer Lauren Godwin**, born 03 August 1983 in Fayetteville, Cumberland County, North Carolina.

2922. Sandra Kaye Spell (Janie Mae[8] Lucas, Eunice Lee[7] Naylor, Susan Lee[6] Culbreth, Daniel L.[5], Daniel Maxwell[4], Mary[3] Holland, Thomas William[2], Unknown[1]) was born 17 December 1954 in Clinton, Sampson County, North Carolina. She married **(1) Gary Hammons** Before 1980. She married **(2) James Alen Long I** about 1983. He was born About 1952 in South Carolina, North Carolina.

Child of Sandra Spell and James Long is:

3301 i. **James Alen Long II**, born 09 March 1985 in Fayetteville, Cumberland County, North Carolina.

2923. Audrey Lynn Spell (Janie Mae[8] Lucas, Eunice Lee[7] Naylor, Susan Lee[6] Culbreth, Daniel L.[5], Daniel Maxwell[4], Mary[3] Holland, Thomas William[2], Unknown[1]) was born 03 May 1956 in Hope Mills, North Carolina. She married **Ronald Stuart Stone** Before 1976. He was born about 1952.

Child of Audrey Spell and Ronald Stone is:

3302 i. **Daniel Lee Stone,** born 26 October 1976 in Fayetteville, Cumberland County, North Carolina.

2944. Dewey Martin Williams III (Mary Amalie[8] Jackson, Olavia Tomzilia[7] Sivertsen, Armelia Bertha[6] Autry, Tomzillia[5] Culbreth, Daniel Maxwell[4], Mary[3] Holland, Thomas William[2], Unknown[1]) was born 08 October 1957 in Roseboro, North Carolina. He married **Mona Celeste Williams** 20 August 1978 in Autryville, North Carolina. She was born 17 February 1957 in Fayetteville, Cumberland County, North Carolina.

Dewey Martin was called "Marty."

Child of Dewey Williams and Mona Williams is:

3303 i. **Ryan Patrick Williams**, born 28 November 1982 in Clinton, Sampson County, North Carolina.

2951. William Travis Mozingo (Edith Juanita[8] Bradshaw, Theodore[7], David L.[6], Eliza Jane[5] Hairr, Stephen[4], Orpah[3] Holland, Thomas William[2], Unknown[1]) was born 28 October 1956. He married **Katherine Lynn Shipp**.

Child of William Mozingo and Katherine Shipp is:

3304 i. **Michelle Lynn Mozingo**, born 21 March 1976. She married **Kenneth Wayne Weeks** 10 June 1995.

2952. Steve Dirk Mozingo, Sr. (Edith Juanita[8] Bradshaw, Theodore[7], David L.[6], Eliza Jane[5] Hairr, Stephen[4], Orpah[3] Holland, Thomas William[2], Unknown[1]) was born 23 September 1957. He married **Mary Cathalene Willis**, daughter of **James Willis** and **Sophronia Daniel**. She was born 10 August 1957 in Clinton, Sampson County, North Carolina.

Child of Steve Mozingo and Mary Willis is:

3305 i. **Steve Dirk Mozingo, Jr.**

2954. Sandra Maria Mozingo (Edith Juanita[8] Bradshaw, Theodore[7], David L.[6], Eliza Jane[5] Hairr, Stephen[4], Orpah[3] Holland, Thomas William[2], Unknown[1]) was born 15 December 1959. She married **Rafty Brown**.

Children of Sandra Mozingo and Rafty Brown are:

3306 i. **Rafty Harold Brown**.

3307 ii. **Dustin Michael Brown**.

2974. Deborah Ann Travis (Della Gray[8] Bradshaw, Owen[7], Franklin[6], Eliza Jane[5] Hairr, Stephen[4], Orpah[3] Holland, Thomas William[2], Unknown[1]) was born 12 June 1954. She married **Vivien Guy**.

Children of Deborah Travis and Vivien Guy are:

3308 i. **Jason Guy**.

3309 ii. **Michael Guy**.

2975. Donna Jean Travis (Della Gray[8] Bradshaw, Owen[7], Franklin[6], Eliza Jane[5] Hairr, Stephen[4], Orpah[3] Holland, Thomas William[2], Unknown[1]) was born 10 October 1956. She married **Tommy Culbreth**.

Children of Donna Travis and Tommy Culbreth are:

3310 i. **Kimberly Culbreth**.

3311 ii. **Jessica Culbreth**.

3312 iii. **Allen Culbreth**.

2976. Mary Jennifer Jackson (Della Gray[8] Bradshaw, Owen[7], Franklin[6], Eliza Jane[5] Hairr, Stephen[4], Orpah[3] Holland, Thomas William[2], Unknown[1]) She married **Kenneth Wayne Tew, Jr.**

Child of Mary Jackson and Kenneth Tew is:

3313 i. **Kenneth Wayne Tew III.**

2978. Romona Diane Thornton (Elsie Mae[8] Bradshaw, Owen[7], Franklin[6], Eliza Jane[5] Hairr, Stephen[4], Orpah[3] Holland, Thomas William[2], Unknown[1]) was born 10 March 1957 in Sampson County, North Carolina. She married **Dale McCullen**.

Child of Romona Thornton and Dale McCullen is:

3314 i. **Regina Kaye McCullen**. She married **Jeffrey Gwyne Allen**.

2993. Luther Columbus Hairr (Hubert Bee[8], William Braxton[7], Isaiah[6], James Thomas[5], John C.[4] Hair, Orpah[3] Holland, Thomas William[2], Unknown[1]) was born 03 November 1945 in Halls Township, Sampson County, North Carolina, and died 29 September 1988 in Smithfield, Johnston County, North Carolina. He married **(1) Mary Alice Wood**. She was born 26 March 1942 in Aversboro Township, Harnett County, North Carolina. He married **(2) Ruby Lee Fisher** 02 June 1968. She was born 01 March 1950 in Halls Township, Sampson County, North Carolina.

Luther Columbus was buried in McGee United Methodist Church Cemetery, Sampson County, North Carolina.

Child of Luther Hairr and Ruby Fisher is:

3315 i. **Kathy Lee Hairr,** born 11 November 1970 in Clinton, Sampson County, North Carolina.

2995. William James Hairr (Hubert Bee[8], William Braxton[7], Isaiah[6], James Thomas[5], John C.[4] Hair, Orpah[3] Holland, Thomas William[2], Unknown[1]) was born 05 December 1949 in Halls Township, Sampson County, North Carolina. He married **Laura Dale Edwards**, daughter of Ethan Edwards and Eunice Daughtry. She was born 03 May 1950 in Roseboro, North Carolina.

Children of William Hairr and Laura Edwards are:

3316 i. **Jeanna Lynn Hairr**, born 08 October 1970 in Clinton, Sampson County, North Carolina.

3317 ii. **Laurinda Glyn Hairr**, born 29 March 1973 in Clinton, Sampson County, North Carolina.

3318 iii. **Jaime Leigh Hairr**, born 09 February 1977 in Clinton, Sampson County, North Carolina.

2998. Ronald Keith Hairr (Floyd Lutrell[8], Spence B.[7], Isaiah[6], James Thomas[5], John C.[4] Hair, Orpah[3] Holland, Thomas William[2], Unknown[1]) was born 08 June 1959. He married **Julia Gautier.**

Children of Ronald Hairr and Julia Gautier are:

3319 i. **Donna Hairr.**

3320 ii. **Stillborn Hairr.**

2999. Shelia Rose Hairr (Floyd Lutrell[8], Spence B.[7], Isaiah[6], James Thomas[5], John C.[4] Hair, Orpah[3] Holland, Thomas William[2], Unknown[1]) was born 11 April 1965. She married **Tommy Jones** in Owens Grove Pentecostal FWB Church, Sampson County, North Carolina.

Child of Shelia Hairr and Tommy Jones is:

3321 i. **Thomas Luke Jones**, born About 1992.

3000. David Patrick Godwin (Christine[8] Hairr, Troy Addicus[7], Isaiah[6], James Thomas[5], John C.[4] Hair, Orpah[3] Holland, Thomas William[2], Unknown[1]) was born 03 June 1950. He married **Sue Hudson Holland**. She was born 10 April 1954.

Children of David Godwin and Sue Holland are:

3322 i. **Jonathan David Godwin**, born 05 December 1978.

3323 ii. **Hilliary Paish Godwin**, born 17 December 1981.

3001. Michael Ray Godwin (Christine[8] Hairr, Troy Addicus[7], Isaiah[6], James Thomas[5], John C.[4] Hair, Orpah[3] Holland, Thomas William[2], Unknown[1]) was born 24 April 1957 in Dunn, Harrnett County, North Carolina. He married **Pamela Florence Parrish** 28 December 1975 in Westbrooks Township, Sampson County, North Carolina, daughter of Joseph Parrish and Lenothal Simmons. She was born 06 June 1954 in Clinton, Sampson County, North Carolina.

Children of Michael Godwin and Pamela Parrish are:

3324 i. **Laura Jennens Godwin**, born 19 January 1979 in Fayetteville, Cumberland County, North Carolina.

3325 ii. **Holly Elizabeth Godwin**, born 27 December 1981 in Wayne County, North Carolina.

The year 1983 is also found for her birth.

3326 iii. **Martha Anne Godwin**, born 05 January 1989 in Wake County, North Carolina.

3003. Houston Lee Lockamy (James Houston[8], Leona[7] Hairr, Isaiah[6], James Thomas[5], John C.[4] Hair, Orpah[3] Holland, Thomas William[2], Unknown[1]) was born 25 February 1944. He married **(1) Judy Lewis** before 1981. He married **(2) Judy Gaye Springs King** 18 January 1992 in Dillon, South Carolina. She was born 12 March 1946. Houston Lee and Judy were divorced.

Child of Houston Lockamy and Judy Lewis is:

3327 i. **James Lee Lockamy**, born 10 October 1981.

3005. Omie Kaye Lockamy (James Houston[8], Leona[7] Hairr, Isaiah[6], James Thomas[5], John C.[4] Hair, Orpah[3] Holland, Thomas William[2], Unknown[1]) was born 09 February 1948. She married **George Henry Cox** 08 March 1969 in Dillon, South Carolina. He was born 08 April 1947.

Children of Omie Lockamy and George Cox are:

3328 i. **Ronald Paul Cox**, born 27 December 1969.

\+ 3329 ii. **Cynthia Kaye Cox**, born 26 September 1975.

3006. Jimmy McThomas Lockamy (James Houston[8], Leona[7] Hairr, Isaiah[6], James Thomas[5], John C.[4] Hair, Orpah[3] Holland, Thomas William[2], Unknown[1]) was born 27 March 1950. He married **Gwendolyn Kay West** 21 June 1970 in Holly Grove Presbyterian Church. She was born 15 January 1953.

Gwendolyn is known as 'Gwen'.

Children of Jimmy Lockamy and Gwendolyn West are:

\+ 3330 i. **June Michelle Lockamy**, born 31 May 1973.

3331 ii. **Amy Nichole Lockamy**, born 29 July 1976.

3332 iii. **Jimmy McThomas Lockamy, Jr**, born 10 July 1979.

3007. Jackie Lou Lockamy (James Houston[8], Leona[7] Hairr, Isaiah[6], James Thomas[5], John C.[4] Hair, Orpah[3] Holland, Thomas William[2], Unknown[1]) was born 26 September 1953. She married **James Guilford Daughtry** 26 November 1972 in Dillon, South Carolina. He was born 14 November 1949.

Children of Jackie Lockamy and James Daughtry are:

3333 i. **James Clifford Daughtry**, born 04 July 1976. He married Shannon Lynn Williamson 17 September 2002.

3334 ii. **Derek Allen Daughtry**, born 02 October 1983. He married Dawn Boone.

3008. Stephen Anthony Weeks (Paul Graham[8], Omie Tera[7] Hairr, Isaiah[6], James Thomas[5], John C.[4] Hair, Orpah[3] Holland, Thomas William[2], Unknown[1]) was born about 1950. He married **Phylis Lynn Jackson** 20 September 1980 in Harnett County, North Carolina. She was born 24 September 1956 in Inglewood, California.

Child of Stephen Weeks and Phylis Jackson is:

3335 i. **Tera Weeks.**

3010. Nelson Cannady (Sudie[8] Hairr, Deames Elton[7], Isaiah[6], James Thomas[5], John C.[4] Hair, Orpah[3] Holland, Thomas William[2], Unknown[1]) was born 22 March 1972. He married **Marilyn Butler**. She was born about 1972.

Children of Nelson Cannady and Marilyn Buler are:

3336 i. **Victoria Paige Cannady**, born 27 February 1992.

3337 ii. **Anthony Glenn Cannady**, born 27 June 1998.

3011. Kimberly Dawn Cannady (Sudie[8] Hairr, Deames Elton[7], Isaiah[6], James Thomas[5], John C.[4] Hair, Orpah[3] Holland, Thomas William[2], Unknown[1]) was born 26 January 1976. She married **Mike Simmons**. He was born 28 January 1977.

Child of Kimberly Cannady and Mike Simmons is:

3338 i. **Fetus Wayne Simmons**, born 06 October 2001.

3012. Wanda Ernestine Warren (Samuel Ernestine[8], Lillie Nadine[7] Butler, Bettie Allen[6] Autry, Allen Merdeth[5], Starling[4], Millie[3] Holland, Thomas William[2], Unknown[1]) was born 10 October 1957 in Clinton, Sampson County, North Carolina. She married **(1) Michael Bryant Sills** 17 May 1980 in Mt. Elam Baptist Church, Sampson County, North Carolina. He was born 26 July 1957 in Germany. She married **(2) Robie Edison Simmons II** 01 June 1990 in Mt. Elam Baptist Church, Sampson County, North Carolina. He was born 22 July 1961 in Clinton, Sampson County, North Carolina.

Children of Wanda Warren and Michael Sills are:

3339 i. **Leslie Michelle Sills**, born 23 April 1983 in Clinton, Sampson County, North Carolina.

3340 ii. **Felicia Anne Sills**, born 13 July 1985 in Clinton, Sampson County, North Carolina.

3016. William Houston Warren (Houston[8], Lillie Nadine[7] Butler, Bettie Allen[6] Autry, Allen Merdeth[5], Starling[4], Millie[3] Holland, Thomas William[2], Unknown[1]) was born 02

August 1956 in Loris, South Carolina. He married **Cynthia McLamb** 28 December 1980 in Mt. Elam Baptist Church, Sampson County, N orth Carolina, daughter of Thomas Avery McLamb and Jackie Delois Spell. She was born 30 June 1959 in Clinton, Sampson County, North Carolina.

"The Heritage of Sampson County, North Carolina 1784-1984," Vol. 2, edited by Oscar M. Bizzell, states on page 653 that William attended Campbell University at Buies Creek, North Carolina and majored in Geology. In the 1980s he was employed in Bladen County, North Carolina, with the Health Department. His wife, Cynthia is/was a nurse with the Bladen County Hospital.

Children of William Warren and Cynthia McLamb are:

3341 i. **Meridith Ashley Warren,** born 02 September 1987 in Dunn, Harnett County, North Carolina.

3342 ii. **Kathryn Leigh Warren,** born 28 April 1989 in Clinton, Sampson County, North Carolina.

3027. Cynthia Sue Butler (James Hubbard[8], Charles Marion[7], Bettie Allen[6] Autry, Allen Merdeth[5], Starling[4], Millie[3] Holland, Thomas William[2], Unknown[1]) was born 24 May 1964 in Clinton, Sampson County, North Carolina. She married **(1) Walter Delozier** 31 May 1981. She married **(2) James Allen House** 10 November 1984 in Herrings Township, Sampson County, North Carolina. He was born 15 January 1963 in Clinton, Sampson County, North Carolina.

Child of Cynthia Butler and James House is:

3343 i. **James Eric House,** born 07 June 1985 in Clinton, Sampson County, North Carolina.

3043. Sherry Ann Tew (James Brewer[8], Doris Gray[7] Holland, John Wesley[6], Alger Rose[5], Stephen Senter[4], Henry[3], Thomas William[2], Unknown[1]) was born 27 July 1966 in Clinton, Sampson County, North Carolina. She married **(1) Kennith Hubbard** 03 September 1982. She married **(2) John Price** 20 December 1992.

Children of Sherry Tew and Kennith Hubbard are:

3344 i. **Michael Hubbard,** born 26 March 1983.

3345 ii. **Scott Hubbard,** born 17 April 1985.

3054. Charles Terry Smith (Charles Davis[8], Jackie Olene[7] Jackson, Roberta[6] Holland, Alger Rose[5], Stephen Senter[4], Henry[3], Thomas William[2], Unknown[1]) was born 17 September 1983. He married **Cherish Nicole Daw** 23 July 2005 in Turkey Pentecostal Free Will Baptist Church, Turkey, North Carolina. She was born 06 February 1986.

Child of Charles Smith and Cherish Daw is:

3346 i. **Charles Dawson Smith,** born 21 March 2006.

3055. Amanda Dawn Smith (Charles Davis[8], Jackie Olene[7] Jackson, Roberta[6] Holland, Alger Rose[5], Stephen Senter[4], Henry[3], Thomas William[2], Unknown[1]) was born 09 October 1984. She married **Dennis Nelson Vann II**, son of Dennis Vann and Brenda Unknown. He was born about 1984.

Children of Amanda Smith and Dennis Vann are:

3347 i. **Madison Page Vann,** born 09 April 2004.

3348 ii. **Dennis Nelson Vann III**, born 07 November 2005.

3056. Michael Allen Smith (Michael Edward[8], Jackie Olene[7] Jackson, Roberta[6] Holland, Alger Rose[5], Stephen Senter[4], Henry[3], Thomas William[2], Unknown[1]) was born 26 January 1986 in Sampson County, North Carolina. He married **Angela Avery**.

Child of Michael Smith and Angela Avery is:

3349 i. **Kimberly Breanna Smith**, born 31 January 2006.

3063. Erica Nicole Smith (Jackie Gregory[8], Jackie Olene[7] Jackson, Roberta[6] Holland, Alger Rose[5], Stephen Senter[4], Henry[3], Thomas William[2], Unknown[1]) was born 18 December 1985 in Clinton, Sampson County, North Carolina.

Children of Erica Nicole Smith are:

3350 i. **Austin Blake** Smith, born 27 June 2003 in Clinton, Sampson County, North Carolina.

3351 ii. **Aaron Gregory Smith**, born 16 September 2006 in Sampson County, North Carolina.

Generation Number 9

3166. Brent Satterfield (Billy[9], Ethel L.[8] Cannady, Annie[7] Lockamy, Onie Vendex[6] Holland, William Wright[5], Thomas James[4], Daniel[3], Thomas William[2], Unknown[1]) was born 10 August 1973.

Child of Brent Satterfield is:

3352 i. **Ian Reid Satterfield**, born 12 December 2002.

3168. Karen Denise Raynor (Barbara Jean[9] Satterfield, Ethel L.[8] Cannady, Annie[7] Lockamy, Onie Vendex[6] Holland, William Wright[5], Thomas James[4], Daniel[3], Thomas William[2], Unknown[1]) She married **Richard Powers**.

Child of Karen Raynor and Richard Powers is:

3353 i. **Lindsey Brooks Powers**.

3178. Donnie Lee Cannady (Diane Marie[9] Tyndall, Doris Marie[8] Ellis, Janie Lou[7] Lockamy, Onie Vendex[6] Holland, William Wright[5], Thomas James[4], Daniel[3], Thomas William[2], Unknown[1]) was born 12 December 1967. He married **Sara Lynn McLamb,** daughter of Jimmie McLamb and Sara Street. She was born 28 June 1970.

Child of Donnie Cannady and Sara McLamb is:

3354 i. **Dalton Lee Cannady,** born 09 August 2001.

3196. Deborah Kathryn Jackson Warren (Herman Denning[9], Ruth[8] Starling, Luther Washington[7], Mary Catherine[6] Williams, Isaac[5], Tomzelle[4] Culbreth, Mary[3] Holland, Thomas William[2], Unknown[1]) died 24 August 1993 in Raleigh, Wake County, North Carolina. She married **Terry L. Moore.**

Professor Rosser, Jr., listed the date of April 30, 1961 for Deborah Kathryn's birthday. However, he gives the year of birth for her mother as about 1961! Deborah Kathryn died during childbirth, or right after and was buried in Raleigh Memorial Park Cemetery, Raleigh, North Carolina.

Children of Deborah Warren and Terry Moore are:

3355 i. **Sarah Elizabeth Moore.**

3356 ii. **Jacob Blaine Moore.**

Jacob is a twin to Isaac.

3357 iii. **Isaac Wooten Moore.**

3358 iv. **Andrew David Moore,** born 24 August 1993; died 24 August 1993.

Burial: Raleigh Memorial Park Cemetery, Raleigh, North Carolina

3207. Lee Ann Spell (Patricia Ann[9] Wrench, Quinton Randall[8], Fletcher E.[7], Lovdie Ann[6] Williams, Isaac[5], Tomzelle[4] Culbreth, Mary[3] Holland, Thomas William[2], Unknown[1]) was born 12 January 1972. She married **Randall Nathan Barefoot** 09 November 1996 in Sampson County, North Carolina, son of William Nathan Barefoot and Sue Ann Cannady. He was born 19 February 1973 in Sampson County, North Carolina.

Children of Lee Spell and Randall Barefoot are:

3359 i. **Reagan Brooke Barefoot,** born 16 May 1999 in Fayetteville, Cumberland County, North Carolina.

3360 ii. **Zana Paige Barefoot,** born 07 April 2003 in Fayetteville, Cumberland County, North Carolina.

3211. Wendy Sue Baggett (Mildred Joyce[9] Draughon, May Dee[8] Tew, Cornelia[7] Wrench, Lovdie Ann[6] Williams, Isaac[5], Tomzelle[4] Culbreth, Mary[3] Holland, Thomas William[2], Unknown[1]) was born 11 May 1961 in Mt. View, California. She married **Arthur Douglas Williams** 15 August 1981 in Baptist Chapel Church near Autryville, Sampson County,

North Carolina. He was born 23 September 1961 in Fayetteville, Cumberland County, North Carolina.

Child of Wendy Baggett and Arthur Williams is:

3361 i. **Allison Suzanne Williams.**

3241. James Roland Sessoms (Billy Roland[9], Roland[8], Mollie[7] Williams, Susan Anner[6], Rebecca Elizabeth[5] Autry, Millzy Adelme[4] Culbreth, Mary[3] Holland, Thomas William[2], Unknown[1]) was born 23 June 1965. He married **Tammy Hall.**

Children of James Sessoms and Tammy Hall are:

3362 i. **Ashley Sessoms.**

3363 ii. **Meagan Sessoms.**

3242. Karen Celester Sessoms (Billy Roland[9], Roland[8], Mollie[7] Williams, Susan Anner[6], Rebecca Elizabeth[5] Autry, Millzy Adelme[4] Culbreth, Mary[3] Holland, Thomas William[2], Unknown[1]) was born About 1968. She married **(1) Donnie Fleet Sessoms,** son of Earl Franklin Sessoms and Sallie Fleet Sessoms. He was born 10 September 1952. She married **(2) Unknown Lucas.**

Child of Karen Sessoms and Unknown Lucas is:

3364 i. **Billy Lucas.**

3243. Deana LeeAnn Sessoms (Billy Roland[9], Roland[8], Mollie[7] Williams, Susan Anner[6], Rebecca Elizabeth[5] Autry, Millzy Adelme[4] Culbreth, Mary[3] Holland, Thomas William[2], Unknown[1]) was born About 1972. She married **Eddie Dryer.**

Child of Deana Sessoms and Eddie Dryer is:

3365 i. **Danielle Dryer.**

3244. Kimberly Ann Sessoms (Jackie Lester[9], Roland[8], Mollie[7] Williams, Susan Anner[6], Rebecca Elizabeth[5] Autry, Millzy Adelme[4] Culbreth, Mary[3] Holland, Thomas William[2], Unknown[1]) was born 01 August 1967. She married **Timothy Farmer.**

Children of Kimberly Sessoms and Timothy Farmer are:

3366 i. **Dustin Farmer.**

3367 ii. **Nicholus Farmer.**

3245. Melonie Denice Sessoms (Jackie Lester[9], Roland[8], Mollie[7] Williams, Susan Anner[6], Rebecca Elizabeth[5] Autry, Millzy Adelme[4] Culbreth, Mary[3] Holland, Thomas William[2], Unknown[1]) was born 03 August 1971. She married **Rodney Hall.**

Children of Melonie Sessoms and Rodney Hall are:

3368 i. **Madelyn Hall.**

3369 ii. **Colin Hall.**

3246. Kevin Earl Tanner (Brenda[9] Sessoms, Roland[8], Mollie[7] Williams, Susan Anner[6], Rebecca Elizabeth[5] Autry, Millzy Adelme[4] Culbreth, Mary[3] Holland, Thomas William[2], Unknown[1]) was born 11 April 1972. He married **Cindy Hall.**

Child of Kevin Tanner and Cindy Hall is:

3370 i. **Kacey Jane Tanner**, born 12 February 2001.

3249. Marilyn Lynette Faircloth (Cyrus James[9], Nina[8] Sessoms, Mollie[7] Williams, Susan Anner[6], Rebecca Elizabeth[5] Autry, Millzy Adelme[4] Culbreth, Mary[3] Holland, Thomas William[2], Unknown[1]) was born 24 March 1963 in Fayetteville, Cumberland County, North Carolina. She married **Seth Alan Avery.** He was born 11 July 1962 in Missouri.

Children of Marilyn Faircloth and Seth Avery are:

3371 i. **Unnamed Child Avery.**

3372 ii. **Unnamed Child Avery.**

3373 iii. **Kailee Rebecca Avery**, born 23 March 1993 in Fayetteville, Cumberland County, North Carolina.

3329. Cynthia Kaye Cox (Omie Kaye[9] Lockamy, James Houston[8], Leona[7] Hairr, Isaiah[6], James Thomas[5], John C.[4] Hair, Orpah[3] Holland, Thomas William[2], Unknown[1]) was born 26 September 1975. She married **Todd.**

Child of Cynthia Cox and Todd is:

3374 i. **Erica Desiree Todd**, born 14 December 2001.

3330. June Michelle Lockamy (Jimmy McThomas[9], James Houston[8], Leona[7] Hairr, Isaiah[6], James Thomas[5], John C.[4] Hair, Orpah[3] Holland, Thomas William[2], Unknown[1]) was born 31 May 1973. She married **Daniel Mark Holland.** He was born 27 July 1971.

Children of June Lockamy and Daniel Holland are:

3375 i. **Dustin Mark Holland**, born 17 March 1999.

3376 ii. **Caitlyn Michelle Holland**, born 24 August 2002.

DESCENDANTS OF SUSAN C. MCCULLEN

I found most of the data for HENRY Y. C. HOLLAND and Susan C. McCullen after I had revised most of the manuscript and thought it best to include it here. Part of it raises questions, but apparently, it supports the marriage of Henry and Susan and a possible marriage to William Holland. See Henry Y. C. Holland earlier in the book, for more notes about him.

Generation # 1

1. **Susan C. McCullen** (Unknown[1]) was born qbout 1838. She married **(1) Henry Y. C. Holland** 29 November 1860 in Sampson County, North Carolina, son of Henry Holland and Mary Tew. He was born 26 March 1836 in Sampson County, North Carolina, and died 15 May 1864 in Battle of Wilderness, Virginia. She married **(2) William Holland** after 1864.

The source for Henry's date of death shows "Holland, Henry Y. C., Pvt., Co. I, Regt. 46, Inf. Born 1838, Sampson Co. Farmer. Enl. 12 March 1862, Clinton. Deserted 11 June 1862 at Camp Drewry's Bluff, Va. Had not been apprehended by 30 Oct 1862." Hit by mini ball in back on 7 May 1864 in the Battle of Wilderness, Virginia; died on 15 May 1864. Most likely, he was buried in Virginia.

Henry's date of birth is difficult to read in the **Old Holland Record Book**; it appears to be the 26 of either March or May 1836. His middle initial "C" was probably for "Chester," and there is no record or tradition that gives any hint about the "Y.," but it is listed in the old recod book and in the Civil War Records.

The following indicates that he married Susan C. McCullen:

"'Fayetteville Observer," Fayetteville, North Carolina, Monday, December 17, 1860 Vol. XLIII #2272:

"Married in Sampson County on the 29th of November, by Jas. A. Warwick, Esq., Mr. **Henry C. Holland** to Miss **Susan C. McCullen.**"

Susan C. Holland, aged 25, was head of household in 1870 in Clinton, Halls Township, Sampson County, North Carolina. Her age should have been about 32. Rhoda J. McCullen, most likely her sister, aged 40, was living with her. In 1880 Susan was again head of household with children and Rhoda was also there. Neither Susan nor Rhoda show up in 1900 indicating they either died or remarried.

The death certificate for L. P. Holland (Loyd Pascail Holland) names William Holland and Susan McCullen (McCullen) for his parents. I have not identified the parents of this William Holland. William may be listed under another given name in census records. In the event that data listed on Loyd Pascail's certificate of death is correct, where was William Holland when the 1870 and 1880 census records were enumerated? I've entered the data as I have found it, but leave the questions for others to answer.

Child of Susan McCullen and Henry Holland is:

\+ 2 i. **Lucy Jene[3] Holland,** born 15 August 1862 in Sampson County, North Carolina; died 16 August 1933 in North Clinton Township, Sampson County, North Carolina.

Children of Susan McCullen and William Holland are:

\+ 3 i. **Lonnie Oscar Holland,** born 13 February 1866 in Sampson County, North Carolina; died 24 May 1932 in Sampson County, North Carolina.

\+ 4 ii. **Loyd Paschail Holland,** born 03 June 1870 in North Carolina; died 04 April 1929 in Westbrooks Township, Sampson County, North Carolina.

5 iii. **Mannie C. Holland,** born about 1873. The following supports his marriage to **Mary Hannah Guthrie** who was born about 1878.

The 1900 census records Mannie C. Holland, aged 27, who was born in February 1873 in North Carolina, and William C. Frost, aged 28, who was born in North Carolina, living in Civil District 3, Stewart County, Tennessee. William Frost was an Evangelistic Preacher and his partner, **Mannie C. Holland,** was an Evangelistic Singer.

In 1910, Mannie C. Holland, aged 38, and his wife Mary H., aged 32, were living in Beaufort, Ward 1, Carteret County, North Carolina. Her maiden name was **Mary Hannah Guthrie.** North Carolina Birth Indexes record Monnie C. Holland and Hannah Guthrie for the parents of **Charles Gehrmann Holland** who was born 12 June 1904 in Carteret County, and M. C. Holland and Hannah Guthrie for the parents of **Lucy Bradshaw Holland** who was born 6 June 1907 in Carteret County, North Carolina..

I have not found any 1920 census record for Mannie using the various spellings of his name. In 1930, Gehrmann was head of household and his two sisters were in his household. Neither their father nor mother were recorded, but apparently, both were still alive.. The Certificate of death for M. C. Holland, aged 49, records that he died of accidental electrocution on 7 June 1922 in Beaufort, Carteret County. He was married and Hannah was named for his wife. He was a Merchant (Fish Dealer) and processed fish and oysters in Southport Packing Company. His certificate also records Sampson County for his place of birth and **Henry Holland** for his father. I have not found any other record to support it, but this may indicate that his father's full name was **William Henry Holland** or **Henry William Holland;** it could also mean that Gehermann, the informant for data on the Certificate of death, did not know the actual name of Mannie's father and may have given the name of "Henry Holland," whom I have listed for his mother's first husband.

Mannie and Mary Hannah had three children: 1) **Charles Gehrmann Holland,** born 12 June 1904 in Carteret County; 2) **Lucy Bradshaw Holland** who was born 6 June 1907 in Carteret County; 3) **Mary C. Holland,** born 1914 in Beaufort, Carteret County.

Generation #. 2

2. Lucy Jene Holland (Susan C.[2] McCullen, Unknown[1]) was born 15 August 1862 in Sampson County, North Carolina, and died 16 August 1933 in North Clinton Township, Sampson County, North Carolina. She married **Matthew James Bradshaw,** son of Thomas Bradshaw and Eliza Carr. He was born about 1858 in Sampson County, North Carolina, and died 1928 in North Clinton Township, Sampson County, North Carolina.

Lucy Jene was buried in Halls Township, Sampson County, North Carolina.

Children of Lucy Holland and Matthew Bradshaw are:

+ 6 i. **George Thomas Bradshaw**, born 02 November 1887; died 05 July 1971.

+ 7 ii. **Vonnie Jane Bradshaw**, born 01 January 1890 in Sampson County, North Carolina; died 16 August 1946 in Halls Township, Sampson County.

+ 8 iii. **Rossie Bradshaw**, born 15 June 1892 in Sampson County, North Carolina; died 19 October 1916.

9 iv. **James Henry Bradshaw**, born 29 April 1894 in Sampson County; died 05 November 1975 in Sampson County Memorial Hospital, Clinton, North Carolina. He married **Mary Britt**; born 24 April 1899.

Henry attended Wake Forest Law School and practiced law in Clinton.

+ 10 v. **Bernice Paskal Bradshaw, Sr.**, born 18 March 1898 in Sampson County, North Carolina; died 06 May 1978 in Sampson County Memorial Hospital, Clinton, North Carolina.

11 vi. **Monnie Ernest Bradshaw**, born 18 March 1898 in Sampson County Memorial Hospital, Clinton, North Carolina; died 06 March 1977. One source names 17 March 1977 in Clinton, Sampson County, North Carolina, for his death. The 1930 Federal census records him in Halls Township, aged 32 with wife, **Rena**, aged 33 and **Ernestine Bradshaw**, 11 months.

12 vii. **Lela M. Bradshaw**, born 16 April 1903 in Sampson County, North Carolina; died 28 June 1970 in Sampson County Memorial Hospital, Clinton, North Carolina. She married **William David Hines**; born 12 September 1899; died 14 November 1968. They had one son.

13 viii. **Vitus M. Bradshaw**, born 18 June 1904 in Sampson County; died 16 January 1926. He did not marry.

+ 14 ix. **Starling Cecil Bradshaw**, born 01 January 1908 in Sampson County, North Carolina; died 19 February 1983 in Clinton, Sampson County.

3. Lonnie Oscar Holland (Susan C.[2] McCullen, Unknown[1]) was born 13 February 1866 in Sampson County, North Carolina, and died 24 May 1932 in Sampson County, North Carolina. He married **Ella Evaline Best** 18 May 1892 in Residence of the Bride's father in Sampson County, North Carolina. She was the daughter of George Best and Celia Butler and was born 13 October 1872 in Sampson County, North Carolina, and died 23 January 1958 in Sampson County, North Carolina.

Lonnie's name is also listed as Loni O. Holland and Lina Oscar Holland. He was known for helping to build Hopewell United Methodist Church and by his donation of timber as well as services. Ella's middle name is also listed as "Eveline." Lonnie Oscar died from cancer of the face; he and Ella Evaline were buried in a Family Cemetery near Newton Grove, North Carolina.

Children of Lonnie Holland and Ella Best are:

+ 15 i. **George Roscoe Holland**, born July 1893 in Sampson County, North Carolina; died 1967.

+ 16 ii. **Irene Holland**, born 15 March 1895 in Sampson County; died 23 December 1972.

17 iii. **Viola Holland**, born 06 September 1896 in Sampson County, North Carolina; died 06 February 1935. She married **William Blaney Holland** before 1935; born 05 July 1894; died 20 May 1959.

The year of birth listed on her certificate of death is 1899. W. Blaney was probably the **WILLIAM BLUEN HOLLAND,** son of **Calton Walker Holland** and **Mary Jelson Sessoms** who married Viola Holland on 21 January 1931 at residence of M. A. Warrick, Justice of the Peace in Sampson County.

18 iv. **Vitus Bethring Holland,** born 20 January 1899 in Sampson County, North Carolina; died 17 October 1904 in Sampson County. He was buried in a Family Cemetery near Newton Grove in Sampson County, North Carolina.

19 v. **Jeronia M. Holland,** born about 1903 in Sampson County, North Carolina. She married **HENRY S. DAUGHTRY** who was born about 1903. Her name is also spelled "Gerona" and "Jerone." Two children are listed in the 1930 census for Halls Township in Sampson County: **Ollie Daughtry**, born about 1926 and **Dixon I. Daughtry** born about 1929.

\+ 20 vi. **Lona F. Holland,** born 20 July 1903 in Sampson County, North Carolina; died 30 December 1991.

21 vii. **James Lisker Holland,** born 02 November 1905 in Westbrook Township, Sampson County, North Carolina; died 21 July 1932 in Westbrook Township, Sampson County. He married Dollie Unknown; born about 1912. James stepped off a wagon in front of an auto, broke his neck, and severed his left jugular vein.

22 viii. **Wade Hampton Holland,** born 28 February 1908 in Westbrook Township, Sampson County, North Carolina; died 16 March 1942 in Westbrook Township in Sampson County.

Wade Hampton drowned and was buried in Family Cemetery near Newton Grove, North Carolina.

23 ix. **Flossie Cleone Holland,** born 30 April 1910 in Sampson County, died 26 October 1910 and was buried in Family Cemetery on Highway 102 off the Dunn Road going toward Newton Grove, North Carolina, about 19 miles from Clinton.

\+ 24 x. **Pauline Holland,** born 19 February 1912 in Sampson County, North Carolina; died 25 October 1981.

25 xi. **Vernon Onslow Holland,** born 08 June 1913 in Sampson County, North Carolina; died 10 November 1914 in Westbrooks Township in Sampson County.

Transcribed cemetery records 10 February 1913 for his birth and 8 June 1914 for his death. His Certificate of Death is interesting: The 10 November 1914 is entered for his birth and the 8 June 1913 for his death. It shows a burial date of 9 June 1914 and it was filed on 8 October 1914! His Certificate of Death shows he lived six months and 28 days. He was buried in Family Cemetery at home of parents in Westbrooks Township, Sampson County, North Carolina

26 xii. **Lucy P. Holland,** born about 1914 in Sampson County.

4. **Loyd Paschail Holland** (Susan C.[2] McCullen, Unknown[1]) was born 03 June 1870 in North Carolina, and died 04 April 1929 in Westbrooks Township, Sampson County, North Carolina. He married **(1) Joanna Tew** 26 November 1893 in Residence of W. B. Warwick, daughter of George Tew and Jewel Naylor. She was born about 1875, and died Before 1896. He married **(2) Molcy Ann Gautier** 12 November 1896 in Residence of T. H. Honeycutt, Sampson County, North Carolina. She was born 04 August 1870, and died 05 May 1948, daughter of **Thomas Gautier** and **Mary Jane Hairr.** "L. P. Holland" and Molcy were buried in Oak Grove Church Cemetery on Warren Mill Road in Sampson County, North Carolina.

In 1880, **Thomas Gotiere** (sic), born about 1830 and **Mary Jane Hairr,** born about 1835 were recorded in the town of Clinton, Sampson County, North Carolina, with seven Children all listed with the spelling of "**Gotiere**" for the surname: 1) **Alexander Gautier**, born 1859; 2) **Orpe E. Gautier;** born about 1862; 3) **Mary F. Gautier**, born about 1864; 4) **John Thomas**

Gautier, born about 1867; 5) **William Henry Gautier**; born about 1869; 6) **Molsie A. Gautier**, born about 1872 and 7) **Nancy J. Gautier**, born about 1874.

SEE MARY JANE HAIRR AND THOMAS GAUTIER ELSEWHERE IN THIS BOOK.

NANNIE HARE (NANCY HAIR), Sister-in-law, was in the household of Thomas and Mary in 1880. The ages of Mary and Nancy (Nannie) support their being the daughters of **John Athae Hair, Jr.**, and **Orpah Holland** and you will notice above that the first daughter of Thomas and Mary Jane was named "**Orpe**" and was probably named after her maternal grandmother, Orpah Holland.

Molcy's Certificate of Death records 4 August 1870 for her birth and notes she died 5 May 1948 at the age of 77 years and 9 months. Transcribed cemetery records list 02 August 1871 for her birth. She died seven days after a cerebral hemorrhage.

Loyd's middle name is also found as "Loyd Paschal Holland." **Paschal L. Holland** was listed for his name in the 1880 census for Halls Township, Sampson County, North Carolina. He was listed as Ford P. Holland in Hall Township, Sampson County, in 1900 with wife, Holsey(sic). Other sources listed him as Loyd Pascal and Paschail Holland. The certificate of death for their son, Paul Palmer Holland, names "Paschal Holland" and "**Malcy Geautier**" for his parents.

His son, Paul, was married and listed as head of household in 1930, but the home was probably the home of Loyd and Molcy as she and her children were in the household.

Jerome D. Tew in his research notes that Joanna's name was "Joanora" Tew.

Child of Loyd Holland and Joanna Tew is:

27 i. **Loyd A. Holland**, born about 1895. In 1920, he was listed with wife, Nannie A. (Maiden Name Unknown), who was born about 1899.

Children of Loyd Holland and Molcy A.Gautier are:

28 i. **Arthur Holland**, born about 1897.

He may be the "**L. ARTHUR HOLLAND**" listed in the 1930 census for Westbroks Township in Sampson County, North Carolina, with wife, Nannie A. about 31 years, **MACK HOLLAND**, 8 years, **HOWARD HOLLAND**, 5 years **and CHARLIE HOLLAND**, 3 years.

\+ 29 ii. **Paul Palmer Holland**, born 21 August 1900; died 13 July 1963 in Clinton, North Carolina.

\+ 30 iii. **Lonnie Harvey Holland**, born 15 September 1905; died 08 February 1975 in Dunn, North Carolina.

31 iv. **Evora Carmie Holland,** born about 1909. Her first name may have been Evona.

32 v. **Dorothy C. Holland**, born about 1910.

33 vi. **Pascail Thurman Holland**, born 12 June 1914 in Sampson County, North Carolina; died 24 January 1975 in Sampson County, North Carolina. He married **LOLA HINSON**; born 19 September 1913; died 10 July 1997.

His first name is also spelled as Paskel and Pascall. Marriage records reveal that "**Paschail Thurman Holland**," aged 21, married **LOLA HUDSON**, aged 18, on 21 May 1932 in Clinton, Sampson County,

North Carolina. If that is the case, perhaps the doctor or someone wrote her maiden name incorrectly on Pascail's Certificate of Death. **Lola Hudson** is listed as the informant for data on the certificate.

Pascail and Lola are buried in Warren Family - Oak Grove Church Cemetery on Warren Mill Road (SR 1647) in Sampson County, North Carolina

Generation # 3

6. George Thomas Bradshaw, Sr. (Lucy Jene[3] Holland, Susan C.[2] McCullen, Unknown[1]) was born 02 November 1887, and died 05 July 1971. He married **Mamie Frances Bell.** on May 1916. She was born 09 April 1895.

Children of George Bradshaw and Mamie Bell are:

34 i. **George Thomas Bradshaw, Jr.**, born 22 April 1917; died 03 September 1917.

35 ii. **Infant Bradshaw**, born 02 November 1919; died 02 November 1919.

36 iii. **James Plato Bradshaw**, born 10 November 1920; died 26 October 1969. He married **Mary Lou Ingram**; born 07 March 1924; died 08 June 1941.

37 iv. **Edna Mae Bradshaw**, born 01 August 1923. She married **LAWRENCE MARSHBURN**.

\+ 38 v. **Vitus Bell Bradshaw**, born 02 June 1929.

7. Vonnie Jane Bradshaw (Lucy Jene[3] Holland, Susan C.[2] McCullen, Unknown[1]) was born 01 January 1890 in Sampson County, North Carolina, and died 16 August 1946 in Halls Township, Sampson County, North Carolina. She married **Elmon M. Hairr** on 13 February 1916, son of William Hairr and Elizabeth Cashwell. He was born 29 March 1884 in Sampson County, North Carolina, and died 31 October 1957 in Sampson County, North Carolina.

Vonnie and Elmon were buried in Keener Methodist Church Cemetery on Keener Road West (SR 1746) in Sampson County, North Carolina.

Children of Vonnie Bradshaw and Elmon Hairr are:

\+ 39 i. **Rossie Marie Hairr**, born 22 April 1917; died 07 April 1987.

\+ 40 ii. **James Elmon Hairr**, born 05 April 1925 in North Carolina.

8. Rossie Bradshaw (Lucy Jene[3] Holland, Susan C.[2] McCullen, Unknown[1]) was born 15 June 1892 in Sampson County, North Carolina, and died 19 October 1916. She married **Allen Duncan Weeks**. He was born 03 May 1894, and died 13 May 1973.

Child of Rossie Bradshaw and Allen Weeks is:

41 i. **Infant Son Weeks**, born 14 October 1916; died 14 October 1916.

10. Bernice Paskal Bradshaw, Sr. (Lucy Jene[3] Holland, Susan C.[2] McCullen, Unknown[1]) was born 18 March 1898 in Sampson County, North Carolina, and died 06 May 1978 in Sampson County Memorial Hospital, Clinton, North Carolina. He married **Mary Lula Weeks** 24 February 1923. She was born 01 January 1905 in North Carolina, and died 10 February 1983 in Jacksonville, Onslow County, North Carolina.

One source names 18 March 1898 for Bernice's birth and 21 May 1979 for his death and notes that he was a twin of Monnie Earnet.

Children of Bernice Bradshaw and Mary Weeks are:

\+ 42 i. **Bernice Paskel Bradshaw, Jr.**, born 03 September 1924 in Sampson County Memorial Hospital, Clinton, North Carolina; died 03 August 1999.

43 ii. **Joyce Freeman Bradshaw**, born 22 August 1925 in Sampson County Memorial Hospital, Clinton, North Carolina; died 24 January 1931.

44 iii. **Vitas Lynwood Bradshaw**, born 21 October 1926 in Sampson County Memorial Hospital, Clinton, North Carolina. He married **Lena Mae Strickland**; born 08 August 1936.

Four children. Lynwood served in the United states Navy from 10 July 1944-30 April 1946.

45 iv. **Charles Bradshaw**, born 26 September 1931 in Sampson County Memorial Hospital, Clinton, North Carolina. He married **Jean Turlington**; born 14 February 1931.

Three children.

46 v. **Mary Anna Bradshaw**, born 19 June 1932. She married **William Dawkins**; born 29 July 1924.

One child.

14. Starling Cecil Bradshaw (Lucy Jene[3] Holland, Susan C.[2] McCullen, Unknown[1]) was born 01 January 1908 in Sampson County, North Carolina, and died 19 February 1983 in Clinton, Sampson County, North Carolina. He married **Maybelle Carter** before 1931, daughter of Murdock Carter and Catherine Hollingsworth. She was born 20 May 1911, and died 30 September 1964 in Route 3, Clinton, North Carolina.

Cecil was living with his brother, Bernice, and his family in 1930. He and Maybelle are buried in Clinton Cemetery, Clinton, North Carolina

Children of Starling Bradshaw and Maybelle Carter are:

47 i. **Mabel Jean Bradshaw**, born 08 July 1931 in Halls Township, Sampson County, North Carolina. She married **NELAS VAN SUTTON** on 21 June 1953 in Keener Church, Halls Township, Sampson County, North Carolina; born 20 September 1925 in Piney Grove Township, Sampson County, North Carolina.

One daughter.

48 ii. **Cecil Clark Bradshaw**, born 09 October 1936. He married **Barbara Stewart**.

He served in the United States Air Force from 1956-1960.

15. George Roscoe Holland (Lonnie Oscar[3], Susan C.[2] McCullen, Unknown[1]) was born July 1893 in Sampson County, North Carolina, and died 1967. He married **Lola Mae Lee**. She was born 1898, and died 1981.

George Roscoe and Lola Mae were buried in Grandview Memorial Gardens, three miles north of Clinton on Hwy 421, Sampson County, North Carolina.

Children of George Holland and Lola Lee are:

	49	i.	**Winnie Mae Holland**, born about 1921 in Sampson County, North Carolina.
+	50	ii.	Roscoe Maurice Holland, Sr., born 05 November 1922 in Newton Grove, Sampson County, North Carolina; died 12 March 1996.
	51	iii.	**Dr. Murray Wade Holland**, born about 1925 in Sampson County, North Carolina.
			Professor in School of Dentistry, Uuniverity of North Carolina, Chapel Hill, North Carolina.
	52	iv.	**Monnie Clifton Holland**, born about 1927 in Sampson County, North Carolina.
	53	v.	**Rev. Oscar Lee Holland**, born 20 August 1931.
+	54	vi.	**Ruth Carolyn Holland**, born 30 January 1935 in Westbrooks Township, Sampson County, North Carolina.

16. Irene Holland (Lonnie Oscar[3], Susan C.[2] McCullen, Unknown[1]) was born 15 March 1895 in Sampson County, North Carolina, and died 23 December 1972. She married **Braston Bass**, son of James Bass and Martha Jones. He was born 08 May 1898 in Sampson County, North Carolina, and died 25 April 1979.

Irene and Braston were buried in Hopewell Methodist Church Cemetery on Church Road near Vanns Crossroads, Sampson County, North Carolina.

Children of Irene Holland and Braston Bass are:

+	55	i.	**Myrtle Estalene Bass**, born 24 August 1918.
	56	ii.	**Braston Onzolo Bass**, born 07 August 1920.
	57	iii.	**Oscar Glenn Bass**, born 19 November 1929.

20. Lona F. Holland (Lonnie Oscar[3], Susan C.[2] McCullen, Unknown[1]) was born 20 July 1903 in Sampson County, North Carolina, and died 30 December 1991. She married **Noah Estel Brock, Sr.**, son of Noah Brock and Nancy Unknown. He was born 23 October 1894, and died 13 February 1974.

Lona and Noah were buried in Oak Grove Church Cemetery on Warren Mill Road (SR 1647) North, Sampson County, North Carolina.

Children of Lona Holland and Noah Brock are:

58 i. **Noah Estel Brock, Jr.** was born 30 October 1924 in Sampson County and died 02 January 1983. He married **Ethelene Barr** who was born 22 November 1929. Noah was buried in Oak Grove Church Cemetery.

59 ii. **Stacy Holland Brock** was born 06 December 1927 and married **Hilda Jones** on 1 June 1948. They both were buried in Oak Grove Church cemetery on Warren Mill Road in Sampson County and their gravestone names three children: **Stacy Ray Brock,** who was born 25 August 1949 in Salemburg, Sampson County, North Carolina, and died 26 November 1996. He was buried in Oak Grove Church Cemetery on Warren Mill Road in Sampson County, North Carolina.

Donna G. Brock was the second child of Stacy and Hilda and **Sharon J. Brock** is the third known child..

24. Pauline Holland (Lonnie Oscar[3], Susan C.[2] McCullen, Unknown[1]) was born 19 February 1912 in Sampson County, North Carolina, and died 25 October 1981. She married **Rastus McLamb.** He was born 03 September 1910, and died 10 February 1975.

Pauline and Rastus were buried in Family Cemetery near Newton Grove, North Carolina

Child of Pauline Holland and Rastus McLamb is:

60 i. **Kenneth Wade McLamb,** born 03 February 1947; died 06 February 1947.

29. Paul Palmer Holland (Loyd Pascail[3], Susan C.[2] McCullen, Unknown[1]) was born 21 August 1900, and died 13 July 1963 in Clinton, North Carolina. He married **Nancy E. Jackson** 08 December 1926 in Westbrooks Township, Sampson County, North Carolina, daughter of Robert Jackson and Mary West. She was born 20 March 1904, and died 11 April 1968.

Paul Palmer and Nancy were buried in Oak Grove Church Cemetery on Warren Mill Road (SR 1647), Sampson County, North Carolina.

Child of Paul Holland and Nancy Jackson is:

61 i. **Robert Pascail Holland,** born 01 April 1931 in Westbrooks Township in Sampson County, North Carolina. He married **Zona Mae Tutor** 07 January 1948; born 13 March 1932 in Sampson County, North Carolina. "R. P. 'Bobby' Holland" was buried in Oak Grove Church Cemetery on Warren Mill Road (SR 1647) in Sampsn County, Nroth Carolina.

Four children:

1) **LARRY MAX HOLLAND** was born 26 October 1950 in Dunn, Harnett County, North Carolina and married **LINDA GAIL PARSON** who was born 29 October 1951. One child: **ROBERT PAUL HOLLAND.**

2) **NELLIE FRANCES HOLLAND** was born 1 September 1954 in Dunn and married 7 April 1971 **JOHN DANIEL BUTLER** who was born 3 October 1952 in Clinton, son of **RAYMOND STANLEY BUTLER** and **UNA DIXIE TEW.** Two children: **JONATHAN ROBERT BUTLER** was born 23 December 1971 in Clinton and **JENNIFER RENEE BUTLER** was born 6 December 1974 in Clinton.

3) **Stillborn Child.**

4) **BRENDA FAYE HOLLAND** was born 3 April 1960 in Clinton.

30. Lonnie Harvey Holland (Loyd Pascail[3], Susan C.[2] McCullen, Unknown[1]) was born 15 September 1905, and died 08 February 1975 in Dunn, North Carolina. He married **Dorothy Jane Godwin** 26 May 1928 in Westbrooks Township, Sampson County, North Carolina, daughter of William Godwin and Bettie West. She was born 01 September 1910, and died 11 August 1998.

A transcribed copy of cemetery records shows "D_____H_____Holland, born 15 August 1905, died 08 February 1975?

Lonnie Harvey was buried in John Godwin Family Cemetery on S.R. 1620 east of North Carolina Rt 242.

Children of Lonnie Holland and Dorothy Godwin are:

62 i. **Janet Holland**, born 06 November 1931 in Westbrooks Township, Sampson County, North Carolina. She married **Nathan Bennett McLamb**; born 20 June 1925 in Herrings Township, Sampson County, North Carolina.

Five children:

1) **Janice Kay McLamb**, born 11 September 1949 in Dunn, Harnett County, North Carolina married 9 May 1971 in Dunn, **Baird Loftis Paschall, Jr.** who was born 14 June 1949. He was the son of Baird Loftis Paschall and Virginia Kelly Huddleston of Siler City. Two children: **Kelly Pachall** and **Trey Paschall.**

2) **Nathan Allen McLamb**, born 8 April 1952 in Dunn, married **Kathy Arthur** 29 April 1973. Two children: **Chad McLamb** and **Tori McLamb.**

3) **Harvey Thomas McLamb**, born 23 September 1953 in Duun, Harnett County, married **Debbie Hamilton** 1 September 1973 and they had one child, **Andrew McLamb.**

4) **Hugh Bailey McLamb** was born 10 october 1954 in Dunn.

5. **Jane Hope McLamb**, born 28 May 1959 in Dunn, married **Walton Whittey** 1 August 1982.

63 ii. **Bettie Ann Holland**, born 20 October 1933 in Westbrooks Township, Sampson County, North Carolina. She married **James Herman Tyler, Jr.**; born 27 September 1926 in Columbus County, North Carolina.

Three children.

1)**James Keith Tyler**, born 30 June 1953 in Clinton, North Carolina, married **Mary Evelyn Jones** 2 July 1972 in Hopewell United Methodist Church. She was born 4 March 1955. Two children: **Tiffany Dawn Tyler**, born 21 October 1975 in Clinton. Unidentified second child.

2) **Unidentified Child**.

3) **Jeffrey Lynn Tyler** was born 30 November 1965 in Clinton, North Carolina.

64 iii. **William Lloyd Holland**, born 27 May 1939 in Westbrooks Township, Sampson County, North Carolina. He married **Peggy Jean Hobbs**; born 03 November 1938 in North Clinton Township, Sampson County, North Carolina.

Four children:

1) **William Lloyd Holland, Jr.**, a twin, was born 19 July 1961.

2) **Renee Holland**, a twin, born 19 July 1961.

3) **Tammie Jean Holland,** born 1 September 1962 in Clinton, North Carolina.

4) **Sherry Holland** was born in March 1969.

Generation # 4

38. Vitus Bell Bradshaw (George Thomas[4], Lucy Jene[3] Holland, Susan C.[2] McCullen, Unknown[1]) was born 02 June 1929. He married **Shirley Autry Odom** 10 September 1957.

Children of Vitus Bradshaw and Shirley Odom are:

65 i. **Frances Ann Bradshaw.**

66 ii. **Brenda Bradshaw.**

Brenda and Linda are twins.

67 iii. **Linda Bradshaw.**

68 iv. **Vitus Bradshaw.**

Vitus and George are twins.

69 v. **George Bradshaw.**

70 vi. **Pamela Ann Bradshaw.**

39. Rossie Marie Hairr (Vonnie Jane[4] Bradshaw, Lucy Jene[3] Holland, Susan C.[2] McCullen, Unknown[1]) was born 22 April 1917, and died 07 April 1987. She married **James Ervin Floyd** 30 November 1939. He was born 13 December 1914 in Columbus County, North Carolina, and died 08 October 1966.

Rossie Marie and James were buried in Keener Methodist Church Cemetery on Kenner Road West (SR 1746), Sampson County, North Carolina.

Children of Rossie Hairr and James Floyd are:

\+ 71 i. **Jimmy Edward Floyd,** born 21 September 1940.

\+ 72 ii. **Jane Marie Floyd,** born 03 March 1945.

40. James Elmon Hairr (Vonnie Jane[4] Bradshaw, Lucy Jene[3] Holland, Susan C.[2] McCullen, Unknown[1]) was born 05 April 1925 in North Carolina. He married **Rachel Phillips** 04 October 1963. She was born in Siler City, North Carolina.

James Elmon and his sister, Rossie, provided the data in the profile on the "Hare Family" in ***The Heritage of Sampson County, North Carolina***, Edited by Oscar M. Bizzell.

During World War II, James served in the United States Army from 25 October 1950 until 29 September 1952. He was stationed on Okinawa Island.

Child of James Hairr and Rachel Phillips is:

73 i. **Joe Elmon Hairr**, born 19 April 1967.

42. Bernice Paskel Bradshaw, Jr. (Bernice Paskal[4], Lucy Jene[3] Holland, Susan C.[2] McCullen, Unknown[1]) was born 03 September 1924 in Sampson County Memorial Hospital, Clinton, North Carolina, and died 03 August 1999. He married **Rachel Boyette** 27 October 1946.

Bernice, Jr., and his son, apparently spelled their middle names "Paskel." He was a barber and was divorced at the time of his death.

Children of Bernice Bradshaw and Rachel Boyette are:

74 i. **Bernice Paskel Bradshaw**, born 16 December 1947 in Sampson County Memorial Hospital, Clinton, North Carolina; died 24 October 1949.

Cause of death was 2nd and 3rd degree burns.

75 ii. **Bonnie Bradshaw**. She married **Bruce Gladden**.

Two children.

76 iii. **Elaine Bradshaw**. She married **Richard Thigpen**.

77 iv. **Kay Bradshaw**. She married **Donel Honeycutt**.

50. Roscoe Maurice Holland, Sr. (George Roscoe[4], Lonnie Oscar[3], Susan C.[2] McCullen, Unknown[1]) was born 05 November 1922 in Newton Grove, Sampson County, North Carolina, and died 12 March 1996. He married **Beaulah Estelle Horne**. She was born 30 June 1922.

Roscoe Maurice was an Attorney with Holland & Poole in Roseboro and Clinton. He and Beaulah were buried in The Clinton Cemetery, Clinton, Sampson County, North Carolina

Children of Roscoe Holland and Beaulah Horne are:

78 i. **Roscoe Maurice Holland, Jr.**, born 28 January 1955 in Sampson County, North Carolina.

79 ii. **Brantley Aycock Holland**, born 03 November 1959 in Sampson County, North Carolina.

54. Ruth Carolyn Holland (George Roscoe[4], Lonnie Oscar[3], Susan C.[2] McCullen, Unknown[1]) was born 30 January 1935 in Westbrooks Township, Sampson County, North Carolina. She married **James Albert Warren, Sr.** 23 August 1952, son of W. Warren and Neta Jackson. He was born 25 September 1933 in Mingo Township, Sampson County, North Carolina.

Children of Ruth Holland and James Warren are:

\+ 80 i. **James Albert Warren, Jr.**, born 17 April 1954 in Charlotte, North Carolina.

81 ii. **Dean Anthony Warren**, born 03 December 1958 in Charlotte, North Carolina.

\+ 82 iii. **Karen Ruth Warren**, born 28 November 1960 in Charlotte, North Carolina.

55. Myrtle Estalene Bass (Irene[4] Holland, Lonnie Oscar[3], Susan C.[2] McCullen, Unknown[1]) was born 24 August 1918. She married **Roy Gibson Williams, Sr.** 30 November 1939 in Westbrooks Township, Sampson County, North Carolina, son of Emmett Williams and Maggie Baggett. He was born 13 January 1916 in Mingo Township, Sampson County, North Carolina.

Children of Myrtle Bass and Roy Williams are:

83 i. **Roy Gibson Williams, Jr.**

84 ii. **Jeffery Glenn Williams.**

Generation # 5

71. Jimmy Edward Floyd (Rossie Marie[5] Hairr, Vonnie Jane[4] Bradshaw, Lucy Jene[3] Holland, Susan C.[2] McCullen, Unknown[1]) was born 21 September 1940. He married **Linda Gray Sutton**. She was born 14 June 1941.

Children of Jimmy Floyd and Linda Sutton are:

\+ 85 i. **Phyllis Renee Floyd**, born 01 October 1960.

86 ii. **Toni Lynn Floyd**, born 12 October 1962.

72. Jane Marie Floyd (Rossie Marie[5] Hairr, Vonnie Jane[4] Bradshaw, Lucy Jene[3] Holland, Susan C.[2] McCullen, Unknown[1]) was born 03 March 1945. She married **David C. Sagel** 03 July 1970. He was born 26 May 1945 in New Jersey.

Children of Jane Floyd and David Sagel are:

87 i. **Carrie Anne Sagel**, born 03 November 1974.

88 ii. **Anna Lee Sagel**, born 20 April 1977.

80. James Albert Warren, Jr. (Ruth Carolyn[5] Holland, George Roscoe[4], Lonnie Oscar[3], Susan C.[2] McCullen, Unknown[1]) was born 17 April 1954 in Charlotte, North Carolina. He married **Brenda Thomas** 15 June 1975.

Children of James Warren and Brenda Thomas are:

89 i. **Carol Warren.**

90 ii. **April Warren.**

82. Karen Ruth Warren (Ruth Carolyn[5] Holland, George Roscoe[4], Lonnie Oscar[3], Susan C.[2] McCullen, Unknown[1]) was born 28 November 1960 in Charlotte, North Carolina. She married **Kevin Marcilliat** 23 May 1981.

Child of Karen Warren and Kevin Marcilliat is:

91 i. **Amanda Marcilliat**, born 14 September 1982.

Generation # 6

85. Phyllis Renee Floyd (Jimmy Edward[6], Rossie Marie[5] Hairr, Vonnie Jane[4] Bradshaw, Lucy Jene[3] Holland, Susan C.[2] McCullen, Unknown[1]) was born 01 October 1960. She married **Anthony Norris** 30 September 1979. He was born 16 July 1957.

Child of Phyllis Floyd and Anthony Norris is:

92 i. **Dustin Edward Norris,** born 10 September 1980.

DESCENDANTS OF MOSES BOYETT

Generation No. 1

1. Moses Boyett died 1780. He married **Anne Maiden Name Unknown**. She died after 1780.

He was probably the Moses Boyt who named daughter, "**Millae Holland**" (Millia(?) Holland," in his 1780 Last Will and Testament. He will also named his wife, Anne, and son, Arther (sic) Boyt, (Arthur Boyet). It was witnessed by Thomas Jernigan, Jonathan Gore, and Christopher Martin. John Gore and Christopher Martin were listed in the 1784-1787 State Census of North Carolina in Capt. Ward's District in Duplin County. Also listed in Capt. Ward's District were, Ephraim Boyet, Lamuel Boyet (Samuel Boyet), and William Boyet. Listed in Capt. Hubbard's Company in Duplin County in this census, were Absolom Boyed **(Absolom Boyet?)**, **Elizabeth Boyet**, and **Jones Boyet**. These same seven individuals were listed on the 1785 Tax LIst for Duplin County.

Several years ago, I found a reference to the Last Will and Testament of Moses Boyt who named a daughter, "Millae Holland," but I had never followed up on it. In the late fall of 2008, Jerome Tew sent me a message about Moses naming a daughter, Millae Holland, in his will. With the greater input from Jerome, the data presented here represents our research on a few of the early Boyets of Dobbs, Duplin, Wayne and Sampson Counties. This resulted from an attempt to find more information about Millae Boyet (Millie). **Millae** is spelled **"Milley"** in the will of her husband, Thomas William. See Thomas William Holland and Milley Boyet elsewhere in this book.

Other Boyts (Boyetts) in Duplin in 1800 and 1810 who have not been linked to Moses, but who were most likely related:

Daniel Boyt.

Jones Boyt in 1800 was 26-44 years of age and with him were one female over 45, one female 10-15, one son under 10 and one son 10-15. In 1810, Jones and one female were over 45 and with them were one female 16-25 and one female 26-44.

James Boyet and his wife in 1810, were 26-44 with one son and two daughters under 10.

Jesse Boyet in 1810 was aged 45 or over with one female 16-25, one female 10-15, one son under 10, one son 10-15, and one son 16-25.

Mich Boyet in 1810 was head of household and he and one other male were 16-25 with one female 25-44 and two females under 10. This appears to be Mich (Michael?) in the household with his mother and siblings and he may have been **Michael Boyett**, the son of William, son of Moses.

John Boyet in 1800 was aged 26-44 with one female over 45 (wife?), one female 10-15, one son under 10 and one son 10-15 in his household. In 1810, this may have been the John Boyet, aged 26-44 with one female 16-25 and one son 16-25.

John Boyett was born about 1763 and died about 1813 in Giddensville, Sampson County, north Carolina; his wife, Mary, was born about 1770 and died after 25 January 1822. Their son, **Nathan Boyett** was born about 1785. Their son, **John Boyett** who was born about 1813, had a grandson, **Nathan Satchell Boyett**, who was married two or three times---the last time he married late in life to **Catherine Grey Holland**, great granddauther of **Thomas William Holland** and **Milley Boyett**. See Catherine Grey Holland and Nathan Satchell Boyett elsewhere in this book.

<u>In Dobbs County, North Carolina, in 1769</u>

Arthur Boyet. Ephraim Boyet sold 57 acres to Arthur Boyet for 57 pounds in 1797. Witnesses were **Benjamin Best** and **John Best**.

Absolam Boyet (Absolom Boyet) (possibly the Absolum Boyet who received 3 Revolutionary pay vouchers). He and his wife, Rhoda, signed a Duplin County, North Carolina, deed to Obadiah Wade in 1787. (150 acres for 125 pounds).

Edward Boyet (and sons **Dread Boyet** and **Edward Boyet**)

George Boyet

James Boyet

Moses Boyet

Thomas Boyet, Jr. 1735-1786

Thomas Boyet, Sr. 1710-1780 (Son, James Boyet was born 1749)

<u>Boyets in Wayne County, North Carolina, in 1790 (Boyet may have been spelled differently.</u>

Amos Boyet 1/4/2

Thomas Boyet 1/2/3

Joseph Boyet 1/0/3

Shadrack Boyet 1/1/5

Benjamin Boyet 1/4/2

Edward Boyet 2/0/2

Etheldred Boyet	1/3/6	

Boyets in Wayne County, North Carolina, in 1800

Micajah Boyet	00100-10100	Born by: 1770
Shadrack Boyet	11001-31202	1745
Thomas Boyet	22010-31110	1750
Joseph Boyet	00011-02002	1745
Jacob Boyet	12010-21010	1755
Etheldred Boyet	01101-21201	1745

One "William Boyt" who may have been a brother of Moses, patented land in Dobbs County, North Carolina, in 1763.

A deed in Sampson-Duplin Deeds Book 3, page 341: Felix Kenan (High Sheriff of Duplin County) to **Moses Boyet**. Dated: 10 April 1771. Trans: 20 pounds 8 pence for 100 acres "Beginning...in Ash Branch.' The 'Supreme Court of the District of Halifax" had ordered 'the Goods and Chattles, lands, and tenements of **Jesse Jornagen** (Jernigan) and(?) **George Calson** (Colsom) in your Bailawick' to be assessed 40 pounds plus 1 pound, 16 shillings, 11 pence for damages to **Henry Eustace McCulloh**. The order was carried out 19 October 1769. Witnesses not named.

Arthur Boyt, **Ephraim Boyt**, and **William Boyt** are found in the 1790 Duplin County, North Carolina, Federal Census; John Boyt is found in the 1790 Sampson County Census. John was mentioned often in the early minutes of Sampson County starting in 1784. He, apparently, owned several hundred acres of land, several slaves, and was very active in the affairs of the county. The Last Will and Testament of Samuel Boyet names John and Hardy for two sons. It appears that Boyt was also entered in records as Boyet, Boyette, Boyd, and Boyed.

Below is my transcription of the Last Will and Testament of **Moses Boyett**:

> "...In the name of God Amen.
>
> "I, **Moses Boyet**, of Sampson County and State of North Carolina, am sick and weak in body, but in perfect sense and sound memory, do make and ordain this my last Will and Testament, This fifth year of Independence ....one thousand, seven hundred, and eighty.
>
> "Item. I give and bequeath unto my dear wife, **Anne Boyet**, one horse bridle and saddle one feather bed and furniture. My land and plantation to her during the time that she chooses to continue thereon or during her life. Also one cow and calf and one mare to have and hold between her and my son, Arthur.

"Item. I give and bequeath unto my dear son, Arther Boyet, my (line may be missing from my copy of the original)... All my land and plantation, one year old colt, one cow and calf, one two year old heifer, one featherbed and furniture.

"Item. I give and bequeath to my dear daughter, **Millae Holland** (or **Millie Holland**?), one shilling (illegible).

"September the 26 1780.

"In presence of Moses (his X mark) Boyette

"Thomas Jernigan

"Jonathan Gore, Sr.(? or Jr.)

"Christopher Martin."

Moses received one Revolutionary War pay voucher.

From Boyt to Boyette, by Wendy Elliot, provides the following information for the family of Amos Boyet: **Amos** was born in Wayne County, North Carolina and he first married **Mary Worrell** and second Elizabeth (maiden name unknown). **Mary Worrell** was the daughter of **David Worrell.** Other records state that Amos was born in Dobbs County, North Carolina, and died in Wayne County. Dobbs County was formed in 1758 from Johnston County, North Carolina, and Wayne County was formed from Dobbs in 1779. It appears that these Boyets moved, but they actually may have lived on the same land or in the same general area for years.

Amos' will was dated April 2 1826 and probated in May 1826. Children listed are:

Moses Boyet, born about 1780, **Dempsey Boyet,** born about 1781, **Mariah Boyet** was born about 1782, **Amos Boyet, Jr.** was born about 1784, **Charity Boyet,** born about 1786, **Micajah Boyet,** born about 1788, **Stephen Boyet** was born about 1792, and **John Boyet,** born about 1795. It is believed all children were born in Wayne County. The **Moses Boyet listed in Amos' will appears to have been younger than the Moses who was the father of Millae Boyet (Milley).** This Amos did name a daughter **Charity** and a son, **Stephen**; Milley Boyet and Thomas William Holland named one daughter, **Charity,** another one, **Mary**, and named a son, **John**; their son, Henry, named one son, **John**, another one, **Stephen Senter Holland,** and named daughters, **Mary** and **Millie**. In fact, Charity and Millie (various spellings) are often found in the early Holland families.

Martha Boyet purchased 48 acres for 40 pounds from Jonathan Thomas in 1810. Witnesses were **Benjamin Best** and **Sarah Best**. It is believed that Martha was the wife of one of the sons of the older Moses. This deed and the one mentioned above for Arthur and **Ephraim Boyet** may indicate a relationship between the Best and Boyet Families. Benjamin Best was in Dobbs County, North Carolina, in 1766 and was married to **Mary Hardy**. Samuel

Boyet had two sons, **John Boyet** and **Hardy Boyet**. It is thought that Samuel's wife, Phereby (Pherebe) may have been a "Hardy."

Children of Moses Boyett and Anne Unknown are:

2 i. **Ephraim Boyet**, born about 1752 or by 1758 died after 1800.

Ephraim was living next to Arthur Boyt in 1800 indicating that they were probably related. He was 26-44 years and one female was 45 or over. Two sons under 10, one son 10-15 and two sons 16-25 were in the household. Ephraim could have been head of household and the others may have been his mother and siblings. He received two Revolutionary War pay vouchers.

\+ 3 ii. **William B. Boyet**, born about 1753 in Johnston, (later Dobbs and then Wayne County), North Carolina; died after 08 March 1834 in Duplin County, North Carolina. He received 5 Revolutionary War pay vouchers.

\+ 4 iii. **Arthur Boyet** was born about 1754 and died in Duplin by 1808. He received three Revolutionary War pay vouchers.

\+ 5 iv. **Samuel Boyet**, born about 1755; died about 1791. He received severn Revolutionary War pay vouchers.

\+ 6 v. **MILLAE BOYET** (MILLEY BOYETT) was born about 1755 and died after 1819. See **Thomas William Holland** pages 3-11.

Generation No. 2

3. William B. Boyt (Moses[1] Boyett) was born about 1753 in Johnston, later Dobbs and then Wayne County, North Carolina, and died after 08 March 1834 in Duplin County, North Carolina. He married **Jane Maiden Name Unknown**. She was born about 1755 in Duplin County and died after 08 March 1834 in Duplin County.

Records also list him as William Boyt or William Boyet. Boyt also was spelled Boyet, Boyett and in early deeds it is found as Boyette. William Boyt sold 400 acres for 80 pounds to Lewis Thomas in 1786.

In 1810, Will (William) Boyet and his wife were aged 45 or over with one male 10-15 and one female 16-25.

Jerome Tew sent me the following from William Boyet's Revolutionary War records:

"Boyet, William, Private, North Carolina Line and Militia, Pension # $1115.

"Soldier was born about 1753 (Johnston, later Dobbs, then Wayne County, North Carolina; Probable son of **Moses Boyt**. One record gives his name as **William B. Boyt**. He married Jane who was born about 1755 of Duplin County, North Carolina, and died after 8 March 1834.

"His brothers are believed to be **Arthur, Ephraim**, and **Samuel.** William was taxed in 1814 in Duplin County, He was between 80 and 89 in 1830 and was still living in 1834 when he applied for a Revolutionary War pension which was rejected. During the war he served from Wayne and Duplin Counties, North Carolina. He was drafted under **Col. (James) KENAN** and **Capt. Hardy HOLMES** for 3 months. He was sent to Fayetteville, then down river to

Elizabethtown in Bladen County, North Carolina. Then served a tour under General (**Thomas EATON** and **Capt. Hardy HOLMES**. Drafted for 9 months, started from Duplin County, he joined the army at Elizabethtown NC, and went on through South Carolina to Augusta, then to Burke County, (Georgia) where he was stationed. During his second term of service, he was a spy in the Creek Indian Nation and fought at Brier Creek (March 3, 1779), but was defeated and swam the river on retreat. In his deposition he stated that he "dropped his gun to save a man from drowning," and saved his life. He managed to catch up with one American officer on the "Duplin side" of the Savannah River in South Carolina. One statement shows that he entered service at the fork of Little and Neuse rivers. He was discharged in Georgia in 1779. During his 3rd term of service, he was drafted for 6 months just before the close of the war. He started from Duplin, met army or joined it at Elizabethtown, marched toward the South Carolina line then towards Brunswick, crossed into North Carolina twice, then marched to the NE River to the big bridge about 10 miles from Wilmington. The bridges were gone, but they stayed there 5 or 6 weeks. Col. MCMUDDAY joined them. Willam was in the company with Major (Abraham) MOLTON, Major James GILLISPIE. They left the bridge area for Duplin County to ascertain the movements of the British, but the British had gone (August 1791) to Newbern. He pursued the British as far as Newbern, then returned and helped mend the bridges. He was discharged soon after "Cornwallis was taken" (October 19, 1781). He deposed that he "never received any pay while in service and was given $50 in continental money when discharged in Newbern "and he gave it for a piper" (Inn). All total he served 18 months. He received no pension prior to 1834. He stated that he lived most of his life before, during, and after the Revolutionary War in Duplin County, except one year when he lived in Lenoir County, North Carolina, on the Tuckaho. He served under Gen. ASHE of New Hanover, Major (Abraham) MOLTON of Duplin, Col. KENAN, Col. Charley WARD, Stephen MILLER, Capt. James GILLISPIE, Maj. James (Thomas) EATON, Col. MALMUDDY, and Major HENDERSON. His neighbors in 1834 were Robert MIDDLETON, Esq. Benjamin COOPER, **Absalom BEST**, **Henry BEST**, **Richard BRADLEY**, and Rueben BLANCHARD. He was the head of household in Duplin County in, 1800, 1810, 1820, and 1830.

"In his deposition dated 1834, he stated his only surviving child was **Michael Boyett**, (his son **David BOYETT** was living in Alabama at the time).

"William died after 8 March 1834 in Duplin County, North Carolina, where his will was probated in 1835. William had at least 7 children: Henry born about 1785, married Elizabeth "Betsey" L., Patsey (?), Dicey who married a **Bradley**, Rebecca who married a **BEST**, Priscilla died before 1784, Michael, born about 1785, William who married Polly, and David who married **Mary BRADLEY**, daughter **of Richard BRADLEY.** It is believed that William had sons-in-law named BEST, GIBBONS, Joseph WARD, BRADLEY, and David JONES.

Children of William Boyt and Jane Unknown are:

6 i. **Henry Boyt**, born about 1785; died about 1831. He married Elizabeth L. Maiden Name Unknown.

7 ii. **Patsey Boyt**.

8 iii. **Dicey Boyt**. She married Unknown Bradley.

9 iv. **Rebecca Boyt**. She married Unknown Best.

10 v. **Priscilla Boyt**, died before 1784.

11 vi. **Michael Boyt**, born about 1785.

12 vii. **William Boyt.** He married Polly Maiden Name Unknown.

13 viii. **David Boyt**. He married **Mary Bradley** and was in Alabama in 1835.

Richard Bradley who married Catherine Taylor may not have been the Richard who was Mary's father. Richard Bradley applied for a Revolutionary War Pension in Sumner County, Tennessee, on 3 April 1822. It was approved and is in Revolutionary War file W # 896. He died 21 August 1827. His widow later received a pension and she died 22 August 1839.

His listed children were: Abraham, David, William, Catherine, Richard and Isaac. Mary was not listed; however, she could have been deceased.

In "2400 Tennessee Pensions" a Richard Bradley is listed as having been placed on pension rolls in 1818 and as having died on 20 August 1821.

4. Arthur Boyt (Moses[1] Boyett) was born about 1754. He married **Polly (Maiden Name Unknown)**.

Arthur and **Ephraim Boyet** were living side by side in 1800. Arthur and wife, were between 26-44 years of age and had two daughters under 10 and one daughter 10-15 years. In 1810, Polly Boyet was head of household and was over age 45 with two females 10-15, one female 16-25 and one male 16-25.

Children of Arthur Boyt and Polly Unknown are:

14 i. **Unidentified Son Boyt**, born between 1785 - 1795.

15 ii. **Nancy Boyt**.

16 iii. **Betsy Boyt**.

5. Samuel Boyt (Moses[1] Boyett) was born About 1755, and died About 1791. He married **Phereby Maiden Name Unknown**.

Samuel's name appears to have been mispelled as "Lamuel" in the 1785 tax list for Duplin County. He was not mentioned in the will of Moses, his father, but in his will below, he names two brothers, Arthur and William.

Below, I have attempted to transcribe a copy of the original Last Will and Testament of Samuel Boyet.

"In the Name of God Amen. I, **Samuel Boyet**, of the County of Duplin and State of North Carolina being sick in body, but of perfect sound memory, thanks be to God for it, and calling to mind the mortality of my body and knowing that it is appointed for all men once to die, I therefore, make this my Last Will and Testament. First of all, I recommend my soul into the hand of God that gave it and my body to be buried in a Christian-like manner at the direction of my Executors which I shall hereafter mention. Also my just debts and final expenses to be paid off.

"Item. I leave to my beloved wife, **Phereby Boyet**, during her life time as widowhood, the maner plantation, one mare saddle and bridle together with all the household furniture, one cow and calf and heifer, and at her death or marriage everything there is which I leave to her is to be equally divided between my two sons. My hogs that are not wanted for my family's use to be sold and all the money equally divided between my two sons, equally share and share alike.

"Item. I give and bequeath unto my son, **John Boyet**, the maner plantation whereon I now live and all the land belonging to it, one mare, one cow and yearling, one two year old steer, and seven silver dollars to him and his heirs forever.

"Item. I give and bequeath unto my son, **Hardy Boyet**, a track of land down Ash Branch below and joining the maner plantation, one cow and yearling, one young Sorrel Mare, seven silver dollars to him and his heirs forever.

"...one line may be missing..?."

"Item. I leave my beloved brother, William Boyett, and my brother, Arther Boyet, Executors to this my Last Will and testament, and revoking all other will or wills, I acknowledge this to be my Last Will and Testament in presence of these witnesses, fourteenth day of May Ano 1791.

" **Thomas Phillips** signed "Samuel (his x) Boyet.

Ephriam Boyt (his mark x)

In the 1800 census for Duplin County, Phereby's name was entered as "Fireby Boyt" and she was between 26-44 with two males 10-15 and one male 16-25 in the household. She was not listed in Duplin County in 1810, but there was a "Pireby Boyt" in Capt Cage's District in Montgomery County, North Carolina. However, I did not pursue the ages of that household.

Children of Samuel Boyt and Phereby Unknown are:

17 i. **John Boyt.**

18 ii. **Hardy Boyt.**

DESCENDANTS OF MARY ELIZABETH BULLARD

Following are the descendants of Mary Elizabeth Bullard; she was a great-great-granddaughter of Thomas William Holland. See her elsewhere in this book to determine her Holland descendancy. Her family data was found after I had revised the manuscript and it was best to enter the several pages of her family descendants separately. Therefore, you will find that **this data does not follow the mathematical relationship as found for the individuals listed under Thomas William Holland.** The relationship for Mary Elizabeth entered here in parenthesis follows her Bullard descendancy.

Generation No. 1

1. Mary Elizabeth Bullard (Giles Mitchell[13], James[12], Barton[11], Thomas[10], Henry Thomas[9], Jeremiah[8], William[7], Issac[6], William[5], William[4], Henry[3] Buller, John[2], John[1]) was born 20 October 1866, and died 17 March 1933. She married **(1) Evander James Cook** 23 January 1889 in Flea Hill Township, Cumberland County, North Carolina, son of Robert Cook and Cathrine J.Innis. He was born 19 May 1863, and died 26 April 1903. She married **(2) Alex S. Wood** 21 January 1914 in Seventy-First Township, Cumberland County, North Carolina. He was born about 1855.

Children of Mary Bullard and Evander Cook are:

+	2	i.	**Ethel J. Cook**, born 13 September 1889; died 21 May 1963 in Fayetteville, Cumberland County, North Carolina.
+	3	ii.	**Andrew James Cook**, born 27 October 1890; died 12 June 1975 in Jacksonville, North Carolina.
+	4	iii.	**Ernest Lester Cook**, born 01 October 1892; died 24 April 1979 in Fayetteville.
	5	iv.	**Della Elizabeth Cook**, born April 1896. She married **Early R. Green** 13 August 1912 in Seventy-First Township, Cumberland County, North Carolina; born About 1891 in Heathsville, Halifax County, North Carolina.
+	6	v.	**Stella May Cook**, born 25 May 1898; died 03 August 1968 in Fayetteville, Cumberland County, North Carolina.
	7	vi.	**Stacy Cook**, born March 1900.
+	8	vii.	**William Blackman Cook**, born 12 November 1901; died 13 June 1985 in Fayetteville.

Generation No. 2

2. Ethel J. Cook (Mary Elizabeth[14] Bullard, Giles Mitchell[13], James[12], Barton[11], Thomas[10], Henry Thomas[9], Jeremiah[8], William[7], Issac[6], William[5], William[4], Henry[3] Buller, John[2], John[1]) was born 13 September 1889, and died 21 May 1963 in Fayetteville, Cumberland County, North Carolina. She married **Frank Beasley** 09 May 1907 in Seventy-First Township, Cumberland County, North Carolina. He was born 06 July 1886, and died 03 March 1976.

Child of Ethel Cook and Frank Beasley is:

9 i. **James Oscar Beasley**, born 01 October 1909; died 10 November 1967 in Fayetteville, Cumberland County, North Carolina. He married **Elma Eatmon**.

3. Andrew James Cook (Mary Elizabeth[14] Bullard, Giles Mitchell[13], James[12], Barton[11], Thomas[10], Henry Thomas[9], Jeremiah[8], William[7], Issac[6], William[5], William[4], Henry[3] Buller, John[2], John[1]) was born 27 October 1890, and died 12 June 1975 in Jacksonville, North Carolina. He married **Lena Bell Capps** 06 August 1914 in Fayetteville, Cumberland County, North Carolina. She was born 02 October 1894, and died 06 September 1961 in Fayetteville, Cumberland County, North Carolina.

He and Lena were buried in Galatia Presbyterian Church Cemetery which is probably on Raeford Road in Cumberland County, North Carolina. This is also where several of his children were buried.

Children of Andrew Cook and Lena Capps are:

10 i. **George Stacy Cook**, born 12 December 1914 in Seventy-First Township, Cumberland County, North Carolina.

11 ii. **Ruby Alyce Cook**, born 26 June 1916 in Seventy-First Township, Cumberland County, North Carolina.

She married and lived in Ellerbe and is said to have died there.

\+ 12 iii. **Dewey James Cook**, born 21 May 1918 in Seventy-First Township, Cumberland County.

13 iv. **Lattie Cook**, born 16 March 1920 in Seventy-First Township, Cumberland County, North Carolina. He married **Rebecca McFadyen**.

14 v. **Robert Herman Cook**, born 16 November 1921 in Seventy-First Township, Cumberland County; died 06 February 1967 in Virginia.

\+ 15 vi. **Andrew Garland Cook**, born 03 August 1923 in Fayetteville, Cumberland County, North Carolina.

\+ 16 vii. **Herbert Lee Cook**, born 10 January 1925 in Seventy-First Township, Cumberland County.

17 viii. **David Leon Cook**, born 14 December 1926 in Rockfish Township, Cumberland County, North Carolina; died 02 June 1951.

He was a First Lieutenant in the United States Army.

18 ix. **Annie Ruth Cook**, born 02 April 1928 in Rockfish Township, Cumberland County.

Did not marry.

19 x. **Catherine Elizabeth Cook**, born 16 November 1930 in Rockfish Township, Cumberland County.

20 xi. **Jeanne Carlette Cook**, born 18 May 1933 in Rockfish Township, Cumberland County.

Did not marry. She died in South Carolina.

4. Ernest Lester Cook (Mary Elizabeth[14] Bullard, Giles Mitchell[13], James[12], Barton[11], Thomas[10], Henry Thomas[9], Jeremiah[8], William[7], Issac[6], William[5], William[4], Henry[3] Buller, John[2], John[1]) was born 01 October 1892, and died 24 April 1979 in Fayetteville, Cumberland County, North Carolina. He married **Ida Mae Lindsay** 03 March 1915 in Seventy-First Township, Cumberland County, North Carolina. She was born 26 January 1890, and died 23 July 1965 in Seventy-First Township, Cumberland County, North Carolina.

Both were buried at Galatia Presbyterian Church Cemetery which is probably on Raeford Road in Cumberland County, North Carolina.

Children of Ernest Cook and Ida Lindsay are:

\+ 21 i. **Ernest Lester Cook, Jr.**, born 02 May 1916 in Seventy-First Township, Cumberland County, North Carolina; died 03 June 1961 in Seventy-First Township, Cumberland County.

\+ 22 ii. **Mary Marguerite Cook**, born 20 February 1918 in Seventy-First Township, Cumberland County.

23 iii. **Armond Mc Cook**, born 30 March 1920 in Seventy-First Township, Cumberland County, North Carolina; died 23 June 1922.

24 iv. **Stillborn Son Cook**, born 10 July 1922 in Seventy-First Township, Cumberland County, North Carolina.

25 v. **William Alexander Cook**, born 15 May 1923 in Seventy-First Township, Cumberland County, North Carolina; died 27 August 1974 in Fayetteville, Cumberland County, North Carolina. He married **Thelda Elizabeth Hall** 28 December 1949 in Autryville, North Carolina; born 06 November 1925 in Bladen County, North Carolina; died 08 July 1968 in Fayetteville, Cumberland County, North Carolina.

Thelda and William were buried at Galatia Presbyterian Church Cemetery which is probably on Raeford Road in Cumberland County, North Carolina.

26 vi. **Edith Cook**, born 16 October 1925 in Rockfish Township, Cumberland County, North Carolina. She married Unknown Abrams.

Edith and her husband are said to have lived in Baltimore, Maryland.

27 vii. **Glen Worth Cook**, born 17 November 1927 in Rockfish Township, Cumberland County, North Carolina. He married **Lilliam Lee Autry**; born 08 August 1935 in Cumberland County, North Carolina.

Glen was called "Toppie." Three children.

28 viii. **Carmen Cook**, born 17 October 1929 in Rockfish Township, Cumberland County, North Carolina. She married Unknown Henderson.

29 ix. **Helen Jenette Cook**, born 20 March 1935 in Seventy-First Township, Cumberland County, North Carolina. She married Unknown Caskey.

6. Stella May Cook (Mary Elizabeth[14] Bullard, Giles Mitchell[13], James[12], Barton[11], Thomas[10], Henry Thomas[9], Jeremiah[8], William[7], Issac[6], William[5], William[4], Henry[3] Buller, John[2], John[1]) was born 25 May 1898, and died 03 August 1968 in Fayetteville, Cumberland County, North Carolina. She married **William Marvin Lindsay** 03 February 1915 in

Fayetteville, Cumberland County, North Carolina. He was born 18 November 1891, and died 07 November 1962 in Fayetteville, Cumberland County, North Carolina.

Stella and William were buried at Galatia Presbyterian Church Cemetery which is probably on Raeford Road in Cumberland County, North Carolina.

Children of Stella Cook and William Lindsay are:

30 i. **Mary Estell Lindsay**, born 31 October 1915 in Seventy-First Township, Cumberland County, North Carolina.

31 ii **Unidentified Lindsay**.

32 iii. **Irene Lindsay**, born 01 January 1921; died 30 September 1944.

33 iv. **William Marvin Lindsay, Jr.**, born about 1922. He married **Patricia Jane Batten**; born about 1938.

Four children.

1) **Camilla Ann Lindsay** was born and died 14 August 1968, is buried in Galatia Presbyterian Church Cemetery.

2) **William Marvin Lindsay III** was born 27 September 1969 in Fayetteville, North Carolina.

3) **John Preston Lindsay** was born 19 December 1970 in Fayetteville.

4) **Patricia Suzanne Lindsay** was born 27 January 1972 in Fayetteville.

34 v. **Eva Mae Lindsay**, born 20 December 1925 in Rockfish Township, Cumberland County, North Carolina. She married **Albert Vernon McLaurin**.

35 vi. **Unknown Daughter Lindsay**, born 28 January 1930 in Fayetteville, Cumberland County, North Carolina; died 31 January 1930.

8. William Blackman Cook (Mary Elizabeth[14] Bullard, Giles Mitchell[13], James[12], Barton[11], Thomas[10], Henry Thomas[9], Jeremiah[8], William[7], Issac[6], William[5], William[4], Henry[3] Buller, John[2], John[1]) was born 12 November 1901, and died 13 June 1985 in Fayetteville, Cumberland County, North Carolina. He married **Bonnie Carbell Lunsford**. She was born 29 March 1907 in Fayetteville, Cumberland County, North Carolina.

Children of William Cook and Bonnie Luesford are:

\+ 36 i. **William Blake Cook**, born 06 June 1925 in Cumberland County; died 07 November 1973.

37 ii. **Carl Vernon Cook**, born 19 May 1927 in Rockfish Township, Cumberland County, North Carolina.

38 iii. **Phillis Juanita Cook**, born 14 March 1929 in Hope Mills, Cumberland County, North Carolina. She married Unknown Davis.

\+ 39 iv. **Martin Luther Cook**, born 25 July 1931 in Rockfish Township, Cumberland County.

40 v. **Robert Giles Cook**, born 23 October 1933 in Hope Mills, Cumberland County, North Carolina. He married **Elizabeth Ivey**.

Four children. Robert is buried in Cumberland Memorial Gardens in Cumberland County.

41 vi. **Margie Alice Cook**, born 21 September 1935 in Seventy-First Township, Cumberland County, North Carolina. She married Unknown Raymes.

42 vii. **Shirley Jean Cook**, born 17 September 1937 in Rockfish Township, Cumberland County, North Carolina; died 08 July 1939 in Fayetteville, Cumberland County.

43 viii. **Vivian Carol Cook.**

Vivian first married **Mr. Brown** and second, **Mr. Lloyd.**

44 ix. **Peggy Joyce Cook**, born 11 December 1941 in Seventy-First Township, Cumberland County, North Carolina. She married Unknown Currie.

45 x. **Bonnie Ethel Cook**, born 09 June 1943 in Seventy-First Township, Cumberland County. She married Unknown Jones.

Generation No. 3

12. Dewey James Cook (Andrew James[15], Mary Elizabeth[14] Bullard, Giles Mitchell[13], James[12], Barton[11], Thomas[10], Henry Thomas[9], Jeremiah[8], William[7], Issac[6], William[5], William[4], Henry[3] Buller, John[2], John[1]) was born 21 May 1918 in Seventy-First Township, Cumberland County, North Carolina. He married **Mary Florence Lindsay** in Seventy-First Township, Cumberland County, North Carolina. She was born about 1923 in Hoke County, North Carolina.

Child of Dewey Cook and Mary Lindsay is:

46 i. **Dewey James Cook, Jr.**, born 18 July 1941 in Seventy-First Township, Cumberland County, North Carolina.

15. Andrew Garland Cook (Andrew James[15], Mary Elizabeth[14] Bullard, Giles Mitchell[13], James[12], Barton[11], Thomas[10], Henry Thomas[9], Jeremiah[8], William[7], Issac[6], William[5], William[4], Henry[3] Buller, John[2], John[1]) was born 03 August 1923 in Fayetteville, Cumberland County, North Carolina. He married **Margaret Lucille Ray**. She was born about 1921 in Hoke County, North Carolina.

Children of Andrew Cook and Margaret Ray are:

47 i. **Andrew Garland Cook, Jr.**, born 15 September 1951 in Lumberton, Robeson County, North Carolina.

48 ii. **Patsey Ann Cook**, born 09 September 1952 in Lumberton, Robeson County, North Carolina.

16. Herbert Lee Cook (Andrew James[15], Mary Elizabeth[14] Bullard, Giles Mitchell[13], James[12], Barton[11], Thomas[10], Henry Thomas[9], Jeremiah[8], William[7], Issac[6], William[5], William[4], Henry[3] Buller, John[2], John[1]) was born 10 January 1925 in Seventy-First Township, Cumberland County, North Carolina. He married **(1) Unknown Boney** about 1950. He married **(2) Jeanette Blease** 03 June 1966 in St. Matthew's United Methodist Church in Seventy-First Township, Cumberland County, North Carolina. She was born 22 January 1936 in Brooks County, Georgia. It appears that Jeanette first married a "Tharrington."

Herbert and his children added an "E" to "Cook(e)."

Children of Herbert Cook and Unknown Boney are:

49 i. **Twin Daughters Cooke.**

50 ii. **Stuart LaVane Cooke**, born 25 May 1953 in Brooks County, Georgia. He married **Debra Arlene Hubbard** 10 January 1981 in Stedman, North Carolina; born 13 July 1959 in Fayetteville, Cumberland County, North Carolina. She was the daughter Eulon elliot Hubbard and Lois Arline Hairr and can be found elsewhere in this history.

Debra and "Tony" were divorced.

51 iii. **Susan Kayreen Cooke**, born 30 January 1957 in Thomas County, Georgia. She married Donald Trent Bain 08 August 1975 in Stedman, Cumberland County, North Carolina; born 23 August 1956 in Fayetteville, Cumberland County, North Carolina.

21. Ernest Lester Cook, Jr. (Ernest Lester[15], Mary Elizabeth[14] Bullard, Giles Mitchell[13], James[12], Barton[11], Thomas[10], Henry Thomas[9], Jeremiah[8], William[7], Issac[6], William[5], William[4], Henry[3] Buller, John[2], John[1]) was born 02 May 1916 in Seventy-First Township, Cumberland County, North Carolina, and died 03 June 1961 in Seventy-First Township, Cumberland County, North Carolina. He married **Loma Beatrice Sowell.** She was born About 1923 in Waxhaw, North Carolina.

Children of Ernest Cook and Loma Sowell are:

52 i. **Unidentified Cook.**

53 ii. **Ernest Lester Cook III,** born 07 July 1952 in Fayetteville, Cumberland County, North Carolina.

22. Mary Marguerite Cook (Ernest Lester[15], Mary Elizabeth[14] Bullard, Giles Mitchell[13], James[12], Barton[11], Thomas[10], Henry Thomas[9], Jeremiah[8], William[7], Issac[6], William[5], William[4], Henry[3] Buller, John[2], John[1]) was born 20 February 1918 in Seventy-First Township, Cumberland County, North Carolina. She married **Clarence Marvin Koonce.** He was born 23 November 1911 in Hoke County, North Carolina, and died 02 June 1986 in Fayetteville, Cumberland County, North Carolina.

Children of Mary Cook and Clarence Koonce are:

54 i. **Clarence Marvin Koonce, Jr.,** born 28 August 1946 in Fayetteville, Cumberland County, North Carolina. He married **Diana Catherine Wilson** who born about 1948.

They had twin daughters, **Shannon Leigh Koonce** and **Robin Michelle Koonce** who were born 19 August 1971.

55 ii. **Debbie Darlene Koonce,** born 06 November 1951 in Fayetteville, Cumberland County.

36. William Blake Cook (William Blackman[15], Mary Elizabeth[14] Bullard, Giles Mitchell[13], James[12], Barton[11], Thomas[10], Henry Thomas[9], Jeremiah[8], William[7], Issac[6], William[5], William[4], Henry[3] Buller, John[2], John[1]) was born 06 June 1925 in Cumberland

County, Maryland, and died 07 November 1973. He married **Helen Jane Bunce**, daughter of James Bunce and Bessie Raynor. She was born 03 April 1933 in Seventy-First Township in Cumberland County, North Carolina.

William is buried in LaFayette Memorial Park in Fayetteville, North Carolina.

Children of William Cook and Helen Bunce are:

56 i. **Kenneth Alan Cook**, born 13 August 1952 in Fayetteville, Cumberland County, North Carolina; died 04 August 1956 in Eastover Township, Cumberland County, North Carolina.

57 ii. **Sharon Rose Cook**, born 06 May 1956 in Fayetteville, Cumberland County, North Carolina. She married **Dennis Martin Pope**; born 26 November 1956 near Fayetteville, Cumberland County.

A son, **Christopher Martin Pope** was born 12 October 1981 in Fayetteville.

58 iii. **Randy Blake Cook,** born 03 October 1957 near Fayetteville in Cumberland County.

59 iv. **Robin Renee Cook**, born 21 December 1965 in Fayetteville, Cumberland County, North Carolina.

39. Martin Luther Cook (William Blackman[15], Mary Elizabeth[14] Bullard, Giles Mitchell[13], James[12], Barton[11], Thomas[10], Henry Thomas[9], Jeremiah[8], William[7], Issac[6], William[5], William[4], Henry[3] Buller, John[2], John[1]) was born 25 July 1931 in Rockfish Township, Cumberland County, North Carolina. He married **Marion Estelle Faircloth**, daughter of Marion Stanford Faircloth and Lillie Gertrude Faircloth. She was born 16 April 1934 in Beaver Dam Township, Cumberland County, North Carolina.

Children of Martin Cook and Marion Faircloth are:

60 i. **Audry Lynn Cook**, born 25 December 1954 in Clinton, Sampson County, North Carolina.

61 ii. **Catherine Rachel Cook**, born 13 July 1959 in Fayetteville, Cumberland County, North Carolina.

BIBLIOGRAPHY

1. Ancestry.com and Familysearch.org. *Electronic.* Birth Records, Federal Census Records, Certificates of Death, Family Trees, and other data posted on these sites.

2. *Bizzell, Oscar M., Editor. A Portrait of Eighteenth Century Sampson County as revealed by Sampson County Court Minutes 1784-1800.* Copyright 1995*; A Portrait of Nineteenth Century Sampson County, as revealed by Sampson County Court Minutes 1800-1810,* Copyright 1990*; A Portrait of Nineteenth Century Sampson County, as revealed by Sampson County Court Minutes 1810-1820,* Copyright 1993;. *A Portrait of Nineteenth Century Sampson County as revealed by Sampson County Court Minutes 1820-1830* Copyright 1995. All four books Compiled and Edited by Oscar M. Bizzell and Virginia Lohr Bizzell for The Sampson County Historical Society.

3. Bizzell, Virginia L. and Oscar M. Bizzell, *Revolutionary War Records Duplin and Sampson Counties, North Carolina, Contributions to Genealogy.* 1997. Transcribed for the Sampson County Historical Society.

4. Bizzell, Oscar M., Editor, Bizzell, Virginia Lohr, Associate Editor, *The Heritage of Sampson County,North Carolina, 1784-1984.* Volumes I and II

5. Bizzell, Virginia Lohr, *1850 Sampson County Census, North Carolina.* (Transcribed for the Sampson County Historical Society).

6. Bizzell, Virginia Lohr, *1860 Sampson County Census, North Carolina.* (Transcribed for the Sampson County Historical Society).

7. Bizzell, Virginia Lohr, *1870 Sampson County Census, North Carolina.* (Transcribed for the Sampson County Historical Society).

8. Bundy, V. Mayo, Professor Political Science & Sociology, Bennett College, *Meet Our Ancestors, Culbreth, Autry, Maxwell-Bundy, Winslow, Henley and Allied Families.* Second Edition. 1978. Media, Inc, Greensboro, North Carolina.

9. Carter or Howell Old Family Bible in possession of Mr. and Mrs. Phillip Smith.

10. "Deeds," Sampson County, North Carolina. Sampson County Courthouse, Clinton. Harnett County Book Committee, *The Heritage of Harnett County, North Carolina, Volume 1*, Copyright 1993.

11. Old Holland Record Book purchased and owned by Thomas William Holland.

12. "Marriage Index (Registers) for Sampson County, North Carolina, USA. Sampson County Courthouse, Clinton.

13. Peterson, Max R., Jr. *Abstracts Sampson---Duplin Deeds. Books 1-3. (ca. 1750 to ca. 1774).*

14. Peterson, Max R., Jr. *Abstracts Sampson---Duplin Deeds. Books 4-6 (ca.1762 to ca. 1779).*

15. Peterson, Max R., Jr. *Abstracts Sampson---Duplin and Sampson County Deeds. Books 7-9. (ca. 1780 to ca. 1794).*

16. Peterson, Max R., Jr. *Abstracts Sampson County deeds. Books 10-12. (ca. 1794 to ca. 1804).*

17. Register, Mrs. Alvaretta Kenan, State Census of North Carolina 1784- 1787. Second Edition-Revised 1971 from records in the North Carolina Department of Archives and History, Raleigh, North Carolina, by Mrs. Register, Norfolk, Virginia

18. Ross, Elizabeth E., *Sampson County Will Abstracts 1784-1900.* Elizabeth E. Ross, 396 Little Creek Church Road, Clayton, North Carolina 27520

19. Rosser, John C., Jr. *Coharie to Cape Fear, The Descendants of John Williams and Katharine Galbreth of Sampson and Cumberland Counties in North Carolina (1740-1990).* Walsworth Publishing Company, Marceline, Missouri 64658, Volumes I, II, and III April 1990

20. Royal, Wanda Gayle, Contributing Editors, Duane Alan Royal and Tiffany Royal Davis, *Royal Family Legacy.* January 2000. Twyford Printing, Dunn, North Carolina. Royal, Wanda., *Royal Family Legacy Addendum*, October 2001.

21. "Vital Statistics," Sampson County, North Carolina. Sampson County Courthouse.

22. West, Bradley Lee, *Nineteenth Century Vital Statistics of Sampson County, 1871-1892),* Volumes I and II.

23. West, Bradley Lee, Kenneth Dale Register, and Phyllis Jeanette West, *Northern Sampson County, North Carolina Cemeteries*, Volume I, Copyright 2001, and Volume II, Copyright 2002.

24. West, Bradley Lee, and Kenneth Dale Register, *Northern Sampson County, North Carolina Cemeteries*, Volume 3, Copyright 2004.

25. West, Bradley Lee, *Sacred To The Memory of The W.P.A. The Works Progress Administration Pre-1914 Cemetery Inscription Survey for Sampson County*, Originally Compiled by Mrs. Thyra R. Ussery, Margaret Jackson, and Mrs. Buck Wilson. Copyright 2004. Edited Version by Bradley Lee West, 8817 Roseboro Highway, Roseboro North Carolina 28382.

26. West, Bradley Lee and Kenneth Dale Register, *Southern Sampson County, North Carolina Cemeteries.* Copyright 1999. Bradley Lee West, 8817 Roseboro Highway, Roseboro, NC, 28382.

27. West, Bradley Lee, *The Clinton City Cemetery.* Copyright 1999.

28. "Wills," Sampson County, North Carolina. Sampson County Courthouse, Clinton.

PHOTOS OF ALGER ROSE HOLLAND AND TWO WIVES

Alger Rose Holland and wife, Ella Jane Howell

Alger Rose Holland and wife, Tomzil Clyde Holland

IMAGES FROM THE OLD HOLLAND RECORD BOOK

On the following pages you will find images from an **Old Holland Record Book**. Soon after I started my genealogical research, Woodrow Smith shared with me what he had copied from The Old Holland Record Book that has been called **The Old Holland Family Bible.** My sister and I were curious and interested in actually seeing the old records. The current owner kindly allowed us to review and copy the records from this old book and loose pages placed in the book. Some of the loose pages also appeared to be from a book, perhaps a Bible. I am grateful to her and to Woodrow for sharing data. The earlier images contain a few blotches, but writing on a few pages is so faded, it is illegible. A few of the old records that I reference in this book do not have images included on the following pages.

The information recorded in these images include names and birth dates for children of Thomas William Holland and Milley Boyett, for children of Henry Holland and Mary Tew, and for a few other descendants. The order of the records made it impossible for me to place the pages in birth or generation order.

"Borned" is written for "born" in the older records.

Recorded in this old record book at the top of one of the images is what appears to be: "Thomas Deceased 8 November _819." This writing is crossed through, but the date of 8 November 1819 probably is the date Thomas William Holland died. The fact that it is crossed through may support an estate sale in which it was sold and later purchased by a member of the Holland Family. (See the paragraph below. See Thomas William Holland's will elsewhere in this book.) The left top corner of one of the images is torn and on the left side of this image, writing from the page underneath it appears. **Thomas Yrarebery**" is written on the facing page and **Yearbary Autrey** is recorded on the left page of the image. **Yarboro, Yarbough** or **Yarbrough** is probably the name the writer attempted to record and I have no idea whether the Yarbrough family was connected to the Holland.or Autry families.

I'm puzzled by more than one entry in this old record book and by the loose pages, but especially by one entry that says: "September. ... Thomas Holland, his Book. Bought of Hugh McPhail for 10 Shillings in the year 1820." This would have been about one year after the death of Thomas William Holland. Perhaps there was an estate sale for Thomas and "a" Bible" or the old record book was sold, and purchased perhaps several months later by Henry Holland; the records are today owned by one of Henry's descendants. Henry would have been aged 19 in 1820. Whoever purchased the book from Hugh McPhail, thankfully, realized its value to the Holland Family. **The loose pages may indicate that at one time, there may have been a Bible and the *Old Holland Record Book.***

This old book holds the key to the family found in the history of descendants of Thomas William Holland. One of these recently taken digital images proves that this book is not an Old Bible. Its title is ***Fifteen Sermons Preached on Various Important Subjects***, by George Whitefield, A. B., late of Pemeroke College, Oxford. Prefixed to the Sermons is "A Sermon, on the Character, Preaching of the Rev. Mr. Whitefield," by Joseph Smith, V.D.M. This book of sermons was published in **1794** by J. Neilson, for J. Gildies, Book Seller, above the Cross Glasgow (England). Rev. George Whitefield (Whitfield) lived 250 years ago and has been called "one of the most passionate evangelists" of the Great Awakening. Theologically, he was a staunch calvinist and it appears that our ancestor, Thomas William Holland, may have followed Rev.Whitefield's teachings.

Of course, we do not know the name of the writing instrument used for the first records in this book, but a "Quill Pen" may explain the blotches found in the earliest recorded names in the book. Those of you who have a computer and an internet connection may find interesting the information you can find on the internet about the history of writing instruments and especially, Quill Pens. After reading only a few pages about preparing the quill pen for writing, I have a grateful "thank you" for those who had the patience to keep their quills and other writing instruments in good writing condition.

Mary Holland was
borned May the 18 18[illegible]

Benjamin J Holland
was borned June the
18 day 1825
Lucinda Holland was
borned November
the 5 day 1826
Mary M Holland
was borned April
the 15 day 1829
Clarkey M Holland
was borned June the 14
Day 1831
Nancy and Milly Holland was
September the 22 day 18[illegible]

Thomas Holland

Henry Holland

Nancy

Mary Holland was
borned May the 18 1824

Benjamin J Holland
was borned June the
18 day 1825
Lucinda Holland was
borned November
the 5 day 1826
Mary M Holland
was borned April
the 15 day 1829
Clarkey M Holland
was Borned June the 16
Day 1831
Nancy and Milly Holland was
September the 22 Day 1835

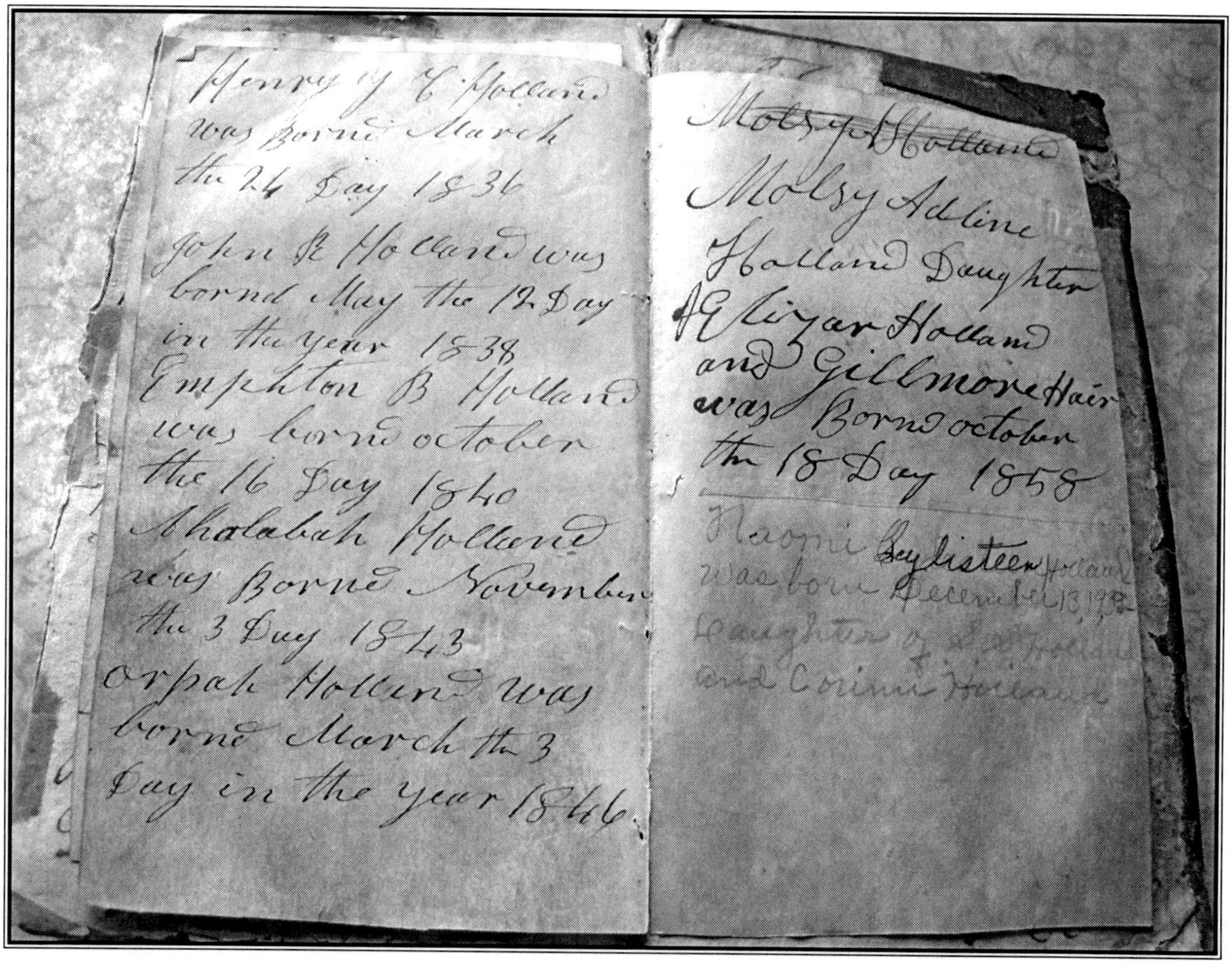

Henry T C Holland
was Borne March
the 26 Day 1836

John R Holland was
borne May the 12 Day
in the year 1838

Emphton B Holland
was borne october
the 16 Day 1840

Shalabah Holland
was Borne November
the 3 Day 1843

Orpah Holland was
borne March the 3
Day in the year 1846

~~Molsy Holland~~

Molsy Adline
Holland Daughter
of Elizar Holland
and Gillmore Hair
was Borne october
the 18 Day 1858

Naomi Seylisteen Holland
was born December 13, 19[illegible]
Daughter of [illegible] Holland
and Corinne Holland

Henry J. C. Holland
was Borne March
the 24 Day 1836

John R Holland was
borne May the 12 Day
in the year 1838

Emphton B Holland
was borne october
the 16 Day 1840

Aholabah Holland
was Borne November
the 3 Day 1843

Orpah Holland was
borne March the 3
Day in the year 1846

~~Molsy A Holland~~
Molsy Adline
Holland Daughter
of Elizar Holland
and Gillmore Hair
was Borne october
the 18 Day 1858

Naomi Baylisteen Holland
was born December 13, 19[illegible]
daughter of [illegible] Holland
and Corinne Holland

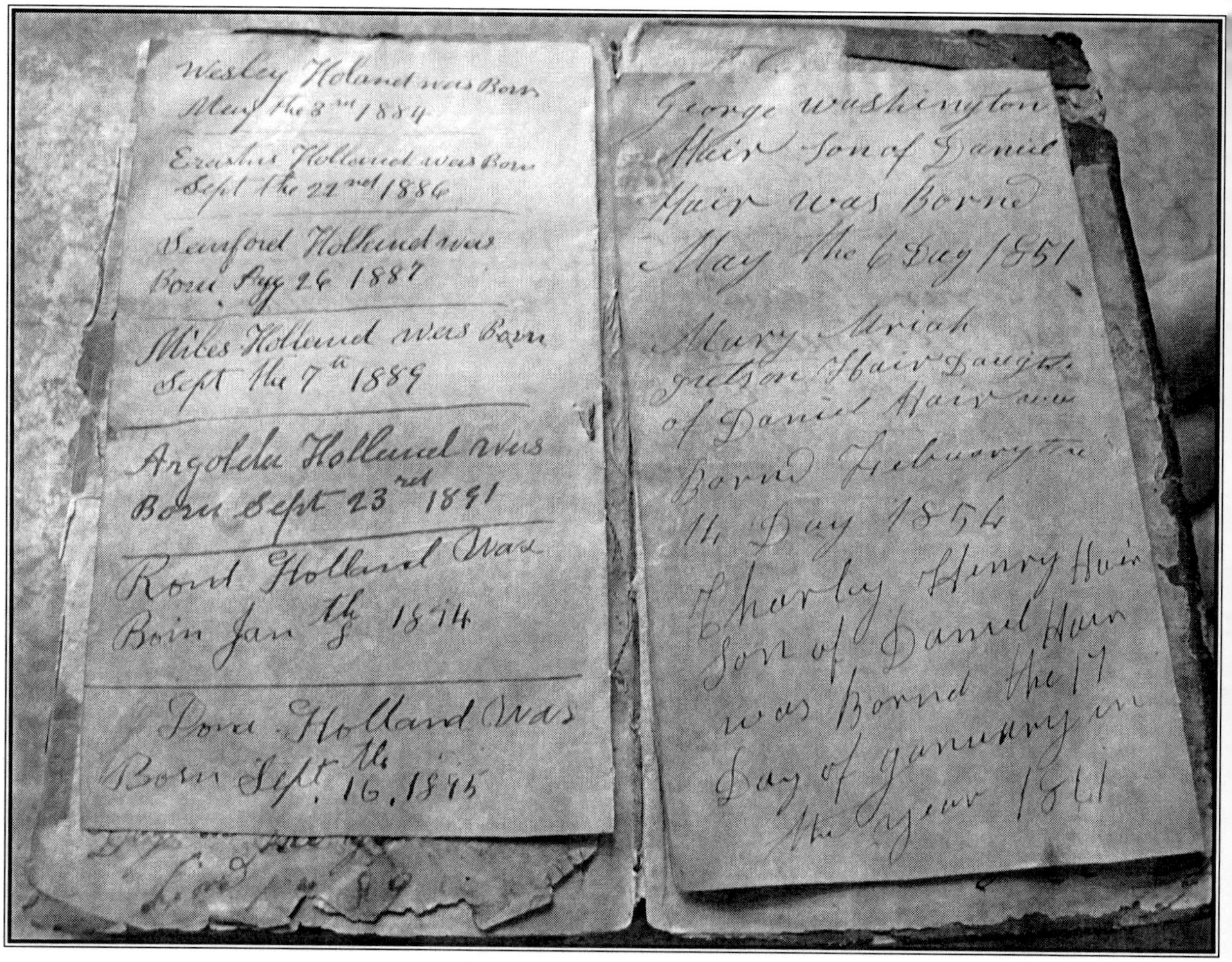
Wesley Holland was Born
May the 8th 1884
Erastus Holland was Born
Sept the 22nd 1886
Sanford Holland was
Born Aug 26 1887
Miles Holland was Born
Sept the 7th 1889
Argolda Holland was
Born Sept 23rd 1891
Ront Holland Was
Born Jan the 8 1894
Dora Holland Was
Born Sept. the 16. 1895

George washington
Hair Son of Daniel
Hair was Borne
May the 6 Day 1851
Mary Mriah
Hair Daughter
of Daniel Hair was
Borne Febuary the
14 Day 1854
Charly Henry Hair
Son of Daniel Hair
was Borne the 17
Day of January in
the year 1841

Wesley Holland was Born
May the 3rd 1884

Erastus Holland was Born
Sept the 22nd 1886

Sanford Holland was
Born Aug 26 1887

Miles Holland was Born
Sept the 7th 1889

Angolda Holland was
Born Sept 23rd 1891

Root Holland was
Born Jan the 8 1894

Dora Holland was
Born Sept the 16, 1895

George washington
Hair Son of Daniel
Hair was Borne
May the 6 Day 1851

Mary Mriah
Jetson Hair Daughter
of Daniel Hair was
Borne Febuary the
14 Day 1854

Charly Henry Hair
Son of Daniel Hair
was Borne the 17
Day of January in
the year 1861

Nancy E. Holland was born June 18th 1857

Stephen Sorter, son of Stephen Sorter & Nancy Holland was born Feb 8th 1878

James Fredrick Holland was born October 3 1925

Elizabeth Inez Holland was born October

... Holland was born Aug 1 1873

Minna Holland was born June 22nd 1874.

Willie Holland was born June 22nd 1874

Alger Holland was born June 20 1875

Jeffrey Holland was born July 18 1877

W. A. C. Holland was born July 30 1879

Henry Holland was born March the 17th 1882

September

Thos. Holland his Book
Baught of [illegible] for 10 shillings in the year 1800

Dont Steal this Book for fear of Shame for over it
[illegible] name

Nancy Holland was Born February the 14 Day in the year of our Lord 17[illegible]9

Stephen Fowler Holland Son of Henry Holland was Born the 24 Day June 1848

Alderman McKay Holland Son of Henry Holland was Born the 24 Day of August in year 1852

~~Naomia~~
Naomia Sylistein Holl[illegible]
Born December 13 19[illegible]
Daughter of [illegible] Holland and [illegible]

[illegible] was Born July 30 1879

Henry Holland was Born March the 17th 1882

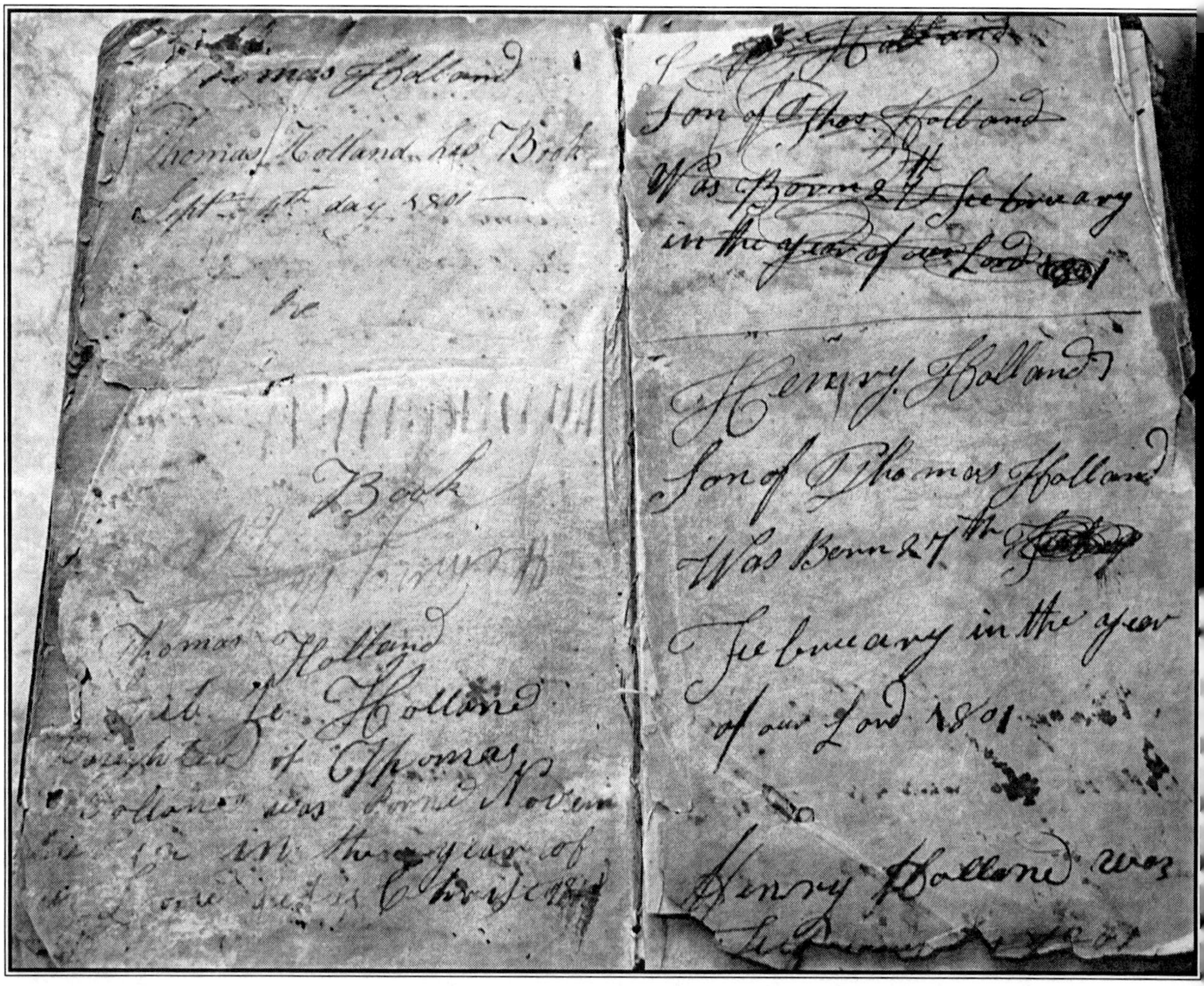

Thomas Holland

Thomas Holland his Book
Sept 4th day 1801

Book

Thomas Holland

Eliz. Holland
Daughter of Thomas
Holland was Borne Novem
[illegible] in the year of
our Lord Christ [illegible]

~~Holland~~
~~Son of Thos Holland~~
~~Was Borne 27th February~~
~~in the year of our Lord 1801~~

Henry Holland
Son of Thomas Holland
Was Born 27th
February in the year
of our Lord 1801

Henry Holland was
[illegible]

[illegible] Culbreath
Was Born [illegible]
17th December 1801
Mil[illegible] Culbreath
Daughter of Daniel
Culbreath and Mary
his wife was Born
[illegible] 180[illegible]
John Colbreath
was born the [illegible]
the [illegible] 18[illegible]

Thomas Hare son of
Jonathan Hare and Mille
his mother was Born
October the 3d day in the year
of our Lord 1812

Henry Williams
Holland Son of Thomas and
James Holland was Bo[illegible]
15th Day of January 18[illegible]

[illegible] Holland was Born
February the 27 Day
the year 1791

Mil Ze Calbreth

[illegible] Son of Cornelius [illegible]
and Mille his mother
Was Born the 30th Day
of December in the year
of our Lord 1811

Henry William
Holland Son of Thomas
James Holland was
Born the 20 January
1810
Clarky Mallet

High and low, rich and poor, young and old, one with another, of whatever sect or denomination, for I regard not that, I beseech you, by the mercies of Jesus, to be on your guard: Fly to Jesus Christ that heavenly bridegroom; behold he desires to take you to himself, miserable, poor, blind and naked as you are; he is willing to clothe you with his everlasting righteousness, and make you partakers of that glory, which he enjoyed with the Father before the world began. Do not turn a deaf ear to me; do not reject the message on account of the meanness of the messenger. I am a child; but the Lord has chosen me, that the glory might be all his own. Had he sent to invite you by a learned rabbi, you might have supposed that the man had done something; but now God has sent a child, that the excellency of the power may be seen not to be of man, but of God. Let the learned Pharisees then despise my youth: I care not how vile I appear in the sight of such men; I glory in it. And I am persuaded, if any of you should be married to Christ by this preaching, you will have no reason to repent, when you come to heaven, that God sent a child to cry, "Behold the bridegroom cometh!" O my brethren, the thought of being instrumental in bringing one of you to glory, fills me with fresh zeal. Once more, I intreat you, Watch, and pray; for the Lord Jesus will receive all that call on him faithfully. Let that cry, "Behold the Bridegroom cometh," be continually sounding in your ears; and begin now to live, as though you were assured, this night you were to go forth to meet him. May the Lord give you all an hearing ear, an obedient heart, and so closely unite you to himself by one spirit, that when he shall come in terrible majesty, to judge mankind, you may be found having on a wedding-garment, and ready to go in with him to the marriage.

Grant this, O Father, for thy dear Son's sake, Christ Jesus our Lord. Amen! and Amen!

FINIS.

Thos James Holland
Son of Thos. William Holland
was Born 30th April
in the year of our Lord
Anno domini 1797

Henry Holland son
of Thos. Holland was Born
the 27th February in
the year of our Lord 18[illegible]

Thos. Holland
his Book

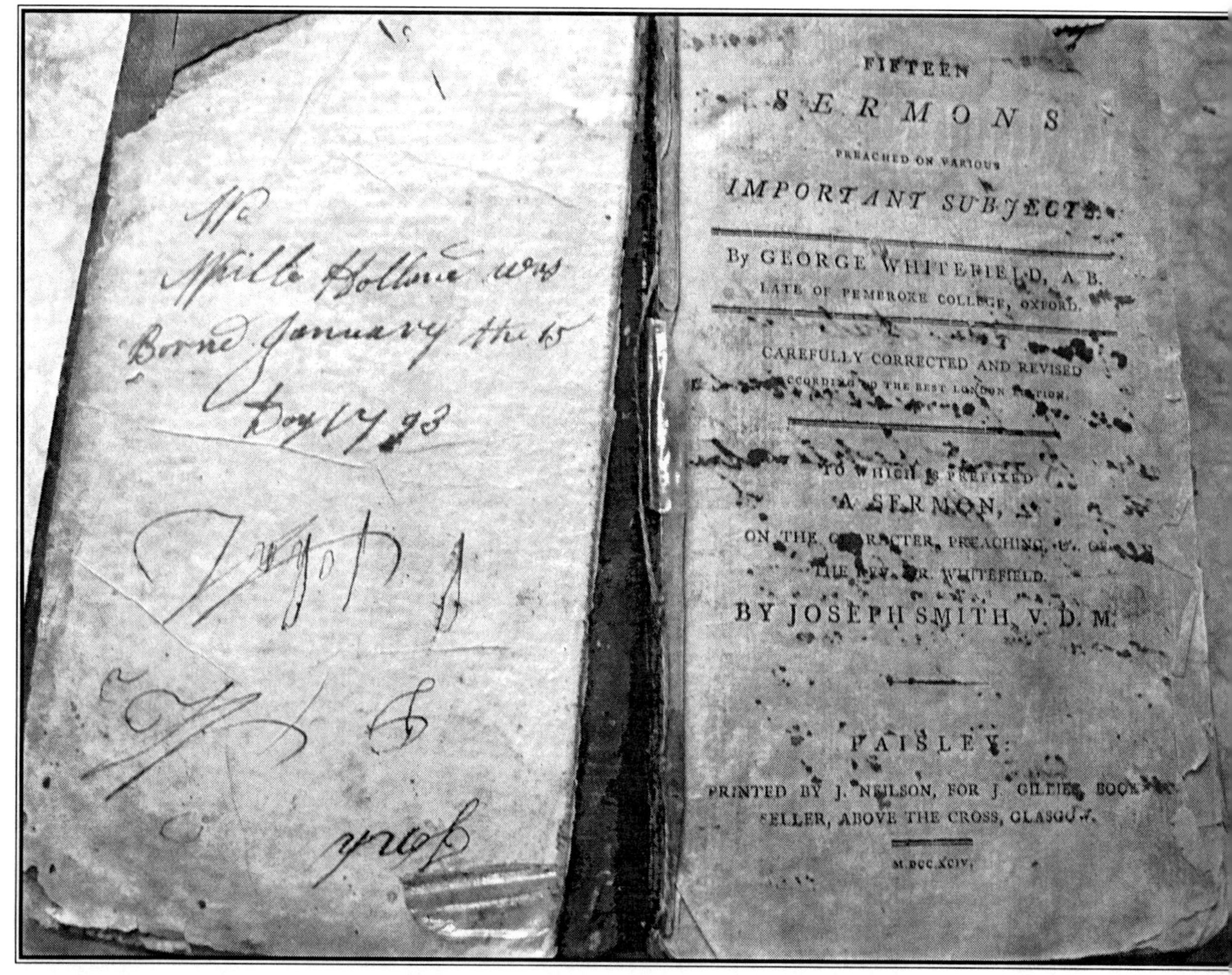

FIFTEEN
SERMONS
PREACHED ON VARIOUS
IMPORTANT SUBJECTS.

By GEORGE WHITEFIELD, A.B.
LATE OF PEMBROKE COLLEGE, OXFORD.

CAREFULLY CORRECTED AND REVISED
ACCORDING TO THE BEST LONDON EDITION.

TO WHICH IS PREFIXED
A SERMON,
ON THE CHARACTER, PREACHING, &c. OF
THE REV. MR. WHITEFIELD.
BY JOSEPH SMITH, V. D. M.

PAISLEY:
PRINTED BY J. NEILSON, FOR J. GILLIES, BOOKSELLER, ABOVE THE CROSS, GLASGOW.
M.DCC.XCIV.

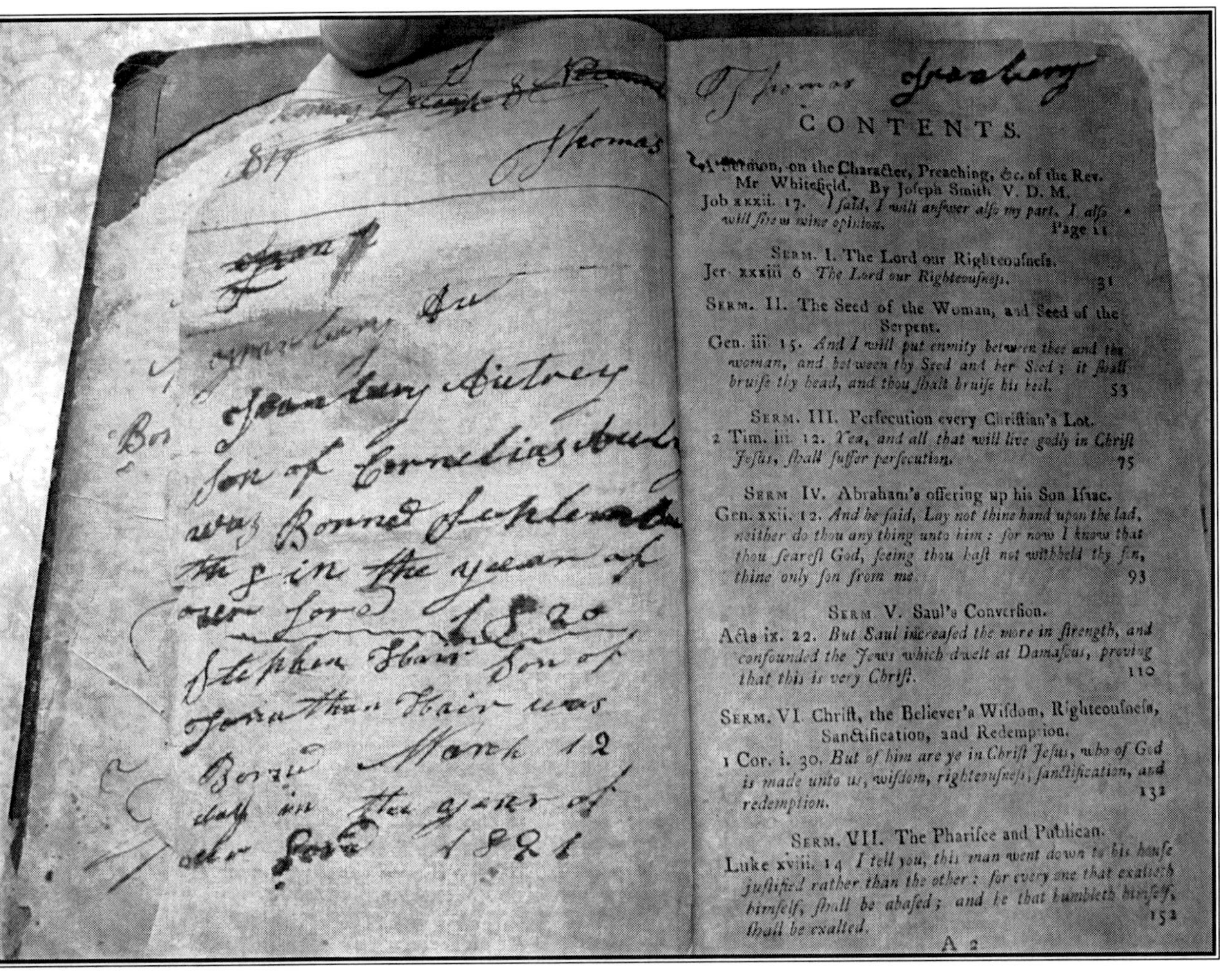

CONTENTS.

A 2

INDEX

LaVergne, TN USA
20 September 2009
158403LV00001B/7/P

9 781438 992624